THE AUTOBIOGRAPHY OF
WILLIAM ALLEN WHITE

THE MACMILLAN COMPANY
NEW YORK · BOSTON · CHICAGO · DALLAS
ATLANTA · SAN FRANCISCO

MACMILLAN AND CO., Limited
LONDON · BOMBAY · CALCUTTA · MADRAS
MELBOURNE

THE MACMILLAN COMPANY
OF CANADA, Limited
TORONTO

THE AUTOBIOGRAPHY OF

WILLIAM ALLEN WHITE

THE MACMILLAN COMPANY

NEW YORK · 1946

Designed by Stefan Salter

PRINTED IN THE U. S. A. BY THE HADDON CRAFTSMEN, SCRANTON, PA.

This Autobiography, in spite of all the pains I have taken and the research I have put into it, is necessarily fiction. The fact that names, dates, and places seem to correspond with such things that may have occurred in real life does not guarantee the truth of these stories. So, in all candor, I wish to warn the reader not to confuse this story with reality. For God only knows the truth. I am hereby trying, in my finite way, to set down some facts which seem real and true to me.

At best, this is only a tale that is told!

Contents

THE FIRST BOOK

About Willie

BOOK TWO

The Story of Will
(Sometimes Billie)

BOOK THREE

Will A. White

(Sometimes Billie)

BOOK FOUR

W. L. White

Illustrations

These illustrations follow page 370.

Dr. Allen White, mayor of Eldorado, Kansas.

Mary Ann Hatten White, mother of William Allen White, in 1909 at seventy-nine.

"Willie" White in 1873, aged five.

"Will" White, a junior at the University of Kansas.

In 1889 a group of college boys from the University of Kansas celebrate July 4th with a beer party.

In 1896: W. A. White, editor of the newly purchased Emporia Gazette.

Will A. White and Albert Bigelow Paine early in the Gay Nineties.

Sallie Moss Lindsay, a young teacher in Kansas City, Kansas, in 1892.

W. A. White, aged thirty, with his staff of ten of the Emporia Gazette in 1898.

Henry J. Allen and William Allen White in 1917, in France for the American Red Cross.

William Allen White in 1914 with his son Bill and his daughter Mary.

William Allen White and Theodore Roosevelt at the White home, in 1912.

Mary White, aged sixteen.

Herbert Hoover and William Allen White in 1935.

William Allen White at his desk in the Gazette office in 1938.

William Allen White in 1940, broadcasting from his study in Emporia.

The last picture of William Allen White—with Mrs. White, in the summer of 1943.

The First Book

ABOUT WILLIE

All that Shakespeare says of a King
yonder slip of a boy that reads in a
corner feels to be true of himself.

Emerson's Essay on History

CHAPTER I

"As It Was in the Beginning!"

I was born February 10, 1868, between nine and ten o'clock of a Thursday morning at Emporia, Kansas. I was born "Willie" though named William Allen, a name which did not occur to me nor any of my friends for long years, even decades afterwards. A few days after my birth, this item appeared in the Emporia News, which referred to my father, Dr. Allen White:

> There is another man in town they call Pap. He wears a stove pipe hat and carries a cane, and weighs (since the event) eight hundred pounds. He talks of sending the "young man" down on "Warnut" to take charge of the branch store.

I, Willie, was that young man, a baby of whom I know nothing except what has been told: that is that I was husky, always fat, with lusty bawling lungs, and that I was a nursing baby. And for perhaps two years, so far as my memory tells me, I was unconscious. When I was a year old I was taken by my parents to live in Eldorado, a little town in the Walnut Valley, "down on the Warnut," southwest of Emporia, then scarcely as much as a wide place in the road. On the journey I came within an ace of my life. It was spring. The creeks were swollen. We were traveling by spring wagon. We were crossing a stream and missed the ford. The wagon lurched. I was wrapped in a big brown shawl and was thrown into the swiftly moving spring flood. For two or three seconds I floated, and in those seconds I was rescued by the driver of the team and went on my way rejoicing, in my deep infantile sleep. My memory tells me that I waked up when I was nearly two years old. I was in my father's arms. Near me was a large round sheet-iron stove in a rather large living room with a bed in one corner and a door leading to the kitchen-dining-room of a frame house, my home. My father, with his pocketknife, was scraping an apple into pulp and feeding it to me on the point of his knife, and I was gurgling in delight, *a-boo, a-boo, a-boo*. This no one told me. I remember it. And after that I remember many things. For life had begun for me on this planet.

3

Now that I have come to this planet, it may be well to explain how I got here. I cannot go much further back in the stream of life than my grand-parents, though my father's people came to this continent in the 1630's and settled in Massachusetts. My first White ancestor was Nicholas White. I know nothing of four generations that followed except that the Whites lived in the town of Taunton in, or near, the village of Raynham. Tradition says that they were farmers or small storekeepers, officers in the Congregational Church and in the township government.

They belonged to the ruling class. A Hannah Bryant, somewhere in the early 1700's, was said by family tradition to be an aunt or a great-aunt of William Cullen Bryant. And my great-grandmother, Martha Keith, who married John White, a Revolutionary soldier, was a Scotch girl, whose brother and father were engaged during the Revolution at Concord Bridge, firing the shot heard around the world. My grandfather, John White, son of the Revolutionary soldier, was born in 1777, and my girl cousins in the middle of the nineteenth century, when the D.A.R. arose, had a terrible time proving that John White, the Revolutionary soldier of Taunton, Massachusetts, was their great-grandfather. For he was stationed on Long Island with his regiment for a year before John White, his son and my grandfather, appeared. It was a family joke, sixty or seventy years ago, that not until those girl cousins were able to run down in the regimental records a furlough, exactly nine months before my grandfather was born, were they able to prove that John White, the Revolutionary soldier, was their duly accredited ancestor.

Of John White, my grandfather, born during the Revolution, I know next to nothing. For my father, who was nearly fifty years old when I was born, was the youngest of a dozen children or more. He was ten years old when his father died. It was nearly forty years after that I came along. And he told me little about his parents. I know from reading and from family tradition that John White, my grandfather, was born in 1777; that his father had an iron foundry, making what was known as hog iron, near Taunton. Andrew Carnegie has a monument in Taunton to the first iron ever produced in America —probably by John, my great-grandfather, the Revolutionary soldier; and in that foundry the second John, my grandfather, worked and learned his trade. In the latter part of the eighteenth century, when he was twenty years old (in 1797, to be exact), he married Fear Perry, of Lee, Massachusetts. Of her I know nothing except that she was a strong woman. She bore thirteen children; and an older cousin, born in the middle of the nineteenth century, told me that every year until she died she celebrated her birthday by carrying a full keg of cider into the house, swinging it on her shoulder. That is absolutely all I know of her. And the little more I know of John White, my grandfather, is that he married this husky Fear Perry, daughter

4

of Content Crocker Perry and William Perry. John went into northern New York at the turn of the nineteenth century, set up an iron foundry, and "went broke." He loaded his family of half a dozen children into a covered wagon in the second decade of the nineteenth century and with all of his earthly possessions migrated to Norwalk, Ohio, where he took a claim, and there, every year until he died, he wrestled with the Indians and was famous miles around for his feats of strength.* That is all I know of John White and Fear Perry, my grandparents, who died in the third and fourth decades of the nineteenth century.

I know even less of my mother's people. They were Irish—Irish Catholics. They came from Longford, Ireland, in the last years—probably the last year—of the third decade of the nineteenth century. Their marriage record was spread on the register of the Catholic Cathedral at Longford, Ireland, in 1828, and it is signed in one handwriting. My grandfather, Thomas Hatten, made his mark, and presumably Ann Kelly, my grandmother, wrote the signature of both my grandparents. My mother told me that her father, Thomas Hatten, was a dour, dark-complexioned man—one of the black Irish; that the family legend said that the Hattens had come to Ireland with Cromwell and they had intermarried with the Irish for a hundred and fifty years. My grandfather, so I was told, was a peasant weaver in the day and time when weaving was a cottage industry. My grandmother, Ann Kelly, was from Dublin, and my mother told me that she came with her father, who was a contractor building the Cathedral where their marriage record is preserved. Dublin has enough Kellys to make me a cousin of all Ireland.

But of Ann Kelly I only know this: that she was a merry soul, with a fair complexion and auburn hair. When my mother was born January 3, 1830, across Lake Ontario from Oswego, New York, they lived in the timber. As little babies came later, my grandfather had to go several miles to his work—whatever it was—and my mother said that Ann Kelly took

---

* When John White died in mid-autumn of 1829 his widow, Fear Perry, and his eldest son, Union White, were made joint executors of his estate. His chattels on the farm where he died were listed thus for probate:

One Steer	$ 6.50	One year-old Steer	$ 4.00
Four Calves	8.00	Five Hogs	12.00
One Cart	9.50	Six Pigs, fifty cents each	3.00
One Grindstone Crank	1.00	Five Shoats	6.50
Two Scythes and Snaths	1.00	Twenty-one Geese	3.23
One Iron Kettle	1.00	Deceased's interest in Six tons of	
One yoke of Bulls	20.00	Hay	12.00
One Cow	9.00	Eighteen bushels of Corn	4.50
One Cow	8.00	Twenty bushels of Wheat	10.00
Two Cows, $6.50 each	13.00	One Ox Yoke and Staple	10.43
One Heifer	6.00	Two Chains	3.50

5

her babies every day several miles to get milk. And when times were hard and Thomas Hatten was away at his work and her spirits were low, sometimes to the amazement of the children and by way of cheering herself up, Ann Kelly used to roll her skirts and petticoats about her hips, clear the meager furniture from the middle of the room, and dance and dance and dance and sing until her soul was refreshed. Living with a dour, dark Irishman required a certain amount of physical stimulation. She died when my mother was a young girl. Her husband had died several years before. Ann Kelly married again a man whom my mother described many years later in a letter as "a worthless Englishman." Then she died, leaving three children of Thomas Hatten.

My mother, the oldest of the children, had not been confirmed as a Catholic. In her teens she moved west with a Congregational family to Galesburg, Illinois. She had the indomitable spirit of the Irish, and the ravening lust of the Irish to get on, and she knew that she must have an education. She spent ten years in Knox College, off and on, earning her way until she finished her sophomore year. Every other year she went out and earned money to go back to college. She learned in those ten years every trade that a respectable woman could know. She served as a hired girl and learned to cook. She was an apprentice to a milliner and learned to make and trim hats. She was a practical nurse and also served as seamstress for a year. I have seen her record in Knox College, and her grades were good. She must have been a good student. She had a strong, clear mind.

While my mother was earning her way, my father was going along with his career. When his parents died in the 1830's he was in his middle teens. He began clerking in a store and teaching school. And somewhere in his late teens or early twenties, he managed to spend two years in the medical school at Columbus, Ohio, a town not far from his birthplace. Most of the money he had saved; but some of it he borrowed from his brother Daniel, who was a prosperous merchant in Clyde, Ohio, putting up, as security, his key-winding, twenty-four-carat gold watch. That debt turned up nearly ninety years later, and I now have the watch back, for the Whites were, all of them, careful about money. He was unable to complete his medical course and went back to work; started a store at Delta, Ohio, where he sold cloth and employed a tailor to make clothing, or associated with him, I don't know which. He advertised in the local paper that he made and sold concentrated lye, which was used for soap making. And then, sometime in the middle forties, he went to a medical school in Cleveland, Ohio, where he was graduated and became a doctor. In the meantime, somewhere along the line of his life, I don't know where, probably

6

in the late forties or the early 1850's, he married his boarding-house keeper, an esteemed woman who had sons almost as old as he.

Naturally it was not a happy marriage. He became restless. He went to Texas looking for a location, leaving his family in Ohio. But after three months in Texas he came back, and family tradition during my childhood, twenty years later, still recounted the horrors of the Texas cooking where they fried everything, didn't know about broiling meat, or roasting it, and used grease so heavily that my father's Yankee palate was deeply offended. He was a Democrat in those days and wanted to live in a Democratic state. But he could not endure the greasy Democratic cooking and fled from Texas as from a pestilence! In the late fifties, early in 1859 to be exact, my father moved with his motherly wife and his ready-to-wear, hand-me-down family of boys to Kansas. He was an antislavery Democrat, and he dearly loved politics.

My mother in those days at Galesburg, Illinois, was a black abolitionist Republican. In 1858, seated in a window of a building still standing on the campus at Knox College,* my mother heard the fifth and best of the famous Lincoln-and-Douglas debates. There she fell madly, platonically, but eternally, in love with Abraham Lincoln. It was here, in their politics, that these two began to live in my tradition and in my consciousness. Never had a child more strongly minded parents, and never had a child parents who were so profoundly different in all their ways of thinking, in all their convictions and in all the passing phases of their political and emotional expression. Looking back upon them and upon the background of each of them, since I came to know it only in my late life, I am amazed that they lived together with an approximation of peace and amity for something more than fifteen years.

From old letters, from newspaper clippings, from the stories of men and women who knew them, from family photographs, and from the family tradition which came to me, I can make a picture of them as they were when they first met. My mother was blonde, with an exceptionally fair skin and dark red hair which she wore in long curls that fell to her shoulder. She was a little creature and weighed less than ninety pounds, five feet three or four inches in height. She had been interested in things of the spirit in those days and read widely. She spoke German as well as English, partly academic German which she had acquired in Knox College, and particularly because she had worked as a hired girl in a German family early in her orphanage. Her eyes were hazel and were not her best feature; but they opened widely and were intelligent. She had a gentle voice and spoke rather correctly, indeed precisely as befitted a schoolma'am. But she was

---

* Known colloquially as "Old Main."

7

absolutely a humorless person. Her idea of quick and devastating repartee to a friend's parry or thrust was then and always, "Oh, so that's it, is it?" —with great sarcasm in her voice!

She gave her heart and soul to the abolition movement. In Galesburg, she sat under the pulpit of Edward Beecher, had heard Henry Ward Beecher lecture, and had listened to the contemporary abolition orators in various Illinois campaigns before the Civil War. She was emotional and most sentimental. She made her way—a hard way—for twenty years before she came west to Emporia. She came to enter the new Kansas State Normal School in 1865; rode in on the stage with the young president of the school, Lyman B. (for Beecher, to indicate the temper of the times) Kellogg, who afterwards became probate judge of the county,* state senator and attorney general of Kansas, a man of distinction. He always said she was a proud little piece, sitting on the box with the driver. She dressed in some taste, as there is a family picture of her in low neck and short sleeves with her curls. It had been tinted on the cheeks by the local photographer, and it reflects an earnest and lovely spirit, also intrepid, with the mouth something more than merely kissable. She was thirty-five when she got off the stage at Emporia; and thirty-five in the middle sixties qualified her as an old-maid schoolteacher. She was not afraid to go into the wilds of Kansas, a hundred miles from a railway, into a pioneer town with wild buffalo and wild Indians roaming less than one hundred miles to the westward. She wore size two and one-half shoes and had even to her last day trim ankles and slim legs, yet she walked on her heels like a captain of artillery. And under her shimmering white skin it was all solid iron in heart and soul.

That was the kind of girl who met my father at a dance in Emporia in the fall of 1865, and this was the kind of man she met. He was forty-six years old; not much taller than she, probably five feet five and one-half inches, he weighed two hundred and twenty pounds. He wore little sawed-off, paintbrush chin whiskers, rather more than a goatee, less than a beard, a smooth upper lip—cleft, as his chin was almost dimpled as I saw it once when he was shaved. He had dark hair, and in his middle forties was just beginning to get a dingy gray. He dyed it, being proud to hold the illusion of youth in his hair as well as his heart. But, of course, the dye fooled no one. It was then, as always to his last day, a bad job of dyeing. But it expressed his vanity. He was quick and nimble on his feet, and old ladies in Emporia long after his death remembered he was a good dancer, as a fat man often is. He had a hard, tough mind. He was a thrifty young man, but apparently he made money easily, saved it without much agony or com-

---

* Lyon County, Kansas.

8

punction. His eyes were gray-blue and his skin was dark, and he had hair like an ape all over him, his legs, arms, and chest. He was rather meticulous about his clothes and, being fussy, gave his tailor many hours of heartbreak. He also was accounted well read, as most of the young fellows were who came to Emporia in the fifties and sixties. They were college men, many of them from the small New England colleges, for this was a Yankee settlement. His nickname—for all of the gentry had names from fictional characters—was Count Fustin, out of a Bulwer-Lytton novel.

His indignation had a low boiling point, but he also was a stayer and a sticker and loved to walk with a minority. He was a Democrat during the war. They called him a Copperhead because he believed in a negotiated peace and thought that Lincoln should have insisted upon a peace conference even after Sumter. He hated slavery, being a northern Democrat, and wanted the government to buy the slaves and free them and set them by themselves somewhere—Texas, Africa, California, anywhere to get rid of them—to run their own civilization. He endured during four years of the war all the contumely that a man must endure in a community where every able-bodied man was a soldier at war and he, who was undersized, overweight and had lost the trigger finger on his right hand and was just over-aged, remained at home. In the town and county they always said, even the G.A.R. boys when they came back patronizing him heavily, that "old Doc White" (and he was "old Doc White" in his thirties) never charged the wife or children of a soldier at the front for any services while the war was on, which made his practice pretty much charity.

He loved medicine but never could make it pay because he did not keep his collections up. So every few years, being a Yankee and a natural trader, he would retire from practice and make some money, pay his debts, get a little ahead, and then go at medicine again. For he was made of the martyr's stuff, though he had in his heart an eternal wellspring of good nature, good humor, and good jokes. He told a story well, and if he ever stopped five minutes on the street he drew a crowd around him by some kind of spiritual gravity. After he had been dead many years I came to know the kind of man he was and learned scores of funny stories that he had told, scores of jokes that he had played, scores of devilments that he was in. He always was the butt of his own joke, the center of his own grotesque tomfooleries. Yet here is a contradiction. He wore a plug hat and carried a cane, to give his short, waddling body dignity. In summer he always wore white clothes, a round white Panama hat that was his great pride. The clothes were called nankeen—white with a greenish sheen. The coat and the trousers and his shirt were starched and pleated, and he changed his outfit overy day; for every day there were one or two, and at most three, small brown tobacco spots on his shirt. He carried fine-cut tobacco for himself in a silver box in the right-hand back pocket of his trousers, and plug tobacco for his friends. I think this was a pose. I think he always offered them the plug tobacco first and then hastily apologized and gave them a pinch of the fine-cut instead —his idea of a joke! Probably this eternal joking was a defense measure against his diminutive height and his rolypoly figure.

The war was over when he met my mother. He had gone through it an antiwar Democrat but, curiously enough, an abolition Democrat. Stranger than all, he had come to respect and admire Lincoln. But when he died I found in the library a Life of Vallandigham, an Ohio Copperhead Democrat, well worn, dog-eared—obviously to him something more than "a volume of forgotten lore."

It was not enough that he should be a Democrat in a town where 80 per cent of the men were in the Union Army. He had to be a "freethinker." Sometime in the midst of war he burst into a controversy in the Emporia News because he had sawed wood on Sunday. The church people attacked him, and he defended himself humorously, but in rather too stately language and deeply involved sentences. He tried to show them that the Sabbath was made for man. The row ran through the columns of the Weekly News for several issues—two months, perhaps; and apparently the editor had to shut it off, for my father wrote with considerable pompous verbosity and consumed a lot of space.*

When my mother tried to enter the Kansas State Normal School in 1865 she was unable to get a room in the town. It was a little town—probably not more than four or five hundred inhabitants—and rooms were scarce. So she went north to the next county-seat town, Council Grove, where she had friends who had known her in Galesburg, indeed the friends with whom she had come west from Oswego to go to school at Knox College. There she had no trouble in getting a school.

Council Grove at that time was known as a nest of southern sympathizers. When she opened the school she announced that colored children in the town would be welcome. Threats were made against her if they came. They came. She took an octoroon girl. When an indignant parent came to protest against the "damn nigger" in the school, my mother told him to pick out the "nigger." The octoroon was sitting beside his own daughter. The angry parent could not identify the "damn nigger" and went away fuming. The little town was in turmoil. Crowds milled around the building. My mother stood her ground. The story spread all over Kansas. An abolition attorney, Sam Wood, of near-by Cottonwood Falls, came up to Council Grove and took her case into court. The colored children stayed. The law

---

* The discerning reader will have a sample of this writing a few pages ahead, to his amazement and delight.

prevailed. But Mary Ann Hatten was a one-term teacher. The episode advertised her spunk and pluck to the state, and, being her son, I can imagine that she liked it. She was a heroine. I fancy she realized that the golden glint of her halo matched her peach and white complexion, and she was proud of the adornment.

So the next term of school she taught was at Cottonwood Falls, the adjacent county seat, and she opened her school and boarded at the home of her protector, Sam Wood. But Mrs. Wood was a statesman also, and the cooking was bad, and the housekeeping, according to the standards of a Yankee Irish old-maid schoolma'am, was sketchy. Specifically, she told me there were bedbugs and unpunctual meals. So at the end of her second year in Kansas, in the late winter or early spring, she left for Galesburg to complete the course which she had hoped to finish at the Kansas State Normal School. Here begins the romance that landed Willie White—a husky, pudgy, squalling, kicking, lusty, red baby—in Emporia between nine and ten o'clock on the morning of February 10, 1868.

CHAPTER II

"Love Comes and We Wonder Why—"

So MATTERS STOOD when 1866 rolled around. My father, a grass widower of several years, was keeping a store to recoup his medical losses. Keeping a store in 1866 in Emporia, Kansas, meant that two or three times a year he took the stagecoach to Leavenworth, or St. Louis, or Kansas City, to buy goods. His was a general store: dry goods and groceries, hats, caps, boots, shoes, and notions, with nails and shelf hardware. This was the setting for the preliminaries to the wedding of Allen White and Mary Ann Hatten. In 1866, she visited in Emporia with a friend from Council Grove, one of those who had stood by her in her desire to admit colored children to the white school. They went into my father's store to buy some knives for the Council Grove home. He waited on them. The slight figure of a woman in her middle thirties who had defied the beasts of Ephesus at Council Grove, the pink and white complexion, the red-brown curls seemed to have impressed the Doctor, though the effect on Mary Hatten of the pudgy little man who sometimes wore a plug hat and habitually carried a cane outside of his store, apparently was just nothing. She left Kansas a few days later with no sort of idea that the man who had sold her Council Grove friend the knives could ever enter her life again.

Apparently he began to inquire about her. The mutual friends in Cottonwood Falls and Council Grove, where she had taught, answered his inquiries. And early in September he sat down and wrote this letter to Galesburg, Illinois, where she had gone expecting to enter school, and then changed her plans:

Emporia Lyon Co., Kans. Sept. 7/66

Miss Mary Hatten

I trust you will pardon me for this unexpected communication after so short an acquaintance with you. Having been favorably impressed with your personal appearance while at my house and learning more of your History by a personal friend of yours, I felt assured that a friendly letter written to you by me would not result in any harm to you or to me to say the least, if written with Sincerity and an honest purpose. My object Miss Hatten in writing you is to make more fully your acquaintance. And in the event that our acquaintance should prove satisfactory to both parties and we felt assured that it would result profitably and happily: Then to unite our fortunes in this world in *Matrimony*. I can assure you that I am not blind to the difficulties and embarrassments, I labor under in attempting to make your acquaintance for such an important purpose. My History pertaining to domestic relations are not as prepossessing as I would desire by no means. But Should you after a carefull and deliberate reflection feel assured that a short corrispondence upon this Subject would not be incompatible with your feelings and unproffitable to your time I would take pleasure in affording you every opportunity of Knowing the true History appertaining to my Misfortunes. I regret exceedingly that you left the Grove so soon after my introduction to you. Mrs. Everett sent me word by Mr. Vigus, I think his name was, she would come and keep house for me this winter. I made a visit to the Grove to get her. But she gave me the *mitten*. Hopeing that this latter will meet with favor I remain

Respectfully yours,
ALLEN WHITE

P.S. I mail this at Leavenworth City Sept. 18th.

ALLEN WHITE

Emporia, Kans.
February 8th, 1867

Miss Hatten

This letter was written last September as you will see from the date. It went to Galesburg and then to Washington D.C. and then to Pontiac Mich. and from there home again. I learned a few days ago that you were in Lapeer Michigan and I now send the original letter to you. Hopeing that this letter will find you in good health and spirits I remain

Very respectfully
ALLEN WHITE

The strange, stuffy, formal letter went to the dead letter office in Washington and then came back. Again he sought to find her, and finally the letter reached her and brought back this answer:

Lapeer Mich
Feb 19th 1867

Mr. Allen White

Your unexpected letter reached me at last and has been read and duly appreciated. It is too bad that Mrs. E would not accept your offer. I think you must have dropped your hat on the blind side. By the way did Miss Streiby give you the mitten too? Please excuse the briefness of this letter. I will write more should we become better acquainted.

Very respectfully
MARY HATTEN

These letters, which I found in an old trunk many years after my mother's death and more than three-quarters of a century after they were written, are reproduced here to show the unromantic background of a strange marriage which brought me into this world. The next letter came right to the point. Notice how my father liked to use big words. The manuscript indicates he could not always spell them correctly, but he has the pompous syntax and rhetoric of an undersized, fat man who wore a plug hat and carried a cane. Where his sense of humor was—how he could have strutted so—only Heaven, that knows the secrets of our heart, can tell. Presently came this declaration, which is certainly sub-Romeo by at least forty degrees:

Emporia, Kans. Feb. 27, 1867

Miss Mary Hatten

Your kind but brief letter of the 19th inst. came to hand this morning. I can assure you that brief as it was it afforded me much pleasure to know where you were; even at so late a date. Having written you on the 7th of Sept. last at Galesburg, Ill. and it finding no one there to own it, then it went to Washington and then back to me again. I then sent it to Pontiac with instructions if not called for in ten days to return to me. Again it came back and I then sent it to Lapeer. I now thank my Stars that it has found a resting place at last. Poor thing, did it not look *fatigued*? As to the side I dropped my hat when in the presens of Mrs. E. I must confess that the embaresment was so great that I have no very distinct recollection about where the hat went to. And as for a *mitten* from Miss Streiby, I think you very *naughty* for asking me this question. You said that you would write more should we become better acquainted. I think unless you write more at length the acquaintance would be all on one side. As it now stands your knowledge of me is better than mine is of you.

But I can assure you Miss Hatten that my object in writing you last Sept. and as well as at this time is to make your acquaintance and in the event that it should prove mutual, then to unite our fortunes together. I am not blind nor unmindful to the objection that you can raise in two very important facts. First discrepancy in age and Second my History touching domestic troubles which no doubt you are familiar with. I take for granted from the tone of your brief little letter that you are willing to write me again. So I now ask you some questions which will furnish you a subject to write about. First, please tell me your age. Second, what constitutes your family connection now living. Third, from your present knowledge of my History, are you willing to persue this investigation and in the event that you should become Satisfied that it would better your condition, would you consent to change your name from Hatten to White. You may think that this question is premature but if you will reflect for a moment it is only to know your present feelings, leaving the matter for future consideration and investigation. Have you at any time since you left the *Grove* thought of returning to Kansas? Do you not think that you could do better in Kansas than in Michigan? The health and climate of Kansas I think is far better than Michigan. Upon looking at the map of Michigan I discern that you are situaated in very high *latitude*. It must have been very cold where you are. We have had a very pleasant winter here in Kans. Except a Good deal of Rain. The two rivers, Cottonwood and Neosho have been very high for the last month. Miss Hatten, I hope you will return to this State this Spring. Please inform me whither you will come back to Kans. I would like to have the pleasure of seeing you soon. If I could be assured that my visit to you would be Proffitable by your permit I would visit you immediately. I hope and trust that you will write me immediately and give me your views and feelings at length. I take it for granted that ether of us are old enough to write with frankness and candor. Trusting in your intelligence and integrity I remain

Very Respectfully
ALLEN WHITE

In answer to this letter, she wrote him very briefly and informally saying she would like to continue the correspondence but not committing herself in any way except that she signed herself, "Confidingly yours." To which he replied:

Emporia, Kans. March 3, 1867

Miss Mary Hatten

In order that our acquaintance may be better facilitated, I sit down to have a little further talk with you tonight, trusting that it will be congenial to your feelings. Will you please inform me why it was that my letters were so long reaching you. . . Failing to hear from you I wrote to Mrs. Sim. . . I recollected the old adage that a faint heart never won a fair lady, so: I then wrote her the second letter, beging her to inform me of your whereabouts. . . . Fearing that I may lose track of you again, with your permit I shall write often. Hoping that each letter will be promptly answered by you.

After Mrs. E. gave me the mitten Miss Jennie Stevenson came to my house to board with Miss Macy for the purpose of attending school. School commenced on the 12th of September and they done the work until the 5th of Oct. when I succeeded in getting a lady which is now with me. Miss Jennie is not with us this quarter neither does she attend School. This term ends about the 27th of this month. The Normal School building was dedicated on the 2nd day of January last. The School is now in successful operation. Numbering some ninety four or five scholars. The Normal School Boarding House will be ready for boarders by the first of June next.

. . . I would like to persuade you to return to Kansas. Assuming as I do from the tone of your letter that you are willing to continue in a correspondence with me, I think it would be better for you to return to Kansas and take a school; this would enable you to know more about the subject you may wish to investigate. Should this not meet your approbation, I would then like with your consent to visit you at Lapeer or any other place you might designate. I expect to visit St. Louis in April for the purpose of buying our Spring and Summer Goods and would like to pay you a visit before or after buying Goods at St. Louis.

. . . After the Spring trade opens I will necessarily be compelled too be at the

Store. I wish Miss Hatten when you answer this letter you will be plain and frank and free to express your honest conviction as you now feel on this important matter. Do not be *timide* in this matter. I have investigated your History and peculiarity since last fall or since I first saw you at my home in Emporia and I am willing to confess that I am well satisfied with the result.

Hoping to hear from you immediately after the receipt of this

I remain
Very respectfully
ALLEN WHITE

Then to this sub-Romeo came back this reply from a puzzled, slightly wounded Juliet. But note the difference in the language, in the use of words, in the something more than maidenly dignity of Mary Hatten:

Lapeer, Mich.
March 11, 1867

Mr. Allen White

Your welcome letter came to hand Saturday evening. I was not quite pleased with it at first, I thought I would send it back but on giving it a second reading I came to the conclusion that I did not quite understand you at first. You are so frank and withall so practical that I humbly confess you do embarrass me. Do you know you are the first one that I could not evade answering a question if I did not choose to. I rather like your style after all and I am going to be just as frank as you are. I supposed from what you said at first that you knew the most of my history. It is very sad and I do not like to dwell upon it so I will only give you a synopsis of it. Let me say right here that I think there are some things too sacred to be canvassed for mere speculative motives. In a word I do not like the idea of setting forth the pros and cons to see if I will do. Perhaps it is all right and proper but I don't like to do it.

Well then my mother and father were Irish of the middle class. My father died of consumtion when I was eight years old, leaving my mother in poverty with three small children unaccustomed to labor and unacquainted with the ways of the world. She married a poor worthless English man in less than a year after my father died. I have taken care of myself most of the time ever since my mother died when I was sixteen years old that was my first great grief for I did not realize my condition until I had lost her love and council. My sister married in about five years afterward and went to Canada to live with her husband's friends. They are well to do respectable farmers. I came west to Illinois, my brother to Mich. We left a little brother behind. I do not know what became of him. I did not know until quite recently what had become of my own brother. I supposed he was in Mich. it was a mear accident through the help of some friends that I found him now. Are you a Mason? I think he is. It was this way that we first heard of him. He had been in the war as Capt. in the 1st Mich. Cav. Several of his men live here, one of them learning my name and thinking that I resembled him went to my brotherinlaw and asked him if he had a brotherinlaw by the name of Frank Hatten, from that beginning we have traced him to Leavenworth Kansas. He is in the State prison. Not a convict however but an over-seer. He was wounded and lost the use of one of his arms. We are looking for him or a letter every day. I am living with my brotherinlaw and sister. They are respectable and in comfortable circumstances. They have two little boys Miron and Eddie. My brotherinlaws name is William H. White. Wight his father spells it. I believe that is all. I will stop to say about my family connection and humble though they be I am just as proud as though I belonged to the most aristocratic family in the land. Now about going back to Kan. I don't remember ever saying or intimating to any one that I ever should to stay. Why do you ask? I like it there much better than I do here notwithstanding it has been the sene of much sorrow to me for that reason and none other did I come away. For that reason perhaps I had better stay away.

And now my dear friend about the name and the age. I should be loath to part with my own name Hatten. It has served me a long time thirty five years. Not so much difference in our ages after all is there? I like the name of White, I think it a very simple pure name. Your domestic troubles I know very little about save that you parted with your wife. I take it that you have a legal right to address me further than that I don't know that I have any particular interest. Should everything else prove satisfactory I don't think that would stand in the way. I think it would be very embarrassing to both parties. It seems to me too that I would be very little help to you in your trying position. Don't you think a more showy woman than I am would suit you better? It seems strange to me with your practical view that you should find anything attractive in so plain a person as me. Now I have written quite a long letter for me, answered all your hard questions I believe. So I will bid you good night. Hoping to hear from you soon

Yours confidingly
Mary Hatten

Then these two letters followed in this strange, punctilious courtship:

Emporia, Kansas, March 19th, 1867

Miss Mary Hatten
  My dear Friend
  Your Kind and affectionate letter of the 13 inst. came to me this morning. . . . Your History is just what I anticipated. The very desideratum (if I may be allowed the fraze in this place) I have sought for over one year past. Your humble and obscure History together with your Self reliance and pride of individuality and desition of character at this time or when in this State has prompted me to my indefatigable exertion to ascertain your address. The desition of character you manifested and carried out persistingly at the time you taught at the Grove when the colored lady was Sent to your School was one act that met my full and entire approbation. . . .
  Your History, together with that auburn hair and those expressive eyes and Pink complexion are sufficient attraction for me. . . . I had always noticed that

choice goods were folded in small packages. . . . Please excuse and pardon me for my jokes for it is my nature.

I to Miss Hatten spring from a very humble parentage. My Father and Mother were borne in New England. My Father's ancestry can be traced to Scotland and my Mother to Holland. My Father died in Norwalk Ohio June 1829. My age was ten at that time. My Mother died at the same place in the year thirty five. At the time of My Mother's death there were then living nine children, I being the youngest, leaving us without any visible means of support. I obtained a very limited education while my parents were living. After their death I availed myself of every opportunity my limited means would allow of to obtain an education. I commenced the study of medicine at the age eighteen Having no means except what I earned by clerking and teaching. I did not enter the Practice of Medicine until I had arrived at the age of twenty two years old. The winter of 44 & 5 I attended one course of Medical Lectures at Cleaveland Ohio. I lived at Delta Ohio as a young man and was Postmaster there when I was twenty-four years old. I have saved my Postmaster's Commission which will probably interest you.

. . . You did not ask me for my History but I concluded to volunteer trusting that you will not deem it improper or egotistical in me. I would here say that I own the house I live in and half of the building and goods that I occupied when you looked at some knives. Would it be asking too much of you to send me your picture. Hopeing you will continue to be prompt with your answers to my letters

I remain your affectionate and confiding friend

ALLEN WHITE

Emporia Friday Eve
March 22d 1867

Miss Mary Hatten
    My dear Friend
    Your kind letter of the 14th came to hand this afternoon about 5 o c, welcoming me to your far off home in Michigan. I will come as soon as I can arrange my matters to go to St. Louis. . . . I shall go via St. Louis but not buy any Goods until I return. Hoping to have Some One with me too help Select Goods. I shall visite you with the full hope that you will be fully prepared to return to Kansas with me. Not from any promis that you have made during our correspondence. But your Kind letters have inspired me with a belief that if we could meet and unfold our feelings to each other, that our attachments would be reciprocal and immutable. . . .

My Dear friend Miss Hatten, I hope you will Sympathize with me in this plain talk. It is not my *Nature* to live alone. I trust you will pardon me for this remark. I possess a reasonable share of the Goods of this world but they are but little use to me without a bosom companion to consult with, too confide with, too love and cherish. . . . Do not laugh when I say that I must and will see you as soon as the 10th or 15th of April Kind providence permitting then I shall expect two lumps sugar one enclosed in an Egg Shell and the other will be encassinated in a small crinoline. Where is the Joke now. If I start to St. Louis on the first day of April an ansur to this would not reach me here. You can answer it immediately and direct it to St. Louis in this way:

Dr. Allen White
in care of L. Levanson & Co.
St. Louis, Mo.

In your letter that you write to St. Louis Please inform me the best Route from Chicago to Lapeer. I would like for you to be very definite in regard to the Rout.

I remain steadfast and confidingly your Friend,

ALLEN WHITE

Then followed several short letters, mere railroad directions and time tables, and then the wedding. The wedding occurred at Lapeer, Michigan, April 15, 1867.

When the happy couple got off the stage at Emporia from their honeymoon they were met by a crowd and the Emporia band, with appropriate cheers and felicitous greetings, and conducted in as good a procession as the town could muster to their home, where a wedding feast had been spread by the neighbors. And it was all very gay. And as a fitting climax, set in the ribald humor of the times, the young married women, whom I met thirty years later as sedate matrons and gray-haired widows, had bedecked with blue and pink ribbons the handles of all the yellow-striped chamber pots. One of them told me about it forty years later, in her late seventies, with reminiscent giggles that flashed back into the modes and manner of the days that have since folded into sunset.

Practical jokers ranged America in the middle of the nineteenth century, and my father was one. Probably these local clowns, who sometimes were most elaborate in their plots and schemes, fed the appetite which the movies now satisfy. But a practical joker like my father, married to a humorless woman, had easy going but, in the end, a hard time. One of my mother's complaints in the early days of her marriage was that "the Doctor" used to bring home from the store the country butter that he had taken in trade. She claimed that it was all bad, that Kansas women could not make butter, and that she wanted her own cow. One noon he came back from the store with a butter bucket, covered with a clean white tea towel.

And he began: "Now, Ma, here is something special."
And she began: "Now, Doctor, haven't I always told you?"
But he cut in: "Now, Ma, just wait—just look at this butter!"
And again her voice lifted: "Now, Doctor—"
"But smell it, Ma, smell it! See how nice and fresh it smells!"
She bent over and cried: "Now, Doctor, haven't I told you? It just stinks!"
Then he lifted the cloth and revealed a bucket of fresh new apples that

smelled like a Garden of Eden; and it was a family joke for many years—a joke my mother until her dying day could not entirely enjoy.

I once asked my mother's sister, Aunt Kate, who was the dancing Ann Kelly reincarnated, why these two middle-aged people ever united, and Aunt Kate twinkled her eye and answered:

"Oh, Will, they both wanted a baby!"

And so I came into this world nine months and twenty-five days after the ceremony was finished. The anonymous birth notice in the Emporia News was my bow to the world.

Soon after I was born my father began looking for a new location. Emporia was getting too thick. A town of five hundred was more civilized and sophisticated than he could bear. So he went sixty miles southwest to what then was known as "the Walnut"! The town was Eldorado. Probably less than a hundred people lived in Eldorado when he opened his store, in a rambling one-story frame-building with a black sheet-iron stovepipe sticking out of the roof over each of the six rooms, and naturally it was known in the countryside as "the foundry." The long procession of settlers moving out of the eastern Mississippi Valley into the western watershed of the Mississippi passed our house every day. We could hear the rumbling wheels far into the night. The dust settled over everything, and my mother, who was a ferret for dust, worked day and night to keep things clean. Perhaps she can describe that little town and that ever-moving procession better than I:

ElDorado, Kan.
Nov. 27, 1870

My dear Mrs. Dunn:

Your kind letter was received. Many thanks for the picture. He is a fine little fellow, looks very much as Eddie did at his age, I think, only he seems taller, he is very much taller than Willie was. I shall not put Willie in pants until spring. I will send you a lock of his hair, he has blue eyes and very fair skin. He talks very plain and knows a good many of his letters.

Your letter was very interesting I can assure you. We are having a very pleasant fall here. There is a large emigration to this portion of the state which makes times lively and money plenty. The streets are full of emigrant wagons all the time, most of them going south. The country about here is nearly all settled. It is astonishing how fast they can build towns out here. We are within sixty-five miles of a railroad now and expect to have one here in less than two years, so you see we are no longer on the frontier. We have a beautiful country and I like the climate much better than Illinois. The winters are more mild and shorter. We have more high winds but I think as the country becomes settled it will pass away. Willie is getting tired of amusing himself and so will not let me write any more. Please remember me to all and write soon.

Sincerely your friend
MARY WHITE

20

I have often wondered how it happened that my father took charge of that town. Everyone agrees that he was its moving spirit. He was a Democrat in a land where the returning soldiers of the Civil War made an overwhelming flood of Republicans, yet he took leadership. A county-seat fight arose with the adjoining town, Augusta. The Eldoradoites built a courthouse with their own funds and turned it over to the county. He headed the subscription list. They hired a man at the county-seat election to commit a palpable election fraud, voting names from the city directory of Buffalo, New York, wrong end to: "Jones, William; Smith, John; Robinson, Harry," and so on down the line. And when the artist who committed the crime was convicted, they paid his family a good round monthly sum while he served his term in the penitentiary, until they could wangle him out. I saw a letter the other day in cleaning up my mother's trunk, from J. R. Mead, long since dead, but then living in Towanda, who said:

Dear Doctor:
Enclosed find my fifty-dollar contribution to the Court House.

The check was his part of the funds paid to the family of the election thief. We were so near the frontier that law and order and the decent amenities of civilization often were but scantily observed.

One night in the midst of this county-seat war, Eldorado had word from its spies that a cavalcade was coming from Augusta, armed to the teeth, to take away the county records. Within an hour a hundred young men with their old army rifles, blue-coated soldiers of the Civil War, were in the courthouse and on the roof and in the windows thereof. The cornice of the roof bristled with gun barrels like quills upon the fretful porcupine as Augusta's procession, headed by an ox team and a great dray to carry the records, rolled into town in serried ranks—a little army of invasion. It was a pitch-dark summer night. My father was in command of the defenders. But as he went out of our house, where he had dropped in on some errand, my mother begged him to take off his white clothes, for he was a shining target in that Panama helmet, his pleated shirt, his light suspenders, and his nankeen trousers. But he waved her aside and remarked gayly:

"Well, Ma, when they are aiming at me they won't be shooting at the courthouse!" And he walked out gayly with his cane over his arm and my little dog following him, a funny, fussy, pudgy little fat man, five feet five, playing grotesquely at Richard of the Lion Heart. I have a notion that maybe he cut such a festal figure, more or less ridiculous, that Augusta could not bear to get a bead on him. For he mingled in the crowd, joking with the invaders—whom he knew, of course, behind their masks. When, finally, fearing to rush the armored courthouse, the grim columns from

Augusta turned tail and marched home in the gray dawn, the mob had an indignation meeting where Augusta had gathered to welcome the conquering heroes. They hanged a little fat figure made by stuffing flour sacks with straw, and vented their anger by shooting it to pieces. And that was the end of the county-seat war in Butler County.

My father's next job was to organize the Democratic party in Butler County.* I can remember, as a little boy, going with him in the buggy for days and days as he rode from one neighbor to another, exhorting the Democrats in the various townships in this county, larger than the state of Rhode Island, to come to a county convention. When they came they put out a full ticket and went home with instructions to trade every candidate on it for votes for Vincent Brown for county clerk. To the amazement of the Republicans, he won and the party had a toehold in the courthouse, and so was duly founded.

---

* Augusta, Kans., Aug. 29, 1871

Mr. White, M.D., Sir: Why can't there be a convention called and get up a good old *democratic* ticket for the fall election? For my part I am tired of voting a Republican ticket and this is the sentiment of all the Democrats in this nation.

Yours respectfully,

L. N. BLOOD

CHAPTER III

"A Child Went Forth"

INDIAN SCARES were common in those days. As a baby, my mother took me into a log house across the street from our home where all the women and children of the town, fearing an Indian raid, were gathered while the men did sentry duty. The Indians, of course, were always in my consciousness from babyhood until boyhood. Not that we feared them—much! But stories of Indian uprisings, of murders and kidnapings, of brushes, skirmishes, and battles with soldiers not so far away, from a hundred to five hundred miles, were often told in the town. Naturally, Eldorado boys knew these stories by heart as they played in the woods. Once when I was a little fellow, probably eight or nine years old, half a dozen of us were playing in the underbrush of the timber half a mile from town, maybe swinging on the grapevines, maybe throwing clubs to knock walnuts off the tall trees, filling our hats with wild grapes and gorging ourselves, or if it was fall, and after frost, eating papaws. Whether it was fall or spring or summer, I cannot remember, but the trees were in leaf.

Suddenly, looking into the road, we boys saw a great company of Indians on horseback, halted in the road where it forked a few rods from us. We did not run into the timber, because they were obviously friendly Indians and we were familiar with them. We walked over shyly to look at the red cavalcade in blankets, one or two of them in feathers, men, women, and children. Why they addressed me, I don't know. Maybe I was farther forward in the group of boys, or maybe they addressed us all and I replied. But they asked how far to town, and I told them. And then one of them, a squaw and a leader, said in perfectly good English, "Boy, will you ride with me and show me?"—and I climbed up and the other boys stood envious. We rode into town, I straddling the horn of her saddle, a little fellow whose bare toes toyed with the mane of the Indian's horse. And as we crossed the bridge to ride up Central Avenue and the town turned from its affairs to watch the Indian procession, they saw me. I knew that I was a person of consequence, and I swelled up. Many is the time I moved in pride in later years, but never in such vainglory as when I rode up Central Avenue and the squaw dropped me gently at the town pump and said, "Good boy!" Often bands of Indians like this passed through town, little more than gypsies. These were Sioux going from their Dakota home to visit their comrades, the Comanches, in the Indian Territory.

Sometimes Indians on the trek from the Indian Territory to other reservations raided smokehouses or begged food from kitchen doors as they passed along, and were not above swiping a calf or a colt on their way, if they thought they could. Otherwise they were friendly, gentle people—grotesquely clad and sometimes painted and bedizened and adorned with feathers. Beside the squaw with whom I rode to glory down Central Avenue, was a chief who wore an old plug hat, his blanket and breechclout, his gaudy moccasins—and little else. For I remember that it was a warm day.

But my clearest memory of the Indians comes when I think of Temple Friend, a boy older than I, who as a baby about a year old had been kidnaped by the Indians—leaving his mother scalped and playing dead in an Indian raid in Texas. When Temple came back to Eldorado, he was ten years old, a tall, slim boy with an Indian figure. He was taciturn. And even after he was home a year, he had few English words in his vocabulary, only the necessary words; perhaps he would not use the other words. But he played town ball with us, and blackman, and he could hit a penny on a stick at ten yards with his bow and arrow and wing a bird in the top of the tallest tree. He taught us to make bows and arrows, though my father was expert at that—having learned it of the Indians in his Ohio boyhood. But Temple's arrows were better than my father's. Temple would take us into his home, and his mother would show us her scalp wound to please him. Tradition says, and I believe this is a white lie, that Temple required a price in pennies or candy or whatever was current wampum among the boys, to take us in to see his scalped mother. It doesn't sound reasonable, but the story lived in tradition long after he was gone, probably because he was not there to deny it.

The boy went to school with his younger sisters. And except when play was good (say, ball, or pullaway, or some rough-and-tumble game—he never took to marbles) he stood apart from the rest of us and seemed sour and solemn. The story of his rescue was one of those things that thrilled us as children, and is worth repeating through these seventy long years. Time after time his grandfather, the Reverend John Friend, who had been a missionary to the Indians when the boy was taken, made a sad journey into the Indian nation looking for him. Of course, the government gave the grandfather every opportunity. Year after year he lined up the little boys of every tribe in a row and went down the line calling one word.

24

"Temple," he would whisper gently, not to shock him. "Temple? Temple?"

But no boy responded. Still, year after year, for nine years the old preacher went down that line all over the Indian country where the reservation Indians were caged. One day, he started down the line, softly intoning his everlasting question to a dozen boys standing beside a wall:

"Temple? Temple? Temple?"

And just as he got to the end of the line, as hope was sinking, one boy slapped his breast and cried out:

"Me Temple!"

We boys had never heard such a story, and I doubt if I have heard many to equal that for the thrill of spiritual adventure. It was a sort of radio back into the realms of a baby's memory into some semblance of eternity. Nothing else explains that automatic response. And here is the other part of the story:

Within a year after he left his Indian home, Temple died; his robust physique crumbled; maybe undermined by too much candy, too much petting and too many clothes, not enough sunshine and fresh air, or the lack of jerked buffalo meat. The Indian environment was stronger than the white man's blood. But Temple left me with a lively admiration for the things an Indian boy could do in the woods and on the prairies and at play. And whenever I think of him I think of his grandfather calling through all the years and at last finding the wave length in the baby's memory that would fit the words "Temple, Temple" and bring that miraculous response.

Prairie fires raged up to the outskirts of Eldorado, and I have no lovelier memory in my heart than the night picture of a prairie fire on the high hill horizon east of town, a great raging fire. We would see in silhouette the little figures of men fighting the fire with wet gunny sacks.

The first emotional disturbance in my life came when I was about two years old, probably a little older. A baby brother was born. I cannot now remember why I hated him. Of course it was jealousy; but I hated him with a bitter, terrible hate. And this I am sure I can remember: I sneaked around the corner of the house to the east porch where his crib was, of a summer afternoon, and began pounding him with my little fists. They caught me when his screams called them. I had no remorse that I remember. I cannot bring back any pictures of his early death and recall nothing of his funeral.

I was three years old then and had a sense of my environment. For me it remained a strange and lovely world. Two elderly, devoted and adoring persons, whom I called "Pa" and "Ma," guided me and bowed down before me; and I knew it and ruled them ruthlessly. I was spoiled, as what child born of parents in their late thirties and forties, would not be? I

25

could draw a picture today of my home, the old "foundry," with its long kitchen where the dining table stood, its attached woodshed with the trapdoor into the cellar. And between the woodshed and the kitchen, in a covered corridor, they hung my little swing where I would swing for hours, singing a little bee song—a kind of long *ah-h-h-h* of sheer delight. I was a happy child and found a thousand things to please me. The world was made to bring me delight. There was a living room, ruled in fall and winter by a big, round, sheet-iron stove. On our walnut table the tall lamp sat, and here always newspapers were piled and books strewn. A spare bed filled a far corner. Our very best room, the parlor, I rarely entered; for it was dark there by day, and I was afraid of it. My own little bedroom and my parents' larger bedroom adjoined the living-room and the parlor. Of course, I went in and crawled in between them in the morning and seemed to give them much delight. They did not quarrel then, at least not before me. I must have been eight or ten years old before I was conscious of family differences. But in that Elysian childhood where I first opened my conscious eyes to the world about me, I was shielded from pain and sorrow and lived, if ever a human being did live, in a golden age. I must have had an early sense of tune, for one of my childish recollections is that I stood on the grocery scales in my father's store where he had me sing about "the old man who had a wooden leg and had no tobacco; no tobacco could he beg," of which the chorus was:

> Oh, buckle up my shoe, Johnnie,
> Buckle up my shoe.

I also sang a ballad about Barney O'Flynn, who "had no breeches to wear and got him a sheepskin and made him a pair!" The customers enjoyed it. But this I also remember—that my mother came often rushing in and said: "Now, Doctor, haven't I always told you?"

And she took me in her arms and headed out of the room with me. I did not like this, for I was a born exhibitionist and loved the applause of the multitude. I seemed to turn everything into song. The little bee song of my babyhood became a long cantata which I made up, perhaps—words and tune and all—as I sat, a solitary only child, in the shade of the morning-glories or, best of all, in the barn at the end of our town lot. That barn was my first enchanted palace. Modern childhood has no equivalent to my barn. I don't know how young I was when I invented the story that it was haunted, and scared the daylights out of other children as I pointed to the barn's high rafters, pretending to see faces and fairies which they also pretended to see; and we scared ourselves and wrestled on the hay of the loft and smelled the nice smell of the horses and the cow. Sometimes we sat in the corncrib and watched the pigs beneath, and the chickens.

26

It was all strange and adventurous. The old pig that woofed at us, and that we were sure would eat us if she caught us, made us feel that we were in the presence of a dragon as authentic as that which St. George went forth to slay.

Of Sunday afternoons, Pa and Ma walked with me to the timber between our creek and its junction with the Walnut River. Pa made me hickory whistles and taught me how to tell different trees by their leaves and bark. It was before they had cut out the buckbrush, the wild raspberries, the blackberries, elderberries, and pokeberries. Above this wood's brush were the one-story trees—the papaws, haws, buckeyes, and the redbuds that I loved. Far above these rose the sycamore, the hickory, the elm, the oak, the walnut, the ash, the coffee-bean tree or locust, and the cottonwoods. Walking with Pa and Ma of a Sunday afternoon, I saw squirrels, rabbits, and once in a while Pa would show me a coon at the river's brim, or a hell-diver. Pa had been born in the Ohio woods and loved timber, and he taught me from earliest childhood to know and love the woods. But the thing that gave the woods their glamour for me was that, only a few years before, the Indians had moved out of this timber onto the prairie lands far to the West and the South. I used to play little games by myself in the woods with mythical little Indian boys. And in some way—I never exactly knew how—I imagined or fancied or dreamed it, and I believed that I turned into a little Indian boy and indeed was one. So I believed, or most seriously fancied, that some day soon the Indians would come back and take me with them. I was scared and happy at the fantasy, which hung about me a long time—maybe a week, a month or half a year.

Then, of course, I had the prairies, the wide illimitable stretches of green in their spring and summer verdure, stretching westward from my front door, with not a dozen rivers or important streams, to the Rocky Mountains six hundred miles away. As a child, I did not know how far they went. To me, they were merely illimitable beyond the horizon and nothing could happen to me except the bite of a rattlesnake; and I never heard of a boy being bitten by a rattlesnake in my childhood. So the woods, the little stream, the prairies, and the dusty road by my door were my playgrounds.

And how I loved the velvety highway dust! It was thick and felt good to my skin, especially to my bare feet. I loved to throw it up in the air, make great clouds of it and feel it fall in my face. And I imagine that no small part of the joy was in being hauled out and scolded by my mother. All mothers along all dusty highways, since little Cain and Abel played in the dust on the road past Eden, have had that problem of children turning primitive in the dust—wallowing in it, kicking it up and heaving it into the air. Like all sweet, forbidden sin, it had its penalties. I had to be scrubbed and scolded at the same time. But it was cheap sin at that.

27

As a little child, before I went to school, I remember the delight of the prairies in the spring and summer when the grass was green and the wild flowers grew everywhere. I used to bring them in little sweaty handfuls to my mother with much delight—foolish little bouquets that I thought were lovely. Two or three hundred yards from our house, where I used to play on these prairies as a child, was a little rock-bottomed creek. In later years they dammed it. But before the dam filled up its channel I was allowed, when I could not have been more than four or five years old, to go down to its banks to play. In the riffle we had a little water wheel which gave me great delight. Here and there, as this brook wormed its way across the prairies, were little pools into which the water ran over the sparkling brown and golden pebbles, and in them silversides, sunfish, and minnows played and could be had with a string and a pinhook. But I caught few. I loved better to watch them, for long minutes, swerving about in tiny schools with tadpoles and sometimes a little turtle, which I brought home and kept in a can or the rain barrel until it got away. I wonder now —I have often wondered—about those little brooks and the courses that they cut in the prairies. For sixty years streets and houses have wiped out those kindly rivulets and springs. In all the prairies across these latitudes, the plow has come and filled the brooks. Even the verdure of the prairies and the pastures is different. The brooks are dry. The land has changed. The white man has come with his presence. The primeval fairyland has gone—fled before the grim reality of man's harrow and his plow, his highway and his house, his horse and his cattle, and all the ugly realities of man's fight to live by the sweat of his brow. The red man, who did not sweat much nor stop to drive away the fairies, knew in some ways how to live more easily in this land than his proud white brother.

As a little child, before they caught and bound me to a school desk, I remember spring, summer, and golden autumn as though I had lived always out of doors. In winter I ranged around the rooms of "the foundry." My mother had pasted copies of the old Emporia News on the kitchen walls to make it warmer there. And while she worked I used to stand and pick out my letters from the advertisements and spell little words and play with my blocks and toys around the big sheet-iron heating stove. The chunks it ate were too big for me to carry, but I cannot remember when I did not have to fill up the woodbox back of the kitchen stove. And there were chips to rake up around the woodpile and bring in for kindling, and cobs to gather. I cannot remember when these duties began, so it must have been early. We called them chores. I am ashamed to admit that the machinations of grown-ups at first concealed from me the fact that they were evil and onerous. I did chores cheerfully in the primitive, savage simplicity of childhood.

CHAPTER IV

The Sophisticate!

BUT I WAS not entirely unsophisticated in those pre-school years. I also had my sly tricks and manners. I knew some way, even then, how to clown, steal a laugh, and avert a crisis. How vividly this picture stands out in my memory! I am sitting by the south window of my bedroom with the sun falling upon me—sitting with my elbows on my knees and my head thrown back, squatting in my little night drawers split down the back, on my little yellow-green striped chamber pot, and I can hear my mother cry:

"Doctor, doctor, come here!"

And both their faces are peering through the door as I lift up my lusty childish treble—I know it was in tune and on key:

"I 'anta be a nangel and with the angels stand."

Whatever cloud hovered over me, I have forgotten, but the memory that I was beclouded remains. Indeed, the sweet and satisfying knowledge that I had come from under the clouds remains with me still. If life chained me to its duties, I also was wily enough even as I toddled out of infancy to pad the chains with guile.

It was about this time, somewhere late in my third or early in my fourth year, when I made my first public stage appearance. I was always speaking pieces or singing lusty songs for my father at the store. But this time the town went to the courthouse for tableaux, and Leila Heaton and I were dressed to kill—I in a little plug hat with a little black coat and a little high-collared shirt, and she in some long doll dress. We appeared as General and Mrs. Tom Thumb, and I first received the plaudits of the multitude while I first felt the vague sweet pain of love. Leila Heaton, so far as I can remember, was the first object of my adoration. Her mother was a widow and ran the millinery store, and Leila had a big brother—old and very tough, maybe seven or eight years old—of whom I was afraid. And she had lovely gray eyes and dark hair, with corkscrew curls that ranged about her shoulders.

I can remember that she called me "Willie" so sweetly that it was a lovely thing to hear. The affair must have been a town scandal. For someone—maybe a big boy or a big girl, it could not within reason have been a grown-up—told me one day that Albert Ewing had taken Leila Heaton into Myer's Candy Store and Ice Cream Saloon. I waited furtively and with the fever of murder pounding in my heart, in the doorway of Ed Ellet's store near by. When the guilty pair appeared, I rushed at them; Albert Ewing fell upon his back, and we rolled together in the board sidewalk dirt—I with the old blood lust of Cain in my heart and he with Abel's fear and amazement in his eyes. The other day Albert and I were talking about it. He insists it was not he, but Theodore Dunlevy, whom I waylaid. I know it was Albert, for I have never quite been able to obliterate the memory of the rage and jealousy with which I pounced upon him—aged four!

My little brother Freddie died when I was still a little fellow. My mother was distraught, and the Ohio family said my father brought her to Ohio to get her away from the lonely home where the baby's little cry in his last illness echoed through the rooms of the old "foundry."

Another thing: I am sure my father went to show me off to his Ohio kin—brothers who were grown-up young men and had soldiered in the Union Army, had reared their families, and heretofore had probably been sniffy with him in his thirties and forties with a wife past the childbearing age, and with only a hand-me-down, secondhand family.

As a final reason for the trip, my father had a formal authorization as a Solicitor of Aid from the Butler County commissioners (it was, in Kansas, a drought and grasshopper year), and a most elaborate document with a red seal and blue ribbon, signed by Thomas Osborn, Governor of Kansas, authorizing Dr. Allen White to collect money in Ohio. He went at his own expense to solicit aid. He brought back two carloads of clothes and provisions.

Anyway, I had my first railroad ride, and looking down from the heights of the passenger-car window, with my child's eyes all untrained and all undisciplined to perspective, I saw strange things. I have the loveliest memory of the weenty-teenty little men in the fields and the tiny little horses and the little bitsy plows I saw when I rode from Florence down the Cottonwood Valley and presently on across into the great land of Ohio. But here follows the story of "man's duplicity and woman's worse than wickedness": I still cherish a picture deeply etched in my heart: I am sitting on a shady, grassy slope, ranging down to a river from a house much, much larger than "the foundry," which then was the largest house in Eldorado—a beautiful house of two stories, with evergreens around it. I had never seen such evergreens. And there were lovely dandelions. I had never known such gay flowers. Their pollen got on my chin and nose when I smelled them. I was sitting there in the shade on that grassy slope, eating wild strawberries with a lovely little girl with dark hazel eyes, flaxen hair, and pink cheeks. I swear that I know I was flirting, untrue to Leila Heaton. And I liked it! I am sure of this picture because nearly fifty years later in Paris, right after the World War, I met a woman in one of the uniforms American girls and women wore there in the war. And when we fell to talking she said:

"Were you ever in Clyde, Ohio?"

And I said I was there as a little child.

She said: "Do you remember a little girl who lived next door to your Uncle Daniel?"

And I answered: "Did she have light brown eyes and yellow hair?"

The woman nodded.

I said: "Yes."

"Well," she said, "some way, God knows how, she has identified you as a little boy who visited there and played with her."

She was my first philandering conquest, and that before I was five. Lord, how deeply in our hearts God has planted that sweet poison.

They were a stern lot, those Whites—and in particular my Uncle Daniel. I remember he tapped on his glass when I talked too much at the table. He made me eat everything on my plate. His eyes followed me around the room, and I knew he thought I was going to break everything in the house. I wish I had known then what I knew nearly fifty years later, when one of the old cousins, in her doddering eighties, told me that all the family knew that Daniel "kept a woman" in Chicago.

About the time that I was first sipping the stolen waters of love in Ohio, I also learned of death. Of course I had seen death many times, though I do not remember it. Neighbors had died, old and young. But no one's death brought the realization of death to me. I seemed to have reasoned it out. Probably I asked questions. But it came over me with a profound shock that everyone must die, and I too; that we are in this life, and the only escape is death. And I was frightened. It was not the fear of heaven or hell. I cannot remember that hell's terms ever bothered me. My father was a freethinker out of a Congregational background. My mother was a Congregationalist out of a Catholic background. I was put into Sunday school as soon as I could toddle. But all I can remember of my first consciousness of death is lying in my bed in the dark night, amazed and frightened at death as the outward portal of life which may not be escaped. Death was a terror, a change from the animate to the inanimate, something that I could not explain and did not understand, and it set a horror in my heart which probably is deep in the race. Thus mankind first stood, baffled and afraid, before his dead. So much for death generic; now for death specific:

One day there in Ohio, when I was a little fellow, they took me to a neighbor's where an old, old man had died, and I stood with my mother looking at him. She went away for a moment and left me in the room with the body. I stood mute and all atremble in my heart when suddenly, without warning, the old jaw on the dead face unhinged, dropped, and the mouth opened. With an agonized scream I fled from the room, and so as a little child I knew and understood as much as any man has ever known of life's two great mysteries—life and death, joy and sorrow, the way we come and the way we go.

After we returned from Ohio, the Aid for the grasshopper sufferers appeared in Eldorado—two carloads of it, transferred in wagons from the railroad thirty miles away. This Aid we kept in a shed at our house called "the aid room." In it were barrels of beans, great stacks of bacons and hams, sacks of flour, sugar all wrapped in five-pound packages, and all kinds of secondhand clothing.

It is to the everlasting credit of the settlers who were suffering—some of them suffering indeed the keen pangs of hunger—that they came for their aid at night and sometimes late at night, not to be seen taking Aid by their fellows. It was a galling thing to take aid, yet it was that or starve. So my father did not keep the Aid room at his drugstore. Often he was wakened late at night to get Aid for some poor devil who begged him never to tell it.

My father was then keeping a drugstore and practicing medicine a little. I cannot remember when the store was in the house except that I sat on the grocery scales there. But it must have been two or three years later, probably in '72 or '73, that my father opened his drugstore. It had great bottles of colored water in the window, five- or ten-gallon bottles, shining red or blue or green. On the left hand as one went in was a soda fountain with half a dozen flavors—lemon, strawberry, banana, raspberry and "don't care," which was a mixture of the odds and ends of all of them. In the top of the screen that shielded the prescription case was a huge mortar and pestle. Bottles, gold-labeled with the names of drugs, stood on one side of the store, and an amazing array of patent medicines adorned shelves on the other side. A short counter of stationery and a case of cigars were opposite the soda fountain.

He made money from his drugstore—and, being Yankee, saved it. A story still is told in Eldorado about the man who came into the store one winter day when my father's cronies were loafing around the stove. The man asked for a quarter's worth of powdered sulphur. My father wrapped it up for the customer, who clicked a coin on the counter and walked out. My father walked to the coin, called vainly after the customer, "Hey, this is only a nickel!" started toward the door, looked out, and saw the man hurrying down the street. My father halted, turned back to the crowd, sighed and told the stove-warmers:

"Oh, well, I made four cents profit anyway!"

My mother once told me that he figured there was a good 40 per cent profit in his drugstore—even counting in the dead beats!

A barrel of whiskey and several barrels of wine ranged along the sides of the back room beyond the prescription case. It was my father's complaint at home that his clerk, whoever it happened to be, was selling too much whiskey; and the town made much fun of him. The town's two or three good saloons should have supplied its liquor demand, but possibly the wine-bibbers and those who desired to be knocked about by strong drinks thought his liquor was better than the saloon liquor. For it was an everlasting fight between him and his clerks to keep down the sale of liquor.

One day a town drunk lay in the gutter before his store, and the town wags, one after another, poked their heads into the store with raucous taunting and ribald remarks to rile up the proprietor. My father got two buckets of water at the town pump on the corner, returned with them, sweating, for it was a hot summer day. He stood over the drunk in the gutter and lifted up a bucket, while the whole town up and down the street cried, "My God Almighty, Doc, what are you doing?" *et cetera,* and with variations.

As he soused one of the buckets in the drunk's face, and lifted up the other, the crowd protested. He roared to the multitude:

"Is freedom dead in this country, that a man has no right to water his own liquor?" So he soused down the other bucket. Whereupon the drunk sat up, rubbed his eyes, and walked fairly sober down the street.

The store was so profitable that within a few years my father was able to trade it for a good farm, and have enough capital to run this at a loss for a year or two.

CHAPTER V

"And Ye Shall Be As Gods, Knowing Good and Evil"

BEFORE I WENT to school I could read in my colored linen picture book about the doings of the cat, the dog, the man, the hen, and other things spelled with three letters. Shortly after, I knew about the four-letter words written on the barn and the fence and the board sidewalk; and about this time my parents uprooted me from the wicked town and I found myself living on "the farm." Until we moved there, "the farm" had been a halcyon place where I had my own little brook, my own little bull calf, my own pigs, and a colt that was growing up to be my pony. A farmer and his wife lived in its little clapboard house, but it never occurred to me that we proud folks, who kept a store and lived in the great rambling "foundry," could go to "the farm" actually to live. But there we went—my mother protesting at the top of her good Irish lungs, but nevertheless going.

For my father had built, on the farm, a large log cabin with a huge fireplace. At first there was no floor; but at this my mother raged, and then, lo and behold, there was a floor. My father's idea was to duplicate exactly the cabin in backwoods Ohio where he was born and grew up. He thought he could go back to the golden days of his youth, when Fear Perry used to carry a keg of cider into the house on her birthday, when John White wrestled with the Indians, when he and the boys—my father's brothers—cleared the land around Norwalk, in Huron County, Ohio. So there was a loft in our log cabin where the hired men slept. And hanging over the rafters, the first autumn, were strips of dried pumpkin, bunches of onions, tufts of sage, and Heaven knows what other nonsense groceries. I remember my father standing at a table, in a lean-to kitchen which we had built on the narrow end of the log cabin, cutting up beef to corn and to dry, and putting away pork to pickle. We had a smokehouse where we cured hams and bacon, and of course a pit where we buried cabbage, turnips, potatoes, carrots, beets, and apples. To carry out his romantic dream of another day, my father had the carpenter build a little trundle bed that rolled under the big bed by day

34

and was pulled out for me to sleep in by night. But clearest of all my recollections is the vast, continuous indignation of my mother at the sentimental tomfoolery of this whole business. Mary Ann Hatten had not spent ten years of her life toiling for an education just to go back to the blanket—two jumps behind a squaw. Her indignation rose from mild, hooting, and fumbling attempts at sarcastic humor, where she was not highly competent, to the direct attack that always began somewhere in a high key with one phrase:

"Now I tell you, Doctor, this thing's just got to stop. I have had enough . . ." And from then on, higher and higher, more and more eloquent—and finally tears.

My father could stand the eloquent sarcasm, but not the tears. It was always that way. My mother, no matter what she was doing, would always sit down just before she began to cry. She seemed to need a rocking chair to release her emotions. When I was a much larger boy and we were back in town, I can remember when moments of disagreement between them arose about matters of domestic policy, and my mother began, "Now, Doctor, I tell you," that my father (let me call him "Pa," as I remember him) would maneuver himself to his cane in the corner and hang the crook over his arm. Then always my little dog Tad, who loved Pa more than he loved me, would appear. Pa would stand for a moment, quizzically smiling and looking at Ma as she sat her rocker, and then he would begin humming a little song— he was a great hummer of little songs under his breath in times of stress and joy. And so, singing just low and sweetly enough for her to understand, he would sail out with his cane on his arm and the little dog at his heels, as the tempest rolled higher and higher from the rocking chair,

> "Sister, thou art mild and lovely.
> Gentle as the summer breeze,"

and so walk out of the room and make for the thick of the town.

But on the farm I was too young to remember in detail how he got out of the log cabin and where he went. Probably it was to the barn. He didn't have his cane nor my little dog there. Yet he just faded sweetly and gently from the domestic landscape. And when he came in, after the storm had cleared, he was smiling. He would open a conversation cheerily, and the episode was closed. But the farm was no place for a woman who was five feet four and weighed even then less than a hundred pounds. Hired girls would not go to the farm even seventy years ago, and my father, being in his fifties, had to hire all his share of the farm work done.

Always there were two, sometimes three or four, hired men about, and Ma had to cook for them. The farmer tenant and his wife in the little clapboard house a hundred yards from ours, of course, helped. But babies were coming there, and the whole weight of the house work fell on my mother's shoulders. She knew, of course, the joy Pa got in reproducing the household of his youth. She knew what a sentimental old codger he was, how he loved the occasional antelope steaks that still were easy to get in the early seventies, cooked on the hickory coals in the open fireplace. She knew that he loved the peaches, apples, and corn dried on the kitchen roof, and the wild-grape jelly and jam. She knew how he loved the pickled pork of his own curing, rolled in flour, fried crisp, and served in cream gravy over boiled potatoes. She knew the thousand little joyous pricks and quivers of memory that came to him as he relived his childhood in his fifties. She tried hard to give him this pleasure. But even I, a child of pre-school age, knew that it was more than she could stand. I sided with her against him, and I think he knew that. But he did not sour at either of us.

I had as much delight on "the farm" as my father. I fed my own pig; I tried to break my own steer calf for an ox; I romped with my pony, and I played long hours by the little brook that trickled through the gravel in the pasture. Sometimes I took a little pinhook and brought home a silverside or a sunfish, or took a can and brought home a tadpole, a little turtle, but Ma would yank them out of the rain barrel as fast as I would sneak them there. Pa did not care. He would always say:

"Why, Ma, let the boy have his fun."

I was always "the boy" in any controversy between my parents, though to each of them in placid hours I was Willie. That was the cast of characters that I came into out of infancy into childhood: the Boy, Pa, and Ma. We were a happy family. Now I believe, chiefly, we were happy because they had me. I was the apple of their eye. No other child appeared after little Freddie died, and you may depend upon it that I did not want one. I knew, being a farm boy and also a town boy who was not without his sophistication, about babies and where they came from, and I had a watchful eye. And I think I would have done murder if I had believed there was a baby on the way. For I was mean and jealous, suspicious and full of deep guile, with the rage of Cain in my heart. I knew, having seen little boys in large families, what tough sledding they had. I wanted my privileges as an only child. Otherwise, I was happy. There on the farm I had only one great sorrow. To this day, across seventy years, I can hear the dying cry of my pig, my own little pig that I had reared, when they killed him to eat and he bled to death; and I hated everybody and went to the brook, stayed there all day, then sneaked to the barn and would not eat ever of his flesh. I can remember few sorrows in my life, no anguished hours so poignant as those that came the day they slaughtered my pig.

I don't know how long we stayed on the farm. I can remember spring there, and summer and late autumn. I know it was a year of drouth. For the prairie chickens and the quail came to the yard to eat with the hens. And once an antelope leaped the stake and rider fence which my father, in his reminiscent folly, had built for the cattle corral, and ate hungrily with the bony cattle in the corral. Way down on the branch, nearly a mile from home, the neighborhood boneyard grew, and I remember in the spring the coyotes had gnawed the bones white, and it was a place of fear and desolation and great offense. Then, as if by a quick flash in a motion picture, I see us back in town.

My father had traded his drugstore for the farm. So, when we came back to town, I could no longer go into the store and get a glass of soda water free from his fountain. I had to ask politely for the empty cigar boxes under the counter. I was no longer permitted to take a handful of almanacs and distribute them among my friends. It seemed strange, and the strange seeming still lingers in my memory, that I could not go into that store and make free of it. So came the sense of property to my childhood.

In the meantime, I was sent to school. What a day! Ma started to take me, but Pa objected. He always objected when she coddled me. Of course I liked to be coddled, and I sided with her; but he had his way. The compromise was that he said, "I'll take him!" And so we started out. She was in the doorway, and I left her with her eyes full of tears, for she knew, having taught school, that I would never come back her baby! She knew that I was gone out of her life as a child and would return that noon a middle-aged young person, out in the world for good and all. Pa took me two blocks on my way to the schoolhouse, still three blocks away, and when he was out of sight of Ma and the doorway he prodded me with his cane in pride and affection and said:

"Now, Willie, you are a man. Go to school!" and turned and left me. He could not bear the shame of bringing me into the schoolroom, shame for him and shame for me, and we both knew it. And I trudged on and was glad. And then, for the first time, I remember Albert Ewing coming along the same way, and he and I walked into the schoolhouse together—my first boy friend. After that day we were inseparable for ten years.

The influx into the western Mississippi Valley, in the seventies, was unbelievable. Every day a score of young soldiers and their wives drove into town, either to settle in the village or to locate land in the Walnut Valley. In the school, new children were entering every day. Albert and I and Leila Heaton and the Betts boys were old settlers there—a haughty aristocracy who lorded it over the newcomers for a few days until they also became scornful of the newcomers; and so it went.

The public schools in Eldorado, and all over the West in those days, were the best that money could buy. We had the largest building in town, a two-story stone one with four rooms which soon afterwards became six—the largest edifice in Butler County. The rooms were well equipped, with good

37

seats and desks and blackboards. We had no pioneer hardships in our Kansas schools. All over the Missouri Valley, the settlers first built a sizable schoolhouse and then built their towns around it. But our school, graded from the primary to the high school even in the seventies, was ahead of the civilization about it.

We sang gospel hymns every morning, and the teacher read a chapter in the Bible, and there was no nonsense about that. For we were all little Protestants, and no one thought of objecting to Teacher reading the Bible. She made us say the Lord's Prayer after the Bible reading, and then we were started off right for the day. At noon we sang another gospel hymn and loved it. The words did not mean much, but it was fine exercise for our lungs. And, a few grades higher than the primary, we were taught to read music and were given secular songs to sing.

As for playgrounds, we had everything west of the schoolhouse to Denver. The prairies came within a hundred yards of the building. And sometimes, when prairie fires rose, we boys—little and big—took our coats off, soaked them in tubs of water from the school well and flopped out the fire, standing with the men of the town. Once the flames almost reached the woodpile that fed the big, potbellied iron stove in every room. Each room had its own water bucket and its own tin cup. And you were supposed to quench your thirst at recess and not bother Teacher between times. At recesses and at noon, we played ball, sometimes one-old-cat, or two-old-cat, town ball and baseball, marbles in season, pullaway, stink base and hide-and-seek. Any new boy had to fight his way into the lodge of boyhood with Byron Snow, Dow Blair, or Ed Dupee, who were ordained to pick a fight for that purpose by the school masonry. A few times—but not often—I was edged into the job; but Albert Ewing, never.

Albert Ewing was held up to me as a little gentleman, which he was. He could do everything better than I could do it. His clothes were always clean, as my mother pointed out—starting me spick-and-span to the schoolhouse every morning. Albert's hair stayed brushed, while mine never did. And he could spell better and write better and draw his geography pictures better than I. We were seatmates and loved each other dearly. And both of us loved Leila Heaton, which was a school scandal. But, being of a wandering and predatory nature in my love life, I again fell away from Leila Heaton and fell head over heels in love with my first teacher, Ida Fitch. I really brought her red apples and really polished them, and really brought her flowers. How fickle I was! The next year I was advanced a grade, and the teacher, Miss Bacon, came to our house to board, and I adored her and hated her beau. And once, very slyly, I dug a deep hole in the path which he passed near our house when he came to see her. I pulled grass and piled on twigs to cover the hole. I hoped in my heart he would fall and break a leg. And this

38

at six! I took love seriously. For me then, it was the greatest thing in the world! It still is!

It was about that time, possibly a year or so later, that politics first entered my young life. Before that, almost as far back as I can remember, I knew I was for Horace Greeley, though I hadn't the faintest idea who Horace Greeley was, nor what "bein' for him" implied. But when Hayes and Tilden ran for President, because my father was a Democrat I had to suffer the flings and arrows of outrageous Republicans—some of the young soldiers; even Albert Ewing turned against me. Only Leila Heaton remained faithful.

She saved my life. I came to school in October, when the campaign was at its height, wearing a little scarf on which were woven "Tilden" and "Hendricks." Naturally the Republicans, the big boys and the little ones, got me down, tied the Tilden and Hendricks scarf around my neck and began pulling it and dancing about with great glee. The world went black. Only Leila Heaton, running screaming to the teacher and tattling on the boys, saved me from garroting, for I was unconscious when the teacher came, loosed the noose, and threw a bucket of water on me. I was a sight to see. No valiant defender of Democracy lay there on the brown prairie grass, but a little pop-eyed, redheaded, freckled-faced, gasping, ashy-blue Democrat, with two teachers and Leila Heaton hovering over him! I opened my eyes and saw Albert Ewing—a renegade to his party, "whence all but he had fled!" But I slowly came to, and grinned. I know I grinned, for they told me so. I know I tried to look brave. Leila Heaton and my adored teacher bent over me, and I was a happy little polygamist, proud of their solicitude.

Sometime between the days when I fished with a pinhook for minnows under the bridge and the time when I suffered valiantly for Tilden and Hendricks, the river east of town was dammed and the water backed up under the bridge, and there was no riffle for a mile upstream. I have no recollection when the dam was built, nor the bridge; it always seems to have been there. Yet there was a time when there was a riffle where the deep green waters stood, where shining golden rocks shimmered in the sunshine, and where little fishes were playing in the stream, and crawdads under the rocks. And then, quicker than the change of scene in a dream, the dam was there and the mill—and we were swimming in the millpond and fishing off the dam, and the riffles were only below the dam. It was all a wonder, full of joy and beauty. The grove around the mill was the town park. And a new bridge spanned the stream. And Eldorado was a big town, maybe six hundred people. We had three saloons; and little boys could pick up corks for fishing bobbers back of the saloons, and sometimes find salable bottles, mostly flasks. Most gay and gorgeous of all, sometimes back of the saloons we could find a drunk sleeping it off and take dares for going closest to him

39

and throwing weeds and other debris upon him. So life was full of dangers. We had two new livery stables in town, and one of them kept a stallion until our mothers complained, thinking we did not know! So then the stallion was moved out of town. And one summer day we discovered a camping place deep in the woods above the town where there was often a covered wagon and some strange girls. We used to peek through the brush at what was going on there until Merz Young, who was the protector of the innocent, came and chased us off with yells and curses, throwing rocks. And the knowledge of good and evil came to us, even as to the Pair in the Garden.

CHAPTER VI

A Changing World

The appletree covered with blossoms and with fruit afterward,
And the old drunkard staggering home from the outhouse of the
tavern where he has lately risen;
These became a part of that child who went forth every day and
who goes now and will always go forth every day.

I WAS EIGHT years old when I stepped out into society. A note in beautiful Spencerian handwriting, on pink paper with gilt edges—I have it yet—came to me, declaring:

Master Willie White is invited to be present at the birthday party of Miss Alice Murdock at their home on Star Street, March 23, 1876.

And so I was dressed to kill in a little blue suit, bound in black braid, with shiny little golden buttons, white stockings, and black shoes. My hair was wet and pasted down, and my neck washed even behind the ears. It was an afternoon party, bright and gay, and little Alice, with her spinal curvature, was the sunshine of it all. And her grand stepmother in flowing robes—she always affected negligee with loose drooping sleeves—and such red lips and such glowing cheeks and such an alabaster skin, looked like a queen, though she had been a schoolteacher before Bent Murdock married her after his first wife's suicide. We played games (kissing games, I think—post office, clap-in-clap-out, and forfeits) and then went on the lawn, shot arrows at a target, and rather wickedly played hide-and-seek in the barn and had ice cream and cake and lemonade, sitting around like little angels eating their ambrosia. It was all very exciting.

In the meantime, at home things were changing. My father, who had been elected to the city council once or twice, and twice was elected city treasurer, had bought a large square of land—a city block—four or five blocks westward from the creek; and we were planting it to trees. He and I used to water them. We planned to build a house there. My mother was happy, for she did not like to live on the street where the "old foundry" stood on the highway, less than half a block from Main Street. Then I think that subconsciously she felt that if we lived on the hill, five blocks from Main Street, the Doctor would not always be inviting people in for dinner. Our house was less than two hundred feet from the stage hotel. It was her complaint that she fed more people from the stage than did the hotel. This meant hard work, for she never would keep a girl. She always said she would rather do the work than bother with one. So when anyone whom my father knew came through on the stage from Emporia, Cottonwood Falls, Council Grove, Leavenworth, or Lawrence—and he knew nearly everyone—we fed them, with Pa, sitting at the head of the table, prouder than Punch of his wife's cooking. He had a baronial air and knew his greatest joy as a host. It was the source of a good deal of bone-picking between my parents after our company was gone. He was always crestfallen when he realized the amount of work he had caused. For he was a kindly man and had been the head of a home too many years not to realize, when he thought of it, how many extra steps company makes necessary. But he could not resist "company."

Then one day the storm broke. My father wanted to sell the lot on the hill; and he wanted to build the big house where "the foundry" was, tearing that one down. The other women of the town lived on the hill, and my mother felt that some sort of disgrace came from living downtown. Only poor folks lived down there in little homes scattered back of the Main Street. She raged and wept, and would not sign the deed for days and days. Times were tough in those days for a little boy of nine or ten, and it sometimes took two or three minutes of play with the gang in the barn, or on the vacant lot, or down along the river, to wipe away the clouds of sadness that hovered over his heart at home. But, finally, the deed was signed, and then we moved across the street while "the foundry" was being torn down and the new house was built.

It was a grand house. Probably my father tried to make up for its location by making it much the biggest house in town. It had eleven rooms and a cellar under all, and one hundred forty-four linear feet of porches, which he enjoyed and elaborately bragged about when he showed it to visitors. The porches made it possible to get a breeze from every angle— north, east, south, west. We also bought a houseful of new furniture from Leavenworth. I found the bill for that among my mother's papers more than sixty years after the goods were delivered. Then we had a big party and housewarming. Whether my father and mother gave the party or whether the town just moved in, I do not remember; but it seems to me it was probably the latter; maybe at a wink and nod from my father, who loved company, reveled in it and was really a glowing host.

After it was all over, my mother had a good cry by herself, and I found her. The big house down in the business part of town some way shamed her. I mention this merely to show that she was sensitive. What others thought, or what she thought they thought, meant much to her. It was the other way around with my father. I have thought, in later years, that probably what success he had in the practice of medicine was due to the fact that he would come bustling into a room, smiling, hand-shaking, and exuberant, just as he always greeted company coming to his home. My mother was polite, but reserved. She always said:

"Yes, Doctor, it's all right for you. But I have to do the work!"

But he always helped her. He always wiped the dishes, made the fire in the cookstove in the morning, and filled the woodbox, with my help even when I was little more than a toddler. I have seen him sweep, fetch, and carry, trying to make up to her for the trouble he had caused. He was an addict to hospitality. He could not take it or let it alone.

I was ten years old when we tore down "the foundry." Eldorado was only a year older, but it had grown by that time to be a town of nearly a thousand people. It was a self-sufficient community. We had shoemakers who made my father's shoes, although my mother's came from St. Louis, where he traded in his merchant days. The town tailor made Pa's Sunday clothes; my mother made his everyday clothes. She, or other women whom she hired, knitted our socks. The food of the town was mostly raised on the townsite, or near it on the farm. A small packing house put up hams and bacon and cured beef. A wagon shop back of our lot made carriages, and one of the town's most distinguished artists was a wagon painter who striped buggy wheels and painted the elaborate designs—cornucopian, or the seal of Kansas—on the sides of wagons. The town had two or three blacksmith shops, which were busy all day. Ringing anvils woke me in the morning and tolled like bells when I went into the house at dusk. Busy places were those blacksmith shops, which mended and made a score of gadgets for house and farm. We had three harness shops, where I loved to play and listen to the stories of the soldiers who sometimes gathered there; for one harness maker was a noted soldier. A little tannery was established, and a small furniture factory made the chairs, tables, and beds of the pioneers. Native lumber—walnut and oak—stood behind these factories curing, and we boys used to play on the lumber piles and hide between them in our games.

Then the railroad came, and everything was changed. I did not know that the smell of coal smoke, which first greeted my nostrils with the railroad engine, was to be the sign and signal of the decay of a town and indeed of pioneer times, when men made things where they used them—all the things necessary to a rather competent civilization.

43

In the boy's world, it meant that homemade sleds and little homemade wagons would pass; that the bows and arrows which boys made by seasoning the hickory behind the stove and scraping and polishing them with glass, would as an art disappear forever out of the life of American boys. The railroad meant that the woodpile would slowly disappear, and that on the far horizon great engines were gathering to wreck the barns, and that the town herd, which I drove for a time, would vanish before the onslaughts of the milk bottles in another fifty years. What a revolution for boys came chugging into the world with that iron horse!

We boys in Eldorado saw colored people for the first time—railroad laborers sweating at their work and singing. We caught their songs and echoed them in our play, building little railroads with whittled ties, imitation rails, grades, and ballast. Our hands were so deft, our imaginations so quick, that we imitated the very things that would rob boys of their skill and their homely work.

Let us look for a fleeting moment at this little fellow just edging eagerly out of childhood. He has been two or three years in school. He is in the second reader, but has read all the readers through to the fourth. He knows the multiplication tables because he was nagged all over the house to learn them—pounced upon at odd times by fierce, merciless parents with "What's nine times three?" or "Eight times twelve?" or "Seven times six?"

And he has drawn fuzzy little mountains on his maps of the United States, of North America or Europe, and colored them after the fashion of schools with red, yellow, blue, and green chalk. He is still sweet on Leila Heaton, sometimes peeks at her and giggles for no reason, and likes to have the boys chalk on the sidewalks:

> The moon is yellar, the sun is bright,
> Leila Heaton and Willie White.

He is a heavy-set boy of medium height, or slightly below it, with one large freckle all over his face, a longish neck, and big, curious, half-scared, bluish eyes. His mother is reading to him every night while his father protests that she is spoiling him; reading the Dickens stories which he understands and the Cooper Indian stories which he loves, and "The Mill on the Floss" by George Eliot, which bothers him a little, and a story by George Sand about a dark pool, which scares him. He knows his Mother Goose by heart. His gospel hymns are engraved on his memory for life. He is going to four Sunday schools for purely social reasons—because the boys are there and he is a gregarious kid. And, because his memory is a malleable tablet, he has learned hundreds of verses and, being a bit of a smarty, likes to show off. His hand is up first when the Sunday-school teacher says:

"Now, boys, who knows the Golden Text?"

And Willie's fingers always snap if Albert Ewing does not beat him—which sometimes he does, or Theodore Dunlevy. In summers at Sunday school he wears a little nankeen suit made of the same material as his father's, of which he is quite proud. And the boys, who nickname everybody, have begun to call him "Doc"; and "Doc White" he is to remain through more than sixty years to a score of oldsters. He is Willie only at home and to his teacher and to Leila Heaton. His love affairs with his teachers have passed. Three of them broke his philandering heart, and then he turned against all teachers. He is rebelling at something—probably discipline. As far as I can learn from honest boys who knew me, and from old people who saw me, this Willie had no exceptional qualities, nothing outstanding in his heart. He knew he was a coward so he did brave things sometimes to prove that he was not, but did them in fear and trembling and always showing off. At an early age, the hired man had taken him along when he took the horses to swim. First off, the hired man waded with the little scared kid to where the current was swift and, holding the little fellow high in his arms, threw him as far as he could and cried:

"Swim, damn you, swim!"

So he had to swim. And the hired man laughed when he came up—spouting, paddling, and yelling. But he learned to swim. One thing he could do so well that all the boys in Eldorado remember even today: he could dive clear across the creek, and sometimes he would dive so far upstream beyond the swimming hole and hide under a stump where there were supposed to be snakes—but weren't—that the whole parcel of young savages at the swimming hole would be scared white, fearing he was drowned. No bathing trunks were ever heard of in that young savage band. They loved to smear themselves with mud and make indecent patterns with sticks upon their bodies and stand near the railroad bridge, yelling when Number Four passed, waving and making obscene gestures at the passengers. For they were dirty little devils, as most kids are when they are leaving the portals of babyhood and becoming boys. He knew ribald rhymes and Rabelaisian catches and catcalls. He and his fellows released their vague, unformed romantic impulses in the venery of the barn and haystack and swimming hole.

Probably four major influences made this child: the home, where there was reading and considerable intelligent guidance which only later did he perceive, as he recalled certain attitudes of his parents; then came the barn, with its ancient lores and skills, its trapeze swinging from the rafter, its haymows full of somersets, forward and backward, where gangs of boys tried to reproduce circus gyrations; after the barn, the river—swimming, fishing, rowing in summer, and skating in winter; and the roaming through the timber, trapping quail and redbirds and mockingbirds and rabbits, and cutting stick horses in spring. Probably the stick horse has passed out of childhood. But this Willie, who developed his acquisitive faculty early, kept a stick-horse livery stable and was a stick-horse trader before he was seven. The woods also yielded walnuts for all the boys who would go after them, and a few hard hickory nuts and papaws after frost in autumn, and coffee beans and buckeyes, which had a certain commercial value in the primitive swapping commerce of childhood. The woods was a storehouse of all boys' treasures.

The woods taught us guile. Once we saw, with shocked amazement, our Sunday-school superintendent sitting in a secluded part of the woods on the creek bank with a young lady who we knew was visiting one of our teachers. They had their shoes off, cooling their toes in the limpid waters, and were obviously returning to nature rather rapidly. Swiftly, silently, the boy who saw them summoned his savage band, and we peered through the foliage at their backs, and then, charged with emotion, let off a yell, and the elders almost jumped into the creek. Like startled birds, we scattered.

Then a strange thing happened. We went about our serious business of filling our little wagons with grapes, and less than an hour later the Sunday-school superintendent appeared with his wife at the same spot. It was a great puzzle. Only years later, when we were in our adolescence, did we learn that the maneuver had saved the good man a divorce. For his wife, when she met the story of the other woman, pooh-poohed it and said that the boys were mistaken: she and her husband were on one of their wild walks. She believed it to her dying day. Thus, in early youth we learned the guile of men.

So Willie White learned to turn and tumble and twist, and to use all the muscles of his body. He even tried to ride bareback on a horse, and fell on his little bottom and jolted his teeth. But Homer Borland could do it even when we made the old gray mare lope a little. But when Homer tried to turn a somerset, he landed astraddle of the old mare. She had a pretty bony back, and you could hear Homer holler for two blocks, and for weeks boys were imitating his uncourtly gestures and his yowl of pain, which wasn't anything like humor—to Homer!

Willie learned to skate and was proud of his achievement, cutting Dutch rolls, figure eights, and fancy curlicues. One winter the boys found an old dead mule imbedded in the ice. They grew skillful in jumping over the carcass as they rushed upon it. And many a little tail thumped hard upon that frozen body when a boy failed to clear the hurdle. The river was a great teacher of boys in that day and time.

Probably marbles and fighting were extracurricular activities attached to and surrounding the school—also foot racing and ball. Willie was a fairly good shot at marbles. His mother lived in the pink cloud of innocence that

46

Willie did not play for keeps. Pa knew better and never betrayed him. But here is a curious thing. The little devil had an acquisitive faculty, and he found, watching the wiles of the older boys, that by setting up a fancy marble for boys to shoot at from a hazardous distance and charging two or three commies or a white alley a shot, then giving the prized marble to the man who hit it, he could accumulate marbles faster by running this thing he called a bank than he could by playing for keeps, although he was fairly deft at that. So he set up a bank. But, alas, one day his father discovered that his child had a whole cigar box full of glassies, potteries, and agates which he had accumulated running his bank. That was the end of the bank. Said Pa:

"Now, Willie, whatever you get playing keeps is yours. It's a fair game. But these are dirty marbles. You didn't win them, and you didn't earn them. Your bank was a swindle."

And so the bank was closed, and the career of a future capitalist was nipped in the bud.

The home, the barn, the river, and the school made this Willie White. The school only taught him superficial things—to read, write, and figure, and to take care of himself on the playground. But those other ancient institutions of learning taught him wisdom, the rules of life, and the skills which had survival value in the world of boyhood.

CHAPTER VII

When Evil Days Come Not

WHEN I WAS SEVEN or eight years old, I fell from a horse and broke my shoulder blade, and after that could never throw a straight ball. My sporting days were done. I was scorekeeper of our alley baseball team. But after my shoulder was healed, my career as a fighter was resumed. As a fighter I was probably repeating the history of the race. I did not want to fight. I did not boast. I did not have wrongs to redress except perhaps in the case of Albert Ewing when I had caught him beauing Leila Heaton to the ice-cream parlor. Even then I was nagged by my elders into that fight. When I fought with Ed Dupee on Ben King's corner, where Ben sold dry goods and groceries, boots and shoes, hats and caps and notions, I was just on my feet and out after a bout with both scarlet fever and measles, which nearly took me off. I kept hoping against hope, as diplomatic relations were swiftly broken between Ed and me there on the corner, that some good, kind benevolent boy in his elder teens would call attention to the fact that I was in no condition to fight. On the contrary, the opinion of Europe— around the pump—seemed to be that now of all times, when I was fresh and keen from rich soups, eggs, and vegetables, I must surely be a gladiator!

So, when I made the inevitable gesture, or spoke the provocative word, and he tried to paste me on the snoot, the fight began. Even then I hoped for mediation, for a negotiated peace, for an armistice, and—being cowardly —I looked for a rock. But no one intervened, and there was no rock. We clinched, rolled, and gouged. Of course, when I got good and mad I always began to cry, which was a great humiliation but a real sign that I was doing my best fighting. How the town enjoyed it! It seemed to me that I must have fought for hours and hours and hours, though probably the fight lasted less than ten minutes. Boy fights rarely do last long.

How that fight ended, I cannot recollect—which indicates that I got licked, but maybe not.

The next fight was with Homer Borland, a dear and beloved friend, who could turn double somersets off the homemade springboard that we set up

48

near his haystack, and could ride their old bay bareback on a lope, and go through hoops and walk on his hands much better than I. We were born on the same day of the same year. And I was heavier than he—much heavier. But he got me down, put his thumbs in my mouth and his forefingers in my eyes, and beat my head on the ground until I yelled—and Nat Long almost died laughing, for it must have been a funny fight. That, I certainly remember. So, after all, it may be that Ed Dupee did not lick me.

The next fight I had was with John Knowles. We fought all the way home from school, wrestling and chasing each other, I suppose, each hoping that the other would get away. And the boys followed us and kept us going, for it was a great sport. And there was no league of nonsense about peace among the boys in Eldorado in the seventies. Whenever I got into any trouble, or whenever it seemed as if the boys could stir up a fight, we all forgot our Golden Text and I suddenly—instead of being Willie—became Bill, and the slogan was, "Bust him, Bill," and "Soak him, John." So John and I fought the good fight for five blocks through Eldorado, and were dear, devoted friends until his dying day when he quit this earth— a district judge of some distinction in Oregon.

My last major engagement, though there must have been scores of skirmishes and minor brushes, was when I was just going out of childhood into boyhood. I know I was beginning to get ashamed to go barefooted, and I had on carpet slippers, being in adolescent love at the time; and my last major battle was with Ive Williams, a colored boy. The few negro boys in Eldorado mingled on terms of absolute equality with the whites. They held their places according to their skills as fighters, swimmers, runners, ball players, skaters, or school playground athletes. His older brother, Albert, was in my class entering high school, and I was immensely fond of him. But one hot August afternoon, at the swimming hole, it became necessary for Ive and me to fight. Public opinion demanded it—upon what grounds, I have no idea. We bore each other no enmity. If an insult passed between us, I do not recall it. We just began to fight under an old spreading elm near the coming-out place at the swimming hole, near the north bridge, even before we were dressed. And we fought naked for a while, and then went back to swim. And then, to satisfy popular opinion, we were forced to it again. He blacked my eye and I dug a nail or two of Ethiopian hide from his face and he bled copiously. Also he had a bloody nose, but I had no marks at the time of the conflict except a scratch on the shoulder which was hidden by my shirt.

The outcome of that fight I do not know. Probably we fought until we began to laugh, which was not an uncommon ending for boy fights. It's a pity the adult sense of humor does not work in the cause of peace. I will guarantee that I laughed first, if it would stop the fight, for I hated fighting.

49

And, as nearly as I can be honest with myself, I fought only because I detected throughout my childhood a lurking suspicion, which sometimes I shared myself, that I was a sissy and a coward. I did a lot of foolish things to show that I was not—things which were supposed to be daring but were nothing but bluff. I knew it then, but I know it doubly now. These fights are mentioned here because they were a part of a boy's childhood in my day. It seems to me now, when I think of war and war's alarms and the vast rigmarole of diplomacy, that we must be in the childhood of the race; though I do not know whether this war now beclouding the world is my battle with Homer Borland or with Ive Williams. Both were savage, bloody, devastating battles which settled nothing in the long run.

At home, after a fight, I knew exactly what I should face. My mother was grimly unreconciled to the degeneration of her offspring. My father was mildly amused and tried to be stern but could not, asking uncomfortable questions which revealed my ardent desire to keep out of trouble. He discovered before I did that I was at heart a pacifist. It did not exactly exult him. I knew that some way he wanted me to tell him that I had won, and my dear mother wanted me to tell the family how I had been put upon and urged unwillingly to combat, which never was true. I just could not say that! Because really I knew I was a bluffer and got into fights because I talked too much and too loud. My father discovered the truth also and offered sage advice which I knew was sane but never could take. It was my mother who put beefsteak over my black eye, where Ive Williams had plastered me, and found odds and ends of work for me to do in the yard for a day or two when she sensed the fact that I did not want to go out and show my shiner. On the other hand, my father devilishly loaded up my little red wagon with garden truck and sent me out peddling it for the pennies I could make—which were my own, of course—and secretly hoped to cure me of senseless fighting by shaming me. I recall the keen poignant sense of injustice I had when he refused to believe that I had scratched Ive Williams' eyes and bloodied his nose. My father even pretended, for my soul's good, that I had been licked, and almost persuaded me of it, which was good for a boy who talked too much before he fought. (Parenthetically, let me recall, across threescore years, that I did not know that Homer Borland was really going to fight until he turned suddenly white, backed off, butted me in the belly, knocking me down, and was on me like a tiger —just as I thought I had him bluffed!)

I wanted my father's good opinion because he was chary of his compliments and shy in his affection. After he was dead I remember my mother told me with what pride he saw me climbing up over the shoulders of a crowd, walking on the mass of shoulders and crawling over it, to get into a railway-car door once. He said to her:

"Well, Ma, don't ever worry about Willie. He'll take care of himself! He'll get ahead!"

But in those days I believe he shared my own opinion that I was a "little gentleman" at heart. His idea was that boys should work. He held no nonsense about child labor and was forever thinking up things for me to do which my mother surreptitiously helped me to avoid—being enlightened beyond her time, or perhaps being just soft, I am not sure which. But I had great pride in Pa. I knew he belonged to the ruling class, though I had not come across the phrase. He sat in the town council. One time he had himself elected street commissioner in order to macadamize Main Street. And I recall with keen pride the picture of him standing at a riffle in the creek below the bridge, with his nankeen trousers rolled up far above his knees, his shirt peeled off, his Panama hat well back on his sweating brow, directing two men with teams who were shoveling creek gravel from the river bed into waiting wagons. He and I rode back to Main Street with the gravel, and he showed the men where to start it, and how to rake it and sprinkle it evenly over the plowed hard surface of the street. For a man who, less than ten years before in Emporia, had been addicted to plug hats and always carried a cane, this incongruous picture of the pussy little man in the Walnut River remains in my proud memory through all the years. I asked my mother once why he did it, and she said:

"Because they said he couldn't, and he showed them."

He loved the path of greatest resistance, and the only thing that ever downed him was tobacco. When I first recollect him, he was chewing tobacco. Later he tried a pipe. It was an ungodly, awfully stinking pipe, and my mother and I protested. Then he returned to chewing, and then he tried to quit tobacco altogether and grew wan and pale and irritable and mean, was ashamed of himself, and smoked mild cigars, was ashamed of himself and, finally, fell back helpless on his pipe. I remember once, in that day of struggle near the end of his life, he called me to him and gave me the only firm advice that I remember. I can hear his fuzzy, soft, self-deprecatory voice crying across the years:

"Willie, let it alone. Tobacco's awful! It's got me! I can't quit it, and I know I ought to. Let it alone!"

Then he offered me a gold watch if I would not smoke until I was twenty-one. I promised. Once, after he was dead a year, I sneaked a cigarette. It did not make me sick, but I hated myself as a liar and a weakling; and I have never smoked since. When I was twenty-one I did not want a watch. I never carried one until my mother died and gave me hers, forty years after his death.

In those twilight days of childhood, just before the beginning of my teens, I had a consuming ambition to be a circus performer. I was in the monkey age, and my father put up a turning pole in the yard for me, and a trapeze and rings in the barn, and let me tumble over the haymow—greatly to the disgust of the horse who some way did not like the hay after boys had roughed it up. But he thought more of me than of the horse, I guess, and gave me every chance to work off my energy and build up my muscles. So I grew physically strong, though never the match for Homer Borland in skill, strength on the trapeze, on the bars and rings, or on the ground. I wonder if my father was wise or just indulgent. For I had everything that a gymnasium could give me, and I kept at it hours and hours; and, as a youth, I could chin a pole twenty times hand-running. Under the fat of my pudgy little tummy there were muscles of more than usual boy's strength. So after my tussle with measles and scarlet fever, I was only sick in bed once, and that was from going swimming too much in dog days. The alga scum on the water poisoned me. They called it catarrhal fever.

When I was getting a little better, but still puny, I lured three or four boys into the haymow and we started a game of seven-up, or cassino. In that far-off day, cards were called "the devil's visiting cards." I do not know how my father felt about it. I can remember seeing him play seven-up or euchre with my mother occasionally. But he caught us in a dark corner of the haymow, made us all come out, get a table, put it on the front porch right where the passing town could see us, and kept us playing there for an hour or so after we tried to quit. He was not stern about it. He just laughed and said: "Oh, no, don't quit!" I think it shocked the town, but it cured me forever of playing cards. There was no longer a secret sin about it, and it seemed a waste of time. So I never have learned cards beyond seven-up, cassino, and euchre. My mother must have been shocked a bit at the exhibition that we gave to the town, for she beckoned my father inside and I could hear her say:

"Now, Doctor, don't you think . . ."

But he didn't think, and came back laughing and told us a funny story. He was full of funny stories. And we went on playing. If my father had ostentation, he was without vanity; and, if he sometimes wore a plug hat, he cared little what people thought.

I never saw him in his plug hat, but it kicked around the house until after his death. He told a funny story about how he had bought it on his last trip East, when he and his brother Daniel went in their plug hats and long-tail coats to Boston to call on their rich White kin. Dan and Allen were fairly prosperous for western merchants in those days. But the Boston kin snubbed them; did not invite them to their homes; let them stay at the hotel. Daniel, who was proud, never mentioned it. But my father told the story of the snub with great glee on the streets of Eldorado, much to my mother's discomfiture. His plug hat, ensconced in its box—a symbol of his humbled pride—outlived him. I think it ended up in a home-talent minstrel show, which would have delighted him also.

Once, at an afternoon performance at the circus, a clown made merry at my father's expense. Pa came back at night expecting more, and maybe with something up his sleeve. But at night the clown pointed his ribald finger at another fat man, who got up and stomped out of the circus amid the cheers of the multitude. My father even led them, to my mother's great humiliation. But I was proud the next day when the story ran through the playground at school, for public opinion on the school ground was with my father, who could outlaugh the clown at his own game. So, though with me he was always a strict disciplinarian, while my mother shielded me, I think I understood him better. But, like any child, I went to her for protection. It was her job to break down the rigors of the stern and rock-bound coast of New England in our family. It was in those days when I was nine years old, or thereabouts, that Leila Heaton, who had left Eldorado for the little town of Chanute, died of scarlet fever. Albert Ewing told me. I carried a heavy heart for days and days, and was probably mean and hard to get along with. I remember this picture of Willie and his grief. It may have been the Saturday after I had the news, which would have been the first holiday when I could go to the woods of a morning. It was a sunny spring day. I was alone, down where the ravine empties into the creek. The berry blossoms, the raspberries and blackberries, were out; and, even now, when I smell them their perfume brings back a poignant pungency. I sat for a long time, as it seemed, but maybe for only a few minutes, in the berry brambles. Then I went down under a hard mud bank to a tree where a pool was backed up into the ravine from the millpond. I sat there, playing with some old pignuts dropped from a hickory tree the autumn before, and found under my hand some coffee beans from a locust tree. I was only thinking, just stringing wandering fancies through my brain about life, and death, and Leila Heaton—a dirty little boy with a bruised scab on his cheek from a fight with John Knowles, not too clean a nose, and very filthy hands. I whispered her name many times and then, looking cautiously about, I said it aloud, and began to make up a little song—with Heaven knows what words. Of course they were silly, but they seemed beautiful. They are gone now. Heaven also may know the tune I used; probably the mélange of all the tunes I knew was my song of sorrow, little above a bee's hum—repeating over and over weird meaningless phrases, lifting my voice sometimes and suddenly muffling it in shame. I can still see the gaudy woodpecker on the dead beech tree across the pool, and hear him drum. Some hogs came down to drink and wallow near me in the mud. Above the fence that hemmed the pond in from the creek, a log had lodged at flood time. Under the bright spring sun came a turtle, and I clodded it back into the water, and so broke the spell of song. In my pocket, among treasures of string and marbles, was a jew's-harp with a bent tongue. I straightened it out, sitting there on my haunches in the spring's sunlight, thrummed the jew's-harp to some sad old tune, and so looked out of my childhood far forward into my teens, and thus through sorrow, at the mystery of life. I felt there in the sunshine of the hog lot something strange approaching, something bright and sad and wonderful. It was youth. And that day and time Willie began to pale and pine away and pass. A boy appeared.

Book Two

THE STORY OF WILL

(Sometimes Billie)

Oh, See the Dude,
His feet protrude
In graceful swanlike attitude.

Song of the Toothpick Shoe (1884)

CHAPTER VIII

"I Dreamt That I Dwelt in Marble Halls"

I was Will White, not Willie, when I came to my tenth birthday. The town of Eldorado had lost its tough pioneer character. Brick buildings were appearing on Central Avenue and Main Street. Substantial residences, with east and south porches, were rising up on the hill beyond the town. The big stone schoolhouse acquired an addition. It was a six-room grade school with a high school, for which I was headed intrepidly. Because our new grand house, all ornamented with jigsaw jimcracks, had six bedrooms—all fancily furnished with washstands, bureaus, and chairs, and covered with ingrain carpet—my father in his pride always invited people whom he knew from Emporia, Kansas City, Lawrence, or from Leavenworth, where he traded, to stay overnight. And my mother tried to look smiling and hospitable. If she failed, my father would say: "Well, Ma, get a girl to help you!" This was easier said than done, for she felt that "help" was more trouble than service. I am afraid I shared my father's sinful pride in the house—in its grained dining-room wainscoting, in the painted yellow and black squares on the dining-room floor, and in the big kitchen and in the parlor with body Brussels carpet and a gaudy parlor suite, most expensive, in the comfortable living room, crawling with half a dozen rocking chairs, large and small.

The house was heated downstairs with three hard-coal base-burners, each glittering with nickel-plated fenders and fancy doodads—glowing household idols! And the house had such a woodshed as a boy prince could dream of in his palace! There was room even for a trapeze. The worm in the bud was that I could split wood there even when it rained, a drawback but not a major flaw. For on rainy days boys gathered there, and, being host, I acquired some prestige, if not quite leadership. In the woodshed I tied my pet coon and kept my trapped mockingbird, also my little lonely bluebird and my voiceless drooping redbird, until my father persuaded me to let them all go though I could have traded them for a king's ransom.

In the woodshed I assembled from the house and from the barn the various tools of my trade, being a boy, what might be called the hereditary appurtenances of Will White: a thick piece of glass that was used for scraping and polishing cowhorns; a drawknife; skates with runners, rubbed with bacon rind to keep away rust; bits of iron that had no use but were potentially of extreme value, for only boys know what reason; a rawhide quirt—an eight-strand, square-braided whip of my own construction, a priceless treasure; rows and ranks of cigar boxes filled with nails, screws, tops, marbles, and Heaven only knows what of the wampum of boyhood. So the place, indeed the entire woodshed, glowed with the warm and comfortable feeling of great riches in my boy's heart. I was an acquisitive kid, with methodical ways, and stored my treasure there in the woodshed with something like a capitalist's delight in great treasure, good investments.

Two events make me remember my tenth birthday: a sheet-and-pillow-case party, at which all the children who went to Alice Murdock's party, that is to say the nobility and gentry, were assembled; and the glorious fact that on my tenth birthday my parents gave me a Mason & Hamlin Cabinet organ, most ornate, most gorgeous, with a chromo of an autumn field on the centerpiece at the top. The other day, more than sixty years after, among my mother's things I found the bill for it, $240, and a receipt. It came from Chicago and was the town pride. That it was the most splendid organ in town, where not more than three or four pianos rivaled it, of course did not make me humble. And probably I needed that black and shiny eye that Ive Williams gave me for my soul's good the next summer. Music, since I can remember, has always been one of my chief delights. I can recall now, after seventy years, hearing the Eldorado silver cornet band playing down in Burdette's grove by the mill. The strains wafted across our creek to our place. I remember even that I was sitting under the grapevines preparing my little stomach for a gorgeous bellyache, eating the half-green grapes and listening to what I felt was heavenly music. It was the first band I had ever heard. I had a little toy brass trumpet with four notes, and I used to make other trumpets of green pumpkin stems. And Charley Harvey and I, from some whatnot, God knows where, managed to sneak two lovely pink conch shells and used to sing in them, and made what we thought were mellifluous noises that passed for music. From that through the twanging jew's-harp to the mouth organ was but a step; and before I had the organ I could play the mouth organ, put it in a tumbler for resonance or put it in my hand and make a grand fortissimo, as I played. At the school organ I had learned to pick out by ear any tune I knew by one hand, and before I had my own organ I could fake some kind of bass for the two or three notes. And I was singing alto by that time and deeply in love with Agnes Riley.

Of course I "took lessons" in music, first from a Mrs. Charley Hobson and then from a most accomplished musician—a Mrs. Fannie DeGrasse Black. In vain she tried to keep me to my exercises; but I could learn by ear almost as well, and certainly more rapidly, than I learned by note. Time and again she would catch me using my ear, and time and again she would try to bring me back to my "one and two and three and four and . . ." So, finally, she yielded and gave me pieces. I never had to be lashed like a galley slave to my practice at home. I was up and at it as soon as I had visited my traps in the morning down in the timber, and probably before I had got my wood-box filled for the day—though the family cow and my calf probably took precedence over the organ, for purely physical reasons. They had to be attended to, and I had to wash up, before I could have breakfast. But I was forever at the organ. Always I had my lesson, for I loved to play the pieces I heard on the street or at school or at the minstrel show or at a circus. The atmosphere of my life seemed to be charged with song and dance. Even though I had to fight my way across town when I went to my music teacher, carrying my music roll, still I did not weary of my delight. I was willing to meet the jeers and rebuffs and the hootings of the boys. Fighting was not the chore it seemed to be. So music threatened to envelop my life. My father saw it a year or so after the organ came. One day he pointed out an old whiskey-soaked failure, whom the town jeered at, a man who gave fiddling lessons and played for dances, drank like a fish as everybody knew, and never paid his debts. Even I knew at eleven or so that he ran after women and had every other fault that beset a man with emotional unbalance. And one day, as he passed, my father called me to his chair on the front porch, where I stood between his legs, and he put his arm about me and said:

"Willie, see old Professor Mechem! Pretty poor pickin's of a man, isn't he?"

I agreed.

"Just about frazzled out and gone to hell."

Again I agreed.

"Do you know what's the matter with him?"

I certainly knew. At least when my father went on I was not surprised:

"Music! Just too damned much music. He wa'n't such a bad feller when he was young. I knew him back in Leavenworth. Kinda dressed to kill and very sporty. But he just let himself go on music. And he's a dead beat and a whiskey sot and everything else that's mean, and it's music. And now, Willie, what do you say that we stop music lessons? I don't want you to grow up like that."

So we stopped. And again my mother sighed herself into a good cry, for she was tremendously proud of my music. I had learned to play—whether by note or by ear, I don't remember—all the old tunes that she could sing. Somewhere she had been exposed to grand opera, and I learned to play airs from "Il Trovatore" by note, and songs from "Fra Diavolo"—those last by ear.

She would sit by the hour when she ought to have been at work, drinking in the crude music that I made by ear and note so slovenly and so carelessly in my ignorant pride. My father was not unappreciative. He heard me play a tune, and he whistled it—and he was a great whistler—with an exact ear; but he would have died before he would praise me openly as my mother did. Nevertheless he was tremendously proud and impressed when I played a tune the circus clown sang:

> She's a daisy, she's a darling,
> She's a dumpling, she's a lamb.
> You should hear her play upon the piano,
> Such an education has my Mary Ann!

Years after, when my father was dead, I found a flute while rummaging in an old bureau drawer. It was his flute, and my mother said that he used to play it before he lost his trigger finger in some accident in the forties. She said the only complaint he ever made about the loss of his finger was not that it handicapped his surgery, but that it robbed him of his flute. Therefore, he whistled. He was not a talkative man around the house. I can remember him sitting for hours either reading or smoking his pipe, meditating like a turtle on a log, perhaps sadly mourning for his flute—his crown of sorrows, "remembering happier days."

Only when my mother got down a book and offered to read to me could I be lured from the organ. She read widely. I would give a great deal to know what became of the two-volume edition of poems by the Tennyson brothers which she owned, and from which she sometimes read to me what seemed like heavenly music. But for poetry, mostly I had Felicia Hemans and verses from selections of poetry that the book agents sold her—good old standard pieces of the early nineteenth century, or maybe the late eighteenth, full of jig and jingle and jump of the sort that I had read over and over in the school readers. And by that time she had gone deep into the file of the Seaside Library, which she must have brought into the family from her college days at Galesburg. They were pirated reprints of English novels whose vogue now has passed, and whose titles mean nothing. But she fed me liberal doses of Anthony Trollope, Wilkie Collins, Charles Reade, after Dickens had played out. She had been one of the founders of the Eldorado City Library, which still functions in the town after more than sixty years. And of course I had my own books from that wellspring. It was there that I ran across "Tom Sawyer," and "The Celebrated Jumping Frog of Calaveras County," and "Innocents Abroad," and loved them. I went stark mad over Mark Twain at a dozen years. My mother was shocked, for Mark

Twain was accounted an atheist. But my father did not care, though they saw that I got to the Campbellite Sunday school at nine o'clock every Sunday morning, and the Presbyterian at twelve, and the Methodist at half past two. Still my father, while he set great store by the Bible as literature and as a code of morals, had very little use for its theological implications. I gathered from their arguments that my mother was still afraid of hell-fire and still hoped for wings. She stood boldly with the angels, "a crown upon her forehead and a harp within her hand"! As an argufier, my father was not a success. My mother could down him. But her responses sometimes grew accurate, and her voice got a keen edge. I remember once when she had him cornered, where he either had to fight or run, he reached calmly for his Panama hat, crooked his cane over his arm, whistled for his dog and marched serenely out of the room, singing sweetly in rejoinder:

> "She's a daisy, she's a darling,
> She's a dumpling, she's a lamb."

As he turned the corner out of the yard, he looked back with a grin and gently chortled:
> "Such an education has my Mary Ann!"

And then we laughed.

But no wonder, when election time came around, this black abolition Republican, who was my mother, and this Stephen Douglas Copperhead Democrat who was my father, still unwashed, still voting for Jackson, had their purple moments. No wonder that I grew up full of complexes, and with a certain lack of conviction which comes from seeing both sides well presented by those you love and knowing full well there are two sides to everything, and that what seems black or white is generally gray.

The other side of the family picture was that often, when he came back from a Fabian retreat, my father would be full of cherubic smiles that fat men love to wear, and try to kiss her publicly before me. And she would pretend to struggle, and say, "Oh, Doctor, why don't you leave that pipe . . ." and it would be all made up again.

I look back upon my boyhood there in the big house, when I was going to school in the grammar department, with a sense of well-being. My father was somebody. Occasionally he took me to Topeka, when there was a Democratic state convention; or when he was delegated from the town to represent it at some state-wide meeting or enterprise, where his leadership rose above his party. And I remember once playing around the naked foundation of the west wing of the Kansas Statehouse while my father, inside at the Democratic convention, was running for State Treasurer. It was then, when we were passing along the streets, that we ran into some sort of city election

61

or informal primary. We saw a long queue of negroes, holding their ballots high so that the checker could read them and pay them when they came out of the voting booth. And my father said angrily to me:

"Willie, look at that! In this state, the year before you were born, they voted a constitutional amendment which gave those men the right to vote and denied it to women like your mother. I voted for woman suffrage, but against this damn shame!"

He wanted me to know it. I have always remembered it. And it is a tradition of family pride that we entertained Susan B. Anthony in the sixties when she was campaigning in Kansas for woman suffrage. And Elizabeth Cady Stanton was my mother's friend. My father also was a Prohibitionist back in the seventies when the issue was pending in Kansas. Democrat though he was, we entertained at our house John P. St. John, the Kansas Republican hero of Prohibition. Senator Plumb, whom my father knew in Emporia, and who had gone to Washington and was a power there, a black Republican, enjoyed our hospitality—as did Senator Ingalls, an erudite Massachusetts man who honored Kansas as a Senator. These house guests gave me a sense of belonging to the ruling class, and maybe I was a little snob, though I hope not. But it could have been, easily.

CHAPTER IX

I Learn of Good and Evil

And I dreamed also, which pleased me most,
That you loved me just the same!

IF I WAS a snob, Agnes Riley took it out of me. She was a farmer's daughter.
In those days, when boyhood was young, my world revolved around her;
and there was no snobbish nonsense about Agnes. She walked a mile and a
half to school. On cold days she wore a scarlet shawl that I could see from
the second-story window of the schoolhouse more than a mile away. And
I watched it come across the prairies with delight and mounting joy. A tall,
thin, black-eyed girl, with high coloring, was Agnes Riley. It seemed to me
her black eyes glowed with a fire I had never known before. I certainly
thrilled with delight when she gave me a smile though I do not remember
that I trembled with fear at her frown. For she never frowned. But after my
birthday party, where I looked for her among the sheeted and pillowcased
ghosts and finally found her, she was the center of my cosmos. So far as I
was concerned, there was nothing in me to attract her. The child had turned
to boy—a pudgy, middle-sized boy who clowned a bit to disguise his awk-
wardness, with at least that much sense of self-defense. He was a boy who
was, according to the preserved records which my mother kept in our old
trunk through all the years until her death, fairly good in his studies, better
in English, geography, and history than in anything else; lower in deportment than anything else, indicating something which his parents called
mischievousness and the teacher probably catalogued as meanness; who
wore the common clothes of his schoolfellows, probably was a bit of a show-
off with his red store sled. Albert Ewing had the only other store sled in
town. This little redheaded boy was the kind who most eagerly and conspicuously pops his hand up and snaps his fingers at the teacher when he
knows the answer. In short, if Agnes Riley saw in this boy anything like

63

the center of her cosmos, it was not in his qualities but in hers. She also, six months younger than he, was passing from childhood into girlhood. It was boy and girl—newborn adolescence moving youth for the first time. It is an exquisite sensation, feeling the blood coursing through strange channels, taking new delightful ways, or running from the heart through life's spring erosions to the brain, reporting there great news of ineffable happiness. We were boy and girl going furtively, almost stealthily perhaps, but eagerly into the new wide land of youth, the promised land of the wicked Canaanites, those grown-ups where all the milk and honey of new untasted joy lay vague before youth to lure it on; boy and girl and youth!

If Agnes Riley, in those first days of my young boyhood, was the center of my cosmos, and if I spent more time than I should, of early morning, plucking my mother's roses and tying them on a wire cross which my own hands made, and if I gathered wild flowers for her and not my mother, and if I watched eagerly in the morning after I had slipped the rose wreath in our desk for the red shawl coming over the horizon, I did not moon about it. I was but playing marbles, probably much of the time, running my bank possibly, running foot races—which was my favorite school-ground sport. But always I had an eye on the main chance. For I was born with an acquisitive sense. My little bank on the clock shelf at home was always well filled. For I was always looking for a chance to run errands for someone with a dime. I remember vividly my father coming up behind me one summer day on Main Street and whacking me with his cane across my upturned bottom, to the astonishment of a stranger before whom I was kneeling, shining his shoes:

"Get up from there, Willie. Not that, by God! You go home!"

And I grabbed my kit, for which I had traded a heavy outlay of marbles that I had won in my marble "bank," and scurried home. How he ever explained it to the stranger, I do not know. But when he came home he called me to his chair and said, very gently:

"Now, Willie" (he and my mother alone were calling me Willie after I was ten—I was Will in school, Will White even to the teacher in her warmest moments), "Willie, there are some things you just can't do unless you have to, and you don't have to shine any man's shoes."

He explained it all in language which I have forgotten. It was the only time in all his life that I can remember when he implanted a sense of caste in my heart. My mother, on the other hand, gave me plenty of it. But I had come into the zone where a boy runs in wild gangs. I was a born gangster. The town was not large enough for more than one or two gangs. Ours dug a cave by the river bank. We stole chickens from a near-by farm, and roasting ears and watermelons and tomatoes in summer. And in fall each of us had an apple stealer, a horseshoe nail driven through a cork, with feathers at one end, tied to the end of a string to keep it upright. We would throw it into an apple peddler's wagon on the street, or into a bushel basket of apples before a grocer's door, spear an apple, yank it, get it into our pockets in the wink of an eye. Then, bulging with apples, we would hie us to our cave and eat in gloating, guiltless glee, proud of our prowess. Old man Young, the city marshal, once took after us with our pockets bulging. Albert Ewing, Bill Betts, Charley Harvey, and I started together down an alley, and with a natural criminal instinct, broke—running four ways; and while the old man hesitated for a moment, before deciding which to follow, we were gone. We made the wide circuit of the town, like hunted criminals, before we rounded up, with panting and beating hearts, to the cave. Old man Howe, whose chickens we stole, reported to my father. He paid for the day's chicken and told me at dinner that night the difference between having fun and being a thief; he said that any time we wanted a chicken he would give me money for it. Even my mother joined him in reprobation, though she did think old man Howe might be in better business than tattling about boyish pranks.

It was about that time when I came running, top speed, home across lots with Bill Burnham hot behind me. I was far enough ahead of him to get around the corner of the house, down into the cellar, pulling the trapdoor on top of me. And when my mother came out, seeing my plight from the window, she confronted him and said:

"You great big stand-up, what are you picking on this little boy for?"

And Bill said: "He can't call my mother that!"

"What?" cried my mother, walking into his trap.

And Bill said: "You know damn well what. And I won't let him call my mother that!"

And I huddled on the top step with the trapdoor over me, listening through a crack to my mother denying that her little boy would use that kind of language. And at dinner that night she told my father about Bill Burnham chasing me, neglecting to explain why, with Pa looking at me hard, and she said, "What did you call him, Willie?" not having even heard about that name I called his mother. But Pa was wise about boys, and he knew that big boys chased little boys only upon extreme provocation.

And I said, "I don't know!"

He answered: "Well, I know. Do you want me to tell Ma what you called him?"

I cannot remember my answer, but this I remember clearly. He said: "Willie, I wish he had caught you and beat hell out of you. You deserved it. You knew he was a lot bigger than you; and you were a coward, and I am ashamed of you."

There for once he would not let my mother take my part. So I ate my bitter meal in silence. But I think I learned something there—instruction in the fundamental moralities of life; these and its decent amenities, which are somewhat the same.

The town changed swiftly. It, too, was going from its childhood into youth. The railroad seemed to shrivel and wither its little industries, though I did not realize it until many years afterwards. The tinshop slowed down. The harness shop was not what it had been; harness came ready-made from Kansas City and St. Louis. The tannery disappeared, and only the tanbark marked where it stood. Even the slaughterhouse was not the busy place it had been when I was a child and gloated and gagged at its stinks and ghastly sounds. The shoe shop seemed to be making no more shoes, only mending them. The plaster-of-Paris hat molds that I had first known around Leila Heaton's mother's millinery, we no longer found around Eldorado's new millinery shop. Hats came in from afar, ready molded. The self-sufficient village was becoming a country town in my early boyhood days. Its population had grown to more than a thousand. It was a bustling place. New houses were going up all over the hill where my father sold his lot. Two-story houses were now becoming common. No one had quite so many feet of porch as we, but wide porches were common; and yards began to be fenced in paling where the cattle had grazed in my childhood. Streets were lined out and bluegrass lawns appeared. Elm trees, moved in from the creeks, lined the streets, and evergreens dotted the lawns. A few women now had time for flower gardens. The wide place in the dusty road where the movers' wagons rumbled, where the movers themselves trudged along, and where the little boys followed herding their cows—all this was going, or was gone.

By 1880, Kansas was fairly well settled, and the era had begun—a time when machinery was beginning to dominate the farm, and the mortgage to buy farm machinery was being plastered over the new state. For there was no economic surplus, no savings to draw on. Credit was easy. Labor-saving machinery piled up in front and behind all the hardware stores. Business was good. Garfield and Arthur were running against Hancock and English. And I, a little Democratic boy, who fought easily and laughed afterwards, had to stand my ground that fall at school and wrestle, kick, fight, gouge, bellow, and bawl, as my passions rose in defense of my father's faith. It never occurred to me to fight for my mother's faith.

It was about this time that my father, who had been enjoying our grand new house with its twelve rooms, its "hundred forty-four running feet of porches," its gorgeous gingerbread ornamentations crawling all over the pillars of those porches and under and around the twenty-two windows and half a dozen doors, decided that he owed it as a public duty to the town to open this house as a hotel. And maybe that did not start a volcano, an earth-

66

quake, and a family cataclysm! I remember the disturbance, but the only sentence of it that hangs in my memory is this:

"Well, Doctor, we might as well have a hotel; they might as well pay something as long as you keep bringing them in!"

My mother meant the interminable list of guests whom he was always inviting: travelers whom he had known in his merchandising days; friends whom he knew in eastern Kansas, passing through the town—farmers chiefly; Democratic farmers from the surrounding townships caught in town Saturdays at mealtime; and, of course, distinguished citizens—the politicians of the time, the governors, congressmen, senators, and judges who came to the town on their political pilgrimages. So my mother yielded. The hotel opened.

I, a little boy of ten or a dozen years, had charge of the cigar stand. I bought and sold my cigars, paid the bills, and kept the profit, under the stern accounting eye of my father. There again arose family discussion. My mother thought, and of course said vigorously, that I had no business in the office, hearing all those traveling men talk. I do not know what my father's return argument was; but probably he knew in his heart that the traveling men had very little to teach a boy who had grown up in a pioneer town around the slaughterhouse and in the livery stable, who had roamed through the romantic woods where the peripatetic strumpets made their camps, who had picked up his sex education from the Saxon words chalked on sidewalks and barns, who had taken his Rabelaisian poetry from the walls of backhouses, and who had seen saloons spew out their back door their indigestible drunkards, swarming with flies, to furnish amusement and devilment for the entertainment of little boys, as it was in the beginning of civilization.

Anyway, I sold cigars and made money, and I stuffed the little bank with the profits. My father turned the pennies, dimes, and quarters into five-dollar gold pieces, and I always had a little money to spend for the fundamental necessities of boyhood, though he made me pay for my first suit of store clothes out of that bank. But I was proud enough not to begrudge the price. He was teaching me thrift, economy, and the rules of business, though I did not know it. Neither did my mother appreciate it. But she was too busy in the kitchen to know, or probably care much, what happened. For while my father preened around the place in his white clothes and Panama hat, on his majestic stretch of porches, greeting his guests, entertaining them, and going to market with his basket like a maharajah to a durbar, she did a husky woman's work—this woman with pink and white complexion and bronze hair which she curled so carefully until we opened the hotel. She wrestled, wrangled, and roughed it, trying to get along with two or three girls in the dining room and kitchen who soldiered on her, knowing that she would rather do it herself than quarrel with them about how to do it. In the midst of it, she was attacked by inflammatory rheumatism. She lost all of her teeth, and they cut off her hair. She kept the curls, all beautifully curled, for many years afterward; and, being sentimental, no doubt she wept over them in secret, for she showed them to me when I was a man and asked me if I remembered them. Before she was up and at work again, we closed the hotel. It was a sad farce, that hotel venture.

My father seemed to have some hidden pride in not making money out of the hotel, though he was a shrewd trader in real estate. Probably he hesitated at capitalizing his hospitality, for he was vastly proud of his table. We used only the breasts of the quail and prairie chickens, generally broiled on hickory coals; and, in season, we had them once or twice a week. He bought only the best cuts of beef. I remember as a little boy going with him many times to market to bring home the market basket, and he taught me where to find the tenderloin, the sirloin, the T-bone, and the rib roast in a beef carcass. He always saved the bones for soup! Not, I suppose, because he liked to save, so much as because he liked to serve good soup. We bought mackerel in the kit, and salt codfish by the case. In rush times I waited on table. I had to learn the bill of fare and sing it off for each of the guests. I also learned how to set the table expertly, and niftily pyramid knives and forks and spoons with a napkin on top. What with my cigar case, my gang, my girl, and the incidental business of going to school, I had a busy and happy time in the hotel, despite the fact that I knew my father was exploiting my mother and her sophisticated cooking. Children learn much more than their elders realize. Yet I suppose the relation between my parents did not harden. She had her pride too, perhaps pride in me and pride that nothing slipshod or sloppy ever went from the kitchen. She made no weeping protest to the hired girls. She rode through that kitchen like a captain with banners. But when she came out of the doors of the hotel, that finally closed, her pink and white skin was gone, her lovely hair was sheared, and she had a set of false teeth which on the whole became her, for before she had had buck teeth which were most disenchanting. That was the weakness of her face, which made her always conscious that she was a plain woman.

It was during or just before our hotel experience that I began my newspaper experience in a curtain raiser, a quick seriocomedy piece that was to forecast my career. When I was eleven years old, or such a matter, my father thought I should work. He was forever singing that ancient father song that came, probably, from Father Adam, telling the boys of the marvelous industry of his childhood. If fathers, when they were boys, really had done all the things they brag about, the world would have been strutted into its millennium ten thousand years ago. So my father is not to be blamed if,

68

when I was ten or a dozen years old, he felt that I should be chained and shackled to the machine of life.

"Now, Willie," he was forever saying, "when I was a boy . . ." Then he was off.

Mothers are different; my mother was. She had had a little brother, as most mothers had, and she knew how naturally reckless and unchainable a little boy is. So she did not want me to go to work. But the Puritan blood in my father, and a vast phantasm of his own industry and exemplary childhood, backed him up when he would harness me to the harsh, hard work of the world. We did not need the money. We lived in the best house in the little town of Eldorado, and he was a country doctor and a storekeeper who had a Yankee seven-devil lust for trading in real estate, which he swapped like horses with the nobility and gentry of the time and place. But, alas for me, he was a Democratic politician and naturally had money invested in the poor little starved-to-death Democratic weekly published in a tiny, unpainted, cigar-box-shaped pine building with a false front, straggling on the outskirts of the mean little business street of the county-seat village that hoped some day to be a city. In order to secure me employment he had only to take me by the hand the day after school closed in the spring, lead me up the street, and present me to the Editor. We shall meet this Editor later.

In the printing office were three racks of type, and a small job printing press—a Gordon, I believe—on which were printed noteheads, letterheads, and small handbills. Near that was an old Washington hand press of an ancient and honorable lineage. It was secondhand—secondhand so many times that no one knew when it had come from the foundry. It had crossed the Mississippi before the Civil War, that was all one knew definitely. Its Kansas lineage could be traced from Leavenworth to Lawrence, to Topeka, to Ottawa, and so, following the stream of immigration, to Eldorado for a few years, after which it was to march westward into the wheat country, and thence into the great desert of the Southwest. A composing stone stood in the midst of the room, on which were the forms of type for the two pages which the paper set up and printed. Its outer pages came from Kansas City, ready printed. The walls of the room were unplastered, as well as unsealed. It being summer, the stove sat—cold and rusty—by the press, with paper sticking out of its mouth and a pot of ancient printer's tableting glue on its top, cold and petrified in disuse. A dejected attempt to cover the rough, splintery board walls and joists of the room with handbills, and so beautify it, disclosed the portraits of a number of stallions and jacks, a Fourth of July bill or two in red, white, and blue, some theatrical handbills revealing the fact that "Pygmalion and Galatea," and "Spartacus, the Gladiator," and "The Hidden Hand," and "Uncle Tom's Cabin" had been played by strolling players—Louie Lord and her company, the Goldens and Spooners, in the

69

courtroom across the street. In the front of the room, near the door, stood the Editor's desk, bestrewn with exchanges, writing materials, and old letters. And beside his desk was the box of sawdust which he used for a spittoon. For the Editor was a meticulous person who chewed fine-cut and respected the amenities of a distant civilization.

Here in this sanctum, twelve years old or such a matter, barefoot, with a clean Monday-morning shirt on, and with pants rolled decently to my knees, I was left by my father. The Editor, the foreman, and the printer formed the dramatis personae of the establishment. I was to be the devil. I have a scant memory of my work in the printing office at that period. I remember picking up type from the floor in the evening, and sweeping out the room. I remember carrying water from a well, down the street and across an alley to the printing office. I remember standing on a box and rolling an ink roller across the type on the bed of the Washington hand press—hard, sweaty work from which, probably because I did it badly rather than because he pitied me, the foreman took me after what seemed a long time, possibly half an hour. I remember folding papers for subscribers which the Editor addressed in lead pencil. And I remember carrying the papers to the post office in a great wash bucket, going several times.

Finally, Saturday night came. I sat around, saw the Editor come over to the printer and make some financial arrangement with him, and saw him slip some paper—possibly a check, possibly an order for groceries, Heaven knows what, but not coin of the realm—to the foreman. And nothing came to me. I was to have had a dollar and a half a week. I was not a brash child, except on the playground. I said nothing. The Editor walked grandly out. The printer winked at me with some cryptic meaning behind his wink, which disconcerted me deeply, for I went home that night full of wrongs; wrongs which my mother abetted. When I went to bed I overhead her upbraiding my father. It seems he had forgotten to leave the money for my wages with the Editor, as per previous agreement. The discovery of this fact, that I was being paid by my own father, was disconcerting. My mother told me the next day that when I had worked a whole week I should have my wages. So I went back—a galley slave scourged to the dungeon—and worked Monday, Tuesday, and Wednesday. Wednesday night I waited— no wages came. I went home surging with injustice and wept, being inside the threshold where tears did not disgrace a boy. Again my mother assured me that I should have my money the next morning; my father had forgotten, or maybe the Editor had forgotten. Someone had blundered.

I went back Thursday morning. The Editor came breezing in, cheerful, happy, and apparently innocent of the great wrong he was committing. It was a hot summer day, in June. The printer and the foreman drank much water. The water in the bucket was two-thirds gone and was stale. The order came to get another bucket of water; this was just before noon. The air was wavy with heat outside. Grasshoppers and locusts were rasping their clatter in the trees and high weeds through which I went for the water. At the well, throwing rocks at the hornets working in the mud around the curb by way of diversion, were my fellow citizens and peers in the free Kingdom of Boyville. I set down the bucket and took a mild detached interest in the hornets. My peers knew that I was no longer of their rank. I had become a bondman not of their caste. And, being boys, they taunted me: "We're goin' swimmin'." "Wouldn't you like to go swimmin'?" "New boy down there says he can take a big rock to weight him down and walk across the creek under water. Betcha he can't." "How many buckets of water do you have to carry?" "Is it hot in that buildin'?" "Who's your boss?" "Does he jaw you?" "Whatja do?" So they twisted the spears of captivity in my entrails. They started up and casually went away, throwing clods at me by way of contempt and derision, and I fired back rocks, looking wistfully at the straggling procession roaming down the path between the high weeds, through the ravine that led to the creek.

All that morning I had furtively watched the Editor for some sign of his intention to establish justice in that shop, as between him and me. I had had no sign; not a flicker of an eyelash. The last tagging toddler of the gang disappeared into the weeds.

And I, lifting my face to high heaven to witness the justice of my cause, kicked the bucket into the mud, swarming with hornets, and went running down the path toward the swimming hole. So fell the curtain on the prologue of my career.

CHAPTER X

I Come Trailing Clouds of Glory

As I LOOK back across the years, my father seems to have been hurrying my education with some kind of premonition that his time was short. He was taking me to places where I should see interesting things—to Kansas City to see steam power engines and the great trotting horse Maud S. or Rarus (I forget which), to the State Fair to see the first electric light when it crossed the Mississippi River. It was on a high pole, a sputtering lavender star which was supposed to light a whole neighborhood. On the same trip, probably at the fair, I saw James G. Blaine. It was in the early eighties. His beard was lighter than an iron-gray. His skin was fair. His smile was electric, even a little boy knew that. His voice was gentle and persuasive. My father explained to me who Blaine was, in language that a boy in his early teens could understand. My father's heroes were few. Even Tilden, whom he thought a martyr, he accepted only at a liberal commercial discount. He came greatly to admire Abraham Lincoln. Andrew Jackson was his ideal. From both my parents I had but scorn for the Republican leaders of Reconstruction days and the things they were doing to the South. In Kansas, in the seventies and eighties, the Democratic party was in a hopeless minority. The soldiers of the Civil War, whom I saw in my childhood coming into Kansas and appearing on high days and holidays in their army blue with visored caps, dominated the state.

Here may be a place where I can set down the photograph upon my child's mind of the first memorial parade I ever saw. It was headed by the Eldorado silver cornet band in splendid regalia—splendid to my child's eye at least. Following that was the volunteer fire department pulling the old pumping engine that took its water from the great cistern at the corner of Central and Main streets. Then in the town's one open carriage sat Peter Telyea, a veteran of the War of 1812—a man well into his nineties who owned the town carriage works, and who toiled amid his lathes and shavings every day until he died. Behind him, on horseback, were the veterans

72

of the Mexican War. Colonel Gibson, our town banker, rode at the head of that small squadron of fifty men or so, all bearded. Then, in order of rank, were the veterans of the Civil War. General Ellet, the hero of Island Number Ten in Grant's campaign on the Mississippi, led the long line. After the general came the half-dozen colonels we had, and captains, all sashed and horsed and panoplied in military pomp; and following them walked the blue-clad soldiers of the lower ranks. Behind them marched citizens on foot, and women's organizations. It was a long parade—a picture I shall never forget. And my father, who had no part in the military glory, held my hand as we stood on the sidewalk. He explained to me the meaning of it all, and left to me no great sense of the pomp and circumstance of glorious war. My Uncle Frank Hatten, my mother's brother, captain in the First Michigan Cavalry, who enlisted and reenlisted three times, and after the war went West to fight the Indians, rode in the parade. My father clapped for him, and so did I; but he dismissed certain sections of the parade with the phrase, "A lot of damn bounty jumpers!" and carefully explained to me that a "bounty jumper" was a man who was paid to substitute for a drafted man, and who then deserted from the army with his bounty in his pocket, turned up in another part of the country, got another bounty, and enlisted again. It was a fairly profitable career in a country which had a wide, unsettled frontier to which the "bounty jumper" could go, and from which he could return to ply his trade in a new and strange community.

After the parade there was considerable bibulous hilarity, and I was struck later with the exact similarity between the alcoholic diversions and the general attitude toward life which the Grand Army of the Republic manifested, in their blue clothes and brass buttons, and the gaudy spectacle of the American Legionnaires, having their purple moments fifty years later. The men of the Grand Army were ten years away from war—men in their thirties and forties, husky, full-throated, happy, carefree, royal American citizens rollicking their way into middle age. Probably Napoleon's soldiers and Caesar's and Alexander's and Xerxes', in the days of their pride, were the same kind of boys who upset the hotel beds and threw the pillow feathers out of the windows, even as the Legion gathered for its earlier conventions in the first decade that followed its return from our overseas expeditionary force. And probably, also, none of those soldiers— from Xerxes' boys to Pershing's—ever realized his fondest dream of shooting a lieutenant. Thus, human hopes dance, beckoning upon the distant horizon, and always recede as we approach them.

I cannot remember (I have often tried) just when it was that our gang of cave dwellers who played "Injun" with our bows and arrows, and shot rabbits with nigger shooters made of rubber bands and forked sticks, came indoors and began to be "housebroke." Somehow I believe the girls got us in. We began to attend parties—somewhere between eleven and fourteen. There also we ganged up, but with the female of the species, and I remember early in our middle teens we who cast ourselves as Indians and desperadoes, bandits and horse thieves, suddenly found ourselves playing post office, dancing the Virginia reel, taking our apples to girls instead of to the teacher, and sending valentines. We called our gang—male and female —the "Spring Chicken Club," and Mr. Murdock in his newspaper in Eldorado named us "Trundle Bed Trash." And we liked the name. Our social diversions, even when we had a party in the town restaurant, could not have cost us more than a quarter, for in those days one could get a fiddler, a pianist, and a cornetist, or any combination of three dance-music makers, for five dollars. But the apex of social distinction was to hire "The Italians," who came from Wichita, or possibly Kansas City, and made the rounds of the country towns. They played on the streets for dimes and nickels and were hired by the young blades of the town, men in their late teens and early and middle twenties, and we Trundle Bed Trash trekked along for a price, and the music—a violin or two, a flute, or a harp—seemed to me exquisite. Hearing "The Italians" was a step up in my musical education. I followed them about the streets. I passed the hat for them among the traveling men at our hotel so that they would play on the porch a long time. I had never before heard such music, and my ears drank it in greedily. When they were gone, I went to my cabinet organ, tried to play by ear the tunes I heard and made some kind of fist of it—probably a pretty poor fist. But it pleased me immensely.

It is curious to note, and I suppose I see more clearly in the perspective of nearly sixty years, how the gang instinct of boyhood changed so swiftly and so surely from the wild life of the male to the mixed society which formed the Spring Chicken Club. Certainly it thought itself the elite, but the same kind of ganging that the boys knew, where there was no line of marked wealth or parental distinction back of the crystallization, governed the unconscious organization of "The Spring Chickens." It was not the rich little boys and the rich little girls in a community where we had few riches, who set the social pattern. Some boys and some girls who were Spring Chickens were dirt-poor. But not all the dirt-poor boys and girls got in, which also was true of our horse-thief gang in the caves. Childhood and youth, left free as we were in a new place and a verdant time, were drawn together in their organized social cliques and clans, somewhat by their natural qualities—their capacity for crystallization. Whatever it may be, I know now and I knew then that we—the elite, the Spring Chickens— were envied. I realized that we were a lot of little snobs and were proud of it. But our parents had little to do with those we admitted or rejected.

We accepted a Jew. We rejected a rich lumber dealer's girl. We took farmers' sons and daughters, even the saloonkeeper's boy and girl; children whose parents our parents rejected. But here and there we drew the line. Why and how, I do not know. I only know that our class lines were not set by money, but they were set. And we thought we were somebodies—this Trundle Bed Trash—and swished our little tails in school with something like social arrogance. Upon it all my father frowned and my mother beamed. And in the meantime, nosing into my middle teens, I made good school grades in the softer subjects, history, rhetoric, Latin, and reading, fair grades in mathematics and the sciences, and often dropped to 80 in deportment, as I began in my middle school years. I was what I was. The pattern was set. I had as Will White, the schoolboy, what was bred in me by Willie White, the child; and he had his forebears in Ireland and New England.

Let us take a look at this Will White, the schoolboy. He is of medium height for a boy, with the one pancake freckle of childhood breaking into crumbs of freckles at his neck under his ears. Here comes his chiefest sorrow—pimples all over his jaw and chin and cheek, miserable disfiguring pimples that he could not help squeezing, pinching, scratching, blackheaded pimples that broke his pride. Other boys teased him and shamed him about them. For there was a boy scandal about pimples which had no reference to a boy's diet. And while his spirit broke under the burden of shame he kept stoking in buckwheat cakes for breakfast, literally by the dozen, and bacon and fried potatoes and sausage or codfish, great hunks and slugs of protein, starch, and other calories. No one told boys then that diet would help with pimples. This pudgy little Eldorado boy was a medium-sized boy, broad-shouldered, rather crescent-vested. He was still a good foot racer and was proud of his straight, hard legs. Clothes interested him. He began to learn to tie a four-in-hand and knew that a made-up tie was not quite the thing. And he tried to learn to waltz.

Square dances, of course, were simple enough; a boy hobbled along and kept some sense of the rhythm of the music in his feet. But waltzes were different. I can see myself now, a chunky, nimble youth carrying in his arms a big brown rocking chair with a cane seat, whistling a waltz, probably the "Kiss Waltz," or the "Corn Flower Waltz," or the chorus of "Pretty Pond Lilies," swinging that big rocking chair around and whirling it along the "hundred and forty-four running feet of porch," which was his father's pride. And I can see (for that picture is etched with the sharp bit of discomfiture) the neighbors stop along the sidewalk, gape and wonder what in the name of all the gods at once had got into the little White boy. But he whirled along, whistling and one-two-threeing, and tried to keep in step while carrying the big brown chair. If the neighbors thought he was going mildly mad, owing to evil ways and wicked habits, he nevertheless

75

whirled on, for in those days he was what might be called an extrovert, who was for the moment impervious to the bad opinion of mankind because in the long run he was so eager to please. On summer afternoons he used to lie in the hammock on the east porch of the big house reading, with maybe another boy or two about, whose nose also was in a book—Albert Ewing possibly, or the new boy, Lew Schmucker, who was very bookish and also very bad, for he brought into the community of boyhood all the dirty stories from a boarding school in Hayesville, Ohio. And yet he could spout poetry, Byron and Hood, whole pages from "Lalla Rookh," and amorous, of course, as befitted adolescence. By way of being human, the other boys played baseball and went out to wallop or be walloped by the Augusta High School team, or the Douglass team, or Towanda, or Benton, or Eureka, or Rosalia. The Eldorado ball players were the Red Socks. I kept score and looked after the bats and catcher's masks, and so learned to be methodical and punctual and precise about material things, while the other boys learned highly laudable skill.

As for girls, even the worst of us—the more venereal-minded—set them upon a pedestal. They were apart, though often in school one of us would sit with a girl to sing in the music hour. All of us beaued the girls to the little dances and to the kissing parties, which still lingered along in the middle teens half surreptitiously in our social life. But on the neighborhood vacant lots girls played with us. Sometimes, if they were tomboys and not afraid of showing their legs, they joined in foot races; and I can remember that Dora Rector, who, because she was husky, commanded our respect, could without scandal do turns on the bar and was not ashamed if her skirt flopped over her head and showed her chaste and ruffled drawers while she hung by her legs and dropped from a knee hold to a toe hold on the swinging broom handle that was our trapeze. Other girls envied her, tried to imitate her, but certainly did not talk about her.

Of course, our society did have its scandals. We had ceased to write on sidewalks and fences the bracketed names of lovers in jeering rhymes. That passed with childhood in a pre-Valentine age of innocence. We played games with girls, like pullaway; and Dora Rector and Vonnie Knowles and half a dozen other girls, whose brothers ran with the gang, would play leapfrog sometimes and walk on top fence rails, practicing for tightrope exhibitions. We all played hide-and-seek together around the barns and high grass behind the woodpiles of our parents' homes. I remember the great scandal that shook the high school when Laura Bassett and I were the center of seething, searing gossip. It happened this way.

A dozen or so boys and girls were playing hide-and-seek. And I had a brilliant idea about hiding. After all the others had sneaked into barns, corncribs or woodsheds, or were crouching in the sunflowers and horse-weeds, I ran into the privy and stood in the triangular space made by the open door and the two walls. I hid so successfully that I hesitated to come out and reveal my favorite hiding place even when they said: "All's out's in free!" When the next round started, Laura Bassett got the same idea that I had. She came in, little dreaming that I was hiding behind the door. She rushed in and swung the door shut. She ran jam into me. In instinctive terror we both realized that we were trapped. The boy who was "it" turned around, opened his eyes, and began hunting for the hiders. We peeked through the cracks in the wall board, trying to find some way to make an exit one at a time. The seconds pounded into minutes. We stood there, ashamed to look at each other, knowing the appalling situation. One by one, the youngsters came tearing and pounding "One-two-three for me" on the base. Then they were all in but us. And they called and called for us and we did not respond, which was not exceptional. The next round began and the next boy, after he had counted a hundred, sang out: "Bushel of wheat, bushel of rye; all 't ain't ready, holler I!" He opened his eyes and went out to look again. We stood there dry-mouthed, frightened. Laura began to cry, and I wanted to, and it was terrible. Finally at the end of the third round, just as the fourth boy was turning around to blind himself and count a hundred, she sneaked out and someone saw her; and, like a fool, I followed her quickly and two or three boys crouching in the sunflowers saw me follow. We only had another round after that. Shame and scandal broke up the game. For days and days Laura and I, who were neighbors and dear friends, but who had no romantic notions or illusions about each other, were linked in a brazen, shameful scandal, though it really was not funny. But laughter rocked in the corners of the schoolhouse, where whispering children started to giggle and ended by roaring as they repeated the story. If the experience did anything to me (and I suppose it did, for I was terribly galled by it) it taught me not to accept circumstantial evidence, but to realize that always there is another side. That lesson submerged in my later years, but rose finally. For the other day, after each of us had been away from Eldorado for more than fifty years, one of those occasional letters we have exchanged came from Laura Bassett. I thought, and I wondered if she thought, of the day when we were branded with the scarlet letter.

But in a week we were all dancing at a grown-up dance, where "The Italians" were playing. The Trundle Bed Trash and young society and the really best people came, and life was lovely. I suppose feeling, as a child, that you have access to the society of the "really best people" does something to you. Of course it makes you a snob, but it gives you confidence. If I had been poor and rejected of men, and deeply cursed with pimples, I would probably have been a criminal with my hand against society and my heart burning with social rancor. But, pimples or no pimples, Agnes Riley smiled back at me. She could either stand them or ignore them, I never knew which. The "White House" hotel closed, and I had my garden and rolled my little wagon full of vegetables through the streets, peddling my wares and making money for my little iron bank. I have that bank today, indicating the persistence of my acquisitive faculty. It is a little fat man in a brown coat, yellow vest, and blue trousers, with his hand extended so that when you put a coin in his hand he flaps the coin into his vest pocket, and it clinks down into his bowels and is safe. It takes a screw driver to get the money out. It was called a Tammany bank in the persiflage of the gay era sixty years ago when corruption was considered funny. Also that summer, my lust for riches drove me to try to off-bear in the brickyard. I was a dozen years old or such a matter. The off-bearer in a brickyard takes the mud bricks from the mold and dumps them on flat, sanded earth in the sun, from whence in a few days he takes them to the kiln. The mold, which contains six mud bricks, is heavy with water. The job was backbreaking, and when I came home I was pale, and whined in my sleep. My mother rubbed me with arnica and alcohol. At the end of the week even my father forbade me to go back. But the three dollars I got for my work comforted me with a warm sense of security like the consolation of a great faith. I bought two dollars' worth of books, took Agnes Riley to the ice-cream saloon, and probably spent the rest of the money foolishly—maybe for a hand-painted necktie or a book of magic. I bought many books of magic, but I never learned a trick.

CHAPTER XI

I Walk with Death

IT WAS in those days in my very early teens that I tried to write what I thought was poetry. Agnes Riley had written a poem "To a Sand Bur," and published it in the Eldorado paper. She had an aunt, Mary Riley Smith, who had published a book of poems, whose name we saw in Harper's Bazaar and other publications designed for women. My first poetical effort was deeply philosophical. I remember writing the title first, "Whatever Is, Is Right"; and I have a notebook now, which my mother preserved, in which I set down a list of words which rhymed with "right": "fight" and "blight," "kite" and "tight." How I must have patted myself on the head in pride when I plunged into the depths of my vocabulary and turned up the word "wight"! A quatrain or so stands there in my little notebook, three-score years, to remind me how well "Lalla Rookh" and Byron and "Lucile" and Whittier and "Hiawatha" and Will Carleton's poems bore their fruit. I had not yet come to James Whitcomb Riley, so I spelled my words correctly.

On the other hand, I could chin myself twenty-two times on the horizontal bar in the back yard. Only Lew Schmucker could beat that. He also could outrun me. But I pitted Dora Rector against him and brought him to shame. I recall today with boyish glee the pride that I had in Dora Rector when she gathered her little skirts and petticoats up to the bulge in her panties, with her eyes set, her jaw fixed, her chin forward, and her head down, the best runner in the east part of town. And I backed her with all the pins, marbles, tops, pennies, and other wampum of boyhood that I could scrape together.

This recollection deserves space here because it marks the passing of a pioneer sport, the foot racer who went from town to town, generally staging crooked races with local runners. He must have been known since the very beginning of man's earthly pilgrimage. In Eldorado he passed on westward with the sun, and we boys and girls merely imitated him—the ancient sportsman who lived on the prowess of his legs. He could not thrive in coal smoke or around the hum of machines. But he was a real figure **in** my boyhood. I was a poor boxer; could not play baseball; was only a passable rider; and the only game at which I could win was foot racing.

The summer of 1882, I crossed the final branch of the Rubicon Valley and came out of childhood ultimately and finally into boyhood. I·was fourteen years old. The carpet slippers which I wore on Main Street in my latter barefoot days were discarded, and they put shoes on me. Two women practically tied me to get them on—my mother and Agnes Riley. Their disapproval of my bare feet lured me into captivity. Maybe as a consolation, I bought, traded for, or received as a reward for soliciting subscribers for the Youth's Companion, an accordion, and mourned through it the passing of the golden days. I wonder what boys and girls today do without the premium list of the Youth's Companion. That little book opened the door to so many desirable things: a scroll saw, which Albert Ewing got; Barney & Berry skates, which later I acquired; musical instruments, balls and baseball bats and masks, books of games and magic, dumbbells, boxing gloves —all to be had for new subscribers to the Youth's Companion. My father caught me crooking it a little by persuading a boy whose subscription was expiring to renew in the name of another family. Pa stopped that swindle. But I worked hard on the Youth's Companion job in those days and captured much loot.

My father seems to have been with me a good deal that summer. I remembered afterwards, and I remember now, that he sat on the front porch in his white summer regalia, trying to coax me away from the natural diversions of the hour to tell me about his boyhood in Ohio: something of his father and mother who had died when he was about my age; how he and his elder brothers cleared the timber from the farm on which he grew up; and the friendly Indians that were around Norwalk, Ohio, in the eighteen-twenties and the thirties. He was pointing morals, which at the time bored me; for a fourteen-year-old boy is essentially amoral. I was probably a little to the left of amorality by nature and disposition. Life had to beat honesty into me by the club of experience. My father's wise saws and modern instances may have sunk deeply into my consciousness, and they may have bobbed up later—I don't know. But I do believe that Solomon's emphasis on the word "old" has not been sufficently understood when he said:

"Train up a child in the way he should go: and when he is old, he will not depart from it."

One certainly departs from that way in youth, also in early manhood. But whatever one has planted inside him in youth, in the way of spiritual and environmental inheritance, comes bursting into his life around forty and thereafter. Probably I did not really appreciate my father nor mourn his loss with real filial piety until I was old in the biblical sense of the word.

It is then that the seeds of decency, implanted by one's parents, teachers, guides, or guardians, bloom and ripen for the real harvest of life. "When he is old, he will not depart from it." Smart old psychologist, that Solomon, for all his petticoat chasing!

One day that summer Pa and I were alone together. I remember I was lying on my belly, idly thumping my toes on the floor, with my nose in a big leather-bound copy of Plutarch's Lives, which Pa had in the bookcase. It was in fine print and I, being a little nearsighted, had my eyes close to it. It was easier to read on the floor that way than to hold the big book in my hand. Pa had been silent for a long while, drumming with his fingernails on his chair the rhythmic skeleton of some old tune singing in his heart. The bee song that he often hummed was silent. I looked up, and his eyes were glistening as he caught my attention. An open letter was on the table beside him. My string-saving mother preserved that letter with the day and date of it: Delta, Ohio, where he lived as a youth, and August, 1882. He saw that I noticed his moistened eyes. He smiled and said:

"Willie, this letter tells me about the death of a girl I knew when she was not much older than you. She was an awfully nice girl, and she thought I was nice too. And she was about your age. She was my girl, and I was her beau; and that was a long, long time ago. And now she is dead! Her sister wrote me here, and sent me a lock of her hair. She said she wanted me to have it. And it's gray! God 'lmighty, Willie, it's gray! It's gray!" He paused a moment, began drumming again; and then:

"Well, I suppose it ought to be really. But it's gray!"

He repeated that phrase like a gentle protest to Providence. Pretty soon he got up, took his cane, and toddled off the porch down the sidewalk to the thick of the town. And Plutarch interested me no more that morning. I looked at my father going down the street, and suddenly realized that once he had been a boy and had had a girl like Agnes Riley—maybe! After that it was as though we were brothers-in-law in the great family of romantic intrigue. So, initiated into that brotherhood, I never told my mother—not to her dying day. But I did tell Albert Ewing, who had Lizzie Ruddick on the string, and Agnes, and we marveled much at the ways of men.

That summer my father took me with him on various trips to Topeka, to Kansas City, and to Wichita, and he talked to me a lot; but what he said is gone from my consciousness. He talked politics with me; that I remember. And, being a rock-ribbed Democrat, he was greatly interested in a young New Yorker who had been a reform mayor of Buffalo, and who was reigning as governor of New York. His name was Grover Cleveland. He was my father's kind of Democrat in those days, and my father so deeply impressed the name of Grover Cleveland on me that later, when school opened and the high-school teacher, seeking to interest us in politics, asked everyone to name his guess for the next President of the United States, I rose and said bravely, "Grover Cleveland!" The schoolroom laughed. They had never heard of him. I suppose that tradition lived in the Eldorado High School for a dozen years. The teacher, who afterwards became a lawyer, never let me forget it. He did not know that I was not abnormally prophetic but merely was echoing the wishful prophecy of an old-fashioned Jacksonian Democratic father.

My father, like most Kansans of substance and some little consequence there in those days, was an ardent believer in prohibition. The saloons in the little town of Eldorado were corruptive, economically, socially, and morally. We children were taught by our parents that they were hell-holes. Not even the glamour of the rowdy outlaw who rode into the saloon on horseback and pretended to light his cigar with a ten-dollar bill—which probably was not more than a dollar—gave the saloon, to our childish eyes, any sound status or real standing. The best we could do for the saloon was to pick up corks for our fish line and bobbers at the back door and swipe whiskey flasks from the saloon's dump heap, to sell at the drugstore. But my father and mother always entertained notables like John P. St. John, who afterwards became a national hero of prohibition—and my father frowned upon the movement, in his party, to make the resubmission of the prohibition amendment its cause in Kansas at the election that year. He headed the Butler County delegation, to the State Convention at Emporia that year. There the Democrats nominated a good old Tennessee silk-stocking Democrat, something of an orator who even then, nearly twenty years after the Civil War, gave his rhetoric the florid flourishes of ante-bellum days, and said "Suh" for "Sir." His name was John Martin.* But in the platform upon which John Martin was to run was a plank denouncing prohibition, promising to annul the amendment by disuse or something of the kind. John Martin took the platform and declined to run with that plank in. Whereupon the convention nominated George W. Glick—a man whom my father called a "whiskey Democrat from Atchison."

He came home heartbroken. He did not whistle. He would lose his cane. All I can remember is that I heard him tell my mother:

"Ma, I lived through the hell of one time when the Democrats stood for nullification, and I just can't stand it again!"

His politics meant that much to him! He finally took to his bed. I did not know it then, nor for many years afterwards, but he was suffering from diabetes or shock, and the worry killed him. He died on October 4, 1882.

His death came to me suddenly. I was not allowed to go to school the morning that he died. I had no idea he was so near death, but I sensed

---

* Not to be confused with John A. Martin, who was elected Governor of Kansas two years later.

something dreadful in my mother's manner and in the fact that two doctors had come. They went away, and I followed them down the walk. I cannot remember what they said; but they shook their heads, and then I was frightened. In the midmorning, my mother called me to the bedside, where she and a neighbor woman were working—rubbing my father's hands and feet and applying hot cloths to his legs and arms. He could not speak. He seemed to be in a coma. I thought it was sleep, though his eyes were slitted, and I too began rubbing his foot and crying and calling "Pa," and looking at his slitted eyes to see if I could get one glimmer of recognition. I was a frightened little boy. Suddenly and desperately, I tried to call my father back. He passed away about noon, and the world grew black for me, though I did not cry much. That I remember. Indeed, I tried to comfort my mother, who mourned with racking sobs and unchecked tears, as we stood alone there by the bedside when we knew he was gone. Then my memory rings down the curtain. I only remember that in the evening I tiptoed along into the room where my father lay upon his bier, covered with a sheet, lifted it up, and saw that his face was bloated and colored with the poison that killed him. I let out one moan of terror and fled, and never looked upon him again. I could not bear, even when they told me that the undertaker had cleared away the blotches, to see him again. I would not go to his coffin when it was opened. But I remember that my mother consulted with me about the hymns they would sing at his funeral. I remember that she said he liked the tune "Rock of Ages" and she also picked a gospel hymn called "When the Mists Have Rolled Away"—the burden of which was, "In the dawning of the morning we shall know each other better, when the mists have rolled away." I knew even then that she was expressing the anguish in her own heart that she had not understood "The Doctor," that she had not realized her dream of love and romance with him.

We had a really notable funeral for the town. He had been elected Mayor the spring before, and Eldorado turned out, filled our yard, and stood far down in the streets beyond. I was not without my pride, looking back as we made the turn half a mile from home and headed for the East Cemetery, to see the long line of carriages and wagons and carts still moving into the procession on Main Street. My pride probably conquered my sorrow for a little while, which is a natural conquest in a boy's heart.

I should have been heartbroken at the loss of my father. I was not. After the first few hours or days of acute grief, I went about my business and resented the tender solicitude of those who supposed I would be mourning deeply. Yet I know now, and probably knew then, that he was a good father to me and a good man in all of his relations. I never saw him lose his temper more than once; and that was only for a second and he was penitent about it for a day or two. He never spanked me or administered any corporal punishment. If I had any, it was when I was too young to remember it; and my mother doubtless did the job anyway, for she flew off the handle easily! I know now that my father was constantly trying to tell me about himself —about his boyhood. Being a boy, I could not realize what he was doing so sedulously. It all slipped away from me, though I am sure that, spiritually, he made me—not by blood inheritance so much as by the unconscious guidance he gave me, the example he set, which I know now I tried to follow, and by the practical ideals he established. He was tolerant but never uncertain of his convictions, which he held courageously but never cantankerously. He hated argument and wrangling. Above everything, he was humorously self-deprecating, perhaps even consciously clowning a bit—an attitude a short man sometimes takes to compensate for the fact that he is a runt. He must either laugh at himself or strut. And I am sure that strutting would have irked him and he would have laughed himself out of his own pomposity. But I have noticed, going through life, that stubby little men are either deadly serious or given to inordinate gayety. Certainly he was gay.

Though he was always objecting in my childhood to my mother reading to me so much, because he said it would keep me from reading myself, he was a man of books and reading, as those things go among pioneers. Going over his papers not long ago, I found carefully put away—for he also was a methodical man, an inbred Yankee—receipts for one year for subscriptions to four daily newspapers: the Topeka Commonwealth, the Kansas City Times, the Leavenworth Times, and the St. Joe Herald. In politics these papers made a fairly even balance between the Republicans and the Democrats. He subscribed also for the Toledo Blade to get the outgivings of Petroleum V. Nasby, who ridiculed Negro baiters and Reconstruction haters and held those Republican Reconstructionists up to blistering scorn. Nasby even hooted at old-fashioned, silk-stocking Democrats, of which group my father was one. Among his books, which included a book on horticulture, another on agriculture, was Plutarch's Parallel Lives, a large volume which he tried to make me read; but for years it was too heavy for me in avoirdupois and in intellectual weight. But I remember that he read it often. He had a book of the essay editorials of "Brick" Pomeroy, another political writer, who jeered at the rapacity of Republican Reconstruction and was given to fine writing. All of his books, which I imagine he brought over from his life before my mother came into it, I read. When I begin to look back at them and to see my father in perspective, I realize that he was in some ways an exceptional man who sought real leadership and tried to keep it anonymous; who loved power but always pretended he had none; who made money easily and spent it wisely and never had a miserly desire to be rich. I know that one of his hidden vanities was to be the first man on the subscription paper with the largest donation. He was a great hand to pass the paper himself to help various causes. He helped to build every church in Eldorado. And there is a little old church in Emporia, built in the early sixties after the New England pattern, with really good lines. An old-timer in Emporia and I were riding by it one day, and he said:

"Your father passed the paper that built that church!"

I know he helped to pay the Eldorado preacher in at least three churches and never went inside a church himself, though he was familiar with the Bible, and its phrases were forever creeping into his speeches, especially in his merrier moments. In the times of tension in the home, when my poor mother was distraught by the eternal hyperbole of his persiflage, his gentle ironies, his everlasting merry, mocking quips and gibes when she broke into storm, instead of raging with her, he always had the soft answer that "turneth away wrath." This man, on the whole, was probably harder for her to live with than another kind who would jower it out.

I am setting down these things here at my father's death. But, alas, I understood their meaning only when I saw him in the retrospect of my own manhood and middle age. A boy of fourteen could not comprehend such a man as he was. But when my memory put him together again, I could mourn him deeply. I have never ceased to sorrow that he did not stay with me for another twenty years, to help me and to guide me from the follies which he may have seen ahead of me. I know now what I did not know then—that I was the apple of his eye. He loved me and hoped for me and maybe, to whatever gods he knew, he prayed for me. And when I was old I did not depart from the way!

CHAPTER XII

I Choose a Foster Father

THE DAY AFTER the funeral, a Sunday, I was wide-eyed beside my mother and her sister, my Aunt Kate, as they talked about my father. And this curious fragment was preserved for me in the amber of family tradition for sixty years. My mother told it to Aunt Kate then and often to the kin; always the same way. For her lack of humor made her mind exact. This is her story:

"Kate, he was not a happy man, though he seemed always to want his joke and he was always gay about the house. You know, Thursday night he didn't sleep. We sat there talking, and he said:

"'Ma, I seem always to get things wrong. I didn't go to scold you a minute ago; I didn't understand you, why you were in the kitchen so long. But I have always made mistakes like that, and life has just been one long lot of mistakes. In the little things I am all right; in big matters, I guess I get things wrong. Of course, when I first got married to a woman old enough to be my aunt, and all that, I didn't have any sense. And I tried to live in Texas, and I couldn't stand the cooking, and I couldn't stand to see the darkies in slavery, so I came back. Then I tried to be a Democrat in Kansas who didn't believe in the war. I thought it could have been smoothed out by buying the slaves, or something. When the hotheads started it I denounced it, and—Oh, Lord, Ma, that was a fool blunder! And I thought after Gettysburg and when the slaves were free, we ought to have stopped the war then. Now I know Lincoln knew better. Anyway, I was a fool about it. I know now we should have built our house on the hill. Of course we shouldn't have started the hotel and worked you to death. And I always tried to mind other people's business, and reform things, and make a better town and a better state than people wanted, and I guess it was better than they deserved. Oh, it's been just one fool thing after another, I'm afraid!'

"Well, Kate," my mother added, "it was just so sad. The tears came to his eyes, for he was sick and he was weak, and he turned over and sobbed for a minute. I was so sorry for him. Then he said:

"'And you, Mary, I guess I made a mistake the way I wanted you to take me. You didn't have a fair chance to know me. And no proper courtship. Well, it's been like that.'

"He sighed, and we fell to talking of something else, and I cheered him up."

And maybe that was why my mother chose for her hymn at his funeral the song which said: "We shall know each other better when the mists have rolled away."

And here is a funny thing—really funny. I can remember that, for many years before Pa died, my mother had wanted a watch of her own, a lady's watch, and had asked for it. When my father went East on some business trip, the year she signed the deed for the lots on the hill, he brought her a mink set, wide collar and cuff, and, I seem to remember, gloves to match. But he did not bring a watch. Always when he went away he brought her some present. I remember after the mink set he brought her a brown silk dress pattern. But a watch, no. He could not understand a woman wanting a watch. I remember he said:

"Why, Ma, you have got a good clock! What do you want with a watch? You never want to know what time it is when you aren't at home."

It was not the money. It was his idea that a woman should not wear a watch. And this, mind you, from a man who voted for woman suffrage and bemoaned, all his life afterward, its defeat in Kansas; this from a man who entertained Susan B. Anthony and Elizabeth Cady Stanton at his house. But a watch for a woman, he could not understand, and refused to tolerate the idea. Also, a woman doctor who came to town the summer before he died, persuaded my mother that she needed an operation. He pooh-poohed and scoffed, perhaps because a woman doctor had advised it—I don't know.

His funeral was on Saturday. And on Monday, at noon when I came home from school, my mother took me firmly by the hand, led me to Main Street and into Charley Richards' jewelry store and bought the best lady's watch he had. She wore it for more than forty years after his death, with pride, even when in her nineties time had begun to blur her senses. I had never carried a watch in all those years. The day after her funeral I picked it up and carry it still. It is a beautiful watch.

My next memorable experience with my mother was a week after my father's funeral, when the circus came to town. I was fourteen, and a circus meant much to me. My mother felt that the neighbors, indeed the whole town, would be surprised to see me at a circus a week after my father's funeral. What the neighbors said meant much to her. It meant, even then, little to me. So I went to the circus, and I heard the old clown sing a sprightly song in a minor key, that ran:

> When the Mayor of the town goes on the street,
>   The ladies at him stare;
> They're going to hitch him up to a buggy next week,
>   For they just found out he's a Mayor.

This scandalized my mother after the circus, when she heard me picking out the tune and hunting for the minor harmony. When Lew Schmucker and I sang it at the top of our changing voices, she took me aside and tried to show me how disrespectful it was to my father, who had been the Mayor of Eldorado. For a woman who defied public opinion by teaching a Negro and standing up to the raging sentiment of a proslavery community, she certainly had queer quirks.

A few weeks after my father's death, she broached to me the matter of the operation. I sobbed so loudly and so wildly, fearing orphanage, that she gave it up, passing thus from the domination of one male to that of another. She was never free entirely, from the day of her marriage.

My father had been ill in bed two weeks the October that he died. The crops on the farm near town, for which he had traded the farm on the West Branch, were ready for harvest—a little wheat, some oats, corn and millet. It was my job to get her share from the tenant. I remember riding on the farmer's wagon to mill when the wheat was threshed, taking the millet to the feed store and the corn to our crib in town by the barn. I got my check from the miller for the wheat, and took it to the bank; but I did not know how to deposit it. The bank clerk showed me carefully how to make out a deposit slip and told me to go and get my father's bank book. I deposited the money in his name, then later changed the account to my mother's name. I collected the rent on the two or three little one-story frame buildings with false fronts that he owned, occupied by real estate men, lawyers, and such like, on the fringe of Main Street, and on one rather nice residence in the best part of town. I put that money into the bank, and my mother and I kept the household account together. But, at fourteen, I was the man of the house. For I took to responsibility as a duck takes to water.

After a few months—maybe by the first of the year 1883—my mother realized that our income would not keep us. My father was always trading. He was a shrewd Yankee trader, and his income from this kept the family afloat. We had lived well. But when he was gone the income stopped except for the rents. So she opened the house to roomers, had two or three families, and charged well for her rooms. And sometime in the spring she began to take her roomers as boarders. Her cooking was famous over the town, and before spring she had the dining room filled with boarders, and at a good price. She was a close buyer and a good marketer. Moreover, she could send me to market, for my father had trained me; and so we did well. But she collected from the roomers and boarders, paid her bills in cash, and only deposited the profits in the bank the first of the month when I collected the rents on the offices and the house. I never remember having a word with her about money. She trusted me, for I was not a spender. So we lived that year and the next in what the town called "The White House," happily and prosperously. The only care I had was my pimples, which grew worse and worse; and the boys told me that they were a sign I would "die or go crazy or be an idiot"! So I wrestled hard under the shadow of the pimples and the devil in my blood.

It was in those boarding-house days that T. B. Murdock came into my life—a man who greatly influenced me, an exceptional man whom my father deeply respected and, I think, held in affection. He ran the Walnut Valley Times, and I can remember him in my childhood as a straight natty figure of a man who sometimes, for full dress, wore his army uniform of blue with brass buttons and his visored cap. He had a short goatee and a mustache which, also for full dress, he waxed at the ends. He was a light-footed, full-faced man, later in life inclined to paunch a little. He had a soft, self-deprecating voice—a bit ingratiating, not exactly a cooing pigeon's; but a voice that pleased women. He and my father had swapped books and read much for busy men in a frontier town. He had no formal education except that which he acquired in his trade as a printer. The thing that gave him distinction in my life was that he could write. My father, though he was a Democrat, supported Mr. Murdock, a Republican, in 1876, when he was elected to the State Senate. He was a notable figure in the state. He was a survival, a holdover, from post-bellum America. He had zeal without moral restraint for holy causes. His amiable casuistry justified doing evil for good. He was a warm-hearted man with a child's love of giving joy, a child's vanity in dressing up, and a wanton's way with him which made his friends trust him further than he would trust himself. For he was never a sanctified winner. He knew too well his grievous weaknesses.

A few years before his election to the State Senate, he and another young soldier, Jim Legate, held brief notoriety when in the Legislature at Topeka, State Senator York rose as the ballot for United States Senator was in progress, held up a package containing five thousand dollars in currency and declared that it had been offered to him to vote for Senator Pomeroy. In the turmoil, the balloting stopped. Pomeroy was defeated, and Bent Murdock and Jim Legate grabbed the five-thousand-dollar package which York had laid on the Speaker's desk, ran out through the Statehouse to the old Teft House six blocks away, pursued by the Sergeant-at-Arms. They ran through the Teft House, up the front stairs and down the back stairs, and in getting over the fence Legate was caught by the trousers and suspended; he gave the money to Bent and delayed the Sergeant-at-Arms long enough for Bent to get away with the loot, to the great joy and delight of Kansas politicians. A legislative investigation was appointed, but the episode was too funny for vengeance; and the story ran that Bent kept his share of the money and a little more, spent it in riotous living in Kansas City on wine, women, and song, and came home to Eldorado with evidence that he had spent nearly a thousand dollars of it foolishly on printing material for his newspaper.

When he was defeated for reelection to the State Senate by the people of Butler County in 1880, he sold his newspaper, left the town in disgust, and took a job writing editorials for the Topeka Commonwealth. Then, after my father's death, he came back, started a new paper—the Eldorado Republican—and lived for a year or so at our house with his family, a new wife and Alice and his baby daughter, Lena.

Across the years, he stands before me, looking down over his glittering bifocal glasses and making humorous self-deprecating noises, not words, more than grunts but less than giggles, framed by funny grimaces, when confronted with some shortcoming. Then he turns airily, sighing, "Well—oh, well—I guess we're all poor sinners!" and shuffles away.

In the seventies Bent Murdock brought his first wife to the wilderness of Kansas from a sheltered little town in Ohio—from a white house with green blinds under spreading elms inside a white paling fence, to a man's world, a tough-shooting, wide-open frontier town, where half a dozen horse thieves were hanged one night in a village near by, where her neighbors might be strumpets or gamblers, and where Mr. Murdock was, with my father, leading a dirty county-seat fight, always verging on felony and often toying with manslaughter. She was a pale, frail, shy, sensitive thing, and one day she looked out of the window of her two-room home on the main street of Eldorado. She saw a group of rowdies carrying a rope and roaring in their liquor that they were "looking for old Bent Murdock"— old at thirty-three! She went stark mad, cut her throat and her son's throat and, still flourishing the bloody razor, fell fainting from loss of blood on her front porch as she was chasing her little crippled daughter Alice (my playmate), who ran screaming to the neighbors. They brought the dead boy and the dying mother to our house, and there held both funerals. I was then three years old, but of this I remember nothing. But the relatives from Wichita and Emporia sat around in our parlor the night of the funeral, and I can see their faces yet though they have long since turned to dust.

That was the tragedy that my father's best friend faced when the town was young and the hot winds of summer blew gales of dust down the gray streets of the bleak, unpainted little frontier town where he had brought his birdlike bride. After only a decent period of mourning, Mr. Murdock married Marie Antoinette O'Daniel—a school-teaching widow who had come out of the Eastern Shore of Maryland to our wilderness to escape Heaven alone knows what little hot hell that was sizzling for her at home.

I must not shorten this Murdock detour in my story. For Marie Antoinette Murdock—later, "Aunt Net"—was one of the women who made a deep impression on my life. I first saw her teaching elocution. She was reciting "The Raven," and scared the wits out of me. And her next selection at the evening's entertainment was a poem with the refrain, "I am not mad, I am not mad—" A long dramatic pause, then in a voice of horror, "But soon shall be!" Woops! but that scared a little tad of six! But she was a lovely thing, that Marie Antoinette—a hothouse flower. She was supposed to be a widow and showed the women of Eldorado—my mother among others—a photograph of her husband's grave in a lovely old oak-sheltered, blue-grass-sodded cemetery in the heart of Maryland. As a matter of fact, she was a grass widow, and the sod was not firmly planted on her departed husband! But, as I hope to die and go to heaven, I believe she believed her story. For she never touched reality. To her, reality was loathsome. She played her life away. I don't think she ever touched dishwater. I never saw her, when she lived in our house, in the back yard on any pretense—any whatever! I lived with her or near her for a long generation and never saw her slouchily dressed, never saw her when she wasn't sitting for her portrait, dressed as for a grand ball.

She read wisely and well. From her, when the Murdocks lived in our house after my father's death, I had many modern books and magazines. She wrote well and sometimes reviewed books for her husband's newspaper. I remember her review of Ed Howe's "The Story of a Country Town," and her review of the first edition of "The Rhymes of Ironquill." A decade before those books were acclaimed across the land, she assessed them for their real value. No fool was Marie Antoinette. Yet her life was folly! A doll of a woman she was, when they lived in our house and I was in my middle teens. Sometimes of winter evenings when the others—my mother and the Murdocks—were out of the way, in bed maybe, perhaps out on some social errand, I used to go to their room and sit with her beside the glow of the glittering base-burner while she read to me beautifully, elocuting elaborately, some tale or poem or magazine article. She was always properly, indeed too conspicuously, well gowned, as if she was expecting royalty. I sat there in the firelight's ruddy glow, fancying that I was Pip to her Miss Havisham! Probably we needed each other: I was the audience she always craved; she was the dramatic actress that I yearned to know. I still can hear her proud voice crying: "The tintinnabulation of the Bells—the Bells, the Bells!" Even now I do not know what the poem meant; but it certainly did something to me that I needed in my business as a teen-age boy who desired to be a sophisticated young gentleman. And so, because "Uncle Bent" and "Aunt Net" added greatly to the sum of x's and y's that is my life, it is only fair to make this wide detour, to tell their story here!

Aunt Net was given to gossamer negligees, filmy gowns, sweeping plumes from her brow to her shoulders. Always at a party or a dinner, she came in last and made an entrance. A few years later when the Murdocks bought a home on the hill above town, they bought one with a circular stairway leading to a wide hallway. It gave her the chance she needed in her life. She never came down those stairs that she did not look like Maria Theresa coming to meet her conquerors. Naturally the women disliked her, and naturally Bent Murdock succumbed to her charms. And certainly the Murdocks were a handsome pair—Aunt Net and Uncle Bent—in their thirties, a distinguished and more than commonly cultured couple. They served the best table in town. They danced well when they led the Grand March at the Firemen's Ball. They read the new books and magazines. They dressed in the latest style. Mr. Murdock bought his clothes even then from Brooks Brothers. At that time he was the political boss of Butler County. He represented the railroads, the packing houses, the bankers of Kansas. They ruled. He governed Butler County for them. And I, a fourteen- or fifteen-year-old boy, seeing them every day and loving their little crippled daughter Alice, of my own age, like a sister, was to all intents and purposes a member of their family. He was my foster father. Because my father held him as his little brother Benjamin, he took me on as his spiritual child. I was proud of him, grafted him into the wound that death had left when my father went, and gave him a son's affection and respect which I never withheld.

CHAPTER XIII

I Walked with a Wizard
Who Is Witching the World—Me Too!

THE WINTER after my father's death, my voice was changing; and, curiously enough, I realize now why I began to be interested in singing. It was the pinfeather rooster starting to crow, though I did not know that my urge to sing, and that of other boys in school, had its biological root. I thought it just happened. Anyway, the next winter half a dozen of us organized what we called a male quartet, though it sometimes ranged from a quartet to an octet, and we did our harmonizing by ear. They learned the tunes; I played them on the organ. Lew Schmucker's brother had a banjo. I could use the accordion. Ed Harvey had a guitar. I forget what Albert Ewing had, but it was something fine. Everything he had, it seemed to me, was something fine.

So we young roosters used to roam about the town at night serenading —chiefly our various "girls," though sometimes singing under windows of prominent citizens for the very joy of it. We called ourselves "The Screech Owls." We sang sentimental ballads of that day, the left-overs from the Civil War, Stephen Foster's folk songs, dolorous ballads like "Marguerite," and waltz songs—"Sweet Violets," "Only a Pansy Blossom," and "When the Leaves Begin to Turn," Negro minstrel imitations of the spirituals of the slaves, like "Golden Slippers," "In the Morning by the Bright Light," and "The Gospel Raft," which had for its chorus:

> Get your baggage on the deck,
> And don't forget your check,
> For you can't sneak aboard and hide away!

And, of course, we used the real spirituals like "Go Down, Moses," "Swing Low, Sweet Chariot," "Nobody Knows the Trouble I See," and "The Old Ark's a-Moverin'." It was a wide repertoire, and anything we heard in a show or on the street we picked up. It was in those years after my father's death that I began to earn my first real money, in terms of dollars, playing for dances with a blind fiddler named Dol Cowley, who was good as fiddlers go, and with a cornettist named George Yonkman. We played at dances in the country, where they took down the beds, moved all the furniture outside except the cookstove, and danced in three rooms— leaving only the cabinet organ, which I played, to clutter up the floor. We played and they danced, chiefly square dances, some polkas, a few schottisches, but rarely a waltz. I remember we had but two or three in our repertoire—"The Corn Flower Waltz," "The Kiss Waltz," and "Over the Waves." Because the fiddler was blind and the cornettist otherwise busy, it was my job to call off the square dances. My changing voice I trained to some powerful register, so that I could unlimber it and throw it, on a clear moonlight night, all over the township as I bellowed the promptings of the dizzy maze. That voice afterwards stood me in good stead in open-air meetings. In those days I got three dollars a night for it, a dollar more than the other two musicians because I called off.

So I had money to burn, and Agnes Riley got more buggy rides than I could have given her earning an honest dollar. But, after all, probably in those days I was more interested in school than in any other one thing. School, to me, satisfied the gang instinct. There, even more than on the prairie with the town herd, more than at the swimming hole where I was only a moderate success, though I was a freak of a diver, more than in the woods or the barn, I was someone. I liked to boss; and always at school a lot of boys not only needed bossing, but liked it. They were the boys who never objected to being the tail end of the line when we played crack-the-whip, the meek little boys who were "it" in playing pullaway and did not object to stooping over and being "it" when we played "slap-and-a-kick" and "foot-and-a-half" (games not like leapfrog, which for some reason or other Eldorado boys never cared for much. My fighting days were over. If they taught me one thing at the end, it was to be careful how you get into a fight; for, once in, no one is going to help you unless it pays him, and your friends enjoy seeing you licked quite as much as your enemies. To know those two things is the beginning of wisdom about war and peace! Unless a boy can laugh off a licking, he should keep out of trouble. That, I discovered in the days of my youth; and the truth has never departed from me.

Two boys in the Eldorado High School period colored my life: Albert Ewing and Lew Schmucker. Both were good at their studies in school. I think Albert Ewing, who was in my class, ranked better than I. He had grown out of childhood a trim, slim, fair-haired youth, with a lot of charm and more than ordinary common sense. He always could do anything better than I. But Lew Schmucker's reading range was wider than Albert's or mine. And, because Lew was a year or so older than I, he led me far afield in books. We both patronized the city library, reading almost exclusively fiction and poetry, as befitted boys in their middle-teen age. We rollicked through Mark Twain. We roared at Bill Nye. Lew could read "Don Quixote" with appreciation, but it stalled me. We bought the current humorous papers—the Texas Siftings, the Detroit Free Press, the Arkansaw Traveler—and read with howling glee the first newspaper syndicated humorist that I remember, who wrote the "Spoopendyke Papers"—pieces which raised their laughs by making grotesque metaphors. Let me pause to add that those comic papers in the eighties had a wide vogue. Their editors must have been the fathers of the columnists of these latter days. But Lew Schmucker and I haunted the bookstores and the news stands and spent our nickels and dimes for that type of literature. Other boys were reading dime novels, stories that filled the place that movie "westerns" hold today: "Deadwood Dick" and "Calamity Jane," "Sure Shot Seth" and "Wild Bill" and "Silver Sam." But Lew and Albert and I—with our Bob Burdette, our M. Quad, our Opie Read, our Bill Nye, and our "Peck's Bad Boy"— looked down with vast scorn on mere vulgar dime novels. Probably it was a bit snobbish. But John B. Alden, the mail-order book dealer who sold cheap pirated editions of British authors, got most of our spare change. We bought his "Red Line Poets," bound in gaudy colors and printed on gilt-edge pages. Looking back and remembering, I have often wondered if when I called on Agnes Riley, hugging under my arm "A Tale of Two Cities" or "Les Misérables," I really seemed to be the little pimple-faced, mild-eyed, redheaded prig that I was. I had a letter from Agnes while I was writing these lines—a letter recalling those very days when I tried to make her a literary sophisticate. She writes:

"You left me no choice about Jean Valjean!"

To which, affiant—squinting down the long line of year-posts, almost sixty of them—deposes and says:

"Ah, no, Agnes—not Jean Valjean, not that slab-sided waxworks poseur. It was Marius and Cosette, Hugo's young lovers, I wanted you to understand, and so to guess what I could not say in my own bashful words!"

I suspect Agnes knew the truth. She had a hard time of it, poor girl, what with listening to the Screech Owls under her window, singing in barber-shop harmonies on nights when I was not playing for country dances, and what with being tied up to the worst dancer in the Spring Chicken crowd, who never could, despite the rigors of the rocking chair out on the hundred and forty-four running feet of porch, learn to waltz, and what with the lovelorn rhymes that might embarrassingly turn up in her dinner bucket, her geography, or, in winter, in a cloak pocket, and most of all what with the strict, mean, mad supervision of a boy who was crazily jealous. The poor girl must have paid heavily for the few buggy rides, the occasional orgies in the ice-cream saloon, and the one or two, or perhaps half a dozen, rides she took to parties on rainy nights in the town's only musty hack. But she was a gentle soul, patient and long-suffering, with most luminous, lovely eyes. So when, in its mid-teens, the Trundle Bed Trash felt that they were a bit too old for kissing games at parties, those eyes tormented me without recompense or adequate reward. But some way, to meet them at school over the top of a geometry for a fleeting second, or over the railing in the hall, or going in the door when the bell rang, paid well for the torture. I was happy. I even made fun of Albert Ewing, who was running the same gauntlet of unrequited affection past Lizzie Ruddick. We talked about the girls a good deal, and Lew Schmucker hooted and gibed us. For he had been to boarding school, and he knew a lot of things about girls that we were not supposed to know—the dirty little devil.

I was sixteen years old when I finished the Eldorado High School. The graduating exercises and the days preceding them are cut deeply in the tablet of my memory. I helped Julia Fulenwider with her graduating essay, and someone else; I think it was Virgil Mayes, a big ungainly boy, a prodigy in mathematics, whose playground name was "Stinkfoot." I vied with Roxy Wilson for grades. I think she beat me by a half of one per cent. Without my perfect attendance and entire absence of tardiness, she would have beaten me by more than one per cent. And Albert Ewing was just behind me or perhaps, Heaven knows, just a point ahead. After we marched out of high school the last afternoon, before the graduating exercises, Albert Ewing and I hung around the building until all the other children were gone, and went up, hand in hand, to stand and look over the little puddle of empty desks, and had a real sentimental souse. We were that kind! But Lew wasn't!

The night of our graduation is burned in my memory, for there, before a whole skating rink packed with people, I had my first public failure—the greatest disgrace that ever came into my life. I had helped the others with their essays. Because I could write fluently and well, I had dashed off my own offering on "the jury system." It was a palpable plagiarism from Mark Twain. When I got going I could not stop in my writing. It was in my own handwriting, which was never good; and, because I had felicity in writing, Professor Olin, the high-school principal, read it swiftly, not realizing its length. So when I rose and began to read, I stumbled with my own handwriting and read on, and on, and on. Someone held a lamp over my shoulder that I might see better. The lamp made me sweat. But I stumbled and mumbled on and on. I could sense that the crowd was restless, but I did not have the gumption to skip and stop. Pretty soon there was a whistle from the rear gallery of the roller skating rink where we were assembled. I knew

Dow Blair and Ed Dupee and "Chink" Green were there, and maybe Byron Snow who was the toughest boy in school. I felt that pretty soon real trouble would begin. Other whistles came. Then someone began to clap his hands. And finally, when only Heaven knows how long I had been on my feet reading that interminable essay, which I once had thought was funny, uproar stopped me and, with my face redder than my pimples, I backed off, sat down, and the crowd laughed and laughed. The day when I am hanged by the Nazis will not bring me such shame as I saw and felt sitting there waiting for Professor Olin to announce the last song on the program:

> Oh, if for me the cup be filled,
> Oh, fill it from the gushing rill!

I do not know what exactly that night's experience taught me—if anything. But I do know that it gave me stage fright and kept me off the public platform for well-nigh a dozen years. Probably that also was good, a gift of the gods. For I might have been a spouter who thought he was an orator.

In summer, after my graduation, I was an idler, a wastrel, for the first time in my life and, sadly enough, for the last time. I flitted like a young butterfly in and out of the county teachers' institute, giving man's natural polygamist instinct full range with the little country girls of my age who had come to town to prepare for the teachers' examination. Lots of girls in those days in Kansas were teaching who were fifteen or sixteen years old, just out of the eighth grade in the country schools. Thirty dollars for an eight months' school meant a lot to a girl whose family was struggling under a farm mortgage. They studied hard, and the county teachers' institute was a place of some distinction then. We had an ice-cream social—sometimes two, one in the midst of the institute, one at the end. During institute, on clear, starlit nights, you could go up to the schoolhouse and shoo couples off the front step, from dusk to midnight. Albert Ewing and I and the other boys of the Screech Owls trod the primrose path with the little schoolteachers and took them downtown and filled them with ice cream, lemonade, and walked home shyly trying to hold their hands—sometimes getting our ears boxed for our trouble, but always in good humor. By day, after the institute was closed, I sat on the porch and read John B. Alden's treasures or, feeling that I was a little too old for the swimming hole and the little tads, sneaked to the creek with my classmates at odd times when we thought the place would be abandoned. For we were now big boys. No longer could we muddy up and go down to the railroad bridge to greet the afternoon train. We had stopped trying to turn somersets from the springboard over the deep hole. And, God save us from vanity, we took towels with us—and Albert Ewing brought soap.

Another thing that I remember: Whenever I went into the barn, especially into the hayloft where my highest, happiest boyhood moments passed, it all seemed strange. I seemed to be looking back into a world that had been. I had passed on and was a disembodied spirit visiting its earthly habitat. Yet only a year or two had gone since that barn was my earthly home. I have had several retrospective glimpses like that as life has moved on and I have come back from the dead into other scenes and times, from another life I have lived in these earthly habiliments. It was Henley who wrote:

> So many are the deaths we die
> Before we can be dead indeed.

Time, with his wizard's wand, had witched many things away. Gone in ten years was the wind-swept village with its self-sustaining industries, its wagon shop, its tannery, its tinshop, its ironworkers, its furniture workers. They went with the coming of the railroad, blown away with its acrid smoke. In 1884 Eldorado was a town of two or three thousand, stretching away up the hill from the river. The new town was all painted and spick-and-span. It had gravel macadam streets which began with my father. Little elm trees and cottonwoods were on the parking, and bluegrass was beginning to grow in the lawns. Smart buggies and well groomed horses went clattering along the streets, and girls and women prettily clad in the cottons, woolens, and silks adorned that period.

I knew even then that Mr. Murdock, editor and owner of the Republican paper, ran Butler County politically. I knew casually that he was a director of the Florence, Eldorado & Walnut Valley Railroad, a Santa Fe branch; often a private car came and picked him up and took him on journeys. I knew that he associated in Topeka with the rich and the great and with the ruling class of our state. I was proud of it. I knew that he had passes for himself and all of his family, and that when the Butler County delegation went to Topeka to the Democratic State Convention he had passes for all of them and their friends, and they had a day coach all set for themselves. I did not connect him in reality, and in his function as leader, with the government of our state and country. I had passed a hundred in Civil Government and still had no idea how our country was really run. I thought the Murdocks were grand people. They took leadership away from the newcomers, college men and women from the East who were settling the town and filling the country—young men, of course, seeking their fortunes in the new land. I did not know, being still a boy of sixteen, how the change in our town was wiping out a civilization in which my father and mother were born and lived, or that those years were introducing a strange new order, something that the world had never seen before—the machine age!

Late that summer my mother and I began to consider college. It must have been in August that a tall, pale, attenuated man, perhaps in his fifties, with an ascetic face, gashed and furrowed with the claws of suppressed desires, showed up at the boarding house one day. He was the president of the College of Emporia, campaigning for students. Because the college was near at hand, and I was timid, and my mother lonesome, we chose it without knowing anything about it. Before I knew it, I was bound for college.

CHAPTER XIV

"And Suddenly There Shined Round About Him a Light from Heaven"

THE COLLEGE OF EMPORIA, in the autumn of 1884, was without a building. It was located on the third floor of a brick structure at the corner of Sixth and Commercial in the throbbing heart of Emporia, which then held six or seven thousand people. There the college opened in half a dozen rooms. Seventy-five boys and girls were herded by six or eight teachers. I met a minor shame on the opening day. I had played the cabinet organ in high school often for singing, and in high school at the organ I marched them out playing "General Persifor F. Smith's Grand March" and "Garfield's Funeral March," so lugubrious but highly popular, and the March from "Lucia di Lammermoor," all of which I had learned by ear. So, when they wanted someone to volunteer to play the cabinet organ for the opening day of college, I took a chance and volunteered. I thought I knew all the gospel hymns, but they rang a new one in on me which was hard to fake. It was "All Hail the Power of Jesus' Name," and while I had a whistling acquaintance with it, the harmony was over my head for a first shot. I knew I was making a terrible mess out of it, which did not help me. But I got through it and learned my lesson. The college marked me for an unmasked smart aleck. It took me a week or ten days to live that down. Only when I showed the boys that I could chin a pole nineteen times, did I restore lost ground.

For the first time in my life I encountered home cooking in another woman's home. I lived with a widow, a preacher's widow, Mrs. Jones, who had a boy my age. She was Welsh and knew how to feed boys. And her son Bob and I kept Mrs. Jones and her two little daughters busy feeding us. I got very little out of that college. I had a year of third-year Latin and my first year of Greek, which I presumed that naturally all college students had to have. There was no nonsense in the curriculum of the College of Emporia to disabuse me. I tried a term of French. I had been through Hill's Rhetoric twice in high school—once to learn it and the second time to enjoy it, and probably to show off my knowledge of it. So I took it again in college, and had advanced algebra and a little primitive physics. There was no chemistry laboratory, and they did not teach chemistry. And, of course, I had English literature, an advanced course over the high-school course, which I enjoyed.

I brought from Eldorado to college a small box of books: my Red Line poets; a pirated edition of Longfellow's early poems; "The Wandering Jew," by Eugène Sue; the Deerslayer stories, and a one-volume condensed copy of the Works of Thomas De Quincey. The last contained the "Confessions of an English Opium Eater," which that year was my favorite literary diversion. And, however poor the college was as an intellectual stimulus, Bob Jones—the preacher's widow's son—was a joy and stimulation to me. He read my books and I read his, for a preacher's son generally has books. And we roamed the woods together Saturdays with our lunch— gay sixteen-year-olders. We carried a sack for walnuts and a club with which to knock them from the tree; also always a book or two. So we rowed on the Cottonwood and stripped betimes and jumped in and stretched out on our bellies, kicking our toes in the mold in the woods, reading Tennyson and Byron, talking bashful big talk that little boys in their teens enjoy. In his diary, after his death, I read an entry of November 1, 1884: "Went swimming with Bill White this morning, thin scum of ice." And, reading it, I recall that it was so cold that my measles came out and I was scared for a bit. But if Bob and I meet again in heaven we can never have lovelier hours than those Saturdays we spent in the woods, on the river, roving the fields, enjoying God's unfolding universe where youth sees so many new, strange, and lovely things.

And of course, despite the fact that Agnes Riley and I had a sweet and bashful parting, as though I were going to the ends of the earth when I left for college, and that I carried her picture in my trunk and put it on the table in my room, still there were fair girls in the College of Emporia. Mostly perhaps because of my pimples, which still bore me down, I viewed them from afar.

But the lifelong blessing which the College of Emporia gave me was a boy—Vernon Kellogg. The thing that brought us together was that he also was buying books from John B. Alden. So far as I know, he was the only boy in the College of Emporia who had much bookish interest. He was my height, a scant five feet seven and five-eighths. He wore the same size hat, seven and a half, and the same size shoes, six and a half on a wide last or seven on a narrower. We both came from the ruling class. It was his father, as the president of the State Normal School, who had ridden into Emporia in '65 on the stage with my mother. The president had studied law, had become probate judge of the county, was elected state senator the year I came to college; and his stepmother also was a lawyer, her husband's partner. And their house, when I entered it to visit Vernon, was the first house full of books that I had ever seen—bookcases around the walls, books on the table. So I walked in the new heaven and the new earth. And I became in the College of Emporia the willing slave of Vernon, a few months my senior. His brother Fred, who was a year my junior, also interested me, but not as Vernon did. The two boys lived in a little house outside their parents' home on the wide lawn under the shading elms and maples. There they had their own way. It was a rule that they should make their own beds, pick up their own things, run their own ménage. And after four o'clock in the day it looked it, though they did manage to get their beds made before breakfast. But to that little house came like-minded boys from all over town, who were interested in books and bugs and birds. Vernon hunted (which I never did), but only for birds to classify and stuff. And the Kellogg boys built boats in the barn, homemade canoes under rules that came out of a boys' book of boats. And maybe because he was slight and well muscled, and maybe because he had no pimples and was not going "to die or go crazy or be an idiot," and because he was lithe and trim and wiry in those days. Vernon had no use for girls, which was good for me, and we cleaved to each other as brothers. When I got home to Lew Schmucker, Albert Ewing, Agnes Riley, and Alice Murdock, I poured forth stories of the prowess and grandeur of Vernon Kellogg. For I was ever a blabby kid and never self-contained—and always loved heroes.

In 1884 I got a lesson that lasted me all my life by scaring the daylights out of me. James G. Blaine was running against Grover Cleveland. I was supposed to be a Democrat. I fought, bled, and died on the school grounds in Eldorado for the Democrats. And I was hoping heartily for Cleveland's election, particularly as I remember standing up in school, amid the hoots of the high-school partisans in '82, and predicting that Cleveland would be the next President. But the day after the election, Blaine seemed to have won. A great crowd surged on Emporia's Commercial Street and Sixth Avenue as the news came seeping in, and the Democrats, for all the Republican clamor of delight, were still cocky, and were still betting on Cleveland. That morning I had received from my mother the twenty dollars to last me through the month of November. It was in four five-dollar bills. Treacherously but greedily, thinking to make money out of the foolish Democrats, I bet five dollars on Blaine and lost. Five dollars out of a twenty-dollar allowance was a burden too grievous to be borne. I have never made an election bet of over fifty cents since. Experience is a dear school, and fools learn in no other; and I have always had to get my experience in the foolish way. I was ashamed to tell my mother that I had bet on her candidate. I just sweated it out!

When I came home for Thanksgiving, I learned a story that shamed me more. When Cleveland's election was finally beyond a doubt the week following, the Democrats in Eldorado put on a great torchlight parade and hired the band, indeed a couple of bands from neighboring towns, and literally tore the roof off of Eldorado. It was their first victory since Buchanan in '56. While I was betting on Blaine my mother had been rejoicing in every way a woman can. But the night of the big Cleveland torchlight procession and jubilee, she was heartbroken. She believed that the rebels were coming up out of the South to run the country. But she knew how my father would feel. So that festive night she put a lighted candle in every one of the forty windows in our house except the kitchen. There she pulled down the curtains, blew out the light, and sat and rocked in sorrow, yet I suppose in a certain proud glamour of loyalty that his house, his big house with a hundred and forty-four feet of porch, where the band stopped three times and serenaded that night, his house was with him—all lighted up in jubilation at the victory. She was the kind of woman who would enjoy the emotional stimulus of that kind of situation.

I remember little about that first year in Emporia College, except that it was fun to get the best of old Dr. Cruickshank, the Greek professor, who slammed us into Xenophon's "Anabasis," six months after we had achieved the Greek alphabet, and I stumbled through the year of Greek as thick-headed a blunderer as ever thumbed a pony. But my Latin was good. And there again I went through Hill's Rhetoric the third time and knew it by heart. Curiously, the quotations and examples of rhetorical forms and figures of speech attracted me as much as the instruction in the book. There I first met verses from Omar Khayyám's "Rubáiyát," and Wordsworth, and Coleridge, and Ossian. And this is funny: In the footnotes where the author's verses were accredited, I found the words "Anon" and "Ibid" and thought they were names of authors also, and not until Vernon Kellogg lifted the scales from my eyes, did I know better. But that year the big thing that Vernon Kellogg did for me was to take me across the street from the college into the second floor of the bank building, where the City Library was housed. The gray-haired librarian, Mrs. Carpenter, who was a glamorous figure for me because her husband had been killed in the Quantrill Raid, let me loaf there and brought me books. In Eldorado I had been thrilled by Emerson's line in the essay on Self-Reliance: "Trust thy-self: every heart vibrates to that iron string." And I asked Mrs. Carpenter for the essay. It was on a snowy February day when I had just turned seventeen; and as I read that essay my spirit expanded as though I had heard the trumpet call of life. I was thrilled and stirred and literally over-turned. I doubt if I have ever been moved so deeply by anything else that I have read. So I read all the essays and other Emersonian books, and was glad to live and proud to feel that I was beginning to understand something of the puzzle of life. The Emporia City Library was a vastly different place from the Eldorado Library; more books, better books, and a fulltime librarian were in Emporia, and all of the magazines that one could want, even from England, and illustrated papers: Harper's, Leslie's, the London Illustrated News, Puck, Judge. To add warmth to the glamour, often across the table sat Vernon Kellogg and we whispered and giggled; and when he found a sentence in a bird book, or bug book, or zoology book that pleased him, he shoved it across the table. And I did the same when a poem or essay pleased me. I found there all the books of De Quincey, who was my especial delight in those days. It made little difference to me whether the college across the street kept or not. I was not bold enough to skip classes, but I doubt if I learned much from them.

But that winter the college students, because there were a hundred of them, could do what the Spring Chickens in Eldorado could not do. Often a sled—a great hayrack on runners—was hired, and we all sat in the bottom, boys and girls, and tangled our legs together and felt very warm and wicked as we slyly held hands, slipped arms about each other, and were quite sinful in our own Presbyterian eyes. I had qualms about Agnes Riley, but I went every time I was asked. Vernon went also, and I often wondered if he got the same kind of fun out of it that I did; but our confidences, though deep in philosophy and science, never went quite that far. I was too shy; he was too wise and canny.

During vacations, of course, I went home; indeed I went home between vacations, sometimes over week ends, and always brought back literally trunks full of food. My mother did not realize how Bob Jones's mother was stuffing me—how good a cook she was. So, to keep my soul and body together, my mother baked cakes and pies and roasted a chicken, and tucked in doughnuts and glasses of jelly. Craftily I widened the circumference of my college influence by inviting boys to my room, where we devoured the feasts that I brought from Eldorado. So I had some distinction in the college which had nothing to do with my scholarship, and other boys deferred to me. I had sense enough never to invite Emporia boys to these feasts, but boys from other towns who keenly appreciated the food. For they lived in cheap boarding houses mostly. Board could be had in that day for from one dollar and seventy-five cents to three dollars a week, half a room for three or four dollars and a fine room for ten.

So, in college, I bribed my way into leadership of a sort as in Eldorado my big barn, my turning pole, my trapeze, my swinging rings, my red sled, and my boughten wagon gave me, from the first, the bribe giver's power over my fellows. In a way I probably knew it and did not take the shame that should have been mine for my advantage. Without these things, which are granted to boys from the ruling class, I would probably have been just a little bashful, measly-looking boy, afraid to say his soul was his own and craven at heart. Instead of which, I read Emerson's "Self-Reliance" and had my first rebirth on earth.

For Emerson seemed to correlate all the world for me, the spiritual world. Deep within me a philosophy was forming. Probably I was just imposing Emersonian transcendentalism upon the theology of the Sunday school of my childhood, and the protracted meetings, pulpit poundings and howling of the itinerant preachers who came along through my childhood at home. Nor did Emerson, who probably justified my rambunctiousness by preaching self-reliance, make me less of a conceited ass. But he did give me courage, always backed up by Vernon Kellogg, to survive a Moody revival which shook the school. Vernon and I were scared stiff that it would get us, and pledged ourselves to stand against it. We were like two mules crossing a rattling iron bridge who leaned against each other and shuffled in trembling timidity through the clamor. But we did come scot-free out of the orgy. It took the town as well as the school, and I can remember Moody yet—a soft-voiced man with a high and lovely tenor singsong to his incantations, a bearded man, paunchy, with fat jowls and wonderful eyes, and with all that a really spiritual face. He looked like a kind of overstuffed angel when he was going well in his exhortations. Of course, Vernon and I heard him time and again. I had two roommates who knelt and prayed every night by the bedside; and, like a soldier upheld by Emerson, I ducked into bed and turned my face to the wall and said my little "Now I lay me's" in secret, scorning what seemed to me the profanation of their public promiscuity with God.

But after the revival I noticed the college gradually slumped back to its normal life. I can remember still the curious spiritual squint-eyed, wordless questioning I put to Rankin Hendy, the president's son, who, being a preacher's son, the devil's dear and mischievous child, proposed to illustrate some precept in our psychology class, wherein we were studying "surprise." He picked up a three-legged chair in the back of the room, a discarded recitation chair, and when I asked him what he was going to do, he went to the open window there on the third floor above the busy street, and said:

"Let me show you some surprise and see how it reacts."

He balanced the chair a minute on the window sill and I stood beside him, wondering what was in his mind. We both looked out and down into the street. It was almost deserted. Fifty feet to the westward of us, going east, was old man Cross, a pompous banker with side whiskers, who wore a high, sawed-off, stiff felt hat and swung a cane which he flicked at dogs and boys who got in his way. And as he approached, Hendy said to me: "Now look!" And he dropped the chair three stories down on the sidewalk, not a dozen feet in front of old man Cross, who literally jumped into the air, threw his cane in the gutter and, hearing the thing crash and seeing it splinter, ran for his life. It was a noble sight, and I can laugh at it yet after nearly sixty years. And I know now how surprise works as a biological process. But a second after we had ducked back from the window I thought: "Hendy's a hell of a Christian." I told Vernon later, and we both laughed and agreed that Hendy was in truth "a hell of a Christian"— a phrase that we preserved in our intimacy as a tag for many years.

The spring semester found me grinding away with the college freshman classical course. I cared little for any of it except English literature, English composition, and Virgil's "Aeneid"; but I was tremendously interested in books and magazines. Occasionally Lew Schmucker and I, in Eldorado, had bought Scribner's and Harper's and the Century; but in Emporia the Atlantic Monthly was placed in my hands by the librarian. And there I had my first taste of William Dean Howells, possibly following an advertisement, or possibly a suggestion of the librarian. I read Howells's "A Modern Instance" and realized that I was opening a new door. Here was a novel different from the Dickens I adored, a novel by a writer whose methods were in conscious opposition to those other writers, Scott and Cooper and the authors of "The Scottish Chiefs" and "Thaddeus of Warsaw," and "The Children of the Abbey," and Eugène Sue, whose "Wandering Jew" I was reading for the second or third time. Mr. Howells some way fitted into the Emersonian pattern of my youthful philosophy. And to look ahead for a few pages, when I got home to Eldorado that summer, I bought his book and tried to get Lew Schmucker and Agnes Riley and my mother interested in the story—but with little success. Lew, who doted on "Lalla Rookh," "Nick Carter," "Tom Sawyer," and "The Pickwick Papers" and "Seth Luvengood," found "A Modern Instance" dry. Agnes could not get interested, and my mother was frankly critical of its realism. But that spring in Emporia I read it and reread it, and some way felt that I had made a great discovery. Mr. Howells was not anywhere near the zenith of his fame in the spring of 1885. I was always proud that I spotted him early. When he came to Emporia I asked him to write in my book, and when I told him how I had found him and taken him to my heart, he wrote in my book: "W. D. Howells—Mr. White's discovery!"

I was a seventeen-year-old boy and was passing out of gangdom and becoming an individual. Looking back now, I know why I made long and lonesome walks into the country. That spring I walked seven miles to Americus once or twice to visit friends, often wandered over the townsite of Emporia; and even Vernon Kellogg, or Bob Jones, whom I got along with so well, seemed to be too much company for me. Probably what I really needed to do was to go fishing; but I never cared to fish. I liked to row the boat and take care of the minnow-pail bait when others were fishing for bass. But, as for fishing alone, neither fishing nor hunting appealed to me then; and they never did interest me. Yet I remember that I was often alone. Sundays I went to the Congregational Church to hear the Reverend Frank Ingalls, brother of the Kansas Senator of that day, deliver his erudite, passionless spiritual essays, rather on the Emersonian pattern, or to hear him tell about his trip to the Holy Land. But also I went to a young men's Bible class in the Presbyterian Church, which had a marvelous teacher. He gave me the first glimpse of a higher criticism when he told us that Jeremiah was probably written by two or three men, that the books of the Gospel were first taken out of tradition into writing probably fifty or a hundred years after Matthew, Mark, Luke, and John were dead, and indicated that Moses had made many mistakes of chronology. All these revelations did not shake my faith; but it interested me, as an Emersonian, to know that my theory of spiritual gravitation toward the triumph of righteousness in human relations was not dependent upon any script or text.

One Sunday night in the early spring I was walking alone, because I felt it was too hot to go to church. I plodded up Commercial Street with my hands behind me, as is my wont today when I am mildly curious and interested about the universe and the immediate environment thereof. Along came a man whom I had never seen before and have never seen since, but have remembered for a lifetime—a slim, good-looking, well dressed, ready-speaking man. I thought he was a traveling man—probably a salesman. He boarded me with some light remark, slowing down his pace and catching step with me, and we began to talk about Heaven knows what. But before we had gone much more than a block we began to talk religion. Because he was a stranger I unbuttoned my heart to him, and he sensed that I was in some sort of conflict. I myself do not remember what it was. For an hour we walked, and he talked and set me right with the world. Whatever religious faith I have is based upon his wise words. And the wise thing he said was that it made little difference how the Bible was put together but a great deal of difference that it had held up through the centuries and for many thousands of years, because its wisdom some way matched and covered human experience. I remember also that he said not to fret too much about the miracles and the story of the virgin birth, that the same stories would be found in many religions. He talked about the tragedy of the life and death of Jesus, pictured him as a young man who found his country and his people in bondage and sought to free them by pointing their way to a philosophy of peace through humility, through tolerance, through charity, rather than by appeal to arms. He held Jesus up to me as the greatest hero in history and asked me to read the story of the two

107

thousand years that had followed his death and to watch how slowly and yet how inexorably the world had changed, veering to human happiness as it accepted little by little, phrase by phrase, the philosophy he preached and made it a part, even a small part, of human institutions. Then my companion turned our talk to a discussion of the futility of force and the ultimate triumph of reason in human affairs. He explained his theory that Jesus died to save the world by demonstrating, through his crucifixion and the symbol of his resurrection, the indestructibility of truth.

My ears had been opened by Emerson. That unknown man turned over the sod of my spirit and uncovered an understanding heart. That, to my youth, was the night of the Great Light. Yet it was only the seed and not the harvest of the truth that came to me as the unknown sower walked with me on that evening's pilgrimage along Commercial Street toward "the way, the truth, and the life"! He may have been a preacher and not a traveling salesman at all. Or, more likely, he was some young divinity student in his early twenties. And I have often wondered whence he came and whither he went. But because I was seventeen, because youth opens its heart in those days to the great mysteries, the faith this stranger preached has been with me through all the years.

So at last I was on the road to Damascus!

CHAPTER XV

Destiny Rolls My Dice—"Come Seven"

IN EARLY MAY of that year 1885, I came to the conclusion that a big, healthy, strapping seventeen-year-old boy had no business to let his mother keep boarders to send him to college. Both of my roommates were working their way through school. One was a janitor in a bank; the other was a printer at the case. So, when I realized the meanness of my position, I sat down and wrote three letters to Eldorado: one to our only Jewish merchant at the time, Cass Frieburg, who kept a dry-goods store; one to George Tolle who ran a grocery, and one to T. P. Fulton, my father's old friend, who ran the Butler County Democrat. I asked all three for a job in exactly the same language and told them why I wanted to earn some money and, more than that, to learn something about a business where I could earn money and go to school. The dry-goods merchant and the grocer replied courteously that they had no job. But the editor offered me a job which he said, with more truth than he realized, would not bring me much money, but would give me a chance to learn a trade that was profitable, and that I could use when I went back to school.

As I took that letter out of Box 10 at the Emporia post office, I did not realize that I had received my life's calling; that I had channeled my entire life without deviation or break from the letter that I held in my hand. Yet there stood destiny pointing over my shoulder, to a road that I should never leave.

The week following, in the Eldorado Democrat, the herald angel sang these two lines:

"Will A. White will return from College June 1, to take a position in the Democrat office."

I had a job. It was in early June, 1885, that I walked into the office of the Eldorado Democrat one fine Monday morning. And as I came in the editor, with a broad and affectionate smile, rose to shake hands with me. I was from college then, mind you, and could be respected as a gentleman. And as he stood with hand outstretched he said:

"Well, Willie, you better bring back that bucket from the well before you go to work again."

So rose my curtain of destiny.

The Eldorado Democrat had moved its office in the five years of my absence. It was housed on the second floor of a brick building on Central Avenue—just off Main Street—over a shoe store. Other brick buildings adjoined, and our hallway ran almost the length of a business block. Lawyers were our neighbors on the second floor, and doctors, real estate men, and insurance peddlers. Indeed, all the gentle professions had quit the little frame buildings on the side streets of the town and had taken offices in the new brick buildings that lined the two business streets of the place.

I stood there among plastered walls; not much of the plaster was visible. On the ceiling it was smoky; on the lower walls it was inky; and from hands-high up to the ceiling it was nearly covered with posters—posters somewhat like those that had greeted my childish eyes in 1880, but new, more gorgeous ones advertising artists of greater renown—Fritz Emmet, Robert L. Downing, Sol Smith Russell, and Modjeska. For we had a town opera house. And the Eldorado Democrat was showing signs of the metropolitan life. Its editor—soon he must walk into the picture in detail—had enjoyed the distinction of a libel suit. He was the hero of a shooting affair. He had chased a gentleman the full length of the main street of Eldorado, popping at him with his gun and gorgeously missing him. And my editor and the rival editor had stood in opposite stairways across the street, ducking from stairway to stairway as they tried to shoot each other to settle certain misunderstandings and differences that had arisen out of a contest for the Butler County printing.

The town disported three bright, shiny, new hacks with rumbling wheels that rattled over the graveled pavements of her principal streets with rich, luxurious sounds, like the lascivious squeaking of the hubs of a circus wagon. The other paper ran a society column. Whist and euchre were gradually encroaching upon seven-up and poker as the evening's diversion of the elect. In the Flint Hills, twenty miles to the eastward, were ranches—real ranches covering five hundred to a thousand acres each, where the sons of the rich from the East and even from England raised cattle and sheep and drove to town in new, strange-looking spring wagons that the farm settlers had never known. These young bucks had the first evening clothes Eldorado had seen. They appeared at the town dances in those swallowtails, and even brought their private liquors, scorning the raw corn liquor of a democracy smuggled even then under prohibition into polite society.

The bankers were busy making farm loans. New town additions were sprawling on the prairie, and the little printing office, which had moved upstairs into a plastered room, employed a foreman, a journeyman, sometimes two printers, an apprentice, and had discharged the devil to give me a chance to learn the ancient art of Gutenberg. The economic revolution that had overturned our world was best indicated by the fact that I, a lowly industrial cub who would have worked nearly two weeks for nothing in my father's day, was promised three dollars a week as devil, with the intimation that four would be forthcoming after the first month's service. But about that I cared nothing. All I was after was to learn a trade and to return to college when I had learned it—a self-supporting young gentleman, beholden to no mother keeping boarders.

Now it is my pleasure and honor to introduce Thomas Parker Fulton, "Tee Pee," my first and dearest boss. Consider: he stands something under six feet and wears a white slouch hat, under it his black hair (for he is only thirty-five), black eyes glistening under black eyebrows, and a military mustache and a goatee surrounding his large, generous mouth. He is of southern Ohio extraction, and possibly has some of the fiery blood that before the Civil War percolated across the Ohio River from Kentucky and the Virginias. He has a loud but caressing voice. He wears good clothes and always a flower in his buttonhole; a black cutaway, or Prince Albert, generally is his coat, and with it gray trousers and shiny shoes. No slouchy sloven is he, but a scholar and gentleman, and also at proper times a judge of good whiskey.

Tee Pee could sling a pen. His was known as a vitriolic pen. And he was always ready to back it up with his trusty gun. It mattered little that he was the world's worst shot. He couldn't hit a flock of barns if they were anchored —chiefly because his hands shook so that he fired with the wide arc of a machine gun. And when he went into action, Sixth Avenue and Main Street and the adjacent alleys sucked in their population, leaving the highways as barren and as desolate as those of Pompeii, save for the object of his wrath who sailed unscathed to shelter. After one of those adventures Tee Pee would come up to the office and weep at his impotence.

He had a beautiful young wife and two lovely little children, whom he adored. His jealousy of his wife wrecked his home, unnecessarily probably, and when the fitful fever of the Kansas boom broke in the late eighties, he was one of its casualties and went outward with the tide—a gay, noble, but futile figure, affectionate to the point of passion, generous to the point of larceny, irresponsible to the point of heroism, the product of an older, more primitive and courageous civilization. He was too young to fight in the great Civil War, but his youth had been shattered by war's warped ideals. After the mad, glad boom of the eighties, sad unromantic pay days came to America. Men simmered slowly down to humdrum living on a cash basis, or thirty days and a 5 per cent discount. Tee Pee, to whom money meant little and credit meant much less, looked about with dazed, hurt eyes at a sordid, grasping world wherein he could not function after the manner of the days of his youth and early manhood. He was the typical country editor of sixty years ago. He was one of the long processes of mound builders who gazed aghast at our new civilization, with its shimmering glossy machinery that tolled the knell of the days of swap and barter, the days when men and communities and nations were self-sufficient, and left it sadly because he could not fathom its mysteries.

In the office of the Eldorado Democrat in the summer of 1885, we were still without a newspaper press. We had two job presses—an old Gordon and a Colt's Universal. They were foot-power presses. On these little presses we printed our job work. To print our paper we went to the office of our less loathed and more highly esteemed contemporary, the Eldorado Republican, and used its cylinder press—a mechanical marvel of that day. In the Democrat office we had four racks of type, and upon each rack was a case of body type in which we set the paper. The editorial was set in bourgeois, and the local items were set in minion. Bourgeois was called a nine-point type, minion a seven—both known as bastard sizes! It was my job to open the office in the morning at six-thirty, sweep it out, and start the day. Theoretically, the printers came down at seven o'clock. Tee Pee generally sailed in between eight and nine, with an expansive greeting for everyone—the foreman, the one or two printers, the other apprentice, and me, the devil.

Sometimes he brought flowers from his wife's garden—roses or lilacs in June, garden flowers as the season deepened. Once in a while, if there had been a particularly good pie or cake at the house, he brought it down to share it with the printers, standing with them—a slice in his hand—expounding upon the glories of his wife's cooking and regaling the gossip of the neighborhood in a broad and Rabelaisian manner.

He wrote rapidly and well. His copy was as meticulous as his clothes and manners. He leaned to editorial rather than news. Our paper still had only four pages; and still the two outside pages, printed in Kansas City, contained news of the world on the first page, a love story and miscellaneous items on the fourth. So the editorials and the local items, on the paper's inside pages, were all that Tee Pee contributed to the news end of the paper. He solicited advertising and, after the manner of editors of his day, as a solicitor he was half blackmailer and half mendicant—from Democratic merchants he begged, from Republicans he mildly insinuated threats! Also he solicited subscribers and job work. He intrigued diabolically for the county and city printing and was in politics heels over head. His little office would not have invoiced more than fifteen hundred dollars; yet with that weapon he wielded much influence in his town and county and state. He was an artist who owned the tools of his trade. "Owned" may be too strong a word, but the men who had bought it and given it to him to run a Democratic paper, and went through the grotesque formality of taking a mortgage for it, had long since lost any flickering hope of interest upon the note or even title to the mortgage. So the weapon rested in his hand, a flaming sword for what he regarded as justice. But his definition of justice sometimes—indeed, often—was the main chance, seethed in his emotions.

In the morning, after Tee Pee came down to work, industry began to hum in the office. The foreman, the printers, and the apprentice, who had idled during the early hours—chatting, standing around looking out of the windows, piddling with the types, possibly throwing them in and filling up their cases—set busily to work. Tee Pee began stuffing the copy hook. At ten o'clock the click of the types in the sticks began to indicate that the long day was well begun.

After I had swept out the office I was supposed to kick the pedals of the job presses, if they were to be used, or to assort the rules and riglet from the forms upon the composing stones, or to run errands for Tee Pee; or, wanting anything else to do, I was put to setting type. Over fifty years later, in the rooms of the State Historical Society at Topeka I saw in the files of the Eldorado Democrat my first piece of typesetting. It was an article about the appointment of Edmund Ross, as Governor of New Mexico, by Grover Cleveland. Naturally the Eldorado Democrat would congratulate Grover Cleveland upon anything he did, for the editor was a candidate for the post office; but this article gave reasons for the congratulations. Edmund Ross, as a United States Senator from Kansas, had defied his Republican party leadership and had cast the one vote necessary in the United States Senate to prevent the impeachment of Andrew Johnson as President of the United States. For this, Ross had been an outcast—a poor political leper for twenty years. He was a printer at the case, a derelict, when Cleveland found him and rewarded him for his patriotism. The item congratulating the President upon his appointment, and the Governor upon his accession to office, was the first item that I put into type.

As a little boy in the office five years before, to my shame, I had during my short apprenticeship been sent around by the printers to borrow a square auger, to get a left-handed shooting stick, to get the italic chases, and upon certain indecent errands which were covered from my innocence. But now, as a young gentleman out of high school, with a year of college behind me, I was too wise to be fooled by the old tricks of the trade. Still I had to be taken down, to be put in my place as the office devil.

CHAPTER XVI

I Get My Comuppens

OF COURSE I was proud of my job, and the printers knew it. I dramatized myself as a heroic young gentleman of the ruling classes, manfully learning a trade years after other young gentlemen had begun their professional apprenticeship. In the evening when work was done, I put on my round-cornered starched cuffs and white collar and sailed out in what was termed, in the vernacular of those times, "high sassiety." Coming out of the largest house in town, I could be a printer's devil and still percolate in society. The Spring Chickens were shedding their pinfeathers. But the journeymen printers, who worked for a living and chewed plug tobacco, had a rather low opinion of their devil. So they laid for me.

Here is the way they brought me low. General Grant died in the summer of 1885. Prohibition was four years old in Kansas then, and at times unsteady on its feet. One could order liquor from outside the state then and have it shipped in by the bottle or case or carload without let or hindrance. So, by way of drowning their sorrow at the death of the General, the printers of the town combined and ordered two or three cases or kegs of beer; they took them to an adjacent grove near town where on the Saturday night of Grant's funeral they proceeded to saturate the beer with a waste basket full of buns, cheese and ham sandwiches. They made the night hideous with their caterwauls. Naturally I went along. Naturally also, being an exemplary young person, after paying my share of the expenses I participated in the orgies rather vicariously. I did not drink, not a drop, which also greatly amused the printers. Then at midnight's stilly hour we collected all our bottles, sent for all three of the town's hacks, loaded the entire printing fraternity of the three Eldorado printing offices into them, and went out baying at the moon, serenading, kicking and rattling the bottles between anthems. Thus we attracted the attention of the sedentary old gentleman with the heavy cane, whom the Grand Army of the Republic had political pull enough to keep in the marshal's office. He piously shooed us off Main Street. Then the war council of the printers' party decided to go out to the leading Presbyterian elder's home and commit some deep outrage on him and his. So we deposited our empty bottles by stealth upon the front veranda of his palatial residence, a long, shiny, gorgeous row which greeted the morning sun. The elder, being a late Sunday morning sleeper, did not know of the shiny jewels glistening on his outer portals. The town next morning filed by, hooting with delight. Now I participated eagerly in all these orgies and, being sober, possibly added certain grotesque details which the befuddled mind might have overlooked. I am quite sure I had more fun than those who were drunk. I have always had more fun in a drunken crowd, being sober, than the drunks—part of the fun being to observe the drunks. Also there is a certain pious joy in virtue, virtue being its own reward in that case. So I hied me, giggling, to the Democrat office Monday morning with my little tin halo of virtue carefully and firmly set above my shining brow. When the first printer came in, he nodded at me cordially and said:

"Have you paid your fine?"

And, to my inquiry, he casually said that the marshal was arresting the participants in General Grant's obsequies, and that they were pleading guilty and paying a ten-dollar fine, with seven dollars costs, for being drunk and disorderly! The second printer and the foreman came in with the same information and indicated that, if I did not go down and pay my fine, the marshal would be up soon to drag me off to durance vile. I protested that I did not take a drink. They protested ignorance and astonishment at my disclaimer. The office was in an uproar of denial and recrimination. The men said they had seen me drink, had even seen me reeling-drunk, and were sorry that they could not testify as to my sobriety. I made an errand to the other office. There I was greeted with the same hailing sign of distress. There also, popular opinion acclaimed me a hypocrite and a liar. I sneaked through the alleys to avoid the good old marshal. With a fear-stricken face, I went about my morning's work, listening for every noise on the stairs as the doomed man listens for the hangman's footsteps.

I could not plead guilty, for I was not guilty. Anyway, I had decided rather definitely to be President of the United States, and I could not see that record on the police-court blotter rising up against me in future years to bar my way to the White House. It was nothing to these other printers. They were not going to be President, any of them, nor even governors. They were just going to wait for General Grant, or someone, to die again, and go out and soak themselves to the gills with hot rebellious liquor and commit their dastardly outrages upon the righteous. I slipped home through the alleys, ate my noon meal in silence, for the cloud of turpitude was on me. I was learning a great lesson—that it is far more shameful to be caught than to be guilty.

That afternoon came the *thump, thump, thump* up the stairs, of the marshal's feet, syncopated with the rattle of his cane. He came in solemnly, walked over to me, put his hand on my shoulder, said that he knew and respected my father and would make it as easy for me as possible, and if I would hand him seventeen dollars and fifty cents he would go down and make the record. I had no seventeen dollars and fifty cents. I knew no one who would lend me that vast sum. To get it of my mother would be to confess. I tried to borrow it in the office. I might as well have tried to get the printer to underwrite the national debt. I begged for time, and that night after work I looked up a young lawyer and laid my woes before him. He also told me there was nothing to do but pay my fine, let the record stand, and turn in the future to a holy life—perhaps take monastic vows instead of going to the White House, which I regarded as a sad compromise. All night I tossed upon a sleepless bed, and came to the office the next morning irritable and forlorn. The marshal came up again.

Again, I begged for time. There I was, caught in the great iron-toothed trap of fate, ruined for life at the threshold of a brilliant career. Another day passed; another conference with the young attorney, and another sleepless night. I grew haggard, and contemplated suicide or flight. And then in the evening again I heard the *thump, thump, thump* of the marshal's step upon the stairs. We were standing around the wash pan, the common office wash pan, and the common, old stinking office towel, when the marshal entered with his gyves and shackles. It was an awful hour. The other printers hooted at me. Then when I had writhed in my torture enough to satisfy their esthete, degenerate, and sadist hearts, with an awful guffaw in which the marshal joined, clanking his spectacles on his belly watch chain, they told me that the whole thing was a practical joke, and indicated in a general way that it would cost me a case of beer for that particular offense, which they would pay for and take from my wages from time to time as I could spare it. I jumped out of the accusation of guilt and rushed into the arms of crime with free and eager feet. I bought that illegal beer, again clinching the great lesson that unjust public accusation brings more shame than undetected obliquity. We are ashamed for the things that men know, not for the things we do. And so, learning this lesson of life, I was put in my proper place as a printer's devil. It was a good lesson anyway.

As the summer wore on, I learned more and more about the printing office. My high-school education and my year at college doubtless quickened my wits. Music had nimbled my fingers. I learned to set type quickly and fairly accurately. I could make up a job for the job press and run it off, adjust the impression, distribute the ink, and my legs traveled thousands of unmeasured miles, kicking the old Gordon and the man-killing Colt's Universal job presses. Occasionally when Tee Pee, a man given to large leisures, left town or felt lazy—being full of politics and a letch for fishing —I wrote local items and cut out reprints to keep the copy hook filled. Joe, the foreman, had no taste for these tasks, which were his by all right; and, because I had some white-collar talent, he drafted me and smoked a peaceful pipe while I worked when Tee Pee was abroad in the county whooping it up for Democracy. Then came a fine, fair autumn day when Tee Pee, in a new and gorgeous suit with rather more scarlet in his geranium boutonniere than usual, sailed down to the office before the morning Santa Fe train went north and told us in his fine, clear, dramatic voice that he was going to Washington to get the post office. He sat down, quickly filled the hook with copy, said he would be back in two or three weeks, waved his hand like a prince's wand at the office, and said:

"Well, you boys get out the paper anyway, and when I come back I will fix it up with you."

It was the post office that made us stay. Without that lure, Joe and the printer would have gone. For Tee Pee had queer ways about money; not that he was dishonest, not that he was careless of our rights. But in those days Saturday night was a hollow, empty form in the office of the Eldorado Democrat. Tee Pee generally put on a Saturday ritual, something like this: He would bustle in briskly Saturday morning while we were all throwing in type at our cases and when there was little need for much copy on the hook, greet each of us cordially, almost affectionately, stand in the midst of his realm and say:

"Well, well, boys, Saturday, isn't it? Saturday!"

Joe Cox, the head printer, being a malignant and courageous spirit, would probably answer back with the voice of the devil's hellions filing a saw: "You're right, it is!"

And Tee Pee would blink at him with a hurt and injured look, then turn to his desk and busy himself getting up copy. In the course of an hour or such a matter, after a subscriber had come in, or a statesman, to discuss the local situation, Tee Pee would rise again and begin the ritual:

"Well, boys, I must go out and see the sheriff. He owes me something for some sheriff sales. And I think I will get a little money from George Tolle, or maybe from Ed Denny, on account. You boys be in this afternoon, and I may be able to make you all happy."

Then Joe Cox, out of the deep malignity of his heart, would cry: "All right, Tee Pee! We'll be here waitin' for you."

And Tee Pee would walk out briskly, with a businesslike air, go clattering down the steps as one who was hurrying to a fire, and the place that knew him that day would know him no more. Late in the afternoon, Joe, the foreman, being a family man, would sneak out on the pretense of ordering some groceries, and we knew he was going to waylay Tee Pee somewhere on the streets and get either money or an order for groceries, or coal, or clothing, or whatever his needs might require. Sometimes Joe Cox, the printer, would sally forth. But as the evening shadows lengthened in the office we would sit in droning and drowsy talk around the cold office stove, smoking and spitting and hoping against hope for the foot upon the stairs that never came.

At odd times, Tee Pee would pass me a dollar, or two dollars, or a five-dollar bill. I kept no account. At first I did not know that he kept no account. But when he went to Washington to get the post office Joe, the foreman, put me in charge of writing the local items and getting up the reprint copy for the editorial page. These duties were loaded upon me in addition to my job as office devil and printer's apprentice, for I was growing rapidly in my knowledge of the trade. Then we four, representing the working class, made a solemn pact that we would take in all moneys and other collateral evidences of wealth that came to the office, keep them, distribute them in proportion to our wages, and make no accounting of it to the boss. We collected what we could and found that he had no books, and that he was none the wiser for our wholesale hypothecation of his funds. We caught up with ourselves a little and, while he was gone, we four thieves enjoyed a degree of prosperity that we had not known before.

The newspaper business in that far day was not a manufacturing enterprise. It was an artistic adventure. The editor, to all intents and purposes, owned the simple tools of his art. The printers were his fellow artists, at least abettors in the art. They lived as artists had lived of old—partly by mendicancy, partly by piracy, but always in joy. I was proud of my job as printer-reporter. It gave me no more status in the office than I had had, but it gave me outlet to the street where I gathered items. The girl clerks in the dry-goods stores greeted me on familiar terms. I was a "person" on the street. And coming back to the office I set my items in type. Naturally I pressed the extraneous matter from my items so that I might hurry back to the street and be a reporter again. There was a flavor in those days about the printing office. Printers were supposed to graduate into editors, editors into statesmen, statesmen into leading citizens, and so rise to empyrean heights in the state and nation. This was the natural road to the White House. No printer ever had gone to the White House, but in general all young printers expected to go there.

Of a Sunday, the printers would gather in the office and read the exchanges, comparing the typographical excellences of other papers and their own and discussing matters of the craft: the secret of glue making, how to mold rollers, how to cast slugs, and how to stop the encroachment of women compositors into the back rooms of the printing offices. Women in that day had acquired no rights in the printing offices. They came in under

protest, remained in scandal, and sometimes left either to marry the foreman or to satisfy the jealous rage of his wife. Every printer in an office
which employed women was looking—indeed, was hopefully, passionately
expecting to trap the foreman in some intrigue with the office printer girl.
Of a Sunday, in our office which was free of the female taint, we gossiped
bitterly and salaciously about the foreman and the printer girls of the other
shop. Perhaps all this was the intuitive fear of a tide of feminism. In our
heart's heart we heard its rising murmur.

CHAPTER XVII

The Dresden Shepherd Rambles into a Revolution

I FIND that I have hurried forward too fast in recounting my prowess as an apprentice. I am forgetting my job as a Dresden china shepherd, with Agnes Riley the Sèvres shepherdess. We two innocents, treading on the pink cotton clouds of adolescence, were enjoying life as an idyll. I remember the night she was graduated from high school in her white muslin with flounces on the skirt and sleeves, and the faintest hint of a V-neck that showed below her Adam's apple, and the hat she wore to match. I can see her yet in all her loveliness, and hear her voice as she read her essay or spoke her piece. I forget, more shame to me, what it was all about. And I remember going bashfully to the spring wagon where she climbed in with her family to go to her home on the farm. I reached for her hand, squeezed it, and told her how well I thought she did. In the telling, this seems like a pretty commonplace adventure; but it took some courage to face the Riley family, and, in those shy words, announce my honorable intentions at seventeen. And as the horses jogged away and the spring wagon faded into the night, I stood there watching her out of sight, a Dresden shepherd with a high saw-edged collar, with a little round straw hat, with a made-up, hand-painted pink necktie, and a suit of store clothes—a funny-looking Dresden shepherd to outward view but most poetically proper in my heart.

That summer, nearly every Sunday, what with playing for dances and with such spare change as I could earn, borrow, beg, or steal, I hired a horse and buggy and went to see her on the farm where she lived; life was as lovely as the picture on the lid of a cigar box. That summer also I made my first excursion into the fine arts. Eldorado gave "The Mikado" by home talent under the direction of a music teacher from Wichita, and I, in the chorus, was a "gentleman of Japan":

> If you want to know who we are,
> We are gentlemen of Japan:

On many a vase and jar—
On many a screen and fan,
We figure in lively paint:
Our attitude's queer and quaint—
You're wrong if you think it ain't.

Also that season I had my first part in the professional drama. James O'Neill came to town playing "The Count of Monte Cristo," in which he was cast upon an island. After destroying his second enemy, he stood tragically holding up two fingers and calling, "Two!" I was in that scene. I played an important part. Lew Schmucker and Bill Betts on one side of the stage, and Albert Ewing and I on the other side, waved a dirty gray canvas in great billows. I was cast as the ocean. Without me and my fellow billow-makers, O'Neill's tragic scene with two fingers up would have been a failure. I hope his son Eugene today realizes that I helped his father in his climb to fame.

One day that summer a young God appeared in the shop. He was a journeyman printer wandering over the state, and was hired in some rush of work, possibly caused by the annual appearance of the tax-sale notices in our paper. His name was Ewing Herbert. He stood six feet, with an olive skin, black eyes that twinkled, and a mop of stiff, raven-black hair that brushed his broad, low, handsome brow. He had an organlike bass voice. He was young and full of gay and malignant adventure. He had been out and around in the great world. He was a swift compositor and an intelligent one. He too had one eye on the White House. Ambition had her prod forever at his back. I became deeply fond of this young knight errant, two years my senior. I followed him about, was his willing slave, accepted his opinion, served him, and probably bored him to a crisp. It was I who, from my meager peculations, bought the watermelon which we ate in the office at the noon hour or after work hours, throwing the rind through the window at leading citizens who passed along the street, and ducking out of sight after letting drive. We once hit the man who was left by his fellow Democrats holding the mortgage. He saw the blank open window and protested to Joe, the foreman, that he would foreclose as soon as Tee Pee came home.

In addition to my excursions into love and the arts, Ewing Herbert and I spent some time of evenings loafing around a big camp meeting that was held a few miles below Eldorado. Revivals, protracted meetings, and, in summer, camp meetings were not new things to me. I had encountered them all my life. As a little boy, I used to sit in the back row of the church with other little boys, pinching one another and passing it on, making disturbances while the preacher pounded the pulpit, and sinners testified, and the congregation sang lustily, and the exhorters, going down the aisles, pulled brands from the burning. But here was a camp meeting larger than any I had ever seen.

Ewing and I used to lie on the grass on the bank that rose above the wooded dell, gossiping and philosophizing. We dressed up for the occasion—Ewing particularly. He had a white suit which, with his olive skin and raven-black hair and piercing black eyes, made him a most romantic figure. I had a hand-me-down seersucker suit, and we both wore gaudy neckties and the mode in shoes. Two young dudes! And through the years I can bring back what we talked about one night. That camp meeting, with its rich and shimmering golden heaven and its glowing, frightful hell, was patronized only by the poor. No Eldorado merchants were there, nor lawyers, doctors, or teachers. Occasionally a clerk came. But here were the workers, the failing farmers and their fading wives. Ewing, who had been reading the meditations of a German philosopher called Jean Paul Richter, the "only one" to match my Emerson, said:

"Will, look at that crowd. Too poor to skin. They've just got to have heaven to square it up with themselves for falling down, and they've just got to have hell for people like us who are having such a good time. They can't figure out a just God without a heaven and a hell."

And it has stuck with me all these years. But our philosophizing did not lessen the joy we had joining in the camp-meeting hymns, considering the camp-meeting emotional upset, the hallelujahs and the imprecations to the Lord for forgiveness—all the outbursts of overwrought minds and burning hearts that made the spectacle so weird, so terrible, so fascinating. So we sang with great gusto:

"Just as I am, without one plea . . . O Lamb of God, I come, I come."

It is a beautiful song if you have ever heard it, packed full of stress and strain and emotion. In the timber, with the arching trees above, with the flickering torches around, and with the great hulking gospel preacher crying aloud, calling men unto repentance out of sin, we found it easy to open our mouths and let the overcharge of feeling come out in song. We were detached young philosophers considering this strange human experience with cold, appraising eyes. Ewing had a beautiful bass voice and sang well, and I was not unmindful of my tenor. Naturally when the singing began we all moved up and joined in and enjoyed it. Then we slipped back and considered the words. I remember one song that repeated over and over again the powerful mental suggestion: "I can, I will, I do believe," and then ended after a mounting climax of melody, "I can, I will, I do believe that Jesus saves me now." And our conclusion was, "That certainly gets them!"— for sinners used to pop up in the congregation after that incantation with great regularity. Another song appealed to women. It was written in a minor cadence, and the chorus ran:

I will arise and go to Jesus,
  He will receive me in his arms.
In the arms of my dear Jesus,
  Oh, there are ten thousand charms!

Ewing and I took a low view of that song and the implications of its power, being pretty well along in our teens and not unfamiliar with the evidence of emotion upon the female of the species.

After camp meeting, we two would trudge back to town indulging in tall talk about the vast mysteries of life, chiefly love and religion, women and God, after the manner of boys who are in the presence of strange forces that they cannot comprehend. We did not realize that our questioning, our bewilderment, our yearning to know the truth of the mystery was as old as the race; that our talk, which had been the chatter of youth since little Cain and Abel walked along the outer garden walls, had bored the angels since time began to tick.

It was I who bought the Century Magazine and sat in the office of a Sunday and heard, with Heaven only knows what delight, Ewing read "Huck Finn," all about the king and the duke and the raft on the Mississippi—a glorious odyssey which fired both our souls. Lew Schmucker and I also bought and laid at Ewing's feet, as upon a shrine, the weekly comic papers of the day—Peck's Milwaukee Sun, the Texas Siftings, the Detroit Free Press, the Estelline Dakota Bell, and others of a score of papers that pervaded the broad and racy humor of the day. We read these papers together, with uproarious delight. When in the fall Ewing went away to the College of Emporia, where I had gone, my heart followed him. But I stuck to my job. I was not swift enough as a compositor to earn a living. I had not learned, in four or five months in that office, what I needed to learn in order to make a living as I went to school. So when Herbert left I went on with my work, torn between the lust to learn and an instinct to slack. The summer deepened into the autumn.

Tee Pee did not receive the post office as a victor's laurel wreath when he went to Washington. He stayed week after week, yet he came back without it—but hopeful! Also, he came back to trouble. No reformer was Tee Pee. It was not the day for reformers. However, his young reporter in a mad moment essayed to run a four-line item about the town poker game, intimating rather broadly that the "officials should do something." Why I did it, I do not know, looking back over the years. That town poker game was an ancient institution. Possibly it was protected by the officials, possibly they participated in its profits. Possibly the ancient and honorable poker game was like the liquor joint in the livery stable on South Main Street where, in a rank-smelling empty box stall in a tub with ice, covered by a gunny sack, one could go on a hot day and get a bottle of beer, or fish a black bottle of red liquor out of the hay in the manger and leave the price in the feedbox. Possibly the town poker game was like the sordid palace of gilded joy down across the railroad track which ran with little molestation as a necessary evil in that gorgeous established order. I do not know. But when Tee Pee came home he found that four-line item staring him in the face, threatening libel, riot, manslaughter, and sudden death.

So I went back to my printer's cases, and Main Street and Central Avenue knew me no more. My career as a reporter was ended. The golden autumn faded into silver winter. Money about the Eldorado Democrat office was still scarce. We had had our seven fat weeks during his absence, had collected wealth beyond the dreams of avarice. He never knew how much nor ever dreamed how our insistence for pay had been blunted during his absence by our own peculations. We still sat around the office stove of a Saturday night. Joe, the foreman, still slipped away during the afternoon. Joe, the printer, still crackled devilishly at the grand, empty pretense of Tee Pee's Saturday performance, and I took a bill, or a silver dollar, or even two to rattle together occasionally, and modestly accepted them, knowing full well that even what I stole and what I got was not enough to cover what I had been promised.

In the meantime, outside the printing office life went along with me in Eldorado in that spring, summer, autumn, and early winter of 1885 and '86 with the changed tempo of the time. We had our opera house. The traveling theatrical companies, which had been going over America since the Civil War, came to Eldorado and gave me great delight. "The Italians" came often, with violin, harp, and flute or cello, to play; and we had dances in the pit at the opera house. Some of the young fellows from the East brought swallowtailed coats, and the girls wore modestly low-necked dresses. Mrs. Murdock, in all her regal finery of lavender and old lace, used to appear with her gallant husband, leading the grand march. Alice kept patiently trying to teach me to waltz, dear girl, and carried corns to her coffin which I made treading clumsily on her feet. Agnes Riley laughed, and so did Albert Ewing; and Lew Schmucker said Alice looked like a little girl trying to move a big house. My big chair on the porch had done me no good. I had played for too many dances when I should have been dancing. Waltzing was out of my life. I never learned. And, so far as I could tell, Agnes Riley never cared. For other boys aplenty came to whirl her about, and I was scowlingly jealous. I harbored a black regret that in my boyish fight with John Knowles I had not broken his head with the whippletree they wrested from me when they stopped our fight.

It must have been a heavy care to Agnes Riley—my dark and jealous heart. I can remember only one of the score of rides that we must have taken together (for I always owed Skinner & Stimson at the livery stable). The ride that I remember was a moonlight sleigh ride. It cost a dollar and a half an hour, and we sped westward over the hard snowbanked roads out into the stony uplands of Towanda Township. Not a cloud was in the sky. The moon glittered. The air was cold. The stars on the horizon twinkled; and we were huddled under a regular haymow of blankets. Old Jerry, my favorite livery horse, was feeling good, and a mere touch of the reins guided him. So we seemed to be speeding through space at an incredible speed, probably up to six miles an hour. All I can remember is that I was very bashful, and I think Agnes was too; but I was approaching eighteen, and she was five months younger, and soon I was going back to college again. She was working in an office and earning money to take her to college too. And we were afraid of college, both of us, and the big new world beyond, which we feared would part us. We spoke of it, that I remember, with dread and nameless terror. But the moon was ineffably lovely. The night was nippy, and the blood of eighteen years was rising—an insurgent sap from our hearts to our brains. We greeted the new life crowding in upon us with fear and delight. When I left her at her door, old Jerry was prancing. I could not leave the sleigh and, getting out, she kissed me a gentle kind of post-office childish kiss and ran away laughing, and leaving the world of snow aflame with a pink delight. If God is in religion, and I think he is sometimes, and if he dwells some way in sex, and I believe he is there too, then Agnes and I that night stood beside our burning bush. It was a long, long time ago.

So came Christmas and New Year's. Then, being able to set a galley and a half of type a day and throw in my case to boot, and two galleys if the copy was flat, I hied me away to college to join Ewing Herbert, and the high gods of the academic Parnassus.

I had, on the whole, a low opinion of those high academic gods. Vernon Kellogg was writing to me from Lawrence about the glories of Kansas State University, urging me to go there. I was torn, perhaps not so much between the grandeur of the university and the shabby ways of the college as I was between Ewing Herbert and Vernon Kellogg. Ewing won. We roomed together; we worked together on College Life, which he had founded. In spare time he earned money as a reporter for the Emporia News, and I went to work as a printer on the third floor of the News office. The College of Emporia had that year left the tall building on Sixth Avenue. It operated in two adjacent frame store buildings on North Commercial Street. It was a measly affair. I had no happy memories of that spring semester at the college. I had studied Latin while I was in Eldorado, under the tutelage of our Presbyterian minister—a bearded patriarch named Anderson, who was an apt and inspiring teacher. He guided me through "The Aeneid" and some of Virgil's "Elegiacs," and together we jogged through Cicero's orations and maybe one or two of the essays; so I kept up with my Latin during the summer, fall, and early winter that I was in Eldorado. My tutor being a Presbyterian minister, a letter from him to the college guaranteed my grades. Probably my home study that year was due to my mother's everlasting nagging more than my own desire for scholarship. She was determined that I should have the education which my father had provided for. As for my other studies, they lagged while I learned the printing trade. But my range of general reading and information broadened notably. My addiction to De Quincey led me, without prompting and guidance, into the work of the other essayists of his time, and I suppose my youth and rather romantic nature shepherded me by the green pastures of poetry and prompted me to try my own rhyming skill. I kept a journal diary or something of the sort at odd times, and I find there that in that hiatus between the college terms I was tinkering with rhymes, trying to set down my thoughts in some sort of metrical form—the squawking young rooster learning to crow.

And now, because I have spent a lifetime as a country editor, it may be well to consider the country newspaper business in that day and time. In the mid-eighties of the nineteenth century, practically all American cities were country towns. In those distant days American towns were driven by factions—political factions based more or less upon commercial rivalries in the town. The banks quarreled bitterly and trivially, but ruthlessly. They generally financed, and virtually owned, the newspapers. The newspapers were beggarly at the best, and mendacious at the worst. A newspaper was an organ sometimes political but, at bottom and secretly, an organ of some financial group in the community which aimed at control of public utilities, or public patronage of one sort or other. Occasionally an editor in a country town, who had a large job-printing establishment, was independent. But his advertisers and subscribers rarely made him independent. He was too often, for all his pomp and bluster, the creature of his banker. The editor borrowed with a prodigal hand, built a grand house in the fashionable part of town; and, having passes, he rode up and down the earth, a dashing figure, and mingled with the rich and great in politics. But too frequently the editor was a pasteboard hero, who, when the times changed and factional fighting ceased in America, caved in and went to the scrap heap—a disheveled, vain, discredited old pretender.

The newspaper business in the middle eighties in the United States was in transit, going swiftly from the status of an ancient craft, where the craftsman was indeed a journeyman who owned his tools, to another stage in his social and industrial progress—the businessman. Tools were becoming expensive. The cylinder press and the new types cost money. The average printer could not pay for them. Capital was needed—not much capital, but those few thousand dollars, where it once required but a few hundred to set a journeyman up in business, were beyond the saving capacity of the ambitious young printer. His case was like that of his friend the teamster, who could save to buy a team of horses, or a yoke of oxen, and a wagon, but who could not compete as a freighter, thus equipped, with a railroad. Machinery everywhere in the last quarter of the old century was dividing and multiplying, making new social, economic, and political patterns, all based on the need of capital. The teamster, the shoemaker, the cabinetmaker, the wheelwright, the tanner, the saddler, all lined up beside the printer at the note counter of the bank to borrow the money to buy the new expensive tools needed to practice their trades as master mechanics in a new, shiny world! When I walked casually into Tee Pee's office to learn my trade, I unwittingly strolled into a revolution.

I went to work as a compositor in 1886 in the office of the Emporia Daily News, a bank-owned newspaper which made faces at the other bank-owned newspaper, and traduced the members of its adversary faction in the town. The composing room of the News was on the third floor of a ramshackle old firetrap. It had a few slim south windows, never washed, and a large stove in the middle of the room. The foreman edited the telegraph news, which came on flimsy sheets of yellow paper with the sentences skeletonized —the conjunctions, the articles, and many verbs being deleted to save telegraph tolls. Half a dozen printers—pale and generally emaciated men hurrying toward tuberculosis from bending ten hours a day over dusty cases of type—stood in their alleys, and two or three inky cubs in various stages of apprenticeship roamed about, dodging the foreman's eye in an industrious endeavor to loaf. A grimy, foul-smelling, filthy place it was. Yet to me, out of the little country printing office where I was a personage, it seemed to epitomize the great city. For Emporia was two or three times as large as Eldorado. I entered the portals of the News office with fear and trembling. I did not dream that I was a discontented proletarian when I grumbled in my heart that twenty-five cents a thousand ems for setting type was measly pay for a high-school graduate and a collegian. I was just a poor devil applying for work, and it was anything to beat the boss. So I told the foreman that I was a journeyman printer, which was not true. The lie was a part of the class struggle, but I did not know it. All I knew was that I could stick type with the best of them. Whereupon my lie stuck, and the foreman gave me what was known in that day as a sub-case. That is to say, I substituted in the afternoon when a printer wished to lay off, or when there was a rush of work. I went to my case. Probably, as I pulled my printer's rule from my pocket and picked up my stick, I showed the old printer standing by his case beside me that I was young and green and nervous.

"You don't know what to do, boy, do you?"

I shook my head.

"Go over to the copy hook on the foreman's desk and bring back a piece of copy, and I will tell you."

The piece of copy I chose was telegraph flimsy, which was without *and*'s *the*'s, *any*'s, *or*'s, and lacked many an obvious verb in the simple indicative mood. It might as well have been written in Greek. Moreover, it was a part of the market report. The old man smiled. The market reports were fat takes, for experienced printers would pick them up already set in type from the day before and correct them for that day. I could not have done this without elaborate instructions. He took my "take," gave me a piece of reprint which he had, easy copy, showed me how to dump my stick and where, and how to identify my take with my own slug, and guided me all through the day. One of the few passionate impulses which have kept me in the narrow path through all these years, is a desire to go to heaven and offer old Slug Nine, who stood beside me that day, the choice of my harp and crown and robe if he needs them.

Work was plentiful that winter in the News office. The industrial revolution was going well, though I did not dream what it was. When Saturday night came, Ewing Herbert and I went to a gaudy restaurant in the town, ordered a thick, rare beefsteak with canned mushrooms, dined like gormandizing young princes, and saw the future shimmering before us—an iridescent dream. Of course the gulf that lay between Ewing and me was unbridged. For he was earning his way through college as a reporter on the News, while I was a mere printer. Moreover, he had won an oratorical prize in the college in a day before football, when intercollegiate oratory made him as important as a football star would have been fifty years later in the college world. Night after night, when he came home from a social gathering in the town, from which most collegians were barred, he pulled the clothing off me to keep me from going to sleep in the cold room, and recited his prize orations to me—gestures, modulations, and all—while I, shivering like a wet dog, coached him. I could say that oration today.

In the spring when the state intercollegiate oratorical contest was held in Topeka, the College of Emporia—with Ewing Herbert as its hero—chartered a special car and went cheering and ballyhooing across the state to support him. I came down from the composing room to the editorial rooms to hold Herbert's place for a few days as a local reporter. Reporters were scarcer then than printers. Also, my brief experience as a reporter on the Eldorado Democrat came more nearly sustaining me than my experience as a printer had at first. I pounded the streets in the afternoons for items, went to the railroad station, rode the fire wagon, chased the runaway horses of the grocer delivery wagon, and made myself generally useful in the literature of the time and the place—prouder than Pontius Pilate of my reporting job in the big-town newspaper office.

At Topeka, the great night came. Herbert, representing the College of Emporia, walked magnificently out on the stage in a borrowed dress suit, a regal figure—black hair, olive skin, black eyes, six feet, oval face, organ voice, magnificent! He opened up, spoke the first sentence with his melo-dramatic manner, paused as was his wont to let it sink in, then moistened his lips, opened his mouth and uttered—not a word. He stood there a few seconds, and the seconds piled into a minute! Then three grew into four awful minutes of stage-struck silence. Finally, with the dignity that befits a thwarted god, he bowed, turned, and walked off the stage. Shame kept him from coming back to Emporia. He could not face the town or the school, and no one today who does not know how the white light of fame glittered upon a college orator should blame him. His college was dis-graced; his town eclipsed. He threw up his job, and I never went up to the third floor of the composing room again. I was a reporter for life.

CHAPTER XVIII

I Dance in My Treadmill

THE NEXT SUMMER I went back to Eldorado and found a job as reporter and city circulator for Mr. Murdock's paper, the Daily Republican. He gave me eight dollars a week, a princely salary. It was my duty to hire the carriers, to collect the monthly subscription from the town subscribers, to solicit new subscribers, and also, which pleased me most, to write local items betimes. Chiefly, I wrote local items betimes. Secretly by bribes, rebates, and subterranean methods I tried to impose upon the carrier boys by making them collect and solicit new subscribers. The carriers were paid a dollar a week. At the end of the first month I was faced with a strike. The whole list of the papers was something like five hundred copies. The month was June; the twilight was long. So I rented a horse at a livery stable and carried the whole list myself. The next night half the carriers came back. The third night they all came back. The strike was broken; capital was vindicated. The proletarian became the tool of capital! I kept on reporting with a casual left-hand attention to the subscription list, which consisted of folding a few papers in the evening, checking out the carriers, receiving their money, looking after the subscribers' complaints, and trusting to whatever gods of luck there are to see that the subscription list kept pace with the growth of the booming town.

As it was in the beginning, so it has been ever after! Always I have taken care of business with my left hand. Money has not been important in my life. Devote to money a certain amount of orderly method along with consistent industry, with such honesty as the times require, and any man need not want seriously for money in this world. Yet he may enjoy the career that beckons to him. But let sloth or inordinate desire for riches creep into his life, and he is hagridden by his job.

The gods at birth gave me two major blessings: energy and pride in my job. Whatever I have done, I have loved to do and have done with all my heart. That summer, working on the Eldorado Republican, was probably the proudest summer in my life. I was eighteen and full of sap. The familiar world of my childhood and boyhood I saw through the eyes of youth. I felt consciously that I was a young man, even a young man rejoicing! I was associating on something like equal terms with grown men and women. I realized that, as a reporter, I had rather ill concealed powers of life and death over my contemporaries. I could wave my wand and bathe them in valuable publicity; or I could withhold the baton and keep them in outer darkness. I was bright enough to realize that my power would vanish if I used it too brashly. I came to know something about Mr. Murdock, my boss, who became my model in many ways. He was the representative in Eldorado, and in Butler County, of the benevolent—at least reasonably benevolent—plutocracy that was governing our land. He had railroad passes everywhere. It was his job to see that the county convention was packed with Republicans who would nominate for the legislature Mr. Murdock's friends, who in turn would vote as he suggested, on what he regarded as major issues and they too often felt were insignificant—for instance, matters pertaining to railroad rates, corporation laws, the control of insurance and banks. Through the county convention he controlled the nomination of judges in our part of the state and, while we were functioning as a representative democracy, we functioned through Mr. Murdock largely. Of course he had opposition which howled lustily and impersonally. But the opposition never questioned the need of some personal vicegerent of the plutocratic gods. The other fellows merely wanted to be vicegerents. As Mr. Murdock was in control, he had money to spend—of course, not his own money, but political money—plenty of it, and I presume he spent most of it. He was no bookkeeper, but I am sure he always knew in which pocket he kept his own money, and in which was the money of the railroads or banks and insurance companies and packing houses, who financed through Topeka and Kansas City the local politics of Kansas in those days. But Kansas was only one among many states in the Union which were run by the same interests. For all my wide reading, I saw no obliquity in this scheme of things, and I was happy to be—through Mr. Murdock—a humble servant in the great creative scheme of government. I was not quite so conscious of it then as I am now, looking backward nearly sixty years; but I knew definitely and with conscious and probably obvious pride that I belonged to the governing classes.

We had few sacred cows in the Republican office in those days. Mr. Murdock was an easy boss. He liked to hear the paper talked about. He liked to have a stir and rumpus going on. So he never pulled the rein on me as I roamed about the town seeking whom I might bedevil, provided he was not a good advertiser, a political ally, or someone connected with the county printing. The county printing was our reason for being. For that, we would sacrifice anything! For that, we wrangled and rowed with the other editors of the town and the county. The county printing was a major objective. In every western country newspaper in that golden day, the county printing, which amounted to five or six thousand dollars a year, was chiefly profit; and it was, as a matter of fact, almost our only profit. For that we lived, moved, and had our being. So the county commissioners who dispensed the county printing were sacred cows. At the weddings of their daughters, we printed the full list of gifts. At the funerals of their families we turned black rules of sorrow. If they dallied with the public funds, we defended them against the onslaughts of the less favored newspapers in the county. The politics of the day was full of intrigue, and the intrigue was greased more or less with corruption. Railroads were being built across the Missouri Valley; legislators were being elected, and governors chosen, who would carry water for the iron horse. The spirit of the times, which we called the spirit of progress, was a greedy endeavor to coax more people into the West, to bring more money into the West. It was shot through with an unrighteous design for spoils, a great, ugly, riproaring civilization spun out of the glittering fabric of credit. Everyone who owned a white shirt was getting his share of some new, shiny, tainted money in those days of the mid-eighties in our boundless booming West. We sought to establish industries and spent much of the investor's money in salaries of promoters. We laid out town additions for colleges and sold town lots to establish these starved little institutions on the prairie half a mile from our towns in sun-baked, rococo stone buildings, without endowment and without reason for being—colleges which struggled along for a generation and then sometimes gave up the ghost, became city high schools, or crumbled into disuse. We voted bonds for anything—schools, courthouses, city buildings, railways, factories without economic reason, streetcars, waterworks, electric lights—anything. Wherever we could borrow capital with bonds we got it, spent it riotously, with never a thought of pay day. So later, when the crash came, the delinquent taxes piled up and newspapers waxed fat in advertising those delinquent-tax sales, and the county commissioners, who awarded tax-delinquent printing contracts, remained as they were in my halcyon days with Mr. Murdock, little tin gods in our newspaper cosmos!

It was in that gaudy civilization—stalking trivial personal items about the nobility and gentry of the times, riding on the rear step of the bedizened new red fire wagon, chasing runaway horses up and down Main Street, running panting to trains that unloaded their daily spawn of suckers, who in turn became a part of the vast swindle that was the Middle West of the eighties—that I, a straw-haired reporter in my teens, began to learn the newspaper business in the fool's hard school of experience. But that summer of '86 was all grand to me. I had no perspective. I was as mad as the craziest, and no better than the worst, when it came to the vast conspiracy of the times.

I had the special privilege of my craft. I rode free to the railroad stations and to public ceremonies in the new varnished hacks that rattled about the streets. I had passes on the railroads. At the eating houses I was a favored guest. All reporters had these special privileges. The opera house opened its door for me when I flashed my old printer's rule. I consorted with the judiciary in return for advertising the dignity and wisdom of the court. When junketing excursions of councilmen started on big drunks, to view municipal improvements in other towns on the taxpayers' money, reporters were taken along and treated as young princes—maharajas of the first class. I had two summers of this in Eldorado.

In the first glorious summer of my reportorial career, Samuel J. Tilden died, and I tried my first editorial eulogy upon him. I was deeply moved by Tilden's death, being so far as I knew a hereditary Democrat. The daily newspapers at the time, which came to the office of the Eldorado Republican, were filled with encomium of Tilden. Even my mother softened her heart toward Tilden after his death. And because Tee Pee was out of town, Joe, the printer, let me come into the office of the Butler County Democrat, mount my old stool, and set up at the case there something that I knew would not go in the Eldorado Republican. And so I composed the following editorial:

It is with feelings of mingled sorrow and unfitness that we take up our pen to chronicle the death of another American hero whose name has been familiarly dear to every American heart. We refer to Samuel J. Tilden of New York. He was a hero without a title, a man who by self-sacrificing acts and noble, fearless espousal of the right, made his friends and followers love his very name and caused his opponents to honor and respect him . . . His name will be enshrined in the hearts of his countrymen and carved deep in the tablets of fame after the echo of other names heralded with tocsin of war and bloody passion will have died away and are lost forever. His life was gentle and the elements so mixed in him that nature might stand up before all the world and say, "This was a man."

It was in the rhetorical style of "Mother, Home, and Heaven" which had been my model when, two years before, I helped Julia Fulenwider with her commencement essay and fell down so hard in the composition of my own. Also, Mark Twain had taught me little—Dickens, nothing. The transcendentalism of Emerson with its short hammer blows affected my rhetorical method not at all. In brief, so far as Emerson really got into me and became a part of my will and affected my conduct or anything like it, probably the Emerson philosophy was for ten years a growing infection before it broke out in my life. It seems to me that many ideas work within the spirit, whatever the coordinated functions of man's mind may be which we call his spirit, a slow-growing virus which appears in life long after the day of infection has passed. At least it has been so with me. That Tilden editorial, so soggy with sentiment and Byzantine with rhetoric, probably photographs the upper layer of my mind in 1886 better than all these pages I have written.

The news of my effort in the Butler County Democrat was whispered around among the printers. Mr. Murdock heard of it. When the Democrat was out, I saw him take up the paper. Mrs. Murdock came in. I heard him read it to her. They did not know I was about, and I heard them laugh at its turgid, florid style. And Mrs. Murdock said:

"Oh, that Willie—that Willie!"

And Mr. Murdock said: "Well, I suppose the old Doc would like it—maybe!"

That eavesdropping was not an exhilarating experience.

But I was learning to write. I was learning that the way a thing was said, even a three-line item, was quite as important as the item itself. Probably I had some facility of expression. Even if the Emerson microbe in my mind was for the time dormant, my reading of Mark Twain and Bill Nye and the newspaper humorists of that day had given me some knack of putting words together grotesquely. And I tried to make all of my items snappy. The printers—this I know, for they told me so—frankly thought I was a smart aleck: an opinion they may have drawn from the town at large. Then one day I learned that language used recklessly was dynamite. It happened this way:

A woman came to town selling corsets. Cass Frieburg, the dry-goods merchant, and one or two others—I forget who—nagged me into assailing all itinerant merchants and making my assault generally, but rather particularly and pointedly, directed at this corset saleswoman. And when I came downtown the next morning, as I started upstairs to the editorial room of the Republican, the devil from the printing office told me that the woman was waiting up there for me with a rather ill concealed rawhide that she had bought down at Jimmie Dodwell's harness shop. So I did not go up to the office, but began collecting my news. The first batch I took up the back stairs and gave to the foreman, and learned that the angry woman was looking for me on the street. Whereupon I haunted the alleys that day, going into back doors of the stores and collecting my news, sometimes standing not more than fifteen or twenty feet from the lady who was laying for me with that "patient watch and vigil long," which controls the conduct of a "woman scorned." For two days and a half this contest lasted, and finally the woman left town.

That was my first lesson in the perils and penalties of indiscretion. I have had many others. It took at least forty years to tone me down. And it still breaks out in me today, as my measles used to come out in the cold water of the creek ten years after my recovery from the disease. I have learned many things in my journey through the dark woods of this wilderness of life, but I am blind sometimes to the dangers of indiscretion. The smart aleck on the Eldorado main street still sometimes leads me into temptation and trouble.

I reported my first murder case that summer. It was a mystery. I helped to solve it, for I had become correspondent for Eldorado of the Associated Press, the St. Louis Globe-Democrat, and the Kansas City Star. Here is what happened: Ten miles from Eldorado a summer flood uncovered the body of a man which had been buried hastily in a ravine. Only one clue was left to guide us to the murderer: a broken spade handle near by, on which were carved the letters "O. L." The man had been brutally murdered, probably the winter before. I wrote the story for the Eldorado Republican and wired it abroad. Several weeks afterward, a sheriff came from North Dakota with a theory about a man named Orin Larriway, who owned that shovel. He was a hired man on a farm. He and the farmer had left their North Dakota home, bound for Texas to buy a farm. A few weeks after their departure the farmer's wife and child disappeared also. The sheriff's theory was sustained by neighborhood gossip that Larriway had murdered his boss, later had sent for the boss's wife and child and that they had gone Heaven knew where. That hypothesis was verified. Larriway was picked up, brought to Eldorado for trial, and I reported the murder case. He was convicted and sent to the penitentiary. Probably I was mean to him, for in jail he grumbled that I had caused his conviction by printing and coloring the evidence.

The Lord knows, he may have been right. For I had no sense of justice then and had great pride in my power. My reporting gave me a little local fame. I sent a day-by-day story to out-of-town papers and was paid for it decently. I was somebody, or thought I was; probably strutted my pride! The incident belongs in this story to indicate how I was getting along as a newspaperman. My self-esteem was growing. It was not yet strong enough to overcome my feeling of inferiority about the everlasting pimples, for my face was still splotched like a pounded beefsteak. Nevertheless, I had my small and, in the case of the Larriway murder, my profitable vanities, even if Larriway's look of burning hate scorched my self-esteem a little as he left the county jail for his life sentence in the penitentiary.

That same summer another significant and memorable episode in my newspaper career occurred. George Gardner, a noted criminal lawyer in our town, helped the new county attorney, Charley Lobdell, try his first murder case. (In parentheses, I may identify Lobdell: He later became Speaker of the Kansas House of Representatives, still later member of the

Federal Farm Loan Board, and later still a figure in Wall Street.) Gardner made an eloquent plea, and I wrote down a column of it, set in what was then called nonpareil and would now be six-point. At noon the next day Gardner met me in the most conspicuous place in Eldorado—at the corner of Central and Main streets, on the lid of the Fire Department cistern—and grasped my hand and slipped a five-dollar bill into it and said, "Will, this is for you!" and hurried away. I went to the office feeling that I had been bribed and corrupted. I went straight to Mr. Murdock with the bill still in my hand, told him the story, and said, "What shall I do?"

The old man looked at me quizzically and broke out: "Tried to bribe my reporters, eh! The damned scoundrel! Hasn't he got any moral sense left?" He saw the bill still in my hand and said: "Willie, give me that bill. By Godfrey's diamonds, plowing with my heifer, eh? I'll show him he can't buy my reporters!" And, slipping the bill into his pocket, he gave me the funniest, quizzicalest, and chucklingest smile and added, "Now go to work!" He kept the bill!

That has been one of my pet stories for years, matched only by one that happened later when I was on the Kansas City Star and Bob Towne, our crack reporter, had been working three days on the story of a new ownership of the stockyards, and the vast changes the new owners were going to make, and the great benefits these changes would bring to Kansas City as a stock market. He came from the Coates House, where the stockyards' nabob was staying, and at the city editor's desk told the gang:

"Boys, I have been corrupted; perhaps polluted. That damned Boston Yankee that's buying the stockyards got me in his bedroom, then took me into his bathroom, and said: 'Mr. Towne, I want to show you my appreciation for all you have done for the company.' And before I could stop him, he handed me a quarter and turned quickly away. I'm willing to put it in a pot, if anyone else will help, and buy the gang a round of drinks. This office is not going to be bribed, without common connivance."

Sometime in that summer of 1886, Vernon Kellogg persuaded me to go to the State University at Lawrence. Vernon came down to Eldorado to attend one of the dances which I was getting up as a budding McAllister of the late Spring Chicken crowd, alias Trundle Bed Trash. He and I talked it all out with my mother and I decided to go to the University. Lawrence seemed to be a long way off. In the end my mother decided to rent our house and establish a home for me in Lawrence.

One Sunday in late August, I went to the livery stable and got my favorite team, Tom and Jerry, early in the morning and set out for Agnes Riley's home, and we two went on an all-day picnic excursion, headed eastward into the Flint Hills. I had never seen them. I had no idea of their loveliness. As we passed Rosalia, on the high tableland that soon breaks into the great ravines and canyons that are gouged beneath this upland to make the rolling hills, we were both astonished and delighted with the beauty that unfolded before us. We were eighteen. I, at least, had never had a consciousness of beauty in landscapes. In music, yes; in poetry, yes; of course in prose like De Quincey's and Emerson's. But beauty in the landscape was a new sensation. The hills were clad in summer green, and in those days the deep ravines were wooded and the road, a dirt road, a farmers' road, ungraded, wound around the contour of the hills, crossing the ravines on wooden bridges which rumbled under the horses' feet and the buggy wheels as we passed. We knew that, when I went to the University and Agnes went to the State Agricultural College at Manhattan, our ways would part. I do not think we ever talked of marriage. And that day we were so enthralled with the beauty around us that life itself suddenly became a part of that beauty. We talked only a little. I think each of us dreaded what we feared was the inevitable parting. At eighteen, a boy with two years before him in college and a deep-seated desire to be somebody, sometime, perhaps a self-centered, little intellectual snob, could feel the conflict of emotions, the dread of a parting, which would make him sad in silence, and also an alternating curve of joy and delight at the new world dawning before him. What Agnes felt, I do not know. But I do know that we were happy and took a deep joy in the loveliness of the soft lines of the hills. They had a sort of vast monotony of curve and lines. The colors in different shades of green, all innocent of the plow, brought us a delight that only youth can have in those first experiences which bring new stimulation to the senses. To see a new world in youth is to approach the ineffable.

So, at noon, we found in a deep ravine a quiet grove and ate our lunch there by a spring. It "were happiness enow"! We rode home through the long afternoon and the late twilight and saw the hills in the new light when the horizontal light lines from the west made strange shadows. The pleasure that had run through the day was turned, at night, into exquisite silence. Thus we rode back across the upland under the stars. And when I had helped her out of the buggy at her father's door I wound the reins around the whip socket on the dashboard, curled up in my seat, and let Tom and Jerry go clattering along their well known beat. I was awakened only when I heard the roar we made crossing the bridge near town. I sailed into the livery barn, yelled at the stableboy, and went home, tired, exalted, happy—with that happiness which is screened through sadness, and purified.

When my mother and I were packed and our furniture boxed for Lawrence, I came into the house that to me had seemed like a grand house, and found my mother sitting on a big goods box all alone, having a good Irish

137

cry. When I questioned her, I found that she had been going all through the house, room by room, indulging in a sentimental debauch, bidding it all goodbye.

She had come to that corner of Eldorado in 1869. It was now well into 1886. In those seventeen years she had seen (and she was deeply appreciative of what she had seen) the miracle of the western Mississippi Valley turning from raw prairie, where the Indians and the buffaloes still roamed, to an ordered civilization. She knew its significance. She had seen the town around her grow from a huddle of unpainted shacks and shanties by the road up from the river to a little city of a smart New England type—all painted white with green blinds, whitewashed paling fences about the yards, and young trees scattered on the lawns just beginning to arch over the narrow streets. She had seen the free school and the free city library appear; the city building rise up, representing municipal solidarity; churches come to symbolize law and order. And while I, a boy of eighteen, had no acute sense of the meaning of these things, to her who had eyes that could see and ears that could hear, it meant what it was. Leaving it, she was surely most upset. She told me that she had always been unhappy in that house. To me, looking back at it now, with its rococo over-ornamentation, in its essentially false economy of that gorgeous settlement of the West, the house seems to stand exactly for that time and place. To me, it had unfolded as an amazing spectacle. But to her, coming there in her late thirties and leaving in her middle fifties, it had all been disappointment, struggle, rancor, bitterness, and sorrow.

I am sure that she was sincere. And I began to see then what life has assured me so well, that happiness is entirely from within, from some quirk of inheritance, some twist of the brain that holds the mind and heart always in the shadow. "My father," she had so often said to me, "was a dour, sour, unhappy man." She was his spiritual daughter. Probably I was the child of Ann Kelly who gathered up her petticoats around her bottom and danced herself out of the dumps. My life in Eldorado had been joyous, and I welcomed Lawrence and the University of Kansas with glowing delight.

CHAPTER XIX

I Creep "Like a Snail Unwillingly to School"

HERE IS THE WAY Vernon Kellogg said I looked when I struck Lawrence. He was writing, in a reminiscent mood, thirty years after:

He was a little taller than a middle-sized boy, with a long neck and what would be called a chunky body. It was clothed in a good, hand-me-down brown suit with braid around the coat edge, and a made-up necktie, hand-painted. In the necktie was a golden bull's head with chipped diamond eyes. Over it all, skimmed-milk-colored eyes, a blond splotched skin, a broad wide forehead, reddish hair topped and crowned with a rather wide white hat with a narrow black band—the type of headgear worn by western cowmen and gamblers. He was not a prepossessing figure.

Yet that was what Vernon had on his hands as fraternity material. For he was bound that I should belong to his fraternity, Phi Delta Theta, and Vernon then and always was a resourceful man, canny, not above intrigue, quietly determined. He set me spinning like a top at the Registrar's office and left me. We had talked over the studies I could take. He saw my grade card at the Eldorado High School, with good grades on it, and from the College of Emporia with rather less than fair grades but passable. And being—as most intriguing, determined men are—a boss by nature, he had mapped my classes, my hours, and the course I should take. We wiped out the classical course which I had started at the College of Emporia and took the literary-scientific course, which required two years of college Latin, two years of German and French, and some balance between the physical sciences—zoology, chemistry, botany, geology—and the other humanities, history, English, economics, sociology, psychology, and political science. And, of course, there were two stiff years of mathematics, which were to be my academic stumbling block and the doom of my college degree.

I had much more to my credit, two college years of Latin, a college year of Greek, and a year of college mathematics, and of course a year and a half of English literature and composition and, I think, six months of French—hardly a smattering, possibly a smear. But with all that credit, I entered a freshman, with nothing to make up and several hours to spare.

That young man under the gambler's hat, with a fairly good suit of hand-me-down clothes and the bull's head with chipped-diamond eyes, eighteen years old—who had worked two years on a newspaper and had been the boss of a dozen carriers and had earned his living as a printer and one summer as a reporter—had considerable self-assurance for his age. Barring his pimples, which still ground deeply in his heart but not deeply enough to humiliate him, he was rather well pleased with himself. He had been accepted as a man among men in a printing office and as a reporter on the streets of Eldorado. He had sent a man to the penitentiary for murder, and could call county officers in the Butler County Courthouse impudently by their first names without being rebuked. Later I heard it said in the university by fraternity scouts who looked me over that I was fresh. "Too damned fresh" was the criticism which the Betas passed upon me; they took William E. Borah, a fellow freshman, that autumn. I made a bee line for the college newspaper called the Courier, and with Vernon's fine Italian hand was installed as one of the local editors and choked the editor, Cyrus Crane, our local college orator, with copy—all sorts of copy. I wrote personal news items, smart-aleck cracks at the various foibles of the university, and dug up some news which other less skilled reporters had overlooked. That did not reduce my hatband either.

Moreover I wrote articles in the Eldorado Republican about the university—bumptious articles, critical articles—with an impudence uncalled for. I signed these articles in brash conscious audacity with the name of a then nationally famous anarchist, Herr Johann Most. The Eldorado Daily Republican in the university library was widely read. One of my "Herr Most" screeds was copied in the local paper. The finger of, if not exactly scorn, at least unpleasant disapproval pointed my way, which pleased me greatly—appealing to my naturally exhibitionistic nature. I strutted inside my black hatband and probably spread a little rooster peacock's tail to the wide world. I was pleased to be a "figure" on the Hill. On the other hand, I was most sensitive, deeply sensitive to the beauty I saw as I stood many a quarter of an hour on the porch of the university on Mount Oread looking over the Kaw Valley for miles and miles. On a clear day, with proper light, one could see the smoke in Kansas City. I had never been so high above the environing plain in my life before, and I had never before seen so much land. It was a lovely prospect and moved me deeply. So I wrote some verses about it. Vernon, seeing the moisture in my eyes which glowed out of my heart, pressed my arm and was happy too. He was that kind of companion.

I herded around in the college for the first few months, finding my place in half a dozen classrooms, letting the faces of my fellow freshmen photograph on my memory. I was soon calling them by their names, without either Mister or Miss to the jug handle of their surname. Indeed I was calling most of the girls by their first names, and I am quite sure I was busy polishing apples for all of my teachers. In high school I was the kind of little boy who stuck up his fingers quickly and snapped them at the teacher when a question was asked which he could answer. The habit did not depart when I donned that gambler's hat and the golden bull's-head tiepin. Cyrus Crane, the college orator and idol and editor of the college local newspaper, who was a senior then, wrote me not long ago that he remembered me as an eager boy, quite independent, who was stubborn when he thought he was right, but easy to order about on reportorial assignments, which suggests to me that I knew the buttered side of my daily bread. I had been in the town but a few days when I went to the office of the Lawrence Journal and tried to make a connection there to report university news. I got an assignment on space, fifty cents a column; not exactly a princely remuneration, but I also managed to land the Lawrence correspondence of the St. Louis Globe-Democrat and, best of all, fell into the carrier's route for that paper and got also the correspondence for the Kansas City News, whose editor was Willis Abbot. He later was to be the head of the Christian Science Monitor in the third decade of this century.

My mother and I installed ourselves in a little five- or six-room house three blocks from the university, where we set up housekeeping and were most comfortable. She, with her leisure time and only one mouth to feed, took up my books and followed me with my classes, and sometimes later, as in the case of German and Latin, helped me with my lessons. For after all she had been a sophomore at Knox College twenty years before, and her mind was always keen and lively. I brought books to her from the university library and, so far as I could see, she was happy.

The Kansas State University in 1886 was an epitome of its environment. It was like a dozen other state universities in the Mississippi Valley. There went the sons and daughters of the squires of the manor, of the gentry and nobility, and of the high lords of politics and business. In their blood was the struggle of the hour—the tremendous desire to make a material world out of raw material, God's great wilderness stretching up from the Mississippi River to the Rocky Mountains. We had been bred in politics, and we took university politics into the academic cloister—not party politics, of course, but student affairs. There we conducted our business under a boss system, with all its chicane, with its terrors and its spoils, much after the manner and methods used by our fathers to rule their little local satrapies and fiefs.

141

Into university politics I plunged with Christian zeal. But I found quickly that unless I expected to be a leader of the nonfraternity world, known as the Barbs, I was barred from leadership in the college political activities which I understood instinctively and loved. So Vernon Kellogg and I renewed his efforts to get me into his fraternity. I had been asked if I would consider invitations to two other fraternities; but my loyalty to Vernon, after consulting with him, made me say no to the other offers, and I was known on the campus, among other fraternity men, as the Phi Delt's errand boy—not a pleasant title, but I was willing to wear the name for the fame. Anyway, Vernon was sure he could swing the fraternity into line for me. So, as he tolled off my supporters inside the fraternity, we took the doubtful ones home to Sunday dinner; and my mother certainly put the big pot in the little one. For I suspect Vernon had told her what was in the air. We fed those boys who did not like the gambler's hat or the milk eyes and the long neck and the brash ways of their fellow student, giving them home cooking in a weary land. So we wore down their natural objections to me as a fraternity brother. And in February, 1887, I was initiated into the Phi Delta Theta and had crossed the first river in my university career.

A week or so before my initiation another belated initiate came into the fraternity. He was Fred Funston, a Congressman's son. Fred Funston was later Major General of the American Army, but at that time he was a pudgy, apple-cheeked young fellow, just under five feet five, who seemed to have decided in his cradle to overcome his runty size by laughing at himself, clowning in short. He was clumsy but nimble. He walked swiftly but not too steadily, indulged in no athletic sports whatever, was a good rifle shot, had absolutely no sense of fear, physical or spiritual, was a poor to passable student, read widely, had vast areas of curious information, loved good clothes which he could not afford to buy, was methodical and rather meticulous in his habits, affectionate by nature; everyone in the fraternity loved him, and I clave to him like a brother. We made three— Vernon, Funston, and I. Just two touches are necessary to complete the picture: he fell desperately in love every six months with a new girl, and could not carry liquor, and he loved it. We used to say that if he smelled a rotten apple he began tearing up the sidewalks. With two drinks, it took three men to hold him. So we—by "we" I mean the fraternity—kept rotten apples, and hard cider and homemade wine, which were the prevailing sinful drinks of Kansas University students of that day, away from Funston. For diversion we encouraged him with his amours, which were always sincere, always decent, and always well directed. He never fell in love with a fool nor an ugly woman. Because of his size he could never hold the kind he loved. But he was persevering, and he never carried a broken heart after the first few days of surging sorrow when he was dismissed. In the national journal of our fraternity his name as an initiate was spelled Timson, instead of Funston, and he became Timmy to the fraternity and the university—Timmy Funston. It fitted him.

I became in the fraternity Billy White. And Kellogg, because he was dapper, wise, naturally bossy and was a born leader, became "V. L."—for Vernon Lyman. We three interacted upon one another. Vernon gave Funston and me a certain academic veneer. We gave him continual delight: Timmy was his wayward child; I was his faithful messenger. He never could teach Timmy intrigue nor interest him in university politics. I was a pointer dog who retrieved beautifully. Vernon schemed. I was the tin cornice behind his political structures. One thing all three had in common: writing. Funston wrote beautifully. His only A grades in six years at the university were in English composition. Kellogg wrote with grace and charm; I, voluminously. Other men in the fraternity—the two Franklins, Ed and Will—became distinguished scientists: Ed, an analytical chemist of international fame and before he died President of the American Chemical Society; Will, a physicist who died after a distinguished career in Lehigh University and Boston Tech. The other boys in our fraternity all rose to decent careers, leaders in their lines of work.

The Phi Delta Theta Chapter in Kansas University in those days was known for its scholarship. It inherited the pious reputation which in my day was cruelly undeserved, but it did lead, or tie, in my day, for Panhellenic scholastic honors, though (the Lord forgive us) Funston and I brought the fraternity far below the Phi Beta Kappa level. He and I were both irregulars —I because of my freshman-plus credits from Emporia, he for some Spanish credits and somewhere, I believe, a surplus of credits in mathematics, in which I recall he was excellent. He cared little for political science, sociology, or history—which he read widely, but as a diversion, never as a task. He wrote as easily as he swore, and certainly, having spent some time in Mexico, he picked up a wide eclectic Spanish-Texan-Kansan-and-Old-English collection of oaths which he loved to juggle with in emotional moments. For he was an emotional creature.

I put down these facts not because Funston became a national hero, but because he typified what I took from the university. My grades were only fair. My extracurricular activities should have given me a Phi Beta Kappa pin, for I poked my nose into everything on the Hill except athletics. And Funston and I, in these matters of extracurricular interests, hunted, ran together like sheep-killing dogs. We held our friendship until death severed it thirty years after we had met. As I look back at it, classroom pictures blur in my memory of the university. Fraternity meetings are clear; political excursions are etched deeply; parties, little dances, picnics, and what, in the student nomenclature of the time, was called "girling," I recall vividly. Also, I was downtown much of the time writing my news items for the Lawrence Journal, taking my copy for the Weekly University Courier to the printer, covering local events for the St. Louis and Kansas City papers. Though I sold at a small profit my Globe-Democrat route early in my university career, I became business manager of the University Review, a literary monthly. Thus I came to know the merchants whom I solicited for advertising. Indeed, downtown Massachusetts Street in Lawrence I knew better than I knew many a classroom, and certain businessmen better than some of my professors.

It was at the end of my first college year that I began carrying Helen Sutliffe's books down the Hill; and the next year, to leap forward a little, I became deeply interested in seeing that the Pi Phis, who were her sorority sisters, got more than their share of invitations to University Phi Delt parties and dances. I became known as a Pi Phi Delt and, incidentally, tried to see that more Phi Delts than Phi Psis and Phi Betas were invited to the Pi Phi parties. As I read this over, it seems a silly jargon; yet it meant much to me—that social leadership that I craved and took in my university career. I suppose, squinting at it through the perspective of nearly sixty years, that social and political leadership, plus the university library, represented the organization interests which stimulated me and promoted my intellectual growth more than the professors and the classrooms—vastly more! But that statement requires important revision.

Three or four men in the university faculty meant much to me. Their guidance and their influence have held through all my life. First of all came James H. Canfield, under whom I took more work than under anyone else. He taught me economics, sociology, political science, and history. He sat at the head of a long U-shaped table, and around him ranged his students. I sat opposite William E. Borah, a solemn, shrewd, rather silent Beta, who cracked few jokes but understood them all; and near us for a year was Herbert Hadley, later Governor of Missouri, who came within a pin scratch of being nominated by the Republicans in 1912 for President of the United States. Canfield asked practically no questions. He promoted discussion. His classroom sometimes was a babble of clamoring voices. He laughed with the boys (only a few girls took his course—but Helen took many of his courses). He set us to reading books and loving him. He was an exceptional teacher, and until he died, twenty years after I left school, Canfield was my political mentor and my dear friend. I transferred my friendship to his daughter Dorothy and so lived happily all of my life.

Another teacher who stimulated me greatly was Arthur Richmond Marsh, who taught English literature and composition. He also asked few questions. His classes were small, and we read—that is to say, he read to us.

He had a mellow, modulated voice with a Harvard accent. He was a big, handsome young fellow, at least six feet, who played a gorgeous game of tennis and sometimes pitched on the university baseball team. He knew so many interesting and important things! He took a shine to Funston's prose, though I think Funston personally repelled him, for Funston rejected him *in toto*. Marsh was the kind of teacher who invited his class to his house, where we had tall talk. I became his willing slave and really tried to make decent grades in his class, though I never got much better than a B or B-plus. But he did chart my path into reading good English and American writers. He taught me to read the New York Nation, which I have read steadily since I first crossed his classroom threshold in 1886. Arthur Richmond Marsh opened the door to a wide field of modern criticism: Arthur Hugh Clough, Augustine Birrell, Andrew Lang, and poets who were modern in his day. He was a civilizer for the red-faced youth from the Walnut under the gambler's hat with the golden bull's-head and the sparkling chipped-diamond eyes. Marsh dropped the corn that led me to the Unitarian Church, where I functioned once in amateur dramatics with some success.

Most of all, there at the university I met William Herbert Carruth, head of the German Department. My class there was taught by his wife Frances. And with Carruth, who was perhaps ten years my senior, I began a friendship which again only death severed. Finally, the other university professor who helped me greatly was Francis H. Snow, who taught the biological subjects—biology, zoology, entomology, comparative anatomy—and afterwards became chancellor. I had few classes under him; but he stimulated my reading, and, because he was Vernon Kellogg's guide and friend, I often met him. Professor Snow certainly gave me a great respect for the sciences and made it easy for Vernon in later years to keep me reading along lines which otherwise I should have abandoned.

But what with the fraternity, the girls, the parties, Massachusetts Street and the businessmen, the Lawrence Journal, the university papers and the incidental university politics which controlled the university papers, and occasionally, by way of diversion, the classes—I took on a heavy load for a western student in the eighties, of what passed for a sort of culture. At least, in my four years there I got the habit of trained attention to the printed page and could read a chapter in a book after dark without falling asleep. Moreover, I could, if the hour was not too late, stand another chapter and maybe a third of a nonfiction book, which capacity for trained attention to the printed page is about the best that any man gets out of a college education. Given that capacity, if he will, any man or woman may keep abreast of his times and know how the world is put together and what makes it click and tick. Without it, the going in the modern world is tough!

CHAPTER XX

I Join a Great Brotherhood!

LOOKING BACK over the years, I am amazed to find the reason for my temerity in attaching myself to the university orchestra as a piano player; compared with the other youngsters then in musical literacy, I did not know a note of music. A letter from a friend a few years older than I who has not seen me since my childhood, before I went into high school in Eldorado, seems to give me a clew to my temerity. She writes:

You were always an ambitious lad and full of curiosity. You would try anything to see how it worked and what happened. I am not sure whether it was courage, a lack of imagination, or pure deviltry that made you take risks which often balked other boys.

In the sixty years since, I have jumped out of various balloons and twenty-story windows, and unnecessarily marched through fiery furnaces. Often I, myself, have wondered why. Whatever it was—brass, curiosity, or zeal to get on—I did offer my services as pianist to the university orchestra and trusted to my ear to keep me going. At first I got along fairly well, for my ear for music and a slight reading knowledge stood me in good stead. On the program the night of our first appearance we were to play a piece called "The Taming of the Lion"—not difficult, with no intricate nuances and harmonies, with no new cadences; and at the various practicing exercises of the orchestra I escaped with my ignorance undetected until the afternoon of the evening performance. Then I caught the leader looking curiously at me. The notes were before me. I could turn the pages with the others. But he came over to where I was playing, and stood listening and said:

"Look here, boy, where do you get those chords?"
I started an argument.
He said: "Play them alone!"
I did, and he began to grin and then to laugh.
He said: "You don't know a note of music, do you?"
And I said, "No."

"Well," he said, "you get down from that bench and scat out of here!"

Which I did to the great delight of the other players, who realized that I was faking my accompaniment to the melody. The story spread over the university and brought out two verdicts: first, that I was a fool; and second, that I had a lot of nerve. Both verdicts were true. Neither did me much harm.

It was in the Christmas holidays in 1886 that I made my first literary pilgrimage. It was to visit Atchison, the home of E. W. Howe. Several years before, he had written "The Story of a Country Town," a Kansas story that had been acceptably received all over the English-speaking world. Mrs. Murdock gave it to me. She was deeply impressed with it. William Dean Howells, my favorite novelist, and Mark Twain, my favorite humorist, had covered the book with warm praise. In Europe, Ed Howe had been received in high literary circles; and he was a notable figure in our part of the world. He was running the Atchison Globe, a local paper, and I can remember that I spent an hour in the Globe office with his star reporter, Joe Rank, talking of Mr. Howe and preparing myself for the visit. His family lived in a large brick house with wide porches in an oak and elm grove at the edge of town. Because his family irked him or bothered him when he wanted to write, he was living in a little house, a two-room affair in the north part of the yard. When I came to Atchison the three children were with him in that little house, and his wife sat sewing or knitting by the stove. Little good it did him to try to find peace outside his domicile.

Possibly he was used to visitors bringing the frankincense and myrrh of flattery, and maybe he liked it, for he was more than kind, and we talked much longer than I should have stayed. I came back to Lawrence walking on the clouds, for I had seen my first literary hero. It was during that same vacation that I went to visit Ewing Herbert, who was editing the Hiawatha World for its owner, "Webb" Wilder.* He had compiled a chronicle history of Kansas day by day from newspaper files from 1854, a real achievement, and I was little less impressed by him than by Mr. Howe. But Ewing Herbert was different. I came to visit him as David ran to Jonathan, and he put me to work on one or another of the outlying towns in his county, writing pieces about the town and soliciting paid local advertising and job work from the banks. It was a happy vacation, and I went home to my mother in Lawrence and found a lot of books by James Whitcomb Riley which I had ordered from Indianapolis.

Then a new horizon opened—the poetry of common things. Emerson made me ready for it, and Mark Twain, I suppose, and Howells with his realism; but when the realism of Howells and the gayety of Mark Twain

---

* Daniel Webster Wilder, a Harvard man and a friend of Bartlett of the "Familiar Quotations."

and the homely philosophy of Emerson's transcendentalism were fused in the lilting rhyme of Riley, I felt a new thrill. I accepted poetry with an added joy. I did not know it then, but, looking back now, I realize that those exciting days of exultation which came to me as I read Riley's homely verses came because Riley's verse fitted into my experience, welded my own experience into man's common joy. I thrilled as I had been lifted up when I first looked upon the beauty of the Flint Hills, and when I first, as a little child, heard the Eldorado silver cornet band discoursing its new melodies and its simple harmonies. Indeed, reading Emerson brought me a similar delight. Later in life, when I saw beautiful architecture, I looked at it with the same eagerness and happiness that had come whenever I had encountered beauty. It was many years before I realized fully that the quickening impulse of eager satisfaction which comes to one who sees beauty is the same kind of gladness, no matter what form beauty takes—poetry, philosophy, music, architecture, love, and delight. Something in the structure of man's mind and heart vibrates with a profound sense of well-being to all the manifestations of beauty that the senses encounter. I did not know it when I was a boy, but I am sure now that beauty of whatever kind one feels is God—the Universal Soul of things—trying to speak the common language to man's heart.

In the summer of 1887 I went back to work for Mr. Murdock on the Eldorado Republican. And there I met for the first time and embraced in delight a friend who has been steadily with me during all these years, a guide and ever-present help in trouble—the writer's friend and companion, Roget's Thesaurus. A few years later, Bartlett's "Familiar Quotations" came rolling across my sky and then Cruden's "Concordance of the Bible." All these years there abide with me these three—Cruden, Bartlett, and Roget; and the greatest of these is Roget. Where would I have been without the trinity? I still have Roget's Thesaurus before me as I write. The copy is inscribed in my adolescent writing, "Will A. White, ElDorado, 1887." I forget what I traded for it to another reporter, but it might as well have been gold and precious stones, for I was considerably interested that year in how I said things. I was consciously, perhaps with a certain smart-aleck fervor, trying to find new twists of language as I wrote the local stories of the little town. I still absorbed quantities of the humorous papers which were displayed on the newsstand at the post office. "Huckleberry Finn" came sailing down the river on a raft into my cosmos and brought a robust gusto to my soul which I tried to reflect in my work as a reporter. Looking back over the files of that paper today, I can see how faint were the flickers of the great light that I thought I had within me.

I was still a boy, and, because I had been away at college two or three years, the fellows whom I had left in the town after high school liked to guy me and make me the subject of practical jokes. They took me out to Sandifer's melon patch on a dark summer night to steal melons, after telling the family we were coming so that they would arrange a reception. So, as we thumped about the melon patch, locating the ripe ones by their hollow sound, one of the Sandifers—the father or his son, I forget which—stood on the haystack twenty yards off and began firing his shotgun. And I, who in childhood's happy hour had been regarded as a good second-class runner by my innocent companions, started out, fleet of wing as Eden's garden bird. Lord, how I ran! And Ed Harvey and Bill Betts, keeping within a decent distance, kept calling: "My God, they're catching up with us!" I put forth new spurts of speed; Ed Harvey dropped back and Lew Schmucker came up, admonishing and warning me that they were gaining on us. When we got to town we swung through alleys and devious courses, not slowing up until we got to Mort Wells' ice-cream parlor. There we rounded up, and there they told me that the drinks were on me. So, taking their gibes, I ordered ice cream and pop and spent a merry, roistering evening, and I think I enjoyed it more than if we had had melons. For I did display a speed on a two-mile track that was the wonder and admiration of my friends. A few nights later they tried to show me a haunted house; I suspected their plot and plans, and when we got out there in the dark I sneaked slitheringly away and left them for half an hour trying to find me to show me the ghost—which gave me some comfort. I set these things down here that men may know the gauntlet which a youth home from college had to run in those days from the boys who stayed at home. I was the only boy in all that town who went to the university. Now, from every little town in Kansas like that, of two or three thousand, ten or a dozen boys and girls go to college. So have the times changed.

Yet we thought it was a pretty good world. Mr. Murdock, who was preparing to run for state senator the next year, was building his fences, and he set them up with the economic and political nails which the system and the civilization in the United States in those times had made and provided. A county convention to nominate candidates for county offices was held, and it was my business as his employee, aged nineteen, to round up voters at the caucuses where the delegates were named. For it was necessary that his friends should control the Courthouse the year before his nomination. Those were the days when the ins of any local politics were called the Courthouse ring from one end of the United States to the other, and Mr. Murdock wanted to be an in. He had plenty of money—contributed, I learned later, by the Santa Fe Railroad. He put me on a hack and sent me out to a stone quarry to round up the boys. Santa Fe money had provided a tub of iced and bottled beer as a rallying point, and cigars were so lavishly plentiful that men grabbed in the box and took two and three and four. Other boxes appeared. And I learned my first lesson in politics under the boss system.

It was simple. A state boss collected money from the railroads, the packing houses, the insurance companies, and the banks in his state. This money he sent to his henchmen in the counties, who distributed the largess to their followers, who controlled the county conventions. The object and aim of all county conventions was to control the nomination of those Republicans who would run for the legislature and the State Senate. When they were elected, as all good Republicans were, they would follow the boss. On most matters they were free; but where legislation touched the banks, the railroads, the insurance companies, or the packing houses, they were bound in honor to vote with the boss, and on his candidate for United States Senator and for the tie-up he made with a candidate for State printer. The two united made a winning majority. So, over the United States, our Senators went to Washington obligated to the large corporate interests of their states. As the railroads were interstate corporations, the railroad lobbyists and bosses in Washington amalgamated their forces. Thus, the plutocracy built its mighty fortress. I did not know those things in that day. Few people thought it through. I am sure, in Eldorado, Mr. Murdock's friends did not see the significance of the fact that he had plenty of money to help him control the conventions which nominated the county attorney, register of deeds, county clerk, sheriff, and the like—"the Courthouse Ring!" But the county officers made the combination that named the Republican candidates for state senator and members of the Legislature. Also, the same convention controlled the nomination of delegates to the judicial conventions and to the state senatorial conventions, where they met the delegates from other counties similarly bossed. It was an intricate system.

Money was easy. The farmers were borrowing up to their ears. The mortgage companies and trust companies had money to lend. No one cared what interest he paid—or promised to pay. Kansas was plastered with farm mortgages. Crops were good, and prices reasonable; times on the boom, and no one watched how the wheels of plutocracy went whirring and grinding, generating the power that ran the land. I was a part of it and never remotely dreamed its significance.

I did my daily stint. I picked up local items, wrote them with a funny twist when I could, and set down the dry and uninteresting facts when I had to. Sometimes I bellied up to a printer's case and set my own items—but only in emergencies. And I bought magazines and the comic weeklies at the post-office newsstand. I took books from the town library, which was in a mangy little room. More than that, I ordered through the newsdealer books which I saw reviewed and advertised. To get funds I called off for dances at night and was a beau around town. I organized our little clique and crowd for formal dances half a dozen times in the summer, rowed a boat under the moon along the three or four miles of the millpond, where the rowing parties would draw their boats together and I would get out my guitar and someone would twang his banjo, and we would all sing the songs of the period—"Marguerite," "Sweet Violets," "Only a Pansy Blossom," "When the Leaves Begin to Turn," and Negro melodies—sometimes real spirituals, more often the gay, galloping rhythms of the minstrel show, imitation plantation songs. Vernon Kellogg came down, and I remember we gave a dance for him, took him out on the waters of the Walnut and lifted up our voices in song, girls and boys, children of what we liked to call "the best" people in our little burg.

It was in that summer that I got a pass from Mr. Murdock, who was the giver of all good and perfect passes, and headed out along the main line of the Santa Fe to Great Bend, where I took a work train and rode on a load of ties a long summer afternoon to Scott City. There was a busy, rough-board town, with board sidewalks and false fronts to the stores, and a Courthouse looming out of the horizon. I went just at twilight to a real estate office. It was open. Real estate offices in those boom times in western Kansas towns were open until nine o'clock. There I located by section lines my destination. It was eighteen miles south and west of Scott City. After loading in a big supper at a restaurant, I started forth with a plat of my destination that I made on a large sheet of note paper, marked and directed by section lines, fourteen miles south and four miles west, with a little oblong marked near the junction of the south and west where I would meet a depression of land called the White Woman's Bottom, one of those queer, dry, sunken prairie lakes which filled up in flood time. The government surveyor, a few years before, had plowed the section lines of all that part of western Kansas wilderness. The land was fuzzed with buffalo grass, and nothing else. Only here and there and now and then had the farmer's plow furrowed a field. But the section lines, fourteen south and four west, were as well marked on the prairie as they were on the map of the real estate office. So I set out in the sunset glow, southward bound on my eighteen-mile tramp, full of food and full of romantic yearnings.

It was a silent journey. The August moon rose at the end of a long twilight and climbed the sky. As she rose she did more than shed the light that revealed the section lines that I crossed. She filled me with ineffable joy. I met no wayfarer, saw a few lights in a few cabins go out at bedtime, and was all alone with the moon and with a boy's desires and dreams on a journey that he thought would end in lovers meeting. So somewhere along about midnight, because I was very happy and too full of romance to be tired, I lifted up my voice in song, as I neared the White Woman's Bottom. Then a funny thing happened. Somewhere off in the distance a coyote, then another and another, awakened by my amorous outpouring, began to yell.

and yelp and howl. They understood me. After a little while I understood them. They had the same trouble that I had. We all belonged to the brotherhood! I had awakened them warbling my young man's fancies. So we all turn lightly to the thought of love.

I crossed the White Woman's Bottom a few hours after midnight and then turned west. At four o'clock, or maybe a little later, I came to the spot on my section line map which I knew was the journey's end. For near the barn I recognized the spring wagon that I could have told among a million. I had seen it come to Eldorado so many times and had watched its maneuvers like a hawk. So I lay me down under the wagon on the hard earth, and slept like a child through the dawn to the sunrise, until the farmer's early rising brought the family out. And I wakened up with Agnes Riley's face bending over me, and saying:

"Why, Will! Why, Will, are you here? When did you come?"

And the family gathered around me, took me in to breakfast after I had washed in the tin basin at the well. Then after the dishes were done, and maybe after I had helped to wipe and put them away, for I did so at home, we walked out under the morning sky into the flat, endless plain, and there, as kindly as she could, she broke it to me that she was engaged to marry another man. So far as I can remember, I had no thought of marriage. I was nineteen and six months over, and she was just nineteen. Marriage had come naturally into her horizon, whereas I, being a boy, and a male with other things around me—an education to get, a profession to cultivate, a living to earn—was just tramping on the clouds of pink romance without path or goal. I understood, and she knew that I understood; and so, without kissing her goodbye, for the family was assembled, and anyway I really was hard hit and emotionally numb, I was loaded in that old spring wagon and the hired man took me southward to the railroad at Garden City. I caught the night train home.

As I walked through that plain in western Kansas—so different from the rolling Flint Hills, really another country from the wide valley of the Walnut—it was photographed in my memory that night under the moon. Years later when I was writing stories of the plains of western Kansas, the things I saw and felt under that August moon on that long and lovely night came out of the etching on my memory. Often I have reached into the etched mirror of that lonely land of the high plains three thousand feet above the sea and brought out images, and have tried vainly to reproduce details of the weird and exquisite beauty which came to me that night, as the coyotes and I lifted our voices in amorous song. The next time we met she was a married woman, with her own duties and her own cares and her own joys. I wrote in the Eldorado Republican the birth notice of her first baby, and so we were happy ever after.

CHAPTER XXI

A Reporter in College

IN THE AUTUMN of 1887 I went back to the university, a fraternity man, a budding college politician with the beginnings of a profession. I was business manager of the university Literary Review. I made a little money selling its advertising and gathering in its subscriptions. I was still reporting university doings for the Lawrence Journal and the Kansas City News, and also now for the St. Louis, Topeka, and Chicago papers. I was an industrious, energetic young fellow, but no great shakes as a student. I continued to be a library hound, and Carrie Watson, the librarian, guided me in my major course, uncharted in the curriculum, through the poets and essayists of England. De Quincey was behind me, and Steele, Addison, and Johnson engaged me, and Carlyle set me afire. Goldsmith, Gray, and, for a few weeks, Pope charmed me.

But as to Shakespeare, not until I heard his poetry read on the stage did I realize the beauty and grandeur, the deep and lovely clarity of his language, the truth of his grasp of human nature. The stage was seriously beginning to interest me. Railroad rates were low, and traveling theatrical companies could move about in the United States so cheaply that every town over ten thousand had a considerable taste of what now would pass for first-class theatrical performances. The regulation of railroad rates has wiped out the drama for a great majority of the American people. Less than half a dozen cities have what country towns had fifty years ago in the way of fairly good contemporary dramatic performance. At Emporia, indeed even at Eldorado in the boom days, and at Lawrence I could see good shows. Stars of national reputation came to all of these towns. Modjeska came. Rose Coghlan, the Drews, Sol Smith Russell, Henry Dixey, Tom Keene, a dear old Shakespearean ranter, Robert L. Downing, Robert Mantell, and a whole troop of traveling Thespians of lesser grade. They brought the current plays and the old standard plays to little towns where the theaters were well patronized. I and my generation received them gladly. That traveling drama was a part of our education. Vernon Kellogg and I often used to stag it together, and in the year 1888 we were both working on the Lawrence Journal and occasionally could wangle a complimentary ticket to the Opera House. We heard Emma Abbott sing "Faust," and Maud Grainger play Juliet to Robert Mantell's Romeo, and were quite overwhelmed by its gorgeous beauty of language and the loveliness of its theme.

In those days, Kellogg and I had grown so close together that we talked a sort of shorthand, rarely finished a sentence, had our own symbols for thoughts, our own gay hyperbole. That was a new experience for me and was altogether delightful—my first real enjoyment of companionship, perfect in all its phases. We complemented each other exactly. I was fat, he was thin. I was a biddable fool—and fearless; he was shrewd and a bit crafty. He was a precise and meticulous scholar. I had to absorb my scholarship somewhat through him, a little in the classroom, largely in the library at odd hours. I seemed to take it through my skin and from the atmosphere of the university. He ended up in Phi Beta Kappa. I quit because I could not get enough points that were usable for a degree, though I was covered with extracurricular honors which his scheming and my audacity brought to me.

I was also bootlegging music. I used to cut classes to go to the fourth floor of the main building of the university to listen to lectures on musical theory, on harmony, and on musical history. And, as a reward for letting me carry her books in my second year at the university, I took Helen Sutliffe to all the concerts of the university course, heard for the first time really good piano music, and was learning to enjoy what we ivory-pounders and catgut squeezers used to scorn as classical music. I had no piano in those days nor access to one. But I had my cabinet organ. When I went home from a concert in a cloud of exaltation that was partly music and partly Helen, I tried to reproduce on the cabinet organ the great melodies and the amazing harmonies that had stirred me so deeply. Incidentally, in those days, I was supposed to be a rather hardboiled, ruthless college politician in glamorous and exciting contests wherein Kellogg furnished the brains and I got the glory. He was a senior and secretary to Chancellor Snow. He was admitted to faculty meetings and was as smug as the cat that swallowed the canary about university politics. Because he had an inside view, I had inside knowledge; and he pulled strings that gave me more distinction than I deserved.

So came the summer of 1888, and Kellogg and I found ourselves working downtown in Lawrence for Colonel Oscar E. Learnard, who owned two papers: a morning paper called the Lawrence Journal and an evening paper called the Lawrence Tribune. The Colonel was an old-fashioned, black radical Republican—radical in the sense that he would go any length for his party. He was a rich man, as the term went in Lawrence. His printing office did all the commercial printing for a railroad. So he had plenty of loose ready money. For some reason of high politics, he bought the Tribune. Perhaps he bought it because it had been abusing him and the Republican Courthouse Ring for a year or so. But at any rate, when he bought it he kept it running as a Democratic paper, though the milk of the word was heavily watered! I was mixed up and bedeviled in those days to decide what party I should join. I was not yet twenty-one. But he made me editor of the evening Tribune, which was supporting Grover Cleveland and the Democratic ticket in Kansas, while Kellogg became editor of the rock-ribbed, staunch Republican morning Journal, supporting Benjamin Harrison and the Kansas Republican ticket. No eight-hour day bothered us. To even things up, the Colonel made me reporter on the morning paper and Kellogg reporter on the evening paper. We began work at eight o'clock in the morning. We left the office after the proofs were read, somewhere around midnight, and often used to go home together with enough gimp and ginger to warble "Larboard Watch" as a duet while we ambled through the night. Our editorial work was light. Sometimes I wrote a ponderous leader, advocating free trade in the world, or a resubmission of the prohibitory law in Kansas. And sometimes Kellogg wrote oracularly about protection or the danger of turning the country over to the southern rebels, emphasizing the fact that Cleveland had traitorously offered to return the southern battle flags to the states that were in the rebellion. But most of our time and energy was devoted to gathering local items. Sometimes we picked up paid items and advertisements, though a man was employed especially for that purpose.

As the campaign deepened that year, our energies doubled and our enthusiasm grew in the contests for local county offices. My impression is that the Colonel, our boss, was more interested in electing the Republican ticket than he was in overthrowing Grover Cleveland. I seem to remember that we treacherously supported the Republican county ticket in both papers. Anyway, Kellogg and I were forever in hot water, partly because we were young folks without conviction about the matters that seemed serious to the Colonel, and partly because all the world seemed very funny to us. We were incorrigibly flippant. So life that summer was just one heat-lightning glow of hectic excitement. I remember one night the Democrats had a great meeting, and the committee, not being able to get enough flag-printed bunting to decorate the speakers' stand, draped it with red, white, and blue bunting and scattered the stars from a few torn flags in and through the bunting. The heading that morning in the Republican Journal on the account of the meeting was "Under the Stars and Bars," meaning, of course, the Confederate flag. Lord, how hot that made the Democrats!

The United States was only twenty-three years from the Civil War. The Union soldiers were nearly all Republicans. The few scattered Confederates we had in the town, of course, were Democrats. Naturally the Democrats were quite as patriotic as the Republicans. And that inference that the Democratic meeting was held under the Confederate flag stirred up such a stink as the town had not known for many years. When we came to the office early that morning, before the Colonel got down, the Democrats were waiting for us—not in squads but in serried ranks! Kellogg and I quietly slid out on the street. An hour later we came back to the office, and a great crowd of wrathful Democrats, some of them leading advertisers, which really counted, had the old Colonel backed in the corner while they demanded that he make amends. When we hove in sight—young innocents grinning like the Cheshire cat—the old Colonel called across the throng:

"Boys, boys, Goddammit, come here and tell these men how it happened!"

And he slid out through a back door, throwing us to the lions. I got behind a railing that marked off the lobby, and I can still feel the impact of air from Jack Watts' fist, Jack being a great husky blacksmith of a man—the impact of the air from his fist on my nose as I ducked just a decimal part of an inch away from it. We tried to laugh it off. The Colonel had tried to cuss it off. But, after stopping subscriptions and discontinuing their advertising while we talked, the mob dispersed.

At another time, in trying to defeat the Democratic candidate for sheriff, we dug up the fact that he had been deputy sheriff ten or a dozen years before when three or four Negroes were lynched from the bridge across the Kaw, at Lawrence. Then, indeed, there was trouble. In the seventies, at the time of the mob, a man named Jerry Gladheart had been accused of being ring leader. Jerry resented any discussion of the issue, though his name had not been mentioned. The rehash of the old story drove him temporarily to drink. Being in high spirits above his rum, he made the rounds of the town and threatened to kill me on sight. Then Kellogg was exempted, I forget how, but I was the target of Jerry's wrath. So, like a fool, the next morning after Jerry's bloodthirsty pilgrimage, I borrowed two revolvers, a .22 and a .32, and, putting one in each coat pocket, sailed down Massachusetts Street to meet death. Jerry had a way of sitting in front of his harness shop in the mornings, on the east side of Massachusetts, the only business thoroughfare in Lawrence in those days.

He used to sit with his chair tipped back, greeting all and sundry in a jovial, democratic way. He had a voice that resounded up and down the street like Gabriel's trumpet. As I came within a block of him on the other side of the street, I saw him sitting there. I tried to screw up my courage to turn from the west side to his side. I could not do it. I walked a half a block farther to a crossing. Then, with superhuman effort, I made myself turn and walk across the street, straight into Jerry in his chair. It was an ordeal. Physically I do not think I have ever known more terror. I gripped my two pistols in my coat pockets tightly, and with my eyes fixed on Jerry like a dying calf I finally came to the curbing. I must have walked slowly. He could have seen my terror—anyone could! He was sober then and grinning—a man in his late forties or middle fifties, and I just turning twenty. The ridiculousness of it all overcame him. His chair tilted back against his harness-shop wall came down with a terrific click, and I jumped like a scared deer straight up in the air. I have since thanked all the gods at once that I did not begin shooting like a fool. As Jerry came on his feet, he was laughing a great guffaw, and I had turned past him, walking perhaps like Shadrach, Meshach, and Abednego of the fiery furnace, slowly up the street to the office. The clerks on Massachusetts Street who stood in their doors awaiting my slaughter when I passed old Jerry, echoed his laughter. Before I had gone the fifty yards between his harness shop and the Journal office, I was chattering with hysterical laughter along with the rest. I got those two guns in the desk drawer quicker than any bad man ever drew a bead, and sat down to tell Kellogg all about it. We both whooped and hurrahed as my hysterical cackle died down, and I never was afraid after that to pass Jerry's shop. He did not mention the matter again.

A few weeks later, Pete Foley, a local Democratic ward boss, taking umbrage at something I had written, came in carrying a club to annihilate me. He was a printer who printed the University Review. I was his customer. He was carrying a load of mean whiskey. He was in a quarrelsome and homicidal mood. I had a ball bat which Vernon and I had brought down from the Phi Delt treasure trove. We had concealed it between our desks from all eyes but our own. We called it our "reserves"! I reached for it, gripped it, and began smilingly talking to Pete. Kellogg, of course, was not the object of Pete's wrath. Vernon was never the object of anyone's wrath. I was the wrath-rouser. Slowly I talked to old Pete, talked him into a grin and then a laugh. Then he put his club away and sat down, and we worked out some kind of correction that made him happy. Kellogg, grinning in the background, began to whistle "See the Conquering Hero Comes."

As I look back upon that summer, it seems one long act from a Gargantuan farce in which Kellogg was the walking gentleman and I the low comedian. We had a particular pest in a preacher who was forever bringing in items about himself. He was a self-advertiser and a pompous little fellow. Never by any chance did he bring in items that concerned anyone else. When he was ashamed to bring them in himself, he sent them by parishioners. Always on Monday morning he had an account of his sermon or something about the Sunday services; and he was devilishly smart because often he dug up things that were of real news value. Still his persistence galled us. The pomp and circumstance that enveloped him like an aura bothered us. So we hated him as much as youths in their late adolescence could hate anyone. Yet our hatred was always watered down with laughter. I remember one day, perhaps late in August, when we were breaking in a new reporter to replace us when we went back to school in September, I was sitting in the office instructing the new reporter. Behind me and the new reporter, yet in front of Kellogg, was a tall wire netting that penned us off from the old Colonel's sanctum, which had an outside door. Instructing the new reporter upon the subject of the pest, I named him, identified him, and described him with malignant joy. I heard the opening and shutting of a door behind me. I noticed casually that Kellogg's face was masked with amazement. I went on dilating upon the theme of that little pompous preacher and all his scheming to get his name in print. I noticed Kellogg's face was almost twitching with hysterical glee and, thinking he was approving my malevolence, I bent to the oar of my ability. Someone back of me in the Colonel's room was making a noise. Instinctively, but not in fear, I turned and found the little preacher, who had been listening to my diatribe, was climbing that netting like a cat. Then it was that Kellogg broke into uproarious and indecent laughter. But it was I, facing the holy man's murderous eye, who turned and ran through the back office like a whitehead, dragging the new reporter with me and leaving Kellogg to apologize and appease and settle the preacher. It was a great hour, and we finished our day's work at midnight and went home treading on clouds.

For we were twenty years old. We had hold of a lever, an Archimedean lever, the same being the control of two newspapers which served a town of ten thousand in a hot campaign. We were in the campaign that elected Benjamin Harrison and defeated Grover Cleveland for his consecutive second term. In Kansas the campaign was notable for piling up the greatest Republican majority that the state ever had registered. The soldiers of the Civil War, in their forties and fifties, were in their prime. They ran the Republican party in Kansas without let or hindrance. The Republican State Convention that summer, held at Topeka, was filled with delegates who wore their old army-blue uniforms with visored caps. The candidates on the Republican state ticket, from top to bottom, were members of the G.A.R. By way of recognizing their duty to the ex-slaves who had flooded into eastern Kansas and made a tidy little vote, a Negro—a university graduate—was also put on the state ticket. Negroes were to be found in Kansas courthouses occupying secondary positions.

When it came to naming delegates to the State Convention and nominating a county ticket at Lawrence, Kellogg and I, being on the paper, took a hand. I had had some experience in Eldorado. I helped to round up in the ward caucus a dozen or twenty university boys who were living in Lawrence that summer and, under the guidance of Charley Tucker who bought chickens and eggs in a small way and had many dealings with the colored people in short-time loans, and who was also a ward boss, Kellogg and I were put on the delegation. In that ward caucus, which was more or less dominated by university boys, were a few protesting and indignant professors and Mr. Tucker's colored friends. It was my duty to tell half a dozen of the boys, and three or four colored men, how to capture the chairmanship of the ward. I gave each a name which he would nominate when recognized by the ward chairman, and each a number indicating his turn to stand and clamor for the floor. And so the poor professors and a few businessmen who were not in the organization stood aside and saw the machine grind, and I was a part of it and so was Kellogg. If we sloshed around in our glory going home that night, it was because we were Somebody. We were young. Life was full of happy surprises, and we laughed easily.

A few nights after Kellogg had poured the unction of his soothing voice on the preacher, a mishap occurred which no one outside the newspaper could explain. In my rounds looking for news, I picked up a few pay locals from a hardware man advertising gasoline stoves. They were to go in the morning paper. In the evening paper, an estimable lady had died and her name formed the heading of her obituary thus:

"Died, Mrs. Julian Hutt."

In the composing room, the printer for the morning paper had taken that head out of the types for the evening paper, intending to throw it away, but he put it over the pay local items I had solicited from the hardware store, and that morning the item in the Journal read:

Died, Mrs. Julian Hutt. My dear lady, the hot weather is at last upon you. Get your gasoline stove ready and save yourself while you can.

But of course it so happened that the lady had been a good friend of old Colonel Learnard, our boss. He was a God-damning boss and swore in a high, monotonous tenor. And when he showed up at the office, it was terrible. Of course he blamed me who, as a matter of fact, was entirely blameless. It was Jim Dennis, the foreman, who had misplaced the head. But the Old Man did not like to cuss Jim Dennis. Jim might quit. He was valuable and probably underpaid. So he lit into Kellogg and me—and me in particular—in that high monotonous, squeaky tenor, God-damning me from hell to breakfast and reciting over and over:

" 'Died, Mrs. Julian Hutt. My dear lady, the hot weather is at last upon you.' " Then he burst again into a volume of tenor profanity, always ending with: "White, you're so Goddam lawless." That was his theme song during all my service under him. The old Colonel was my third boss: first there had been Tee Pee, the Democratic editor who never complained because he rarely paid me; then Mr. Murdock, who was a soft-soaping boss with a gentle voice, and who always laughed with us at my blunders and made it hard for me to repeat them, and who always called me "Bill Allen"; and now the old Colonel, a volcano of emotions, a director on a railroad who made his living not off the newspaper but because he got the printing for that railroad and did most of the job printing in his own office, and made enough money to support two newspapers. Kellogg and I knew this. It did not bother us. Life was too gay and salubrious for us to look into first causes. The only editorials the Colonel ever wrote himself were in support of the railroads in general, and because his handwriting was poor, his grammar worse, and his construction verbless and impossible, we had to recast his editorials. But because the Colonel owned the two newspapers, he was consulted by the local ward and township bosses, and was a power. Kellogg and I got our standing in the ward where Charley Tucker was the czar because we worked for the Colonel.

Sometime during that summer of 1888 I went to Eldorado for a few days in the midst of Mr. Murdock's campaign for state senator. Of course, I did not care particularly whether Harrison beat Cleveland, or whom we elected governor of Kansas, though I did have a real interest in the Republican county ticket at Eldorado that year. But Mr. Murdock was different. He was charged with being a rich man. Poor devil, even I knew that was silly; for he had to borrow money from the bank to keep his paper going, which he rarely repaid and never earned. So he was indeed "an absent-minded beggar"! He had a lovely home on Walnut Hill, and one of the charges he had to meet in the campaign was that it was full of quarter-sawed oak and hammered brass, and that he had bought a piano out of his ill gotten gains from the county printing. Most people of any intelligence knew where his money came from. They realized, without blaming him much, that he distributed, in Butler County politics, the funds sent down from Topeka by the ruling classes to the governing classes. But it was not charged that he kept any of it, or that he used it other than honestly after the morals of the time.

It was not quite so simple as that. Mr. Murdock and his kind did take the money of the men who owned the tools of industry and agriculture— whether they owned these by fee simple, deed or under mortgage—and distribute it to the electorate to keep the governing classes in power, that they might serve the ruling classes. But, because all men had their right of conscience, and assemblage, and free utterance, and because they had the writ of habeas corpus and the further right of trial by jury in trouble, Americans did not understand how their government was turning into a plutocracy. Certainly, when I saw with pride how Mr. Murdock won in that election by scorning demagoguery and turning for aid to what we called railroad money, I was not shocked. No one but a lot of cranks—ex-Greenbackers, third-party Prohibitionists, and visionary socialists—complained. They were ne'er-do-wells—the rag, tag, and bobtail anyway. So who listened to them!

Other candidates that year wore their army blue uniforms as they campaigned, but Mr. Murdock scorned that demagogy; he preferred to use money in his campaign. It was a nice point—his choice. He was a poor speaker. He talked in the vernacular instead of in oratorical phrases. He had a thin, high, strained voice. But he rode over the county with Alice in the family phaeton with the tasseled top. Or he and other candidates on the ticket hired a livery team and went yammering away in the schoolhouses, at the old settlers' picnics, at G.A.R. reunions—wherever he could get a crowd. He talked common sense, and some way he won. To me, it was a glorious victory. After that Eldorado visit I began to realize that sooner or later, probably fairly soon, I should have to make the great decision about my political alliance. I had no special feeling for either party and was confused between allegiance to my father and fear of my mother. So I was in considerable conflict that fall of 1888 when I went back to the university.

CHAPTER XXII

I Garner the Wages of Sin!

IT WAS in those days and under those circumstances that I decided to be a Republican. I had been talking it over for a year. When I sat in the Republican Douglas County convention as a delegate that year, my mother saw my name in the list distributed on slips at the convention. She was perturbed. She must have been torn between pride and duty. She said to me sternly:

"What would your father say!"

Then we talked it out as Kellogg and I had talked it out, as Dr. Canfield, professor of political science, and I had talked it out, and as Helen (whose books I carried) and I had talked it out, and even as the old Colonel at the office, who really loved me when he was not swearing at me, had talked it out. I told them all the cold truth—that I did not care particularly for either the Democratic or the Republican party, but I had to make a choice. Canfield agreed with that. I remember he said:

"Well, White, I don't know. I have tried to be independent, and I have got nowhere politically. I know you dislike and distrust the protective tariff, which ought to make you a Democrat. But in Kansas, as a Democrat, it is hopeless for you. You probably can do more harm to the protective tariff by going into the Republican party and fighting it there."

That seemed sensible. My mother, of course, wanted me to be a Republican, but her loyalty to her dead husband was strong even after six years of absence; yet she hated the Democrats, feared the rebels who would capture the country; and her dead Union soldier brother also gave her an emotional bias toward the Republicans. Still she was fair with me. I knew even then that I did not want office. In Eldorado I had seen men hanging around the Courthouse because they had taken county jobs; that fact had removed them from their first business of earning a living by their trades or professions and spoiled them for normal usefulness. Even then I had a low opinion of politics as a livelihood. In Lawrence I found the same kind of people in the county offices that I knew in Eldorado, corrupted by the easy money that came with a county salary. In the county convention, that summer of 1888, I saw the horse-trading, saw the men like my old Colonel, before the convention met, getting together and putting up a combination of the friends of the various candidates for county offices, so that the local bosses might control the nominations for judge and state senator and members of the Legislature and Congressmen and United States Senators. And I knew how the wheels went round, and I also knew that an effective citizen in politics had to be a party member. Then one day, perhaps it was after the county convention, I talked to my German professor, William Herbert Carruth—afterwards known nationally as a minor poet, who wrote some verses with the lilt:

> Some call it Evolution,
> And others call it God.

He said this in a long and serious talk: "White, your job in life, so far as politics is concerned, is to make your private sentiment public opinion. You are going to be a newspaperman. You will have a great opportunity. Remember, that is what you are here on earth for."

Professor Carruth was in the city council fighting for all sorts of local phases of righteousness and the Will of God, like honest city scales and the proper location of the City Library, and macadamed streets. Let me detour a moment and say that in that talk about politics he gave me this other pearl of wisdom which was good for the 1880's, and shone with luster through the nineties and into the first decade of this century:

"You know it's vastly more important than many pious prayers and tons of highfalutin aspirations, to get a street in a country town made wide enough so that two loads of hay going in opposite directions still leave it possible for a woman to drive a horse and buggy between them without getting hay wisps on her buggy top. There is righteousness and the Will of God incarnate for any man in town politics."

Those two pearls of wisdom probably have been beacon lamps for my feet through all these years: Make your private sentiment public opinion, and see that the streets of the town are wide enough for safe and decent driving. But it does not make much difference how you get these things done if they are really achieved.

So what with Kellogg, whose father was elected to the State Senate that year as a Republican, and with Canfield, who told me how to creep up on the protective tariff to throttle it, and with Helen and "Dear Old Vermont," and my mother, loyal to her dead husband and still a black abolitionist Republican who feared the rebels, I crossed the Rubicon and became a Republican without deep conviction, purely as a means to an end:

163

to make my private sentiment public opinion, and to see that all the various kinds of streets in my journey through life were wide enough for two loads of hay and women driving cleanly and safely and decently between them. Now at the end of nigh onto sixty years, in which I have consistently voted for Republican Presidents and Republican governors, I have about the same idea of party politics that I had when Ben Harrison was defeating Cleveland, and Vernon Kellogg and I were wielding at Lawrence the Archimedean lever that moves the world; at least we wielded it when Jim Dennis, the foreman, did not gum it up. We loved Jim. Yet he was always our enemy, for he bossed the composing room and he wanted his copy in early. He was our only editor. He revised our copy, corrected our spelling, put in the right initials, and above all he wanted the paper to make money. He had a theory maybe that his salary depended on such a remote contingency. The Colonel trusted Jim where he did not trust us. He merely loved us and cussed us and took pride in the fact that our bedevilments were increasing the circulation, making the paper talked about, cussed, and discussed.

Well, anyway, Kellogg and I had aspirations, noble ideals about the profession, that amused Jim. We tried to stop the habit of printing, at the end of a wedding notice, a list of all the gifts that the bride received. The bride's family and friends liked to see it in print; but Vernon and I thought it was unethical. Jim, because the lists of bridal presents came in early and helped him get up the morning paper in time to quit shortly after midnight, loved them; and we had to fight with him to keep them out.

One evening the Houses, who ran the clothing store, put on a big wedding for their daughter. They were Jewish people, and to them a wedding was a great ceremonial. Vernon and I, representing the press, were invited to the wedding, at their home; and they rented the Odd Fellows Hall for a gorgeous dinner and a dance afterward. We heard three days ahead about that dinner from the grocery boys and their hired girl friends, and from the expressman who was bringing delicacies from Kansas City to the home: a crate of lobsters, for instance, and venison and molded ice cream—a new confection in the eighties—and a wedding cake four feet high. Kellogg and I hurried through our evening chores, omitting the wedding at the home and getting to the Odd Fellows Hall about half past nine or ten, in time for the dance and dinner. Socially, we were innocent youngsters. Kellogg's father had been a college president, a probate judge, and now was a state senator. My father and mother had entertained Susan B. Anthony and Elizabeth Cady Stanton. They also had entertained John P. St. John, the father of Kansas Prohibition in the seventies, who had run for President in 1884 on the Prohibition ticket and had taken enough votes from Blaine to give New York to Mr. Cleveland and so win the election for him. I set these things down here because they paint in our background, Kellogg's and mine, in Bacchic knowledge. It is hard to believe, but, having grown up in Prohibition Kansas and in families devoted to that cause, we hardly knew beer from whiskey, had not yet identified brandy, knew no difference between the various kinds of wine. We understood that wine was the product of the grape. It was all rum to us, or maybe gin—sinful alcoholic tools of the rum fiend, low products of the grogshop.

Anyway the Houses were good advertisers in the Lawrence Journal. They turned in their list of wedding presents and, with Spartan determination and Puritan resolve not to be bribed by advertisers, we carefully omitted the list of wedding presents from our wedding notice, which we sent to Jim, the foreman. When we showed up at the Odd Fellows Hall we were hungrier than she-wolves with cubs, ready for the lobster and the venison and the molded ice cream, little thinking that the devil was lurking in the dark windows of the Odd Fellows Hall waiting to bring us to shame.

By the time we had got to the dinner, the bridal party and the guests from all over that part of Kansas were seated at two long tables running the length of the room. We had two end seats, down near the front doors of the hall. Just beyond those front doors were our good friends, the Lawrence hack drivers on whose boxes we rode in proud state by day, to and from the railroad station where we collected the names of those who were coming into and going from the town. These hack drivers, in an outer vestibule, saw us sitting together at the end of a table. They were a few feet from Vernon and me. They ate vicariously with joy the viands that the waitresses were passing to us.

We noticed that the waitresses poured into our tumblers some new kind of soda water, which went tingling up our noses and was not so very good. But we were tired and thirsty after a day's work, as well as hungry. And the waitress filled our glasses again with that belchy stuff. Also, we noticed that, the third time our glasses were emptied, the hack drivers in the hall signaled to the waitress to fill them up again, which we felt was mighty decent of the hack drivers. Again, as we stowed away the venison and the lobster and the cakes and the exotic fruits that loaded the table, we drank that new soda water—clear and sparkling. As the meal grew old I noticed that Kellogg, ordinarily a gentle soul with a soft ingratiating voice, was talking raucously, and it seemed to me perhaps a bit bawdily, to the bride at the other end of the hall, making great merriment. I don't know whether or not he noticed any symptoms in me, but that soda water was taking hold of both of us. I wanted to play the piano and was restrained by Kellogg, who always had a maternal influence upon me. The next thing I recall, after these more than fifty years, is that the tables were gone and the orchestra from Kansas City, which included a harp, a flute, two violins, a cello, and a bass viol, was playing what seemed to me the most exquisite waltz music I had ever heard. And I wanted to dance. But because I had always played for dances, I had not learned to waltz. I could not, but I saw Kellogg floating down the long hall and in his arms rested Mrs. House, the bride's mother —a large lady whom Kellogg's arms only partially encircled. She was having the time of her life, and Kellogg was struggling nobly to do the honors. It was a great occasion. I believe I made a short speech, and I know that I tried to get to the rattletrap old piano on the platform where the orchestra stood, and was persuaded by Kellogg, and perhaps by the bride's father, to join a square dance at which I was good. I took the bride out, and the bride's cousins, and a very pretty black-eyed girl from Kansas City—a veritable sylph, a wood nymph—and I danced on air with her two or three times.

At least Kellogg and I were having an altogether deliriously happy time. Only Kellogg, whose sense of duty was always keener than mine, seemed to have a seven-devil lust to do the right thing by the Houses, who were good advertisers. So he took the bride's two aunts, one after the other, and each more ponderous than the other, down the hall in a schottische— a military schottische where you ran two steps, clinched, turned around a couple of times, and ran two steps more. And Kellogg was the belle of the ball, and the hack drivers, still standing in the door, laughed noisily, even rudely it seemed to me, at Kellogg, who obviously was doing the honors of the Lawrence Journal. What there was to laugh at, I could not see at the time; I stepped up to rebuke them in a loud voice, and they laughed again. But I didn't care. Who was I to rebuke them! Perhaps that was Mr. House's duty. He was the host. So I hurried off to the houri of the melting brown eyes from Kansas City and gave her a whirl in "Old Dan Tucker." It was long after midnight when Kellogg and I, realizing that we had a day's work ahead of us, beginning at eight o'clock, withdrew from the merry party, parted the wall of hack drivers in the hall as Moses smote the waters in the Red Sea, and started down Massachusetts Street for home.

It was a moonlight night, and the street was deserted. I wanted to sing, and Kellogg said, "Hell, yes, let's sing!" We walked for half a block, arm in arm, singing "Larboard Watch, Ahoy," and then turned out into the street and lifted our voices in another duet, "Oh, Alice, Where Art Thou?" and then "Bye, Baby, Bye, Oh, Why Do You Cry, Oh!" and then yodeled at the moon. And as we turned west to leave the street, old man Phillips, the town night marshal, in his blue army uniform, came running to catch up with us and said, tapping each of us on the shoulder:

"Oh, my dear young gentlemen, don't you think you could sing as well if you stayed on the sidewalk?" And then he added, deprecatingly, under his breath: "Don't you boys know you're drunk?"

We had been drinking champagne, and, God help us, we thought it was soda water! So we went home and to bed, only to wake up in shame and sorrow. For the wages of sin is death. Old Jim Dennis had slipped down to the reporters' room, fished the bride's list of presents out of the wastebasket, and run it in spite of us, knowing from the hack drivers late in the evening that we were too happy to return to see the proof.

In my shame at seeing the list of the bride's presents follow the wedding notice of an advertiser—certainly a special privilege flaunted before the town—in the dejection of a raging headache, it was borne into my heart's core that there is a moral government of the universe.

CHAPTER XXIII

I Become a Republican and a Sinner

I ENTERED the university again the autumn of 1888. It was to be my last year. I carried a heavy load of history, sociology, political science, English and American literature, the physical sciences, stressing biology because that was Kellogg's field, German which I disliked, and French which gave me delight. I dropped mathematics entirely. I had failed in sophomore mathematics somewhere between spherical geometry and trigonometry—failed signally and ignominiously. The dear old head of the mathematics department, Ephraim Miller, told me I had no head for mathematics, which was true—nor any desire to have such a head. I was so irregular in my classification, that third year at the university, that my name was not in the catalogue. They had not been able to place me in any of the classes—freshman, sophomore, or junior—and, while puzzling on it, accidentally left me out. But I was there happily and energetically making fairly good grades, probably a B average to please Kellogg, and wandering all over the place in extracurricular activities.

Athletics did not interest me remotely in the intramural contests of the various university fraternities. I kept the bats and the rackets of the Phi Delta Theta Fraternity. We had no uniforms. The players fastened their trousers at the ankle with rubber bands and twine string and played in their shirt sleeves, with their hatbrims turned down—if they were exquisites, they wore caps. I was not interested in university poker, which was a flourishing diversion. Not that I thought it immoral, but I was naturally tight and did not get enough excitement out of penny ante to pay for my losses. I had the same attitude toward the small doses of beer or wine that seeped into the college life. I needed no exhilaration. Four decades later, Heywood Broun said of me that I started life with four cocktails and a highball, meaning probably that life always seemed gay to me—a dazzling adventure, always new, strange, puzzling, and delightful. So I have saved on my liquor bill all my life, not having the need of it. Moreover, any time I did look upon the wine when it was red, it made me sleepy.

Now, Fred Funston, who shared with Kellogg my affection in those days, was gayer even than I. He was always scintillating, talking in hyperbole, clowning to overcome his five feet four. Yet sometimes, though Heaven knows why, he felt the need of a bracer; and then he just could not carry his liquor. One drink of hard cider at the liquor dives in the colored section of Lawrence would set him wild: his favorite diversion was to go around silently, solemnly, alone, overturning the board sidewalks of the town. I never saw him tight, but the fraternity is full of legends of his hard-cider excursions, funny stories of a laughing man suddenly serious, solemnly doing strange, weird, unnecessary things. My own diversions probably were less spectacular but equally extravagant in time and money. I liked parties. I consumed gallons of convivial oyster soup with the boys and with Helen and her sorority sisters, indulging in the talk and the gay hyperbole of youth, blowing bubbles of great visions, also forever clowning. I had a stunt—an imitation drunk—that was popular in student societies and got me in bad with the faculty, who sometimes took the imitation for reality.

I had straightened out some of the crooks and quirks that I had brought up from Eldorado. Gone was the white, wide-brimmed cattleman's hat. Gone were the ready-made, hand-painted neckties; gone the bull's-head tie pin; gone the pompadour haircut and the massed freckles; not gone, but going, the pimples which had been my cross for six long years. I acquired a mandolin and achieved some skill with it. We had a fraternity guitar, banjo, and mandolin outfit, and six or eight of us used to sing in the moonlight on the steps of the fraternity boarding house and serenade our girls. I suppose I might be called a leader in those activities. Kellogg had retired from college politics into the chancellor's office, as assistant secretary. He was a senior. He continued to energize and direct my political strategy. The Phi Delts allied themselves politically with the Barbs (the nonfraternity men), and I was the fraternity figurehead—a conspicuous young rascal who delighted to foment political trouble on the hill. We once had a riot in front of the chancellor's office when the regents were in session, roaring, clamoring, and hooting because they were trying to suspend or expel the editor of the college paper for criticizing a professor. We had a big college contest and college lawsuit, with the faculty for judges, over an election in the oratorical society, and I was rather too conspicuous in the ruckamuction. At the end of the year I had the most important political place on the campus. I was editor of the university annual, a rowdy college publication that rounded up the year's events in the college.

Incidentally, during that year I had become "Billie"—"Billie" to Professor Canfield, "Billie" to the boys in the fraternity and the girls in the sororities, except Helen. I think I was always Will to her. In the university publications I was Will A. White. That name was signed to the verses I wrote, the pieces I submitted for publication, and that should have been my name in the catalogue if they could have classified me. But I was "Billie," wore the best clothes I could afford, and studied neckties in clothing-store windows. I was careful to see that my collars were properly moded. Certainly I was careless about my grades, often cut classes for more important matters, crammed all night many a time for examinations which I passed fairly well. I headed student committees, was proud of being included in the lists of downtown parties, glad to play the piano at any informal dances and leave Helen to the mercies of my fraternity brothers, liked to cut up and exhibit myself, tried to fraternize with the young professors, was never happier than when I was organizing boating parties on the Kaw or picnics to Blue Mound, or moonlight skating parties. I debated a little, wrote essays for the literary societies, liked to lead in all kinds of pranks or capers. And there you have me.

Anyone who knows anything about coeducational college life in the last two decades of the old century, or the first decade of this, has spotted me by now: the college sport; a poor student; a good mixer; a bit of a smart aleck; hail-fellow, not afraid of being caught and taking the blame, come-easy-go-easy; half student, half roisterer, who knew the students by name and catalogued the faculty by their weaknesses, tried to be friends with them out of class and was, when he made so poor a showing in their classrooms; college editor; college politician; figurehead for the fraternity; brother-in-law to the sororities; out always to make a dollar here; pick up five dollars here or there, and spend it as fast as it was made. By all the rules of the game I should have been in debt; but instinctively I was a tightwad. My Yankee father and my mother, who had always been poor, had branded on my heart the motto "There are only a hundred cents in a dollar."

But the strange thing is that a boy so sentient of his surroundings should have been so insensible to the real world about him. I knew in a general way that Kansas and the West in general were living on borrowed money; but I did not understand that I was living in a debtor land, nor what that signified. Every town was bonded for its public improvements, its macadam paving, its waterworks, and, in some cases, its light plant. Every business was more or less mortgaged. All the railroads were heavily bonded. The utility companies erected their plants on borrowed money. The banks did a thriving business in renting out cash, and they had a lively hope that some way, in some far-off day, interest would come back and mortgages be paid. But we were all insensible, all of us over the western Mississippi Valley, of the fact that what goes up must come down. And while I sat in my political economy class, my sociology class, my history class, making fairly good grades, I did not relate what I was studying to the realities around me. It was strange. But I suppose I was like all the rest of that world—hypnotized by its shimmering surface of false prosperity.

The election of 1888 in Kansas, with its smashing Republican majority, was a thankful prayer and paean of praise to the God of prosperity and his hidden debt for this new civilization that he had nickel-plated across our land. I did not know, we did not know, that all this debt would bring its pay day and calamity. For I was a Republican, Heaven help me, a Republican and a sinner—a blind sinner in a blind world.

CHAPTER XXIV

I Find "The Hills Whence Cometh My Strength"

IN THE SPRING and early summer of 1889 I worked for a month for Colonel Learnard, in order to get a round-trip pass to Loveland, Colorado. My job for the Colonel was to get in a rattletrap buggy with a sway-backed old horse which he furnished (trading advertising to a livery stable) and go up and down the countryside in Douglas County, Kansas, soliciting subscribers to the daily and weekly editions of the Lawrence Journal; also to sell job printing, letterheads, billheads, handbills, and the like in the various little towns and incidentally to write pleasant things about each neighborhood in which I worked. As I remember it, he gave me five or six dollars a week for expenses. But my mother put up my lunch, and I managed to get the horse into the Lawrence livery stable every night, and so kept my expense money. I turned in a decent amount of business. The Colonel was satisfied. I must have been a curious sight in that old buggy with the sleepy old horse going up and down the hills and dales of Douglas County. But I had my railroad pass. One memory of that month has remained:

I stopped at the home of a girl whom I knew at the university but slightly. I could not rouse the family at the front door, so I walked around the house to the kitchen porch, where she stood with her back to me, ironing. I said, "Laura," and without a word she whirled and literally jumped into my arms, crying, "Oh, George!" She blushed to a crisp when she found her mistake. I see her every year now at commencement. We are old folks, and George—Heaven knows where he is. But he was never loved in his long life as that little girl must have loved him.

I spent that summer in Colorado. Vernon Kellogg, who also had been working for the Colonel in Lawrence to get a pass, went with me. Thirty miles from the railroad, we joined a group of university boys, mostly members of Phi Delta Theta, with three Phi Psi's who were camped in a cabin by the Big Thompson River in Moraine Park, a valley above Estes. It was the most notable summer I had ever had, notable for the fact that I was associating every hour of the day with men who were intellectually my superiors, including the two Franklins, who in their thirties were to become scientists with international recognition; Fred Funston, who within a decade was to be a national hero and a major general in the Army; Herbert Hadley, who in a score of years was destined to be attorney general of Missouri and then governor, and still later stand for four days under the national limelight in a Republican national convention as a possible nominee for President—all young fellows in their late teens and early twenties. We lived there blissfully happy, reacting upon one another, stimulating one another, literally fertilizing one another with ideas and visions, entangling one another's destinies in that mysterious fabric which is the skein of fate.

We were not a serious crowd. We lived simply, gayly. We had two rules, only two, as the laws of our republic: every man must clean his own fish, and no razor would be allowed in the camp. So we grew whiskers. Mine were red and upturned from under the chin—an Irish mustache. We cooked when the Franklins told us to cook, for they were our elders, and washed dishes without rancor or friction. Every man made his own bed, which was on the floor, of the one-room log cabin, for we all slept in a row over spruce boughs and under our own blankets. And every man looked after his own kit—a change of underwear, his store clothes which he never wore in the park, a book or two or three or half a dozen which he brought, and his gun if he had one, which I did not, and his fishing tackle—ditto with me. (In parentheses, here and now, let me say that that summer, when we lived largely on the fish we caught and somewhat on the game we shot, I did not once cast a line, nor once fire a shot—and I have not fished since, nor shot a gun! Nor, let me add, have I played a game of cards, or ball—nothing. In sport, the fun is too expensive physically; in games, the stakes and prizes are not worth the winning. It is a make-believe world.)

Vernon and Funston and I were an inseparable trio. I went with them when they hunted, sometimes. I often loafed along behind them within yelling distance. I liked to gather the wild red raspberries and strawberries in the canyon, which the Franklins put into delectable shortcakes. I was willing to cook and wash dishes. I made a passable flapjack, fried fish with reasonable skill, helped to cut up the contraband mountain sheep which Funston shot, took my turn and probably had more than my turn in hauling down wood from the mountain for our cabin. I hung a hammock in the pine woods above our cabin and went up there many an afternoon to read.

I should define life that summer as hilarious. It was a roar of laughter at me, somewhat as a poky fool, or at Funston who could not walk a log across a creek, and had to coon it. But once he took his rifle all alone, and marched all alone down the road to where some advertising painters were smearing huge boulders with admonishings to use somebody's sarsaparilla. Literally Funston chased them down the road, largely by his unique and convincing profanity, supported somewhat by his cocked rifle. We laughed also at Wilmoth, a Phi Psi who baked for us excellent bread of which he was justly proud and one day, leaving it outside to rise in the sun, came home and baked it; when he started to cut the loaf, found a chipmunk in it. He was a pious man, a Y.M.C.A. person, and when the knife struck the chipmunk he swore. He said "Dammit." And we made a ring around him, chanting over and over: "Wilmoth, he said 'Dammit.' He will go to hell!" Then we laughed at Bill Franklin, who was continually quoting Goethe in German and expounding German philosophy and literally raving over its beauties, which we, because he spoke his own academic patois of German, could not entirely comprehend. Also we laughed at Kellogg because he was so meticulous, placed everything exactly where it belonged, had a place for everything.

We were not a drinking crowd. On the Fourth of July we had one case of beer for twelve boys on an all-day celebration. Two or three days later, we had our picture taken with the empty case, all pretending to be very drunk. The picture, printed in many a newspaper and magazine later when we were grown into man's estate and somewhat celebrated, has frozen us there as the young devils we were not.

But we lived well on grouse and sage hen and bacon and a few ptarmigans tougher than boiled owls, rabbits which were plentiful, and trout—thousands of mountain trout in streams which had scarcely known a fly before. We saw, forty miles from our camp, a deserted mining town—a marvelous picture like Pompeii. For twenty years before a rumor had come of a rich strike forty miles below on the Grand River; and overnight, it seems, the thousand inhabitants had pulled out. There was the post office, with the letters in the boxes; the saloons with the empty bottles on the shelves; the billiard tables with their green baize, moth-eaten and rat-gnawed; the stores with their shelves like grinning skulls empty of their fleshly furnishings; in the cabins the cookstoves stood in the kitchens, and iron safes standing open, too heavy to be moved. It was a dramatic picture—that little town of Lulu down on the Grand.

Twice that summer, Kellogg and I climbed Longs Peak: once with no one else along; and once with a party which included Funston, Hadley, and Ed Franklin. It is a hard, long climb, impossible by any machine that man has yet made. Of its 14,500 feet you go up 2,000 on all fours, creeping and climbing along crevices and cracks in almost perpendicular rocks. You come down on all fives until you strike a level 2,000 feet above timber line. Then you walk a mile over huge boulders, jumping from one to another. When I got to the summit the first time, we could see across the plains the smoke of Pueblo two hundred miles away. We could see over into Wyoming. It was a beautiful sight. But when I started down that precipice I was frightened, literally scared numb and stiff, and Kellogg had to coax me down.

The summer passed—certainly the most profitable two months I had ever spent in my life, for I learned to live with others. Proteus, who changes us from decade to decade, with some kind of transmigration of souls as the years pass with their ceaseless mutations, worked his miracle on me. If I ever grew up and became a man, it was in the summer of 1889, in Colorado, in a little log cabin filled with a dozen boys on the Big Thompson River.

CHAPTER XXV

I Finally Quit "Creeping Like a Snail Unwillingly to School"

I WENT BACK to the university in the fall of 1889 and tried to hold my job as a reporter for the Journal and do my class work. It was unsuccessful. Some way I had ceased to be a student and had become a reporter. I cut classes, depended on my native wit too much to get by in the class when I did attend. The boys in the fraternity used to say:

"Billie is majoring in ventilation and acoustics."

I tried again the mathematics examination that would take the academic skeleton out of my class record. It was no good. In December I had an offer from Mr. Murdock of the Eldorado Republican—eighteen dollars a week to take charge of his paper, hire and fire, write the locals and editorials, run the bank account, and get out the paper. Said he to me, when we talked it over:

"Now, Bill Allen, I am on a Senate committee to codify the laws of Kansas. We are on per diem and expenses. I am going to be away a long time. I want someone to take charge of this shop."

The eighteen dollars he offered me seemed to be beyond the dreams of avarice. I had been working much of the time for eight dollars. The most I had ever had was ten, in the gay and fleeting summer of 1888. In the university the requirements for mathematics were strict, immutable. I never could graduate. I figured it out that I might as well quit when the quitting was good. I had had all the honors I could get out of the university. The class had elected me class poet. I was on good terms with the faculty, partly because as university reporter I had some influence and partly, I suppose, because I was easy to get along with. The word "Billy" defined me. I was a "Billie" to the fraternity and, in private, to the faculty, to the girls, and to Massachusetts Street downtown. Professor Canfield advised me to stick it out. Professor Marsh, of the English department, bewailed my going; so did Helen; and so did my mother, who had missed her own college degree at Knox.

But I was headstrong. I made the decision. My mother and I put our little household traps into a freight car and went back to Eldorado. We moved into one of our smaller houses, ousting the tenant who had been there more than ten years. It was a small house—six or seven rooms—on a tree-shaded street, in the best residential part of town. She liked that part of it, did my mother. And I think while we were there she was happy, except at moody moments when she remembered that I had missed my degree. She did not realize that since walking out of the high school in June, 1884, I had been for the better part of five years and a half in and around college, reading when I was not studying, playing the college game every hour in my academic career that was not occupied by reciting, writing, or reporting. If ever a young man was exposed to an education, I was—even though I did not carry an academic degree. Books and reading had become a major part of my interests and habits. Indeed books and reading were the main things in my life when I got off the train at Eldorado the first day of January, 1890. I had written verse which had been reprinted in the Kansas City Star, and from there had gone over the country. I was known to the re-porters in Topeka and Arthur Capper and I had begun our friendship that was to run through a lifetime. Among the newspapermen of Kansas City, I was a marked young man. Fame, so far as I was concerned, was a cradle snatcher. She flirted with me early! I was a figure in college life. I was well known in the town of Lawrence. I was beginning to get my nose above water in the current of Kansas journalism. The trademark "Will A. White" was signed to verses and short articles clipped from the Lawrence and the university papers. And my head swelled accordingly.

When I moved into the Republican office, I took Mr. Murdock's desk. He came down the first morning and saw me there and began to laugh. "Well, Bill Allen, you are a chip off the old block. Your father never hesitated to boss things. Where do you think I am going to sit?" After that, whenever I heard his footsteps upon the stairs, I sneaked over to another desk.

He was a tall, well built man in his late forties. He was self-educated, and spent much time with books and papers. He wore heavy bifocal glasses, gold-rimmed and scintillating. He drew a pension for partial blindness which he had incurred as a young soldier after the Civil War, fighting Indians in Colorado. He wore a mustache and a little goatee on his lower lip—not on his chin, which was cleft. And he had the full, round, ruddy face of a man who loved good living, and the soft voice of one who per-suaded rather than commanded.

Looking back at the campaign which made him a state senator, I can see that it was symptomatic of the economic and social change that had come into the country. He was supported in his candidacy by the Santa Fe Railroad and opposed by the Missouri Pacific. The Missouri Pacific had crossed the county in '83. Kansas was veined by railroads running for the most part east and west—the Union Pacific, the Rock Island, the Santa Fe, and the Missouri Pacific. And each railroad had become, in its own territory, a political overlord. When two railroads crossed a county, often in those days the railway overlords struggled for domination, which was both unethical and wasteful. Even worse, it became revealing. For people, lined up on each side, knew the masters on the other. The system spread pretty well over the Mississippi Valley and the South. New England may have had its own way of political life; but we—in the vast rural areas—we still were a rural people. With us, the great public service corporations, which of course included the railways, the telephones, the banks, the insurance companies, and the packing houses, took charge of politics. The trust problem appeared in the seventies, waxed strong in the eighties, reflecting the deep change in American life and economic habits.

Mr. Murdock's state senatorial campaign in 1888 was a symptom of the world change. The Missouri Pacific backed the Republican newspaper which opposed Mr. Murdock. The opposition attacked Mr. Murdock personally as a plutocrat and put up a farmer against him for the Republican nomination. The fact that he bought his clothes from Brooks Brothers in New York was advertised and used heavily against him. The truth—that he was the candidate of the Santa Fe and was opposed by the Missouri Pacific—did not come out in the campaign. If it had, it would have disclosed the fact that Kansas, along with the other American states, was no longer a republican democracy but part of a plutocratic republic. The ballot box was reasonably clean. The conventions were not corrupted by money. Mr. Murdock used a little money, and the Missouri Pacific spent a little money for cigars, for buggy hire, for workers in the party caucuses in the various wards and townships. But personal corruption was not an important part of the plutocratic control. If Mr. Murdock had been attacked seriously as the candidate of the Santa Fe, it would have made him stronger. For the people were for the railroads. The people favored the control by those corporate influences which had built up their civilization. If they stopped to think of it, the voters realized that the bonds of the corporations that governed them were not unlike their own farm and home mortgages. For it was a civilization whose capital was its credit. That capital still was independent. It was still furnished by banks acting almost as individuals. Pools and wells of capital were scattered over the country. They made not one great pool but many little ones! Even in New York, where the pools were deepest and widest, there was competition among the Morgans, the Rockefellers, the Goulds, and the Vanderbilts. Naturally, our plutocracy in Eldorado stemmed back through the bondholders of the railroads to the capitalists on Wall Street, Broad Street, and lower Broadway, where the great sharks played each in his own tadpole pool of capital which he controlled.

So Mr. Murdock, standing there at the desk which I with the natural complacence of my inner vanity had assumed, and looking at me over his heavy glasses, was the symbol and the instrument of the new world that had come to replace the world of the sixties and early seventies in which he and my father as young men had set out to make their fame and fortune in the Walnut Valley, still innocent of railroads—still the land of little masters who made their own wares and peddled them to their neighbors, the printer, the tanner, the carpenter, the saddle maker, the tinner, the blacksmith, the baker, the butcher, and the candlestick maker.

That first morning, Mr. Murdock pulled from his vest pocket a leather case and threw down an engraved card—very nifty. It read, "Thomas Benton Murdock, Senator from Butler County," and in the lower corners, "ElDorado," and "Member of the State Senate Codification Committee." It was impressive.

He was going to Topeka on the noon train. He was arrayed in his Brooks Brothers suit, had on an expensive but subdued necktie and his stylish, sawed-off, semi-plug hat. He saw me invoicing his sartorial outfit and he laughed softly.

"I'm going to the Coates House tonight, and tomorrow I'm going to send that card with a note to Ogden Armour. And, by Godfrey's diamonds, he'll come and see *me*!" Then, squinting up his eyes and puckering his face, he said: "And he'll pay for it!"

At this point I should have been shocked; but I was not. He well knew I would not be. We lived in the age where the sort of thing he was explaining needed no defense, required no apology, was accepted as the way life was. However, as manager of his newspaper, I was not supposed to use corruption in soliciting business. If in a deal with the county commissioners, it was necessary to give one or two of them a percentage of the gross returns from the county printing, Mr. Murdock would do it surreptitiously or through the bank where he did business. It would not appear on my books. It would not be a part of my job to inquire about it. But when he went forth, up and down the earth on his railroad passes, to the packing houses, to the insurance companies, and to the Kansas City banks and mortgage companies, seeking whom he might devour, that was a matter of common knowledge among the governing class; and I was born into that governing class. I accepted its heritage. I knew that my father was one of those who had paid the wife of the ballot-box stuffer who had located the Courthouse at Eldorado as the county seat, while the scapegoat was in the penitentiary. I was rather proud of it. I might even have boasted of it in the Sanhedrin of the local government. So when Senator Thomas

Benton Murdock, of Butler County, told me about his scheme to blackjack Mr. Armour, I wished him well.

I was solicitor of advertising, in addition to being local editor, editorial writer, business manager, and once in a while I had to use strong-arm methods with reluctant advertisers. In that day there were three ways to get advertising for a newspaper: to sell it as a legitimate commodity; to beg for it as help for the paper which was booming the town; and to hold a more or less obvious gun in the ribs of the advertiser while a salesman, politely if possible but firmly if necessary, explained why it was to the intelligent self-interest of the advertiser to put an advertisement in the salesman's medium. So I got business from the merchants. So Mr. Murdock got business from Mr. Armour, *et al.* Probably he had no more qualms about his task than I had about my job. As an Episcopalian vestryman, he came home every other Sunday. Certainly he was not a pious fraud in his own view, but a good solid citizen upholding the church as a pillar of a rather felicitous society—the Republican plutocracy, giver of every good and perfect gift, distributor of justice to the rich and benefices to the poor. And if sometimes Mr. Murdock, whose wife still was an invalid, had an eye for a pretty girl with a well turned ankle and a come-hither smile—well, God was just and, after all, you could not expect perfection in weak flesh and blood.

In that day and time I began my real life, in January 1890, as a responsible head of a country weekly with a circulation of something under three thousand in a town of two thousand five hundred and a county of twenty-five or thirty thousand people. Here I was at home.

I had come from the university not quite under a cloud because I did not bring home my degree, but in a nebulous haze of uncertainty as to why I had quit in mid-term. I played the guitar, the mandolin, the accordion, and the cabinet organ, and the piano if necessary; and that spring I bought me a black and gold blazer jacket, white trousers, and a black sash which was most fashionable for young gentlemen. And after work I splashed around on the bosom of the Walnut in boating parties, and was quite the young beau in the long summer twilights. In that blazer suit I would sit on a bench by the tennis court and watch the young nobility and gentry play, take them to eat, either out to my mother's home or downtown to Mort Wells' ice-cream salon. After that I probably went back to the office, wrote local items or editorials or, if I was in a particularly mellow mood, wrote verse—and printed it in the Republican. It was promptly reprinted in the Kansas City Star and began to circulate over the country. People in the town, the few people that really amounted to anything, knew about it. So I was mildly famous and certainly happy.

CHAPTER XXVI

I Become a Blind Leader of the Blind

THE YEAR 1890 opened God's perfect world, so far as the ruling classes were concerned, in the western Mississippi Valley and in the South. The Republicans two years before had swept everything north of the Indian Territory. The Democrats in the South had returned to Congress and put into the governors' mansions the Confederate veterans from the big houses, or their sons. It seemed to the people in the towns, and to the better class of farmers all over the two regions west and south, that life would go on about as it was for those whom hard work, good luck, and God's mercy had assigned to places in the upper social stratifications of a classless democratic society. Obviously, the distribution of wealth which nature and nature's God had written in tablets of stone would be undisturbed through all future ages. Revolt, reform, progress, change—all were unthinkable. At the post office, waiting for the evening mail to be distributed, in a thousand ways in all the implications of the gossip, indeed in their fundamental interpretations of life, men said serenely:

"Here is the land of pure delight!"

Then out of the nowhere into the here came trouble. We laughed at it, of course. I remember one day in the midst of spring, when Senator Murdock came home from one of his predatory excursions to Topeka and Kansas City, I told him with glee about a meeting in the Courthouse of the county committee of the Farmers' Alliance. They were arranging to call a mass convention to put out a county ticket. It was funny. I listed the leaders of the meeting. Among them were all the town and county malcontents who had been blowing off since the days of the Grangers and the Greenbackers, and who had supported Ben Butler in '84 and the Union Labor party in '88, which polled less than 10 per cent of the vote. We knew that the Farmers' Alliance had been organizing in the county, and presumed it was just another of those farmer cooperatives which would start a store and maybe build an elevator, last two or three years, and then dry up and blow away—such things had been happening since the beginning of the settlement of the county.

Mr. Murdock listened to my story, grinned complacently, and pretty soon lit out for the bank, to talk it over with his cronies. (He had an anomalous relation with the bank. His account, before I came there, was always overdrawn. Everything he had was mortgaged, and occasionally the bank would wipe out the mortgage. Maybe he brought some money down from Topeka; and sometimes he sacrificed the juicy rewards of printing for the county the delinquent tax list, in September when we were paid for it. Or sometimes, though rarely, he paid the interest on his debts. But because he represented the powers in the state, and because the private cars of the rich and the great stopped at the Eldorado station to take him on, he was accepted at the bank as an oracle and an equal, as few men were who had such a low rating at the note counter.) When he came back from the bank later in the day, he took up the subject of the farmers' ticket with me. It was his opinion that it was another fly-by-night political disturbance which was of no great consequence, and of course I felt the same way. How could a group of incompetents that were not able to get into a county convention of either party, a group that for twenty years had been the laughingstock of the countryside for its visionary nonsense—how could they get anywhere in politics? So we paid no attention to the platform upon which they had called the county convention.

The Democratic paper printed the platform, but it was generally jeered at in the conclave that crowded the post-office lobby every evening after the arrival of the five o'clock train. If one of the group came in, he was assailed with good-natured raillery. He fired back as good as he got from the banker or the lawyer, or the judge, or the old doctor, or the leading merchant; and the crowd had some good laughs. For generally the rascally reformer had a sharper tongue than even the old judge—certainly sharper than the banker—though sometimes the "Old Pounder," who presided at the banker's note counter and was known as a wolfhound far and wide, could be pretty rough with the hayseed rebel who could not even afford a glass-fronted box in the post office and got his mail "general delivery." I remember one evening, the Old Pounder got a big laugh out of the town atheist, whose wife took in washing while he did nothing more important than deliver the clothes to her customers:

"I suppose you are going to run for sheriff again. I notice you always do when there is a crazy man's ticket in this county! A hell of a sheriff you will make! You would spend your two years trying to collect the judgments against you piled up down at the Courthouse! God'lmighty, man, do you think we are going to turn the Courthouse over to a lot of blatherskites who can't pay the interest on the back interest on their wives' debts!"

I laughed with the crowd. The scatterbrained reformer took his medicine. I wrote gay, ribald, and possibly subtly Rabelaisian editorials, directed at the whole fly-up-the-creek, rag, tag, and bobtail movement.

When they had their convention, it filled the Courthouse. And the size of the convention, symbolized by a dado of backsides sticking out of the courtroom windows, bothered for a moment the Olympians who ruled the county. I told Mr. Murdock about it. As a news item, we printed the county ticket which the rabble rousers had chosen, and made supercilious and obliquely scurrilous reference to the kind of candidates they had chosen. For we prideful ones considered the Alliance candidates as the dregs of Butler County society; farmers who had lost their farms, Courthouse hangers-on who were glad even to serve on a jury, economic and political scapegraces who had been turncoats, first Republicans, then Greenbackers, then Union Laborites, then Democrats again, and schoolteachers without schools, doctors who were seedy and sometimes had questionable practices. But the convention stuffing the Courthouse was annoying, if it was not quite ominous. But the bankers, the lawyers, the good deacons of the churches who passed the hat, and the Past Grands or the Noble Knights in the lodges still laughed at the Farmers' Alliance, and still, even after the convention, I wrote editorials in the Eldorado Republican jeering at the uprising.

Naturally, because the editorials were pretty mean, I acquired some distinction with the ruling class. I still do not see why and how they took me seriously that summer, running about in the evening after work with a mandolin under my arm, or a guitar, or even at best stopping after the mail was distributed to buy at the newsstand half a dozen comic papers or maybe one of Mr. Lovell's pirated copies of Kipling or J. M. Barrie's outgivings. I was crazy about Kipling, and a gibbering idiot about "A Window in Thrums." The other day I had a letter from one of those Eldorado girls, Addie Miller, now a great-grandmother, who wrote:

Will, do you remember the time when you came out and sat me in the hammock one evening and put me sound asleep trying to read or recite to me, I don't know which, one of those Kipling poems about soldiers? As I went under, I remember the line:

Waiting for the Sleary babies to develop Sleary's fits!

Sometimes if I had the mandolin under my arm, or the guitar, I would assemble a local fiddler who had not a note in his head, but who could play by ear "Hear Me, Norma," or "Sobra la Soras," or "The Blue Danube," or another boy who had half a dozen mouth organs in various keys that he could play, and a banjoist or guitar player, for an evening's serenading orgy. But if the crowd in the post office saw me without the mandolin, it was a fairly safe guess that I would go upstairs from the post office to the Republican office, to write an editorial, to clear my notebook of local items, to prepare the copy for the advertising I had sold during the day, or to sit there writing verse which I signed "Will A. White."

As the summer deepened, the Farmers' Alliance began to assume serious proportions. We who followed politics professionally with anything like sensitive ears knew its county ticket was amazingly gathering strength. Mr. Murdock would come to the office from the bank and caution me about the intolerance of my editorials. Sometimes he wrote an editorial himself. He astonished me one day by attacking the Republican leadership of the state. It was a sacrilege, but he owned the paper. I apologized for Mr. Murdock under my breath to the bankers and the post-office moguls when the paper was out, and he had gone out of town on his codifying trips. His idea in attacking the Republican leadership was to placate the rebels. The word "appeasement" had not come to prominence, but he was an appeaser. During this first summer of that Populist uprising, he used to go about town in seersucker trousers, a spotless white shirt, red suspenders, and a Panama hat out of George Tolle's stock on Main Street. He was a great hand to go through the stores on Saturdays when the farmers were in town, talking with everybody, particularly the rebellious farmers; maybe not about politics, maybe about crops, religion, business, or gossip. He wore his thick bifocal glasses at the end of his nose and looked over them rakishly. He never lifted his soft voice in argument. He avoided controversy. He was just Old Bent to the farmers—Old Bent to his enemies, who always softened when he was around. He knew the names of their wives and their children, their dogs and their horses. And when he was electioneering he carried fine-cut tobacco in his silver tobacco case which he chewed gingerly and passed freely among the farmers in the Saturday crowd. And so he came to me one Saturday in midsummer with the truth:

"By Godfrey's diamonds," he said, "something's happening, young feller! These damn farmers are preparing to tear down the Courthouse!"

It was about this time that he and his brother Marshall, who edited the Wichita Eagle, and his brother-in-law, Jake Stottler, who was running a paper at Emporia or Wellington, started a counterrevolution known in the state as "the Murdock rebellion." Its chief demand was that the Republican party in Kansas clean house. How the crowd at the post office hooted about the phrase "cleaning house," the day the paper was out, considering the past record and position of Mr. Murdock.

For, after all, he had been for at least twenty years the chief fugleman of George R. Peck, who "handled" the legislature for the railroads and the other interests which feared reform legislation, and desired legislation in its own behalf. George R. Peck was the general counsel of the Santa Fe

Railroad. To him, the general counsels of other railroads, the attorneys for the packing houses, the bankers, and the insurance companies, turned over their legislative funds. In today's parlance he would be known as the general counsel of the Associated Industries. Peck generally had about twenty thousand dollars, sometimes thirty. Mr. Murdock told me this himself. Peck was supposed to maintain a room at the political hotel, the Copeland, where entertainment for man and beast was free to all who came. He was supposed to distribute anywhere from five hundred to two thousand dollars each to ten or a dozen leaders of the legislature. If they were lawyers, they got it as retainers. If they were not lawyers, they got it to help them with their expense money for, after all, the legislator drew but three dollars a day. Room and board at a hotel would cost him from three to six dollars a day if he lived among the nobility and gentry of the legislature. When Mr. Peck distributed his largess, nothing was said of any return from any recipient. It was just a pleasant social gift. A funny story was extant in those days about Senator Blivens, known as Old Bill Blivens. He was an attorney. He got his two thousand at the beginning of the session, and he came back toward the end of the session for more. An important bit of legislation in which the railroads were interested was before Blivens' committee. As chairman, he had power of life and death over it. Mr. Peck remonstrated that he could not go back in good faith or good taste to the donors and ask for more. It was a gentleman's understanding all around. But Old Bill said:

"Well, George, I have had to buy some of my own whiskey and I have had to sit in some poker games to keep my standing. Now you know how it is with these girls around the capital here. That accounted for fifteen hundred of it. I may have spent the rest of it foolishly. But anyway it's all gone! I tell you, George, she's all gone!"

Again Peck remonstrated that he had no excuse for going back to the railroads for more money. What would they think of his giving money to friends who would betray him by greedy insistence? What excuse could he give? Old Bill looked at him innocently, batted childlike eyes of faith, and then, as inspiration surged into his intelligence, he put his arm around Peck and said:

"George, I tell you now, George, now you go back to your fellers and say sort of mysterious: 'Old Bill Blivens is acting kind of queer.' Just that! And see what they say."

The story was known of men in politics pretty generally over the state, and that night in the post office, after the Murdock counterrevolution started, the banker said to the lawyer, and the lawyer said to the doctor, and the doctor said to the merchant, and it went tittering around the post-office lobby while the evening mail was being distributed:

"Old Bent Murdock is acting kinda queer! Just that." And it was a gay session.

None the less and howsomever, "the situation"—which in political jargon means the environing developments—was getting serious. The Farmers' Alliance in midsummer put out a state ticket. It was supposed by Republicans to be, of course, the riffraff, rag, tag, and bobtail, the scum of the earth politically. Nevertheless there it was. And in Butler County and all over Kansas townspeople riding out at night noticed that once or twice a week the schoolhouses were all lit up. In Kansas, schoolhouses are used for political meetings. The Republicans had not begun their campaign. But the Alliance people had. And right square in mid-July, almost without notice, certainly without any clamor in the Republican papers, a procession two miles long moved down Main Street in Eldorado. It was made up of protesting farmers, their wives, and their children. There were floats on hayracks filled with singers crying political protest to gospel tunes. There were mottoes: "Special Privileges for None; Equal Rights for All," "Down with Wall Street," "Kill the Great Dragon of Lombard Street," "Let Us Pay the Kind of Dollar We Borrowed."

That was the core of the issue which had crystallized the political strength of the Farmers' Alliance. Said they: "We borrowed money in the seventies before the resumption of specie payment and the return to a gold basis for currency. Now we are asked to pay in a gold dollar which is worth much more in crops and cattle and farm produce than the dollar we borrowed." It was the free-silver issue, a form of fiat money. Heretofore, in our politics, the only issue since the days of Reconstruction, save in the seventies when the Greenbackers and the Grangers were rampant for a few years, had been the protective tariff. But here came something new, and Mr. Murdock, senator from Butler County, henchman of George Peck, a member of the Temple of the Pharisees, was alarmed. A counterrevolution, which was beginning to find a few adherents in other editors than the Murdocks, was attempting to head off the Farmers' Alliance by taking its issues. Senator Plumb, the titular head of the Republican party, was a free-silver man. He advocated free silver in the Senate. It was claimed that he owned a silver mine! Because Plumb and the Murdocks came from Emporia and had drunk from the same canteen in the army during the Civil War, it was supposed that Plumb was back of the Murdock rebellion. I set all this down because it vitally affected my editorial writing, the first serious editorial writing I ever did on the Eldorado Republican. I was not a high-tariff man. Professor Canfield had made me immune to that poison. But I was for the gold standard. Looking back over fifty years, I can say that the gold standard is the only economic principle to which I have consistently and bitterly adhered.

I had a low opinion of the Farmers' Alliance credo, and a still lower opinion of the leaders of the movement. So my editorials in the Republican were biased by the fact that I wanted to please Mr. Murdock. He was my little tin god at the time. Yet I was satisfied, being what I was, that the whole Alliance movement was demagogic rabble-rousing, with no basis in sound economics. How intellectually snobbish I was about "sound economics"! Alack and alas, I took no account, absolutely no account, of the tremendous fact staring me in the face, that the short shimmering day of mass borrowing which had built a civilization in the West and the South, from Appomattox to the nineties, was done! Its sun had set. The railroads were all built. Sound economics should have warned me that another day had dawned. All the free land was taken. All cities and townships and counties were laid out—all bonded to the limit for public improvements, public utilities and, in some rare instances, to give rascals a chance to steal public funds. The flood of credit that had been following the star of empire across the world suddenly was dammed. The day of the great boom of the seventies and eighties—a day which had seen railroad pirates rise and become captains of industry, a day which had seen all the great industries organizing with capital gathered more or less by the same proud captains of industry, the packers, the steel men, the oil men, the railroads, a day which had seen the play of free, competitive industrial capital—that day was at its sunset. Those rumps of seedy farmers sticking out of the Courthouse window in Eldorado, Butler County, Kansas, as the Farmers' Alliance county convention met, cast the shadows of a great twilight. In another three years came the night—the collapse, and the depression of '93. But I was a young fool. I sat at night in the office of the Eldorado Republican, writing reactionary editorials about Sound Economics which I had learned from Francis Walker's college textbook, just one of ten thousand other fools across the land who thought that classic economics could be fitted into the social and political upheaval that was closing a brilliant era in our national history. And we had been looking at one of the great treks of the white race across a continent building a civilization on borrowed money—capitalizing credit; and it had slowed down now for a long stop! Being what I was, a child of the governing classes, I was blinded by my birthright!

CHAPTER XXVII

We Have "an Infant Crying for the Light" on Our Doorstep!

IN THE LAST PARAGRAPH I wrote, "Being what I was." Well, what was I? Look: Among my contemporaries, the boys and girls who had graduated from the Spring Chicken Club but had not gone to college, high-school alumni of my own age in town, I was "Billy" as I had been in college. I read voraciously, loved formal society in the town, organized dances, loved serenading the girls and rowing them up and down the three- or four-mile mill dam of the Walnut. I was given to conspicuous clothing, was not afraid to wear the first pongee silk shirt that came to town. Before I had been back from the university six months, I had bought, at a price, a states-man's double-breasted Prince Albert coat with mouse-gray trousers—hand-me-down! There was a sight for gods and men. A young fellow, a bit fat, five feet seven and five-eighths inches tall, wearing a Prince Albert coat that came almost to his knees, with bell skirts which flared when he swung on the corner in the "grand right and left." There was a funny figure for a man aged twenty-four or twenty-five, who was writing editorials in the Eldorado Republican that goaded the Populists to wrath. That kind of dude was foreordained and predestined to hang in effigy in the Populist parade with the title "Silly Willie" painted across his capacious cartooned posterior.

How that figure amused Mr. Murdock! We stood together watching the parade. And when the wagon containing my dangling effigy passed, Mr. Murdock looked at me over his glasses and laughed his soft, ingratiating laugh. "Old Doc White, by Godfrey's diamonds! It's Old Doc White! Eh, Bill Allen!" And he was proud. Perhaps he was proud that I was his bondman. Certainly I was proud that he was my master.

We both told Alice, his daughter, at different times how proud we were of the attention I had received from the farmers in their parade. It was no new thing for Mr. Murdock to be caricatured as "Blind Bent" stealing money from the Pension Fund. But I had been in town less than six months and had achieved this fame. The hanging effigy gave me leadership among the young Republicans of the town and county, in spite of my mandolin and striped blazer and sash. Even in my pompous Prince Albert with the mouse-colored trousers—God help them!—they accepted me. I used my talent for verse-making to write rhymes for the Republican Glee Club: ribald rhymes, hooting at the Farmers' Alliance, deriding its leaders, jeering at the ragged nobodies who were its followers; silly rhymes which we Republicans in those days thought were grape and canister in the entrails of our adversaries. We who had eyes and saw not, and ears and heard not!

By the end of the summer, Mr. Murdock and the Republican county committee realized that they were up against a real political revolt. The Farmers' Alliance in Kansas had put out a ticket. Also, the Alliance had tickets before the people of Nebraska and the Dakotas and Iowa. In Iowa the movement was led by General James B. Weaver. He had been a brave soldier in the Civil War, and had led the Greenbackers and Grangers in their political sorties in the seventies. In the South, a great industrial boom had started from the ashes of the Civil War, building railroads, new towns, new enterprises, building everything on borrowed money which was now due. Economic conditions were much as they were in the West. The South was aflame as the western Mississippi Valley was, and the party that had struck the shackles from four million slaves, that had saved the Union, that had built up the West, was on the run. Its plight and its flight had come in six months, and a panic was in the air. The political bandwagon, for the first time since Appomattox, had left the soldiers who had worn the blue. Debt, in a land where everyone was in debt, where every township, city, and county was bonded to its limit, was making a great issue and shaking a Great Old Party to its core.

Through it all, there at Senator Murdock's desk, I was writing all sorts of things. I had become the Eldorado correspondent of the Associated Press, of the Kansas City Star, and of St. Louis, Chicago, and New York papers. I was writing syndicated articles for the American Press Association, a concern which sold stereotyped features to small dailies and weekly newspapers, and I was forever writing verse which appeared in the Republican and then was scattered like leaves upon the wind. It was imitation, of course, imitation of James Whitcomb Riley, or Will Carleton, or Eugene Field. But I did not realize that it was imitation. Perhaps after all I got my inspiration from the pioneer people around me—farmers of the Alliance in their desperation, moving in the cloud of debt. But at any rate I was working hard, even though Alice Murdock and I did a lot of social catering in the town. We sometimes went together to dances at Wichita or to functions in Emporia. The fact that we were from a little town did not lower our flag. I am satisfied that there is no social snob so sure of himself, and no social queen quite so arrogant, as the social leaders who dominate a little snide country town. They stand before kings, unblinking. So Alice and I lived in a world quite fenced off from the seething social, economic, and political unrest that was boiling down the Walnut Valley and across the western prairie plains. I had a mask in each pageant. But they were two masks, two people, two distinct careers. Also, as I was by way of being a poet, I courted other poets. Fort Scott had two: Eugene Ware, whose "Rhymes of Ironquill" have been more widely read than those of any other Kansan, and Albert Bigelow Paine, who had come there as an itinerant tintype photographer in a van, married a rich girl, started in the wholesale photographer's supply business—the while, writing verse which he sold to magazines in New York. (He died, the official biographer of Mark Twain.) Ware, whom I idolized, was a Civil War veteran who learned the saddle-maker's trade to support him while he studied law, married a Vassar graduate, became a state senator, was defeated for Congress because his verse was not regarded as orthodox in that far-off day of the seventies and early eighties. He was one of the most distinguished lawyers in the Middle West, and, in the early part of the first decade of this century, was appointed United States Pensions Commissioner by Theodore Roosevelt. Ware was a person and a poet of real distinction, whose verses are still read and sometimes are credited to "Anon" in anthologies and suchlike collections. To me, those two—Ware and Paine—were persons of much consequence. Their careers represented to me, as I wrote in the office over the post office in Eldorado, realizable ideals.

So summer slipped by, and the November election came. It was a close election on governor. Probably the Republicans stole it. But in those days United States Senators were elected by the Legislature. The State Senate was a holdover body, chosen in the Republican triumphal election of 1888, while the members of the House of Representatives were overwhelmingly, almost unanimously, Farmers' Alliance, elected with just one purpose, to defeat John J. Ingalls. He was the shining figure of western Republicanism —a national figure too, for he was a polished orator, a graduate of Williams College, and had helped write the Kansas Constitution and had designed its seal. He was elected to the United States Senate in the seventies. Ingalls, because he was a distinguished writer, became the gadfly of the rebel brigadiers who came out of the South to the Senate. He was erudite, arrogant, cynical; tall, thin, with iron-gray hair, dark olive skin, piercing black eyes and iron-gray goatee, a mustache after the military fashion of the hour, with a voice like iron strings, resonant and terrible. In season he wore a long gray overcoat, and under it a gray Prince Albert coat with always a flashy tie, generally red. Imagine that figure, then give him talent for vituperation, for oratorical castigation; add a narrow partisan viewpoint and a scintillating mind! One can see why the Democrats in Kansas lined up with the Farmers' Alliance to defeat John J. Ingalls whom they hated implacably.

Economic issues had no place in politics in 1870 and 1880, at least not in the major parties. A "good government" was the ideal of reformers. "The best citizens" were supposed to desire honest men in office, men who would not take bribes, men who would appoint high-minded men as their subordinates, men who would look after the public interests, see that the public charities were well supported, insist that public service was maintained at the highest level component with party success, and men who would have as little as possible to do with the machinations of the local boss. Ingalls, in Kansas, was the typical product of good government in the later days of his senatorial career. He never discussed economic issues, leaving that for demagogues. Consideration of patronage irked him. His cronies at home were the kind of men whose political ambition was satisfied when they were appointed regents of the State University. It was inconceivable to me that the people of Kansas should be seriously interested in issues touching on the realities of the economic situation. When Ingalls realized, late in his campaign, that the Farmers' Alliance was serious, he got up in the Senate and made a speech for free silver—a scholarly, futile, rhetorical performance. He could not realize how tragically real to the Kansas people, and especially the farmers, was the deflation of the currency. He could not understand why mortgage foreclosures got into politics; how ten-cent corn could affect Republican majorities; why deflation was scattering devastation across an agricultural state like Kansas. He was set by nature and polished by circumstance as a shining mark for political death in 1890. And about that time he preened his political plumage and declared impudently that "the purification of politics is an iridescent dream." That bright saying—erudite, arrogant, cynical—deeply offended hundreds of thousands of Kansans who were struggling against debt, taxes, and a shrinking dollar to maintain their homes and uphold their self-respect. Was it coincidence that erected for the people of his state a man so exactly personifying all that they hated, or was it some impish prescience in the times that made Ingalls' defeat symbolic of all the anguished yearnings of a distressed electorate? Chance, or fatal circumstance dramatizing the issue —whichever it was, like a lightning flash the fall of Ingalls revealed the political realities of the hour in understandable terms.

When it was found that the joint session of the Legislature would defeat Ingalls by half a dozen votes, the Republicans, without consulting him too carefully, set Cy Leland—the local boss who handled the details of Kansas politics for George R. Peck of the Santa Fe Railroad, and the financial interests thereunto appertaining—to buying the votes necessary to rescue Ingalls.

Mr. Murdock, at the time it happened, told me this story; Mr. Leland afterwards verified it: It would take ten thousand dollars to buy the ten men necessary to Ingalls' election. They, of course, were a scabby lot. Their reputation in the state as mercenaries and worse was known to those who dabbled in Kansas politics; Leland knew it, and Ingalls had to know it. Leland called on him in his hotel bedroom, and handed him the list. Ingalls rose and paced the bedroom floor like a caged panther, snarling, as he looked over the list, up and down. Finally, he burst out with imprecations, curses, and such profanity as a scholastic vocabulary could readily improvise:

"Oh, the dirty, slimy bastards!" he cried. And he repeated the thought in all its variants.

Leland stood it for a while. He was a practical, little sawed-off cavalry officer, with chin whiskers and no nonsense, who faced the realities of the situation. He grew tired of Ingalls' vituperations:

"Ah, shut up!" said he. "Do you want to do it, or don't you want to do it?"

Again Ingalls began attacking the maternal genealogy of his mercenary supporters.

"Damn your stinking Massachusetts pride—hush!" cried Leland. "Of course that's exactly what they are. But do you expect me to take ten thousand dollars and go out and buy you a lot of Goddam Sunday school superintendents?"

Ingalls stopped before Leland and dramatically handed back his list.

"No, Cy, no! I have my family and my name, and I won't take the risk of disgracing them to hold this job." And, buttoning his long gray coat, he strolled out of the room into oblivion.

This happened in January, 1891. I set the story down here that the reader may know something of the politics of that time and the atmosphere in which I attained my political majority. If I had known that Ingalls rejected a seat in the Senate that was tainted, probably I should have had enough moral sense to applaud him. But I should have had my qualms, and certainly should have wished with all my heart that his decision had not been necessary.

These are nice points and must be recorded here as a part of American life at the beginning of the last decade of that century. We Kansans were at the base of the political pyramid. Over us were the railroads, which were at that time America's largest interstate industry. Just above the railroads, were the insurance companies; then, in the West, the packing houses (in other states, the liquor interests); and above them, great individual bankers. Beside the bankers, not yet under government control, stood the industrial captains—Stanford, Huntington, Jay Gould, Jim Hill, the Vanderbilts, and their kind. These leaders of industry were still comparatively free men.

That is to say, they assembled their own capital, dominated the banks that lent them money, and were not creatures of their bankers. American capital was amalgamating in 1890, but still was assembled in little pools. Ownership of an industry meant ownership and control, and there was no control without ownership. And this system, still mildly competitive in its upper zones, needed political sovereignty to hold its sway. So we had in every state someone who furnished the legal sinews that moved men in the politics of the state. Generally and typically, such a man was a big railroad attorney and was known as a scholar and a gentleman. He was the suave toastmaster at formal dinners. He made erudite and eloquent speeches on formal occasions. He was often chairman of the board of trustees at the state university, and bestowed honorary degrees with aplomb on whitewashed rascals and such poets and pastors as were subservient to the plutocracy. In larger states sometimes there were many divergent, but not often rival, political satraps who battled for senators in the legislature and for control of legislation. In Kansas, George R. Peck was Allah. Perhaps his garments stank with brimstone in the nostrils of the pure in heart. But not in mine.

I sensed these things more or less. I knew them when I was in college. I realized when I chose to be a Republican that the Democrats in Missouri, or in any Democratic state, controlled their politics with their local Pecks like ours in Kansas. There was no choice between the two parties so far as their moral turpitude was concerned. And I, alas, was not clearly and definitely conscious that there was any moral turpitude in the established order which had built the railroads, assembled the packing industry, gathered the capital for the insurance companies, and turned Kansas from a desert into a human habitation with a name, all in three decades—less than a generation. It seemed to me—and I think it must have seemed to all well placed, well fed, well clad young men in those days—quite an achievement for Divine Providence. Now, who were we to scoff at the Lord's servants, to sniff at those who held power and basked in the glory of the great work. So Peck and Cy Leland ruled, and their scurvy crews were often beyond the pale.

When my father's old friends in Eldorado realized that I had followed my mother's Republican footsteps, they were heartbroken, but I think not too deeply surprised.

"Oh, Willie, Willie! What would your father think? How could you!" they said, and let it go at that, realizing that I had taken, on the whole, the wise course if I wished to live in Kansas politics.

The fall of Ingalls, the rise of the Farmers' Alliance, the first wave of the shock troops of a revolution that was to gather force as the years went by—all this did not disturb either the Spring Chickens or their parents at the high-five clubs, the formal dances at the opera house given for the firemen, and the town charities. Life went on in that far day a half-century ago as it had been going on for at least a hundred and fifty years on this continent. As for the revolution, we were conscious of some disturbance, and quoted Tennyson's lines at it,

> An infant crying in the night:
> An infant crying for the light:
> And with no language but a cry,

and let the little misbegotten creature bawl his lungs out on our doorstep. He was no concern of ours—but we were rather proud of that quotation.

I had the lines first from Professor Canfield when I wrote him a letter after the Farmers' Alliance state convention—a bewildered letter asking him what was causing the upheaval. He sent to me, or at least referred me to, Richard T. Ely's book on "The Labor Movement in America," and a treatise on American Socialism, which I read—still more bewildered than I had been. In his letter he used the Tennysonian lines. Later, George R. Peck, our state satrap, who probably next to Ingalls was our most scholarly politician, used the lines in a speech perhaps to the Unitarians, perhaps to the teachers' association, or the bar. The quotation epitomized our general attitude toward the farmers' rebellion.

Vernon Kellogg came down to Eldorado to see me in the winter of 1891, and we had long talks about this agrarian rebellion. Vernon was inclined to treat it as an interesting nuisance and diverted the talk to biology. He gave me some books to read; among others, I remember distinctly a book on biology by Edward Clodd, and some of Professor Cope's. But, when Vernon came visiting, Alice and I rented a meeting hall of one of the fraternal insurance companies, brought down a drayload of rugs, floor lamps, parlor furniture, and dishes, hired a fiddler, two cornettists, a cellist and a first violinist, as an orchestra, and we put on as pretty a party—with punch, ice cream, cake and trimmings—as you ever saw, with one end of the hall looking like a pleasure's bower.

Later, Ewing Herbert came to town for a visit. He and I discussed the Farmers' Alliance. He frankly regarded it as treason and was for hanging the lot. Mr. Murdock's general idea was to stay close to shore, keep out of the wind, and lie low. He had seen the Greenbackers rise and fall, the Grangers march forth to defeat, and the old order finally triumph. And, anyway, he would not be up for re-election for two years, in which time a lot could happen—and did!

CHAPTER XXVIII

I Go Mildly Mad and Become a Changeling!

IN THE SPRING of 1891 I bought "Leaves of Grass" and became for the time inebriated with Walt Whitman's philosophy. I don't know how I came to buy that book. I had known of Whitman casually as a student of American literature knows a poet. Maybe some of the boys in the fraternity chapter, or most likely of all Professor Canfield who was a beacon of light and leading in my life, may have turned my mind to Whitman. I don't remember. But the amazing thing about my madness was that I did not in any way connect the Whitman democracy with the Farmers' Alliance. For here, parading down Main Street, was a barbaric yawp if ever there was one—a pure Whitmanesque picture! I was ten years making it all out! In those ten years two poets, entirely different, almost antagonistic, held me enthralled—Walt Whitman and Rudyard Kipling. I fear that Kipling's philosophy, rather than Whitman's, colored my mind in its practical attitudes toward life. But the two must have jangled and left me disturbed and uncertain. Later I tried to imitate Kipling, but in the early nineties what I wrote still was a pale moonlit shadow of Riley and Eugene Field. My mother, who loved Tennyson and Whittier, exposed me to her favorites, left them in my room, sometimes read them. I liked them. I was polite to them. Often I sat alone browsing in them, sometimes reading a page or a poem; but I was bound to my idols—Whitman, the great democrat, and Kipling, the imperialist. These I took under my arm when I went out girling under the spring moon, which was often. What a pest I must have been to three or four girls in that town, who had something else on their minds as they should have had! The wonder is they did not all fall asleep, as Addie Miller did. But it was a lovely world. A horse and buggy still could be had for a dollar and a half on Sunday afternoon, and a boat on the Walnut for fifty cents an evening. I still could make two dollars and a half for playing the organ, or the piano, at a country dance and calling off the same. That occasional windfall in addition to my eighteen dollars, with a pleasant comfortable home and my mother cushioning me with kindness and rich cooking, made life idyllic.

It is no wonder that I often sat on the front porch of our home in the twilight, tinkling my mandolin and trying to whistle also to its tunes, or perhaps took out my guitar and thumped it romantically in the gathering dusk. But also do not forget this: I was writing bitter editorials about the Farmers' Alliance, getting ready to help my friends in the odd-year election who were running as Republicans for county offices, and keeping a decent balance for Mr. Murdock at the bank, meeting the Republican's pay roll, getting up its local news items, soliciting the advertisements, and, in rushed afternoons, working at the printer's case or feeding the old Cottrell press for half an hour or so in the back room.

That year, well into the summer, I first met a young prince whose life was to be linked with mine fairly closely for more than two score years. He was Charley Curtis. He came down from Topeka to campaign the county, sent by the Republican state central committee. His job was to fight the Farmers' Alliance. He had a rabble-rousing speech with a good deal of Civil War in it, a lot of protective tariff, and a very carefully poised straddle on the currency question (which, I was satisfied then—and still think—that he knew little about, and cared absolutely nothing for). For his politics were always purely personal. Issues never bothered him. He was a handsome fellow, five feet ten, straight as his Kaw Indian grandfather must have been, with an olive skin that looked like old ivory, a silky, flowing, handlebar mustache, dark shoe-button eyes, beady, and in those days always gay, a mop of crow's-wing hair, a gentle ingratiating voice, and what a smile! There his French grandfather showed, Louis Papin. When his mother died, his Indian grandmother sent him from the reservation to live with his father—a not very enterprising ex-captain home from the Civil War—who let Charley work at a livery stable and ride horses as a jockey, until a lawyer friend took the boy out and put him to studying law. He won his way by his smile and hard work, was admitted to the bar, twice elected county attorney, and was headed straight for political glory when I saw him.

Butler County is larger than the state of Rhode Island, and he and I, with a buggy hired by the county Republican committee, rode over the county together for three days. He made the speeches; I introduced him. A glee club went with us and sang ribald doggerel, lambasting the Farmers' Alliance. In those three days when we were together most of the time, we explored each other's minds. He must have thought me a silly, sentimental person, and I felt that he was a wonder with his winning ways. I never saw a man who could go into a hostile audience, smile, shake hands, and talk before and after the meeting so plausibly that what he said on his feet as an orator was completely eclipsed by what he was as a human being. We got onto a "Will" and "Charley" basis which would last through our lives. Neither of us believed anything that the other held fond and dear, yet we trudged through life without a serious quarrel. Our friendship survived many bitter antagonisms without stress or strain, for it had few emotional roots. I have known married couples that had the same relation, not founded on affection, hardly friendly, but pleasantly amiable, tolerant and perhaps a bit supercilious here and there on both sides, yet plodding through life without serious altercations. When Charley and I threw dishes at each other it was in a purely Pickwickian sense!

In Kansas the young Republicans have a way of organizing. In the process of organization, youth gets acquainted. Youth pretends that it is organizing to reform the world. As a matter of fact, it is organizing politically to get jobs. After the Republicans were defeated by the Populists in 1890, we young Republicans hustled into an organization. We were going to do big things, and did. In the next decade we got elected to a lot of offices. But in the state organization I met other young men whom I had known from the other Kansas colleges, whom I had met in the political battles of the State Oratorical Association, also many K.U. alumni of my own day and of the decade before. So I was at home in the organization of the Young Republicans. I did not make speeches. I took no office. I knew enough even then to realize that he who seeks honors loses power. To help an up-and-coming young fellow become chairman of a committee, gave me more power on the committee than he had, if he was grateful. And I suppose most of a man's luck in politics depends on his ability to keep away from ingrates. This ability to smell an ingrate and avoid tying up with him, is a really great talent in politics and elsewhere. So, as a young politician who knew more young fellows than most of his associates on the floor of a state convention of the Young Republicans, and as a writer, I was a figure in the state. The editorials in the Eldorado Republican were read by three or four score of editors who knew that I was writing them for Senator Murdock. Sometimes when those editorials were copied they were credited to me personally. In verse and in prose, the trademark "Will A. White" was becoming known. When I went to that state convention at Topeka I had sense enough not to appear in the girling clothes I wore in Eldorado, and left behind the long-tailed Prince Albert coat with striped trousers, and the white trousers, the dark crimson sash, the black silk shirt, and the flowing crepe tie in which we young beaus of Eldorado disported ourselves after the fashion of 1891. I seem to remember my convention regalia as a giddy straw hat, a seersucker suit, a pale blue four-in-hand, and—of this I am sure—patent leather toothpick shoes. I paid seven dollars for them, prodigal that I was!

I swung the Butler County delegation in the Young Republican convention to the support of the state chairman. I think it was Ed Little. So we became friends for life. When he went as consul general to Cairo, and buddied around with Richard Harding Davis, when he was private secretary to Governor Leedy, when he was lieutenant colonel in the Philippines, and a member of Congress, he was loyal to me, consulted me, and we were useful to each other. By that time I had become a full-fledged Republican with some enthusiasm—if not for my faith, at least for my friends! The more the local Populists denounced me, the surer I was that this was the best possible world, and that any attempt to remake or reform it was folly bordering on treason. So I wrote for Senator Murdock's paper with ardor, with force, and with considerable plausibility. Because he taught me more than anyone before him to write short sentences, to use simple common words, to say exactly what I meant in the vernacular, and because I was young and full of youth's vigor, I carried conviction and attained some little fame.

After returning from the convention I sat down at the big desk in the Eldorado Republican office one afternoon and wrote my first piece of fiction. It was the story of an old-soldier Republican who returned to the Republican fold for purely personal reasons. It was all emotion, all sentiment, and probably all nonsense. It was called "The Regeneration of Colonel Hucks." It was a column and a half long. The Kansas City Star copied it. So did the Kansas City Journal. All the Kansas daily papers published it within a week after it appeared in Eldorado. The Republican state central committee saw it, and Senator Plumb, who had been my father's friend, read it. I am sure he was telling me the truth when he said it brought tears to his eyes; for he was a good politician, and his tear ducts were loosely valved. Anyway he saw to it that the Republican state committee issued the story in stereotype plates the next week and sent it to every Republican paper in the state, credited to me, "Will A. White, in the Eldorado Republican." It fitted into the other western states where Populism was rampant—Nebraska, the Dakotas, Colorado, Iowa, Minnesota—and the Republican state committees there used it. For a month, perhaps, straggling letters, four or five a week from all over the region, came in thanking me for it. I have no doubt that my head swelled, for I was twenty-three and had more than a vague notion that I was a hell of a fellow. The crowd in the post office, waiting for the evening mail to be distributed, knew about my little flickering flame of fame. My father's Democratic friends jeered. The Populists laughed. So, naturally, the Republicans defended me, and I, who never argued but always grinned and took it, enjoyed the situation hugely. Before the summer was over my good opinion of myself was strengthened by two offers of editorial jobs in Kansas City. One was a letter from Colonel William R. Nelson, editor of the Kansas City Star, offering me twenty-five dollars a week to come to Kansas City and write editorials for the Star. The other was from Charles

S. Gleed, whom I had known in my Lawrence days, for he was an alumnus not only of the university but of the Lawrence Journal. He read my foolishness when I was working on that paper in the summers. He was the receiver, or something like that, of the Kansas City Journal, representing the Santa Fe Railroad of which he was a director, and which had in some way taken over the ownership and managership of that paper. Gleed offered me the same salary that Colonel Nelson offered me. Taking my Republicanism seriously, I chose the Kansas City Journal, thinking I should be happier writing for the Republican organ than for a mugwump Independent newspaper that had supported President Cleveland.

Between the time I decided to go to the Journal and my departure from Eldorado, I had nearly a month. I was afraid I could not hold the job, and my mother and I decided that she would stay in Eldorado while I adventured. She was proud that I chose the Republican paper and not so doubtful as I was about my holding the job. I gave myself one final farewell social toot in a dance in the Fraternal Insurance Hall. I went fishing with two visiting Kansas editors all day one Sunday and wrote a piece about it for the Eldorado Republican.

Whenever I wrote anything which I regarded as particularly flossy, my laurel wreath crowned my brow. Now Mr. Murdock came shuffling up to the desk and looked over his glasses to say: "Well, Bill Allen, I see you've spread yourself and writ a piece!" Then he grinned at me above his bifocals, looking a father's pride and affection.

I was proud of my fishing piece. Mr. Murdock was a greater fisherman than I—as a matter of fact, I never cast a line. I merely rowed the boat for my guests; but I enjoyed being out on the river and in the woods.

"Well, young feller," he said, "that'll be your last piece. They'll tie you up there like a mule to the treadmill, and you'll grow old and gray in the city, a hired man, a nobody." He paused. "When you get your belly full, come back." Another pause. "Gawd, what a life! Your father wanted always to push West where he could be free." He half turned away, then said sadly: "Old Doc White, good old Doc White!" Then he grinned and chuckled: "Well, go it while you're young, Bill Allen. When you're old you can't!"

My farewell with the boys and girls of the town was rather hilarious, though I can remember a funny thing. I was going stark mad at the moment over William Dean Howells' novel, "A Hazard of New Fortunes," and I remember what little success I had cramming it down the throat of a dear girl who for the summer was good to me. Looking back over the fifty years and seeing her a grandmother now, I am amazed that she kept her face straight while I tried to set her afire with Howells, when I should properly have been making arrangements to be the grandfather of her grandchildren. Which did not occur to me. But I did assemble the fiddler and the guitarist and another youth with a banjo, while I tinkled my mandolin and went around serenading the female members of the Imperial Club (successor to the Spring Chickens) and others whom I loved. Some way the whole season of my farewell seems to be threaded on a new tune we had learned— the theme aria of Flotow's ancient opera, "Martha." And when I think of the hiatus between Eldorado and the world, even now I begin to whistle that old tune. I must have emotionalized my farewell in that melody.

One other thing I remember—a strange thing and quite mad. The August harvest moon, under which a few nights before I had come home feeling most poetical from my day's fishing with my visiting editors, was still shining high in the sky when I walked home another night, either from the Imperial Club dance or from our serenading, or from an evening on Walnut Hill with Alice Murdock, her family and maybe two or three young people sitting on the porch, not unconscious of the night's splendor. I turned in and slept deeply. Then I remember waking up, when the moon's beams were slanting and the dawn must have been but two or three hours away. Now this is sure: I did wake up. Something—it seemed to me the sound of distant music—came to my ear. The head of my bed was near a south window, and I looked out. And I will swear across the years during which I have held the picture, that there under a tree—a spreading elm tree—I saw the Little People, the fairies. I was not dreaming; at least I did not think so then, and I cannot think so now. They were making a curious buzzing noise, white little people, or gray, three or four inches high. And I got up out of bed and went to another window, and still saw them. Then I lay on my belly on my bed and kicked my heels and put my chin in my hands, to be sure I was not sleeping, and still I saw them. For a long time, maybe five minutes, they were buzzing about, busy at something, I could not make out what. Then I turned away a moment, maybe to roll over on my side or to get up on my knees, and they began to fade away; an instant later they were gone. And there I was, like a fool, gawking at the bluegrass under the elm. I got up and sat in a chair. I was deeply upset, bemused, troubled. I thought maybe I was going crazy! I knew well enough of course, even then, that what I saw I did not see; but when you are cold sober, and have the conviction spread over you that you are mad, you are bothered—and I have been bothered ever since. It is not impossible. Nothing is impossible. Many years later I heard of transparent fish; with other eyes, other creatures see other things; with other ears they hear much that escapes our human ears. Perhaps in our very presence are other beings like the transparent fish, which we may not feel with our bodies attuned to rather insentient nerves. Heaven knows! For an hour I thought I was crazy. And when I recall that hour, and am so sure that I was awake, I think maybe I am still crazy.

But, the marvel or the hallucination, or whatever it was there in the moonlight before the dawn, was no more puzzling than the thing that actually happened to me a week later when I left Eldorado on the morning train for Kansas City, to make my fame and fortune in the big world. For all of the familiar world—the fairy world in which I had lived, the ancient order in which I was born, the self-sufficient little town with its little self-sustaining industries which changed overnight when the railroad came, vanished. Gone also was the boom town with a hundred houses rising on the hill above that wide place in the road that was Main Street, with its sophisticated troop of young married people that came merrily in, filling the stores with strange store clothes, store shoes, store food, store plumbing, bathtubs, electric lights, gas, and all the miracles of the machine age—fading just as the fairies went. Instead of that gay village, Eldorado was a town of paintless houses, of vacant stores, of debts coming due on the borrowed capital that had built the shimmering prodigy that was Eldorado in the eighties. Indeed, that day when I took the train for Kansas City, the whole countryside was shabby, drab, and shopworn; the farmers were in revolt; the townspeople were bewildered and down at the heel, and the politicians were aghast at the terrible thing that was happening. Change and decay were about me. It was as though some transmigration of souls had come, the pioneer spirit had been born into the phantasy that was the boom. That had died, and the same spirit had appeared again in the town, in the state, in the whole Missouri Valley, which was reborn in the twinkling of an eye into an old battered, hopeless, dejected creature, mildly mad, singing strange songs, swearing strange oaths to strange gods, while the old gods, the sturdy gods of the pioneers, the smiling gods of prosperity, were crumbling idols in the past. And when I shook hands with my friends there at the station platform and climbed aboard the little plug train that took me out of my home town to what seemed like the great city—a town over a hundred thousand then—I stepped as it were out of one body and one environment and one old chain of circumstances into another, a new body of thinking and feeling, a new life.

When the train stopped at Kansas City that evening, a young man whom I seemed to know, but who some way was strange to me, got off. He was a bit ashamed of his clothes. He was not sure how to get around or what to do. He went, at first bashfully, through the crowds of clanging cablecars to the heart of the great city, to the tall six-story building where the Journal was published, a countryman, probably quite as scared as was young St. George when he first lifted his spear to the dragon. But was I, who had been so confident, so cocky, so brash in Lawrence, Eldorado and Topeka, that timid youth walking for the first time down a new road into a strange world?

And so Will White, who was sometimes "Billie" in his late teens and early twenties, became rather definitely Will A. White of the Kansas City

Journal, with his nervous, trembling hands tightly squeezing, more in fear than in pride, the shaft of the spear that would slay the city dragon. It was as though he had burst from the cocoon of childhood and youth, and had suddenly become a man!

Book Three

WILL A. WHITE

(Sometimes Billie)

CHAPTER XXIX

A Gilded Metropolis

THE KANSAS CITY of 1891, to which I came as Childe Roland to the Dark Tower, was an overgrown country town of a hundred thousand people. It was consciously citified, like a country jake in his first store clothes. It had one ten-story building, and a score of buildings from five to seven stories. Its business area comprised a dozen blocks in something like the center of the town. To the west of the business area were the packing houses, which were inflated replicas of the stinking town slaughterhouse in Eldorado. Around them were the small industries of the city and the stockyards, which smelled to high heaven. And of course fringing these were the shabby, unpainted homes of the workers. North of the business district was the red-light area, segregated and properly policed. South of the business area lived the ruling class in lovely homes surrounded by green lawns, with spreading elms, massive oaks, a few walnut trees, and young evergreens. There, in great ten- or fifteen-room houses, surrounded by hundreds of feet of deep porches, in houses that bulged with the tumors and warts of the ornamental architecture of the jigsaw period, lived the bankers, the merchants, the lawyers, the doctors, the teachers, the preachers, now and then a prosperous gambler or a corrupt politician. These worthies were generally boycotted by the respectables, who were too nice to accept socially those whose business they tolerated, and whose immoralities were acknowledged as a part of the necessary social order of a boom town.

But in 1891 the Kansas City boom was deflated. That year saw the collapse that had begun on the farms of the Missouri Valley in the late eighties. Mortgage companies in Kansas City were tottering. Several banks were unstable, and everyone knew it. The merchants were having a hard time making their collections. It was rough going for young lawyers and young doctors. The fat pickings had vanished, and only the stark white bones of many a financial and mercantile structure, of many a small industry, were left for the young cubs. So life in Kansas City, in the autumn

205

of 1891, instead of being hectic and regal, as I expected it, was beginning to be a bit drab.

But I was too green really to know it until I saw it in retrospect at the end of a decade. Probably no young professional man who had been exposed to six years in college was ever so raw and unsophisticated in a city as I. I had visited Kansas City but a few times. The cablecars that ran up and down the hills around the Missouri River, where the town was staked out, were marvels to me. I had used the telephone a little at Lawrence and at Eldorado, but always with the consciousness that I was tampering with a miracle.

I got off the train and went to the Journal Building, where they were expecting me. The managing editor had arranged that I should board out a defunct advertising due bill, and led me to the Centropolis Hotel, a third-rate hostelry down near the edge of the red-light district, but still the haunt of old Missouri cattlemen who remembered it in the days of its royal prime. We walked south from the Journal office and passed the Keith-Perry Building, which loomed above me seven or eight stories. I knew that Keith and Perry were coal operators, and when the managing editor said, "Mr. White, that building is made of coal!" I took him literally and touched my finger to its cyclopean dark, smoke-grimed sandstone masonry. Then I looked down and away so that the managing editor would not detect my ignorance.

Along other lines I was not so innocent as I looked. I had not been in Kansas City a month before I discovered that, by working it right, you could get a streetcar pass; and I worked it right, and the managing editor did not know it. But he would not have cared—much!

Mr. Gleed had discharged a man for drinking too much and put me in his place as editorial writer. My predecessor, like many men who drink too much, was a charming fellow, much beloved by the reporters and the executives of the Journal. They had done his work for him to shield his negligence. So I was not popular. But I sensed the trouble. One night when I had been on the paper for two or three months, the managing editor, an old boy in his sixties, the telegraph editor (in his fifties), and the dramatic critic, who for some reason had really become fond of me, knocked off after the paper was up and started out casually to roam down Grand Avenue, drinking as we went from bar to bar during the midnight hours. Early the dramatic critic left the party, and we three prowled around the saloons until three or four o'clock. My drinking experience was slight. It did not occur to me that I was taking on much. I knew I was talkative; but so were the others, and I stood up with the nerves of youth and no experience behind me.

I noticed as the night grew old that the other two were wilting. We chartered a hack somewhere on lower Main Street, and I helped the managing editor to his door, rang the bell, and held him until it was opened. I took the telegraph editor to his boarding house and put him to bed, then went home and turned up the next afternoon fresh as a daisy. Dean, the dramatic critic, who heard the story, greeted me with cheers. It seems it had been agreed in the office that I was to be taken out and gotten wildly drunk, so that the story could be told around that I was worse than my predecessor. It was my first bacchanalian triumph, and probably my last; for liquor never interested me. I acquired much face in the office by my prowess that night, for of course Dean whispered the story about; and the managing editor, after that night, felt kindly toward me, perhaps as he felt my arms about him climbing the stone steps to the terrace and the wooden steps to the front door of his home.

The eternal row between the business office and the news department, familiar on every newspaper, gave me standing in the business office, for the advertising men and the business boss heard the story that I had put my enemies to bed—their enemies also; and Charlie Gleed, my sponsor, eventually heard the story and was proud of me, for his judgment about me was vindicated. So, when I had been in town less than a month, I was taken out of the Centropolis and promoted to the Midland Hotel, a first-class caravansary where I ate out a due bill in state and style, of which I shall tell more later.

For some strange reason I attracted the attention, and was honored with the friendship, of Colonel Robert T. Van Horn who was nominally editor-in-chief of the paper—but only nominally, poor fellow. If ever our profession knew a scholar and a gentleman, it was Colonel Van Horn. He had been a brave soldier in the Civil War. He had come to Kansas City before the Civil War and had started a Republican paper when it took courage in that proslavery stronghold. He had served several terms in Congress, and —being an old-fashioned man chary of his intimacies and proud to be called "Colonel"—disliked and distrusted James G. Blaine, who had called him "Bob" the second time he met him. He seemed to me to be an old, old man though he was only in his late sixties. He had a scraggly, snow-white beard, and a pink complexion which shone through it, and kind, wide blue eyes. The Journal, in his heyday, was of course a political organ that depended somewhat for its patronage and prestige upon the Republican party. The tide had turned, and newspapers in the larger cities were becoming business enterprises, with their politics quite incidental to their prosperity. The old Colonel probably could not sell gold eagles for tin dimes. He had no salesmanship. He had little business sense. He was a stalwart, wool-dyed, black radical Republican who still was fighting the battles of the Civil War, so his circulation shrank. The advertisers, even

Republicans, were leaving him for the Star. The mortgage on his paper grew. As he could not pay the interest, his equity wore thin. Santa Fe Railroad interests bought the mortgage and kept the old Colonel in his rather stately editorial room—an exhibition piece without power, though he did not know it; with no authority, though he would not have used it if he had it, and with only the privilege of seeing his name at the paper's masthead and occasionally contributing an editorial in highly involved sentences, and what to him was the precious boon, a Sunday editorial.

That Sunday editorial was the town joke and the office mystery. Every Saturday morning, promptly at ten o'clock, Colonel Van Horn appeared in the office where I sat writing the editorial for the next day. He generally chatted for a moment with me about some episode of the Civil War, or perhaps of the border war around old Kansas City, then went into his office, pulled down all the blinds, turned out all the lights, made the office as nearly pitch-dark as he could, and then, with his eyes closed, he took his pencil and wrote his editorial. He told me, in the self-deprecatory, apologetic voice of old people who know they are eccentric, that his son guided his pencil. He adored his son, who had died in his youth. And the old Colonel some way or other, wearing heavy bifocal glasses to see when he wrote in the brightest light, managed by some automatic writing to get out that Sunday editorial. Always it was a column long, sometimes two columns. His son may have controlled the pencil, but the long and involved sentences were the Colonel's own. To me and to most of the readers of the Journal, the editorials did not make sense. They were mystic and seemed mildly mad. I used to see the copy and always the proof. Sometimes I chopped them into short sentences or did what I could, without telling the Colonel, to make his stuff "read sense."

But he liked me, and we established a kind of camaraderie. He was such a gentle man, so unworldly in his estimates of men and his judgment of events, so kindly and sweet withal, that I could not laugh at him. I could not even smile at him. He took me to his heart, as some sort of a link perhaps with his dead son, and I grew fond of him and have held him always in affectionate remembrance. His stooped figure, his frank, mystical blue eyes, his shabby untrimmed beard, his baby-pink skin, and his mild ingratiating voice remain with me across fifty years a vivid and lovely picture of age.

He had a way of patting me very gently on the shoulder when I came into the office in the morning, perhaps in lieu of a word of greeting. He heard when I was promoted in my hotel due bill from the Centropolis to the Midland, and stopped one day at my desk to say that the proper appreciation of food was a part of a gentleman's education. Looking me over, perhaps observing the youthful rotundity of my torsal curves, he added: "You like food, don't you? Well, learn to know about it."

So I did. At the Midland Hotel I took my Master's degree in the gentle art of consuming groceries. My father was a good liver. My mother was a good cook. But our table, in a pioneer household, was fairly primitive. We broiled and roasted our meats, took pains with game and fish; but, except in the summertime, we had few vegetables. It was dried and preserved fruits nine months in the year, and our dietary range was necessarily limited. When I got to the Midland, as a natural adventurer I ate my way straight into a new, strange culinary realm I had not dreamed of in my philosophy.

My due bill limited me to the table d'hôte meals; but "limited" is a grotesque word to use. In the eighties and nineties, the table d'hôte menu of a first-class hotel in a town of a hundred thousand or over was a labyrinth of delight. And every dish that I had never heard of, I took. More than that, I asked the head waiter about it. Willie was a large, double-jowled, good-natured colored man, and quickly discovered that I was good for a tip. Because I came in late, he used to stand by my table and talk to me about the food, tell me what it was, how it was prepared, where it came from. He loved to serve me and watch me eat. I think he got a vicarious thrill out of it, for I certainly was a sincere and competent eater in those days. On the breakfast menu were baked oysters, and broiled oysters with strange sauces. I learned to like them even for breakfast, along with pancakes, fried potatoes, and fruit. At lunch and at dinner I wandered through the bill of fare as a Sultan might stroll through his harem. And Willie, like the Sultan's eunuch, followed me and picked out delectable bits and pieces for my comfort and joy.

When I went home to Eldorado, I told my mother about these strange dishes, and tried to tell her how to prepare certain gravies, sauces, and soups. I even brought a bottle of curry to Eldorado, on which she faithfully experimented until she achieved success with curried lamb, or veal, or chicken. For she, though naturally Republican and conservative in all things, even things culinary, was a doting and devoted mother; and she would have tried fried babies if I had asked her to do so.

At the Midland, which was the headquarters of traveling salesmen and visiting capitalists, I also learned about clothes. For I had the quick eye of youth in looking at well dressed men. I remember distinctly that when I left Eldorado I had three casual ambitions: to own a typewriter, to have a swallowtailed evening suit, and to own a soft-spring, tufted, leather couch in my office. That was the acme of my physical desires. The week after I came to town I got the typewriter, also on a due bill, paying a dollar a week on a secondhand machine. I ordered a suit of clothes on tick by taking the managing editor to the tailor to vouch for my credit. And when I was fitted for this first tailored suit the tailor showed me a gorgeous suit of evening clothes which had been left unpaid for by a customer of somewhat my figure; he was taller, but the coat and vest fitted with a few alterations. So I blazed out in evening clothes before I had any place to wear them. The leather couch remained an iridescent dream for ten long years. But it did not fade.

Thus went my first three months in Kansas City. In addition to writing editorials, I started a column. Every young newspaperman in the last sixty years has wanted to write a column before he could write a three-line item, and my column was probably as bad as any of them. I filled it with Kansas politics, my own verse, literary allusions, and personal gossip. Probably it did not amount to much; but it got my initials and sometimes my name, Will A. White, on the Journal's editorial page. Among the Kansas Republican politicians, the Journal was still a party Bible; and I grew a little in Kansas fame and grace—but not much.

I had three roommates that year. I managed to get a room over on McGee Street, north of Twelfth, with two double beds. Frederick Funston had come back from Central America, where Charley Gleed had staked him for a share in a sugar and coffee plantation, and was on the paper as a police reporter. He had part of my bed. Lew Schmucker of Eldorado, who was my dearest friend after high-school days, shared a bed with Fred Vandergrift, a city editor of the Star—a man ten years our senior. Harve Hoover, a railway postal clerk who was running with Lew Schmucker, also slept with Vandergrift. The railway postal clerk occupied only half a bed, for neither of them ever was at home the same night. So I was never lonesome, and in that company of rollicking hellions I was never homesick nor sad. But because it was a gang I was happy, and someway the girl proposition did not bother me—at least not seriously. Dean, the dramatic critic, who was my best friend in the Journal office, saw that I had theater tickets when I wanted them. In those days America had a national theater, and Kansas City shows were as good as New York's. While I used to run around with Dean much at night and dropped in on shows most casually and with great urbanity, still I did appreciate a couple of tickets and managed to find girls that first autumn who would go out with me. From which inference the reader may assume that Eldorado was sloughing off like a skin, and I was taking on the big city.

Again I fell into the trio which, in my youth, always seemed to be surrounding me. In the autumn of 1891, in Kansas City, it was Funston and Schmucker and I. We three roamed the city like sheep-killing dogs after my work was done. I generally finished by half past ten, my proof were read, and my troubles over. Whereupon I made a bee line for the north-end police station, where Funston was on dogwatch. We would sit around there or wander about, seeing the wicked life of what to me was a great city, making friends with the cops and the dopes and the toughs, male and female, who ranged the streets at midnight. Generally at one o'clock Funston called it a day, and we two, because streetcars ran infrequently and legs were easier to use than nickels to get, walked a mile home, indulging in tall talk, sometimes lifting our voices in ribald song. I remember Funston always liked sea songs; "Blow the Man Down," he would roar in solo. And we sang together, "The sailor's wife the sailor's star shall be," and howled a song that had for its refrain:

> And we poor sailors go skipping through the tops,
> While the landlubbers lie down below, below, below!

Across fifty years I can hear Funston roaring raucously: "Below, below, below," and hear the admonitory voice of the good-natured cop:

"Here, you boys, do you want me to call the wagon and run you in?"

For generally, having loafed around headquarters, we knew the cops, and anyway, being newspapermen, we were of the privileged class to the cops.

But I had two tremendous toots, jags, emotional outbursts. The first was when I heard Pat Gilmore's band, the first professional band of any competence that I had ever listened to. He played a concert program in the Warder Grand Theater. The music overwhelmed me. I had not realized before what man could do with instrumental music; and a sixty-piece band was like something from another world, created by other creatures than the human beings I had known. I reveled in its memory for days. The clarion notes entwined in the harmonics from the various instruments kept calling in my heart—for the first time—tunes that I could not whistle, airs that I could not even hum. After that, while I worked on the Journal, I heard good music wherever I could, and Dean, who covered the theaters as well as concerts, was forever taking me around with him to see good plays and hear good music. What with the beneficence of Dean and the due bill at the Midland, the stimulation of Funston, and Lew Schmucker the link with Eldorado where I had been so happy, life was certainly one round of joy in Kansas City; and the keenest joy, I think, was in my job. I was writing verse in odd moments. I seem never to have been rushed for time on the Journal. And my verse was being printed, and I was having the acclaim that follows a little local fame. I felt I was somebody.

The second emotional rousement I had came when I heard James Whitcomb Riley. He packed the old Warder Grand chuck-full, and recited his verse. He was an actor first and a poet incidentally. He had a flexible voice, and his whole body—hands, head, arms, and legs—was synchronized in the song that he sang, the rhythm, rhyme, and cadence of his homely verse. It got me. I went raving mad. I kept saying over and over and with variations, the whole long way home: "I can do that! I'm going to do that, I tell you! I know I can do that!" So I bent to the oar myself for some time after that night, writing dialect verse with all my might and main. I saw many shows with Dean that winter, and have forgotten them all. But Pat Gilmore with his band and James Whitcomb Riley with his poetry come back to me across the long generations vividly today.

Only with an effort do I remember that Kansas City in those days was growing shabby; that the Farmers' Alliance in Kansas, Nebraska, and Missouri was rising in its might. Politics, which had been so much a part of my life in Lawrence and Eldorado, seemed to fall away for a time. Yet I must have been keenly interested in it. The Journal, being railroad-controlled, of course stormed at the agrarian revolutionists. Though curiously, in his mild, husky little senile tenor, old Colonel Van Horn deprecated our impatience. He even wrote a few mild conciliatory editorials which were gently killed by someone before they got into print, even though his name was carried at the paper's masthead as its editor-in-chief. He was as unreal and altogether mystical as his ghostly son who guided him. If he had his heartbreaks, I did not witness them. If he felt his humiliation at all or realized his position as the shadow of a once vigorous past, I had no way of knowing. Perhaps I was too preoccupied with my own ego, with the echoing music of Pat Gilmore and the intoxication of my ambitions to be another Riley, to sense very clearly what a mauve tragedy in the background, set in old age's shabby pastels, was passing across the stage before my very eyes.

CHAPTER XXX

"In the Spring a Young Man's Fancy . . ."

IN THOSE DAYS, doing editorials on the Kansas City Journal, I had little time for reading. Magazines? Probably an armful every month. And newspaper exchanges from all over the country I literally wallowed in, seeing for the first time papers I had read about for years—New York papers, Philadelphia papers, Boston, Atlanta, New Orleans, Los Angeles. I wolfed them down. I would glance casually at the news pages; carefully scan the editorial pages, looking for editorial ideas; glance at their poetry, and take account of the current books in capsule by reading book reviews. I read carefully the New York Nation, first because in classrooms at the university I had been taught to consider its style, and secondly, because I liked its editorials. It barked so circumspectly at the status quo in this world, with which in a high and mighty way, as a youth of twenty-three, I was not entirely satisfied, even though I was a Republican and proud of it. Perhaps my uneasiness at the way the world was made was a reflection of a restless conscience. I do not know.

Ewing Herbert and Albert Bigelow Paine came to town at least once a month, and we had tall talk, which wearied Funston and altogether amused Lew Schmucker to the hooting point. But we three sat around in bars, sometimes the Midland bar, sometimes the Coates, or sometimes bought a big thick steak at Wosslick's over on Baltimore Avenue, garnished with potato chips, and washed down with beer which I hated so—sometimes taking lemonade instead, Heaven forgive me, or soda pop. We ate and drank until the fat on the steak congealed, then ordered sandwiches and continued far into the night. Only God, who smiles on youth, and the devil, who protects fools and drunkards, knows what we talked about. But it was good for us.

It was in those days that Walter Armstrong, whom I had known in college as a brother Phi Delt, told me he had a mighty pretty girl who would like to meet me. His suggestion did not interest me greatly, for in college

I had noticed that his idea of a mighty pretty girl was a rattlehead; but he was a persistent cuss, and one November evening we went over to Kansas City, Kansas, which was then Wyandotte, to see this mighty pretty girl. The girl proposition at that stage in my life was not so important as it had been in Lawrence and Eldorado; but Walter's girl made me bat my eyes. I agreed with him that she was a knockout; for she had brains—something that Walter accounted as of little consequence in young females. My surprise at his girl and my admiration for her made a dent in my self-sufficiency. And, as if to set a dent permanently, she served us cake and maybe coffee. Anyway it was nice food. Her name was Sallie Lindsay. And as we left the Lindsay portal, I hit Walter a grateful wallop on the chest and made noises of delight. Within a month I went back. She wore, I remember, a red dress. A contemporary magazine story called "Miss Devilette," which we both had read, started us off. She produced a volume of Kipling's poetry which we read together, and then a book of Richard Harding Davis' stories. And then again, food—good food in man-sized lots, on a tray in front of an open-grate fire. Deep in my heart, though I did not know it because I did not want it, something was happening. If there was anything decent in me at that time beneath the vast complacency of the silly senility of my adolescence, Sallie Lindsay hailed it, and it spoke to her as a lovely ship in passing. I did not go back for another month; but I went carrying a book, which was a sign of surrender. I did not know even that. But the picture of "Miss Devilette" by the fire glowed in my heart and kept shining out at odd and most inopportune times, and so late in the winter I went back again, and maybe again. With each visit the dent that she had made when Walter took me, deepened and strengthened and became a part of my life and destiny.

It was in the late winter, maybe in February or in early March of 1892, that I persuaded Charley Gleed, who was the big boss of the Journal, to let me go to Topeka and fill a vacancy as Topeka correspondent of the Journal —a job that was quite as dignified as that of editorial writer. For a Topeka correspondent of the leading Republican newspaper organ of the Southwest made me practically an ambassador to the Republicans of Kansas. And I strutted in my job. It was a Presidential year. Cleveland and Harrison were facing each other, each running for a second term. The Populists were sweeping over the Missouri Valley and through the South. There was talk of Populist fusion with the Democrats in Kansas. As in every fusion, respectable minorities of both parties were fighting it; but, on the other hand, those in both parties who wanted the fleshpots favored fusion. It was the business of a Republican ambassador to Topeka to stop the fusion, so that the Republicans might defeat the divided forces. That was part of my job. For that I colored the news, but did not realize that I was doing so. For that

I connived and conspired with men twice my age, and became the devil's errand boy. But the job had its compensations. I had to attend political conventions of the Populists, of the Republicans, of the Democrats in every one of the seven Congressional districts. I had to attend state conventions. I knew what was going on in all three party councils, and of course sat in the councils of the conspirators in each of the minority parties who were opposing fusion. The Republicans naturally took me in as the Journal's vicegerent. So that year I left the blue lodge of county politics and learned to put on the work from the grand lodge of state politics, with a touch now and then of national affairs. I was going to school, taking a course in practical politics as it was played in the last quarter of the nineteenth century in the United States. I saw the game as one who watches the cards from back of the player.

And, curiously enough, I did not know the stakes on the table. It is clear enough now in the perspective of fifty years that all this pulling and hauling, all this political conflagration fed by the sordid ambitions of designing men, was but the reflex of economic conditions in the Missouri Valley to the south. Debtors who could not pay, overwhelmed with their personal calamities, each of which seemed unique, were organizing with great vigor to redress their wrongs. The farmer who was losing his homestead, the jobless laborer, the town merchant or professional man who felt business slipping away and his debts overcoming him, even towns and counties that had voted bonds for improvements—railroads, waterworks, electric lights, paved streets—all felt the black hand of despair dragging them down. All of these things produced a mass psychology which manifested itself in the growing Populist movement. That movement, being one of opposition to the Republican dynasty of those days, had a chemical affinity for the Democratic party and tore into it with the ruthlessness of an elemental force.

Heaven knows, I tried to understand it. I wrote letters to Jimmie Canfield, my mentor, with whom I had studied political science, history, and sociology at Lawrence. He did not clearly know what it was about, but he had his inklings. So he sent me more titles of books to buy and read on American socialism. Vernon and I tried to make heads or tails of the whole mess, but vainly. Ewing Herbert's idea was simple: these men were traitors. They should be treated as such. They were in rebellion against the United States. Ewing's idea was the Republican idea, and the best they could do was to yell "Socialism" at the Populists and predict a recurrence of the French Revolution. The charge against the Populists that they were Socialists had more basis in fact than we Republicans understood; for, after all, Populism stemmed back to the creed of the Grangers and the Greenbackers, who were led by the old Abolitionists, those who proclaimed the rights of men—Greeley, Garrison, Wendell Phillips. All that the Populists were doing and saying boiled down to this: By their clamor against the trusts, by their demand that the railroads be regulated and that the currency be inflated, that an income tax be established more for justice than for income perhaps, that inheritances be broken up again for justice rather than for income, that a score of minor irritations against the common man be removed, these reformers were trying to use government as an agency of human welfare. They were trying to establish economic as well as political equality, to help the underdog, to cut down some of the privileges that wealth carried by reason of its size and inherent power. It was all Karl Marx, highly diluted; and the Republicans, who did not realize how true their indictment was, continued to cry "Socialism" at the top of their lungs without really believing it.

So, in the midst of all this hullabaloo in the spring and summer of 1892, the silk-stocking Democrats, hungry for victory but jealous of their self-respect, permitted the more practical Democrat politicians to fuse in Kansas and elsewhere with the rag, tag, and bobtail—the political adventurers who were the only people the Populists could get to press their claims. All over the state and adjoining states, it was arranged that Grover Cleveland, an anti-Socialist if ever America bred one, should get the Presidential votes of the Populists, in return for which the Democrats would vote for the state and Congressional tickets of the Populists. It was an unholy alliance, crazy and practical; and it worked.

There I was in the midst of it, fair, fat, and twenty-four, a supercilious young Pharisee, blinder than a bat to the great forces that were joining issue in our politics, forces that would be in combat for fifty years and more and finally would tear up modern civilization by the roots in devastating wars. I wrote jeering pieces about the Populists. Unwittingly, I lied about them and their motives, and derided the intellectual scarecrows who led them and sensed their wrongs. I sat in the seat of the scornful and larded my ribs with the fat of their altars. I had my typewriter paid for. The last payment on my evening clothes was made before I left Kansas City. I lived well—a pampered young prince of plutocracy—on the milk and honey of privilege. Incidentally, in Topeka I was beginning to get the hang of the social blue book, the "Burke's Peerage," if you will, of Topeka society, and was meeting some Very Nice Girls. Sallie Lindsay, in the back of my head and in the core of my heart, was an embryonic passion, slowly gestating as we exchanged casual letters that spring, more intellectual than emotional, but regular enough to be a pulse throb of what was to become a glowing body of affection before we knew it. While I was snubbing my way into the nobility and gentry of Topeka, I was still writing dialect verse, trying to portray the heart of a sturdy peasantry, though I did not recognize it as peasantry. My dialect verse was supposed to reflect the colloquial idiom of midwestern middle-class people, presumably well-to-do and substantial farmers, out of New England by the Ohio Valley. In my rhymes was no touch of the wide sense of rancor in the hearts of those people which was flashing out in the conventions that I attended and manifesting itself in the elections of the day. One would have thought, from reading that verse, that the Kansas people were all prosperous, contented, emotional, smug, and fundamentally happy. As a poet, I was deaf to the cries of a bewildered people as I was blind in politics to their assemblage in serried ranks that did not break step for fifty years. In those days I met and formed a casual acquaintance that became a lifetime attachment—my first literary man—Hamlin Garland. I had read his "Main Travelled Roads," and other slight books describing the farm people. I had accepted his political heresies, his sympathies with the farmers' wrongs, yet I accepted these heresies in a rather highty-tighty mood. But when I talked to Garland for two hours on a train, as we were going to a Populist meeting some place in Kansas where he spoke, his passion for his cause disturbed me. It did not quite upset me. But it was strange, I thought, that a man with such competent literary powers should be so deeply touched with the political insanity of the hour. Also in that year I met and talked to Ignatius Donnelly, a Populist from Minnesota, a scholarly man who had written a most elaborate thesis to prove that Bacon was the author of Shakespeare's plays. He proved by a secret code which he discovered in Shakespeare's writings. I had read his book. It arrested me but did not move me deeply. And when he, with burning eloquence, defended the Populist cause, again I was bothered that one I had come to respect should have such a soft place in his brain.

Of course I made friends with the Populist leaders in Kansas. I was a friendly dog by training and by breeding. Jerry Simpson, a self-educated man ten years or so my senior, I came to respect deeply. He was smart. He had read more widely than I, and often quoted Carlyle in our conversations, and the poets and essayists of the seventeenth century. His talk, as we rode together on trains or sat in hotel lobbies, or loafed in hotel bedrooms, was full of Dickensian allusions, and he persuaded me to try Thackeray, whom I had rejected until then. Jerry Simpson was not a sockless clown. He accepted the portrait which the Republicans made of him as an ignorant fool because it helped him to talk to the crowds that gathered to hear him. They expected little and got much, and that helped Simpson. He had been a Lake sailor in his boyhood and youth. He was Yankee to the core of his bones, a tough-skinned man, brown and bronzed with crow's-feet at the corners of his eyes, which deepened when a smile twinkled there. He wore gold-rimmed glasses that fastened over his ears, and he beamed through them with benevolence and wisdom. His hands were big and gnarly, and he shook hands with warmth and sincerity. He stood slightly above the middle height, spare of body and lean of limb, without an extra ounce on his cheeks. When he went to Congress, his natural capacity for debate and his wide reading gained for him the friendship of the most sophisticated and erudite man in Congress at that time—Speaker Tom Reed. Years later, because the young man, Jerry Simpson, regarded me kindly and accepted me as a sort of Nicodemus, the rich young man who turned away sadly, Tom Reed was ready to talk with me at odd times and take me into the sanctuary of an old man's admiration for an acolyte. Jerry Simpson was that much of a person. He was intelligent enough to know that, the more his silk-stocking opponents portrayed him as "Sockless Jerry," the quicker the discontented and the underprivileged citizens of Kansas would give him their vote. He was opposed in this first victorious campaign for Congress by a Wichita railroad lawyer who went around campaigning in a private car and was known as "Prince Hal." In a contest wherein the bidding was for the farmer staggering under his mortgage, it is not strange that "Sockless Jerry" defeated "Prince Hal" in the race for Congress in the Seventh Kansas District. "Sockless Jerry" became a national figure. The real Jerry Simpson profited by the fame of his own effigy.

Another, perhaps the only other, really strong and conspicuous figure in the Populist movement was "Mary Ellen" Lease. Her real name was Mary Elizabeth Lease, but the nickname "Mary Ellen" stuck. She was the complete antithesis of Jerry Simpson, a woman with a voice. I have never heard a lovelier voice than Mrs. Lease's. It was a golden voice—a deep, rich contralto, a singing voice that had hypnotic qualities. She put into her oratory something which the printed copies of her speech did not reveal. They were dull enough often, but she could recite the multiplication table and set a crowd hooting or hurrahing at her will. She stood nearly six feet tall, with no figure, a thick torso, and long legs. To me, she often looked like a kangaroo pyramided up from the hips to a comparatively small head. Her skin was a pasty white; her jowls were a little heavy; her eyes, the most expressive feature of her face, were of a nondescript color but capable of everything except spoken language. She wore her hair in a psyche knot, always neatly combed and topped by the most ungodly hats I ever saw a woman wear. She had no sex appeal—none!

Once, at a great outdoor meeting, I was sitting by Jim Orr, a Kansas Democratic politician, a railroad attorney, who loathed Populism but was not beyond getting its votes for Grover Cleveland. On the platform, speaking with Mrs. Lease, was General James B. Weaver, a Civil War general who had led the Grangers and the Greenbackers in Iowa in the seventies. He rose when Mrs. Lease came back from the rostrum, and helped her on with her coat. The General was about sixty, Mrs. Lease about forty. She had moved him deeply, even as she had moved me and as probably as she had moved Jim Orr. But Jim saw the old hands of the General rest for a moment or two on her shoulders when she had her arms through her sleeves. The gesture was obviously inspired by the affection of an old man for a young woman who had stirred his heart deeply in a sacred cause. Jim saw it, and I saw it. He winked at me, and I burned with a hot desire to hit him on the nose. The wink bothered me for a long time, and Jim Orr died before I could forgive him. For Mrs. Lease, who, I am forced to conclude, was sometimes a bit of a demagogue and was not without a letch for money and the fleshpots thereunto appertaining, was at least as sexless as a cyclone. She was married to a mild and apparently gentle man who provided her with children. When they were nursed and educated and ready to leave the home, she was ready to leave it also. Apparently that part of her life was done and finished. She was an affectionate mother; but either her home-making qualities had been frustrated or they had come to some calamitous close, for she took to the highway and was really a great exhorter. She was not so quick and intelligent as Jerry Simpson. She knew much less than he about the fundamental causes of the uprising; but she knew it was an uprising, and she rode the waves.

After the tide washed out, she left Kansas and made an honest and honorable living in New York City and died a respected citizen. But she flashed across Kansas in that day of turmoil, a harridan in the eyes of her enemies, a goddess to her friends. Looking back across a generation, I think she was a little of both.

The other Populist leaders were mostly incompetents of one sort or another, sometimes moral misfits but more often just plain ne'er-do-wells, with here and there a visionary staring at his utopia, wandering in a dream with the marching hordes of the discontented, the disinherited, the poor. And we, the Republicans, knowing they were poor and maybe consciously realizing that they had a grievance, hid behind the words of Jesus, "The poor always ye have with you!" and so went on with our business of guiding the Republic in the profitable ways of a ruling plutocracy.

CHAPTER XXXI

I Learn the Rules of Politics

WHEN I TOOK the Topeka job my mother moved up from Eldorado, and we established a home there. Again she helped me. I set up my little bookcase which I called my library, and began reading books; and she began cooking for my men friends, mostly politicians or Topeka newspaper ambassadors from the Kansas City and St. Louis papers. Sometimes a traveling correspondent of note and consequence appeared in Topeka. If I could, I snared him and took him home. And if we could afford it, for my mother never was one to go in debt, we bought a heavy beefsteak, garnished it with canned mushrooms, and spent an hour "beholding how the world was made." I had to spend many hours on trains, attending conventions, and many duller hours in hotel rooms, so I bought books, mostly new books, and read while I worked. It was that winter of '92 that Ewing Herbert, Harry Frost, who edited a little society newspaper in Topeka, and Charley Harger of the Abilene Reflector, all young fellows in their mid-twenties, and I formed what afterward became a potent political society, the Kansas Day Club. We issued the first invitations. We guaranteed the hotel for the first fifty guests. Eighty came and paid two dollars for a tenderloin beefsteak, fresh mushrooms, *au gratin* potatoes, ice cream, and cake. The speakers at our dinner became the Kansas roster for Congress, for we were the young crowd. We were ostensibly hostile to the old soldiers, then at the apex of their political power in Kansas, who were soon to cross over to the sunset side; but we did not know that. We were just greedy for power—young buffaloes horning the old bulls out of the old herd. Let us take a look at this young bull with all his assurances, with all his lusty vision of coming power.

He had grown in stature, if not in grace, during the six months that he had spent at the Midland. The waistband had expanded. He was pussy. He weighed two hundred ten pounds, as against one hundred eighty-five at Eldorado. His mat of soft brown hair was just beginning to thin and he was using every variety of hair restorer that the broad continent of his country could afford—frightened, panicky, but determined. His jowls were fat, but his neck was long and heavy; and he walked on his heels with no catlike toe tread in his gait or manner. He was calling older men, veteran politicians, by their first names. He was still writing much verse and printing it in his column in the Kansas City Journal, maintaining his fame as a young Kansas poet. After fifty years, it is obvious that poetry never was to be his passport to fame, for while his rhymes were true and his rhythm good enough, that verse had little back of it but false sentiment, colloquialized in a decent cadence. The young man was given to haberdashery hats of the proper form, neckties of the proper shades, shirts with collars of the proper cut. Later in the spring he went to his Kansas City tailor, who was the best in town in those days, and got him a gaudy light gray spring suit, much lighter and much more conspicuous than other grays that young men of more circumspection were wearing. He bought him a rolling Byronic collar, a loose, drooping crepe necktie, gray shoes, and, to top all, a hat made by the tailor of the same piece of cloth from which the suit came. He was tremendously proud of himself. All together, this paunchy young ambassador from the Kansas City Journal to the Kansas Republicans, walking on his heels and swaying his bottom like an elephant, with bold, immodest eyes, was a spectacle for gods and men. Here is the finishing touch, from Sallie Lindsay:

"When I married you, you had a big head that you were forty years catching up with—deserving!"

I was virtually a traveling man that summer. Often I would be absent from home from Monday until Saturday night, attending district conventions of the Populists, Democrats, or Republicans in various parts of Kansas. The automobile had not come to shorten distances. So, to get from one convention seat to another I might have to travel a hundred miles east and west to reach a town fifty miles away. I rode on passes, of course. Sometimes I had Pullman passes, as befitted an ambassador from the Kansas City Journal to the Kansas Republicans. I was a reporter, and I hope a good one. At least I had the confidence of the leaders of all three organizations. Which would seem to indicate that as a reporter I was fairly honest. That surprises me now, with the feeling I had then about the Populists; for no one had taught me the modern ethics of sophisticated journalism. I was seeing Kansas as I never had seen it before, from one end to the other, up and down and crisscross, on slow trains and fast, in miserable little hotels, and sometimes as the guest of the "best people." I did not see the state again in such a way for many years. I found out from trial and error what in Kansas politics was regarded honest and what dishonest. The code was something like this:

In politics a man may take money if he earns it.

He is dishonest if he takes money from both sides or if, taking money from one side, he deserts for any cause to the other.

A man must be as good as his word and go down with his fellows, take a licking with his gang and wait.

If, in a convention, a leader makes a slate and his favorite candidate wins, he must help to victory the other minor candidates who agreed to support his losing candidate.

If a man really has principles, he must not take money even to do what he was going to do anyway.

If a man takes money, he must keep his mouth shut. Otherwise, the paymaster will have to buy others whom he could easily fool.

A scoundrel is a man who swindles his friends. It is, however, permissible to cheat your enemies.

It was in the spring or early summer of 1892 that I formed my admiration for Cy Leland, a local factional boss, and established a friendship that lasted for twenty years until his death. In the Republican state convention he was supporting for governor a candidate named E. N. Morrill, a congressman. The game to nominate a governor was to tie up enough votes in a combination by getting the delegates, friends of candidates for minor state offices —secretary of state, treasurer, attorney general, and auditor—pledged to a slate in which all would combine to make a majority and nominate a state ticket. Leland formed his slate. He apparently had a majority; but some of his candidates for state offices could not hold their supporters for Morrill, and he lost the nomination. The other crowd had its slate, including Smith for governor, but as soon as he was nominated for governor, its leaders disappeared from the convention hall. They had too many promises out which they could not keep. I watched Leland in his defeat. All the afternoon he moved about the convention, guarding the Morrill slate. He nominated the entire state ticket below governor, without a miss. He even stayed to nominate state superintendent of schools, generally a consolation prize that the convention was left to choose without let or hindrance. I was reporting the convention, making a running story as the events unfolded. When the last nomination was made and Leland's candidate for state superintendent was nominated, not even one-fourth—perhaps not one-fifth—of the delegates were there. But Leland was there. The other reporters were gone. I was there. After the convention adjourned, he stopped for a moment or two to console or comfort a few of his more intimate defeated followers. He saw me sitting alone at the reporters' desk when he turned to leave the hall. It was absolutely empty. The janitor was locking the doors. Leland and I walked out together. And so down the primrose path of politics we strolled to the end. I gave my heart to a man who would stay in the game, protect his ante, and play his cards, even after he had lost his major stake. I was a Leland man after that.

Cy Leland was a little, gray-brown, hickory nut of a man, five feet six, with graying hair, ruddy brown skin, and brown chin whiskers and mustache neatly trimmed, always meticulously dressed, always stingy of language, monosyllabic, who never loafed, rarely laughed except with his eyes, walked straight along some invisible crack, loved the mystery with which he surrounded his movements, was given to Indian feints, sorties, and ambushes, liked to fool his enemies almost as much as he loved to best them, and had an elephant's memory, of which more later.

It was late in the spring of 1892 that I began to be more than vaguely conscious that Sallie Lindsay was something more than an awfully nice girl. Our letters had become more than fortnightly, and probably in her circle over in Kansas City, Kansas, I was known as Sallie Lindsay's new beau. Wishing to show off, I invited her and a group of her girl friends to lunch at the Midland one day. Before the luncheon I consulted Willie, the head-waiter, told him that I could not afford to go more than seventy-five cents a head for those girls; and we picked out what we thought was an elegant luncheon—elegant in its simplicity. It was built around chicken gelatin, and Willie without extra charge got me a private dining room on the mezzanine floor. He dropped in himself to take the order, when the girls came in. I can still remember the show-off flourish with which I looked down the card most casually, and repeated the menu that Willie and I had so carefully decided upon. Willie, for the tip which he knew was coming, put on a few frills and trimmings. It was really something in the way of a luncheon. When Sallie told me the next time we met that I had knocked the girls cold and stiff, I had to confess the truth that Willie had coached me. I am good as a show-off up to a point, after which I always have to laugh.

It was not long after that that Sallie and I had our first and really only tragic experience. We were scheduled by letter to meet at the gathering of the Western Artists and Authors at the Midland at Kansas City, late in the spring. The Western Artists and Authors Society was just what its name would indicate—a lot of us who were trying to be artists and authors, maybe a hundred from Kansas, Missouri, and possibly Iowa and Nebraska —newspaper poets, newspaper artists, painters of china dishes, writers of unplayed plays, but none the less striving nobly and hoping wistfully to rise. I put on my brand-new gray suit with the gray hat which the tailor had made of the suit material. As I swung into the Midland Hotel that morning of the meeting, I ran into Albert Bigelow Paine, my poet friend from Fort Scott, a few years older than I, and Eugene Ware, his friend, whom I was proud to know. Ware was a Civil War veteran, and that was

1892—twenty-seven years after the war. He was gray, but his ardor was uncooled. He was writing verse copied all over the country, perhaps the only authentic author at our Midwest gathering. Passing the door of the bar, he suggested a drink, and I, to show my sophistication, took a sloe gin rickey. The other two took highballs. Then after ten minutes or so, as we stood at a table near the bar, Paine ordered a round. Again to show my worldly wisdom, I ordered what I called a "calico drink," a "pousse café," a long, thin, striped drink with a streak of vermouth, a streak of port, a streak of sherry and a streak of green mint; a pretty little drink with some kind of fuzz on top of it, sprinkled with powdered nutmeg. What they took, I do not remember. Then as the talk was good for that first half hour, I bought a round of drinks and counted the cost like a Scotchman. I remember, to save myself, I took beer. And we lingered over that round, tearing the world apart and gluing it to suit ourselves. I had no sense of having too much under my belt. I felt good as I always did. I was going to see Sallie Lindsay, and that made me feel a lot better. I did not realize that I was unnaturally exuberant, and maybe I was not. Maybe the liquor had not caught up with my naturally high spirits yet. Anyway, through the lobby we went, arm in arm, Paine and Ware on either side of me. We stepped gayly into the elevator and came out in the mezzanine parlor of the Midland, where the Western Artists and Authors had assembled in chairs well down the spacious rooms. I had about twenty feet of clear space to go and, feeling good, did an old trick that I had learned from a circus clown in my boyhood: I twirled my hat—my prize gray hat that matched my new gray suit—high in the air and poked my head into it as it came down. This I did twice, and the Western Artists and Authors applauded. It was a neat stunt, and I was proud of myself. I sought out Sallie with my eyes and rushed over to see her. She was cool. When I sat down, she moved. I was amazed and bewildered. I could not imagine what had happened. After the session I tried to take her to the dinner, called a banquet, which was part of the Western Artists and Authors program. She eluded me. I pressed. She refused me. I was paralyzed. At the end of the dinner I followed her and asked if I might take her home. She probably maneuvered so that we were out of earshot of the others and said:

"Now listen, Mr. Will White! I am not going home with a man in your condition!"

The liquor, whatever it did to me, had had two or three hours and a big dinner to tromp it down. I was cold sober and I gasped at the words "in your condition," realizing quickly that the exuberance of my entrance and maybe idiocy of my stunt might have deceived her. Also I realized that maybe I was just a bit high. She saw my questioning astonishment and went on:

"If you are ever going to see me again, we must understand each other."

There was no love light in her eyes, but cold, implacable reason, as she went on:

"Unless you are willing to quit, absolutely stop, drinking, let's understand it now and quit."

Whereupon she turned and went down the stairs with the elderly woman who was taking her home, with the whole universe sinking below the pit of my stomach. I stood there an instant; watched her at the turn of the stairs. She did not look back. I followed her quickly from the mezzanine floor to the lobby, followed her to the carriage. As she got in, I said:

"All right, all right!"

She smiled, and the world went on rolling again.

That must have been in late May, for I took a night train from Kansas City to a convention and did not get back to Topeka for three or four days. Somewhere I must have written her a letter trying to square myself, and somewhere I must have had an answer that was good. But after all, no words of pledged affection had passed between us. We were just "going together," rather more than casually but not quite anything else.

In early June, out in western Kansas, three conventions came. I left home Saturday night with my mail unread. The Journal office sent me all the Kansas papers to read, as a help with my Kansas column. My letter mail and the papers were piled in a corner in the room I called my library, and my mother treated them as holy objects, never daring to touch them. There was a two weeks' pile when I came home, and on Sunday sat down and began to go through the letters and papers. There I found two unanswered letters from Sallie Lindsay, one telling me that she might have to go to the hospital for a major operation, the other written in the hospital a few hours before her operation. It was a sweet, gentle goodbye, and the thing grabbed my heart. It was five days old. Without waiting for the meal that was on the table, I hurried to the railroad station, went to Kansas City and, thence to the hospital, where I was allowed to stand for a moment and smile, at the door of her room. And she smiled back.

God was in His heaven, all was right with the world. I hurried back to Topeka and returned at a date when the nurse said I might see her. The nurse suspected something that might disturb or arouse her patient. It was a week before they would let me call, and during that week the seed of a great passion that was in my heart grew and blossomed, rooted and consumed my life, and made it part of something fine, something different, something I think divine.

I mooned around the bookstores of Topeka, trying to find a book to take to her. I finally bought four books with blue bindings and silver lettering, French short stories. I don't know how or when I had read them;

but I knew what they were, and knew they were light and lovely and gay and wise. So, when the day came that I could visit her, armed with those four books, I hurried to Kansas City, went straight to the hospital, found her waiting for me with my telegram on her bed; she smiled as I went in, and I kneeled and kissed her, and it was all over. I read the stories to her for a little while, and the nurse, when I came again, said she kept them under her pillow. And so, August 13, 1892, we began our long life's happy journey.

I do not know how it happened. Perhaps she was telling the very truth when she said:

"You were ripe for some girl. I only had to spread my apron and shake the tree, and you fell into it."

CHAPTER XXXII

I Change Jobs Overnight

In 1892 the Kansas Populists for some reason delayed their state convention to nominate state officers until August, and held it at Wichita. The date, nearly three months after the Republicans had put out their state ticket, made the Populist convention big news for the Kansas City Journal, and indeed for all of the Kansas papers. The question of fusion with the Democrats was to be settled. The convention was to nominate or refuse to nominate, as it chose, the Democratic Presidential electors who were to vote for Grover Cleveland.

But Cleveland was no Populist. He loathed and publicly spat upon the whole fiat money and reform programs of the Populists. The Democrats and the Populists had nothing in common except the desire to beat the Republicans. But the fusion was not a fact accomplished when the convention met, and much significance was attached to the Populists' nominee for governor. The Democrats had not put out a state ticket. The left-wing Populists had a candidate whose name would be an offense to the Democrats, a rabid advocate of fiat money and social reform. The right-wing candidate would not hold even the Populist vote, though he might get the Democrats'. It was a dramatic convention. After balloting all day on governor they adjourned until night. Of course reporters were there from all the region, from as far east as Chicago and St. Louis. The other Kansas City and Topeka papers were represented by men with whom I had been working for three or four months. The Journal had sent as my associate one of Mr. Gleed's friends, Tom Norton, who was studying law in Gleed's office, after having edited the Newton Republican as I had edited the Eldorado Republican for the owners. Apparently Mr. Gleed regarded the convention as most important, for he asked Tom and me to do a good job and not to spare the wire if we needed it. The night session was our big second act. It was in the Toler Opera House, a big barn of a place that was crowded from pit to dome when the chairman's gavel clicked. I went back of the stage, just before the convention opened, and there I ran into Jerry Simpson, leaning against the wall and whittling. He looked up from his whittling, caught my eye with his shrewd Yankee quizzical glance, and said:

"Well, mister, she's settled."

Like a trout, I leaped at the bait. To my question he replied:

"It will happen after the third ballot tonight. We are going to give the old rabble-rouser his chance"—meaning the militant, anti-fusion Populist—"and then we are going to nominate Lewelling."

Lewelling was in the balloting, but far down the list. He was a Populist state senator from Wichita. Simpson's news floored me for a minute. I knew that he was a man of few words. He was honest. He was my friend and would not deceive me. Moreover, he was one of less than half a dozen leaders who would have decided upon the way to break the deadlock.

I asked: "Am I safe to use it? I mean, to begin filing now Lewelling's biography and an interview with you, telling how and why it happened. I can wire in the lead the moment the nomination is made, and have the story out for the first edition."

Jerry whittled for a minute a long, curving sliver, and said: "All right!"

Then he told me the story of the combination that released the deadlock. I hurried to Tom, told him my news, then rushed to the telegraph office while Tom stayed in the convention and filed, first, the story of the combination; second, the biography of Lewelling, who was an utterly unknown man, and finally some comment on the significance of the combination and the nomination of Lewelling. It was then nearly nine o'clock. Two ballots had been taken, but I had filed enough to hold the wire, the only Western Union night wire into Kansas City, while the ballot slowly ground along. Then I went back to the hall.

Tom Norton had his running account of the ballot ready, and he left the reporters' desk and went to the Western Union office to file it ahead of my background story. I continued the story of the ballot where Tom left off, and when finally, just before ten o'clock, Lewelling was nominated, I had the story of the ballot finished and a short, possibly fifty-word, lead concerning the result of the final ballot. I filed that while the man at the wire was still on our stuff. Tom and I were happy, for we had caught the first edition of the morning Journal, and by the time our story, a matter of fifteen hundred words, was cleared from the wire, it was too late for our rivals. They knew we had beaten them. We were smug and wrapped the mantle of our couch about us and lay down to pleasant dreams.

The next morning Tom and I and the other newspaper correspondents took the morning train at Wichita, eager to get to the main line at Newton and see our story. No newspaperman is so casehardened that he does not like to read his own stories in print. At Newton we bought the copies of the Journal. So did our rivals. Quickly we glanced at the first page. The story was not there. Up and down the passenger coach, half a dozen other reporters were opening to the second page, glancing quickly at the third, the fourth, and the fifth for editorial and departmental pages. We all turned to the seventh and eighth—no story. Finally, on the tenth or twelfth page, tucked in with the markets, we found our story mauled down to six or seven hundred words, hidden and, we felt, deliberately played down. Whereupon our rivals and contemporary reporters hooted, jeered, mocked, and Tom and I set our jaws. We rode eastward from Newton to Emporia, through Topeka, and on to Kansas City—he and I getting madder and madder, nursing our wrongs. At Lawrence we bought the evening Star, with a long story of Lewelling's victory and how it came about—the story that we had written nearly twenty-four hours earlier. We went from the train right to the Journal office. It was then around seven o'clock. We knew the telegraph editor would be on his job. We walked into his office, turned the latch on his door, and began on him. Each of us had a fairly good livery stable vocabulary. We poured it on him; dared him to fight; promised that he could have either one of us, and that the other would get out of the room. We bent over his desk jawing him, roughing his hair, slapping his jaws, but there was no fight in him. We left the room, hurried down to the business office, and then and there I quit my job, drew my pay, and hurried to Sallie Lindsay to tell her what I had done.

Tom took the evening train for Topeka to tell Charley Gleed he was through with reporting so far as it touched that city editor. Sallie Lindsay helped. She had just learned that Roswell Field, brother of Eugene Field, an editorial writer on the Star, was going to New York to work for the New York World. And the next morning I showed up in the Star office, found the man who had offered me a job a year before, told him my story, and particularized about our defiance of the telegraph editor, who was unpopular in newspaper circles in town. By ten o'clock I had a job at twenty-five dollars a week, all that I was getting on the Journal and a good salary for 1892. I was to write what was known as minion editorials. That phrase meant gay editorials—stuff about literature, the stage, frivolous comment on unimportant events of froth and foam on the daily newspaper's editorial tide. In addition, I was supposed to turn in a serious editorial every day or two, write the Kansas notes, and also to mark over from the daily paper the material that went into the Weekly Star. It never occurred to me that it was a heavy assignment, and I was so happy to have a job and at the same time to have my full free say to that telegraph editor that I went back to Sallie Lindsay, rejoicing as a strong man to run a race. Also I wanted her to be proud of me; and she was.

My mother moved down to Kansas City, and my real life began as a working newspaperman on a first-class paper. The Kansas City Star, twelve years old in 1892, even then was rated one of the dozen best and most influential newspapers in the country. It was honest. Politically, it was independent. It was the daily expression of William R. Nelson, to the office sometimes "the Colonel" but generally "the Old Man," though he was barely in his fifties. He was a great hulking two-hundred-sixty-pounder, six feet tall, smooth-shaven, with a hard, dominating mouth and a mean jaw, high brow, and wonderful eyes, jade in color, which opened with wide frank cordiality or squinted like the lightning of Job. He became my idol. Although I saw him every day most casually, I did not work with him nor know him well for nearly a year; but he began at once to mold my life. Every man on the paper, from top to bottom—in the advertising department, the circulation department, the news department, the editorial room —was convinced of his own absolute freedom, his right to express himself unhampered save by the truth as he saw it. If I wrote nonsense the managing editor, Tommy Johnston, or the editor-in-chief under Nelson, Mr. Runyon, carefully explained why it was nonsense, and I had a right to talk back and defend myself. In a newspaper that is heaven. I wrote my head off, and from the men who chopped my copy—competent, free, honest editors—I learned every day much that helped me. I was seriously writing. I turned in verses once or twice a week. I was growing away from dialect rhymes. Sallie and I were reading the New England poets—Whittier, Aldrich, Lowell—and of course the verse I wrote was colored by their minds and manners. Poor stuff it was; but I was proud of it and in a year became a sort of office laureate, was called upon even by the Old Man to celebrate this or that gay and festal occasion, or funny local episode. I remember that on the birth of Kipling's first baby I wrote a rhyme that went the rounds of the United States, with the refrain:

> They are walking baby Kipling in the morning.

Rudyard himself, through a mutual friend, sent back some word of approval.

Now don't get an idea that the Old Man, Colonel Nelson—called Colonel just because he looked coloneliferous, without any reference to a war record —was no angel. His clay foot was Grover Cleveland, who could do no wrong. We who wrote the editorials—Alex Butts, who had owned the Emporia News just before I came to Emporia as a student, and Noble Prentis, a Civil War veteran who wrote like an angel and seemed to reincarnate Oliver Goldsmith, and I—all hated Grover Cleveland; and when Cleveland did something that required incense we took turns at swinging the incense pot and gagged behind the Old Man's back. Once when I had been there over a year Cleveland did something, Heaven knows what, that required heavy buttering and, in our disgust, we three decided to go the distance on the Old Man. Alex Butts, then in his late fifties, wrote an encomium of Cleveland, comparing him to Washington. The next time we had to write on bended knee about Cleveland, Noble Prentis compared him to Lincoln. And I in turn wrote a veiled editorial indicating that Cleveland had many Christlike qualities. When even that got by we felt better. By *reductio ad absurdum* we had purged our hearts of sin. The Old Man was mad and let it go at that. But, otherwise, we were happy. I was particularly happy because I agreed with the Old Man about the protective tariff, and he turned me loose to say my say.

CHAPTER XXXIII

Here Comes the Bride

I WAS TWENTY-FOUR when I walked into the Star and talked Tommy Johnston, the managing editor, out of this job. About all I had to commend me was boundless energy, a facile style, a love of books, music, and the theater, a liking for good food and plenty of it, and a competent knowledge of Kansas politics—brought up to the minute by my experience that summer with the conventions. Politics was my meat and drink. So I wrote Kansas politics. The other two editorial writers—Butts and Prentis—were from Kansas, and the Star, printed in Missouri but really for Kansas circulation in those days, was top-heavy with Kansas affairs. It was a Kansas daily newspaper, the leading Kansas daily. And living in Kansas City, somewhat aloof from the contemporary battle, I had better standing in Kansas on the editorial page of the Star than I had had when I lived in Topeka and loafed at the Copeland Hotel, the political arena of the state's Republican politics. When I visited Topeka, or any considerable Kansas town, as an editorial writer on the Star and the author of its Kansas notes, I was treated with the royal acclaim of a visiting statesman.

But my vanity was cloying fast. I had pretty nearly enough of the sense of political distinction. I went to Kansas fairly often, but I did not realize the change that was coming into Kansas politics. George R. Peck, who had been the Kansas vicegerent of the god of things as they are in Kansas politics, with whom all the privilege-seeking corporations pooled their political corruption funds, was moving his office to the Santa Fe general offices in Chicago, where he would take charge of the region along the Santa Fe Railroad from Illinois through Missouri, Kansas, Colorado, and New Mexico to Albuquerque. Beyond that point the general counsel of the Santa Fe at Los Angeles controlled politics for the Santa Fe in California and Arizona. But in Kansas the other railroads, with Peck gone, were setting up rival satraps. M. A. Low, of the Rock Island, represented Rock Island territory. Major Richards of Fort Scott and Balie Waggener of Atchison controlled politics along the Missouri Pacific lines. Loomis, the attorney for the Union Pacific, directed Union Pacific political activities in Kansas. These rival railroad attorneys clashed. They sometimes battled in a convention to control the nomination of a governor, or fought with one another for the right to name a United States Senator. Of course, it made scandal. In the Star we knew what was going on at Topeka. The same thing was going on at Jefferson City, the capital of Missouri. The railroad lobbyists, who were also attorneys, were directed in each state by their general counsel somewhere outside the state. It was the twilight of the gods for the railroads. Competition and skulduggery in rate-making were reflected in corruption and shenanigans in state politics, all directed from railroad offices—sometimes in St. Louis, sometimes in Omaha or Chicago, often in Wall Street. The day of competition in American industry was doomed to close because it was clumsy, scandalous, and indecent. Yet when I went to Topeka, as I often did, to cast an appraising eye for the Star over the political landscape, I did not realize what was happening at the heart of things political and economic. I could not say that within another decade this flagrant flouting of democracy would end partly in the rise of outraged public opinion, expressed in cramping legislation, and partly in the natural coalition and amalgamation of capital which had sense enough intuitively to stop the waste and downright wickedness that came from the political pulling and hauling of the railroads in the various state capitals.

Wealth in those early nineties, when the Populists were clamoring across the land, was learning that the fear of the Lord was the beginning of wisdom. So the forces of economic privilege were amalgamating the great banking houses, were consolidating ownership of the bickering railroads in a pool of railroad capital, while the steel trust was being welded under Carnegie, oil was flowing into one vast tank under Rockefeller, the copper interests were forming interrelated corporations. The day of the trusts was dawning.

Kansas politics was reflecting the iridescent colors of the dawn. I saw the gorgeous picture. I wrote about it. But I had no idea of its meaning, of its real significance, and for those who were aware of some vague shadow of the truth, men like Jerry Simpson, Ignatius Donnelly, Thorstein Veblen and Edward W. Bemis, a Chicago economist who was to come to Kansas State Agricultural College—for all those astrologists and seers who were trying to give some account of the forces that were moving the world, I had the deepest scorn. It seemed to me then that honesty and good government— that is to say, tax-saving, the purification of politics and personal integrity— were enough to save the world. I fancy Colonel Nelson had somewhat the same idea, except that he held in profane contempt those men around him and near him who were assembling fortunes by what he regarded as shady methods. At the head of the list he would have put tariff beneficiaries, then men who watered public utilities stocks, then those who fostered political corruption for the sake of political privilege; but neither he nor any of us around the paper in those days had any idea of the deeper currents of life that were shaping events and directing the destiny of our country. It was enough for the Old Man on the Star to Goddam the protective tariff, suspect the gas company, look at the street railway company and the light company with a baleful eye, trust in God and Grover Cleveland. The rest of us around the office—including Republicans like Butts, Prentis, Phillips, the telegraph editor, and Tommy Johnston, the managing editor—were willing to draw our salaries, hate old Cleveland, regret the frigid ineptitude of Benjamin Harrison, hoot at the Populists, and sputter for the relief of our frustrated spirits. A perfect example of our attitude in those days was revealed by Fred Vandegrift, then city editor, my roommate the year before. One afternoon when the national ball games were closing in climax and an important local story was gathering on the horizon, the telephones from all over town began piling up on his desk. We had no central telephone system in our office then. He was trying to edit the big local story. The telephone bells jangled and jangled. Finally he got up, red-faced in wrath, went to the basement, came back with a hatchet and chopped off all the telephone wires that connected with the office, and went on calmly with his work. All of us on the Star were using that hatchet more or less to shut out the warning voices that were clamoring to know the truth or to tell it to us. Old Van at the city desk might well have been the god of our machine.

But my chief source of education and delight was Sallie Lindsay. Together we saw the pageant of the theater. Every Saturday afternoon we went to a matinee. I managed either to wangle complimentary tickets or to raise the necessary cash. And we saw the best of the contemporary American theater in Kansas City in the early nineties. For the New York stage in that day was only the preview of "the road." The stars and the better grade of stock companies generally opened in New York, played a short season, and left on tour, spending a week in larger cities and at least a week end, Thursday, Friday, and Saturday, in smaller cities like Kansas City. And the stage weaned me from politics for a time.

Together we heard our first symphony orchestra, conducted by Walter Damrosch. It was to both of us a momentous experience. It was as far above Pat Gilmore's band, which had set my spirit aquiver, as Pat Gilmore's band was above the Eldorado silver cornet band. That night with Damrosch, I heard for the first time Wagner with a full-throated orchestra. And Sallie and I nearly squeezed our hands off with delight as we listened. We read books together, the novels of the day, and browsed in bookstores at odd times before and after Saturday matinees. She lived over in Kansas City,

Kansas, and was not teaching school that year, 1892, because she was recovering from the operation which had devastated her.

I remember with what trepidation I brought Sallie Lindsay to see my mother, and how my mother and I spruced up the house and did everything we could to put our best foot forward. We had a three-story house in a long row, two rooms on each floor—kitchen and dining room in the basement, parlor and back parlor on the first floor, two bedrooms on the second floor. In the parlor we had furniture of great pride which my father and mother had bought for the new Eldorado house in 1878, heavy walnut, Victorian, with fringed lambrequins and heavy curtains at the windows, marble-top tables, pimpled all over with jigsaw ornamentations, stuffed chairs and a sofa to match, with a patent rocker of the same design, and a body Brussels carpet that had been cut and recut. We were proud of the room, and its whatnot in the corner adorned with shelves and oddments. We had under a glass in a velvet-lined box a wax representation of an angel on a rock clinging to a flowered cross. But we kept that hidden. I think it was my fear of its good taste. Into the back parlor we had moved my bookcases, two of them made from oak of the tables in the old dining room at the hotel. I also had there some kind of desk. This I remember clearly: When I began to talk about bringing Sallie Lindsay over for dinner, my mother became all fluttered about a plain, black walnut rocking chair with the simplest lines, almost crude. And she began hunting downtown for a covering, and upholstered it herself and wrapped it so heavily that it was hard for anyone to squeeze into it. This was done for Sallie Lindsay. It was the only piece of furniture that my father had brought from his home in Ohio. His mother, Fear Perry, had had it at her marriage in Lee, Massachusetts, to my grandfather, John White. My mother liked to believe that his mother, Martha Keith, had rocked him in that old chair as a child during the Revolution. Certainly Fear Perry had used it. My father and Mary Hatten had rocked me in it, and I think my mother, with that feminine instinct for breeding which makes a woman yearn in the spring to set a hen, had some designs on Sallie Lindsay and her son with that old walnut chair. We have it still in an honored place in our house, and my mother's son's son's wife may use it for her child some day. Anyway, I watched the little byplay of my mother fussing with that chair. I tried to dissuade her, but she was set on it; and, to avoid a spat, I let her have her hour of romance, lining the nest, even if the lining made the nest uninhabitable.

Of course my mother was jealous of Sallie Lindsay. She had even looked with a baleful eye on Alice Murdock, the little cripple whom I had grown up with as a sister. Any girl at whom I looked twice ruffled her feathers. But she tried to be sweet about Sallie Lindsay, knowing probably that I had come into the zone when men married. So she scrubbed, dusted, swept, burnished and pushed the furniture around for days before the visit, and I believe she was happy. Her indomitable energy was finding an outlet for her inner fear, and maybe unconscious rage, at losing the apple of her eye, the one thing she had to show for a dream of romance that was always a bit drab and had not quite come true. She accepted the inevitable probably, but with reservations. She was determined in her heart to show Sallie Lindsay the schoolteacher that she, Mary Hatten the schoolteacher, was "folks," somebody—the wife of Dr. Allen White who died mayor of Eldorado. So when Sallie Lindsay crossed her threshold, my mother was determined that this young lady should meet a paragon of Yankee housekeeping. Above all, she wanted to flaunt her cooking.

So I bought a thick beefsteak. We had soup with brown barley in it made from the recipe which I had brought back from the Midland Hotel. It was our show piece. Sallie, who was only twenty-one, was shy, and my mother and I were most circumspect. It was a trying but happy hour, I think, for all of us.

CHAPTER XXXIV

Behold the Bridegroom Cometh Forth

IN THE STAR OFFICE, for the first time in my life, I was learning practical ethics. For the Star was an honest newspaper. I saw it from the inside. After I had been in the office five or six months, I came in almost daily contact with Colonel Nelson, who was the directing force of the paper. I never saw his handwriting more than two or three times, and then only a dozen words. He wrote nothing for the paper. We men around the office understood he could not write, could not put ten words together on paper. Yet he bought writing talent and directed it. After I had been there six months or so, he called me into his office one day and asked:

"Billie, what do you know about gas?"

I told him gayly that I knew absolutely nothing.

"Well, by God, you are the man I am looking for. You have a virgin mind. I have an idea—maybe I am wrong—that this town is entitled to dollar gas." The price then was much higher. "I'll tell you what I wish you would do: read up on gas. Here's a lot of stuff."

He handed me some publications of various associations and researchers, mostly loaded heavily in favor of the gas companies.

"Read this, and then go down and look over the gas plant and see how they make it and where the stuff comes from, and see if you can get some kind of a squint at the cost of the stuff in the storage tanks and delivered at the outlets. Don't write anything about it for three or four weeks, and then come back and talk to me."

When I had learned all I could of gas, I went in and talked to him. He said:

"All right! Now write a local story—write a series of articles about gas in Kansas City, and we will see where we get. Don't editorialize about it. You don't know enough yet. I don't either."

So we studied gas again. And I wrote my stories. They did not amount to much, but they set folks talking; and from then on for five years the Star kept hammering away for dollar gas. It made no difference that Colonel Nelson's friends owned the gas stock. It made no difference that the bankers who were financing the gas company were his dear friends. He was absolutely incorruptible on his social side, and one of the few publishers I have ever known who did not yield to the lure of the country club. He was making money in real estate as well as with the Star. He bought tracts of farm land, laid them out in subdivisions, walled off in stone from rock picked up on the premises, large plats, acre plats, planted the stone walls to honeysuckles, constructed six- or seven-room houses beautifully designed, built by the day and not by the contract, with no skimping and jerry-carpentering, and sold them at a decent profit. He started a love of beauty in Kansas City suburbs.

On another occasion he called me into his office and assigned me to write an article about a series of slums called the McClure flats—terrible places. I made a horror story which pleased the Colonel, though his friends—the owners of the slum property—were boiling-hot. The hotter they got, the more he pounded on his desk, and God-damned them around and made them ashamed of themselves. The tenements were either improved or torn down to be replaced by better buildings. He tackled the corrupt elections that were conducted by the local Democratic city machine, and gave me the job of bedeviling a poor election crook named Pinky Blitz, whom we sent to the penitentiary later; and we pounded a county officer named Owsley rather mercilessly for what we felt was his responsibility in the election corruption. This, in face of the fact that the Colonel was supporting Grover Cleveland almost abjectly. He had no more use for corrupt Democrats than he had for corrupt Republicans. He was absolutely independent politically, and in every other way I knew. My admiration for him rose, and I tried to make his ways my ways. I felt that all the men in the office swore by him. It was one of the few newspaper offices I have known where the boss and owner was actually respected.

One spring we conducted a mayoralty campaign, and not long afterward the victorious opposition candidate for Mayor, whom we had treated rather roughly, came stomping into the office. The Colonel's room and the rooms occupied by the editorial writers were on the second floor. My room was directly opposite the Colonel's. The floor was reached by a grand stairway sweeping upward out of the lobby on the first floor and branching north and south—left and right—into the telegraph room and the editorial offices. I saw the double-breasted, Prince Albert coat of the aggrieved statesman sweeping past my door and saw Tommy Johnston, the managing editor, and Ralph Stout, the city editor, follow the raging people's tribune into the Colonel's office. I was writing with my face to the door. I heard the loud voices and in a minute, maybe two, I heard that unmistak-

238

able thud of fist on flesh and looked up to see the Colonel lying on his back and the mayor bending over him. Phillips, the telegraph editor, who chewed gum in his front teeth and wore a dark green celluloid shade over his eyes, came mousing out of the telegraph room as I looked up. He too had heard the voices and identified the swat. In an instant Stout and Johnson, both good-sized six-footers, had hold of the assailant. While the Old Man was getting up, they rushed the mayor out of the room and into the hallway, where they kicked his feet out from under him. Phillips grabbed a leg. I grabbed a leg. Johnston and Stout took an arm each, and we literally threw the mayor down the first flight of that grand staircase to the landing. I was located so that I was the first man to reach him after he fell. As he got up, I started to rush him. He pulled a revolver from under his Prince Albert coat and stuck it in my face. It was the largest, most terrible-looking circular aperture I ever beheld. His eyes were glaring. I put my hand over the banister, and God knows why I said it, but I cried, half in hysteria and half because it was funny:

"Excuse me!"

I vaulted over the stairs and landed on a circular desk below where a white-haired Danish boy named Siested, brother of the business manager, was working on a row of circulation figures. He did not know of the row above, and as I landed on his papers he nearly passed out from fright. This also was a funny thing: as I went over the banister I saw down in the newsroom a thing that greatly heartened me. Old Campbell, the stockyards reporter, with one arm resting on the top of a tall desk, had a dead bead on the mayor and a mean glint in his hard old eye. I do not know whether the mayor saw that bead or not, but as I landed the mayor began to walk slowly down the grand staircase to the first floor with his pistol drawn and cocked, bellowing something. As he made his exit all hands began telling the story of the assault. It was in time for the first edition, and we had it on the streets in no time. The Colonel was proud to omit no detail.

At another time, another politician brought a roll of greenbacks up to Tommy Johnston's office and tried to buy him. Some say it was five hundred dollars, some say it was five thousand. I never knew. Anyway, Tommy let the man tell his story with his package of bills in his hand, then let him put the bills on his desk. Very politely, not lifting his voice, with quiet, meticulous courtesy, Tommy broke the band and threw the bills out of the window, smiling.

"I beg your pardon. I fear we can't do it."

The people on the street had a grand time grabbing for those bills, while the statesman ran madly down the stairs and across the lobby into the street, trying to rescue his spoils.

Generally speaking, our cloistered lives on the Star were calm, and we were happy. I mingled with the reporters downstairs because they were my age, but I was deeply fond of the older men I worked with. They read my copy and cut it wisely. They taught me much about editorializing. They were men of books, all self-educated—Mr. Runyon, the editor-in-chief, was the only college man in the lot—but I never mingled with a more cultivated group. Butts, the senior editorial writer, a bachelor in his sixties, who loved formal society, was heartbroken when he found that I was engaged to a Kansas City schoolteacher. He wanted me to get out into Kansas City society, and he said:

"Billie, it's just as easy to love a girl with a million as it is a schoolteacher!"

There was real heartbreak in his protest. But when I brought the schoolteacher to the office and old Butts met her, he sighed and gave up! And Tommy Johnston, who had an eye for skirts, laughed at Alex and paid me some compliment about luck and taste, while Prentis, who always reminded me of Goldsmith, put his arm around my shoulder when Sallie had gone, and told me to stick to her and not let Butts seduce me with the fleshpots.

Prentis loved James G. Blaine as all Union veterans of the Civil War loved him, though Blaine had never been a soldier. Prentis followed him with an abject devotion. When Blaine died, Tommy Johnston came in gently and said:

"Mr. Prentis, will you give us something for the telegraph page about Blaine, and then maybe an editorial?"

That was in the afternoon. For three hours Noble sat writing that biography of Blaine. Then he straightened up with a sigh and wrote the editorial obituary, a beautiful tribute. When he had finished, he straightened up again, and I remember seeing his face begin to twitch. He buried his face in his arms on his desk and began to sob and sob, shaking his pudgy little body with his racking grief, and coming up in two or three or four minutes swearing like a pirate at his weakness. He did not speak to me, but toddled over, took his hat and coat from the hook behind the door, and shuffled down the hall, down the stairs into the street, and trudged homeward— plodding under the burden of his grief.

CHAPTER XXXV

Wedding Bells

VERNON KELLOGG came down to stay with me the night before the wedding, which was April 27, 1893; and he went over to the Lindsays with my mother and me. He was shocked to know that I had not bought roses for the bride, and so we stopped in at the florist's and bought a dozen white rosebuds. He was my only guest. I had invited Ewing Herbert, but he failed me. Lew Schmucker was out on his railway run. Funston was in Alaska, botanizing for the government.

Ours was not a formal wedding. Kellogg was not my best man. Sallie's friends, perhaps a dozen or fifteen, gathered in the little parlor of an eight-room frame house at 330 Waverly in Kansas City, Kansas. Kellogg's step-uncle, the Reverend Charles B. Mitchell, a fashionable Methodist preacher over in Kansas City, whom Kellogg had persuaded to come and take the five dollars that I could afford to pay the preacher, performed the ceremony. Sallie, the eldest of ten children, had risen at dawn, scrubbed and bathed the three little ones, helped her mother with the breakfast dishes, seen that her four brothers were dressed in their Sunday best, helped her father with his necktie, and made herself useful that morning before her girl friends of the neighborhood came to dress her in a simple gown. Then we all sat to a lap breakfast, and we two—in a blaze of splendor—went away to the station in a hack which cost a dollar and a half, quite a hole in our gross savings. But it was the only hack that drew up in front of the Lindsay house that morning. The neighbors were proud of it. Hacks were no casual adornment of the landscape on Waverly Avenue.

My chief anxiety was quieted at that high hour, for my mother behaved beautifully. I was afraid she would cry—she did easily under emotion. And the Lindsays were splendid. I was taking away a wage earner, for Sally had taught since she was sixteen and, with her older brothers, had turned in her wages to the family fund. Her father was superintendent of the yards at Fowler's packing house, and the family had the job as sexton at the cemetery near by. The frame house, one in a row on Waverly Avenue, was a neat, scrupulously clean home where every little stroke, every little picture on the wall, every article of furniture represented loving planning, careful arrangement, affectionate savings. The Lindsays were Kentuckians out of Virginia in the early nineteenth century. Sallie's father had been a rebel soldier in the Civil War; he had ridden with Morgan in the Ohio raid and was one of Jeff Davis' bodyguards until an hour before Davis surrendered. Then Captain Lindsay rode away, leaving the wagonload of Confederate gold and silver which was divided later among the other guards as the Federal troops drew near. Money meant nothing to him. He was a gentle soul, blue-eyed, fair-haired, with a kindly face, a soft voice, and evidence of good breeding in every line of his body. Mrs. Lindsay, small, black-eyed, straight-haired, of olive complexion, was a throbbing dynamo of energy, with a strong, earnest and eager face; and she bore her ten children and kept the family together with a managerial talent which women often develop when the need of it comes, that surpasses understanding. I remember that when Sallie and I entered the mood where we thought we ought to be looking for a house, and were setting the date for our wedding, she told me quite firmly that I should talk to her father. So I went down to the stockyards, and he and I had probably the most embarrassed moment of our lives. I came headlong into the subject of our marriage, and of course he was expecting me to talk about it. I had memorized my opening remarks. We stood in the stock pens with our feet on the rails, looking at a drove of hogs passing through, and I spoke my piece.

He spat desperately into the pen, turned his wide, sweet blue eyes on me that were watering, and cried: "God 'lmighty, man, God 'lmighty!" That was as far as he could get for a moment. Then he added desperately: "I don't know about these things. Why don't you go and talk to her ma!"

That ordeal was over, and we had a good talk about hogs, and the run of the market, and the hard times that were coming on us in that terrible day of depression, and finally shook hands and parted. When I went to Sallie's mother, the next time I called on Waverly Avenue, she took a practical view of it. I told her how much money I was making, that my mother had a little income from our rentals in Eldorado, that we could not afford a separate household. This naturally but also obviously bothered her a bit, and she said:

"Well, if you must, you must. Sallie generally has her way."

In Mrs. Lindsay's eyes I was not much of a match for her beautiful daughter, who had had many better prospects. After looking at me for a second, she laughed gayly and said:

"Well, Mr. White, I always told Sallie she would go through the woods and pick up a crooked stick."

And so I laughed. We called Sallie, and were very happy for a moment together. Which episode defines the Lindsay family—mother and father. At the wedding Mrs. Lindsay was so busy that she had no time for tears. Only my mother and Mr. Lindsay were in danger of spilling.

It was nearly noon when Sallie Lindsay and I stood on the wooden platform of the old Kansas City Union Depot waiting to take Train Number One to Santa Fe. After a bright sunrise, it had clouded up in midmorning. We were quite alone—we had forbidden our families to come to the station —she in a modest tailored outfit and I in my best Sunday suit, when three old bachelors from the Star office appeared: Alex Butts, the chief editorial writer, Tommy Johnston, the managing editor, and Ralph Stout, city editor. They brought with them as a wedding gift a brown alligator traveling bag, quite scrumptious. And as they came toward us under the trainshed the sun suddenly burst out of the clouds, and they formed a little ring around us and sang, "Happy Is the Bride That the Sun Shines on," in high glee. And so we went away, waving to our friends in the trainshed, on a journey whereon we have truly lived happily ever after.

The train—Santa Fe Number One—rolled out of Kansas City at midday of April 27 with the buds a little more than green-brown on the elm trees, with the bluestem staining the hills and pastures of eastern Kansas, with the wheat finger-high and the alfalfa a deep, lovely green, the meadow larks all singing on the barbed-wire fences, and the first Johnny-jump-ups showing on the north banks of the railroad cuts. At Emporia, my friend, and classmate, Dale Plumb, son of the late Senator, brought our wedding present—some books—to the train, and at Florence we stopped at the Harvey House for dinner at twilight. The Harvey Houses in that day, and for thirty years after, were famous for their food. They were Santa Fe railroad eating places of great distinction. That evening they passed great platters of meat, beef, spring lamb, and roast pork. I took the lamb, being rather sophisticated with my Midland Hotel palate, and Sallie reached for beef, a conventional pink-sliced roast.

I cried: "No, try this lamb. You'll find it gorgeous with the mint sauce." As it was.

"No, thank you, I don't eat lamb. I never eat lamb," said Sallie in her gustatory simplicity.

I turned and looked at her with amazement, shaded perhaps, but just a glint of disappointment.

"You don't eat lamb?"

"No, no, I don't care for lamb."

It was a trying moment—do or dare, then or never. I knew the kind that "never eat lamb." With rare presence of mind, taking our life's happiness in hand, I answered as sweetly as I could, "Oh, yes, you do, yes, you do, dear!" and helped her to the lamb.

And so on the 27th of April, for forty-nine long and lovely years, we have had lamb on our dinner table, to celebrate that triumph of mind over matter.

Of course we were riding on railroad passes. We were in the privileged class. I had made it my business, even on the Lawrence Journal, to know the passenger agent and the advertising manager of the Santa Fe. When they heard I was to be married, they wrote asking where we would like to go on a wedding trip, and sent us passes to Santa Fe, New Mexico. More than that, the Santa Fe had an interest in a hotel called the Montezuma, at a mountain resort at Las Vegas where there were sulphur springs and a great barn of a hotel with roomy porches, nearly a quarter of a mile of them, which we walked like the deck of a ship. And they gave us rates at that hotel—I think ten dollars a week for two weeks for the two of us, with a room and board included—which we could afford. The Montezuma was in the New Mexican mountains. We hired a burro and walked over the hills. Sallie, still convalescing from her operation the summer before, rode. I was engineer and fireman to the burro. We drank, at least I drank, quantities of the terrible sulphur water, and other guests at the hotel sometimes invited us in their carriages, and we rode through the irrigated fields of that lovely region. But, best of all we enjoyed the table d'hôte meals. We acquired a waiter, by reason of modest tips, and he led us in the green pastures of that great menu, great even for breakfast where there were steaks and mackerel and bacon and eggs and ham and eggs, and—even as at the Midland—baked oysters, and a cornucopia of canned fruits and pancakes and waffles. The waiter's name was Louie, bless his memory, and may he rest in peace. Of course we were always a little late for breakfast, and we had to choose between a rare steak with mushroom sauce and a rare steak with tomato sauce. It was a great adventure, that morning choice. But most of the day was spent hunting the sunny angles of the porches for reading. We had brought a lot of books, and read by the hour; or at least Sallie read to me, for she read beautifully. And I fingered out, on the hotel parlor piano, the popular melodies of the day. I can remember one, "Oh, Mollie, Oh," a melody which I traced first in three fingers, harmonized, and got pretty well in hand to my delight and Sallie's pride; for we both were easy to divert and amuse—we still are—and the Montezuma was a pleasure palace beyond compare.

No one ever was happier on a honeymoon. I wrote pieces, one or two a week, back to the Star about the country. I had never seen an irrigated country before, nor an ancient land where now and then a church, an old water mill or a deep irrigation ditch dated back two hundred years and more to the Spanish occupation. The Mexicans squatting against the sunny sides of buildings at noonday, sleeping with their sombreros pulled over their eyes, sometimes wrapped in gaudy serapes, sometimes just clad in blue overalls and shoes without socks, seemed to us like denizens of another day and time—ambassadors from another world. We were seeing foreign parts and were gravely impressed with our privileges.

After two weeks of that we went to Santa Fe, where my mother was visiting old Eldorado friends. We stayed with them in what was known then as the Bishop's Garden, the home of the archbishop made famous by Willa Cather's story. It was altogether lovely, an ancient adobe house surrounded by a formal garden which was bordered with high cottonwoods with shining shimmering leaves, and willows nearly a hundred years old. A mountain brook ran through it, with flowers neatly bedded along its banks, and the vegetable garden was bearing even in May. The low, one-story adobe palace of the governor of New Mexico, occupied by General Lew Wallace when he was writing "Ben Hur," and the great curio store where we saw for the first time Indian blankets, Indian jewelry, and Indian pottery and baskets, gave us a sense that we were far from home, from the middle western, middle-class America that we had known all our lives.

When we left for Manitou, Colorado, my mother went with us. It was the first honeymoon I ever knew where a mother-in-law tagged. But she was a strong-minded woman, had her own income, and paid her own way. At Manitou Sallie's little brother Milton, aged thirteen, who was frail and needed a summer's outing, joined us; and after a week or ten days, we went in June to Estes Park—a bridal party of four. There we rented for five dollars for the season a log cabin on the banks of the Big Thompson River, far up in the canyon a mile and a half from any human habitation, in the heart of what became, many years later, Rocky Mountain National Park. We bedded on spruce boughs, cooked over an open fire, and Milton furnished the fish. He was a wonderful fisherman. We picked red raspberries and wild strawberries and had watercress unlimited for salads, bought fresh beef from the ranch house when they butchered, and fared sumptuously if roughly.

I had been sending editorials back to the Star every day. But sometimes they arrived rather late, and were cold potatoes and could not be used. They were paying me my salary, which was generous of them; now they wrote to me to come back. But Sallie was getting so strong, and life was so beautiful, that I stayed on. Then one day, by wire, they fired me, and the next day the bank at Denver, which held all of our money, one hundred and twenty-five dollars, failed. That was a dark day. I got ready to go to Denver to look for a job, as a printer, a reporter, an editorial writer, or an advertising salesman, all of which I had been, or even as a solicitor of subscriptions. I knew I could land a job, one way or another, even in the midst of the devastating panic that was sweeping over Denver, as other banks went down in the national depression. Some way, being penniless and fired at twenty-five did not seem to bother me, since I had a trade and one or two professions. And then Providence was good to me, for it gave Mr. Prentis, the other editorial writer on the Star, a light stroke, and the Star wired me to come home and help. So I took the stage two days after I had been fired, and two days later was at work. The rest of the bridal party trailed in later in the summer. On the whole, even if the wedding journey became a caravan, even if calamity came upon us in its direct form this side of death, we were happy; and, as a memento of those rough days, I saw the other day among poetry books on our library shelves a copy of Andrew Lang's "Ballade in Blue China," all properly inscribed as of August 27, 1893, to Sallie from Will, indicating the sort of thing that we thought was precious and available for a present to celebrate the fourth month of our happiness. The book measures the character and quality of our joy—a joy that has lasted for half a century.

CHAPTER XXXVI

A Statuesque Statesman

FOR TWO YEARS there in Kansas City, on the Star, I worked hard and we were most happy. It was about that time that Colonel Nelson decided to establish the Sunday Star. Being a good general who knew what his troops could do, he decided to establish it without hiring much extra help. Moreover, he decided that most newspaper features were made for sale rather than for reading. So he put the men who were working on the Daily Star to writing features—chiefly local features in which they were interested—for the Sunday Star. We editorial writers had to get up Sunday editorials which would avoid politics. The old Colonel made that much of a concession to a religion which generally he ignored in his cosmos. In addition to the Sunday extra editorial, the managing editor assigned a feature article to me every week about some phase of Kansas City: the stockyards, a gypsy colony, the Greek neighborhood, and so on. He sent me once to Fort Riley to write about the cavalry acrobats, who were being trained like circus equestrians. Sometimes I wrote interviews with prominent citizens, not political interviews but interesting stories of their lives. Maybe I was too realistic. I put this down because often my feature stories made trouble in the office.

A story I wrote about the Kansas City stockyards made a lot of trouble. The Weekly Star was being sent under a stockyard subsidy to ten thousand Kansans, and my article was so flippant and so generally highty-tighty that the stockyards threatened to cancel the subsidy. Tommy Johnston, who loved me but knew my weakness, said after the stockyards delegation had been mollified:

"Bill, you can conceal more dynamite in three or four innocent lines than any man I know. How do you do it? Just tell me that."

So I began to learn a new trade. For feature articles I began to write fiction, short stories with the background of Kansas City and Kansas. Most of these stories appeared two or three years later in a little book called "The Real Issue." Before they appeared I read some of them at a rather unique institution in Kansas City known as the East Side Literary. It was a fairly authentic revival of the old country literary society, except that all of us, something like a hundred, participated. We thought we were pretty smart. I read short stories and poems. The town's newspaper dramatic and musical critics wrote and read comments on plays and concerts. Our local fiddlers fiddled, and our sopranos and tenors sang their prettiest, and the town's pianists played Chopin, Liszt, and Rubinstein with here and there a jigger of Beethoven or Debussy. And the wealth, beauty, and fashion of Kansas City's smart neighborhoods came out to grace the occasion. The East Side Literary in Kansas City was a shadowy ghost of an institution that passed with Hayes and Garfield.

The young people of Kansas City, who mingled in the society of the nobility and gentry, did not show any consciousness of the economic storm that was passing over the Missouri Valley and America. Occasionally a bank failed in the business district, and we heard from a reporter in the Star office the story of the long queues, during the runs which smashed the banks, and the tragedies that these queues revealed. Once in a while a suicide, with a financial angle, splattered over the first pages of the papers. I was conscious of many vacant store buildings and of cloth signs fluttering outside bankrupt establishments. But the White household had a hard time finding a detached house in what we regarded as a decent neighborhood for the twenty-five dollars rent that we could pay; and a year later we had to pay thirty dollars. Groceries were cheap, and we managed to live on our income and without debt. Sallie Lindsay had a horror of debt, like my mother. So we lived simply, entertained occasionally, and generally had a little money ahead—not much, sometimes a hundred dollars, sometimes a little more, enough for happiness.

Through 1893 and 1894 the depression held its blighting hand over the country and especially over the Missouri Valley. Railroads were going through bankruptcy, the big ones swallowing the little ones. Financial institutions were reorganizing after failure, or to avoid it. The whole structure of American business and finance was being recast before our eyes. Yet I doubt if any of us in the Star office, which should have been a watchtower, knew even in rough approximate what was going on. The merchants advertised the growing literacy of the population coming out of the Kansas schoolhouses under compulsory education, which was furnishing the Star more and more subscribers. The advertisers found these literate subscribers good customers. The paper grew and prospered. As a side line, I began to write advertising for the Jenkins Music House, adding a few dollars a week to my salary, and felt most important.

I kept my connection with Kansas politics vital. Often I saw Cy Leland, the local Republican boss. He had plans for Kansas politics, and because I was in a place of power where I could further his plans he talked with some candor to me. The Colonel, who distrusted all politicians, listened while I unfolded Leland's plans; and, as they seemed to be a decent way to overwhelm the Populist state administration, he let me play Leland's game. The Republicans nominated Congressman Morrill for governor. We supported Morrill during the campaign and shared his triumph in the election in 1894. That year another gubernatorial election marked the rise of an Ohio politician who was to dominate the close of the century in national politics—William McKinley, a friend of Cyrus Leland. Leland undertook to see that the Kansas delegation in the national Republican convention was for McKinley. After the nomination, McKinley set forth under the tutelage and with the financial support of Mark Hanna, fronting for Wall Street, to tour certain Republican states.

When he came to Kansas City he had a private car attached to one of the Sunday trains, and the Star sent me again as its ambassador on the train. I was to report the doings of the Kansas statesmen and to send a running account of McKinley's speeches by wire to the Star as he proceeded in his double-breasted, Prince Albert coat and white vest up the Kaw River, over the ridge into the Neosho and Cottonwood valleys and along to the Arkansas River Valley at Hutchinson—a long day's journey. It was the best reportorial assignment I had ever had, and was a part of Colonel Nelson's idea about an editorial writer. He must, first of all, be a good reporter and, so far as possible, make his editorials news.

Here is the way a leading candidate for the nomination of a major party, in the middle of the last decade of the nineteenth century, wooed his way to place and power. The royal train left Kansas City about eight o'clock in the morning. We were scheduled to stop for short speeches a minute or two at Holliday, ten minutes at Lawrence, a quarter of an hour at Topeka, three or four minutes in Osage County, ten minutes in Emporia—and so on through the afternoon to Hutchinson, where a great meeting had been arranged in an agricultural hall at the fair grounds, with McKinley as the speaker of the evening.

Mr. Leland was in charge of the train. His political friends were invited to come on at certain stations and get off at certain other stations, so that the private car never would be crowded but always would be comfortably filled. McKinley was the looming candidate of the Republican party. He was a high-tariff man. The Republicans offered a high protective tariff as the solution for the depression. The Democrats, except the waning Cleveland faction, were offering the free and unlimited coinage of silver, as their cure-all for hard times. On that train only Republicans of the strictest high-tariff cult were accepted as Mr. Leland's guests. Half a dozen reporters from as far away as Chicago and New York, and reporters from the St. Louis, Kansas City, Topeka, and Wichita papers, had a baggage car. Here we set our typewriters on mail racks, chairs, and boxes, and hammered out our stories of the regal triumph as it made its way across Kansas. We were always welcomed in the throneroom—an observation parlor at the rear of the private car. It was interesting to see how craftily, during that long jaunt through Kansas, McKinley handled the Kansas statesmen. He sat most of the time in a large, cushioned wicker armchair in the rear of the observation car and back of the door, where the swing of the rear doorknob would catch anyone who was standing up before him right between the back suspender buttons. As that door was swinging frequently, it was unprofitable to stand long before the Presence in the chair, and of course no chair could wedge into the door side of McKinley's corner. He carefully kept any chair from his right-hand side. The politicians who drifted in and out of the car and on and off of the train had to be satisfied with an introduction and a few formal words. The great man rose for the introduction, stepped into the midst of the arriving pilgrims, shook hands, pleasantly chatted for a few moments, most formally, and then retired to his inaccessible throne. Cy Leland, during the journey, explained to me with great pride that this was McKinley's strategy: he did not want to talk to any man personally before a crowd. No man could say on that journey that McKinley had made any deal with him, that any man had his confidence. It was written on the wall that Leland, and only Leland, was McKinley's vicegerent. And with the rise of McKinley, Leland waxed stronger and stronger in Kansas.

One of the more purple moments of the day came as we stopped at Florence, a railroad division point, for a short talk. There, when the train started after McKinley's deliverance, in the midst of the little lobby of the private car, was my old boss, Bent Murdock, adorned in a brand-new Brooks Brothers cutaway coat with diplomatic braid binding, gray trousers, a purple Ascot tie most fashionably arranged, and a shiny, brand-new, bell-crowned plug hat styled down to the split second of the day. He made the other grass-fed statesmen look like rustics, and I caught McKinley's eye going over him, appraising everything—McKinley was a master politician, given to those hunches which are the result of keen, quick, accurate observation through eye and ear. I was standing in the appropriate niche at McKinley's right hand, after he had greeted Mr. Murdock and looked through those double-lensed, bifocal, gold-rimmed glasses into the old man's gray-blue smiling eyes—the ingratiating eyes of one who lives by his own charms. McKinley, who knew that I was a reporter and Leland's friend, asked, under the roar of the train, who was our Ward McAllister friend. I told him and, in telling him, buttered it on pretty thick for I loved old Bent. McKinley smiled complacently and put a period to my remarks, closing the interview with an "Ah!" And in that "Ah!" he let me know that he had catalogued the specimen, pasted him in the golden book of memory for life.

As a postgraduate education in Kansas politics, the McKinley train was valuable to me. I worked like a horse between Kansas City and Emporia, and filed three thousand words with the telegraph operator when the train stopped at eleven o'clock. It did not show up in the Star office until after six o'clock. Of course, I had an alibi but no story, and a reporter does not get his standing on his alibis. The Western Union took the blame for mislaying my story, but that did not make it any better for me at the office. I filed another good three-thousand-word story that night at Hutchinson, but the next day it was cold potatoes. Being an editorial writer in my midtwenties among reporters who were generally older, I knew what they were saying, and it was true. I should have done or said something to that telegraph agent to make it impossible to mislay or misread the instructions on my story.

So, the net of my journey was to watch two master mechanics of American politics—McKinley and Leland—handle the procession of Kansas statesmen faultlessly. Each of the statesmen wished to have an inside rating with McKinley. Some of them were two-faced, some of them were sincere in their admiration for the Presidential candidate. But, because his bread and butter depended on knowing how to reach men, size men up, and handle each according to his worth rather than his outer invoice, McKinley had been able to survive twenty years in Ohio politics, where survival values combined the virtues of the serpent, the shark, and the cooing dove. McKinley, for my taste, had a little too much of the cooing dove in his cosmos. He was too polite, too meticulous in his observation of the formalities of the political Sanhedrin. He used too many hackneyed phrases, too many stereotyped forms. He shook hands with exactly the amount of cordiality and with precisely the lack of intimacy that deceived men into thinking well of him, too well of him. His Prince Albert coat was never wrinkled, his white vest front never broken. His black string tie, or a dark four-in-hand, was always properly tied but never attractively. He was well tailored but not fashionably dressed. His smooth fat face made the casual observer feel that it was a strong face. It was not. It was a wise face, wise with the ancient lore of politics, crafty with the ways that win men and hold them. He had a sweet, but not cloying, manner; gentle but always, it seemed to me, carefully calculated. He weighed out his saccharine on apothecary scales, just enough and no more for the dose that cheers but does not inebriate.

I came home to Sallie Lindsay the next day and poured out my heart about this statesman—the first of a major size that I had met with any degree of familiarity. And I made her see why I rejected him. He was unreal.

McKinley was to influence my life in the years to come rather definitely, and I saw him often. But I never changed my opinion of him—the one I formed that first sunny day riding on his train through Kansas. I respected him. I admired his tact and aplomb. I watched the manifestations of his loyalty to those who had served him, and the way in which he kept himself at a decent distance from all men. I felt some way that he was rather finicky about keeping out of political debt. On that train he was only a few degrees warmer to Mr. Leland, who was taking his own political life in his hands for McKinley, than he was to the casual visitors on the train. We had in Kansas City in those days what was known as the Santa Fe hug —an affectionate arm over the shoulder, which George Peck used to bind his henchmen with hoops of steel. Certainly McKinley never gave even Mr. Leland the Santa Fe hug; and, for all his virtues, I did not respect his mind. It seemed to me that the whole diplomacy of his spirit was to conceal how little he really knew—how little about the real essentials of life and generous living and thinking.

CHAPTER XXXVII

I Cross the Rubicon

As I LOOK BACK on those years in Kansas City when I was on the Star, and try to patch together some picture of that youth in his mid-twenties, his chief characteristic seems to have been an eager ardor—like that of a friendly pup. Probably that is why the old Colonel sent him to represent the paper on one of those chamber of commerce good-will excursions which cities used to give in those days.

The chamber of commerce hired a special train and sent it south to the Ozarks and east almost to St. Louis, skirting eastern Kansas, northern Arkansas, and passing through west and central Missouri. We were on the train a week or ten days, and I came to know some of the businessmen of Kansas City as I knew those of Lawrence and Eldorado. We had our dining car, and because the train was fairly hilarious some one of the twoscore passengers was tight most of the time, giving us a continual source of uproarious delight. And we ate where chambers of commerce in other towns would invite us.

The businessmen made speeches and contacts with prospective customers; and, going through the peach country of southern Missouri, we took home a lot of peach brandy as baksheesh to our families. We organized a chorus, sang a good deal, and got to know one another's favorite stories and what our orators would say at every dinner in the towns where we were dated. The eager pup that I was, was accepted so heartily that later, when the chamber of commerce gave a minstrel show in Kansas City to raise funds, I was made an end man; did a turn of buck-and-wing dancing, sang a song, and thought myself quite a figure in Kansas City affairs. I have a notion that it amused the Colonel to have this monkey on the string—such an amiable monkey with so many tricks. For sometime along the line I got a five-dollar raise without asking, which Sallie and I saved for the most part.

It was in those years that Albert Bigelow Paine and I put together a volume of our verses and Ewing Herbert wrote the introduction. It was printed

253

in Fort Scott and rather festively decorated with drawings by two Fort Scott artists. Paine and I had no definite understanding about the publication. The publishers sent me ten copies. Paine took upon himself, without my authority, the distribution of the press copies, and left off many of my friends. I felt that I had the right to send as many press copies as he. We quarreled. The book sold out quickly. We could have had another edition, and maybe a third, if I could have resumed relations that would justify the title "Rhymes by Two Friends." But it was impossible. Eager and ardent as I was, I had my pride; and after the publication of the book I saw little of Paine. He went east, kept on writing, became editor of St. Nicholas Magazine and, through his connection with Harper & Brothers, became Mark Twain's official biographer and did an exceptional job; for he had real ability and great energy. When he became famous twenty years later, "Rhymes by Two Friends" became a collectors' item. I knew a man who paid twenty-five dollars for a copy. I have never known a copy to sell for less than ten since the first decade of this century. The book got pleasant notices, only pleasant in the proper places. In the East, where it was a curious visitor to the editorial desks of critical magazines, their pleasant reaction toward the book was probably, in part, surprise that such a book should come out of Kansas.

I suppose the quarrel with Paine was good for me. It taught me to be more definite in business relations with my friends; and it certainly pared down any bumptiousness I might have acquired as an author. For years, every time I thought of the book, it was with humiliation and regret: humiliation that my newspaper friends in Kansas were slighted through my inability to buy my own books for them, and regret that I could not continue a pleasant friendship with a man who had great talent and who I was sure, despite the wrong he had done me, had real affection for me. The net effect was good for my head, keeping it from swelling.

I was taking on fat. We lived well. We started the day with the old-fashioned, mid-Victorian breakfast: in the winter, buckwheat cakes, bacon and eggs, fried potatoes, some kind of fruit, generally apple sauce; and in the six warm months, pancakes or toast and jam. I had a streetcar pass and came home for lunch. Always we sat down to our meals—there was no nonsense about eating in the kitchen; and once a day we had a square meal of some dimensions, usually three courses. We all enjoyed it. Because I enjoyed my meals, took them with gusto, and regarded the table as a place of high emprise, Sallie, a Kentuckian by birth, made an adventure out of cooking. Her mother cooked well, and my mother had learned cooking before her marriage in the school of hard knocks. So Sallie had good instruction, really enthusiastic support, in her culinary quest, and she made of her table a real adventure. But I suppose we gave the same thought and delight to making our home, as we quested through Kansas City second-hand stores for old mahogany. Each piece of furniture that we brought in was bought after we had saved the money for it. We still have around the house pieces which we bought in those days. We are eating at the mahogany table that we bought when we started housekeeping, and the cherry chairs that came with it are still brought out when we have extra company. We are bound to our idols. Home meant much to me. It always has meant much more than any other part of my life. I approached it at noon and night with warm anticipation always. I liked to think in those days that I was quite somebody downtown. At the office I was, in the vernacular, "a hell of a fellow." There I knew all of the reporters, all of the men in the telegraph room, and most of the advertising salesmen. The circulation man was a dear friend. On the streets of Kansas City I spoke to many people. It pleased me to dress as well as I could afford to. Sallie and I liked to go out always to the Saturday matinees, sometimes to dinner and to public gatherings; but I had no nonsense in my head about going downtown at night. The happiest place I knew was home. Poker games did not lure me, nor stag parties—ever. For I had always home work to do, and it bound me with golden chains. We were reading together, and often in Kansas City I wrote on the dining-room table the stories for the Sunday paper that brought me praise in the office, and some little fame outside. Then, of course, I was always tinkering at verse, and Sallie was always reading to me the books of the hour and the magazines of the day. There were hours of tall talk before I wrote, and afterwards while we were revising what I wrote. I went to Kansas maybe once or twice a month, spent hours in smoky bedrooms with politicians going over that interminable, intangible, and eternally changing thing which politicians call "the situation." When I came back to Kansas City the Colonel let me talk over "the situation" with him much as a fat Buddha hears the prayers of the temple acolytes. Occasionally he would let out a crashing, jovial laugh or an indignant "Bigod," but otherwise he was as a god should be—a bit detached, self-contained, imperturbable. But I wrote largely what I pleased about Kansas. We supported Morrill for governor in the campaign of '94, which brought me again into the counsels of Cy Leland, who had many of Colonel Nelson's qualities except that they were pickled in vinegar. Cy never had a belly laugh. His "Bigods" were staccato, pianissimo—not fortissimo or crescendo. And I think he liked me. I know he trusted me, and I am sure I served him well.

But I am sure of this: if I served Cy, this service was at the Colonel's pleasure; and that irked me. Other things around the Star were beginning to gall me. I had to submit my Sunday stories to a Sunday editor named Richardson. He was a major cross. Also, Saturday matinee tickets were becoming harder and harder to get, and they meant much to me. And then probably, in the core of my heart, I was a countryman. Ever since I had touched that Keith & Perry Building and looked at my fingers to see if it really was built with coal, the city had disturbed me. I detested city ways. I subscribed. I bent the knee. I played with the chamber of commerce. We went to the East Side Literary. I wrote about gas and Pinky Blitz; but my heart was in Kansas and I wanted to be my own master. Most likely, what I really wanted more than any other spiritual thing was independence. I could not be happy as a hired man. The fact that the Colonel was my boss made it impossible for me to give him the affection he deserved. I could only give it to him as an equal.

It was in those days, and for such reasons, that I began to hunt for a Kansas newspaper, one that I could afford to buy. I talked it over with Sallie—and, at the proper time, with my mother. She had a little property at Eldorado. She had hung onto the real estate my father had left her—the big house where we lived, the farm near town, another good residence on a fashionable street. These brought her a little income. She could have lived on it. With that capital in the back of my head, Sallie and I began to talk over various locations. And we were this smart: we knew we had to live in a college town. Whatever talent we had, whatever freedom I yearned for, could thrive and take root only in a town where there was a considerable dependable minority of intelligent people, intellectually upper middle class. These I could write for. These, I felt, understood what I was trying to do. These people, being in the leadership in a college community, would afford me an insurance which instinctively, even then, I felt that I must have. So I tried to buy the Lawrence Journal. It cost too much. I tried the Manhattan Mercury. It was not for sale. I tried an Ottawa paper. It was making too much money and was beyond my reach. So it narrowed down to Emporia.

Two papers were slowly starving to death in Emporia in the hard times of the middle nineties, the Daily Republican, which had absorbed the Daily News, and the Gazette. The News had been established in 1857 with the founding of the town; the Republican, in 1880. It was a staunch, rock-ribbed party paper. Its rival—the Gazette—had been established in 1890 by the Populists, who could not get advertising support nor much cash from circulation. So they sold it to W. Y. Morgan, who had helped me with my first job on the Lawrence Journal as he was retiring from the university. Morgan was financed by Major Calvin Hood of the Emporia National Bank, and after much dickering we agreed on a price of three thousand dollars. Offering my mother's property as security, I borrowed a thousand from Governor Morrill, who was a banker, and a thousand dollars from the Plumb estate—somewhat because my father and Senator Plumb had been friends, and

256

somewhat because his oldest son, A. H. Plumb, and I had been fraternity brothers. And each of them had good security. George Plumb, a brother of the senator, lent me two hundred fifty dollars on my personal note, and Major Hood transferred to me a seven-hundred-fifty-dollar note which Morgan had carried. I was three months making the deal, at odd times when I could get away from the Star. Cy Leland helped me persuade Morrill to lend me the money, though the security was ample; Ewing Herbert helped me with Hood; and I had no serious trouble persuading the Plumbs, particularly as they were covered by a good real estate mortgage.

Sallie and I had a hundred dollars or so in the bank, which was spent mostly on moving and the thousand little incidentals that come at such times. I only know this: Sallie and my mother did not come with me to Emporia when I took charge of the Gazette; and after I bought my ticket on the afternoon train, the Saturday before June 1, I had a dollar and twenty-five cents in my pocket. It seemed ample at the time.

I was happy. I still can remember with what joy I rode across Kansas into the sunset and through the long twilight. The train went by way of Ottawa, and I still retain the picture of the ride through the Marais des Cygnes Valley. The grass was lush. The trees were in first foliage. The prairie flowers were abloom in the pastures and in the wood lots. Mostly blue flowers, they were. The streams were full. The ponds were full. The hour filled me with a delight that I have held through nearly fifty years. I have forgotten what visions of conquest I had; they were probably lively enough. I only remember that the road across eastern Kansas into the sunset and through the twilight was ineffably beautiful and gave me a deep joy. This also I remember: when I stepped off the train at Emporia it was into a considerable crowd of idlers who in that day came to the station to see the two plug trains come in from Kansas City. The announcement had been made that I had bought the Gazette. I was a fairly familiar figure on the streets of Emporia—from my student days and my occasional sorties into the town as a gay young blade who danced in Jay's Opera House. Also I was spotted when I made the many visits to Emporia completing the deal with Morgan to buy the Gazette. I knew many of the faces that greeted me. I had a moment's indecision: Should I lug my heavy baggage uptown to the boarding house where I was expected, and establish a reputation as a frugal, thrifty young publisher, or should I establish my credit in the community by going in a hack? The hack was a quarter. I decided, as a credit-strengthening act, to take the hack. I piled in. I never regretted it. I was never the kind who could have made my money by saving it. But if the crowd had known that when I paid the hackman I had just a dollar left (a fact which was nobody's business) the opinion of the town would have been divided about me. As it was, no question arose in the mind of the town about my financial ability. A good front is rather to be chosen than great riches.

I was twenty-seven years old. Just ten years before that May evening that landed me in Emporia, I had left Emporia to take a job in a printing office. In those ten years I had learned the printer's trade and had made a living at it. I had become a reporter. I had been in charge of the circulation of a small daily. I had earned my way through college, at least partially, by writing. I had managed a weekly newspaper, the Weekly Eldorado Republican, hired and fired the help, solicited the advertising, written most of the editorials and all of the locals. I had taken charge of the bank account, and had made twenty-five hundred dollars a year, for Mr. Murdock and left his credit A Number 1.

I had written for the Kansas City Journal and for the Star, and had published a book which had sold out in sixty days. My stuff—prose or verse—had been copied across the country. I had had a little nibble of fame. I was not afraid of the Emporia Gazette. I was not uneasy about the mortgages on my mother's property. I had fitted myself to do everything, from sweeping out to writing the editorials and keeping the bank account, that I could ask any other man to do. So I was not afraid to plank down twenty-five cents to the hackman and go on a dollar over Sunday until the money from the Gazette began to come in. Which is another way of saying that I was a brash youth with a lot of assurance, who took considerable satisfaction, even pleasurable delight, in getting in a tight place and wiggling out. I never played poker but I did enjoy throwing dice with Fate that May evening as I rode regally through Emporia with the top of the hack down, a dollar in my pocket, and in my heart the sense that I had the world by the tail with a downhill pull.

CHAPTER XXXVIII

The Gazette: 1895

I HAD CROSSED the Rubicon—that border line in this world between the hired man and the boss. I waked the next morning, which was Sunday, scared. I had the key to the office in my pocket. After breakfast I went to look at it, all alone.

Here's what I saw: a room twenty-five by sixty with a smaller cubbyhole ten by fifteen, subtracted from that floor space. In the cubbyhole were three chairs and a pine-board table built into the wall. There I and the two reporters were supposed to do our writing, to keep the books and get out the copy generally for the paper. It opened into the street. The walls of the cubbyhole were covered with theatrical posters, campaign pictures of statesmen pasted on the wallpaper; and a few photographs of local celebrities and crooks were tacked above the desk. There was a swivel chair—presumably mine. A second chair had a large cane bottom and arms, and the third was a common kitchen chair. The oilcloth on the floor had been scuffed into holes beneath each chair. So much for the editorial department.

The rest of the sixty-by-twenty-five floor space was the composing room and printing office. In the middle stood the cylinder press on which the Gazette was printed: a Cottrell equipped with a water motor which in drouthy seasons was disconnected and replaced by a colored man who turned a crank. Half a dozen racks for type cases were strung along the walls of the room, and three composing stones stood in the center of the floor. A heavy lead roller, weighing seventy-five pounds, stood on one end of the largest composing stone. That was the proof press. And that was all of the machinery that went with the Emporia Gazette.

I wonder if God has yet forgiven me for my sinful pride in it all. I knew what everything was—how good it was, or how bad from misuse or wear and tear. As a printer, I looked over the various cases and was pleased to find they were full. There had been much thrift in the organization of the shop. The floors were swept, and everything was in order, which was another good omen. But I fear that the tidiness was for the new boss. I must have spent an hour in there, gloating over my treasure. The foreman, Jack McGinley, a six-foot, two-hundred-forty-pound, curly-headed, black-eyed Irishman, with a goatee and mustache, showed up in midmorning, and he and I talked until noon about the paper, the pay roll, and business prospects generally. Jack was a dozen years older than I and was a good printer; he had at one time owned his own paper. I did not know it then, but he was a periodical drinker and had sacrificed his position on the right-hand bank of the Rubicon to his lip for liquor. He took me in hand like a father, and I have never had a wiser, more loyal friend than he. He came to be my refuge in many a storm. Why he liked me, I do not know. He had every reason to dislike me, for I was younger than he, and was the boss. I seemed to have smart city ways; very likely I was most opinionated. But he realized early how much I trusted him.

The paper was supposed to have between seven and eight hundred subscribers. Jack told me that there were only four hundred and eighty-five in the town of Emporia and fewer than a hundred in the county, and that the county collections were far in arrears. Jack seemed to have helped Mr. Morgan with the books. In the seesawing and horse trading, Mr. Morgan had given me certain of the May bills and the arrears in certain other collections. It was a fair trade. Jack knew about it and helped me to straighten out the accounts. He and I, being somewhat of the same blood and of an ardent nature, dropped our guards in that hour alone in the office, and when noon came we stood at the front door. I offered him my hand. He looked me over from head to foot, quite formally, a heavy-set young fellow whose pudgy hands had never known toil heavier than typesetting, a youth with evident, even maybe a little conspicuous, modesty in his voice and mien to hide an inner self-esteem. Jack surveyed that figure with intuitive Irish appraisal, then smiled a beaming, possessive, fatherly smile and said:

"You'll do. I guess we'll make it!"

I hope I blushed when I thanked him, and we shook hands warmly. The binding tie was welded.

Sallie and my mother did not come to Emporia until the end of the first week. Sunday afternoon I wrote my salutatory editorial. Reading it the other day, after nearly half a century, I am amazed to find that it stands up. It still represents my ideals, realized with such a sad and heavy discount in approximate. But what I wrote I tried to do. Here it is:

ENTIRELY PERSONAL

June 3, 1895

To the gentle reader who may, through the coming years during which we are spared to one another, follow the course of this paper, a word of personal address from the new editor of the GAZETTE is due. In the first place, the new editor hopes to live here until he is the old editor, until some of the visions which rise before him as he dreams shall have come true. He hopes always to sign "from Emporia" after his name when he is abroad, and he trusts that he may so endear himself to the people that they will be as proud of the first words of the signature as he is of the last words. He expects to perform all the kind offices of the country editor in this community for a generation to come. It is likely that he will write the wedding notices of the boys and girls in the schools; that he will announce the birth of the children who will some day honor Emporia, and that he will say the final words over those of middle age who read these lines.

His relations with the people of this town and country are to be close and personal. He hopes that they may be kindly and just. The new editor of the GAZETTE is a young man now, full of high purposes and high ideals. But he needs the close touch of older hands. His endeavor will be to make a paper for the best people of the city. But to do that he must have their help. They must counsel with him, be his friends, often show him what their sentiment is. On them rests the responsibility somewhat. The "other fellows" will be around. They will give advice. They will attempt to show what the public sentiment is. They will try to work their schemes, which might dishonor the town. If the best people stay away from the editor's office, if they neglect to stand by the editor, they must not blame him for mistakes. An editor is not all wise. He judges only by what he sees and hears. Public sentiment is the only sentiment that prevails. Good sentiment, so long as it does not assert itself, so long as it is a silent majority, is only private sentiment. If the good, honest, upright, God-fearing, law-abiding people of any community desire to be reflected to the world, they must see that their private opinion is public opinion. They must stand by the editors who believe as they do.*

It is a plain business proposition. The new editor of the GAZETTE desires to make a clean, honest local paper. He is a Republican and will support Republican nominees first, last, and all the time. There will be no bolting, no sulking, no "holier than thou" business about his politics—but politics is so little. Not one man in ten cares for politics more than two weeks in a year. In this paper, while the politics will be straight, it will not be obtrusive. It will be confined to the editorial page—where the gentle reader may venture at his peril. The main thing is to have this paper represent the average thought of the best people of Emporia and Lyon County in all their varied interests. The editor will do his best. He has no axes to grind. He is not running the paper for a political pull. If he could get an office he wouldn't have it. He is in the newspaper business as he would be in the drygoods business—to make an honest living and to leave an honest name behind. If the good people care for a fair, honest home paper, that will stand for the best that is in the town—here it is.

In the meantime, I shall hustle advertising, job work and subscriptions, and write editorials and "telegraph" twelve hours a day in spite of my ideals. The path of glory is barred hog-tight for the man who does not labor while he waits.

WILLIAM A. WHITE

---

* I have lost some faith in this lot; but I have gained some faith in just plain folks.—W. A. W.

I slammed that editorial on the copy hook when I left the office that Sunday night, and the next morning came down to take charge. Nothing new confronted me except the sense that I was actually boss, not a sub-boss for someone else, which was more frightening than exhilarating. But I had this comfort that first day. I met scores of my father's old friends who had known him twenty-five years before in Emporia. They were mostly substantial citizens, many of them old-line, anti-Populist, silk-stocking Democrats. And they heartened me. Mr. Morgan, my predecessor, took me up and down Commercial Street, introduced me to all the merchants and most of the lawyers and some of the doctors. I picked up local items as I went, talked advertising to advertisers, and did a good day's work. We had two reporters, one of whom helped keep the books, and we all solicited advertising. The total pay roll of the office was forty-five dollars. I had to find that much money before the next Saturday night.

The ravens brought it. It may be well to give the reader something of the economic picture of the times, to set down what the wages of skilled labor were in Emporia in 1895. Jack, the foreman, got twelve dollars; later a raise to fifteen. The best printer got eight dollars a week, and four girls set type at from two-fifty to four dollars a week, according to their skill. The office devil got two-fifty, and Mr. Morgan told me he was entitled to a raise to three dollars the first of July. The reporters got eight and ten dollars each.

But living costs were low. A frying chicken cost fifteen cents, steak ten cents a pound, bacon eight and nine cents, flour two dollars a hundred, sugar twenty pounds for a dollar. Sallie and I paid eighteen dollars a month for a six-room house. It did not have a sign of a pipe or a wire in it, either for water or for light. We laid aside five dollars, and no more, for our grocery and incidental budget, and lived within it. We kept no maid, but we could have gotten one for from a dollar and a half to three dollars a week. Those wages and those commodity prices represented a hangover from the old days when communities, even homes, and certainly farms, were self-sufficient, when craftsmen in many trades set their wages on the basis of a self-sufficient home, a small farm and garden, cows and chickens and pigs as one of the props of every family.

But the world had moved on in the quarter of a century before 1895. Railroads and other machines had wiped out all but the skeleton of the old self-subsistent civilization, and the catastrophic maladjustment between the two epochs was evident all around Emporia, and particularly on the farms. Unemployment had beaten down the price of corn, wheat, hay, hogs, and livestock until farming was unprofitable. The protest of Populism was the political phase of the unpainted farm houses and barns one saw all over the midwestern country, the run-down fences, the fallow, weedy fields; and in towns, the vacant stores and bankruptcy sales. One of the town banks, though I did not know it at first, was slowly sinking into insolvency. It was not Major Hood's bank.

Yet in the big houses, ten or twenty of them, people lived well. The bankers and some of the doctors and lawyers drove spanking teams to carriages that cost as much as three hundred dollars. The Whist and High Five clubs, attended by the best people, had gay parties. Dances were given with some style and éclat, perhaps in the third-floor garrets of the baronial rococo mansions built in the seventies, or maybe in the skating rink or the hall of some fraternal insurance society. People who had money were living well in Emporia; others, hanging on by their eyebrows. And Populism was raging across the state, across the Missouri Valley, and through the South.

I did not realize during those first days in Emporia why our town was divided, as were most towns in the western world, into bank factions, deeply divided, bitterly feudal. But now I see across the years that those two factions in Emporia—the faction gathered about Major Hood and his bank and the faction gathered around Charley Cross and William Martindale and their banks—arose and thrived as local clans bound by purely monetary interests, and somewhat made necessary by the fact that storekeepers, professional people, and the owners of the little industries around the town could not live without credit. This, the banks furnished. The use of credit was made widely necessary by this transition from a simple self-supporting and self-sufficient economy to the new economy in the machine age. Capital, as represented by the banks, was still tribal, feudal, competitive. The banks fought for business. Their customers lined up behind the banks, and all over this part of the world in the nineties as the economic scenery of the world was changing. Factions, feuds, internal bitternesses, wicked and sometimes bloody rivalries were fostered at the front doors of the banks in towns and cities across the land—at least across our western land. I only know about that.

So when Mr. Morgan took me up and down Commercial Street and Fifth and Sixth avenues, calling on our friends and customers, I went unwittingly wearing the collar of the Emporia National Bank, Major Hood's bank, the bank which Plumb and Hood had founded twenty-five years before. This civic brawl, typical of the day and time, was a sad reality in the life of a young editor who took his pen in hand that Sunday afternoon to write his salutatory to the town of his birth.

That night, in the Emporia Republican, "our loathed but esteemed contemporary," a two-line item appeared thus:

"Will A. White, of Kansas City, has bought the Gazette from W. Y. Morgan. Next!"

The editor of the Republican was a man in his sixties who had served

263

the town in the legislature, who had secured the location of the State Teachers College in Emporia, who was an acknowledged leader of the Republican party in Kansas, and vicegerent of the Santa Fe Railroad, which named a town for him on one of its branches in an adjoining county. He was a dignified man with a rather large head who covered the bald frontal area of his skull with long hair from the side and dyed it, and who always wrote the resolutions at the Republican county convention. He was of the samurai caste in Kansas Republicanism, receiving remuneration from the Santa Fe as needed for his paper's pay roll, and was a spokesman of the other bank, the Cross-Martindale bank. When it was closed, a few years later, a sheaf of the old editor's blank notes, accommodation paper, was found in the bank which they slipped into the note case to polish up the record for the national bank inspector. He did not realize it, but I was the young bull who had come to horn the old one out of the herd. Toward the end of his career, as was the fashion of the day, he devoted much space to abusing me. The Gazette never replied. Not a line in our paper indicated that we even knew he was on earth; and that—his reporters told ours—galled him more deeply than anything we could say. He was used to every form of abuse but contempt.

Sallie and my mother came to Emporia the week end after I arrived. Sallie came down to the office daily, and we worked together—she on society items and other local items, I writing the editorial, soliciting advertising, taking care of the bank account. Soon we invited Lew Schmucker to quit his job as a railway postal clerk and come to the Gazette as bookkeeper, reporter, and advertising salesman. To him, it was a dream come true, for he had always wanted to be a newspaperman.

So we jogged along six months or so, with nothing more serious to cloud our happy lives than a weekly overdraft at the bank Monday morning, which was wiped out by Wednesday evening. Then one Saturday night we rocked the town with laughter in one of those sheer accidents which the devil, in his ingenuity, sometimes contrives for newspapers alone. Sallie had made the announcement in the society column of the wedding of Hortense Kelly, daughter of a Methodist elder, a man of great political power in the state, and George Crawford, son of a former governor and brother-in-law of Arthur Capper, of the Topeka Capital. It was quite a wedding. For a week, at odd times, Sallie had been at the Kelly home with the other young women of the town, helping to draw blue or pink baby ribbon through the bride's trousseau, and she was an intimate of the house. Saturday morning she wrote a funny story about John Martin, the laundryman, who had taken his son Charley to Kansas City. Charley came home saying that his father had given him a dollar to call him Uncle instead of

Papa when the girls were around. She had prefaced her story about John Martin with a Kipling quatrain:

> This is the sorrowful story
> Told as the twilight fails
> And the monkeys walk together
> Holding their neighbours' tails!

And then, the devil only knows why, the make-up man on the paper put a separating dash between that quatrain and the John Martin item and tacked the verses on at the end of the Kelly-Crawford wedding, which concluded thus:

"This marriage unites two of the oldest and most important families in Kansas, the Crawfords and the Kellys."

Then followed: "And this is the sorrowful story . . ."

When old Jack saw it after the last paper was out and the carrier boys were gone, he began to roar with laughter, and within ten minutes the barbershops of the town were churning with hilarity. In an hour the town was giggling its head off. In three hours the town was divided. Nine-tenths of the burghers thought we did it on purpose and that it was a dirty shame. The other tenth realized that it was one of those devil's accidents which come to newspapers in spite of all their care. But on the whole it was good medicine for the Gazette. It had never made such a deep and widespread impression on the town as that which came in that item. As for Sallie, she went to bed in tears; and when she tried to explain to the Kellys she was greeted by cold, rebuking unbelief. If the Gazette gained circulation and attention, it was the woman who paid, and paid, and paid.

CHAPTER XXXIX

The New Editor and His Town

IT IS A LOVELY THING in youth to have "the valor of ignorance," to have no other cares than a weekly overdraft at the bank and to have hold of a lever—the Archimedean lever that moves your world—and to be overwhelmingly in love and be able to laugh at the accidents of fate and turn the barbs of misfortune with the armor of an invulnerable self-confidence. We two—Sallie and I—walked to and from work every day, chattering, honking our laughter, billing and cooing like birds—perhaps equally brainless, which was a good thing also, for we did not realize how precarious was our lot. Times were unbelievably hard that first summer. The overdraft began to mount Friday, sank into a dark abysm Saturday night, and, strain as we would Monday, Tuesday, and Wednesday, we rarely got it entirely wiped out. Once in a while Major Hood at the bank would call me in and remonstrate. Twice that summer we had to give our note for fifty or a hundred dollars to cover the deepening overdraft. But we went on cutting our paper dolls at the office most happily. I printed two stories in the Gazette for filler which Richardson, the Sunday editor, had rejected on the Star. One story was called "The Court of Boyville"; the other was the story of "Aqua Pura." Both appeared later in a book, as you shall see. But from the Gazette they were copied and got around the country. So, in the winter or early spring of 1896, we had two offers from legitimate book publishers, asking if we had any other stories like that, enough to make a book. We had! We chose Way & Williams, Chicago publishers, largely because they were western; and we turned down Henry Holt & Company chiefly because they were eastern. We were loyal westerners without much sense. So we began gathering up our stories for The Book. A five-hundred-dollar advance came from the publishers with the contract, and we slapped that advance on one of the mortgages. Which made us still happier, and carefree. We screamed our delight like jays as we went about our work and through the town. That five hundred dollars seemed to cheer the old Major up. At least it strengthened our credit so that we could deepen the overdraft a little when we had to; but we could not get rid of it. Let me paste in a picture here of Major Calvin Hood, our banker friend, known in the town as the Little Major.

Major Hood was in his late fifties then, a slight little figure beginning to bend just a bit at the shoulders. He had sharp brown eyes, a clear skin, gray hair thinning at the brow, and gray whiskers always immaculately trimmed. Behind the barrier of those whiskers he kept a hard cruel mouth, rapacious and hungry; yet he smiled easily, laughed gently, very gently when he smiled—the refinement of his face appearing. He was another man. It was this man who always headed the subscription for every good thing. It was this man who lent students money, who bought beautiful pictures for his home when he went to New York, and good ones too, who patronized the arts in Emporia, gave generously to the library, kept a box at the Emporia Opera until he fell out with the owner of the theater, had a spanking team of well matched sorrels hitched to a magnificent phaeton which adorned the streets. Compared with all other carriages in the town, the Little Major's equipage was a Rolls-Royce beside a T Model. He was generous to his friends and ruthless to his enemies. He had a thin, long-fingered, bony hand. I never saw a palm that cupped so deeply nor a palm that seemed so dry and crinkled. His voice was soft, and he always cleared his throat with a little "Ahem" when he spoke of interest, which he could compound in his head quicker than another banker could look it up in his interest book. Yet he was loyal to his friends who were loyal to him, and for twenty years he treated me as his son. He was a type, a product of his day, the banker who was a free man, who ran his own bank in his own way, deferring only slightly to the nonsense of the federal bank inspectors. In his town and county, that typical banker was the sheik. The Little Major was one of fewer than a dozen men who, with the railroad attorneys and the old heel-walking captains of industry who owned the packing houses, were the ruling class of our state. Every state had its rulers like these. Although he was known in Emporia as the Little Major, the pioneers knew that at the time when he set up his bank in Emporia he used to carry tens of thousands of dollars in a money belt buckled around him down into the wilds of Texas, with a pistol almost as large as himself, to buy cattle, and sometimes pulled the pistol and stood off bandits with a nerve of steel. Only his enemies saw that side of him—or his friends when they were in trouble and needed him. He and his kind have disappeared, as have the Mound Builders. The banker of 1943, hag-ridden by the comptroller of the currency, walking between the state laws and the federal restrictions, like Eugene Aram, "with gyves upon his wrist," is another creature, certainly neither the residuary legatee nor the heir-at-law of the Little Major and the Mound Builders. Yet, in his suzerainty over the business world around him, Major Hood was typical of the banker in that day of metamorphosis when the old self-subsistent economy of America had passed and a new order had come, all confused because it was uncharted, highly competitive in everything, yet more or less manacled by trusts which were themselves somewhat competitive, and by a growing subconscious feeling among men in control that their competition was wasteful, and that some kind of amalgamation was necessary. The Major—in little—was Jim Hill, Jay Gould, Henry Villard, Andrew Carnegie, John W. Gates, the elder Morgan, old John D. Rockefeller and all the heads, organizers, and owners in trust of the nation's industrial and financial institutions. The Little Major, there in the back room of his bank, spinning his web (his enemies used to call him the Old Spider), dominating the politics, controlling the business, bossing his church, financing and directing the local college, was my friend, loyal, generous, and understanding. I had no sense that he was corrupting our newspaper. When we talked over local or state politics, I had the feeling that we were two free men. He never gave orders, and, in many minor matters, I suppose he took advice. It was years before a major matter appeared to threaten a division between us. I just happened to think his way most of the time in those first years as a young editor, and maybe sometimes, because I was young and he was old, he deferred to me. Certainly he was an easy boss. I doubt not that they all were easy bosses in the big world which he symbolized. They too went with the current of the times, walking sturdily on their heels or stealthily on their toes, thinking they were going their own way. They were really guided, guarded, led unconsciously in the pellmell rush of the times.

The first real knock-down-and-drag-out fight I had in Emporia was with the Grand Army of the Republic. The Union veterans literally packed and controlled the Courthouse. They had majorities in the city council and on the school board. The Republican county convention and the Kansas state Republican convention were their private parade grounds. When I came to town I determined to cut down extra words in the Gazette and boil down the items to the bone. The G.A.R. had two posts in Emporia, and every week their notices came to the newspaper office in the form of a military order. It took twelve lines to say that P. B. Plumb Post of the G.A.R. would meet in its hall, as usual, Wednesday night. I cut the twelve lines down to exactly that many words—eliminating all the military phraseology, the names of the commander and the adjutant and the corporal—and the G.A.R. blew its head off and boycotted the Gazette. I explained to the people that I was not refusing to give the news of the G.A.R. meeting, but was refusing to clutter up the paper and take the space that real news would occupy by printing every week a lot of military jargon; and the boycott disappeared impotently after a few weeks. My competitor, the old editor of the opposition paper, faunched wildly because I was insulting the men who had saved the Union and had struck the shackles from four million slaves; but little good it did him. We stressed local news and printed a number of items that ordinarily would not have been printed in a strictly conventional newspaper. We were chatty, colloquial, incisive, impertinent, ribald, and enterprising in our treatment of local events. Looking back over it now, I can see that much of it was based upon a smart-aleck attitude; but the people liked it. Circulation grew. The Gazette was generally abused in conservative households. A few prudish people sighed that they could not allow the Gazette in their homes on account of their children, which I felt was silly. So did Sallie.

Editorially, from the very first week the Gazette was a conservative Republican newspaper. I had no use for the protective tariff, but I tolerated it because I wished to advocate the gold standard. Kansas was sadly bitten by the fiat money theory. Senator Plumb, who had bossed the state and led it politically in the seventies and eighties, had been for the free coinage of silver. He owned silver mines in Colorado. Most of our Kansas statesmen toyed with the free-silver idea. They hoped to beat the Populists by making fun of pure fiat money, and at the same time advocate the free coinage of silver which was 40 per cent fiat. So, when the Gazette advocated the single gold standard, it was politically a pariah in Kansas. It is not unlikely that occasional editorials in the files of the Gazette, speaking well of the theory of protection, were my defense weapons against attack upon my gold-standard flank. But I set no great store by the editorial page. I believed that local news, if honestly and energetically presented, would do more for subscriptions and more for the Gazette's standing in the community than its editorial page. Indeed I believed then and believe now that a newspaper that prints the news—all of it—that is fit to print, can take any editorial position it desires without loss of prestige or patronage. People choose their paper not because of its politics but because of its integrity, its enterprise, and its intelligence. They want an honest paper, well written, where they can find all the news to which they are entitled.

Except for occasional boycotts, which were noisy, but highly incompetent, our editorials never got us in trouble. It was the news items that brought in irate subscribers. Our policy, for instance, was to drop the word "lady" and substitute the word "woman." A lady who had paid a fine for streetwalking came in to protest not the publication of the news of her fine, but the fact that we called her a woman, and she assured us that she was as much of a lady as any of the other girls in this town. And from that hour to this, the Gazette has referred to all females as women except that police-court characters were always to be designated as "ladies."

One time a colored man who had been in the penitentiary twice for crimes of violence threatened that, if his name ever appeared in the Gazette again, he would cut my heart out and show it to me. He was known as Razor Billings—commonly accounted by the orderly colored people of the town as "a bad nigger." He got in trouble again. We used his name. The next morning I knew he would appear. So did the two reporters and the people in the back room. He was a big, lean, lantern-jawed chimpanzee of a man whose wild, bloodshot eyes had a lot of white in them—a loud-talking person. He began bellowing as he left the side-walk. I had wrapped a lead window weight in a newspaper rather deftly, waiting for him, just in case. He did not know what it was. It lay on my desk, and my hand toyed with it. He began shouting to work up his temper as he stood there before me. I looked through the door into the office, and my eye caught sight of the monumental figure of old Jack McGinley wrapping in his apron a steel sidestick from the forms, which weighed ten pounds at least—a deadly weapon if there ever was one. Billings could not see Jack, though Jack was less than ten feet from him. Jack was "reinforce-ments." I got suddenly brave and assumed a cold, deadly manner which belied my inner fear and trembling agitation. With my hand toying with the window weight, and with Jack armed to the teeth with the sidestick, I exhibited a courage that I certainly did not feel. But it was terrible and deadly enough for me to make Mr. Billings sit down while I read him a riot act, and then get up and walk out of the office. As he got to the sidewalk I followed him to the door, and then, with the window weight unsheathed, herded him verbally down the street. As I turned to go back, old Jack put his arm around me and said:

"I said you would do, and you'll do!"

After that we had a good laugh which was 98 per cent hysterical. Jack went back to his work, and I sat down at my desk, with the window weight before me as I went on with my morning's job, whatever it was. Of course through Jack, through the reporters, through the printers, the story of Razor Billings' rout from the Gazette office spread over town that day. We went on printing whatever news came up, and in our own way. In his heart Jack knew that my intentions toward Mr. Razor Billings were hon-orable; that I meant to stand my ground with the lead window weight, and that I had spoken my lines like a little man—and he took a father's pride in me. That night he got very drunk and told the town a tall tale of my courage, which had small foundation in fact.

One noon, when the office was deserted, old Jack came upon me swing-ing a chair in defiance at some irate customer who had come in to bulldoze me, backing him out of the office, down the steps, clear onto the sidewalk and into the street, after the subscriber had angered me beyond endurance and had tried to bully me with mere words. After that, Jack accepted me as an equal and wiped out the years that might have stretched as a bar between us. Often of a summer evening we sat outside the office door, our chairs tilted against the building—he smoking and talking and telling me old stories of the craft, of his odyssey up and down the land as a journeyman printer, of his light loves and major adventures in romance, of his hopes of the future and his philosophy of the present, smoking, spitting, meditating in long silences and looking at the stars. Twice I sent him to the Keeley to be cured of the drink habit, and twice he came back penitent, serene, and sure of his salvation.

Once, when I sentenced him to the Keeley, appointed the hour and the train by which he was to go, and called up the Keeley Institute at Kansas City telling them to get him off the train, old Jack decided to go on one last, long, lingering drunk. So he dressed up in his best, borrowed a plug hat from one of the printers who kept it sacredly dedicated to his moments of inebriation, hired one of Marshal Tom Fleming's best hacks, and rode up and down the four or five blocks of store buildings, which is our business area, calling on the merchants and telling them of my virtues. This was the burden of his song:

"Willie thinks I should go to the Keeley. Willie's my boss. Willie, God damn him, is trying to save me from my personal devil. Be good to Willie while I'm gone. He's a good boy, and he'll fight. But, God damn him, he don't know as much as he thinks he does. But I love him just the same, for Willie's my boss."

Lew Schmucker brought this story back to the office, roaring with delight. Sallie and I took great comfort from it. It was affection's garland on my brow. Jack went away to the Spanish War, a captain. What a figure he was, and what a captain he made! And when he came back, what tales he had to tell! To know Jack was to understand why God loves the Irish. They teach such tolerant joy in the weakness of men, and such affectionate amazement for man's strength.

It was that year and the year after that I traded space with the man who owned the billboards. Whenever one was vacant, the town read in flaring red type:

"All right! Cuss the Gazette, but read it!"

Whatever figure I may have cut on Commercial Street as the intrepid man-eating editor, our lives at home were simple and gentle and sweet. At night we read, or Sallie read to me. I remember that about that time we read "The Crowd," by Gustave Le Bon, which impressed me. We were reading the current Howells novels as they appeared in the magazines, and, of course, Kipling, every line of him; and were taking excursions into the English minor poets like Henley and Andrew Lang; but my heart was still true to James Whitcomb Riley. We went to Kansas City to see him again when he was reading there. He was a little, elfin man, a slender blond creature whose reddish hair was beginning to thin and gray, and whose eyes, light blue-hazel, were keen and twinkling. We had breakfast with him at the Coates House and went away stepping on air. But I had almost ceased to write imitations of Riley, and the verse I was writing—which was not much, for I was tapering off—was mostly serious and was beginning to take a social cast. Problems of life were interesting me. It was about this time Sallie told me that any of a thousand men in America could write as good verse as I, but that I had a chance to do something with prose which might really carry me. And I knew she was right. I had an idea for a novel in those days which was to deal with a county-seat fight in western Kansas, full of the beat of horses' hooves, the crack of revolvers, the tense rivalries of towns, massacres, and sudden death. It never came off, but many is the hour I sat in the dining room at the table at night writing page after page of that story while Sallie sat by, reading a book or a magazine. Even with our scanty means we had Scribner's, Harper's, the Century, the Atlantic, the Nation, the Outlook, and the Independent. Some of them, we got by swapping advertising. The others, we paid for. We had no time for bridge. We seemed to be out of the dancing zone. Probably we did not go out to parties more than two or three times a month, for we were an extra couple at cards and had to work too hard in the daytime to dance very much at night. It was not that we were pious. The Lord knows it was not that. We were just busy. What a strange couple we must have made in those dear and dizzy 1890's in Emporia, when, even though a depression was blighting the land, the townsfolk with their social diversions—Colonel Whitley's Opera House occupied three nights a week by passably good plays, the lecture course at the Normal crowding them in to hear the year's celebrities in lecture or song and all the gayeties of the Feast of Belshazzar—were making the night merry through those sad, drab times.

CHAPTER XL

A Battle of Giants

It was in the winter and early spring of 1896 that we put together that group of stories, most of which had appeared in the Star, in the Eldorado Republican, and in the Gazette; some of them had never been published, but we sent them all to Way & Williams to make a book which we had entitled "The Real Issue"—which proved to be a bad title, a confusing one. Over and over we revised those stories, boiling them down, recasting the sentences for clarity. But when we sent the book off, some time in the early spring, we were proud and happy. We had sense enough to know that "Rhymes by Two Friends" was a most amateurish enterprise, but we felt some way that "The Real Issue" was in a way professional.

In the meantime the campaign of 1896 was opening. Mr. Leland was selecting the delegates to the national convention from Kansas, instructed for William McKinley for President. I did not care for McKinley. I supported Thomas Reed, who was Speaker of the House and had declared emphatically and unmistakably for the gold standard. McKinley, even during the campaign, was silent on the currency question. Mark Hanna, who had taken charge of the national campaign for him, was more interested in his candidate than he was in his platform; but, being an industrialist rather than a banker, he would have made the campaign on the tariff. Our Kansas statesmen were all for the tariff because it gave them a chance to take the wind out of the sails of the fiat money Democrats and Populists by advocating the free coinage of silver, an inflationary proposal. The young Kansas congressman from our district, my friend of Butler County days, Charley Curtis, was an advocate of free silver. I remember his breezing into Emporia that spring—straight, slim, with a certain virile grace that came from a lithe and supple figure. He wore a blue suit and a straw hat and a loosely tied bow tie, and was too handsome for words. He shook hands up and down Commercial Street and had everyone for free silver before the national Republican convention. I had a chance to report that convention for the Kansas City World. I went to St. Louis, where the convention met, in a crash suit that cost me five dollars, and I was proud of myself. I filed a story every day, a thousand or fifteen hundred words which I wrote in an hour or so, and had the other twenty-two hours for sightseeing, for hobnobbing with other reporters, and for running about with Ed Howe who, being an old stager, knew the good places to eat. We discovered Tony Faust's restaurant, then famous all over the Midwest, and went to comic opera in an outdoor beer garden. I remember I saw "The Bohemian Girl" for the first time. Though I knew all the tunes taken from that old opera, it gave me an added thrill to hear them in their proper setting. Ed Howe was ten years older than I, but we roamed the city together, good comrades. In addition to Ed Howe, I saw the other Republican heroes of the day and was particularly interested in Mark Hanna, a human sort of man in his late fifties with a barrel chest, slim legs, a fleshy mobile face that looked Irish; he had a way of twitching his upper lip and nose sideways like a horse, that was most expressive. I saw him, asked him a few questions which he answered politely but with great discretion, and got a fine impression of him as an earnest, honest, courageous, though somewhat hotheaded and impulsive man, not like the politicians who hid behind the mask of imperturbability and veiled their designs like Florentine conspirators. Hanna sputtered on, even God-damned. He was forthright. But, compared with Cy Leland, who was my ideal politician of that day, Hanna talked too much.*

I reported the superficialities of the convention, chronicled the events without real knowledge of what was going on. Actually here was the first real cleavage in the Republican party, if one omits the slight crack that occurred in 1872, when Horace Greeley, Peter Cooper, Wendell Phillips, and Garrison formed a minor rebellion against Grant and the reactionary corruption of his administration. But here in St. Louis, the issues of the new times first appeared. The battle was over the inclusion of a straight, unequivocal stand on the currency. The East, and particularly the eastern bankers who supported Reed, had no faith in McKinley; they demanded that in the platform the currency plank should declare, "We favor the single gold standard." After that, they did not care what chicken feed was thrown to the fiat money birds. Of course, all Republicans believed in the theory of protection. Upon that theory Hanna had planned to nominate McKinley and conduct his campaign, hoping, because he loved McKinley, to avoid a clash between McKinley's platform and McKinley's straddling record.

---

* At that time I wrote a picture of Hanna in action at that convention, which my paper did not use. I afterwards included it in "Masks in a Pageant," Chapter XVIII, p. 211. It revealed Mark Hanna, who controlled the destinies of American politics for more than half a decade, as he really was.

The West generally was opposed to the gold-standard declaration. Most of the western Republicans were for free silver. The Rocky Mountain states were rampant for it. The economics of the depression of the nineties found their expression in the politics of the times. The debtors who had borrowed to build a trans-Mississippi civilization believed that an inflationary measure would relieve them. In the East lived the creditors, the holders of western farm mortgages, the owners of railroad stocks and bonds who also had in their strong boxes the state, municipal, and county bonds of those western communities which had borrowed to build their cities, to make state improvements, and to enjoy the new, shiny gadgets of American civilization introduced by the public utilities—light, gas, and water.

In that Republican convention, the creditor and the debtor in American life stood toe to toe in massed forces in their first great battle in a major party.

It was apparent early that Hanna, by controlling the southern delegates and by hard work in the Ohio Valley and Great Lakes commonwealths, had a majority for McKinley. Tom Reed made a sorry showing in delegates, but his friends and supporters dominated the platform committee and forced upon Hanna a plank that was at first odious to him, then became more and more acceptable. Finally he surrendered. The Republican party was committed then and there to the doctrine that prosperity in a land is the first requisite for justice. The Hanna-McKinley surrender on the currency plank wrought deep, widespread turmoil among the delegates in St. Louis. A bolt was organized. Leland had trouble to keep the Kansas delegation from joining the mountain states in revolt. The eastern Missouri Valley, Kansas, Nebraska, and the Dakotas were all fiat money states. Most of them were controlled by the Populists or the fusion between the Populists and the soft-money Democrats. In the Rockies and westward, the free-silver sentiment was overwhelming; but these states were sparsely settled. The delegates from the South, many of whom were conventionally corrupt, joined those from the eastern and middle states in supporting the gold standard. The plank, as the New York bankers wrote it, came out of the platform committee into the convention. Between the publication of the committee report and its adoption, rumors of the silver rebellion in the party swept through the hotel lobbies. I reported those rumors; but I did not know essentially why the western Mississippi Valley and the mountain states were raising their outcry against gold. Only vaguely did I sense that the drama I was to see in the convention, when it met to adopt the platform, was the opening scene of a great political morality play which would hold the boards for more than fifty years—a play of which the long procession of Populists winding through the Kansas streets, hanging me in effigy in Butler County and rising in wrath in Emporia, was but the prelude. It was a revolt of the man with one talent or with five talents against the man with ten, who was hoarding his gains in unfair privileges.

Wednesday morning of the convention, we knew that Senator Teller, of Colorado, was to lead a bolt after the adoption of the gold-standard plank. No one knew how many delegates he could call around him in the march out of the convention. The moment was tense because of the uncertainty. Mr. Leland was not quite sure of three or four of his delegates, and the Nebraska and Iowa leaders, and Senators Davis of Minnesota and Spooner of Wisconsin, feared the silver heresy would split their delegations. When the reporters tried to interview Mark Hanna that morning he was gruff and wrathy. I wanted to see how he would take it when the big scene was staged with Senator Teller as the hero; so I quietly slipped a dollar to a colored delegate from North Carolina, and occupied his seat immediately in front of Hanna and the Ohio delegation. This is the story of the play upon which the curtain rose after the committee on resolutions had asked for the adoption of the gold standard and it had been voted to put gold into the Republican platform.

When the platform had been reported by the committee on resolutions, and the clause endorsing the gold standard had been read, Senator Teller, advocating the free and unlimited coinage of silver at the ratio of sixteen to one, made a speech favoring the adoption of a minority report of the resolutions committee which eliminated the gold-standard declaration. While Teller spoke, a pudgy man, broad-shouldered and of robust girth, sat fidgeting in his narrow chair among the Ohio delegates, but one row removed from the aisle. The man was Mark Hanna.

The loose muscles about Hanna's mouth twitched irritably as Teller's silver swan song rose and fell. Occasionally he lifted a broad hand to a large, bumpy cranium, as if to scratch. Instead, he rubbed the rich, healthy, terra-cotta hide on his full, firm neck. His bright brown eyes took the orator's mental and moral measure with merciless precision. But with the rise of passion in the speech his expression changed from a mobile smile to a vicious iron glare. When Teller sat down weeping, Hanna grunted his relief; but he was nervous. He kept rubbing his jaw. His long upper lip twitched from side to side. The muscles under his eyes quivered. Others spoke in favor of the Teller resolution—perhaps an Idaho man, maybe a Montanan, from a chair behind the Ohio delegation. Then a young chap, with a boutonniere on his perfectly fitting frock coat, came chasséing down the aisle and received Chairman Thurston's recognition. "Who's that?" asked Hanna of Congressman Grosvenor of Ohio.

"Cannon."

"Who's Cannon?"

Mind you, it was Mark Hanna who was asking these questions—Hanna,

276

who was popularly supposed to be omniscient and omnipotent at St. Louis that day. Yet here was a United States Senator whom Hanna did not know—Hanna, who really held the convention in the hollow of his hand.

"How did he break in?" growled Hanna.

"Senator—Utah," replied Congressman Grosvenor of Ohio.

The westerner opened his mouth to read his address.

"Well, for heaven's sake, goin' to read it! Lookee there!" And Hanna's broad, fat head waved toward the orator. "Perty, ain't he?" His eyes slitted, and he sneered: "Looks like a cigar drummer!"

The orator soon abandoned his manuscript.

Hanna showed a wise serpentine tongue between his thin lips and snapped, "So that's Cannon!" After appraising the dapper young man, he jeered to Governor Bushnell beside him: "Why, it's a regular stump speech. Listen there!"

The man on the rostrum made an acrid reference to the gold standard.

A small-boned, fat leg flopped across its mate, and Hanna changed his weight from one hunker to the other. "They ought to admit a lot more of those little sand patches and coyote ranges out West as States. We need 'em!" he said by way of sarcastic persiflage to Grosvenor.

Cannon's remarks were growing more and more luminous. As the orator proceeded, Hanna's brown eyes, which had been twinkling merrily at his own humor, began to glow in heat lightning. His mouth twitched two or three times, as if to cut off the tail of a truant smile, then spilled its rage in grunting imprecations. The rhetoric of the Utah man was telling. He referred to the Republican party as the party of oppression, and began to threaten to leave the party.

Then Hanna's harsh voice blurted out across the multitude, "Go, go!" He stopped, then renewed his courage and grumbled in a lower voice: "It's an insult. It oughtn't to go on in the proceedings of the convention."

Grosvenor swore a couple of bars. Bushnell carried the bass. Finally Cannon, shaking a flamboyant head of hair, put the threat to bolt in a rococo period of rhetoric, declaring that the Republican party had seceded from the truth. Hanna, uncoupling his short, fat legs from behind his chair, stretched out in nervous wrath. A steel sneer wired its way across his face as he groaned in a flat, harsh snarl:

"Oh, my God!"

There was a tragic half-second's silence. Ten thousand eyes turned toward Hanna. Evidently he could feel their glances hailing on his back, for his flinty auburn head bobbed down like a cork. He was still the businessman in 1896, and this blab was unbusinesslike. It was political. Hanna, the ironmaster, ducked. The orator on the rostrum had used the phrase, "the parting of the ways"—famous through the whole campaign to follow.

It was Hanna's voice that cried out, "Goodbye," an instant later. The whole convention was firing the word "Go" at the rostrum. Then Hanna, the politician, rose proudly from the small of his back, and got on the firing line. After that the Utah man was in the hands of a mob. Hanna devoted himself to the pleasurable excitements of the chase. He stormed and roared with the mob; he guyed and he cheered with the mob. He was of it, led by it, enjoying it, whooping it up.

Then, when it was all over, when an hour or so later the gold-standard platform had been adopted, Hanna climbed into his chair, clasped his hands composedly behind him, threw back his head, let out his voice, and sang "America" with the throng. Where he did not remember the words, his dah-dah-de-dah-de-dums rang out with patriotic felicity, and his smile of seraphic satisfaction was a good sight for sore eyes. For Mark Hanna was giving an excellent representation of a joyous American citizen with his wagon hitched to a bucking but conquered star, jogging peacefully down the Milky Way of victory.

When I came home from the convention Sallie was ill, and the doctors had told her that there was a spot on her lungs. Passes being easy to get, we went to Colorado, where my Aunt Kate was running a hotel. She took Sallie in. I returned to Emporia and sat at a telegraph desk while the story was going through of that great day in Chicago when William Jennings Bryan was nominated by the Democratic party as its Presidential candidate. That story, even on the wire, thrilled the nation. Here was a new figure. Here was a young man. Here was an intrepid advocate of a cause which he proclaimed as that of the downtrodden. It was the first time in my life and in the life of a generation in which any man large enough to lead a national party had boldly and unashamedly made his cause that of the poor and the oppressed. The story coming through in bulletins, even detached and sometimes overlapping and out of chronological order, pictured a scene that some day will be a part of a great drama. It was the emergence into middle-class respectability of the revolution that had been smoldering for a quarter of a century in American politics.

I saw the story in no such perspective as I do today. I was moved by fear and rage as the story came in. I had never heard of Bryan. To me, he was an incarnation of demagogy, the apotheosis of riot, destruction, and carnage. A little group of us were standing around the ticker as the story came in, and I can remember someone—and oh, if I could only remember his name—cried out as the drama climaxed in Bryan's nomination:

"Marat, Marat, Marat has won!"

It was with those words echoing in my heart that I entered the campaign of 1896, full of wrath and inspired with a fear that became consternation as the campaign deepened. It seemed to me that rude hands were trying

278

to tear down the tabernacle of our national life, to taint our currency with fiat. So, swallowing protection as a necessary evil and McKinley's candidacy as the price of national security, I went into the campaign with more zeal than intelligence, with more ardor than wisdom. The ardor of Kansas was more than a fever. It was a consuming flame. After the nomination of Bryan, which seemed like the swinging of a firebrand in a powder mill, people argued on the streets. The Republicans cried, "Socialists," which would have been a reasonable indictment if they had not immediately followed by calling the Democrats nihilists and anarchists. In offices, on the front porches of the town homes, everywhere the clamor of politics filled the air. I remember one day in July going to Topeka, where in Eugene Ware's office I sat with delight and heard him deliver a diatribe which rang the changes of what ails Kansas or what's wrong with our state. I sat chuckling at his poetic eloquence and told him that I was going to use that in an editorial sometime. He waved his hand and cried:

"Go to it, young man, with my blessing!"

At home I could not walk up Commercial Street without being pulled and hauled by the Populists. I hated wrangling. I never debated anything orally. My answer to argument all my life has been a grin or a giggle or a cocked eye, anything to avoid an acrimonious discussion. Anyway, I have always had to work too hard to bother with the futilities of debate for its own sake.

The Gazette kept me at work twelve hours a day. I was writing the editorials, a good share of the local items, soliciting the advertising, and looking after the subscription books. Subscriptions, in spite of the Populist boycott which had been clamped on early in the summer, were growing. The Republicans were rallying to the Gazette. The other paper, Lieutenant Governor Eskridge's Emporia Republican, had been a protagonist of free silver. The Governor, being a man in his sixties, could not take his political medicine without a wry face. All summer he was sputtering and spitting out, and the Republicans did not like his attitude. He was on the losing side. The Populists remembered his years of abuse. And, anyway, the young bull was strutting through the party herd with the old bull on the fringes thereof. In mid-August the proofs came to me for the book of short stories, "The Real Issue." When I opened the package, I was inordinately proud. I remember that I stopped in the midst of my work to look at the type and examine the make-up and form of the title page. It was most exciting. Being what I was, there was no alternative. I must take those proofs right out to Sallie Lindsay, and we must read them together. So came Saturday, August 13. I had decided to take the evening train to Colorado with the proof sheets. I hurried through my morning work. I got up some editorial for Monday, clipped out some editorials from other

Republican papers, wrote the day's local stories, and broke it to Lew Schmucker that he would have to run the paper for four or five days. Early that afternoon I went to the post office for the mail. It was before the days of mail delivery in the town. I remember that I had on my crash suit, which my mother had washed and ironed as she had so many times laundered my father's nankeens. I was dressed to go to Sallie in my best bib and tucker, and I probably looked like a large white egg as I waddled down the street to the post office, and came back with my arms full of newspaper exchanges. A block from the office a crowd of Populists tackled me. I was impatient and wanted to be on the way. They surrounded me. They were older men—men in their forties and fifties and sixties—and I was twenty-eight. They were shabbily dressed, and it was no pose with them. They were struggling with poverty and I was rather spick-and-span, particularly offensive in the gaudy neckties for which I have had an unfortunate weakness. Anyway, they ganged me—hooting, jeering, nagging me about some editorial utterances I had made. I was froggy in the meadow and couldn't get out, and they were taking a little stick and poking me about. And my wrath must have flamed through my face. Finally I broke through the cordon and stalked, as well as a fat man who toddles can stalk, down the street to the office. I slapped the bundle of mail on Lew Schmucker's desk and sat down to write for Monday's paper an editorial, and I headed it, "What's the Matter with Kansas?" And I remembered what Eugene Ware said and added frill for frill to his ironic diatribe, and it came out pure vitriol:

WHAT'S THE MATTER WITH KANSAS?

Today the Kansas Department of Agriculture sent out a statement which indicates that Kansas has gained less than two thousand people in the past year. There are about two hundred and twenty-five thousand families in this state, and there were ten thousand babies born in Kansas, and yet so many people have left the state that the natural increase is cut down to less than two thousand net.

This has been going on for eight years.

If there had been a high brick wall around the state eight years ago, and not a soul had been admitted or permitted to leave, Kansas would be a half million souls better off than she is today. And yet the nation has increased in population. In five years ten million people have been added to the national population, yet instead of gaining a share of this—say, half a million—Kansas has apparently been a plague spot and, in the very garden of the world, has lost population by ten thousands every year.

Not only has she lost population, but she has lost money. Every moneyed man in the state who could get out without loss has gone. Every month in every community sees someone who has a little money pack up and leave the state.

This has been going on for eight years. Money has been drained out all the time. In towns where ten years ago there were three or four or half a dozen money-lending concerns, stimulating industry by furnishing capital, there is now none, or one or two that are looking after the interests and principal already outstanding.

No one brings any money into Kansas any more. What community knows over one or two men who have moved in with more than $5,000 in the past three years? And what community cannot count half a score of men in that time who have left, taking all the money they could scrape together?

Yet the nation has grown rich; other states have increased in population and wealth—other neighboring states. Missouri has gained over two million, while Kansas has been losing half a million. Nebraska has gained in wealth and population while Kansas has gone downhill. Colorado has gained every way, while Kansas has lost every way since 1888.

What's the matter with Kansas?

There is no substantial city in the state. Every big town save one has lost in population. Yet Kansas City, Omaha, Lincoln, St. Louis, Denver, Colorado Springs, Sedalia, the cities of the Dakotas, St. Paul and Minneapolis and Des Moines—all cities and towns in the West—have steadily grown.

Take up the government blue book and you will see that Kansas is virtually off the map. Two or three little scrubby consular places in yellow-fever-stricken communities that do not aggregate ten thousand dollars a year is all the recognition that Kansas has. Nebraska draws about one hundred thousand dollars; little old North Dakota draws about fifty thousand dollars; Oklahoma doubles Kansas; Missouri leaves her a thousand miles behind; Colorado is almost seven times greater than Kansas—the whole west is ahead of Kansas.

Take it by any standard you please, Kansas is not in it.

Go east and you hear them laugh at Kansas; go west and they sneer at her; go south and they "cuss" her; go north and they have forgotten her. Go into any crowd of intelligent people gathered anywhere on the globe, and you will find the Kansas man on the defensive. The newspaper columns and magazines once devoted to praise of her, to boastful facts and startling figures concerning her resources, are now filled with cartoons, jibes and Pefferian speeches. Kansas just naturally isn't in it. She has traded places with Arkansas and Timbuctoo.

What's the matter with Kansas?

We all know; yet here we are at it again. We have an old mossback Jacksonian who snorts and howls because there is a bathtub in the State House; we are running that old jay for Governor. We have another shabby, wild-eyed, rattle-brained fanatic who has said openly in a dozen speeches that "the rights of the user are paramount to the rights of the owner"; we are running him for Chief Justice, so that capital will come tumbling over itself to get into the state. We have raked the old ash heap of failure in the state and found an old human hoop skirt who has failed as a businessman, who has failed as an editor, who has failed as a preacher, and we are going to run him for Congressman-at-Large. He will help the looks of the Kansas delegation at Washington. Then we have discovered a kid without a law practice and have decided to run him for Attorney

General. Then, for fear some hint that the state had become respectable might percolate through the civilized portions of the nation, we have decided to send three or four harpies out lecturing, telling the people that Kansas is raising hell and letting the corn go to weed.

Oh, this is a state to be proud of! We are a people who can hold up our heads! What we need is not more money, but less capital, fewer white shirts and brains, fewer men with business judgment, and more of those fellows who boast that they are "just ordinary clodhoppers, but they know more in a minute about finance than John Sherman"; we need more men who are "posted," who can bellow about the crime of '73, who hate prosperity, and who think, because a man believes in national honor, he is a tool of Wall Street. We have had a few of them—some hundred fifty thousand—but we need more.

We need several thousand gibbering idiots to scream about the "Great Red Dragon" of Lombard Street. We don't need population, we don't need wealth, we don't need well-dressed men on the streets, we don't need cities on the fertile prairies; you bet we don't! What we are after is the money power. Because we have become poorer and ornerier and meaner than a spavined, distempered mule, we, the people of Kansas, propose to kick; we don't care to build up, we wish to tear down.

"There are two ideas of government," said our noble Bryan at Chicago. "There are those who believe that if you legislate to make the well-to-do prosperous, this prosperity will leak through on those below. The Democratic idea has been that if you legislate to make the masses prosperous their prosperity will find its way up and through every class and rest upon them."

That's the stuff! Give the prosperous man the dickens! Legislate the thrift-less man into ease, whack the stuffing out of the creditors and tell the debtors who borrowed the money five years ago when money "per capita" was greater than it is now, that the contraction of currency gives him a right to repudiate.

Whoop it up for the ragged trousers; put the lazy, greasy fizzle, who can't pay his debts, on the altar, and bow down and worship him. Let the state ideal be high. What we need is not the respect of our fellow men, but the chance to get something for nothing.

Oh, yes, Kansas is a great state. Here are people fleeing from it by the score every day, capital going out of the state by the hundreds of dollars; and every industry but farming paralyzed, and that crippled, because its products have to go across the ocean before they can find a laboring man at work who can afford to buy them. Let's don't stop this year. Let's drive all the decent, self-respecting men out of the state. Let's keep the old clodhoppers who know it all. Let's encourage the man who is "posted." He can talk, and what we need is not mill hands to eat our meat, nor factory hands to eat our wheat, nor cities to oppress the farmer by consuming his butter and eggs and chickens and produce. What Kansas needs is men who can talk, who have large leisure to argue the currency question while their wives wait at home for that nickel's worth of bluing.

What's the matter with Kansas?

Nothing under the shining sun. She is losing her wealth, population and standing. She has got her statesmen, and the money power is afraid of her. Kansas is all right. She has started in to raise hell, as Mrs. Lease advised, and she seems to have an over-production. But that doesn't matter. Kansas never did believe in diversified crops. Kansas is all right. There is absolutely nothing wrong with Kansas. "Every prospect pleases and only man is vile."

I remember even across these years that I slammed the editorial above on the copy spike with a passionate satisfaction that I had answered those farmer hooligans. I was happy and turned to something else for the afternoon. Before I left I had read the proof on it, which meant that I probably revised it two or three or four times, as I always do even now when I have for the paper an editorial that I am proud of. And so, late that afternoon I gathered up my proofs, a book or two that had come, the magazines of the week, and took the train for Colorado to lay my treasures before the feet of my lady love, fancying myself a romantic figure. And so there at the little red-stone depot of Manitou, where she came running down the platform to meet me, and I hurried with all my treasures for her, the book of our pride, the papers and magazines which would bring us together so happily, a journey ended in lovers' meeting.

I Awaken to Fame

SALLIE AND I began that very Sunday morning reading the proofs of "The Real Issue," a joyous job—our first book. We read steadily that afternoon and the next day. On Tuesday, the Monday Gazette came with the editorial "What's the Matter with Kansas?" in it. Sallie was shocked. She feared I had gone too far: that it would make enemies, and enemies would make trouble in Lyon County. So now I was scared. I thought in my heart:

Well, there is another of those foolish impulsive things that I do which seem all right at the time but which I know when it is too late are inspired in a habitual unwisdom in me that amounts to a major weakness.

But we went on with the proofs until the middle of the week, and returned them to the publishers in Chicago. The next Sunday I took the train for home. Lew Schmucker wrote during the week that there was quite a lot of mail for me about "What's the Matter with Kansas?" and I was frightened. When I came into the Gazette office there was a fat stack of letters from all over the country about the editorial. A few of the letters were abusive. Most of them were laudatory and asked for extra copies. One which pleased me most was from Thomas B. Reed, Speaker of the House of Representatives, who declared:

"I haven't seen as much sense in one column in a dozen years."

I have kept that framed in my office over my desk now for forty-six years —my proudest trophy. Reed did not then even know my name. In his own handwriting, he had addressed it to "The Editor of the Gazette." Day after day those letters kept coming. We reset the editorial and printed it by the thousands. The Republican national committee reprinted it as a circular, and state Republican committees reprinted it in many forms. Mark Hanna told me a few months later that he had used it more widely than any other circular in the campaign. Suddenly, I—the Editor of the Emporia Gazette —a country paper with little more than five hundred circulation, was a somebody. The dimensions of my world were enlarged. Papers from all over the country asked for exchanges. Charles Curtis, now a member of Congress, came into the office early in September, two or three weeks after "What's the Matter with Kansas?" had struck the world, and offered to get me the Associated Press franchise and to buy two or three thousand copies of the paper to circulate in his district. It was done, though a little while after the election, of course, I stopped taking the telegraphic press news. I had to hire a part-time stenographer to handle my correspondence, and Lew Schmucker used to hoot and gibe at me as I dictated letters. To him, it seemed ridiculous. And he told Sallie to watch me sometime as I dictated and see me swell up. It was then, I think, that she said gayly: "No matter how important Will gets to be, he could never swell up. He has already swelled beyond the dimensions of any ordinary fame." Which was probably true. I grew up to my head that year.

The Bryan-McKinley campaign came to a noisy and highly emotionalized climax on election day. Bryan carried Kansas. The Democrats swept the State house and the Lyon County Courthouse. But McKinley won in the nation. I do not believe, as the academicians have said, that McKinley won because Hanna spent so much money. Few votes were actually purchased in that campaign. McKinley won because the Republicans had persuaded the middle class, almost to a man, that a threat to the gold standard was a threat to their property. Incidentally, labor as a class was persuaded to the point of coercion that if McKinley was defeated industry would shut down, and that if McKinley won prosperity would return because capital had confidence in the Republican party, and because the gold standard and the protective tariff as national policies would be established. The coercion was bald, unashamed, and effective. Hanna had more money than probably was ever spent in a national election before. But Bryan had enough to present his case fairly to the people. It was the case of the debtor, and he carried the debtor states—the South—perhaps automatically; the West also, in the face of a generation of traditional Republican allegiance. That campaign of 1896, in which I had a minor and not particularly creditable part —for I only aroused bad blood and bitter feeling—was the first national campaign in the United States in which the debtors were for the most part on one side and the creditors on the other. No one can doubt that labor sympathized with Bryan, even though it was persuaded more or less with crass coercion to vote against him. It was our first class-election. McKinley's victory was due to the fact that he could unite to a political solidarity the American middle class.

In Emporia, the day after election, the Populists and Democrats, for all their county and state victories, were sad, disgruntled, and discouraged. I felt at once that the pressure of opposition to me, to which I was extremely sensitive for all the success of "What's the Matter with Kansas?" had been relieved overnight. It was then, in their national victory, that the Republicans of our town rallied to me. As a national figure, I had their respect; and my ancient competitor, Governor Eskridge, who had before McKinley's nomination been a free-silver leader, could not quite claim a share in the Republican victory. All of which was rather unfair. The Governor, despite his free-silver heterodoxy, was at heart a better, more loyal party man than I; for to me partisanship, in the sense that it really governs men's thinking and directs their conduct, seemed always a political folly. I have always believed that parties were but a means to an end. A good partisan believes that partisanship and a party victory is an end in itself. Nevertheless I crowed editorially in the election for my party, and was much more bitter on our editorial page than I was in my heart. Probably my bitterness was to convince myself that I was right. But it did not work. Politically I was a poor sinner in the temple, wearing the broad phylacteries of a Pharisee and ashamed of my pride. Perhaps if I had known the real significance of that election, perhaps if I had realized that it was the beginning of a long fight for distributive justice, the opening of a campaign to bring to the common man—the man lacking the acquisitive virtues, the man of one talent—a larger and more equitable share in the common wealth of our country, I should have been more consciously ashamed of my political attitude than I was; for I was constitutionally and temperamentally, by blood and inheritance on both sides of my family, a friend of the underdog. But some way, in those days, I was blind to the realities. My college education, my reading in sociology and in science, to keep abreast and be worthy of fellowship with Vernon Kellogg, did not teach me to see the truth all about me in the middle nineties. I saw the mange on the underdog and did not realize its cause. Perhaps if Bryan had won and the underdog had been fed up a little and had been top dog, I should have respected him more heartily. I wonder. I doubt it. Perhaps I shrink from the truth, even now, looking back at those days.

One incident of that hour of triumph in November, 1896, has stuck vividly in my memory across the years. It was a sunny winter day. The Gazette office door was open. In walked Frank Frazier, an old banker friend from Eldorado. He was a cynic. It was said of him in Eldorado that he never made a loan without assuming that his debtor was a deadbeat and letting the debtor know it. He had a wiry voice—not high, but low and deadly. He was my father's friend, and was one of those who represented the Santa Fe in Butler County politics but kept entirely out of the limelight. He stood looking at me the way he appraised his customers in the bank, with a cocked eye, hard, mean, then began abruptly:

"Well, so you think you are a hell of a fellow. Maybe you are. At least you rung the bell in this election. Now let me give you one thing. Your father was my friend. I want to help you. I owed him something for things he did for me. And here's what I am paying you on that debt!"

He paused for a moment to gather himself.

"Young man, around town they say you are paying your bills. Major Hood says you have been getting out of the red recently. I guess you're on the upgrade. I know you put old Bent's Republican on its feet. But a damn sight of good that did! Now here's your inheritance from your father. I'll tell you, if for the next five years you will run your paper so straight and square and necessarily mean that you'll make every faction in this town hate you and every man in this town fear and despise you, then you'll know that you never can have any hope to run for office. You'll know you can't be elected to anything any time, and so you'll keep away from running for office. It kills any editor. Editors who take offices lose their influence and wreck their business. You've got to take the veil of absolute chastity, so far as political office goes. Boss it, if you can, but don't ever let them talk you into running for anything. And if you're mean-honest for the next five years, your paper will make money and you'll know you can't get an office. That, by God, is because I owed your father, not money, but many kindnesses."

He stared at me for a moment; and then the fat, chunky, hard-featured little county boss waddled like a potbellied god, out of the office without another word. But what he said sank deeply in my heart.

In mid-autumn after "What's the Matter with Kansas?" came the publication of "The Real Issue," a book of Kansas stories. It had the tremendous lift of the campaign editorial. But the campaign editorial could not have given the book the kinds of reviews that it had from the kinds of reviewers who praised it. For the book had nothing to do with the politics of the campaign of '96. The stories in the book were stories of Kansas life, mostly under three thousand words. Probably the average length was two thousand. The stories were modeled on Kipling, Davis, and Frank Stockton—on an American last but with a little of the French influence, Maupassant, Coppée, and Daudet—tear-jerkers most of them, though some were just ebullient Kansas spirits. Before the book had been out a month, a letter came from McClure's Magazine asking for the right to publish the story called "The King of Boyville," and ordering half a dozen others at five hundred dollars each. It was enough to lift one's hair and fit one's head into the dimensions of something approaching success. But the real thrill came in the late autumn when I went into the corner bookstore where Vernon Parrington and Frank Miller, who drove the oil wagon, and John Van Schaick, a young college professor, were loafing in the "Amen Corner." They yelled at me:

"Hey, Bill, did you see the review of your book in Life?" And, "My God, man, you've hit it!" And, "How did you wangle that out of them?"

I bought Life, which was then a critical journal with a humorous slant, and hurried with the magazine unread to Sallie who was in the office. We walked out, to be free of the slings and arrows of Lew Schmucker and the other reporter, and read it as we walked home on the sidewalk. It was a beautiful review written by Robert Bridges, who was one of the editors of Scribner's Magazine in its best years. He was the top-ranking literary critic of the country. Even a pleasant notice from Mr. Howells did not go so far nor mean so much as the review by "Droch," which was Bridges' nom de plume. Our eyes filled with tears and our hands met in a passionate grip as we walked under the falling leaves of the elm trees, along Sixth Avenue, toward home. It was a moment in life never to be forgotten. It was indeed the journey's end of our struggles and hardships. We had entered into a new life. We were breathing another atmosphere. The printer, the reporter, the editorial writer on the Star, the country editor wrestling three days a week with his pay roll, with his petty cares and troubles—all these skins which I had worn were cast aside. I was a young author. It was indeed journey's end and lovers' meeting.

That fall, amid great preparations at home which included a new suit of clothes, I crossed the Missouri River, headed eastward for the first time. I went to Chicago. Waiting at the station was a man who for ten or twenty years meant much in my life: Chauncey Williams of the firm of Way & Williams, publishers of "The Real Issue."

Behold Chauncey! Six feet, with a long fat face, a wide brow, kindly, gentle eyes, good sturdy nose, a pleasant mouth which reflected his capacity for affection, and a dimpled chin. He was twenty-six years old. His father had left him a hundred thousand dollars. He was of the University of Wisconsin and had found a book collector who loved rare books and first editions—Irving Way, who had been secretary to the president of the Santa Fe Railroad. He was Way, and Chauncey was Williams, of the publishing firm; and with an earnest, honest patience they were spending Chauncey's inheritance on publishing fine books. Another publishing house in Chicago, Stone & Kimball, was engaged in the same artistic task, though Stone & Kimball had a wider list of books which were more imaginative. Way & Williams went to London and bought the plates, or books of sheets, of dilettante books which they bound sumptuously and tried to float on the commercial market. Around these two Chicago publishing houses a group of authors had grown up: George Ade, Finley Peter Dunne (Mr. Dooley), Maurice Thompson, Elia W. Peattie (mother of Donald Culross Peattie), Hamlin Garland, and Henry B. Fuller. These people were found often in the big living room with a wide, hospitable hearth at one end, of Chauncey Williams' house. It was built by Frank Lloyd Wright, a young architect still, who was just pursuing the harlot goddess, Fame. And we used to sit around that hearth of his own envisioning, with Chauncey and Helen, his lovely wife who looked like a creature out of Rossetti's poems, and there was tall talk there, and sometimes a gaunt, loose-skinned, fiery-eyed rebel, Clarence Darrow, sat in the fireside circle, and sometimes Hamlin Garland came, always serious, always a rebuke to our ribaldry. And once in a while "Octave Thanet," a short-story teller from Iowa, a huge two-hundred-pound marshmallow of a woman who smiled easily and had a twinkling mind, was in that fireside group at Chauncey's.

It was all new to me that November, 1896, a new world with a brand-new set of angels, rather different on the whole from the Imperial Club, the Pan-Hellenic group at Lawrence, and the Pi Phi girls, and the Trundle Bed Trash at Eldorado. I was moving in a rarefied atmosphere, and my toes were just barely touching the insubstantial clouds beneath my feet. I used to pinch myself sitting there, or perhaps lunching with Chauncey and the literary nobility of some Chicago club which was rich and sumptuous beyond my imagining, and ask myself how that bellyful of Walnut Creek water, which had started the steam in my engine, had sent me so far! But I was always conscious of the Walnut Creek water and never pretended I had any other kind of steam in my pipes. The Chicago experience into which Sallie soon came was a definite step up in our lives to a place where we could see wider horizons and lovely visions. Chauncey's prodigality—and it was princely—brought us much that was dear and lovely in our lives. It seems, looking back at it now, that it was really a loftier rise, as indeed it was, from Emporia to Chicago than from Chicago to New York, or London, or Paris, or Moscow, or Rome, or Peking, where our journeys led us. The Chicago of the late nineties, provincially conscious of its new literary aspirations, was much more than New York a center of eager, earnest artists. Even then, I led a double life. I had to speak at the Marquette Club, the official Republican organization of the Middle West; and, best of all, that winter I went to a feast at Zanesville, Ohio, whereat Mark Hanna was the host. It was given for the men who, he publicly announced, had helped to win the battle of 1896. But the story of that journey is too long for this chapter.

CHAPTER XLII

There Were Giants in Those Days

AT THE ZANESVILLE, OHIO, victory dinner in the political hotel of the town, I met Mark Hanna. Chauncey Williams went with me. Hanna was the first national political boss the country had ever seen—a man who at that time held national power in a victorious party by reason of his control of its organization. We had had Congressional bosses who dominated Congress. We had had local bosses who dominated states and who, through the horse-trading power of states in conventions, sometimes for a day or a week or a month or season, rose to national eminence. Hanna, garbed by his cartoonist enemies in a dollar-marked checked suit, represented—with full authority and power to act—the amalgamated wealth, the merged and associated fears of the American middle class and its allied plutocracy.

When I came to him across the tiled lobby of the Zanesville Hotel, a medium-sized man, a little inclined to corpulence, not over five feet nine or ten, with a fading bronze complexion and a radiant, smiling, kindly face, he turned upon me his glowing brown eyes, reached for my hand, put his left hand on my shoulder, looked at me steadily from top to toe for a moment, twitched his loose lips and his nose in a funny grimace of pleasure, and said confidently: "Well, my boy, I am mighty glad to see you." Then quickly he added: "I owe a lot to you." Then, after a second's deliberation, he said: "Come on up to my room. I want to talk to you."

And so I met the most powerful man on the American continent. We went to his bedroom. In that day and time the political bedroom was the throne room of American politics, and this of Hanna's was typical—a small room with a narrow passage past the bed and the washstand to the window; at the other side of the window, a deep, fat chair at the foot of the bed and beside the chair a bureau with a mirror. Another chair, a small bedroom chair, completed the furnishings of the room, which was in black walnut, crawling with rococo decorations that meant nothing. On the washstand were the china bowl and pitcher. In the drawer of the washstand, or at the sides on a towel rack, were the towels. Under the washstand drawer the occupant of the room generally kept his whiskey or, if he was sophisticated, a flask of brandy. When the doors opened into the bottom of the washstand, the political ritual of the meeting had begun. Hanna affected to open the washstand doors and said: "Want something?" I shook my head. He said: "I thought so." He made me sit in the big chair. He took the little one. A third man would have sat on the bed, or a fourth. But there was no third; just he and I were there. Hanna began:

"Well, young man, I suppose you know now that I used your 'What's the Matter with Kansas' all over the country. I suppose we must have printed more than a million copies."

I do not remember how I replied—maybe I did not say anything; maybe I just sat and grinned, which is very likely. Then he went abruptly at it:

"Well, what do you want?"

I did not parry. That I remember well. And I came back at him as bluntly as he had come at me:

"Nothing, absolutely nothing. You couldn't give me an office if you wanted to, and I guess you do."

Hanna looked straight into my eyes for a second or two and then began to laugh. "That's all right, young man; that's all right. You'll come to it." Then he said quickly: "Is your paper making any money?"

I answered: "A little. Enough."

"All right, all right. When you change your mind, just come around to me. I'm kinda glad you take it as you do. Have you been down to see the Governor yet?" (He meant, of course, McKinley.)

I answered: "No."

He snapped back: "Well, you've got to go. He'll be glad to see you."

I had not planned to visit McKinley, probably because he did not interest me. During his long front-porch campaign, even when the Kansas delegation went to Canton, McKinley's home town, I did not care to go, though my expenses probably would have been paid. I hesitated for a moment and Hanna looked straight at me and said:

"Nevertheless, you must go!" and sat there at the washstand where he had pen and paper, and with his own hand wrote a letter beginning: "My dear Governor," then identifying me with "What's the Matter with Kansas" and adding and underscoring, "He wants no office!" He read it, then showed it to me, then put it in an envelope with the proper inscription.

He then began to ask me about Kansas politics, Cy Leland, and also of J. R. Burton and Governor Morrill, the new Populist victors in Kansas. And then after he had assembled a little information, he rose and steered me out of the room. Probably five minutes was all the time he gave to me. But in that five minutes he convinced me that, personally, Mark Hanna was an honest, just, ever generous man who had no frills, no side, no nonsense about him, a man with a sense of humor and a sense of loyalty; and I have not changed that opinion in nearly fifty years.

I remember little about the dinner except that the Democrats called it the Feast of Belshazzar. I made my speech. I had written it in Emporia and memorized it, and I may have gotten it off at least fairly well, because it was gay, to the point of festivity, as became a victory dinner. I had my share of applause. I remember that I sat beside Booker Washington, the negro president of Tuskegee Institute. I sat there by choice. I may have moved my place card, or may have asked to have it moved. At any rate, I saw that the man who was placed there did not sit down, and I landed at Booker Washington's side. He may have seen the maneuver. He said nothing about it. (Once at a Hamilton Club banquet, in Chicago, the same thing happened. George Peck came to me and said: "Will, you and I must flank Booker Washington," and we did.)

The day after the Feast of Belshazzar, Chauncey and I went to Canton armed with my letter. We sat in the anteroom, ten or fifteen minutes, then I went in, taking Chauncey. My letter was lying on McKinley's worktable. Our interview was short. McKinley sat in his chair. I sat at his side. While we were talking, I picked up the letter and had it in my pocket. I do not think he saw me, for I stood where he could not see my hand. I treasured the letter more than I valued the audience he gave me. The audience was most perfunctory, cordial enough but I felt the heat was regulated by a thermostat. He gave me just the degree of warmth I deserved. He thanked me for "What's the Matter with Kansas," but even though Mark Hanna had told him that I wanted no office, he had that inner shrewdness, that bland cynicism which distrusted human nature, and he left no opportunity for me to change my mind, then or ever. We just were not meant for each other—William McKinley and I. He was destined for a statue in a park, and was practicing the pose for it. When we got out of his presence, we hurried into our coats in the anteroom, and on the front porch Chauncey reached down and got a handful of snow and rubbed the hand that had clasped the hand that held the scepter of his country. And then we both ran roaring down the steps to the hack that was waiting for us.

That day Chauncey and I visited "the trade" in Ohio, to stimulate the sale of "The Real Issue." We went into the Methodist Book Concern in Cincinnati, called on Burroughs in Cleveland, somebody in Toledo, and then went down and spent a day with James Whitcomb Riley. We invited him to lunch at our hotel. He dined us at his club. And that day also I met for the first time off his Presidential pedestal, Benjamin Harrison, and chatted with him for half an hour. He left me with profound respect for him—a man of erudition, of real culture, a wise and kindly gentleman who never could wear the courtesan's scarlet mantle, and so in his Quaker gray of reserved sincerity, seemed cold and repellent to the politicians who were used to those manners which the second oldest profession in the world—the ruler's cult—learned from the oldest profession many thousands of years ago.

I came home from that swing around the circle with Chauncey Williams to begin the "Boyville" stories, which afterward became a book. As they went out and the money came in, it went directly to pay the mortgage on my mother's property, which in a few years was released. As 1897 opened and as the Republicans came back to power nationally, a post-office row arose in Emporia, and patronage rows arose all over the state. Mr. Leland's leadership was being challenged by his factional opponents, the followers of J. R. Burton.* Our Congressman, Charles Curtis, in the local post-office fight arrayed himself with the Emporia faction that opposed Major Hood. Curtis recommended a candidate for postmaster, and Major Hood's ally—United States Senator Baker—recommended another. It was a bitter fight. I favored a third man who had no chance and, finally, I supported the Major's candidate. By June, even with Leland's support and the Senator's endorsement, our candidate was having a tough time at the White House because after all the postmaster is under Congressional, not Senatorial, patronage and the gentle McKinley was playing the game according to the rules. A letter came from Senator Baker to the Major saying that Curtis would compromise on my appointment as postmaster at Emporia. I had just one card in my hand, Mark Hanna's promise to stand by me. So I got passes for Sallie and for me and the Major came tiptoeing into the office before I went, and handed me a hundred dollars, for which I afterward gave him a note and later paid it.

At the train, as we passed through Topeka, Cy Leland came in, handed me an envelope and said, "This ought to help you out a little," turned quickly, and went away.

His appointment as district pension commissioner had been made, but I believe had not been confirmed. He said nothing about it. But he knew well that he did not need to. So Sallie and I made our first trip across the Alleghenies. She was twenty-six and I was twenty-nine. We were young and scared. We had railway passes; we probably had a shoebox full of fried chicken and deviled eggs, which lasted us two days for meals. We went to a little hotel known as the Normandie, infested with congressmen, judges, and statesmen, some of high degree. Across McPherson Park was the Arlington, where Senator Hanna was housed in regal splendor. We paid $3.50 a day for our room with bath, and ate out of the hotel at little restau-

---

* Mr. Burton may be identified as the Kansas statesman who later became United States Senator and ended his term in jail for irregular practices.

rants and holes-in-the-wall, where for a quarter one could substantially stoke one's physical furnace. Those holes-in-the-wall thrive, but country editors no longer eat there.

We had arrived early in the morning and by half past eight we had had breakfast and I was in the lobby of the Arlington and the boy who was paging Senator Hanna led me into the dining room, where he was at breakfast with his secretary and some Ohio politicians. He saw me and knew me as I came across the room and rose with his napkin in his hand, to meet me half way to his table. He turned his fine, glowing brown Irish eyes on me and with his nose and loose lips twitching in mischievous gayety, called out:

"I knew it. I knew you would be back. I knew you would change your mind. Well, I'm as good as my word."

And he sat me down among the statesmen and told them who I was.

I blurted out my story, the object of my journey. I wanted his help, I said, to keep out of office and told him about the Curtis-Baker compromise. When I had finished he asked quickly, almost abruptly:

"What can I do?"

I told him that I wanted him to take me to the President and wanted him to ask the President in my presence to promise never to sign my commission. I must have spoken awkwardly and with some emotion, for the crowd at the breakfast table laughed and Hanna threw back his head, put his hands on the table and said:

"Gentlemen, witness this marvel. I have had all kinds of requests from all kinds of people in the last six months, but this beats them all. This boy puts me on the griddle and wants me to promise to keep him out of office. Well, I'll be damned."

Half an hour later, Hanna and I were in the White House. They were repairing it. The President was in a downstairs office. As we approached, the Senator, with his arms in fatherly affection around my shoulders, smiling like a locomotive headlight, his eyes dancing and his nose and mouth twitching to indicate merriment, the President at his desk looked up and saw us. It was clearly obvious to me that all Hanna's gayety and the obvious turning on of charm, which was a bit conscious, bespoke a surprising relation. McKinley, not Hanna, was dominant in their friendship. Hanna—the nation's first big boss, Hanna of the dollar-mark suit, Hanna who ruled his party with a rod of iron—was just a shade obsequious in the presence of the bronze statue in the double-breasted Prince Albert coat and in the unwrinkled mask of a face. His greeting, whatever words he used, amounted to:

"Well, what can I do for you two?"

And Hanna waggishly began: "Mr. President, this is my boy."

A shocked, humorless batting of an eye showed Hanna that the President did not understand. McKinley looked at the two of us. We were the same shape, about the same height and had much the same moon faces. And Hanna, who was quick, perceived the question in McKinley's heart.

"Oh, no, Governor, no, no! I mean he's my spiritual son."

McKinley was not too sensitive to show his relief, and Hanna went on: "The only promise I have out is to help this young man, and I ask you to heed his request for we are both indebted to him."

The President withheld any assent to Hanna's question. His eyebrows raised in interrogation and I cut in: "Mr. President, I want you to keep me out of office. I do not want to be postmaster at Emporia."

There the President was on solid ground. He knew then what I wanted. It was plain that the Curtis-Baker compromise had been presented to him. With conspicuous judicial poise, he said:

"Well, I don't see what I can do if the congressman and the senator agree to it and the commission comes up from the Postmaster General."

Hanna cut in rather sharply: "Well, you can refuse to sign the commission. Mr. White is in earnest about this, Governor, and I think we owe it to him."

The President looked up slowly to see if Hanna was really in earnest and caught unmistakably the true ring in his voice and the sincerity stamped on his countenance. The President paused a moment, fingered his desk, shut his jaw, registering judicial composure, probably counted five or maybe ten to save himself, then replied:

"Well, Mr. White, so long as Mr. Hanna insists, I see no reason why I should not grant your request."

I then presented Mr. Leland's compliments to the President, got exactly to the pennyweight the return of cordiality which a national committeeman is entitled to for his message, and after a few most perfunctory remarks Senator Hanna led me away. He saw by my face, when we were in the anteroom, just what I thought had been revealed in those few moments there at the President's desk about the attitude of the two friends. Hanna, looking at me askance, grinned and said:

"When you know the Governor better, you'll understand him."

Now I have forgotten my reply. It is unimportant. We stayed around Washington, doing various chores which I knew Mr. Leland wanted and which I could do easily: among other things, securing the confirmation of Glen Miller, nephew of Leland's old friend, Sol Miller, as United States Marshal of Utah. Glen Miller was a Kansas University alumnus who had been to Europe and had written letters from there for the Kansas University Weekly Courier when I was one of its editors—letters which I read with envy and pride.

He was now waiting here in Washington until Hanna could act. Hanna was Miller's champion and a long factional fight, involving the intrigues of Mormon politics, had to be won. Miller had moved down from the Normandie to a boarding house, where for a dollar a day he had a room and three meals. He glorified the place until, one day when I was out of town, Sallie moved us into another boarding house of its class and kind which Miller recommended, his house being full at the moment. The room was comfortable enough, but the meals left something to be desired for a husky, full-feeding Kansan. After a day or two of sojourn in the respectable atmosphere of that boarding house, I acquired a jumpy, nervous, irritable hunger, and Miller—having suddenly had a great streak of luck (Hanna had finally promised him the job)—took Sallie and me out to a resort near Washington for dinner, called Cabin John's. We rode out on a street car. Senators and Congressmen also used that vehicle, and also crowded the precincts of Cabin John's. It was a gay, even festive, resort of the aristocracy; and Miller, who was a familiar of the place, ordered the dinner with a magnificent wave of his hand.

The preliminaries came, possibly oysters, celery, olives, young onions, whatever was seasonable and proper, and then the waiter brought in a large Potomac River shad, planked. Now let us look at the stage setting of that shad. Consider three days at a genteel boarding house: one small chop with parsley on a plate as the hero of its dinner, with little side plates dancing around it decked with a few feeble beans, stewed tomatoes, a pallid pat of mashed potatoes; then a salad course consisting of a forkful of cabbage and some shredded lettuce; and for dessert a saucer of bread pudding or an acute angle of pie—and that for a husky, corn-fed youth of twenty-eight with something of an abdominal tendency, who at home was addicted to thick, rare beefsteaks or heavy roasts on weekdays, and piled platters of fried chicken of a Sunday.

I was so hungry that I nearly howled. When that large planked shad came on, I noticed that the others helped themselves to it sparingly, after which I took one whole side, accoutered with shoestring potatoes. I wolfed my large portion down, growling beatifically, and urged the others to come on. Sallie was polite; Glen Miller was the host. Sallie signaled a negative, but my blood was up. I lunged forward with my weapons and rescued the remains of the fish. The waiter took away its skeleton and I leaned back at the end—a giant refreshed. I wondered how the others could eat so sparingly. I was stuffed, at peace, sated, complacent, fuller than a tick.

And then I had the shock of my life, for the waiter brought in two huge, tender, delicious-looking, golden-brown, charcoal-broiled chickens. My face showed my consternation. I had not known it was a table d'hôte dinner. He flanked this with an alligator pear salad, but I could only pick at it.

Even the gorgeous slab of strawberry shortcake found me cloyed, inept and incompetent, while my companions gloated in the feast. Subsequent proceedings interested me no more, and I was full of shame.

Now these details are set down somewhat to reveal a major tragedy in my life, but largely to indicate the size of the dollar in those days. That dinner with all its effulgence, served with acres of white linen in a lovely woodland setting amidst the powerful and noble of the earth (a senator and two ambassadors were there), cost Glen Miller one dollar and fifty cents a plate, and he gave the waiter a forty-cent tip and made him a willing slave. But five dollars in that far day was a king's ransom. Miller spent it like a Persian prince. It brought homage and fame, commanded vassels and serfs.

It was on that trip to Washington that Congressman Charles Curtis introduced me to the man who, more than any other in my twenties, thirties and forties, dominated my life. Curtis said one day, after he knew that my name as a compromise had been withdrawn and that he was probably licked in the Emporia post-office fight:

"Will, there's a man down in the Navy Department that has been asking for you. He knows you are my constit—a young fellow named Roosevelt. He read 'What's the Matter with Kansas?' He knows about your book. He heard you were in town, and he wants to meet you."

So we arranged an appointment. I met Theodore Roosevelt. He sounded in my heart the first trumpet call of the new time that was to be. I went hurrying home from our first casual meeting, in the office of an assistant of the Navy Department, to tell Sallie of the marvel of the meeting. I was afire with the splendor of the personality that I had met, and I walked up and down our little bedroom at the Normandie trying to impart to her some of the marvel that I saw in this young man. We were to lunch together the next day at the Army and Navy Club, where I went stepping on air, as one goes to meet an apparition. It was a rather somber old barn in those days, that club, and we sat there for an hour after lunch and talked our jaws loose about everything. I had never known such a man as he, and never shall again. He overcame me. And in the hour or two we spent that day at lunch, and in a walk down F Street, he poured into my heart such visions, such ideals, such hopes, such a new attitude toward life and patriotism and the meaning of things, as I had never dreamed men had. We had this in common: neither of us could work up any enthusiasm for McKinley. I remember the first shock of pain with which he revealed not only his scorn for McKinley and his kind, but his disgust with the plutocracy that Hanna was establishing in the land. For Hanna, he had a certain large, joyous tolerance as a man, but for the government he was maintaining, for the reign of privilege he was constructing, for the whole deep and damnable alliance between business and politics for the good of business, Roosevelt was full of vocal eloquence and ironic rage. That was the order which I had upheld, to which I was committed, to which I had commended my soul. Yet so strong was this young Roosevelt—hard-muscled, hard-voiced even when the voice cracked in falsetto, with hard, wriggling jaw muscles, and snapping teeth, even when he cackled in raucous glee, so completely did the personality of this man overcome me that I made no protest and accepted his dictum as my creed. Presently we launched out into Heaven knows what seas of speculation, what excursions of delight, into books and men and manners, poetry and philosophy—"cabbages and kings!" After that I was his man.

It was not the ten years between us. It was more than the background of his achievements in politics. It was something besides his social status which itself might have influenced me in those days, something greater even than his erudition and his cultural equipment, that overcame me. It was out of the spirit of the man, the undefinable equation of his identity, body, mind, emotion, the soul of him, that grappled with me and, quite apart from reason, brought me into his train. It was youth and the new order calling youth away from the old order. It was the inexorable coming of change into life, the passing of the old into the new.

I was only functioning after the manner of my kind. All the youth of that day was leaving the nineteenth century and hurrying into the twentieth. And this was one of the episodes of a spiritual migration as definite, and yet as marvelous, as that which came when our grandfathers and fathers poured over the Alleghenies into the Mississippi Valley and built their homes there. We were building our homes too—mansions not made by hands. And so came the new order.

To think that the difference in the size of a dollar, a mere dollar, measures so much of the difference between the world of the 1890's and the world of this latter half of the third decade of the new century, is a doleful thought. We should like to think, being men who have put a life of aspiration and struggle into the generation, that we have done something for humanity. That new world, which came into being with the new century, seemed while we were making it to be a new heaven and a new earth. The thing that happened was the shrinking of the dollar, and with that shrinking came the enlargement of our needs. Maybe the miracle of change was something like this: our dollar would buy less; our lives required more. Hence, the world turned inside out and upside down.

Theodore Roosevelt and I, walking that summer day under the elms on F Street in Washington, going from the lunch at the Army and Navy Club, visioned a vast amount of justice to come in the cruel world. Much that we visioned has come.

A few months later he sent me his book "American Ideals and Other Essays." I read it with feelings of mingled astonishment and trepidation. It shook my foundations, for it questioned things as they are. It challenged a complacent plutocracy. I did not dream that anyone, save the fly-by-night demagogues of Populism, had any question about the divine right of the well-to-do to rule the world. But that book was filled with an unsettling arraignment of the more predatory representatives of our American plutocracy. As a defender of the faith, I had met my first heretic.

CHAPTER XLIII

Home in Clouds of Glory

I CAME BACK to the hotel from my luncheon with Theodore Roosevelt, literally thrilled with his personality. I burst in on Sallie with the story of our luncheon at the Army and Navy Club, including my first double mutton chop. All of this I poured into Sallie's ear that summer afternoon, and the next day or so she bundled me up and sent me on my pass to New York City—my first trip to the great metropolis.

I had seen cities, Kansas City, St. Louis, Denver, Chicago, but even in 1897 the New York sky line as I ferried across to the Twenty-third Street slip, made my country eyes bug out with excitement. I put up at the Netherlands Hotel, as it was in those days a rather gorgeous rococo place. And after I had stowed away my grip I hurried downtown to the office of McClure's Magazine, somewhere around Twenty-third Street and Fourth Avenue. There, for the first time, I met in the flesh real magazine editors —Sam McClure, John Phillips, his guardian angel; Auguste F. Jaccaci, the art editor of the magazine, and Ida M. Tarbell. They had bought my "Boyville" stories. They were gracious beyond words to me. That night John Phillips, Jaccaci, and Ida Tarbell took me far uptown on a street car amid an unbelievable squirming army of bicycles to Grant's Tomb, where we had a gorgeous dinner and much tall talk about the magazine business and current literature. These people knew Rudyard Kipling. They knew Robert Louis Stevenson. They had dealt with Anthony Hope Hawkins, whose novels were quite the vogue. The new English poets were their friends.

And during the day they had made an appointment for me to see William Dean Howells, who had written pleasantly about my book. He was living somewhere south of Twentieth Street between Third Avenue and Broadway, in an apartment, and I remember that they were all packed up to leave for the summer. He was a gentle, sweet-voiced, keen-eyed, stoop-shouldered, stocky man, then, I should say, about sixty years old, and I remember that he sat on a trunk and tattooed his heels against it as we talked quite informally. He poured honey into my ears about my book and a "Boyville" story that he had read, and his sparrowlike wife kept flitting in and out of the room, perhaps to remind him that he was holding me too long. At least I thought so. And after a few minutes, maybe twenty, or perhaps half an hour, I hurried away and, as Jacob must have left the angel after the wrestle, quite out of breath spiritually and greatly exalted. I became a literary acolyte in his temple. Many times afterwards we met but, looking back on that day, I am still proud and happy when I think that amidst the crowded hours of packing for a journey, this kindly man who meant so much to American letters in the eighties and nineties, and the first decade of our century, was so patient with me, so altogether lovely and forbearing. He tolerated fools gladly, which I suppose is a test of human kindness.

The McClure group became for ten or fifteen years my New York fortress, spiritual, literary and, because they paid me well, financial. They were at heart midwestern. They talked the Mississippi Valley vernacular. They thought as we thought in Emporia about men and things. They were making a magazine for our kind—the literate middle class. This group had real influence upon the times from McKinley to Wilson. It is well to pause here for a moment and consider them.

Enter Sam McClure: blond, tow-headed and mustached, blue-to-hazel eyes, oval face, short, that is five feet seven or eight, with a wire voice which had come down from some Scotch or New England ancestry. He talked like a pair of scissors, clipping his sentences, sometimes his words; gave the impression of a powerhouse of energy. He was full of ideas. Sam McClure was graduated from Knox College. He had married the president's daughter. His wife's people knew my mother, and that was a tie. When my mother was a student at Knox College, Mrs. McClure's father had been her teacher and friend. Sam McClure, during my first half-hour in the office, swamped me with assignments, piled ideas all over me for stories and articles. If I had taken them all, I should be working yet on them. And a lot of them were excellent. Some of them I took, after John Phillips had gleaned them from the pile of chaff. Being a fellow midwesterner, I probably called him by his first name and he called me by mine after the second meeting. He was always Sam to me and John Phillips was always John, and Miss Tarbell was always Ida M., and Jaccaci was always Jack. And I loved them all. There was no New England repression in our relations. They were cordial to the point of ardent. I know that I was Will when I left the restaurant at Grant's Tomb to go to my hotel and pick up my grip to go to the ferry that night.

To be fathered by Mark Hanna as a son, even if McKinley was shocked at the feeling for a fleeting second that I might have been an illegitimate son; to have met Theodore Roosevelt and to have walked with him under the young maple trees of F Street between his club and his office; to have met even casually, as a part of my errands for Mr. Leland, a dozen Congressmen and Senators; and to have shaken hands and had the glowing brown eyes of Tom Reed beaming upon me from his height, a great hulking blubber of a human figure; to have seen the skyline of New York from the ferry at early morning; then to have seen William Dean Howells sitting on a trunk and scuffing his heels on it as he talked so gently and so wisely to me; and then to have walked with the high gods that sat as a Jovian rabble around Sam McClure, surely that eastern trip for a young couple in their late twenties was enough glamour for one year. "Mine eyes have seen the glory" of the seven hills of Olympus.

When I came home to Emporia and strolled into the corner bookstore where Vernon Parrington and Will Griffith, a painter who had studied in Paris and later was to have his own fame on the Pacific Coast, and John Van Schaick, the young English Professor at the College of Emporia, John Madden, who had once run as a Populist candidate for Congress, and maybe Vernon Kellogg—if he was home that year—were loafing, I had a story to tell. The tall stack of McClure's Magazines there on the magazine counter meant something to me. For days I was a Marco Polo in that amen corner of the bookstore, telling of the wonders and delights of my trip to the East. I hope yet, with something more than vague uneasiness, that I was not a prig and a bore. For years that corner in the bookstore there on Commercial Street was a hangout for the young fellows around town, young fellows too proud for pool, too wicked for prayer meetings, too lazy for baseball (though Vernon Parrington pitched a mean outcurve on the Emporia Browns), too sophisticated for the local poker game, and too young and full of visions to let the world go by without trying to understand it. Though certainly we were as blind as anyone. How could we know that the syncopated puff-puff of the gasoline engine in Kincaid's cabinet shop and at the mill of the Cottonwood and in Sprague's planing mill was the machine gun of an impending revolution? We stood one day in the door of the bookstore, at the turn of the century, and watched, in a parade that was passing, a buggy drawn by two mules, with a great sign over it "Horseless Carriage," and we laughed with the others. We talked there in the bookstore about the Klondike. Three or four young fellows left town for the Klondike and we read the story in their letters, published in the Gazette, of their adventures through snow and ice. How could we know that the Klondike gold mines and those of South Africa would solve the problem that Bryan had set, and make the issue of free silver at sixteen to one a dead cock in the pit? A gold inflation of the currency was on the way. After the election of McKinley and the year following, the Democrats thought it was smart to ask a Republican:

"By the way, have you seen the General?"

"What General?"

"General Prosperity! Haw, haw, haw!"

But at the end of 1897 and the beginning of '98, that joke grew stale. The wheels began to turn partly through confidence that the plutocracy was safe, partly to catch up with the production which lagged in the long idleness of the early and middle nineties, and partly because the currency was slowly expanding, as Alaska's gold flowed in. It was madness. We young visionaries there in the alcove at the corner bookstore, who thought we were so smart as we took the world apart and put it together again, were as dumb as the boys in the pool hall about the realities that were coming into our world. The Gazette's editorials in those days were partisan and on the whole, I suppose, rather foolish. But we did brag about prosperity. We did chortle as Populism and the fiat money democracy faded from our politics. Another thing: Cy Leland, the state boss, had been appointed pension commissioner for thirty-four states, including Kansas, Missouri, and Nebraska. The pension blanks sent to him from Washington had to be partially reprinted, and he gave me the job. I bought a Gordon press, later two, started a small job office, and the income from printing the pension blanks amounted to nearly three thousand dollars a year—all velvet. The mortgage faded in a year or two, and prosperity around the Gazette office was a reality. I paid all the notes at the major's bank.

Advertising, which had been sold largely as a subsidy in 1895, when I took over the paper, began to sell as a commodity as the circulation grew and as storekeepers enlarged their stock and learned that there was magic in a quick turnover.

The whole world about us was changing. Our prosperity, Sallie's and mine, at the office and in our home where we kept adding this stick of furniture and that picture, rug, or bit of linen, moved along like a tide, so slowly that we scarcely noticed it. Yet looking back we could see how surely it came.

It was in those days, before we realized that the hard days were over, that Charley Curtis came to town on some kind of electioneering trip. We were in his district. I was scheduled to pick up a horse and buggy at the livery stable and take him out to Plymouth and maybe up to Allen, little towns built around a schoolhouse, a general store, or a blacksmith shop, where he was making speeches. I remember that with some trepidation we stretched our budget to include a can of mushrooms and a two-inch beefsteak when Curtis came to our house for dinner.

A steak-and-mushroom dinner was an event in the White household, and we were tremendously proud of the landscape on the dining room table when the pièce de résistance appeared in all its glory of garnishing with canned mushrooms. I carved it like a little man. It was just pink rare. The mushroom sauce creamed it with pastel gray. The au gratin potatoes were browned to a turn. The expensive French peas, all shiny and green out of a bottle, were served with pride. As we began to eat, Sallie and I noticed with consternation that Curtis—scion of the proud and noble red man of the forest—carefully picked off and laid aside on his plate those precious mushrooms, our sign of culinary triumph and social distinction.

He did not eat one. I had served him more than his share. My mother's hawk eye caught his gesture and I feared that she would tell him what she thought of him. But she restrained herself and at the end of the meal, after he had gone, with one voice we cried in our trepidation and disgust:

"The next time that Injun comes to our table, we'll serve him dog!"

Another thing I remember about Curtis on that trip: a mile or two before we got to Plymouth, he pulled out a little book on which were the names of the Republicans of Pike Township, surrounding Plymouth, and like a pious worshiper out of a prayer book he began mumbling their names to impress them on his memory. It was a curious rite, I thought, and funny, and I giggled. But it was dead serious to Curtis. He had a little book like that for every township in Kansas, and carried the county's Republican poll list when he went into a county. In that way he survived politically for forty years. No matter what the issue was, it did not concern him. He knew that if he could call a man's name in a crowd, shake hands with him and ask him about his wife and children, whose names were also in the little book, he had that man's vote. Whether Curtis was for free silver or the protective tariff, the railroad regulations or what not, the voter was hypnotized by the fact that the Congressman knew him as an old friend.

And what a congressman he was: Well on to six feet tall, sturdy but not fat, with that raven mop of black coarse hair, that silken mustache, those glowing black beady eyes that were kindness electrified, that warm hand-shake, that ingratiating smile, that strong, warm, cordial voice—he was a kind of animated figure of political seduction whom few voters could resist. The old soldiers of the Civil War, members of the G.A.R. whose cause he championed and defended on the stump, called him "Our Charley" because his father had been a Civil War veteran. He "Our-Charleyed" his way in Kansas politics and in the Republican organization of the nation for more than thirty years, a man who after his one blast for free silver never let the expression of his conviction affect in any way his rise in prestige and power. Thus, statesmen are made and wax strong through the years in our democracy. And, strange as it may seem, the Republic stands. God moves in a mysterious way, his wonders to perform.

I write this, not irreverently but in amazement that approaches awe. As the year 1897 drew to its close, America was approaching the forks of her road to destiny. We had been trudging along to that crossroad for five years. When I was on the Star, part of my job was to make up a page of world news for the weekly, and in 1893, '94, and '95 our difficulties with the Spaniards in Cuba began to occupy more and more space on that news page. The Spaniards were having some sort of a war with the Cubans. It was probably one of those long drawn-out rebellions which the natives everywhere in the nineteenth century were making against Spanish rule. But because Cuba was only a few hours from our coastline and because many hundreds of millions of American dollars were invested in Cuban industry, largely sugar and rum, and then because we were a soft-hearted people, hated tyranny and loved justice, those who had the dollar invested were making it plain to the tender-hearted people that Cuba was being oppressed. No doubt of that!

No doubt also that the oppression was related to American business, politics and health, for yellow fever was one of the Cuban exports that affected American life. I saw this story of Cuban oppression spreading wider and wider across the United States and sinking deeper and deeper into the national consciousness. American sympathy for the oppressed was following the American invested dollar and beckoning the American flag. Charley Curtis made some speeches, as did most of our Congressmen in Kansas, about the oppression of the Cubans, and he waved his flag along with a lot of other statesmen across the world because it brought applause and made votes, and who would have thought that there was much more to it than a little temporary enthusiasm? "Our Charley" knew nothing about the deeper currents of imperialism that were sweeping the world in the nineteenth century. He was out after votes to hold his job, and "free Cuba" was a vote-getter. I wrote editorials about "free Cuba," just as casually as Charley Curtis wrote speeches. I do not remember which side I took, but whichever side I took was taken in ignorance of the deep movements of the heart of man all over this planet that were moving toward freedom and the protection of the invested dollar of free men, the thing called imperialism which, like a lodestone, had pulled humanity across the earth in iron ships and steel, over rails across vast deserts, through jungles and over mountains, building up the structure of a world commerce: a structure that within three decades was to bear down so hard upon our political institutions that they began to creak and crack and sag and snap for the tangled rights of nations, and the snarling skein of human freedom began to mess and mix up that vast structure of world credit based upon the pledges of many nations, mortgaging the souls and bodies of millions upon millions of men. And we in Emporia, and "Our Charley" in Washington, thought we were free to spout and jower and jangle about the atrocities of the "brute Weyler" without in the slightest affecting the reality of our lives. We were as little boys making snoots across the fence, throwing rocks into the next yard, but innocent of the fact that we were starting wars that would last far into the next century, threaten all that we loved and wreck much that we cherished.

Our little immediate, intimate part of it came when Fred Funston sat around the big baseburner in our little parlor and told us about his adventures in Cuba. He had gone there after a job had run out as an auditor of the Santa Fe, wherein he signed his name on many a bond and mortgage for the company, after he had gone into Central America with some friends in Lawrence and wasted their money and his in a coffee plantation, had come back to New York without a job and had helped a friend in a New York boarding house set up a machine gun which a Cuban General had bought to send to Cuba.

Funston and the friend went with the gun. He fought in the Cuban rebellion for two or three years, twice was wounded, once through the chest, and lay on a bullhide hammock stretched in a Cuban forest for three months; then had risen to the rank of Major; then came home to America on sick furlough and was lecturing in Kansas. He talked in Emporia. The boys whom he knew in the university in the eighties made lecture dates for him in their home towns. He was charging fifty dollars and would take twenty-five—and was living happily ever after, except once in a while he would spit up a bit of blood. But the story he told there at our fireside, as the hard coal glowed in the big baseburner, was a story that might have been told in the sixteenth or seventeenth century when an adventurer came home from distant lands bringing the tale of his wonders to his admiring friends. In Funston's case it was told with chuckles, giggles and vast modesty. He debunked his own heroism. He exalted and generally guyed the courage of his comrades and depreciated their sorrows and selfishness by multiplying their joys when the day's fighting was done.

Funston had become something of a figure in Kansas. His father was in Congress. We talked over that, around the baseburner, considering whether or not it might be wise for Funston to run for something. But I insisted that nominations were pretty well controlled by the Republican organization and that the obligation of the organization to men who had run its errands was paramount to the claims of a hero. We felt that we had a Republican majority in Kansas and we did not need heroes. And Funston understood that. So he went over the state telling his story in churches to help the missionary fund, or in the Odd Fellows Hall or the Masonic Temple, to raise funds to pay the interest on their debts. And the shadow of imperialism rising on our southern horizon did not dim the happiness, tarnish the glory, nor cloud the rising sun of prosperity under which America was basking in that halcyon day. The Democrats had quit asking, "Have you seen the General?" The old fellow with all his opulence, brass buttons, jangling hardware and hearty bluff and bluster, was marching across the United States like an army with banners. And so, 1897 passed into history.

I was writing "Boyville" stories for five hundred dollars apiece at night on the kitchen table, getting them ready to make them into a book. The Gazette's payroll still was a problem, lasting from Thursday until Saturday, and sometimes a headache with the Monday morning overdraft. But we felt, as I wrote the "Boyville" stories at night and as Sallie sat reading the magazines or a Barrie story or a Kipling poem, that we could see the light on ahead through the wilderness.

Book Four

W. A. WHITE

CHAPTER XLIV

Middle Age

In 1898 I attained the age of thirty. My name now appeared on the Gazette's masthead as W. A. White. I felt that there was something irrevocably sad in being thirty—middle-aged. I felt impatient at the futility of my life, that I had done so little and now it was about over. Willie White, the little boy who skipped a rock across the creek in a serpentine curve and died to become Will White, the youth who devoted himself to love and combat and music and became a slave to John B. Alden, the book publisher, and then passed away having begot Will A. White, the young printer, the reporter, the budding poet, the bridegroom—those three dead ancestors of mine seemed to be mocking me; seemed to be asking me what I had done with the visions they had seen and given me, what had become of the man they had brought forth.

Those were haunting, disturbing questions. When I heard them coming suddenly into my consciousness in the still watches of the night, they prodded, wound up my energies, rehabilitated my ambitions and probably thwarted my vanity. Also Sallie helped in that a lot—a very present need in those days, and always. That little, chubby, blue-eyed, redheaded kid, with one big grand freckle on his blond face, who thrilled with delight when he was allowed to strut with Leila Heaton in the tableau with Uncle Tom, always was around the corridor just backstage of my consciousness, wanting to strut again.

Sallie and I were in Clover Bend, Arkansas, in mid-February, visiting "Octave Thanet"—the pen name of Alice French, who was one of the best short-story writers of the nineties. She was from Iowa but lived in the winter on this southern plantation. There survived the civilization of the old South. The freed men were only nominally free. They lived with the land and on it, virtually serfs, and because she was passing rich Octave Thanet lived in feudal splendor. There, for the first time, we had high-class southern cooking—turkeys stuffed with chestnuts, and roast pig stuffed with apricots and almonds, quail fried exquisitely, and all manner of gorgeous pastry. Chauncey Williams, who was about to publish one of Octave Thanet's books, also was her guest, and for four days she put on a real gastronomic parade. Miss French, who weighed something over two hundred forty pounds in her six-foot stature, enjoyed stuffing us much as a taxidermist loves his art. We sat after dinner before her great log fire and talked far into the night about everything in God's wide lovely world. It was one of those nights, I think the night after my birthday, when the news came upon us suddenly, I don't know how, of the sinking of the Maine. And we realized that sooner or later it meant war.

What we did not comprehend was that the war would lead us into an imperial realm where the Monroe Doctrine would become virtually a protectorate over this hemisphere, and where we should take an excursion into the Far East and find ourselves established in the Philippines as one of the great world powers. We did not realize that as we talked on and on by the smoldering log fire that night. But we did know, all of us, that the explosion of the Maine had jarred something fundamental in our own way of life. We were afraid, dreading what the war would reveal. Probably millions of our countrymen in those days, who had accepted the vain, glorious vision of America's manifest destiny and all its pompous nonsense, were sobered when they saw the anchors of the Maine clipped as though they were part of our ship of state, "the Union strong and great," setting forth under sealed order to do combat for only God knew what. Whereupon the next morning we ate a late breakfast of orange juice, country sausage, fried potatoes, scrambled eggs, and buckwheat cakes with honey. This also was the typical, old-fashioned American breakfast that Uncle Sam took the morning after he had been so deeply stirred and strangely moved by the dawning of a new destiny that came out of the explosion fires of the Maine. No sackcloth and ashes, no purification of the flesh did your Uncle take that next morning. He was up and going then, raring to go, an imperialist Yankee—doodling like a gamecock, and proud of it.

In those days I was of two minds about the rising issue of imperialism. My editorials revealed my uncertainty of purpose—not so much that, as an uncertainty of those I saw in my daily walks—the boys in the bookstore, "Old Jack," and Lew Schmucker, the "Little Major" cat-walking daintily down the street, important Populist friends who were fading back into their old shabby insurgency of the eighties, the silk-stocking Democrats who loved Jefferson and Jackson, distrusted McKinley, loathed Hanna, and backed off in doubt when they were faced with the issues that rose from the sinking of the Maine.

Sallie fell ill that summer and the doctor sent her to Colorado. I commuted back and forth on our pass and took the stories that I was writing for her criticism and correction. Robert Bridges, who was then an editor of Scribner's, wrote to me asking me to write some political stories, and George Lorimer, editor of the Saturday Evening Post, commissioned me to do an article or two. I was like Shakespeare's Thane of Cawdor, "a prosperous gentleman," no longer conscious of the pay roll until Saturday morning and then only mildly fidgety about it. Lew Schmucker kept the books and generally told me, about Friday, how our balance was. Sometimes we stirred our stumps and made a few collections, but mostly the Gazette ran on an even keel. A new drygoods store had come to town. It was buying page advertisements, putting on special sales. The hardware dealers were realizing that advertising would bring results, so they told about their buggies, farm implements, kitchen gadgets and paint, in quarter-page and half-page lots. The newspaper business in country towns passed definitely in those latter years of the nineteenth century out of its character as beggar and blackmailer, and became one of the major industries of every little town. It was in the earlier part of '98, when we held an election for mayor in Emporia, that I printed after the election a mean three- or four-line item along with the election returns, about a defeated mayoralty candidate, Colonel Luther Severy, who had bolted the Republican ticket and had gone down to defeat. In his defeat, I twisted a stick of scorn in his sore entrails. The next morning I went on the street, entirely forgetting that mean swipe I had taken at the Colonel. I had no grudge against him. I was just a young smart aleck, and he was a man of seventy. I know now how my gibe had cut him and hurt him—but not then. We passed on the muddy street crossing. I smiled at him, touched my hat, said, "Good morning, Colonel." And the next I knew, I was coming to, lying on my face in the mud at that intersection, and the old colonel was dancing around me waving a broken cane and men were trying to lead him away. Back of my ear was a bleeding welt which became a bump. As we passed, he had whirled and hit me, felling me like a log. And here is a funny thing: I felt no anger toward the old man. I got up grinning, rubbed the mud from my vest and trousers, which in some way had been slit at the knees as I fell. And by that time my friends had gathered and his friends had gathered, and they led us apart and I went back to the office, cleaned myself as best I could. Sallie dressed the bump back of my ear, and I wrote a funny account of the incident, appeared in police court, preferred no charges, and the next day, or maybe the day after, the old colonel met me on the street. I saw his hand fluttering and quickly reached out to grab it. There we stood, he with tears in his eyes, and I tried to say quickly that I was sorry, then he said it, so we both said it—and it was all over. It was a case of temper with him and idle meanness with me, put into rather cutting and unjustified rhetoric. I think it taught me a lesson.

I hope so. It was worth what it cost. And the old colonel and I were friends until his death, as men are sometimes who have been dumb together, made fools of themselves, know each other's weaknesses, and perhaps each other's strength. It was a pleasant relation anyway.

That summer I had occasion to borrow two or three hundred dollars for thirty days or so, and because I was conspicuously on my feet in the town financially I strolled into the other bank, the Major's rival, where I had two good friends. My two good friends in the bank were Charley Cross, the cashier, and D. M. Davis, the vice president. Davis was a squatty, roly-poly little Welshman with a beard over his jellylike jowls, a pleasant, soft and modest voice. And Charley Cross was a big six-footer. He had lived in the town thirty years—since his boyhood. He was then a man in his early forties. As a boy he had had the first Shetland pony the town had known. He went away to an expensive military boarding school, which set him apart from the common run of boys. He was the town beau in the early eighties, married the prettiest girl in Kansas, and took her to a beautiful home which he had built and around which he had planted elms. He was the glamour man of Emporia. I met him in Kansas City sometimes, loafed around at the clubs with him, enjoyed him, for he was a good fellow, an easy spender. He owned the finest Hereford cattle-breeding ranch in Kansas and entertained cattle kings from Texas and editors of the great livestock papers from the East. Also he bought my book "The Real Issue" in large lots, and sent it away to his friends in pride. When bank examiners came to town, Charley Cross telephoned for me to come over to the bank. I was his prize exhibit, next to his famous bull, Wild Tom, a national character in the breeding world. I talked to the examiners, told them all my best Kansas stories about Lane and Chester Thomas, stories that Noble Prentis had told me. We passed many a merry hour together. Charley mixed up drinks for the examiner, which I did not care for. I know now, which I did not know then, that too often the examination of the bank was made rather perfunctorily.

Late that summer, I began to hear rumors about Charley Cross's bank. The Major told me that special examiners had been sent out from Washington. The Major knew all about it. His bank was a rock. He was able to garner the new crop of prosperity that was coming with the gold inflation. But Charley Cross had his Hereford-breeding farm on his shoulders, with a staggering debt. The bank had for its President a shrewd old polly-foxing politician who had financed too many statesmen in Kansas, bought too many shares of stock in boom propositions, hotels that never paid, light and power companies set up in towns that waned and faded, and the assets of the bank were shot through with bad paper. The story of that bank is the story of the Middle West in that day of returning prosperity. Its sins were finding it out. It was in politics to the hilt, and to the last note in its note case. I, who in three years had risen to be a leader in my ward, found the bank taking away from me delegates that I had put into the county convention because they were borrowers at the First National. I thought that friendship would hold these delegates, but the bank fooled me.

Only once, however.

In the autumn of 1898, the "Major" at the other bank, the Emporia National, confided to me that the First National was in grave difficulties with the Federal Comptroller of the Currency. Now when bank examiners came to town they were special examiners from Washington, stern men whom Charley Cross could not wheedle into slackening their duties. I learned afterwards that he dictated letters to the department which were signed by all the directors, with only the last page, where the signatures were, genuine. He rewrote the other pages, which presented an entirely different set of facts from that to which the directors attested. But he was fighting for his life.

This is fairly axiomatic: that no banker whose bank has failed should be held to strict moral accountability for anything he does in the last sixty days before the failure. His motives are mixed. He wants to save his bank. He desires to save the depositors and stockholders from loss. And perhaps more keenly than that, he feels that he must save himself. So he lapses into crime and justifies his crime by the danger he is running, the responsibility that burdens him.

The stories that the "Major" told me about the Cross bank were confidential. I could not warn my friends. One day in early November, the "Major" said that the crash was inevitable. He was in politics, owning a considerable interest in a United States Senator and being himself a candidate for governor that year before the Republican convention. He was a first-class power in Kansas. The bank examiners leaped to the "Major," in fact were sent to him as their adviser. One day when November was a week or ten days old, he came to me, took me into the back room of the bank, closed the door, sat down, spread his arms on his desk, began drumming with his fingers on its glass top, and said:

"Will, you can save the First National. You can keep Charley Cross out of jail. He is in a tight place. He cannot escape. They have pinned a criminal shortage on him of about seventy-five thousand dollars. I want you to go to him. He's friendly with you. Tell him that I will buy his bogus notes and free him of criminal responsibility for a majority of his stock in the bank. I can swing it for fifty thousand dollars."

He was not as direct as that, but that was the substance of a ten-minute talk. I was frightened. I felt the job was too big for me. Charley Cross was ten or a dozen years older than I. He was a man of substance, and I still trembled a little in the presence of money. But I went out on that errand.

I could not go into the bank—perhaps because I did not have quite the courage, but also because I was afraid that the other bankers there would see me and suspect my errand. It was necessary to deal with Cross alone. His criminal shortage was unmistakable, and he knew it. So I loafed around the outside of the bank, in stores and offices, until I saw him come out. I hailed him on the north side of Sixth Avenue, headed toward Commercial Street. I stopped him casually and tried (Lord, how I tried!) to make my lips say what the "Major" had told me to say. I started in to talk about the bank examiners. Charley gayly threw off that grappling hook. I started to talk about the bank, and he had some flippant and ribald remark to make about the bank, and the times. He was a proud man, proud as his old father who was a strutter, which Charley was not because he hid his pride. But there it was. We started to walk east together, and I could not get my nerve up to deliver the message. I was a coward and knew it, and went to the "Major" in humiliation and told him I just could not do it, that I had tried and it would not come. The next day, early in the morning, I saw the "Major." He said:

"Well, Will, they'll be closing in on Charley today. Jobes, the bank examiner, has wired to Washington for authority to shut up the bank."

After a few words I left and went on my rounds through the stores and offices, gathering news. I saw my friends taking their deposits to the bank that morning. I could not stop them. To have stopped them would have caused the run that would have closed the bank even if Washington had delayed. I was tied to the track. The train was approaching around the bend.

About half past eleven I saw Jobes, the bank examiner, coming across the street from the Western Union office to the bank. I could not bear to look at the bank as he went in, and a few minutes later I crossed the street to the bank, expecting to see it closed. Instead, I saw Charley Cross standing by the front window of the bank. What a handsome figure he was! He had his hands in his pockets and as I came across, he waved his hand gayly at me. He was looking at the street—his street, his town. He had a quizzical smile on his face. As he watched me crossing the street, I could not quite interpret it. I thought that the bank would have been closed. Five minutes later, it was closed, and Charley Cross went out the back door of the bank, never to return. I think the quizzical smile on his face as he waved his hand to me was his way of saying:

"Well, Will, in another hour you'll have such an item for your paper as it has never printed before."

For he went directly to his home, harnessed his trotting horse to his red-wheeled trap, hurried across the town, out through the fields of his stock farm—and within twenty minutes of the time when I saw him, I picked up the telephone at the Gazette office and learned from Sunnyslope Farm that Charley Cross lay there dead, a suicide. The two stories, the story of the suicide and the story of the closing of the bank, swamped us in the Gazette office that day. Sallie came from the house. Everyone around the Gazette office worked on the story. At four o'clock we had two pages full of it, fairly well written too, it was—a good story, the biggest story the town had ever seen. In my heart as I wrote, and I certainly worked hard with it, was that agonizing self-reproach that I, through my weakness, had brought death to my dear friend and misery to hundreds of our citizens. The "Major" would have saved Charley. He would have had the bank, and have paid the depositors in due time. Even in a year, while the bank was going into receivership, the tide of the times changed and the depositors received about as much as the "Major" could have given them. It was not the financial loss but the shame of it in my own heart—the death of my friend.

After the bank closed, one day the receiver showed me the wreck there, where thousands of dollars were wasted in stock of boom enterprises—a big barn of a hotel in Cascade, Colorado, an electric light company in Salina, stock in an interurban railway, mortgage bonds, and little jerkwater railways that were never built. Then accommodation notes, pads of them, signed by the bank's satellites—cattlemen to whom the bank granted credit, old Governor Eskridge, editor of the Republican, merchants whom the bank held in its power. These blank notes were slipped into the note case when examiners came along and the books were tampered to indicate that the notes were bearing interest; so for a year, perhaps for two or three years, the bank had remained open—a fraud and a swindle. Charley Cross, a night or two before he died, had written a pathetic letter, taking the blame for the bank's failure and explaining that he had inherited a criminal shortage from his father, who had died suddenly—a suspected suicide—a dozen years before. He had shouldered the criminal shortage and then had gone in deeper and deeper, kiting checks, appropriating deposits, tampering with accounts. It was all terrible, but it was a typical picture of one side of America's gay, careless journey out of the day of the self-sufficient economy into the corridors of the machine age. There, in little, were Wall Street, the great boom industries, the moments of folly which were paid for by the people's money. There were the western star of empire moving over the cesspools and swamps, the tangled labyrinth of good and evil that marked men's way as they went out of the old world into the new, the years of deception, intrigue, and corruption which accompanied and probably were necessary to the changing times which, on the whole, changed naturally, wholesomely, honestly. All were revealed in the back room of the First National Bank in Emporia when the receiver one day spread out the burglar's tools, the forger's kit and accouterments, the swindler's paraphernalia, which kept the bank open through the days of depression. Here was one pilgrim, this poor, crippled bank going along with millions of others, most of which were honest earnest travelers following that star of empire, that way of progress, that unfolding of the human spirit which we call destiny for short, a way of life from the simple to the complex, the abundant life of man.

CHAPTER XLV

Emporia at the Century's Turn

IN THE MEANTIME, the Spanish War was raging. Theodore Roosevelt was in Cuba, leading the Rough Riders. The country was excited. Emporia was thrilled to the core. We celebrated the fall of Santiago with a big public meeting outdoors at the corner of Fifth and Commercial, and Ike Lambert, our leading lawyer and most accomplished orator, spoke to the multitude. He rang the changes of noble patriotism, the band played "The Star-Spangled Banner," we sang "Hail Columbia," threw out a full-throated hymn to imperialism with the verses of "America," and were most pleased with ourselves. We had two companies in the war—one from the state normal school and the college, and one from the town and county. When the Spaniards surrendered in Cuba and gave us Puerto Rico and the Philippines to conquer, America had turned down that fork of the road which led to world domination. American imperialism was planted on this globe. We were committed to a new way of life.

Probably it was inevitable that the machine age, having triumphed in our land and covered our United States with the insignia of its power and the trophies of its suzerainty, should have to burst beyond our borders. For we needed an outlet for our goods; we needed raw materials to feed our machines; we needed international commerce to market our finished product. Imperialism was in the stars. We thought in those days that the glory we had won and the lands we had taken over had come to us because of the valor of our soldiers and the blessings of liberty which we were showering upon the dark places of the earth. We did not know that America, our United States, was just a guinea pig in the vast planetary experiment that the spirit of man was making with the many inventions springing out of the human heart and the human mind. Ike Lambert's oratory told us of the glories of Bunker Hill, the triumph of Appomattox, the victory of Dewey in Manila Bay, our naval prowess at Santiago. And we patted ourselves on the shoulders here in Emporia as our citizens were congratulating themselves across the land. We were the chosen people; imperialists always were—from Moses to McKinley. The Emporia Gazette was just as crazy as any of the newspapers, no better. I hope not much worse. For I, in my heart's heart, had my doubts that sometimes squeaked through in a questioning editorial. But Kipling sang of the white man's burden in those days, and the English-speaking people were keen to hear just that soothing message to justify their conquests. At least this is the way it stands in my memory, and in the editorial files of the Gazette.

In the meantime, the "Boyville" stories which I wrote for McClure's Magazine were appearing in book form and selling well, and were better than pleasantly greeted by the book reviewers. By the time I was thirty-one, I was working on another series of stories for Scribner's Magazine, political in their background. Before the century turned they were to appear in a book with the title "Stratagems and Spoils," of which I gave a copy to Theodore Roosevelt—and many years later he was still giving it to foreign diplomats, inscribing on the flyleaf that it was the best picture of American politics that he knew. He told me almost at the last that he thought it was my very best book. It was not. But Mr. Howells praised it, which was enough for me. It did not sell well—eight or ten thousand, I think; maybe a few more or less. Three books in four years was not going too fast. But they were enough to give me a minor place and bring in magazine orders at astonishingly good prices. The magazine articles, of course, sooner or later turned up in books, and the money from the books and the magazine articles was invested in the Gazette, finally cleaning up the mortgage and erecting a new building. When I announced that we were putting up a Gazette building, I happened to be in the bank the next morning and the cashier said:

"I see you are putting up a Gazette building."

I nodded.

He said: "Come in here!" and took me by the arm and showed me my bank balance. I was five dollars in the red. He grinned and said: "How are you going to pay for it?"

I said: "Red ink."

He had been carrying that account, mostly in the red oozing into the black for two or three days, maybe a week, or maybe a month, and then popping into the red again, for five years. He looked at me quizzically and said:

"Well, you've got your nerve!"

I had. We paid for the Gazette building. I think it cost six or seven thousand dollars. Within a year it was opened.

If the "Little Major," in his spider hole at the Emporia National, thought that the bank fight would end when his rival bank was closed and its surviving officers indicted, he was sadly fooled. The town row warmed up. The indicted officers had their liberty to fight for, and nothing much else to do, so that the air was thick with lawsuits and countersuits. Lyon County politics was conducted largely with affidavits and lie-nailers, anything from libel to mayhem. I was in the thick of it. Indeed I took the brunt. I became precinct committeeman in my ward. It was my job to return a delegation that would stand by my side in the county convention. Legally we held a caucus. Let me describe this one so future historians may know how a party caucus worked in a highly literate state like Kansas, with 95 per cent of the voters American-born and 85 per cent American-born of American-born grandparents; how these people ran their politics in the interest of the prevailing plutocracy. The night before the caucus my cohorts met. We agreed on our ticket. I assigned one man to nominate a certain other man on the ticket until I had enough men who would stand up and nominate other men as delegates to fill the delegation. Then I gave my nominators their order from one to, say, twenty-eight, the number of delegates we had in the convention. I then proceeded to memorize in their order the men whom I would recognize the next evening. That next night, the little room where the caucus was held was packed full. My men, by order, were standing as far front as possible. I opened the caucus on the tick of the clock, stated the purpose of the meeting and set the chairs ready to receive nominations for delegates to the Republican county convention. Then I shut my eyes and recognized Number One amid the clamor of voices. Number One put the name he presented, which generally received an overwhelming viva voce vote, with scattering negatives, and so it went down the line to Number Twenty-eight. At about Number Ten, the crowd saw what was up and the row began. But we went through with the program. The delegation to the county convention was elected—my crowd. I remember that Mort Allbaugh, the chairman of the state committee and sub-boss under Cy Leland, also being at the time receiver of the First National Bank, stood in the back of the room and watched me perform. He came forward after the meeting and looked at me for a moment or two and said:

"Well, you fooled me. I thought you was one of them long-haired, literary fellows. God!" He paused in awe and reverence: "You pretty nearly got away with murder."

In the county convention, of course, the big prizes were the nomination of members of the legislature, for they elected United States Senators. For these legislative offices, we who controlled a convention swapped anything that would make a majority slate. Generally we could combine the delegates who were eager to name, let us say, sheriff, county attorney, county treasurer and one other county officer in the convention to make a majority. We put our slate through in order to control the nominees to the legislature. And generally the organization succeeded. That is why I was in the organization in those years of the late nineties. I ran with the machine. We controlled our state senators and our members of the house of representatives at Topeka. We named United States Senators. We gave color to the legislation. I was making my private opinion public sentiment, and occasionally when I wanted something that I thought was particularly decent, I was able to get it in Kansas politics even then. I did not stand aloof and sniff. If, as Senator Ingalls had said, "the purification of politics is an iridescent dream," I had some control of the nightmare.

But in 1899, in the town of Emporia, I took my first long step forward in public affairs by putting on a street fair. Ed Howe had been doing the same thing in Atchison for a year or two and, copy-catting him, I went into the street fair business in Emporia. It was a three-day festival. We had booths in the main street and also a flower parade, a mile long, wherein buggies covered with gorgeous paper flowers and harness similarly adorned drove up and down the street, parading for prizes amounting to something over a hundred dollars. Then we had a lot of little colored boys in G-strings, or less, carrying stalks of kaffir corn, brown-tipped with the ripened corn —gorgeously colored stalks that looked like spears—and we put a band at their head, playing the jungle jazz of that day; they did look splendidly barbarous until their mothers, catching sight of them parading down the street in their shiny skins, raided the procession and spanked the kids out of it, to the delight of the multitude.

We had a tribe of Indians from the Pottawatomie Reservation giving Indian dances. The highlight of the fair was the first automobile that ever crossed the Missouri River. It came from Chicago from a friend of Chauncey Williams' friend, Sam Clover, of the Chicago Evening Post, who persuaded his friend—a rich, young mechanical engineer named Ed Brown —to send it. The Santa Fe gave him a freight car free from Chicago to Emporia and back. And what a crowd that first horseless carriage drew! It was the marvel of the fair. People came from a hundred miles around to see it. And then we rented a big circus tent and had all sorts of shows and entertainment going there. The first colored photography that had been seen in Kansas appeared one evening. And another evening we put on a baby show. We had a colored section and appointed three old bachelors as judges. If anyone ever saw a pretty sight, it was those colored babies competing for prizes. They were dressed to kill, and their mothers stood bursting with pride near the platform when the exhibit began. And Lew Schmucker, the old devil, who had a sense of humor, told the band—we had six bands from neighboring towns on duty in that street fair—to play "All Coons Look Alike to Me," as the judges filed by in solemn plug hats;

and you can bet the colored mammas knew what that tune was and grabbed their offspring and marched out of the tent in wrath, and broke up one of the finest features of the street fair.

But the fair gave me prestige. I collected the money, most of it at least. Mit Wilhite, owner of the hotel, George Newman, owner of the drygoods store, and I collected it together and paid for everything. It cost nearly four thousand dollars. I stood for it, hiring the bands, paying the prizes, taking care of the payroll day by day, guaranteeing the attractions. People knew that I was responsible for the show. It was called "Will White's Street Fair." And Emporia also began to realize that the editor of the Gazette was not one of them damn, long-haired literary fellows.

It was about that time that our arch enemy, old Bill Martindale, of the busted bank, who was leading the fight on the "Little Major" and his crowd, gave a stranger who came to town this admonition, and it came first-hand to me:

"There he is," said Martindale, "over there by that pillar, in front of the desk."

This was in a hotel lobby.

"Look at that face, pink and white, fat and sweet, as featureless and innocent as a baby's bottom! But, by God, don't let that fool you!"

That first street fair, which made the merchants a lot of money, did more for me in the town than "What's the Matter with Kansas?" did for Mark Hanna. Our daily subscription list already had doubled, and was more than a thousand. Our weekly was growing in the county. We tried to do, and were doing, a little business in our job office, besides the pension printing which Cy Leland had given us. My income, including my royalties and magazine earnings, after paying the Gazette bills every month, must have been seven or eight thousand dollars a year when the century turned.

It was in July, 1899, that Sallie and I moved into the house where we now live. We bought it of the man who held the mortgage, who took it out of the bad debts of an eastern insurance company. It was a ten-room house made of red sandstone from Colorado and pressed bricks. It was covered with towers and turrets and fibroid tumors and minarets and all the useless ornaments that an architect in 1885 could think of. An Emporia lawyer-politician built it. The story ran that his wife had inherited three thousand dollars from an estate. The lawyer-politician was at the time a member of the state board of railway commissions. He grafted the stone, freight-free from the quarry. When he started the house he was, as many well-to-do western lawyers often were, a heavy investor in cattle. Before the house was completed, cattle prices dropped and he went broke. Mechanics' liens covered the house. It cost eighteen thousand dollars, in a day when carpenters worked for a dollar and a half a day, stone masons for two dollars. His wife was well beloved. She wrote poetry after the fashion of Felicia Hemans, Jean Ingelow, and Ella Wheeler, which was widely reprinted and gave her some distinction. She died just as the house was finished, amidst the filing of liens and while he was staving off the foreclosure of the mortgage, which was plastered upon the place. In his desperation he remarried six months after his wife died, thinking he would recoup his fortune. He brought a bride from western Kansas who thought he was rich. It was a sad awakening. The town refused to call on the new bride. The lawyer's three daughters had a sad time of it. It was a house of heartbreak. But after two or three years of battle against the town, he left Emporia for Kansas City, and when we bought the house the colored people, who lived not far off, called it the haunted house. It was accursed. Two or three tenants had died in it. And the man who sold it to us for six thousand dollars thought he had a famous bargain. Through some prejudice of the builder, it did not have a wire or a pipe in it—nothing modern—no furnace, no water, no gas, no electricity.

But Sallie and I were tremendously proud of it—towers, turrets, tumors and all. We used to walk up and down the sidewalk in the summer twilight admiring it with "wonder, awe and praise." Here we have lived ever since. Here the children were born. Here we have seen the major pageant of our lives pass. Here we have lived, indeed, happily ever after.

CHAPTER XLVI

Roosevelt Moves Toward Power

THE YEARS at the turn of the twentieth century were vintage years if I ever had any. In those five years from 1898 to 1903 I stepped out into the big wide world. Geographically, I went westward to the Pacific, north nearly to Canada. Politically, I met two living Presidents and two ex-Presidents, and had become a member of the executive committee of the Republican state central committee in my state. And I had definitely become a member of the governing, if not the ruling, classes of my country. I was awakening to the deep spiritual truths in the Christian Bible. Its theology did not interest me, but the wisdom of the ages there moved me deeply. I discovered the New Testament about this time. I had been buying for several years separately bound books of the Old Testament, with notes and commentaries. I loved its English. I was moved by its mystic wisdom. Job, the Psalms, Proverbs, and Ecclesiastes seemed written on purpose for me. But it was not until the turn of the century that I began to understand the New Testament.

I have no recollection that I ever traveled on the road to Damascus. But Theodore Roosevelt and his attitude toward the powers that be, the status quo, the economic, social and political order, certainly did begin to penetrate my heart. And when I came to the New Testament and saw Jesus, not as a figure in theology—the only begotten son who saved by his blood a sinful world—but as a statesman and philosopher who dramatized his creed by giving his life for it, then gradually the underpinning of my Pharisaic philosophy was knocked out. Slowly as the new century came into its first decade, I saw the Great Light. Around me in that day scores of young leaders in American politics and public affairs were seeing what I saw, feeling what I felt. Probably they too were converted Pharisees with the zeal of the new faith upon them. All over the land in a score of states and more, young men in both parties were taking leadership by attacking things as they were in that day—notably Mark Hanna's plutocracy and the political machinery that kept it moving. And literature was rising. Novelists were making fictional exposés of plutocratic iniquity. Magazines were full of what later was to be called muckraking, uncovering cesspools in the cities and the states, denouncing the centralization of power in the United States Senate which assembled there through the dominance in the states of the great commodity industries—railroads, copper, oil, textiles and the like. So I, opening my New Testament and reading wide-eyed the new truths that I found revealed there, began to relate my reading to my life. Dickens, Emerson, Whitman came alive, and I saw things as they were.

Incidentally, I should add that I was reading many books on biology which Vernon Kellogg suggested to me and, of course, I read the popular pseudo-sciences of the day, such as "Anglo-Saxon Superiority," by Edmond Demolins. The better known works of Herbert Spencer also stirred me up. When Herbert Spencer died I wrote for the Saturday Evening Post an account of his life and works, one of the few things I ever asked George Lorimer, the magazine's editor, to print. Herbert Spencer, along with Whitman, Emerson and Dickens, became at the turn of the century one of my spiritual inspirations. At that time I was also reading rather widely, with a questioning mind, the literature of abnormal psychology. My questions were never answered.

Physically I looked like a big, blond bartender, with brown hair, a complexion that sunburned easily, large blue eyes, a big mouth wherein three baby teeth never were replaced, giving it a snaggle-toothed appearance, a long neck capped by two double chins. I tried to give it the appearance of power and consequence by walking nimbly. I know now that I fooled no one. I was just a fat slob who was trying to hide, under the exuberance of youth and its strength and force, an oleaginous complacence which was satisfied with beaming and grinning and not above a little clowning now and then, more or less conscious, in an attempt to hide my obvious shortcomings. I was an extrovert, glad-handing my way through a vale of tears. Mrs. White kept my clothes down to something like a decent exterior, though I remember that I had a black hat with a slightly too wide brim, and was given to ascot ties, rather rich and luxurious in color and in texture, which I pinned together with a baroque pearl surrounded with diamond chips which she had given me to my delight, probably to keep me out of something more dazzling. In summer I bedecked myself in white, following an inherited paternal tendency. I must have looked like a skinned elephant. Looking back at myself in those days, I wonder how that inner self who worshiped at the shrine of Emerson, Whitman and Herbert Spencer, must have looked at that paunchy figure of a youth rigged out like Solomon in all his glory.

At any rate, as we go on with the story of this young man who was getting a little mild fame as William Allen White outside the borders of Kansas, wherein he was known as Bill, I should make it plain to the reader who will follow me through these next chapters, just what kind of a man inside, and particularly outside, he was. In those years, at the turn of the century, he had written three books which had a most flattering sale and received most encouraging reviews. His name was in the popular magazines, attached to articles upon current matters of politics, literature and passing events of human interest, and it appeared oftenest in "editorials from the Emporia Gazette," which even then were passing through the exchanges of the United States in a thin but fairly steady stream. Ten months out of the year that young man could be found in Emporia, going to his work at eight o'clock and coming home at six. Or if he were engaged upon a magazine article or book, you could find him at home in a little book-lined workshop, hammering out of an old Smith-Premier double keyboard typewriter the surging thoughts that flowed rather too voluminously from his mind and heart. There is William Allen White turning out of his twenties into his mid-thirties while the old century moved back into history and the new one rolled on toward its tragic and calamitous destiny.

When Theodore Roosevelt returned from Cuba, after the Spanish-American War, I saw him several times and, because each of us was a rather voluminous letter writer, we exchanged our views and he gave me some confidences about his intentions. He did not want to be governor of New York. He wanted to be President of the United States. Of course, I hoped he would be President, and I saw the New York politicians take him up in 1898 and make him governor rather against his will. But he surrendered coyly, and even then when we met I was consulting him about the way to capture the delegates to the Republican national convention when his time should come. He knew that McKinley was entitled to his second term, but even in 1899 we were planning for 1904. I knew something of the factional Republican line-up in each of a group of midwestern, trans-Mississippi states bordering upon Kansas and Colorado; for instance, Nebraska, Missouri and a little bit about Iowa and something of Dakota. I could at least make a factional map for him, and did make one. I was tremendously impressed by the personality of Theodore Roosevelt. I felt he had something extraordinary, some unusual power, some plus quality which made him a man of destiny. So I followed in his train.

It was in 1900 that I met William Jennings Bryan for the first time. McClure's Magazine asked me to write a character sketch of him, and I journeyed to Lincoln, Nebraska, where he lived, to see him. We spent the greater part of a day together. The picture I held of him in that day is still with me. He was a tall, at least a tallish, young man who was, as I was, beginning to get too opulent a crescent on his vest. He had a mop of black hair and a tawny complexion. His eyes were large, expressive, kindly. In all things he was a gentle person, I felt. He was kind to me, though I could see that he suspected me of no good motives because I was a Republican and because he knew I had written "What's the Matter with Kansas?" which he thought had been rather devastating to his Presidential career. Nevertheless we were both extroverts and got along gayly. Bryan, even in that day, was too much of a professional politician to suit my tastes. He was getting what all politicians get, a lively sense of his ability to influence people individually and in the mass by charming manners, meaningless courtesies, pleasant words, outworn phrases. A politician who is professionally trying his lures on the people, seeking to gain their confidence and thus secure their votes, gets into bad habits. He develops a technique—the fatal ability to so assemble and spread his particular charms that they will attract the admiration of his fellows. I suppose a courtesan falls into the same routine of bad habits and becomes a professional charmer. I felt that Bryan, who in 1900 was about forty, was too definitely conscious that he was an extraordinary personality, that he knew too well that he had many graces. In short, he was dramatizing himself with a skillful art as William Jennings Bryan. This did not offend me, but it did steel me a little against him. So when he left me for an hour in his library and told me to look around and I would find there the foundation of his faith, I was saddened to find it was founded not upon a wide reading in general economics of accepted credibility. I found instead that most of the books dealing with the currency and with the tariff were written by partisans of a theory and published by groups interested in propaganda. The Bimetallic League published many of the volumes that I saw on his library shelves; the various free-trade associations put out books on the tariff; and so on down the line— books written not by scholars but by partisans of the creeds that Mr. Bryan preached. It was a shabby library and, to me, revealed much.

Bryan's conversational voice was not particularly pleasant. Only when he stood on the platform did he display that quality of voice and manner which belongs to the born orator. On the platform he was another man, not the shirtsleeved, folksy, hail fellow, a bit of a back-slapper and handshaker, cordial, even lovable, whom I met at Lincoln. There also I met Mrs. Bryan, who was a born Phi Beta Kappa, a student, an introvert who surveyed me, and I think everyone around her husband, with a fishy eye of distrust. At least she held the presumption that we were guilty of subversive intentions toward him until we were proven innocent. I doubt if I ever proved my innocence. But she was exactly the kind of woman he needed. God had been good to him there. Such a woman must always have stayed his hand when he was too magnanimous, checked him when he was too gracious, stopped him when he was too impulsive. The two personalities, and she was as strong as he, rolled together made a well-balanced person, and through the most of his life their lives were mingled. She was with him almost until the last. And after she went, he made his greatest blunder.

The article which I wrote about him was coldly objective but not deeply critical. How she must have disliked it!

On the other hand, the next time I met Bryan he was as cordial as he was when we parted at his doorstep. But that article, for some strange reason, pleased Theodore Roosevelt immensely and he seemed to take me more closely into his heart because of it. He was trying earnestly and I think absolutely honestly in the spring of 1900 to avoid nomination as the Republican candidate for Vice President. He wanted a second term as governor of New York and felt that he could get into the White House more easily from Albany than from the Vice President's chair. He was not in agreement with McKinley and his ideas. He liked Hanna personally, as I did, but was opposed to all his works and felt that he would be tied under his foot as Vice President in the McKinley administration. But Senator Platt, the Republican boss of New York, wanted to get Theodore Roosevelt out of the governorship. He was wrecking the Platt machine quietly, almost stealthily—but certainly. Hanna had as low an opinion of the Roosevelt cast of thought and way of politics as Roosevelt had of Hanna's machine. On the other hand, Platt, who had backed Reed for President against McKinley in 1896, represented the bankers in the Republican convention of that year, as Hanna represented the industrialists. Platt was in the cabal that forced the gold standard into the Republican platform, and Hanna cordially despised Platt. So when the latter tried to dump Theodore Roosevelt, the *enfant terrible,* into McKinley's lap as Vice President, Hanna was wroth. And because the majority of the convention, any Presidential convention, which has to take without debate and without question the Presidential nominee, revolted and did the thing that would rile Hanna most, they obliged Platt by backing Roosevelt and at the same time putting a fly in Hanna's ointment. So Roosevelt was nominated for Vice President— and received the nomination with considerable inner disturbance. It humiliated him to know that Platt, the boss of New York, had removed him because he feared and despised him.

After the election Roosevelt began definitely to organize the Republicans of the country to nominate him in 1904. I was torn between two obligations. I admired Hanna, though I was beginning even then to question his philosophy. I was grateful to Hanna for his consideration of me. It had been valuable. But my heart was with Theodore Roosevelt, and I joined his camp. Hanna knew it, and was appreciative of my position. And he let me know it once or twice when I saw him—in a gay, half-rueful way, after he had spit out his protest. All of this, of course, was behind the scenes and under cover, as politicians ply their trade. As Vice President, Roosevelt sat presiding over the Senate with a reasonable amount of dignity for him, and went on trying with what small power he had in the Senate to gain the friendship and support of various senators, and so capture state delegations to the Republican presidential convention three years ahead of him.

In the summer of 1901, a number of Roosevelt's friends in the Middle West, say in the trans-Mississippi country and the Missouri Valley, began meeting with him and discussing ways and means to organize that part of the country in his behalf. He came to Colorado Springs in midsummer and, at the house of his friend, Phil Stewart, a Harvard man, Roosevelt held a conference of leaders. I was there representing Kansas. In those days Roosevelt had to do business with the local political machine in each state. It was before the primary was widespread, and so the Republican machine in the various states had power of life and death over a Presidential candidate. So the politicians gathered in Colorado Springs—as fine an assemblage of political gangsters as you would meet on a journey through a long summer day. I sat with men who, ten or a dozen years later, were to be denounced by name by Roosevelt as enemies of the Republic because they stood by Taft in 1912. But we did make proper plans and we did give due pledges, with our political lives as hostages, for those promises, to return Roosevelt delegations to the Republican Presidential convention of 1904 from Colorado, Wyoming, Kansas, Nebraska, and Missouri—and, we hoped, Iowa if Senators Dolliver and Allison could be rounded up.

I was tremendously swelled up, of course. Teddy Roosevelt was the Vice President. I rode on the train with him and brought to the train half a dozen Kansas politicians. The train stopped at various stations and Teddy made speeches from the rear platform. And I stood by him, swelling like a poisoned pup, and was proud and happy. When we came to Emporia, he got off the train and there were Sallie and little Bill, and Roosevelt kissed them both and visited with us a moment in the midst of the crowd. It was honey in the comb for us.

We parted with a promise that I should come to Oyster Bay in early September with reports on Iowa and Missouri and, when the train moved out with him standing on the platform waving at us and a good-sized Emporia crowd, I was somebody, or thought I was, and beamed on my fellow citizens with pride and complacence.

When I got back to my desk I found there a letter from McClure's Magazine, asking me to write a character sketch of President McKinley. The Bryan sketch had pleased the editors of the magazine. They had also asked me to prepare a sketch on Senator Platt. With those two orders in my pocket and my appointment with Roosevelt in the back of my head, I left

Emporia in late August with an appointment to see both President McKinley and Senator Platt. After I had gathered the material for the two articles I was to meet Roosevelt at Oyster Bay to discuss that indefinite, interminable, ever-changing political kaleidoscope called, in the parlance of politics, "the situation."

CHAPTER XLVII

Exit McKinley—Muted Trumpets

IT WAS IN LATE AUGUST that I met William McKinley for the last time. I had met him three times before. I had spent a long day with him on a railroad train, watching him reportorially for many hours. I had made a pilgrimage to his home in Canton after his election to the Presidency, and had talked with him there half an hour or so. I had seen him in the White House, where Mark Hanna took me for another interview of perhaps half or three-quarters of an hour, early one morning in the autumn of 1897. I was familiar with his political record and his political views and attitudes and public methods and manners. I had read everything biographical about him that was available in books and magazines before I went to see him to prepare the article about him for McClure's. I took the order reluctantly after one or two letters of mild protest. My reluctance arose from the fact that I did not care for William McKinley as a man or as a public figure. His political honesty was irreproachable, as the honesty of politicians goes, which is based upon a code of its own. Personally, he was an agreeable man. He had been more than courteous. He had been kind to me wherever I had approached him. We were two human beings who could not develop any intimacy founded upon anything like mutual respect. His personal technique in meeting strangers, and even friends, seemed to me carefully studied, formulated and more habitual than genuine. He smiled pleasantly, casually, and with friendly grace, upon everyone. He had, or seemed to have, the fine condescending manners of a squire, though Heaven knows he was anything but that in blood or background.

The time I entered his home at Canton I had one purpose: to find out if the man was entirely a public mask or if he had any private life whatever. I wanted to find the real man back of that plaster cast which was his public mask. I can remember that I wished: if I could only see this man in his shirt sleeves, with his suspenders down, in slippers, with unkempt, tously, really friendly hair and a two-day beard, what would he be like? So as we walked through his modest home that hot August day, I kept an appraising eye upon him all the time. A photographer came along from McClure's Magazine to make a portrait, and I wondered if the story was true that he always laid aside his cigar before the camera. It was true. He smiled and said, as he always said, quietly, sweetly and gently:

"We must not let the young men of this country see their President smoking!"

When the photographer had gone, we took chairs on a side porch opening into a little garden, a pleasant, shady spot, and began to talk. I explained that I was not seeking an interview, did not desire to quote him, but merely wished to get his views and understand his position on certain passing public questions without in any way presenting these views as officially his. He was wily. He had heard reporters say that before. He mistrusted all reporters who came with that attitude, but his mistrust was sweet and friendly and was revealed only by the guarded complacence in what he said. He refused to tousle his hair politically. He was the statue in the park speaking. I tried him on reminiscences, and his reminiscences were as intimate as a newspaper biography, not pompous of course but consciously conventional. He had no stories of his boyhood or youth that would not fit into the Fourth Reader. In our hour's talk, he was completely guarded. Other reporters had told me what I would find, confirming what I had seen at the other times I had met him. I knew that somewhere behind the bastions of his fortress of reserve a real man was hidden. Again and again I charged the fortress, only to find myself most engagingly and, I felt, almost unconsciously on his part, repulsed.

He sat there in a large cane veranda chair in a lightweight, dark alpaca coat and trousers, with a double-breasted immaculate white vest adorned only by his watch chain, with a dark purple four-in-hand necktie meticulously arranged, a heavy man five feet ten or eleven inches tall but never paunchy, with a barrel torso, a large head and face, deeply cut though not finely chiseled features—but without spot, blemish, wrinkle, or sign of care or sorrow upon the smooth, sculptured contour of his countenance. I was sweating, for it was a hot day. He was stainless, spotless, apparently inwardly cool and outwardly unruffled. I thought then, and I think now, that he sensed what I was seeking and guarded it from me, maybe consciously. I also thought that his bland and amiable manner, his array of politician's tricks—to enchant acquaintances and to hold friends—was somewhat consciously used upon me as we talked. As the first hour closed and he could see that through my mushy affability I was not caught, he was not exactly worried or irritated but puzzled—that the spell did not work—and I caught his slight bewilderment as we chatted. Finally, as I knew my time must soon be up, though his body gave no signs of restlessness or anxiety, I said as gayly as I could:

333

"Now, Mr. President, there is just one thing I really want to know."
He smiled pleasantly and said: "Well?"

"It is this: Your strongest quality, the characteristic which I think has been the source of your strength, has been your capacity, your ability, sure and instinctively certain, to pick honest men for important places. How do you do it? What is your method of testing and balancing human characteristics? How did you know, for instance, that General Porter was a strong man? How did you sense a dozen years ago Mark Hanna's impregnable loyalty? You sent my old friend Joe Bristow to Cuba, the one man in the post office department who could clean up the Cuban mess. How did you know Joe was a bulldog? He looks like a setter."

McKinley smiled and put in an aside that he was glad to know that I knew and admired Bristow. And I went on:

"You must have some way, some series of tests, some invariable compass that points to the lodestar of honesty and capacity in men you have chosen for important and disagreeable jobs. Can you tell me how you go at it?"

McKinley rose and stood before me as I sat there with a leg over an arm of my veranda chair. He smiled down at me as he would to an audience which he was about to address. The audience was one fat, moon-faced, heavy-jowled young man just entering his thirties, with a canine eagerness on his face, red and sweaty and with the glint of a fading hope, but still a hope, in his eyes, that the truth at last would come from the sculptured lips of the hero. Our eyes must have conveyed the inner antagonism of our hearts, though we were both most polite, even warmly cordial. The President put one hand under his buttoned alpaca coat and in the other held his cigar and began to make a speech. I was audience. It was an address. His speech had no answer to my question. It was the thing he might have told the Canton High School at commencement. He stood there—a public man on an occasion. I do not remember what he said. After he had spoken a minute or two, I closed my memory. He was saying nothing that interested me. Perhaps he knew it. Probably he did. If he knew it he could not help it or perhaps feared to help it, feared to loosen his spiritual collar, feared to reveal the real McKinley, even the strongest lineaments of the man imprisoned in the fortress of his public life. When he had finished he said:

"Is that what you wanted?"

And I said: "Yes." And thanked him. A moment later we were out on the front steps of his house. He was cordial. His handshake was genuine. His hand on my shoulder was kindly, I should say simulating and probably approaching an affectionate warmth. He told me if any other questions occurred to me, to let him know and he would answer them as best he could, which I think was an honest affirmation—"as best he could." He had somewhere back in his youth or young manhood, possibly as a soldier in the war, buttoned himself up, and had become almost unconsciously the figure that stands now in Canton not far from his front door—William McKinley in bronze.

From Canton I hurried on to New York, where I had appointments which would give me the material for the Senator Platt story. Colonel Roosevelt had made these appointments with some ancient and some recent enemies of Platt who had once been his intimates. Most of my material I got from Lemuel E. Quigg, a New York statesman who for a decade had been Platt's eyes, ears, and legs. Platt was a typical Republican state boss. He deserved attention only because he was the Republican boss in the greatest Republican state in the Union, and the story of intrigue, corruption and the sordid amalgamation of plutocratic self-interest and political power was typical of American politics in the North at that time. I tried to tell an honest story. It was to the credit of Theodore Roosevelt that he always wanted that kind of a story about his own party printed, because he felt that the more the people knew about his relation between politics and business, the sooner they would wreck the machines that ground out its product in plutocratic government. I worked hard on the Platt story for several days in New York. Then to make my picture intimate and personal, I saw Senator Platt in his office downtown, a frowzy little cubbyhole that had not been tidied up for years. Papers, books, pamphlets, records—mildewed junk —lay around it everywhere; on top of his desk, on tables, beside his desk, along the walls. And when I went in and saw him, he looked to me like a little old mangy rat in his nest. He was not so old as I am now, but his face was blotched with brown spots, his bleary eyes were rummy, his jaw was uncertain. Yet there was a power behind his eyes, and a curious electric quality in his rather noncommittal handshake, that I cannot describe. It was the deep personal source of his power and he impressed me, even in the adolescence of his senility, as a powerful man. He held his power not by chance but by conquest, and it was held by an indomitable spirit. What he must have been in the days of Conkling and Garfield and Arthur and Blaine explains what he was that day I saw him in his rat's nest in New York—a little, old, frightened man who saw death around every corner and who blinked at it a rather cowardly defiance. I wrote the Platt story on that basis. It was in the midst of my work on that story that William McKinley received the assassin's bullet at the Buffalo fair. I had seen him in all his strength and physical pride, for he was a handsome man with a matinee idol's virility, though not at all sex-conscious. When he was stricken down, I was shocked. I read in the papers that the vice president, Theodore Roosevelt, was hunting, or fishing, or roughing it in the Adirondacks, and I wondered how the attack on McKinley would leave our appointment.

For a day or two McKinley seemed to rally from Czolgosz's bullet. Then he suddenly sank, and the newspapers carrying the story of his death described it as curiously like a stage deathbed. They said that as he sank out of consciousness, he was humming "Nearer, My God, to Thee," and that he reached an affectionate hand to Mark Hanna and parted with him in a well set, school reader deathbed scene. I wondered then if that was the truth —if the tremendous force of a lifetime of conscious dramatics, stage-play and character-acting had really persisted thus in death—or whether the power of his life's drama had written the story, as the reporters unconsciously tried to round out the heroic figure that he had envisaged in his heart, and carried into his career. Certainly McKinley died—in truth or in accepted fiction—in character; the statue in the park was expiring.

The day of his funeral I had a most astounding experience. I sat in the Century Club with Thomas B. Reed, former Speaker of the House of Representatives in Congress. We ate lunch together. He was the first national character who wrote to me about "What's the Matter with Kansas?" and we had built up a friendship in those six years. I saw him often. It was decreed that for five minutes in the afternoon during the McKinley service in Buffalo, the whole nation should pause. Every wheel in every factory stopped. All across the land, workmen stood at rest. Trains paused. The nation held a session of silent prayer. It was in the early afternoon in New York when Reed and I, sitting at the dining-room window on the third floor, looked down and saw the cabs and drays suddenly halt. We realized that this was the hour of prayer for the spirit of McKinley, which also was as he would have written the script for his funeral. McKinley and Hanna had ousted Reed as Speaker of the House when it held an overwhelming Republican majority. It was done behind the scenes, and anyone knew it who was at all familiar with the inside workings of the party. Reed resigned, making it fairly plain to the American people that he could not go along with the kind of government which Hanna would establish—the open liaison between American politics and business, particularly industrial business rather than finance. Hanna was the apotheosis of industry rather than banking. Incidentally, he hated the New York bankers as Mr. Reed scorned the upstart industrialists.

Reed was a great porpoise of a man. He must have weighed three hundred pounds. He stood six feet of blubber, and yet power exuded from his excess adipose, his triple chin, his big, jowled countenance, like visible electricity. He was a man of wide erudition and exceptional culture—New England Brahminism blowing a hundred miles an hour.

As the cabs and drays pulled up and stopped in the street below our win-

336

dow, Reed literally hauled off, smacked his flapperlike hands heavily on the table, stiffened up and began—not a prayer but a diatribe. He cursed McKinley and Hanna for what they were. I have never heard such exquisitely brutal, meticulously refined malediction in all my life. It was an experience out of the bitterness of a life that had been thwarted, for Reed, under the rules of the political game, had deserved the Presidency in '96 and had been deposed as Speaker behind the scenes because he did not believe in the divine alliance between business and politics which was cemented by the protective tariff; because Reed cried out for the gold standard when McKinley was wobbling. Reed had reason for his bitterness, and justification for his contempt. He poured it out in a torrent of wrath, a cold, repressed New England cascade of icicles. I was a fairly good reporter in those days. I tried to reproduce it. I could not. It was rage, chilled into sarcasm and frigid contempt. The man's bleak glacial passion—New England understatement freezing in invective—flowed in that icy Yankee drawl across that histrionic moment, shattering the drama of the hour. For Reed spoke as a man who knew for a fact and in deep truth what a terrible thing was happening to his country. And, as a patriot but mostly as a wronged man, he spoke for ten minutes, even after the clatter in the street had resumed, with such force and in such beautiful language of power, and with such chaste, simple diction, that I realized that I was the witness of a great occasion. Alas, the only witness! If I could have reproduced those words! But there was a great figure, a huge, angry face livid with petrified rage, and there was the quiet of the club and the deserted dining-room tables, and the melodramatic pause below the window which set the scene. I could never regain that moment or recapture words that would reproduce that mood. It was a philippic. If only it could have been reported, what a speech it would have made for the school reader, on the opposite page from the story of McKinley's stage deathbed and stage funeral!

CHAPTER XLVIII

My New President

IN NEW YORK I had received word from Theodore Roosevelt that he would be in Washington the night but one after McKinley's funeral. We were to meet, according to his suggestion, at the home of his Navy brother-in-law, Captain Cowles. So in the morning after McKinley's funeral, I went to Washington and at seven o'clock, in my tux and black tie, hurried over to the Cowles residence. It was one of a row of houses on a quiet side street not far from Connecticut Avenue; a tree-lined street with a postage stamp of a lawn, and a front stoop—one of those square houses built in the eighties or nineties, with a front hall from which the stairway ran to the second floor, and a rather formal parlor off the front hall, connected with folding doors to the back part which led to the dining room, making four square rooms set like four cubes in a larger square. Each room had its carved-oak mantel and tile-trimmed grate. It was typical of the middle-class urban residence in America at the turn of the century.

When I came out of the square hall into the square parlor, another young man was there—perhaps six or eight years my senior, a handsome young fellow with black hair, keen searching eyes and a strong, full, eager face. I was introduced to him, and thus first met Nicholas Murray Butler. We dined with the Cowleses, who gave us an ordinary rare-roast-beef, mashed-potato dinner. The captain carved, the servant passed the plates, and Mrs. Cowles and her brother, the young President, kept the conversation rippling brightly through half an hour. He was to go to the White House the next morning. I was filled with curious excitement to know a President as well as I knew Theodore Roosevelt, to hear him talk about the McKinley funeral, to know in my heart how low an opinion he had of the things Mc-Kinley stood for. These things kept stirring in my mind as I listened to the dinner table conversation, the best I had ever heard. I did not make much out of the young schoolmaster, Mr. Butler, and he made less out of me.

Years later, when he told the story of the meeting, he forgot that I was there.

After dinner we went through the square living room into the square parlor. Mrs. Cowles disappeared. The captain sank into one of those large, tufted Sleepy Hollow leather chairs in a corner at the left of the fireplace. The new President sat in an armchair, part of the walnut suite. The schoolmaster and I sat on smaller chairs of the same suite. And I remember that in the midst of it I was most uncomfortable sitting on a chair, my hands on my knees, agape probably as I heard the young President, who was in his very early forties, tell of his plans and his hopes, his dangers and his fears. Theodore Roosevelt was a most candid man, and I was shocked at the casual way in which he considered affairs of state. I could not get used to it. What he said I do not remember, except that he feared Hanna and was frankly out to beat him for the nomination in 1904. That would stick in my memory. And one other thing which the schoolmaster and I both recall through forty years: he was worried about what he would do when he left the White House. He would be barely fifty, a strong and vigorous man who had had every political ambition satisfied, yet was wedded to the political life. He said:

"I don't want to be the old cannon loose on the deck in the storm."

He knew himself so well. No man who could make himself the butt of his own jokes could fail to see himself after he had left the White House, still in the midst of American politics.

As I sat on the edge of my chair and Nicholas Murray Butler, with more dignity and aplomb, sat back in his chair, I noticed early in the evening that the captain's eyes were drooping. He was not much interested in the talk, chiefly his young brother-in-law's gabble. He was used to it. He refused to be excited about the young man coming to the White House. He had heard many times Theodore Roosevelt rattle on, and the good dinner had lulled him to rest as we two young fellows sat with wonder, awe and praise in front of our prophet and ruler. And in the midst of one of Roosevelt's more dramatic sallies into the intimate affairs of the nation, I glanced at the captain. His hands were linked across his paunch. His eyes were closed, and he was gently snoring through it all.

Undoubtedly Nicholas Murray Butler discounted the young man and his enthusiasm more heavily than I did, for always in Dr. Butler's veins ran a few drops of the blood of doubting Thomas. But I swallowed it all, and it was a heady wine. I walked back to my hotel, the old Normandie on McPherson Square, on clouds of moonshine and amazement that I could see such things as I had seen, and hear such tall talk as I had heard. I did not go to the White House the next day, I remember that. I hurried home and wrote my piece about Senator Platt. Platt had scorned my hero. Unconsciously, or perhaps consciously, I used my best and most burning adjectives in that article expressing my scorn of Senator Platt and his machine, and contempt for the things it represented. It was a bitter piece. I could not write that way now. I realize that Platt was a senile old man who held his power because those about him had to keep him as a symbol, and use his name and fame to hold his machine together. But I was proud of the job, and the editors of McClure's seemed to like it, and we put it into the hopper in mid-September for publication in the early winter.

I came back to Emporia to be a country editor. We were trying about this time to promote a railroad from Emporia to Omaha, a north-and-south interstate line that would use a branch of the M. K. & T. to connect with that road going south to the Gulf. It was a pretty dream. We were in the midst of a boom then, an upward spiraling wave of business activity that began early in McKinley's administration and for five years rose lustily and spread out over the land before the tide went out a year or so later. Our railroad dream seemed all but reality. When the receding wave of depression came, it washed away. But I was busy with it after the Platt article was finished, and also was taking part in Kansas politics. The election of 1902 was not so far away but that we who were somewhat on the inside of Republican politics were busy setting up the pegs to control the state conventions of that year and so to elect a governor and a United States Senator.

I must have been an odd, perhaps funny is the word, figure in Kansas in those days when the new century was unfolding. I smiled easily and, I am afraid, too consciously. All the stories that Noble Prentis had told me as we worked together in the little cubicle on the Star, were at my tongue's tip. I tried to make speeches, political speeches and sometimes occasional speeches at dedications, cornerstone layings and the lot, and I was tongue-tied and stuttering and must have given the impression of a very young bullfrog trying to lift his voice. It was pretty terrible, but I did not know it; and Sallie, perhaps realizing that I was struggling to do my best, was kind and let me struggle. But I was headed for the executive committee of the state Republican central committee. I was committeeman in my ward and functioned in the Republican organization in my county. It was really college politics all over again. I learned no new talent that I did not use when Vernon Kellogg and I were pulling the strings and manipulating our fraternity vote at the university. The talent of politics is much the same, whether it works in affairs of state, church, school or business. The same qualities win or lose in all the formal relations of men.

In the late autumn of 1901 I went back to Washington—I think it was at Roosevelt's suggestion—to talk over his candidacy for 1904 as it had been

340

going since he became President. The Roosevelts had moved into the White House, bag and baggage. I remember that Roosevelt said:

"You know, Will, Edie says it's like living over the store!"

I ate a meal or so with them, luncheon, and I remember a breakfast at this time, at which half a dozen Senators, after devouring scrambled eggs and buckwheat cakes, discussed the Platt Amendment, which concerned the government of Cuba and the attitude of this country. The Platt Amendment was introduced by Senator Platt, of Connecticut, no kin to the New York boss. The discussion was good. Roosevelt had assembled men on both sides of the controversy, and he really let them talk—though at the last he took the floor and set forth his views with great positiveness and clarity.

The Roosevelts lived in middle-class simplicity. At family meals the children came to the table. The President, of course, was served first and in the early years of his office he used to apologize for it, indicating that he did not see any sense in the formality, but declaring that he could not overrule the servants. Roosevelt never was fond of sophisticated foods, but he took two helpings of meat generally, and they always had at least three vegetables. Potatoes in those days were standard dinner equipment, generally mashed. He liked gravy, but au jus. At dinner he ran the table—not that he talked all the time but he primed others and pumped them to talk about what they knew best. I remember once, when John Sargent was painting Roosevelt's portrait, and we three were at lunch together, the colonel made me talk about clubwomen in the Middle West and how they read papers on John Sargent's work, and I gave a picture of western town culture that I am sure John Sargent never imagined and could scarcely believe for, having been Anglicized, he thought that the West was a bleak, wind-swept semidesert, where the best white men still married squaws. Roosevelt sat chuckling and prodding me on, and I don't think John Sargent much cared for the picture I was making. It was too homely, too folksy, too civilized for his idea of the Middle West.

At another time, when Mrs. Roosevelt was in Oyster Bay on some errand and Mrs. White and I were in town, he assembled a fairly small tableful of personal friends. Justice Holmes was there, and Elihu Root, General Leonard Wood and John M. Parker, of New Orleans. And a good-looking, most intelligent woman in the party, whose name I did not catch, was seated in Mrs. Roosevelt's place as hostess. Roosevelt fished the table like a fly fisherman, throwing to each guest. As, for instance, he asked Parker to tell the story of the lynching of the Mafia in New Orleans, where the good citizens raided a jail, cleaned out and knifed a blackmailing secret society that had defied the courts, and Parker told a fine story. Then Roosevelt baited Holmes with a professor fly and got him to talking about his father, the poet. I caught his eye and he was asking me to tell some story or other, Heaven knows what, and I launched out. The story led into the life and character of James G. Blaine. I knew that both Roosevelt and I had a low opinion of Blaine. As I approached the subject of Blaine under a full head of steam, I noticed across the table that Sallie gave me the dirtiest look any woman ever shot at a fool husband making a *faux pas* in public. I felt at my shirt buttons to see that they were all right, fumbled at my necktie, went on talking and could not think what was wrong. Then the dirty look got black and I just plain stopped short, as though I had been choked, and my tongue all but hung out. The Blaine thing was coming— my deep dislike for Blaine and his kind. Roosevelt may have sensed it. He may have seen Sallie's look of horror and warning, for he took the conversation away from me and later, as we were going out, he and Sallie and I drifted together and she cried:

"Will, Will, when you were getting ready to scalp Blaine, didn't you know that the hostess at the other end of the table was Mrs. Beale, Blaine's daughter?"

And I nearly fainted.

But the Roosevelts' meals and the Roosevelt household were always riotous. And he gave them their rambunctious character and keenly enjoyed it. Mrs. Roosevelt once said to Sallie:

"How Theodore loves a party!"

It was beautiful to see him with half a dozen guests at his table, with the children there cutting in, for they were never repressed children, and once—in a lull during the meal, perhaps before the main course—someone asked the youngsters:

"Who are your father's favorite cabinet members?"

As if they were trained to it—and maybe they were—they took their knives and forks by the handles and drummed on the table and piped in something like unison, "Mr. Root and Mr. Knox." Which made a great hit in the Capitol after the story got around; indeed the Capitol was scandalized at the Roosevelt children.

But they grew up into decent, useful, self-respecting men and women, and the liberties they had as children gave them a sense of duty later in life. The Colonel and Mrs. Roosevelt were good parents, though Alice was a handful. She smoked a cigarette once at a ball game or a horse race, and nearly brought down the public, for cigarettes in America were then used only by painted ladies. She once jumped into a swimming pool with her clothes on—to the consternation of the Republic, which should have expected it, for politically her father was always doing just that. She was her father's child. But the atmosphere of the White House, which bewildered diplomatic circles by its general informality and occasional dis-

342

regard of usage, was nevertheless typically middle-class American—sincere, wholesome, a bit boisterous, but always well bred in the deep sense of the word, which makes kindness the soul of manners.

Now to go back to the autumn of 1901. In our Kansas politics we had elected a crooked senator whom Roosevelt afterwards sent to jail. He was my particular black beast in the politics of Kansas. He was a flashy dresser, flashily equipped intellectually, full of flashy demagogic works in politics. He had reason to hate my guts, and did. At that time he was trying to get my old friend and boss, Cy Leland, deposed as pension commissioner for the Missouri Valley district. When I saw McKinley, a few days before his death, he told me that he was going to reappoint Leland, which was natural. Leland had been his early supporter for the Presidential nomination in 1896. Leland headed the Kansas Republican faction that fought the crooked Kansas senator, and Leland was implacable in his hatreds. The first thing that the new senator from Kansas asked the new President for was Leland's head on a platter, and I, recounting McKinley's promise, asked that Leland be saved from the senatorial fury. The other Kansas senator was a Democrat and a decent man. Two or three other national politicians, including Hanna, told President Roosevelt that McKinley had plainly indicated his desire to reappoint Leland. But the senator had much power. He was not to be checked. He had National Committeeman Mulvane back of him, and half of the Congressional delegation followed the senator. The fight was publicly staged. I was fighting the senator. Kansas knew it. The Civil War veterans generally lined up with Leland. He was one of them, and they felt deeply the senator's attack on Leland. The senator picked a Spanish War veteran as Leland's opponent and that also galled the Civil War veterans, who regarded the Spanish-American War as mere fly-swatting and its veterans as upstarts. Those Civil War veterans had passed the peak of their power and, in their hearts, they knew it.

The knowledge was bitter medicine. They were beginning to huddle together, gathering in their old blue coats and brass buttons in reunions and in politics, like bluebirds preparing for flight. The day that Roosevelt yielded and appointed the young Spanish War veteran to Leland's job, the members of the G.A.R. in Emporia came out on Commercial Street like a swarm of bees, buzzing their anger. I remember Tom Fleming, city marshal for years, a kindly, gentle person who mothered the drunks and roisterers of Commercial Street, picked them up, brushed the flies from them, took them to the cooler, locked them up, bathed them, sent them out to their families refurbished; he always warned the evil-doers for the first offense and arrested them for the second. Tom was getting old and walked with a cane, but like a grenadier. And when the news came that our crooked senator had triumphed, Old Tom met me on the street, led me two blocks aside and into his livery stable, took me into the boxstall where he kept his prize hearse horses, pulled the door to and hissed into my ear, "Well, Bill White, what do you think of your goddam Jew President now?" and stalked out, beating his cane on the dirt floor; and, like Pontius Pilate, he would not wait for an answer, but left me standing speechless in the encircling gloom.

CHAPTER XLIX

A Literary Explosion

THEODORE ROOSEVELT came into the White House as the country was going into an ascending spiral of prosperity. Credit was expanding. The debts of the depression of the middle nineties were settled either by readjustment or by payment. The country was prospering. The tide of immigration was flowing steadily into the high plains area east and west of the Rocky Mountains. Little cities were springing up; great ranches were opening; irrigation was extending to farm lands. Money was easy at first. Every promise that Mark Hanna had made in '96 about the return of prosperity was fulfilling itself abundantly. The alliance between business and government seemed to be profitable to the parties of both the first and second parts, and voices of protest were few and far between. Speaking broadly, interstate corporations, chiefly the railroads, were controlling legislatures which elected United States Senators who, in turn, had the appointment of federal judges, so that reforms in the legislature, the governor's chair, the Congress, or the White House, had a hard time of it. The courts took care of that. The federal constitution was strictly construed to free the *status quo,* so that banks felt secure in loaning money to industrial corporations; industrialists felt secure in expanding their business on credit.

Theodore Roosevelt in the White House, having peculiar ideas about the divorce of the great alliance that Mark Hanna made, was creating a sensation in highly respectable circles, where he had been acclaimed a few years before when he publicly denounced Bryan, with his inflationary ideas and his socialist program.

But Theodore Roosevelt liked a fight. Also, as a man of wide viewpoint and with reason behind his knowledge, he knew what the Populists and radical Democrats only felt in their bones. Moreover, he had written in books, talked around club hearthstones and spoken at anniversary occasions so many times against the evils that were concentrated in Hannaism that he could not retreat, for he was met by the echo of his own voice which he always feared. So while he made a great show of carrying out McKinley's policies, at heart he was their deadly enemy. His lip service to his fancied duty to the dead President did not bring him any change in fundamental conviction. So the air, even in the first year of the Roosevelt administration, began to be electric with suspicion and alarm in high places. And that alarm began to spread to Wall Street, and to the little Wall Streets peppered across the country in cities and towns where the bankers and industrialists controlled local government.

Curiously, Robert M. La Follette, then governor of Wisconsin, the only national leader who was fighting Roosevelt's enemies, distrusted him profoundly. It was temperamental. Roosevelt would take a half a loaf. He loved to compromise. If he seemed to seek martyrdom, it was a delusion. La Follette wanted the whole hog. He would dramatize his cause by a tragic failure, so that it might revive in triumph in another day. It was curious to watch the two men rise in the decades that followed, each struggling to take his country to the same goal, each bitterly scornful of the other's methods, and probably deeply suspicious of his inner aims. I happened to be a friend of both. I had a genuine affection for both. I trusted both. I worked with both.

I was working hard at the Gazette office every day from eight until six. At night I worked until midnight on magazine articles and stories, and on the proofs of books I had written. I had seen four books go through the press by December, 1901. I had got as much as a thousand dollars for one article, and for a year or so had been getting five or six or seven hundred dollars for stories and articles. I was writing for the Saturday Evening Post at that time, and George Lorimer, its editor, was my dear friend. I felt that it was wise to own a good house. I do not suppose Sallie and I consciously capitalized our hospitality, but when magazine editors and politicians of all sorts visited us, they knew we were people of substance. The politicians treated us with respect that did not come to starvelings. Magazine editors knew that we were in a good bargaining position when we demanded high pay for what we wrote. The rising spiral of prosperity took us along with it, and we saved as we rose. We have never had more than one debt at a time. It is a good rule for a young man. Too many equities in too many properties is the ruination of many a man.

In December of 1901, McClure's Magazine printed my article on Thomas Platt. He read it. His friends read it. The enemies of Theodore Roosevelt in the senate read it. They all raged. It was fairly obvious that I, who had been a familiar spirit around Roosevelt for four years, must have garnered much of the information for the article from Roosevelt, or from his friends. This was true, though I was cautious enough never to print any story that Roosevelt gave me without getting the story from another source. Generally he told me where to find the other source. For he loved intrigue. So when the story of Platt infuriated its hero, he went to the White House and made a scene there, accused Roosevelt of abetting the article and demanded, as a senator from New York, that I be barred from the White House. He came out of the President's office and told the reporters that I had been barred, which made a fine story. It helped the sale of the magazine. It boosted the market value of my writing. For a few days it revived the author of "What's the Matter with Kansas?" as a national figure, which was fine. But Platt started, or threatened to start, a libel suit for six figures against McClure's Magazine. Also against me. It scared me to death, and by Christmastime I was going into nervous exhaustion. One day in the Gazette office I was dictating a letter ordering a carload of paper. I began to sweat and tremble. The order was a formal one, routine in its nature, but I just could not finish the dictation, and came home and went to bed. The doctors hustled me out of town. I went to Colorado, then to California, and did not come back until May. For hours together, Mrs. White and I sat on the beach on Catalina Island off Los Angeles, I lying down speechless, dozing in and out of sleep with my hat over my eyes, she beside me watching me, shooing off the children who might disturb me, reading and sewing. We had a little cabin where we lived like kings. It was the mushroom season on the island and we ate great saucerlike wild mushrooms with beefsteak, and learned to cook them with fish. The island markets were filled with all sorts of delectable sea food, and Sallie was always avid to learn new dishes. Books came from Emporia, and she read to me. At first I could not bear to open the mail. She told me casually what was in it and, without asking me directly, got my reaction and, using her own common sense, replied to all the questions that were raised in the mail. By mid-April I was well on the mend. We had left Billy, our baby, at home with his two grandmothers. One grandmother will spoil a baby. Two working together will bring him up in the way he should go, for each will suspect the other of spoiling him and will check it. This should be put somewhere in a book of advice to parents.

While I was gone the papers controlled by Senators Burton, Mulvane and Curtis, my factional enemies in Kansas, printed a story that I had gone mad. So when I returned to offset the story, dear old Major Hood, the Little Major, God bless him, hired the Emporia silver cornet band, rounded up a congregation of my friends who crowded the depot platform and as the train came in the band began to play "See, the Conquering Hero Comes." Sallie and I got off the train, and what did we care for the band, and what did we care for the crowd, when little Billy in his grandmother's arms came to us and spoke his first two words very slowly and astutely— "band boys"? Our cup ran over. I was well. Of course, the newspapers carried the story of my return and told about the band and the crowd, and swiftly a letter came from the White House congratulating me upon my return. The President had sent word by mutual friends before I left for California, to pay no attention to the rumors that Platt was spreading. The editors of McClure's wrote even before I left not to let the Platt lawsuit worry me. And when I was in California I saw a story in a New York paper that McClure's had hired Tom Reed to defend them. They said afterwards that the story was without foundation, but it had frightened Platt so that he abandoned his libel suit. It was never filed.

Sometime in early June, 1902, I went to Washington and, for want of a better time for a talk, the President invited me to breakfast with a number of statesmen who were wrangling with him about some bill before the Congress. I think he wanted these Republican politicians to see me in the White House, whence Platt had banned me six months before, and of course I was happy.

Roosevelt's zest for what may be called euphemistically a prank, is illustrated by this letter which I find in my files. The letter should be supplemented by a phrase from another letter given me a few months before, introducing me to Charles Dawes. Closing it, he said of me: "I trust him as I trust few other men." And now after more than forty years, it seems to me that the record of this gay bedevilment may be printed, to give historians a peep-hole insight into the heart of Theodore Roosevelt, who loved danger for its own sake and if he could combine danger with a frolicking intrigue, would get an inner joy out of it that was like the consolation of a great faith. Such was the infantile, or perhaps adolescent, hangover in his heart that never entirely left him. In the White House, it rendered him inexplicable to men of solemn and somber maturity. The following letter is an answer to my request to him to give me some kind of a "line" on how to get to Platt. We had talked over the Platt article that I wanted to write. This had been his reply:

The Vice President's Chamber
Washington, D.C.

Oyster Bay, New York, March 20, 1901

Mr. William Allen White
  Emporia, Kansas

My dear White:—
  I have your letter of the 16th inst. Be sure to come out and stay with me. I will tell you all about Platt and how to get a letter to him.
  Give my warm regards to Mrs. White.

Faithfully yours,
THEODORE ROOSEVELT

A funny thing happened that was most characteristic of Theodore Roosevelt's love of danger and intrigue. Following this breakfast, six months after Platt announced I was barred from the White House, he maneuvered me away from the retiring statesmen and said:

"Did you meet Platt when you were writing your story?"

I said "Yep!"—snapped it out just like that.

He said: "How long did you talk to him?"

I replied, consideringly: "Let me see, probably ten, possibly fifteen or twenty minutes."

"All right, he won't remember you. Come along with me if you want to have a good time."

I had no idea what he was up to. We went into his private office. He put me in a chair just back of his. He looked at his clock. It was nine-thirty. The office doorman announced Senator Platt of New York. I started to go. The President with his hand made an almost mandatory gesture, and said:

"Stay where you are!"

In tottered old Platt on some minor errand about New York patronage. He glanced at me. I meant nothing to him. He was an old man, and my twenty-minute interview with him ten months before had not registered in his memory. He supposed I might be some Harvard friend of the President, and went on with his errand. He and Roosevelt talked for ten minutes. Roosevelt walked with him to the door. It shut. He turned to me, beaming with delight, and squeaked in the falsetto that indicated his pride in himself and his keen love of danger:

"Didn't I tell you? I knew he wouldn't remember you. Did you enjoy it?"

And then he burst into high, happy, nervous laughter and we both giggled. I went out of his office following Platt. The reporters were there. They saw us coming out of the White House only a few moments apart. They made a good story. Platt was too old to protest. When he read the story, his friends did not care to take the matter up. My stock advanced. And then, to give me still more prestige on Commercial Street, the President named my candidate for the Emporia post office, ignoring the recommendation of the Congressman. Roosevelt was that kind of a friend. When he could, he would. When he could not, he said so and it was all right.

The death of Mark Hanna dropped the curtain on the first act of a tragic comedy. Mark Hanna was well cast in the morality play as Plutocracy, the plutocracy of a blithe, irresponsible immorality. The plutocracy which rose out of the last quarter of the nineteenth century was not greedy and circumspect, not in the least aristocratic. It was the plutocracy of boots and whiskers which cavorted, danced and pilfered with a certain fine impudence that was not immoral. It was merely a whimsical bias against the cramping respectability of the Decalogue which liked to filch pennies, make millions thereby, and scatter them either on beneficences or mistresses—ignorant of or oblivious to any social obligation. I suppose my belief in plutocracy in those first ten years of my emergence from school came from a conviction that it was a diverting frolic to let the public be damned. My admiration and devotion to Mark Hanna probably was based on some such idea in his heart which formed his character and career. If he had lived perhaps he too would have seen how evil was his rollicking economic lechery; how badly those whom they robbed of pennies needed the largess which those accumulated pennies made. But in the puckish impudence of his poaching, he did not live to see its sad consequences. If he could have lived another decade, he might have died the death of the penitent thief, for he was a tender-hearted brigand and, on the whole, he meant well. I, who loved him as a father, was blessed with time to repent and, I hope, do works meet unto repentance.

When Hanna died in 1904 Theodore Roosevelt had no serious opposition for the Republican nomination. He was a vigorous man who knew the game as it was played. He had a powerful political weapon in his hands, the patronage of the White House, and he used it. He was nominated by a convention which disliked him and was beginning to fear and scorn his so-called Roosevelt policies. They knew that with the election of 1904, Roosevelt would abandon any pretense of carrying out the McKinley policies. In the meantime, during the winter of 1903, I learned how states elected their United States Senators under the old plan, which made Senators elective by legislators. An account of that election in Kansas in January of 1903 should be preserved, not because it was important but because it was typical and sometime historians may wish to know how the forces operated which named United States Senators.

I spent most of the month before the senatorial election in Topeka and was a part, and a fairly inside part, of one of the groups which was striving to name a Senator, and I was acquainted with the inside workings of the whole procedure. I think I can testify as an expert. This is the story:

The legislature of 1903 was overwhelmingly Republican, as it had generally been since the admission of the states to the Union. Only two or three times between 1860 and 1902 had the Republicans failed to carry the legislature. Senators were elected by a joint ballot of the legislature. Under ancient precedent, the nominee of the Republican caucus was made the nominee of the party, so the struggle in the election of the United States Senators was to control the Republican legislative caucus. To do that a slate had to be made which would elect the speaker of the house and also vote for the state printer, who in those days was also elected by the legislature. Friends of the speaker and of the state printer had to get into a combination of the friends of a senatorial candidate. Rarely did a speaker or a state printer go it alone. In 1903 each side of the senatorial contest picked its own candidate for speaker and for state printer. On one side were friends and forces of Charles Curtis, a member of the national House of Representatives. Opposing him was a coalition between the friends of Representative Chester I. Long and Governor Stanley, each seeking to control what was obviously a majority anti-Curtis faction in the legislature. Curtis' tactics were to break the Long-Stanley alliance.

The railroads of the state, represented by their political attorneys, had great power. But they could not agree. The Rock Island Railroad was supposed to be for Curtis. The Santa Fe was neutral, with leanings toward the anti-Curtis crowd and in particular toward Chester Long. The Missouri Pacific was divided, but finally swung into the anti-Curtis crowd. These railroad attorneys had great power to negotiate on their own, but they were nevertheless controlled by the railroad managers and owners in Chicago, St. Louis and New York. The switch of the Missouri Pacific from Curtis to Long was made in St. Louis. The power of state railroad attorneys lay in the fact that they could issue passes. Practically every member of the legislature came to Topeka on a pass. Generally the pass included members of their families, and if the legislators had any power, they could demand passes to and from Topeka for their friends at home. Imagine how the railroad passes controlled state politics in the last quarter of the nineteenth century and in the first decade of this century! Little money passed in the election of the United States Senator, but passes talked the same language that money talks.

Yet scores of legislators were influenced more by personal friends than by railroad attorneys. I was among the supporters of Stanley, and I worked on my friends to support him. I was one of half a dozen of Stanley's friends who worked upon the legislature. Long had as many friends, and Curtis had more. We all descended like wolves on the foe. Cy Leland was in charge of the anti-Curtis forces. He said frankly that in the end he would support the man who could get the most votes to beat Curtis. Both sides had faith in him, and probably with reason. Both Long's friends and organizers and Stanley's reported to him, and the friends of both Long and Stanley united on a candidate for speaker and a candidate for state printer. That union, in the parlance of the day, was called the slate. When we lined up the friends of the speaker and the friends of the state printer, who were more interested in them than in the United States Senator, and then lined up the friends of two United States Senators who were more interested in the Senate than they were in the election of the speaker or the state printer, we easily elected a speaker and quickly elected the state printer. After that the patronage of the speaker was ours, a powerful weapon, for it meant the appointment of committees in the House, of doorkeepers, postmasters, janitors, and the like. I remember one day going with Henry Allen to round up a member of the legislature from Rooks (or maybe it was Decatur) County who had come down to the legislature with just one aim and ambition. He was a Civil War veteran. He wanted a job as janitor for a broken comrade, a one-legged man, to whom the three dollars a day for three or four months made quite a little nest egg, and the legislator was willing to swap a speaker and a state printer to be assured that his old bunkmate could have that little contact with the public tit. Of course Henry and I promised him, as we were authorized to do, what he wanted and we brought him into the campaign, triumphantly. He chose Stanley rather than Long, but we knew he would go with Long if it was necessary. At the end of the day I walked into Mr. Leland's room, a Holy of Holies, and told him about my conquest.

"What did you have to pay?" snapped Leland.

"Assistant janitor, and we have got it. Assistant janitor," I repeated, "for old Jim Higginbotham, the representative's comrade."

Leland looked up quickly and snapped: "Jim who?"

"Jim Higginbotham," I repeated.

"No, by God, no, by God!" he shouted. "Jim Higginbotham double-crossed me in the Osborne convention [convention of 1876] when I needed him. No, by God!"

The Osborne convention had been thirty years before, but the elephant remembered the man who had given him the red-pepper peanut. When I broke into a laugh, Leland looked at me for a second with flashing anger, which cooled, and he smiled grimly: "Nevertheless, we won't do it!" and turned away. So Leland let the member from Rooks or Decatur County go to Curtis, badly as we needed him.

That's the way the game was played. The Republican caucus deadlocked for a week. Finally the Missouri Pacific moved its cohorts from Curtis to Long, on the promise that Long would support Curtis in the next senatorial campaign, with all the railroad attorneys concurring and affirming the bargain; so that the next senatorial election was decided in advance. The people had nothing to do with it. In order to get the support which elected him, Long went to the office of J. Pierpont Morgan in New York and pleaded his case. Morgan's railroad connection gave Long the backbone of his strength. Long in the Senate was known as a railroad Senator. The rank and file of the Kansas people had no way to break up the plutocratic control of their state, except to join the other states and change the federal Constitution to provide for the direct election of United States Senators. Those Senators elected in that way in the days when machines and the ownership of machines were passing into the hands of a class-conscious, organized plutocracy, had no obligations to the people of their state. They were obligated to the machine owners in other states. In Kansas, it was the railroads. In western Massachusetts, it was textiles. In eastern Massachusetts, it was the banks. In New York, it was amalgamated industry. In Montana, it was copper. But the power which developed and controlled any state went to New York for its borrowed capital, and New York controlled the United States Senate. Mark Hanna's plutocracy seemed unbeatable. The grade of Senators, as far as intelligence went, was higher than the grade which the people selected, but on the whole and by and large it was not representative government. Only a minority of the people of the United States had any control over the United States Senate. And that minority was interested in its own predatory designs. I saw it work in Topeka. I ran with the machine, and I realized at the end of that session what a tin-cornice front for organized wealth our sham election of United States Senators was. The day after Long's election my dear little friend, the old Major, came walking on his toes into the Gazette office, and after a gentle cough clearing his throat, said:

"By the way, Will, I loaned Stanley and Long fifteen hundred dollars each to pay their own personal expenses at Topeka this month. I wish you would go to Long and ask him to take care of Stanley's note. Long will understand."

And he did, for the note was paid. The Major was playing safe. He was a good banker. But that, my dear posterity, in another day, is the way we chose United States Senators when the state legislature elected our Senators. The organizing capacity of keen, selfish minds in this country cannot be trusted to organize except in their own self-interest. Power breeds arrogance. Arrogance breeds cruelty. And any institution in government which gives great power without responsibility to a few is merely building up tyranny, oppression, greed and the lust for more power at any price. This is quite as true in organized labor as it is in organized capital. It is true in any field of human endeavor. Even the church has its proud bishop, the schools their mad dictators, the cities their bosses. But now I must close this chapter by recounting the sequel to the senatorial election of 1903. I was in Washington a year or so later. I was sitting by the fire one evening in the White House with the President, talking over some casual matter, when he said:

"By the way, what do you know about Judge Blub Blub [which, of course, was not his name] of St. Louis? I have decided to make him a federal circuit judge. He comes highly recommended by all the Senators in the district and seems to be a man of parts and consequence, though he is a Democrat."

I knew Judge Blub Blub. He was a man to whom the Long forces appealed when they took the Union Pacific from Curtis. Judge Blub Blub always came to our state conventions in a private car and participated in Republican and Democratic politics with equal keenness and perspicacity. He was Jay Gould's political fixer for the upper Mississippi Valley—the very type of man who represented that "predatory wealth" which the President was denouncing. He knew the game—did Theodore Roosevelt— as well as I. So I told him the truth: that Judge Blub Blub had not appeared in a courtroom as an attorney for twenty years; that he handled the money for Gould in all the shady political transactions that Gould needed to perpetuate his empire. Then I explained, and Roosevelt got it before I was through explaining, why all the Senators in that federal circuit came clamoring for Judge Blub Blub. Roosevelt snapped his jaws, showed his teeth and cried:

"Well, by George, I almost bought a gold brick."

My answer to that was to advise him to talk to some of the honest congressmen of that circuit district, and particularly I said:

"Talk to Representatives Joy and Bartholdt, of St. Louis. They are honest. They will tell you the truth."

Roosevelt assented and I sent Joy and Bartholdt to the White House. I saw the President the next day. He had scratched Judge Blub Blub's name off the available list. However, later I ran into the Magnificent Chester I. Long, whom I had known for a dozen years and I said:

"Well, Chester, Judge Blub Blub is out of the running."

The Senator smiled patronizingly, "So?"

And I said: "Yes, I saw the President scratch his name with my own eyes. Go talk to him."

Long literally jumped into the air with amazement. He cried out in sudden wrath:

"Why, you, you, you—"

He couldn't quite use the name. I grinned, and he whirled around and headed for the White House. And the next day when I saw the President, he said:

"I had a lot of fun with Long."

And then someone came in and interrupted him. But Judge Blub Blub was out.

It is easy to see, when a system of corruption begins to mildew any section of government, how hard it is to check the blight. The nomination of Judge Blub Blub would have been secure and he would have held the rights of property in that Federal Court like Leonidas at Thermopylae. But Theodore Roosevelt, when he had the truth, was not afraid to defy Senators, nor to discredit his party when it was wrong. He had courage and knew the game.

CHAPTER L

Three Aging Gladiators

THE GAME of politics in that far day at the beginning of the century was in-stitutionalized by those who played the game—politicians seeking office, politicians seeking no office but power which controls the giving of offices, businessmen who wanted either to be let alone under the rules of business as it was conducted or who wanted special privileges from government, such as tariff benefits, municipal franchises, advance information about this and that, and the edge or inside upon a thousand matters and things wherein money would be made by inside knowledge.

But one must not presume that this was an unhappy country, oppressed by special privilege and extra-legal power. It was indeed a prosperous coun-try, and the prosperity filtered down pretty well toward the bottom of the middle class. Millions of foreigners, coming into the country to take the rough, hard jobs, probably depressed wages and made the living standards of workers too low. But those foreigners who came in during one decade, either by their wits or by their strength rose out of the lower ranks, and their children had something approaching equal opportunity with the children of the better placed parents in their community. Caste lines were not set. The flow up and down was unimpeded, from the top to the bottom of the scale.

In Emporia we were rebuilding the town. We had been building square houses, two stories with rather wide eaves, sometimes square houses with brick or stone for the first story and wood for the second story. They were called shirtwaist houses, and were right fancy. They were six or seven or even eight-room houses, and that meant a servant—sometimes two serv-ants. The scale in Emporia in the days of McKinley and Roosevelt ran from $2.50 to $4 or $5 a week. But the living costs were such that those wages seemed fair. At least one never heard a servant bewailing her hard luck. What she did was to marry a clerk or a railroad man, and pretty soon she was living in her own square house. And her children in Emporia were

355

going to college before the end of the century's second decade. Our opera house was open three or four nights a week the year around. Generally the shows were cheap, ten, twenty and thirty cents—traveling stock companies, and a good theatrical attraction appeared three or four times during the season. The automobile was just around the corner. Emporia had three in the first half of the first decade of the century. The moving picture was a freak entertainment. It was installed in vacant store buildings twenty-five feet wide and maybe fifty or seventy-five feet long, with folding chairs for the spectators. It was a ten-cent show, often a five-cent show; the theater was called the Nickelodeon and the pictures were terrible. No one who amounted to very much liked to be caught in the Nickelodeon. All the automobiles did in those days was to scare horses and provoke laughter. Major Hood's spanking sorrels, George Newman's big bays attached to their family carriages, and the scores and perhaps hundreds of one-horse phaetons, buggies and traps rode around Emporia and went spinning along the dusty country road of a fine summer evening. When, at the end of the first half of the first decade, we put in a few blocks of paving in the town, the whole cavalcade rode up and down that paving in the summer twilight with relish and delight. There was even talk of good roads. People played bridge, which then they called bridge whist, and the town supported several layers of whist clubs with naturally The Club which rotated around the Hoods and the Newmans and the Warrens at the top. And the news of their parties, indeed all in all the whist club parties of those days were chronicled in the Gazette, the names of the guests and prize-winners and sometimes we noted the prizes—chiefly cut glass and hand-painted china, most elegant and estimable. In the summer the town's baseball team played the teams from other towns in Kansas, in Soden's Grove. And of a late summer afternoon, the town gathered at these games with noisy loyalty and great excitement, the women in their best big hats and high sleeves and wide skirts, the men in what then were called shirtwaists, tailless shirts gathered with a rubber string under the waist just inside and below the trouser top— quite fashionable and exciting. The ball game was the only public summer sport. We had a small swimming pool in a vacant building, for men only, and they wore no bathing suits. As the summer closed, the horse races at the county fairs round about attracted the populace, and half a dozen men in Emporia owned fast-steppers which often they drove themselves—doctors, lawyers, merchants, railroad men. And the ownership of a good pacing horse gave a man distinction in the town. We were ten thousand. We owned our light and water plants. We were beginning to use gas for cooking. The sewer was going down every alley. The old-fashioned privy was becoming extinct. Thus, another sign of social distinction was being wiped out. But the barn and the chicken house still survived in the town. The town herd still was gathered in the morning and brought home in the evening, and still old Tom Fleming, the city marshal, found most of his summer troubles rising from chickens that destroyed their neighbors' yards, flower beds and lawns. It was only twenty years before that the town had been rocked to the circumference by an ordinance which compelled householders to stable their cows, which before had run loose on the streets. But the stable and the housefly still were one and inseparable all over our town, and for that matter pretty much all over the United States.

The poor, and Emporia had its submarginal ten per cent, of course lived meanly. But they were dismissed with Jesus' apology: "The poor you have always with you." No one thought of organized charity or social work in our town in those days. Whatever justification our callous negligence had, may come from the fact that today, among the old settlers, at least twenty-five per cent of the prosperous citizens who run the town came from those same ranks of the poor who are "with us always!" The exercise of the virtue of thrift and diligent persistence in the old century gave the children of the poor who lived below the tracks, qualities which made them dominant in the town. But, on the other hand, those families who did not develop those virtues, who still are on the townsite, have filled the ranks of the WPA the last ten years, and their children will be the chronics on whatever poor list we have for the centuries to come. A few breed out of it, but mostly the handicap of blood holds them in low estate.

It was out of that environment, which we were proud in those days to call American, that I went forth from time to time to conquer the big wide world. I was writing stories about it and the people that made it, for McClure's Magazine and for the Saturday Evening Post, character sketches of from three to six thousand words about prominent contemporaries, mostly in political life. My method was the reporter's method—first to read as much as I could about them wherever I could find it, in newspapers, in magazines, in books and on subjects correlated to the works of my particular hero, then to see the hero and talk to him as long and as often as he would let me. He knew, of course, what I was up to. Public men, if they move or even reflect their times, often either take on the protective coloring of those times or are selected by the spirit of the hour because they, in their qualities, harmonize with the times and appeal to the motives, ambitions and tendencies of mass humanity at the hour when the leaders rise. It is hard to say which is the cart and which is the horse, whether the spiritual color of the people choose leaders of their own cult or whether leaders, by the sheer dominance of their natures, impress qualities upon the populace.

Three men, particularly, seemed to me at the time, and looking back a quarter of a century seem more and more, to embody the spirit of the last decade of the old century. They were Benjamin Harrison, Richard Croker and Grover Cleveland. These men were poles apart in their qualities of heart and mind save one, strength; each appealed to some major instinct of the people, each epitomized some broad facet of the times. Benjamin Harrison was physically a little man, five feet six or less, bearded, soft-voiced, small-boned, gentle-eyed, meticulous of dress and in manners, in speech, in thought. He always spoke in completed sentences and often in rounded paragraphs. He finished his thought. He left nothing in the air. His desk was cleared at night, not as the desk of a captain of industry, for there was nothing brusque, vigorous or overwhelming about him. His desk was cleared as a gentleman's desk is cleared, with a certain deference to tomorrow. Personally he was shy, most diffident and unassertive in his personal relations. The rough, noisy, elbowing multitude of temple acolytes who guarded the political arc of the covenant in Harrison's day, regarded him as a cold, unsympathetic, conceited snob. He was indeed the last of the aristocrats in American politics—using the term "aristocrat" to define that repressed and self-contained gentleman who sprang out of the hereditary background of the eighteenth century in our colonies, of which Washington, the Adamses, Madison and Marshall were typical.

Harrison had been United States Senator and had served upon an important commission in the early eighties. He came into the White House largely because he lived in Indiana, a doubtful state. But he brought to leadership in American politics the incarnate nobility of what his party would have been, were it not for its partisans. I remember sitting with him in his library a few weeks before his death, indeed he was kept indoors that day—a fine, soft day in late winter, or perhaps it was an early spring day—by a cold which later developed into the fatal pneumonia that took him. We had walked home the night before under the stars, while I listened and he discoursed on the nobility of man and so established our relation upon a certain plane of dignity. And that day, musing by the fire, he spoke of our Kansas Senator Preston B. Plumb who, when Harrison was President, was the dominant figure of the Middle West; a pioneer printer who set up the first printing office in Emporia under a tree before he could build a roof over the first building in the new town—a soldier and a colonel at twenty; quick, nervous, a dynamo pounding his way through to his end, generating force by his own incessant action, hard-headed, tenderhearted, big with purpose, impatient of formalities, a very tumult of a man. Harrison told of the nomination of Justice Brewer of Kansas to the United States Supreme Court. Plumb was for Brewer. Brewer was a judge of the federal circuit court. A vacancy in the Supreme Court made Brewer a possible candidate for the Supreme Court. Plumb, whose henchman Brewer had been in Kansas, sent Brewer's name to the White House as a candidate.

Brewer was equipped for the place. He was a Yale man, a student of the law, a scholar, and a gentleman according to the methods and morals and manners of his time. Plumb had spoken to the President once or twice about the appointment. President Harrison had regarded it as a matter of the utmost consequence. He was going slowly, thoroughly investigating the qualifications of each candidate.

Plumb's method was different. A situation was created in the Senate in which Plumb controlled. Harrison needed Plumb's support. Quite independently of that need, the President had made up his mind that Brewer, everything considered, was the best fitted candidate for the place upon the Supreme bench, and he had Brewer's commission made up. It lay on his desk several days. He was anxious to be sure. His mind, however, became more and more settled, and then one day Plumb burst into the President's office. He seemed to have heard some gossip about another candidate, and was raging like a bull. Up and down he paced before the President's desk, demanding the appointment of Brewer, threatening vengeance in the Senate, flinging insinuation, innuendo, insult at the calm, pink-cheeked, gray-whiskered, gentle-eyed, husky-voiced, unperturbed little aristocrat, master of himself to his fingertips, sitting drumming with his fingers on the polished mahogany of his desk, looking betimes at the commission of Brewer lying on the green blotter before him. He made no answer except a perfunctory response, let Plumb run down, rose when the Senator left, gave no hint of the Presidential intention, and bowed him out of the room.

"I think," said Benjamin Harrison, rising from his chair and walking to the fire, turning slowly from it and standing with its heat upon his back, "I think that one of the great moral victories of my life came when I put that commission back on my desk that moment after Plumb had left, and conquered a despicable temptation to tear it up and throw it in the basket. Your Senator never knew Judge Brewer's commission lay there at my fingertips while he was showering me with his gratuitous insults. If he were not dead, I should not tell the story now. I could not bear to think that he would ever know that his fulminations did not produce that nomination. It would be a surrender to have given him that knowledge of one of the finest victories in my life."

There was Harrison revealed—"a gentleman unafraid." He embodied all the nobility which was latent in the American heart, which boomed in its patriotic bombast which was beaten down by the curse that a punitive victory after a great war put upon a blind and aspiring people, that nobility Lincoln sensed and voiced, that chivalry Grant and Lee, the soldiers at Appomattox, dramatized. But alas, it vanished with the rise of the carpet-bagger, the symbol of the bloody shirt in politics. All the altruism in our politics was diffused in the heroic adventure that came when men poured pellmell, helter-skelter over the Alleghenies into the Mississippi Valley and up the slopes of the Rockies, dragging railroads, cities, colleges, factories, farm houses and equipment—all the impediments of a new civilization —behind them. Harrison rose when that adventure was over, and for a moment glowed, a cold, thin, white little flame of aristocracy in a sordid day. Grover Cleveland overcame him, and he respected Cleveland. McKinley and Hanna, to a certain extent, obliterated Harrison, and probably he despised them. That day before the fire he spoke of a certain weakness, a certain flabbiness, a certain propensity for unhealthy intrigue which he had found in McKinley as they met during the eighties in a Republican national convention. Harrison had a low opinion of Hanna also, but it was higher than his opinion of McKinley. For the robust Roosevelt, who in the last days of Harrison's life seemed to be shaking the pillars of the temple like a young Sampson, Harrison had no sympathy. He did not understand the new purpose, the doctrine of righteousness, the philosophy of the rediscovered Ten Commandments for a reconstituted world which Roosevelt was preaching. Harrison was of the old order. He saw the government of the fathers; the structure that was visioned before Lincoln, and in him glowed a holy faith in the constitution of the fathers as it was in the beginning, the great dream of a young republic.

Grover Cleveland, in his strength and through his virtues, was the antithesis of all that was fine in Harrison, whom Cleveland preceded and succeeded in the White House. Cleveland was what in after years we liked to call a he-man, handsome with a certain bull-like pulchritude, which was the outer symbol of his inner courage, his direct purpose and stubborn aspirations. He came from the muck of American politics. He ran with the gang in Buffalo, was sheriff, then mayor, knew all the tricks and ways of political corruption, all the fumbling futility of those who followed political ideals.

The professional old soldiers of the Grand Army of the Republic loathed Cleveland because they believed he hired a substitute during the Civil War. Also they claimed he went fishing on Memorial Day when he was President. Now if he wanted to, he did go fishing on Memorial Day in spite of the fact that the old soldier had made it a sort of political Good Friday. Cleveland was never bullied by the mob. Harrison stood aloof from the mob, avoided contact with it, despised it. Cleveland challenged it, defied it, walked over it roughshod. After a generation of fake patriotism, which had created a lot of fetishes in government—for instance, Civil War pensions, a high protective tariff, a chronic genuflection toward the silver dollar—Cleveland came along and insulted the mud idols of his time. He was candor incarnate, with a lust for iconoclasm. But he made his doses too large. The people in '88 turned to Harrison, the aristocrat the gentleman in politics who had as little faith as Cleveland in the mud idols and the mob and the arc of the covenant, but who gently, coldly and with terrible purpose ignored what Cleveland had challenged and defied; so then the country turned back to the more vigorous character.

I visited at the Cleveland home in Princeton and there saw the ex-President for the first time. He was then in his sixties. The years had stripped some of the fat from his neck and jowls; the full bull face of the man in his forties, who had charged the great god Demos, was down. But his eyes still carried the fine flame of their ancient courage. He was kindly, cordial, tremendously human without reservations, and he loomed as a human being quite apart from his record as a statesman. We fell to talking about the slanders which had been heaped on him in the White House. He was bitter—frankly, profanely bitter—about the New York Sun which was a sort of picador, throwing dirty darts at the old bull to anger him during his entire public career. Even then, five years removed from public life, he lowered his head, shook his horns and roared at the New York Sun. Thus:

"They lied about me. What infernal lies they told! Said that I was drunk on the *Mayflower*. That was their favorite slander. Hell, young man, do you think as President of the United States that I would get drunk? I took a drink—maybe two, maybe three or four if I wanted them—when I was in the White House and when I was on the *Mayflower*, but I never got drunk. I could handle my liquor. And the Sun . . ."

The ex-President then lit off his fireworks and in the pyrotechnics of language which played upon the effigy of the Sun, which he had conjured up, there was such virile hate, such courageous scorn, such blustering bull-roaring indignation as would have made Washington or Jackson in their profanest moments lift reverent hats in humble awe.

"Why, the damn ghouls even entered my home and told vile stories of my domestic relations!"

The big man's eyes glared and yet twinkled, encouraging his interviewer to prod in: "Yes, they said your wife was going to divorce you."

"And that wasn't all they said. Do you remember they said I kicked her downstairs? Think of that. And if ever there was a happy couple in this world it was Mrs. Cleveland and I. We had our differences, as what married couple doesn't, but we were happy. Why, I never—kicked her downstairs!" His eyes danced partly in glee, partly in wrath—they had that quality. But his mouth smiled as he roared, "Kicked her downstairs! Why, I never laid a hand on her!"

Then he shook his sagging old paunch in glee at the hyperbole, rose from the chair, kicked out a leg as a sort of he-gesture of comfort and, with beaming face, added a skyrocket of lovely invective—the short and simple language of the poor. For he was, despite his scorn of the mob and his joy in defying it, an old-fashioned Jeffersonian Democrat in his personal contacts, his deepest instincts. He had a broad, sardonic joy in standing off and looking at himself as a grotesque figure. Never was he a park statue while breath came through his nostrils. During the summer afternoon, for some reason finding a paper for a reference while he was telling how the New Jersey politicians tried to fool him and foist unfit men into office, we went up to the second floor, where in the hall stood a lovely old colonial piece—possibly a highboy or chest. His interviewer stopped to admire it, to touch the satin softness of the wood with a loving hand.

"Like that stuff?" Cleveland asked, turning around quickly, and added: "Know anything about it, or just like the looks of it?"

His companion indicated that he had such knowledge as an affection gives one for old furniture. Grover Cleveland stood, hands in his pockets, running his eye up and down it, his mouth twitching humorously, his hand rubbing an itching nose, then he exclaimed:

"Well, I suppose if you like it, you like it. Frank liked it. She went down to an island off Maine last summer." He named the island, for he was an exact man with a powerful mind for details. "A little while after she came home," he resumed, still walking up and down the hall before the mahogany piece, "a great, damn vanload of junk came rolling down the avenue toward the house. She was in New York that day. I went out and said to the man: 'What in the hell have you got here?'

" 'Old furniture,' said he, 'for Mrs. Cleveland. It came from some place up in Maine.'

"I asked him what he thought he was going to do with it, and he said he supposed he was going to bring it to our house. And I took a look at the old junk pile. God, you never saw such dilapidated, secondhand-store stock—old chairs and bureaus and beds and battered desks. And I said:

" 'Like hell you're going to take it in here. You turn around and take that damn kindling pile back downtown.'

"And he did. And then I forgot all about it. And one day I had to go down to New York, maybe two weeks after, and I came home and saw this piece here, and I said:

" 'Frank, where'd you get that? Where'd that come from?'

" 'That? Why, we've always had that. We've had that for years.'

"And I grunted and went on. And the next time I went away for three or four days, a big chair showed up down-stairs, and I said:

" 'Where'd that come from, Frank?' All polished up, pretty good-looking, it was. And she said:

" 'Oh, that old chair, we got it out of the attic; we've had that for a long time.'

"And then one day I went in the spare bedroom and there was a new bed, shiny and polished, and I took a look at that bed. I had seen it before, and I knew it. Then I suddenly remembered that damn bed was on the kindling pile that I sent away. But I didn't say anything, not a word. It was a good-looking bed, and I just waited. And in six or seven months, what do you think? Frank had slipped every damn sliver of that furniture into the house, one piece at a time, and she thought I didn't know it. And one day I told her, and we had a good laugh. I suppose it is all right; if that's the sort of thing you like, why, you like it!"

His hands were behind him; he was happy. His pride in his young wife was beautiful to see. It was any husband bragging about his wife—a most human performance. Of course, none of this dialogue appeared in the rather tight and circumspect article which I wrote about him for the magazine, but something in the article—some reference to his obvious humanity and to his Buffalo beginnings, some undercut that I did not intend to land, angered him. I remember in the closing sentence I spoke of his "mild Presbyterian eyes." That phrase stirred the bowels of his wrath, and he referred to me once in an interview with another newspaper man who suppressed it, and once in a letter which his biographer quoted, as "that Kansas coyote," all because of those "mild Presbyterian eyes" and some implication that he attached to them.

Richard Croker's face and green-gray eyes mirrored a low, incessant, gnawing greed—greed for power, for money, for destruction. They epitomized all that the politics of our city was revealing in those days. The word "graft" was coined at the latter part of the old century, to define that quenchless hunger for raw, quick, dirty money in American politics, which hardly sugar-coats its bribes, which glazes over its most iniquitous corruption. Croker, the boss of Tammany, who made his millions in speculations and investments as he skirted just outside the dirty waters of politics, was a calm, wordless man whose greed must have functioned mechanically by some deeply intuitive logical processes beneath the surface of his upper consciousness. He was strong—as strong as Cleveland or Harrison—but with a certain innocent malevolence, whose import he did not realize. I saw Croker in the last year of the century; tried to talk to him. He was patient, devoted time enough to the interview, but we had no common denominator of speech, of ideal, of background, and the interpreter who brought us together found it difficult to keep the talk going. I was a young reporter just over the line into my thirties, probably brash, and very likely I bored him to extinction, but spurred in him an amazing curiosity. I know now that I was talking to a great thirst, a quenchless desire for material things, unhampered by any nonsense about justice or beauty or any of the things of the spirit. And that, for thirty years and to a certain extent, was the attitude of politics in our big cities at the close of the era of conquest that followed the Civil War.

Men went into the rural West with the desire for material things, but also they went in the high and beautiful adventure of him who seeks a home, which is the symbol of all that is noble in our racial hope. They were greedy too, these men of the rural West, ruthless also in their empire building, but at least with a certain outer armament of righteousness which they polished even if by self-deception and which finally became, to an extent, their real reason and defense for conquering the wilderness. But this city exploiter who was not just Croker, but who also lived in Cincinnati, in Pittsburgh, in Boston, in Philadelphia, in Chicago, looked through the dead gray eyes of Croker, and in truth the Tiger of Tammany was a symbol of one phase of American life.

Here I was—a young fellow in my early thirties. I had met pleasantly and professionally all the great figures of my country in my day and generation. I had talked with them as a self-respecting reporter and had written honestly, as honestly as I could, about them. Probably I had offended most of them. But I hope I had not, for I have always shrunk from giving pain. "What's the Matter with Kansas?" written a few years before, was a sesame to open many doors, but probably I took something across the opening threshold besides rhetoric and fame. As things went in those days, among writing people, I was accounted a success. I saw my name blazoned on express wagons and in elevated railway stations in New York, advertising my article on Croker in McClure's. It was a real thrill. I was asked to speak, in evening clothes, after occasional dinners. I spoke badly. Through my friendship with President Theodore Roosevelt, I was meeting most of the Congressional leaders upon good terms. The President's friendship, and a knack for politics, gave me in Kansas a kind of leadership. Certainly I was not a first-rate leader, but a good third-rate perhaps. With all this money from writing coming in in large chunks, with my debts paid, with a house almost paid for, with my office building paid for, is it any wonder that I grew complacent with the status quo, that I wrote editorials defending the boss system as an institution which created the most responsible government? Is it strange that I still felt a distrust of the people en masse? Reading the Gazette files of those days between 1896 and 1905, I am always shocked, but never amazed, at the intrepid complacency with which I viewed the universe. I was an incurable optimist, with a sort of spiritual hydrocephalus.

CHAPTER LI

I Discover Reform

I SAW A LOT of the American continent in the decade of my thirties. Writing, of course, took me East. But I went into North Dakota once to write about wheat. Illness took me to California and brought me back by way of Portland and Seattle through the Northwest. Of course Sallie and I were riding on passes, and occasionally we rode in private cars with railroad officials. I remember in those days meeting Senator William A. Clark, of Montana, a curiously little, dried-up, shriveled man with a wizened face hidden by brown whiskers that I suspected were dyed, with brown eyes like a snake's, with an unconvincing toothy smile, false teeth, I think—I could all but hear them click—with a mean little voice and more arrogance than I had ever met assembled under one hat. I rode in his car for an hour or two with some other western railroad officials. The mountain states were opening up in those days. Irrigation projects, mostly financed by private capital, were appearing on the great rivers of the West.

Big money-making projects colored our thinking and our talking, and one afternoon, riding on the Oregon Short Line across Idaho with some officials of the road in their private car, we cooked up a scheme to buy some desert land which in a year or so would be under irrigation, and to start there a cantaloupe farm. We made a jackpot. The ante was low—less than a thousand dollars, as I remember. And the first thing I knew, I was in Boise and with the others was buying an entry-right for one hundred sixty acres of desert land. A former Governor of Idaho transacted the business, and I was puzzled to learn when I offered my check, that the money must be paid in gold. Now about that time Theodore Roosevelt began prosecuting the western timber thieves. With others there was the Barber Lumber Company, who had bought these entry-rights from unimportant people. And suddenly my hair rose in amazement and genuine fear when I found they were sending men to the penitentiary for doing exactly what I had done. I had my moments of anxious pause, and was scared stiff. Here I was, fighting the United States Senator from Kansas as a crook. Here I was, working with the forces of righteousness in New York State—attacking Platt and Croker—and I myself had certainly violated a Federal law and was liable to go to the penitentiary as a dirty corrupter of morals who had illegally acquired a quarter section of Uncle Sam's good rich land almost under the irrigation dam.

I did not know what to do. But finally I wrote to Senator William E. Borah, whom I had known in my student days at Kansas University. He knew Idaho laws and Federal laws, and I told him the whole story as I have written it here and asked him what I could do to get out of the net. He replied quickly, seriously and with affection that the best I could do was to deed the land back to the man who had deeded it to me, and he dictated a letter I was to send with the deed. I did it, and breathed below my collar button for the first time within a year. But I think I understood crooks better after that, and lambasted them less cruelly. It was a great thing for me. Nothing is so good for an uptious person as a consciousness of guilt. It is the father of tolerance.

Also, in the middle of the first decade, I took my first real political licking. It came about with the election of Charles Curtis to the United States Senate. He was my sworn factional enemy. Curtis was a Gould man, as I knew Chester Long was a Morgan man. But Chester was of my faction. Curtis was not. So my indignation boiled quickly at the subserviency of Curtis. I went to Topeka with the crowd that tried to defeat Charles Curtis. Two or three young Congressmen—Dan Anthony, Phil Campbell and Victor Murdock—were opposing him, but our crowd was working against the promise of all the railroads to support Curtis. We were nothing but starry-eyed reformers. The railroads cleaned us up in short order. And along about that time, in the files of the Gazette, will be found my first reform editorial.

It was an editorial directed at the evil of railroad passes. I certainly knew what I was talking about, for when I wrote that editorial I carried a system pass on the Santa Fe, a state pass on the Missouri Pacific, the Rock Island, and the Union Pacific, a telegraph frank, and an express frank and, as symbols of my thirty-third degree in the Sanhedrin of the boss's temple, a visiting card from Fred Harvey, directing all Harvey hotels on the Santa Fe System to give me of its flamboyant nourishment. But I knew that the system was wrong, and for all that I had that hump on my back like a camel made from the big book of passes in my hip pocket, I sailed into that reform with fine indignation. It was in that movement against railroad domination of politics that I came across the trail of the elder Robert M. La Follette. He had just gone through a successful fight in Wisconsin, leading it as governor, for the primary system, for the state control of railroads, for the reorganization of state government, for a state anti-pass law and for reform taxation. And he was the hero of the young hopefuls of American politics. It was curious that two men so entirely different as Theodore Roosevelt and Robert M. La Follette should hold the allegiance of hundreds of thousands of men of both parties—chiefly, however, young Republicans north of the Mason and Dixon line. They were mostly college men, and they rejected Bryan. Because he was highly emotional, his widest appeal was to the young South, but in the North the young liberals felt that he was shallow. Bryan had prescience. He was, in those days, instinctively for justice. Always he felt more deeply than he knew. Seven times out of ten his diagnosis of evil was true, but his prescription too often was futile.

So these young liberals of the North who followed Roosevelt and La Follette in the first decade of the century, responded to low emotional content in their leadership. They were thinking things through. Probably this was typical of the whole lot. They had grown up conservative and they had reaped in full measure the benefits of the conservative plutocratic democracy, with its convention system of nominations, its reactionary ballot laws which made it easy to vote a straight ticket, and thus control cities and states. They were a growing power in this democratic plutocracy, after they had come into it—and become a part of it—and tried its institutions and saw its evils.

But friendship, association with Theodore Roosevelt, and an intimate relationship with the governing powers in my state and, when my horizon widened in the nation, gave me, as it gave hundreds of thousands of young men in their twenties, thirties, and early forties, a quickening sense of the inequities, injustices, and fundamental wrongs of the political and economic overlay on our democracy, which was keeping too large a per cent of its citizens below average participation in the blessings of our democracy. It took a licking in the Curtis senatorial fight to open my eyes. The fact that from the private car I had walked straight to the threshold of the penitentiary also disturbed me deeply. About this time I had another shock. I had gone into the Thunder Mountain region of Idaho to write a series of articles on the new gold boom that was rising there. Gold was found free there in talc. But it was hard, and later proved unprofitable, to sift it out. Great interest in the high-grade ores of the Tonopah region developed about that time, and the bottom fell out of Thunder Mountain. But I was cautious enough in my Post articles, though I told the truth about the unsolved difficulties. Then one day along came an offer from what looked to me like a reputable mining journal in New York for two thousand dollars for another article about Thunder Mountain. I wrote it, and was amazed and ashamed—ashamed that I should have been such a sucker, and ashamed of my profession when I read the article in that mining paper which had entirely distorted my viewpoint, which had even inserted puffs for certain mining enterprises that I did not believe in, and otherwise again mixed me up in scandalous proceedings. That men of wealth, if not of standing, could do such things, soured me on wealth, made me suspicious of the whole system which was institutionalized in the prestige and power of wealth. I narrowly escaped disgrace. Only luck and the fact that I answered scores of letters denouncing what the mining journal had done kept me from real trouble, but I was sore clear through at myself—and at the social stupidity that was the foundation of many of my political views.

So by the middle of the first decade of the new century I was a champion of the new rebellion. That rebellion was spreading across the country in every northern state. Little La Follettes and little Roosevelts were appearing in city halls, county courthouses, statehouses, and occasionally were bobbing up in Congress. Two or three or half a dozen had appeared in the Senate. Reform was in the air. Political reform appeared first in the demand for the primary system and, a few years later, for the recall, for the initiative and referendum, which spread to considerably more than half of the states north of the Ohio, and for ballot reform. These were the weapons of democracy. We who were in the revolt of those days and who at first called ourselves insurgents, felt that if we could get elbow room to fight and weapons to break down the convention system and the control of the railroads in our city councils and legislatures, we could forthwith institute economic reforms which we cherished. So in Kansas, as in every state in the Missouri Valley and in many states in the Lake district, the Ohio Valley and westward of Kansas to the coast, the young insurgents were coming out hammer and tongs after the election of Roosevelt in 1904. He also threw off the cerements of McKinley and became President in his own right, advocating his own reforms. He surely was a bull in the plutocratic china shop. What a time he was having, and what a zest he put into his contest! He seemed to court opposition with ardor. And he had his worthy foes. The whole set-up of Congress was conservative. Much of it was deeply reactionary. Cannon, the Speaker of the House, and Aldrich, the Republican leader of the Senate, who became the black beasts of insurgency in those days, were probably the most reactionary leaders along political and economic lines that were ever given command in Washington. They were not crooked or corrupt. They were deeply convinced that the rule of the dollar was by divine right. As a young insurgent, I had taken a black oath against them. Ten years had seen a complete revolution—perhaps I may haltingly use the word evolution—in my attitude toward government and organized society. I no longer believed that whatever is, is right; but I did believe that it could be right. And, as a sort of shibboleth in my heart, then arose the words of Professor Carruth, of my Kansas University days, who said to me:

"Will, the job of a good citizen is to make his private opinion public sentiment."

And how I went at it! It was as though the two narrow escapes from humiliation, disgrace, and worse had cracked the foundations of my beliefs in the established order, and overturned the house of my political faith.

So when I went into that battle of insurgency, I knew full well that I had to walk circumspectly, that I was under the merciless eyes of a powerful enemy. And whatever virtue of word and deed I have developed in the last forty years of my life has not been, I fear, so much a deep and righteous conviction as it has been a lively sense that I had to walk straight or be tripped—and tripped to destruction. Time and again, in those first years, when I walked with the insurgents, I have caught myself withholding an itching hand. Time and again, I have painfully retracted a course that I began which might have brought quick gains but also might have cost more than it came to. I am not naturally a good man, but I have been scared to death so many times that I have learned regretfully but definitely that honesty is the best policy.

Kansas politics during those first years of Roosevelt's elective term were in a turmoil. A redheaded reformer, named Stubbs, was chairman of the state central committee; later he became governor. Under his leadership and that of Governor Hoch, who preceded Stubbs, while Stubbs was Speaker of the House, Kansas abolished the anti-pass system. Kansas recast her institutions and made them as unpolitical as was possible thirty years ago. Kansas, after a desperate struggle, adopted the primary system. Kansas began to try to regulate interstate commerce, and tried to establish a state oil refinery; but the courts checked that. Kansas gave her cities the commission form of government, with the initiative and referendum included. Kansas tried to do everything that La Follette had done in Wisconsin, as other states from New Jersey west to California were doing. And in those days I spent much time in Topeka, more than I have ever spent since, working for the Kansas reforms. I was the problem child of the state committee, that was about four years behind the governor and the legislature. Political organization always is sluggard. I remember one day, sitting at a meeting in a committee, bubbling with carbonated ideas and getting set upon heavily by the chairman. It was in the days when Alice Roosevelt in the White House was going strong. Mort Albaugh, the chairman and regular to the core, looked over at me and said:

"Bill White, sometimes I know just how your friend Roosevelt feels when he sees Alice coming his way!"

Life was not all politics with me; not even chiefly. In the century's young days, I was still writing verse which was published in the Kansas City Star and in the Gazette. I was writing short stories which appeared in Scribner's and the Saturday Evening Post. I was reading myself blind, keeping up with Vernon Kellogg, who was becoming an authority on insects. I was a regent of the state university, devoting two or three days out of every month to that job. Sallie and I were enjoying our baby Billy and, before long, Mary—our second child—was coming. We generally had a current novel on hand; Sallie read aloud to me at night, and the Gazette was with us always. We walked together to the office, worked together there, and were busily engaged in being head-over-heels in love. How I could have had time for all the politics and the political writing which I have recounted in these last chapters, I do not know. I enjoyed it. It was, however, anything but a major interest in our lives.

When Vernon Kellogg was writing to me about his bugs and biology, he put in a few purple lines now and then about a young woman author, Mary Austin, with whom he was enamored for the hour. She had written two books, "The Land of Little Rain" and "The Flock," and he sent them autographed to us; we were greatly stirred by them. In a few years I met Mary Austin. She had written what I considered, and still hold, to be one of the great American novels—"A Woman of Genius." I was excited about it, and when I met her in New York at the National Arts Club down in Twentieth Street off Fourth Avenue, we ate together often, talked interminably and I was convinced that she had a tough-fibered brain. She was vainer than a wilderness of gargantuan peacocks, a strong, overbearing woman. When she entered a group of friends, she at once took charge of the meeting and began to monologue. She was a mystic and believed a lot of interesting and uncanny, nonsensical things that were easy to discuss if one did not care to keep his feet on the ground. For years after, when Sallie and I went to the National Arts Club, Mary Austin was there. She was addicted to gaudy shawls and the most God-awful hats that made her look like a battleship. She grew into a bottle-shaped woman and wore long dresses because her legs were cylindrical and without form and void. Her face grew strong, plain, and commanding. She was known about the place for years as "Old Sitting Bull."

But Sallie and I loved her and took her to our hearts. Until the end of her days, nearly forty years later, Mary Austin was a familiar in our house and held a high dear place in our hearts. She was a thwarted spirit, a frustrated person who needed her man and her babies, and took it out in books and in many love dramas—some of which were written in her books and others graven with scarcely more reality than fiction upon her warm tender heart. But she talked well, lived honorably according to her code and

Dr. Allen White, d. in 1878. He was then Democratic mayor of the Republican frontier town of Eldorado, Kansas, and father of Willie White, aged ten years.

Mary Ann Hatten White, mother of William Allen White, taken on her return from a European trip in 1909 at seventy-nine. When she spoke of the old soldiers' parade on the Fourth of July in her girlhood, she referred of course to the veterans of General Washington's army. She is here wearing her "Paris dress."

"Willie" White in 1873, aged five, in blue flannel with
black braided stripes. His father was able to afford a
colored india-ink enlargement of this daguerreotype.

"Will" White resplendent in evening dress and gold
fraternity pin, a junior at the University of Kansas.

In 1889 this group of college boys from the University of Kansas, on a camping trip in what later became Rocky Mountain National Park, celebrated July 4th with a beer party. Thirty years later all had succeeded in their fields. From left to right: Vernon Kellogg, director of Belgian Relief in World War I and secretary of the National Research Council; (2) Henry Riggs, professor of civil engineering, University of Michigan; (3) Frank Craig, president of the Oklahoma Bankers Association; (4) William Allen White; (5) Herbert S. Hadley, Governor of Missouri; (6) William S. Franklin, professor of physics at M.I.T.; (7) Edward C. Franklin, professor of chemistry Stanford University and president of the American Chemical Society; (8) Frederick Funston, major general; (9) Schuyler Brewster, attorney general of Oklahoma.

In 1896: W. A. White, editor of the newly purchased Emporia Gazette and author of "What's the Matter with Kansas?" with which Mark Hanna covered the nation in the McKinley-Bryan campaign.

Will A. White and Albert Bigelow Paine early in
the Gay Nineties, when they became joint authors of
"Rhymes of Two Friends." Following a quarrel over
which should distribute press copies, the two friends did
not speak for several decades.

Sallie Moss Lindsay was a young teacher in Kansas City, Kansas, in 1892, when she met William Allen White, an editorial writer on the Kansas City Star. They were married a year later. This picture was taken the next year, after they had bought their own paper in Emporia.

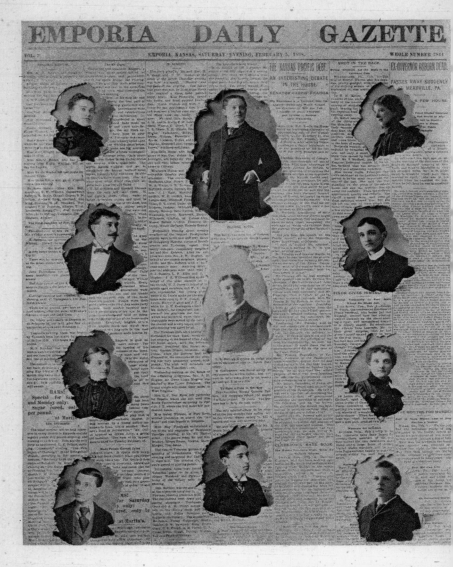

W. A. White (top center), aged thirty, with his staff of ten wrote, edited, set up in hand type, and printed the Emporia Gazette in 1898. All are now dead but Miss Laura French (top left), who came back in 1945 to help read proof during the Christmas rush.

Henry J. Allen and William Allen White in 1917,
resplendent in lieutenant colonels' uniforms when they
toured France as observers for the American Red Cross.

William Allen White in 1914 with his son Bill, aged fourteen, and his daughter Mary, aged ten.

William Allen White and Theodore Roosevelt at the
White home, where Roosevelt, as the Progressive
nominee, spent a night in the heat of the 1912 Presidential campaign.

Mary White, aged sixteen, on the grounds of the Emporia
High School, a few weeks before her death in 1920.

Herbert Hoover and William Allen White, who as a delegate to the 1920 (Harding) convention cast his vote for Hoover, and later supported him during his 1928 and 1932 campaigns. The picture was taken in Emporia in 1935.

William Allen White at his littered desk in the Gazette
office on his seventieth birthday in 1938.

William Allen White in 1940 as chairman of the Committee to Defend America by Aiding the Allies broadcasts from his upstairs study at home in Emporia. With him is Mrs. White.

The last picture of William Allen White—with Mrs. White in the window of their summer home near Estes Park, Colorado, in the summer of 1943. At the foot of the distant mountain was the log cabin in which they had spent their honeymoon just fifty years before.

thought strongly and as logically as a mystic can, was on the whole a most interesting, stimulating, and lovable person. Always we left her presence feeling that our minds and hearts had been kindled with new energy and refreshment. Some way her books, which gave out that same energy and delight, passed away when her body perished.

Happy Days

ALONGSIDE this turbulent, boiling stream of politics in the life of that young, fat, apple-cheeked political insurgent ran another current. The pleasant life in Emporia, at 927 Exchange, had produced in those days of the first Roosevelt, three books and almost a hundred profitable magazine articles. And then, of course, the Gazette was growing. The little four-page paper which we took over in 1895 with a circulation of less than five hundred, now by the first half of the first decade of the 1900's had over two thousand circulation. It was a six-page paper now every day, and eight once or twice a week. Our family was growing. Bill, the baby, was four years old when Mary was born. She was a frail baby. In the years of 1904 and '05 and '06, we lived all the summer months in Colorado, at Manitou near Pikes Peak. And of course I shuttled between Colorado Springs and Emporia many times. Bill sometimes lived with me and his grandmother White; sometimes he was with his mother and Mary. There never was a better little boy or a more satisfactory baby than he. He tried so hard to make it easy for us. He was so gentle and considerate that his mother and I were afraid that God might be shy of angels someway and send for him. But he was a robust youngster and full of joy and mischief and insatiable curiosity, and most affectionate.

In 1904 or '05, when I was alone in Emporia, I began writing a series of short stories reminiscent of my life around a newspaper shop. Each story was complete in form, yet they all strung together as an account of country newspapers in the eighties and nineties. When I sent two or three to George Lorimer of the Saturday Evening Post, he wrote eagerly for more and paid well for them, a thousand dollars each for most of them. For one story, I forget which, he gave me twenty-five hundred—the most money I had ever received for an article. In the end, as the Gazette was paying well, we were never in need of money. The truth is that never once in my life have I felt needs, personal needs covering necessities, comforts, and a mild taste in luxuries, needs for money when I did not have it and could not get it. Poverty never has gnawed at my vitals, indeed never has snapped at me. In those days, we were living in a good house—one of the ten best houses in town. We were able to keep a hired girl, who was not called a "maid," and who lived with us in considerable familiarity which maids are not supposed to have. We had bought a horse and buggy. The horse was a big-footed old Morgan horse whose grandmother had had an unfortunate affair with a Clydesdale, and you could hear him klop-klop-klop for two blocks coming down the street. He was old and gentle. We bought him in his early teens and kept him at a livery stable in luxury, and almost in idleness, for I generally walked to and from the office, little better than half a mile, two or three times a day. In the evening we harnessed Old Tom to the surrey with a fringed top, joined the parade around Emporia and its environs, and were exceedingly happy and proud to be accounted among the gentry and nobility. We set a good table and enjoyed our meals. Our clothes were decent when we went East or West, and I hope our table manners were reasonably endurable. We traveled together—we two, Sallie and I—whenever she could leave the children at their grandmother's, and we tremendously enjoyed the rollicking fun of each other's company. I think we have never lived a bored minute together, and incidentally as I was writing those stories and all the other articles, books, and suchlike word-carpentry, I wrote out the job and we read it over and corrected it together, revised, rewrote, and revised again.

After the publication of the stories about the country newspapers in a book entitled "In Our Town," which had a considerable sale and more than passing vogue—Howells and all the critics reviewed it with some enthusiasm and Mark Twain wrote me a letter about it—we decided rather formally, walking one day through the Garden of the Gods in Colorado in February, 1905, to tackle a novel—a full-length, man-sized novel. For three or four months we talked about the mainspring, the central theme of this novel, for we knew then that the first need of a man who is writing fiction is to have something to write about—a story to tell with a meaning, a fundamental fable which has "hic fabula docet." My favorite story of all the Mother Goose and Andersen fairy stories and Bible stories was the story of the prodigal son, the young man who got too big for his breeches, who took his inheritance and went out into the big world and realized that he was not as smart as he thought he was, then got on his uppers, living among swine of various kinds, and finally arose and went back to his father's house. I suppose unconsciously that was the story of my own inner life. I was the young man who was spiritually puffed up, pretty materially minded, the young fellow who scorned the truth and beauty and essential moralities which make for happiness, and started out on my proud way to live my own life as I pleased—an inflated, young, materially minded reactionary. And then I also came to myself. I realized, not suddenly but gradually, through the natural processes that open men's hearts through duties, that we are the fathers and guardians of rights. I came to remember, as the prodigal son among his swine thought of his father's house, and I wrote slowly, stumblingly, haltingly in those first years of the century with a sense that there was something in the world really better and lovelier than success, as it was expressed in terms of wealth and power in those days.

So our first novel became the story of the prodigal son. The hero was John Barclay, son of a pioneer Kansas mother; and her faith in some kind of moral law of gravitation toward righteousness took the place of "his father's house" of the parable. He went into life seeking money and power, and he got it. And in his prime, John Barclay saw that the money was husk and that the money-grubbers were swine, and he rose and returned to his father's house. That is the plot of "A Certain Rich Man." We were four years working on it. Four times it was rewritten and revised from start to finish, and condensed. It was over two hundred thousand words when we finished it, even the third time. We worked at home in Emporia at odd times. We worked in Colorado steadily for one whole summer. Every morning I was in my little room with my typewriter hammering away right after early breakfast, and every afternoon I pounded away on that old Smith Premier until dinner. But it was a joyous job. We were all together that summer—Sallie, the babies and I, and my mother all of the time, her mother some of the time, her brothers and sisters a good deal of the time—a full house and a gay one. But I was shielded and shut off from the family current all day. At night we rollicked and roved and rambled, and if ever two people drained the cup of life to its last good drop, it was we.

It was in one of those summers in Colorado that I had a strange visitor on a strange errand. The visitor was my college friend, William E. Borah, of Idaho, who had just been elected United States Senator. Then after the election he had been indicted for timber frauds. He was the attorney for the Barber Lumber Company. The Barber Lumber Company probably had been most irregular in grabbing timber tracts in Idaho and other places in the Northwest by the use of exactly the same device by which I got the cantaloupe land—which I deeded back to the man who sold it to me when I found it was illegal. But Borah, to me, protested his innocence. He said that he could not go to Washington until he had been tried, and he was convinced that a fair trial would acquit him. What he wanted from me was this: to see President Roosevelt, tell him that the United States Senator was under indictment and wanted an immediate trial, and also ask that the Attorney General send from Washington an assistant general who would watch the proceedings and guarantee that Borah should have a fair trial.

He explained that the district attorney of Idaho was his bitter political enemy, which was true. I wired the President, made an appointment to see him in Oyster Bay, dropped my work and went there. With me was the Attorney General and I think an assistant, who had charge of the land fraud division of the Attorney General's office. I made my plea, explained my friendship for Borah, my belief in his honesty and the facts surrounding his indictment. The President and the Attorney General agreed that in the case of a United States Senator making such a request it should be granted, and when Borah came to trial, an assistant was there. Borah introduced no evidence in his behalf, made no plea to the jury, which was out less than five minutes, and when Borah was acquitted, the fire department, the town militia, the Boise band and a great crowd celebrated his acquittal in the street before his office, and they told me that the town got gloriously drunk. It was a great day. Yet Borah afterwards told me that they had him framed up tight. The judge and the district attorney could have made rulings as to evidence which would have been overthrown in the higher courts, but which might easily have resulted in a hung jury or a conviction which would have made it impossible for him to go on with his career in the Senate. Naturally we two, who had saved each other from jail, lived happily ever after—disagreeing deeply about many public questions, but dear friends to the end. I recite this story because it is one of the things which I have been proud to do.

One day about this time, in came W. T. Soden, an old-timer contemporary of my father in the fifties. He was a director of the Major's bank, a man of considerable means and substance, an Irishman with a long black beard and an ineradicable twinkle in his eye. He owned most of the gas company stock and the electric light company. When we had private ownership of the waterworks, he owned a good deal of that. He must have known that my canceled notes had come through the bank. He came in, sat down and evidently had brought his knitting. Something was on his mind. He came to it quickly. Said he:

"Well, Will, I have got a story to tell you, and I guess I can tell it now pretty freely. Listen: when I was a young man, just about the time of the outbreak of the Civil War, I was a young buck on the turf, and I had a little water flour mill here. [He was still the town miller, with flour dust on his clothes and in his black whiskers.] And your father, a man in his early forties, a dozen years older than I, lived here too. He kept store in addition to practicing medicine and used to go to Lawrence two or three times a year on a marketing trip. Well, one day, the federal soldiers—they were under Buchanan then and were generally hated in Lawrence—were occupying the town, and either some soldier or some camp-follower raped a girl in the ravine down back of what is now the Eldridge House, and the town was pretty mad about it. And by God, they thought I did it and they grabbed me. I expect they had some circumstantial evidence because, as I say, I was a young buck on the turf. But I didn't do it. I didn't have to in those days." And he smiled across forty years of not unpleasant memory. "Well, the crowd kept swelling and yelling: 'Hang him, hang him!' And I was scared pea-green. But I noticed at the edge of the crowd your father, in his white nankeen suit and his panama hat, elbowing through the crowd and coming straight to me with blood in his eye. He got on top of something, maybe it was a wagon, and began waving his hands, nodding his head, and cried:

" 'Hear ye, hear ye, hear ye!'

"And he took over the crowd. 'I know this man; he is a loyal Union man. He is a Republican and he runs a mill in Emporia and is a decent man. He didn't do this. He is not that kind. Let him alone. Give him time. Hear his story.' And after talking three or four minutes, I'll be damned if the crowd didn't break up."

Soden paused and looked at me and grinned: "You're doin' all right. I notice you got your notes all out of the bank; your account's in good shape."

I forget what I said in assent but I remember that, pounding my desk for emphasis, he said:

"Well, by God, Will, I have watched you, and many's the time down there at the bank I have put my name on the back of your note, standing good for it. What less could I do? And now you don't need me, and I'm damn glad. You are your father's Yankee son. You've got money sense."

By that time he had put his hand on my shoulder as I sat at the desk and without another word he said:

"Well, I'll be going," and walked out. I had never heard of the episode he related. I had never dreamed that I had two friends in the Little Major's bank.

It was curious how the turn of this century marked such a strange, quick change in our country. In those days the old machinery seemed to go with a rush. By 1901, the Gazette press was operated by the gasoline engine. We had six girl compositors in the new century, who were getting from three to five dollars a week; and we worked on an eight-hour schedule, sometimes overtime ran it to nine, rarely ten. Within a year or two after the century turned, we put in a linotype to save money. The girls married or found other jobs, and we helped them relocate, and we set almost a third more type for about the same money we paid the girls. The paper was growing. Our circulation at that time was around twenty-five hundred, and we bought a new press—a web press—which cost seventy-five hundred dollars, printed papers five times as fast as on the old press, and the town and the county came in to see the wonder. Within three years after the first linotype, which I paid for by the month, we had bought a second linotype and were paying twice as much wages for setting up type as we were when the girls were doing it. But a new thing was happening in the business world. Advertising was multiplying as fast as machinery was coming into the office, and Emporia merchants who ten years before had spent twenty-five or thirty dollars a month for an advertising card, which remained standing often for a month, now were spending fifty, seventy-five and a hundred dollars a month. They were proclaiming bargains. Page advertisements were frequently in the Gazette for special sales. Drygoods men, hardware men offering new machinery and labor-saving gadgets, but who were still advertising buggies and wagons, were our best customers. The people of Emporia and of Lyon County, our twenty-five hundred subscribers, someway were finding money to buy things which their fathers— the pioneers—did without and lived most comfortably. The milk separator on the farm was passing out. Milk, as a farm product, was coming to town in great cans, to be distributed by milk dealers. The hen was helping the cow, and farmers were learning the value of breeds in all their livestock. Farming in Lyon County was becoming not a way of life but an industry. Hired men could no longer be had for ten or fifteen dollars a month and keep. Twenty dollars was the going price, and the farmers raged at the injustice of it. But the hired man demanded the keep of his horse, and bought a buggy and came to town spruced up in store clothes. The whole face of life in Emporia and in the world was changing. Nothing better illustrates the thing that happened in the world than what happened at the Emporia Gazette. When I walked into that office in 1895, I could do everything that I asked anyone else to do. I had swept floors. I had set type. I had made up the type in forms. I had put it on the press and had fed the press. I had even turned the press if needed, back in the Eldorado days. Ten years later, when I walked over the threshold of the mechanical room of the Gazette, I could do not one process that led from the copy desk to the printed page. The change had come swiftly as that. But one thing I could do: I could take the heavy lead roller of the proof press, which weighed fifty pounds, and raise it above my head, straighten out my arms and repeat it ten times, which was more than any other man in the office could do—and I had that much physical prowess to back my right to speak in that office. It was little, but it was something. The gymnasium of the woods and fields and water that had hardened me in my youth held its strength during my manhood. All my life it has stood me in good stead. A man gets something from living near the earth, from running barefoot on the earth over the open field, and the waters of the creeks, and the sunlight on the prairie—something real yet something indefinable, which gives him a life inheritance in physical reserve.

377

CHAPTER LIII

I am Sought by a Lady

PROBABLY the large storage tank of surplus energy in my body gave me a capacity for indignation. I liked to call it righteous indignation. It might have been. But, specifically, I am sure those who did not care for my works and ways called it sticking my nose into things that did not concern me. I, with considerable complacence, called it making my private opinion public sentiment. And in the early part and middle of the first decade in this century, I became involved in the ancient Emporia town row. When I came here, and for twenty years before, it was a row between the banks. It made politics out of everything, bank politics. A school board election could not be held without dragging in the town row. The prize there was concerned with the treasurer of the school board, who would deposit the school funds in one bank or another. The city election always involved the two banks or the two factions and every county convention to nominate county and district officers seethed with the political feuding of the bankers. They must have spent a lot of money in one way or another, promoting that feud. It attached itself to things outside of politics. One of those things was a quarrel which was started by the county medical association against a doctor whose practice was irregular and whose personal and professional conduct offended them.

In this particular row, the doctors went to the preachers, the Ministerial Association. They also went to the state board in Topeka to demand a revocation of the enemy doctor's license to practice in Kansas. That, of course, threw the contention into state politics. The doctor involved deposited in one bank. The bank rallied its factional forces to him and the other bank wheeled into line and, before I knew it, I was the spearhead of the fight. I was supposed to take the matter to the governor and the state medical board, and did. The license was revoked. It took nearly two years. And that quarrel, which, of course, brought the doctor's patients rallying round, stirred the town to its foundations. Scandals were circulated in the form of affidavits. It was bitter and wicked on both sides. And because I had a lot of energy and no fear and a capacity for indignation which I called righteous, I was more or less the figurehead of the fight. And of course the little old Major and his bank stood by me. The doctor appealed his case to the United States Supreme Court, trying in the meantime to spot machinery that would answer the appeal by getting dirty affidavits on his opponents. I was threatened, but gave the doctor's friends the laugh. However, one day in the heat of it, I saw the Little Major and one of my dearest friends in town approaching the Gazette office from the south. I knew that my friend had been attacked with a blackmailing affidavit, rather terrible in its accusations. I felt in my bones they were coming to see me. When they appeared in the office, the Little Major sat down beside me, put his warm, hard, bony hand on my knee—a favorite gesture of his in the technique of his seduction of adversaries—cleared his throat, and spoke in his softest, most self-deprecatory voice.

"Now, Will, here's a little matter in which you can help our friend." He nodded to his companion, and went on: "Our good friend, the doctor [which was bitter irony], has got out an affidavit about our dear friend here and threatens to use it, and has told us that if we could just persuade you to drop the fight and let his appeal to the Supreme Court go unopposed, he would be glad to forget this affidavit!"

I had had just five minutes as I watched them through the window to make up my mind, to arrange my answer and take my stand. It was the hardest thing I have ever done. I must have hesitated, moistened my lips, and managed to get out without much emphasis but feebly and finally, so that the Major knew it was final:

"Oh, Major, I just—I just can't! I mustn't do it!"

I looked at my dear friend. His face was distorted with fear and pain, but I shook my head. I did not dare trust myself to further language. I was tempted of the devil. The Major tried again:

"You know, Will, you wouldn't have to do anything. All you would have to do, is to do nothing more. You have done enough. You have shown the town and the state where you stand!"

He ended on a rising inflection like a question, and I knew all I had to do was shake my head. I did it—and finally got out a "No, no!" and I grasped the hand of my friend and said:

"Old man, I just—I just—I just can't do it!"

And that ended the interview.

The United States Supreme Court finally, a year or so later, rejected the doctor's appeal; a rather important decision had been made that in matters of public health and public morals the state has a right to control finally the decisions of its boards and commissions. It was a fight worth making.

Then a funny thing happened. We printed the news of the court's decision in the Gazette. I tried to eliminate bitterness, and thought I had done it. But probably the decision itself enraged the doctor and the sense of defeat angered his friends, for they persuaded the divorced wife of the doctor to lie in wait for me that afternoon with a rawhide. I saw her in a stairway about seventy-five feet from the Gazette office. I had the start of about twenty feet of her. She was handicapped by skirts. I grinned at her, giggled at her, waved at her, and ran like a whitehead. She never came within a rod of me. And the next day (November 18, 1904) I inserted this account of the episode in the Gazette:

Last evening at dusk as the editor of the Gazette was starting for home, a few yards from the office door he met Mrs. Delta Meffert, divorced wife of William Meffert, of whom mention was made in these columns recently. She was accompanied by a lady friend, and as the Gazette man started to pass, Mrs. Meffert pulled from her cloak a small but effective-looking whip. The editor of the paper side-stepped and did what every true gent would do; ran forty yards like a whitehead back to the office by the back door.

That calm dispassionate communion which a man holds with a situation in the sixteenth part of a second convinced the man in question that when a lady challenges a gent to an athletic contest of any kind, he cannot win a sparring match with any grace, nor be the victor in a wrestling match with a lady with any credit at all; but that a foot-race is the one event in the sporting calendar in which any gent may vie his prowess with any lady. And how he did run! Shooting the chutes, leaping the gap, or looping the loop are clumsy dilatory tactics, compared with the way that fat old codger hiked the hike around to the back door of his office.

That was the only way to handle the episode. But I must have made a funny figure covering those hundred-odd feet in three or four seconds flat, with the lady trying to take long steps in her hobbled skirt, waving her rawhide. When I got back to the office, a telephone call came from a lawyer friend, telling me to watch out because he had just heard the lady was lying in wait for me, and he tried to warn me. Afterwards, though he was a Democrat, I did what I could to see that he had a term as county attorney, and later two or three terms as district judge. I tried to show the same degree of gratitude to my friends as I gave in indignation to those whom I made my enemies.

That episode and the uproarious ending I gave it, strengthened me in the town. Of course, in a little town like that, everyone knew that the Major had failed to call me off from the fight and everyone knew how much it cost me to say "No" that day. And the attempt of the lady with the rawhide to avenge her friends, of course advertised the victory over the doctor all over Kansas and even across the country, for of course the episode and my ribald editorial were used by the Associated Press. And I established a reputation for competent and determined righteousness in a local row that I probably would not have had except for the desire of the doctor's friends for revenge.

In those days, McClure's Magazine was a militant organ of political reform, and its editors—Sam McClure and John Phillips—and its associates, Ida Tarbell, Ray Stannard Baker, Lincoln Steffens, and David Graham Phillips became my warm friends. I saw them whenever I went to New York, and was with them much of the time. It was in those days that I met Mark Twain. John Phillips, one of the editors of McClure's, and Auguste F. Jaccaci invited Mark Twain to a luncheon and took me along, one autumn day in 1907. I had had a letter from Mark Twain about my book "In Our Town"—a beautiful letter which, in my vanity, I framed and kept on my workroom wall.

The luncheon was at the Aldine Club on lower Fifth Avenue, an organization of publishers, writers, and master printers. And Mark Twain came in white flannel and a white hat. He wore a contrasting plain black bow tie. His hair was a fluffy halo of white around his head, and a heavy, drooping white mustache slightly colored by nicotine arched above a firm strong mouth. During the meal sprightly talk went around the board. The table was set in a little private dining room fifteen by fifteen, near a window looking down on the avenue. After we had finished, Mark Twain lighted a cigar rather formally, with what seemed to me theatrical ceremony, puffed it a few times and then rose from his chair and began to talk. Of course I was a young man and did not quite comprehend what was going on. Our guest was putting on a performance for us. He paced the vacant area of the room in tracing rectangles, and diagonals across the rectangles, for two solid hours, and recited contemporary magazine articles which he had written and which heroized himself pretty strongly as a man who could not be imposed upon. He stuck closely to the text of his articles, which I had read and which I afterwards reread. It was an amazing thing to do—to give a two-hour humorous lecture about himself to three comparatively unimportant people. We had other appointments that afternoon. Phillips tried to stop Mark Twain, but he roared ahead like an engine on a track. His hands were behind him as he walked, slightly stooped, and he droned on—sometimes laughing at his own humor and sometimes indicating by facial grimaces a place for us to laugh. It was a conscious performance and greatly shocked me, though Phillips and Jaccaci had heard of our hero staging such acts before. But while we appreciated the distinction he was conferring upon us, we certainly were eager to get back to our afternoon's work. He did not realize that he had bored us. We parted pleasantly and I am sure he felt that he had greatly honored us and entertained us.

Men who knew Mark Twain—particularly Mr. Howells, whom I afterwards told of the incident—said that the oratorical habit was growing on him and declared that in his earlier days his sense of humor would have saved him from making such a spectacle. I am sorry, but that is the only memory I have of the greatest figure in American letters which the last quarter of last century produced. I had read his books in adoration. I still believe he is a monumental figure in American life as a philosopher, as a story-teller, as a representative and expounder of the real American democracy. But my ideal, Mark Twain, was a little battered as we parted there at the doorstep of the Aldine Club and walked out into Fifth Avenue together in the late autumn afternoon.

I was seeing more and more of William Dean Howells in those days. Once he gave a luncheon for me in his studio apartment on Fifty-seventh street, and after lunch I remember that he took me down on Third Avenue to see little grocery and fruit stands there. He chatted amiably with the Italian keepers in their language and seemed to know them and understand them, and obviously they had great respect for him. He wanted me to see these gentle people and to know them. I wish he could have written a novel about them, but alas, they were beyond his depth and he was not enough of a reporter to learn about them and write about them superficially.

The book of mine which he liked the best was "In Our Town." It was a newspaper story and it revived for him his newspaper days in Ohio before the Civil War. He used to tell me what fun he had writing editorials that would stir the rich southern blood across the Ohio in Kentucky. He was probably a homeopathic abolitionist, intellectually persuaded rather than emotionally, and that kind made the southerners rage perhaps more than emotional protagonists like Wendell Phillips or William Lloyd Garrison. He must have had an amazingly good time as an editor. He was graduated out of the printing office without much schooling, and his sense of humor was larded through his mind and heart so that he could not feel too deeply without a smile at his own rising intolerance. As he moved about New York in the last ten years of his life, a struggling, bustling, raw, contentious place literally popping with the dynamic progress of the new century, he seemed to be detached and aloof from it all. He loved it but could not quite comprehend it; but was immensely pleased with it and hopeful about the picture. He was a Swedenborgian, a mystic, an addict of optimism, who could not take it or let it alone. His was an orderly mind, and to the last his vest was always properly buttoned. No spots came on his clothes. No slovenly habits crept upon him. He was always spick-and-span, and he stood out among his cronies who were not so meticulously watched and tended. Often he put me up at the Century Club, and there I met many writing men of renown—men who had lingered over from another day and time. A score of these Centurions used to lunch around a long table down the center of the dining room. They looked like elder statesmen. Their whiskers still lingered. They were generally well fed, well kept, and prosperous. But their gray beards wagged as they ate and talked. We entered the dining room one day—Mr. Howells and I—and he said in a soft, merry voice:

"You know, Mr. White, the Century takes its name from the fact that it represents the average age of the members!"

Howells, when I met him, must have been in his late fifties, possibly his early sixties. He was heavy-set, with rounding, slightly stooping shoulders, a short neck, a heavy but not a paunchy torso, and rather short nimble legs. His voice was low and gentle. I never heard it rise even when he was moved deeply. It was a self-deprecatory voice which did not provoke argument. He was gay, sometimes happily ironic, never pugnacious. He would ward off disagreement with a smile and a patient gesture. Yet he was, in the 1890's and the 1900's, an arbitrator—perhaps the chief arbitrator of American letters. He had almost ceased writing novels when I met him, yet he has a fat sheaf of them to his credit, and they do portray American life east of the Mississippi and north of Mason and Dixon's line accurately, with solid honest realism, even though they do not give much space to the short Saxon words which pass for realism now in the middle of the twentieth century. He discussed love in its rise, its glow and its decay with a decent biological sense of the earthy texture of his subject. He was more, it seems to me, than a novelist of manner. He left a picture of the American scene that was revealing to his own generation and will be valuable to those who will return to his day and times. Through it all he was as fine and sweet in his writing as he was in his personal relations. In his later days, when his legs were tottering, his daughter Mildred used to bring him to the door of the club, and the colored boys inside saw that he moved about as he would. He was a mild, gray, amiable wraith at the last, and seemed to look out of wise old eyes eagerly upon a generation which amazed him but did not discourage him.

One more Century Club memory, and then I quit those ancients and honorables of the nineteenth century. It is of Brander Matthews. He was of the literary type. He taught English at Columbia University. He wrote critical articles. He was what might be called a magazine columnist and sometimes picked up an honest dollar by writing short stories, and maybe a novel or two. At any rate, he was quite a person. Sometime in the early nineties I had written a story called "Rosemary, That's for Remembrance," a short sketch about a letter written by a doomed young wife and hidden among the family relics for her successor, telling the next wife about the care and feeding of her husband—what he liked, how to wheedle him and please him. A year and a half later, Brander Matthews used that idea —plot if you will—in a story printed in the Cosmopolitan Magazine. I wrote him a note—maybe it was indignant, but I hope not—calling his attention to the obvious plagiarism. He did not reply. One day, at the Century, in a circle of the oldsters, he called to me across the room and said:

"White, I want to apologize to you across twenty years. I did swipe your idea. It was a good one, and I thought I could tell it better." He threw back his head and laughed, and then said: "After all these years I am now rather sure that I was wrong."

Then he told them the story of "Rosemary" and, as the group was made up chiefly of fellow craftsmen who at one time or another had "taken what they might require," we had a laugh and maybe a mild drink to close the episode.

CHAPTER LIV

I am Taken Up on a High Mountain

THE DISTANCE was short in time and space from the Century Club to the Century Magazine office on Union Square where Richard Watson Gilder resided in a frowzy old office, book-lined, paper-strewn, charming, or to the office of Harper's Magazine far downtown, which seemed to be covered with the mold of Harper's antebellum antiquity, or to Scribner's office where Robert Bridges gave me my first leg to literary standing, if I may venture to call it that, with a review in the middle nineties. Scribner's, in those fin de siècle days, was brighter, more alert, less covered with the hoarfrost of forgotten winters. But even so, those magazines—the staid old standbys of upper middle-class America in the middle 1900's—were still printing reminiscences of the Civil War, articles on archeology, stories of the old western ranchers and Indians, and novels by Mr. Barrie, Robert Louis Stevenson and Hardy. Each magazine was produced after its own formula, discovered sometime in the seventies, edited by men in their fifties and sixties, and some who had reached their fourscore years and ten. I had sold a series of stories to Scribner's Magazine, and the publishing house had published a book, "Stratagems and Spoils." I wrote articles once in a while for Harper's.

I was fond of Mr. Gilder, and sometimes Sallie and I dined with him and his family down near Twelfth Street in a lovely museum of a house, furnished with rosewood furniture, rather scantily upholstered, and where we ate on heavy damask linen, with beautiful silver and exquisite china, all out of the reconstruction days. Gilder was one of the last living survivors of the New York mugwumps whom Theodore Roosevelt secretly adored and openly scorned. They rallied around Grover Cleveland, and he was a familiar of the house. At dinner with us there, one found the poets and novelists of the eighties. I cannot think where I met Mary Murfree, a Tennessee romantic novelist of the eighties, but it might have been there. I can see her—a prim little old lady with a spinster look, properly mincing her food, spacing her words gently and living, even then, it seemed to me, in the trailing clouds over mountain sunsets, patronizing most exquisitely her southern mountaineers and incidentally washing behind their ears before presenting them to us Yankees. She wrote under the pseudonym of "Charles Egbert Craddock," and in that prim and proper day she passed for a rather masculine writer. I have often wondered what she would do if she could read the books of our modern southern writers who gloried in obscenity, reveled in profanity and brought up to us out of the south the stinks of the sordid poverty and the meanness and anomaly to which men drop when they fall below the line of economic self-respect. Today, when I read their books, I think of Mary Murfree there at that Gilder dining table, serene in her maiden reserves, gentle but a bit snobbish at times, with her eager birdlike face under the candlelight in the dark walnut-paneled room, with all of us about her in most respectable evening clothes, and considering a world that was about to blow to-hell-and-gone.

And when in my New York visits I left the sweet serenity of the Century Club and its literary hereditaments, and I walked across Fifth Avenue and up into Twenty-third Street to go to the McClure's Magazine office, it was as though I had stepped out of some "ancient volume of forgotten lore" into an unexpurgated dictionary of tomorrow. McClure's was housed much as a wholesale silk or hardware office would be housed. There were glass partitions reaching only halfway to the center. There was clatter, noise, and bustle. There was method and every known gadget of managerial efficiency. There editors talked about new presses and new processes in printing. One saw blueprints. And if occasionally there were on the walls pictures of Mr. Kipling and other writers who were about to recede into the imperial past of a fading era, there also was Sam McClure. Look at Sam McClure in his early fifties, a Swedish blond with a yellow mustache, big, sensitive but challenging eyes, and a sharp, hard but still ingratiating high voice snapping orders like a top sergeant, conscious—Heavens, how conscious—of his power and glory, yet concealing his complacency by self-deprecation. Sam McClure from 1900 to 1907, who was selling his magazine by the hundred thousands, who was a partner in a thriving book business that was conducted like a compromise between a broker's office and a textile mill—Sam McClure was among the ten first men who were important in the American scene. He was the pioneer of a reform that was to surge onward in American life and run for forty years as the dominant note in our political, social and economic thinking. We used to say around the office, where I was a familiar spirit and most happy with the editors, and associate editors and art editors, that crystallized around the blond dynamo, with the name S. S. McClure on the frosted glass door—we used to say that Sam had three hundred ideas a minute, but J. S. P. was the only man around the shop who knew which one was not crazy.

J. S. P. was John S. Phillips, a complete antithesis of Sam McClure. If Sam was the crackling motor, John Phillips was the governor and power belt that conveyed the force and drive of the motor to the manufacturing machine that turned out the finished product of the McClure corporation. John Phillips was perhaps half a head taller than Sam. Both were educated in Knox College at Galesburg, Illinois. John Phillips had gone on to Harvard. He and Sam formed a partnership, first at writing and selling advertising. Then they organized a literary syndicate and bought novels from the great figures of the nineties—from Howells, from Hardy, from Kipling, from Stevenson, from F. Marion Crawford, from Frank Stockton. Sam put them in a pack and peddled them personally to newspapers across the land. Sam was a born salesman, a fast talker, a go-getter. William Dean Howells, in his novel "A Hazard of New Fortunes," put Sam like a bug on a pinpoint in the character Fulkerson. John Phillips spoke softly but he carried a big stick, and the power of his club was his wisdom. Sam knew it; generally accepted it. But John was a man of books and vision and deep fundamental honesty of heart and soul and body, whereas Sam blew where he listed, and had few restraints. He did not entirely realize where he was going nor know exactly what he was doing, but he was conscious of his hunches and that one in many was good. He had—and knew it—a spark of genius. John Phillips could blow on that spark and make it burn and set the land aflame with a strange new light, for John Phillips knew what it was and deeply respected it and consecrated his life and work to it. As McClure came into power he began to reject John's influence, to be irked by the bit and rein. When the rift between them came it was over what seemed to us, who followed John over to the American Magazine, a question of common honesty. Sam could not see it. That kind of insight was not his gift.

But in the middle of the decade we had left, John and a few of the others, with a little help from some of us, bought Leslie's Monthly, called it the American Magazine, and started out to carry the torch of an evolutionary revolution to the world. Around him, John Phillips gathered Ray Stannard Baker, Lincoln Steffens, Finley Peter Dunne ("Mr. Dooley"), Ida Tarbell, John Siddall; and what with the investments large and small of a few other eager souls with bank accounts like Charles R. Crane, Walter Roscoe Stubbs of Kansas and a dozen others whose eyes saw the glory of the coming of the Lord, we had a magazine. It was an organ of propaganda wrapped in the tinfoil of a literary quality which at least reflected the temper of the times.

Among the Centurions as Mr. Howells' guest, the fat young Kansan who was always tempted to call his elders and betters by their first names, the

Kansan who occasionally got under hat brims too broad and who wore his clothes perhaps just a trifle too conspicuously, the Kansan who clipped his g's and was unashamed of his western brogue and lingo, must have been an amusing exhibit. But with John Phillips and his crowd, or even with Sam McClure, the brusqueness, the breeziness, the colloquial metaphor and hyperbole of the brash young man, a familiar at the White House and a member of the National Institute of Arts and Letters, who was beginning to hang honorary doctors' degrees around his neck and who enjoyed talking to the advertising salesmen of the magazine as much as he enjoyed talking to the poets who sometimes clustered about the place, that Kansan was not out of key or focus with his New York environment. For I had become in Kansas politics a bleeding reformer. I was working with what was known at that hour as the boss-buster crowd, and before we knew it old Cy Leland, a boss, had joined us and was giving us the benefit of his organization and his counsel. So we formed our own machine.

The machine in politics is the thing which a defeated candidate uses as an alibi for his own shortcomings. A machine which lacks both coordination and power after his defeat, becomes a noble band of patriots seeking to serve a glorious cause. But unfortunately if the victorious group, which the defeated and disgruntled call the machine, tends to bind its organization together to repeat its victories and consolidate its gains, it becomes in the end a real machine. Probably we Kansas reformers who were in the saddle for a generation finally became more conscious of our means than of our ends. But in those days in the middle 1900's we were zealous, and I was proud to be among the leaders. We were all fighting for a better world. We in Kansas were off the same piece of goods that Sam McClure was, and John Phillips and two or three other monthly and weekly magazines— Collier's, for instance, and Everybody's, which was blazoning across the sky Tom Lawson's book on Wall Street. We were all the inevitable products of our environment. We were doing what we had to do.

I think, looking back nearly forty years to those days when Roosevelt and La Follette and a thousand little Roosevelts and La Follettes in state houses and legislatures, in city halls and country towns, were cleaning those dirty economic and political stables of the ancient giants who followed the Civil War, we were part of a world movement. We were—all of us in New York, in Washington, in Kansas, in the forty-eight states—doing and thinking what men all over Christendom were doing and thinking; we were trying to establish all over the civilized world more equitable human relations. We were trying to distribute the economic surplus of the machine age, and curiously, we thought that if we took the surplus away from the rich and gave it to the poor, we would be achieving our aims. Those of us who saw a little further ahead thought for instance that if we could only change the system of distribution which would automatically give more to the poor and the under dog, and therefore systematically take it from what Theodore Roosevelt called "predatory wealth" or "aggrandized capital," we could bow in our Utopia and leave the world to a long sweet twilight of tranquillity.

It was in those years that I first met Albert J. Beveridge, a young United States Senator from Indiana. He was an eager young man, so earnest that he could not smile easily and never giggled or tittered. His ambition was obvious and sometimes a bit ridiculous, but always innocent and shameless like a child's indecencies. His was a warm personality, gentle, kindly. He liked to talk sometimes sensuously and seemed to be stroking himself on the back with a pride in his oracular wisdom that was not offensive—at least not to me, for I knew that inside he was a noble soul. Sometimes he irritated President Roosevelt. The grand manner that Beveridge assumed so theatrically forced Roosevelt to swallow his risibles, and his regurgitated chuckles sometimes soured into annoyance.

One day in Beveridge's room I met a slim, handsome, silky-mustached, clear-eyed young man, a friend of Beveridge, George W. Perkins, a young political representative of the House of Morgan in downtown New York. Beveridge told me in Perkins' presence that Perkins was his political godfather. The two of them had lived in Kansas in the middle eighties, and Beveridge had tried to practice law at Dighton, Kansas, while Perkins had tried to sell life insurance at Wichita. A few weeks after that meeting I spent an hour or so with Perkins in Beveridge's apartment. Beveridge tackled me with:

"White, why don't you go to the Senate? It can be arranged. Perkins likes you."

And I recall that Chester Long told me he had gone to J. Pierpont Morgan to make his senatorial "arrangements." I was scared. Whatever I was to be, I did not want to be in the United States Senate under "arrangements" made in Wall Street. There was no use saying this to Beveridge. It would only start an argument in which he would justify his suggestion. So I laughed at the absurdity of the idea and the matter dropped there. And in the end Beveridge said:

"Well, don't ever forget what I have told you."

So I haven't, and here it is. I had come to Emporia for that self-respect, even bumptious self-respect, even for considerable conceit which comes with freedom, and I knew enough to know that servitude to the House of Morgan, even with padded golden chains, would be servitude. Freedom is one of those things that are absolute or nothing.

The under dog bothered us all. We were environmentalists. We believed faithfully that if we could only change the environment of the under dog,

389

give him a decent kennel, wholesome food, regular baths, properly directed exercise, cure his mange and abolish his fleas, and put him in the blue-ribbon class, all would be well. We reformers who unconsciously were sucking at the pabulum of the old Greenbackers and Grangers and Populists were intent upon making wholesome dog biscuits for the under dog. We did not know that we were merely treating the symptoms. We and all the world in those days were deeply stirred. Our sympathies were responding excitedly to a sense of injustice that had become a part of the new glittering, gaudy machine age. Machines of steel and copper and wood and stone, and bookkeeping and managerial talent, were creating a new order. It looked glamorous. It seemed permanent; yet, because someway the masses of the world, not the proletariat but the middle class, had qualms and squeamish doubts about the way things were going, discontent rose in the hearts of the people and appeared in world politics. The German Kaiser, Lloyd George, the French Socialists, Lenin, Trotsky and the Russians who had left their blood upon the snow in January, 1905—all of us were protesting against something we could not define, against iniquities that we sensed but did not comprehend.

So reform magazines and reform books made towering piles every month at the corner bookstore of Emporia. And the boss-busters arose and the devil was to pay and no pitch hot, all across this lovely land of the free, this home of the brave. And I, who had no more sense than the others as I whanged away in the Gazette—demanding anti-pass laws, clamoring for a primary system, advocating a workmen's compensation law, clamoring against child labor and the ten-hour day, insisting upon the initiative and referendum in our constitution—was just a little oleaginous molecule with a red round face, waddling in a dog-trot from God-knows-whence to God knows where, but obeying an impulse that was moving humanity across the world. God helping me, I could not do otherwise—being half Irish and full of emotion, half Yankee and full of the visions of the young men.

CHAPTER LV

I Join a Rebellion

ALL OF MY LIFE I have had on hand at the same time two or three major jobs, and it is always easy for me to switch off from one job, without bringing its cares, to the other. So in the summer of 1907, leaving the turmoil of politics, Sallie and I picked up the family—the two children and my mother—and set off for Manitou, Colorado, to finish our novel. Clamorous telegrams from the Kansas politicians, Governor Stubbs, Senator Chester Long, Joe Dolley, the state chairman, fell on our hearts like the gentle patter of rain on a tin roof. These things did not sink into our consciousness. But when Senator Bill Borah appeared on the front steps, wan and anxious, I pulled out for a week, did his errand and came back. All day long I went into a little alcove on the porch that ran around our two-story cottage and hammered away on my Smith Premier typewriter, working on the story of my hero—John Barclay, the prodigal son. It was mainly set in the politics and economics of the last half of the nineteenth century. But it was more than a political novel. It is outmoded now and has only historical interest. But the spiritual decay of John Barclay and the wreck it made of him and the world about him, was the real theme of the book. I knocked out over two hundred thousand words that summer. And to me it was a delight and a joy—all of it. Bill and Mary were little folks, one eight and the other four. They were good children and they and their mother and my mother shielded me and muched me. I had no physical cares or interruptions. I ate well and slept well and lived well and worked like a horse, and was happy. "Heaven," says Thackeray somewhere, "is the place where all the parents are young and all the children are little!"

One day, in mid-July, a letter came from Vernon Kellogg, if about fifty words of explosive epithets of delight can be called a letter. In those fifty words he told us with exuberant and elided joy that he had found the girl —the very girl—a goddess, and that they were in love. Follow love with three dashes and add "God, it is great," and you have some idea of

Vernon's single-sheet message of his journey's end and lovers' meeting. He added: "She has gone to Europe to get away from me. I am off for Europe. Goodbye." More exclamation points, a few stars, and his initials, "V. L. K." Then ten days later came another envelope addressed in Vernon's hand: "What in the name of God are you using for a secretary in Emporia. Read this letter I got this morning." Then below:

Dear Mr. Kellogg:

Your letter received and contents noted. Will say that Mr. White is in Manitou, Colorado, for a complete rest. When he returns in the autumn I will show him your letter.

It was signed: "Gazette, F.F." We had had his letter, but some way the gorgeous comedy of these two letters gave us titters for the summer.

We remained in Manitou until frost, then returned with a novel, "A Certain Rich Man." We spent a whole long year revising it and recopying it for the third time.

We went to New York in the early winter and spent nearly a month there seeing the shows, visiting friends, mostly among the writing people in the book and magazine world, and absorbing the joy that comes to country people in a great city. I have seen New York grow from the little old town of the nineties to the imperial city that stands there now. It is a soul-shaking spectacle, this American metropolis—our capital in everything but politics, and once the home of our ruling class. But I never saw it gloomier and shabbier, nor did I ever see the nation droop and wilt as we saw it wither under the panic of 1907. Factories that had been booming turned glassy-eyed windows to us. Inland towns in the Ohio Valley and Pennsylvania showed us crowds of idle workers on the streets as we whirled along. Cloth signs on store buildings in the little cities and villages advertised bankrupt sales. The banks were closed. Towns were issuing script in lieu of cash. Commerce and industry stopped dead-still. It was a terrible time. Before we left home, the town bankers called me in to a meeting. They wanted the cooperation of the newspaper in establishing their script as temporary legal tender. Someway I feel that it was more dangerous while it lasted, which was but a few months, than the panic of 1933, or perhaps my eyes were keener and my heart more sensitive than they were nearly thirty years after this panic.

It was dangerous because it came in a time of transition. Industry was slowly passing out of the hands of owners into the hands of banks. The banks, controlling minority stock in great industrial corporations, began to hire the operators and managers—presidents and other executives. The banks had the responsibility of the amalgamation of industries, sometimes called the trusts. And of course the owners who in the last quarter of the

392

nineteenth century operated the industries did some consolidating themselves. Carnegie and Rockefeller, Heinze in copper, were notable examples. Their policy of buying out competitors was somewhat predatory, but largely defensive. The banks, in taking over the industries, established a policy of consolidation. It made management easier. It made control more centralized and certain. But in 1907 Theodore Roosevelt was fighting this consolidation, or what he called "predatory wealth." His Attorney General was instituting suits and prosecuting them vigorously against the promoters of trusts. When the panic came, the friends of President Roosevelt contended that the bankers made the panic of that year an answer to the Roosevelt trust-busting policy. Probably the panic came for other reasons—inevitably. It was an economic phenomenon that followed overspeculation, extension of credit too far and too thin in the financing of industry. But the panic did menace the security of the nation. It was charged that Roosevelt made terms with J. Pierpont Morgan, the elder. He probably consented to certain consolidations that Morgan was planning, but the gun was in the President's ribs. If he did connive with Morgan, it was because he had to.

When Sallie and I went to New York that autumn in the midst of the panic, we found no serious hindrance to our comfort and happiness. We went about the town as usual. The theaters were gay and the dinners were good. We knew many of the young reformers of the press and the magazines whom Roosevelt about that time was calling muckrakers, and they were busy and cheerful. One night on that trip Bob Collier, of Collier's Weekly, gave a dinner down at Martin's, a gay restaurant near Madison Square. There we had our first meeting with nobility, real British nobility—no one less than the Duchess of Sutherland—a famous beauty and a leader in high society in the England of that day. The Norman Hapgoods were there, and the Finley Peter Dunnes (Mr. Dooley), and Mrs. John Jacob Astor, another famous beauty; also Helen Hay, daughter of the Secretary of State. It was a grand dinner and Bob Collier summoned entertainers—a juggler who did curious things, and a spiritualistic clairvoyant who told the guests intimate things about themselves. He was blindfolded, sitting in a chair. He rose, still blindfolded, came over to me, and, with his hand on my shoulder, said:

"A man who calls this man Willie says: 'Willie, I was there that evening when I told you I remembered you at the last when you were rubbing my feet.'"

So far as I know, Sallie is the only human being to whom I have ever told that episode. It may be that in the mediums' international union my name was catalogued with that incident. I know of no other normal explanation. But after the jugglers and the astrologers and the medium were gone, we had a gay time until well toward morning. Our first Duchess was a curious person. As we went home we wondered how she would fit into Emporia. We could not see her in the young bridge club. We certainly could not see her in the college faculty group. The bankers' wives would have rejected her—too much make-up! Her clothes were rather out of line for the best dressmakers in our town. But it was all lots of fun.

We were glad to get home for Christmas where the stockings were hung over the fireplace in the workroom, where we gave everyone in the office a present and they all gave us presents and then all came out to the house and we had a big romping party and ended by gathering around the piano and singing. It was good indeed. They were our kind of people, and I was entering the last year of my thirties. We both felt young—Sallie and I. At the holidays we always had a houseful of kin, and the panic, which had then passed its peak in Emporia, did not darken our doorway.

We had four linotypes in the Gazette office. We had bought a new press for the job office. Business in our line was good. Merchants were trying to get rid of their stocks, to pay their debts, so they advertised right along. The subscription list was growing and the pay roll was mounting—a good sign in a sound business. I was at work every morning revising "A Certain Rich Man," and it was beginning to shape up. Politics was growing lively. In January, 1908, Governor Hoch, under pressure of the left-wing Republicans, of whom I was one, called the legislature together to enact a primary law. The fight at Topeka was lively, and at times embittered. But the primary law came, and with it a law that got around the election of United States Senators by the legislature. The law provided that candidates for the legislature could register their preference for candidates for United States Senator before they were nominated. And the preference was a pledge to vote for the man named. The people therefore, in voting for a pledged member of the state senate or the house of representatives in Topeka, voted directly for United States Senator.

In 1908 Kansas had her first state-wide direct primary and had her first direct vote for a member of the United States Senate. There I entered the game of Kansas politics as a leader. United States Senator Chester I. Long was up for reelection. He and his friends represented the conservative faction in the Republican party. Governor Stubbs was the leader of the liberals, who in those days were called insurgents. Kansas rejected the word "Progressives," which La Follette had coined for his Wisconsin party. The Kansas insurgents were after Long's scalp and senatorial seat. Long had a friend named Joseph L. Bristow. Long's friends encouraged Bristow to enter the fight for the United States Senate. They felt sure that Governor Stubbs also would be a candidate. With two candidacies definitely against him, those of Bristow and Stubbs, Long could win easily. It fell to my lot to eliminate Stubbs, and to get him to run for governor—a job he did not care for. I knew Bristow could not be dislodged from his candidacy. Chief Justice Johnston, of the Kansas Supreme Court, was my patron saint. He called Stubbs to his office, and Stubbs and I, sitting on the leather sofa in the chief justice's room, went at it. We were there for an hour. I wore Stubbs down. It was one of the hardest things I have ever done. The chief justice was sitting in a little workroom off the main office. As soon as I got Stubbs to agree with me, I called in the chief justice and said:

"Justice Johnston, I think Stubbs will run for governor."

Stubbs twisted a wry smile across his gnarled Quaker face, moved his biceps muscle a moment before he spoke, and said:

"Well, I guess that's the fact!"

The chief justice gave us his blessing, and Stubbs went out and announced to the reporters in his office that he would not run for the United States Senate but that he was a candidate for governor. It was a body blow to the Long forces. Henry Allen and I, a few hours later, saw Senator Long going out of a conference surrounded by his satellites—certainly a commanding-looking man, handsomer than a bird-dog pup but with an anxious face in that hour. They huddled together and trudged down the corridor, and Henry giggled:

"The retreat from Moscow."

From that hour I made it my business to support Bristow.

Stubbs, in his gubernatorial fight, was fairly well assured of winning, for his opponent was on the wrong side and was the wrong man for the wrong side. But Senator Long was backed by Federal patronage, so it was an uphill fight for Bristow.

That was 1908, but a similar fight was going on in a dozen northern states in that year in the Republican party. Nationally, La Follette rather than Roosevelt was the leader of the revolt against the Republicans in the United States Senate in 1908. The story may have some historical value. The Kansas campaign against Senator Long was typical of other campaigns in the party that year. I went to La Follette and asked him to have his office compile the voting record of Chester Long in the House of Representatives and also in the Senate. It was a bulky document. There, by page and chapter, La Follette had recorded a long list of unbroken conservative votes which Representative Long, and later Senator Long, had cast in Congress. It was a black record in the eyes of the Kansas voters. I took it and tried to give it vitality. I explained the significance of each vote. I prepared the manuscript in triplicate, divided it into three sections and sent it to the Kansas City Star, to the Topeka Capital, and to the Wichita Eagle. I wrote a stirring introduction and a rousing closing for each article, and ended every diatribe with an address to the voters, which closed with this paragraph:

"Will you help?"

I began publishing that record in the spring, and by June I had collected enough money to make boiler-plate stereotypes of my three articles and send them to friendly country daily and weekly papers. I covered the state. It cost three thousand dollars. Most of it I put up myself. Heaven knows I could not afford it, but I did.

Certainly it aroused Kansas. I had been Long's affectionate friend. When Stanley failed of election to the United States Senate in 1903, I was one of those who persuaded Stanley's men to go to Long. I had cautioned him against making too conservative a record. He thought I was mildly mad in those days; so, when the record was made, my attack was savage, I suppose, and he felt its effect. Moreover, Bristow was going over the state, a long figure, making speeches on street corners, in opera houses when his friends in a town would hire them, in schoolhouses at crossroads—covering one county after another. He also was reciting that record to the people. It was new tactics. It was winning.

Long came home from Washington. A rich banker at Wichita had lent him a big, black, shining, brass-bound automobile. He toured Kansas in it. Charley Knowles, the editor of the Leon Indicator, lent Bristow his old bay mare and a rattlety-bang buggy when he campaigned in those counties. A similar shabby equipage took Bristow from town to town. He was a tall, lean, gaunt, Kentucky-bred creature, hungry-faced, fiery-eyed. He looked like an animated cadaver. He had a long arm and a long bony hand, with a point on it like Banquo's ghost. When he directed it at the well kept, well tailored figure of Long as he orated, he challenged him to answer. That also was a new figure in Kansas. The contrast between that lean hungry figure and the fine, florid, broad-browed, deep-voiced, well fed Senator Long was damning, for the Kansas people had just been through the panic of 1907. The tide was turning against Long. He came to Emporia to meet me, and asked me to go on the stage and respond to his reply to my charges against him. Of course I accepted. The opera house was crowded. His defense mainly was that he had voted in line with the recommendations of the Republican party caucus—a defense that pleased only those who were ironclad Republicans. Senator Long could not conceive that the state was in the midst of an insurgency and, with that, defense was anathema itself.

La Follette had made three mistakes in compiling the record. They were Long's trump cards. He faced me with them. There was nothing for me to do but rise and admit they were mistakes—three out of nearly fifty in the indictment. The others stuck. By my admitting my wrong and thereby apologizing for those three mistakes, Long's friends thought they had scored a triumph. They were exultant. Their papers said I had withdrawn my charges, which everyone knew was untrue. I was terribly cut up the next day to think that even three of the counts in my indictment had to be withdrawn. But with my humiliation came wrath, and I went at it hammer and tongs. I loaded the papers full of the general charges, withdrawing absolutely the three mistaken counts.

Roosevelt, in the White House, did not dare to give us encouragement. He had to get along with the Congress; and the Republican Representatives and Senators, many of them, were under attack. To join the foes of these Congressmen would have precipitated a fight on the President in Congress. While he gave me many a cheer behind his hand in Washington, he did not say the word that would have helped me to defeat Long. But La Follette did.

I rented a circus tent in Kansas City, pitched it in our high-school yard, brought La Follette to Emporia, gave him a great meeting there, took him to three other similar meetings in the state the week before the primary. Standing under the tent on a hot afternoon, La Follette held a chunk of ice in a towel to the back of his neck while he spoke, held the record in the other hand, and waved it for gestures. He talked three hours. And certainly La Follette read Long's record and all the changes thereunto appertaining, to an eager, serious, sweaty multitude.

Long, knowing of Bristow's raucous voice, his awkward manner, his halting speech, challenged him to a series of debates. That was a terrible mistake. The crowds were with Bristow. Long struggled to keep a front, but his courage waned. The last debate was Bristow's from the start. The retreat from Moscow ended in calamity. In the primary, Long was defeated for United States Senator; Stubbs was nominated for governor, and a number of Kansas papers hailed me as the new boss.

If I was a boss, I had no desire to be one; I was not in the least interested in patronage. I cared nothing and never have cared for organization. But I did believe in the mass appeal. Obviously, I could make it; and I took my place among those of the first rank in Kansas politics when the old convention horse-trading system went out and the new primary, with its direct vote for nominations, came in. I had functioned fairly well under the convention system, and with the legislative election of the United States Senate, but it all irked me. I did not like it. And when the pass system was outlawed, the convention had to go with it. The primary was a new boon in Kansas. I knew how to swing it, and I was of the younger generation. We, who had begun as young rebels in 1890, two decades later in the prime of our manhood were in control of the State, and we dominated the state house. We were in the majority in the House of Representatives in Washington. Now in 1908, we had the governor and the United States Senator in Kansas. It was our day of triumph. I record this only because similar contests were going on at the latter part of the first decade of the 1900's in Iowa, in Illinois, in Indiana, in Michigan, in Pennsylvania, in Massachusetts, in New Hampshire, in Wisconsin, in the Dakotas, in Minnesota, in Colorado, in Wyoming, in Montana. The fight was spreading to the Democratic party, where Bryan led the liberals. The primary system gave the liberals an effective weapon against their conservative opponents. Fights like our Kansas fight were being won in those years, everywhere.

CHAPTER LVI

I Crow in Victory

I HAD a pretty good opinion of myself after the defeat of Chester I. Long. He had patronized me as I sat on the stage at his Emporia meeting, ruffled my hair, called me a nice young man, but said I didn't know much about politics. And he had lost the town, the county, my own Fourth Congressional District, and had been defeated in the state. And I was the cock of the walk, a young radical, but not so young—I was just out of my thirties, with something of a literary reputation and about to finish my first novel. It had been retyped for the third time and had gone to New York, where the elder George P. Brett, head of the Macmillan Company, had accepted it with what for him, a rather cold-blooded Englishman, was mad enthusiasm. He even wanted to come to Emporia and talk it over with me. So I thought I was bearing down heavily on an Archimedean lever that was moving my world. If I strutted a little I should not be blamed too heavily. If I put a little too much complacency into my smile, that also should be granted to me, considering how blind I was. I was a bubble on a swiftly moving current.

I was helping to send to Washington a United States Senator who would attack social and economic privilege. I was working with the governor of the state, who, along with a hundred other leaders in the land, was welding new political weapons—we were eager to try the primary, the initiative and referendum, the recall, the commission form of government, and lastly ballot reform—taking eagles, roosters, and clasped hands off the ballots so that illiterates would be confused in "voting-'er-straight." All of my associates at home and everyone I knew or worked with in New York ranged in political opinion from liberal to radical. I often sat down at lunch or dinner with men who were called advanced for those days, even Socialists. Once at that time, Peter Dunne (Mr. Dooley) invited me into a small group to meet John Burns, the leader of the labor movement in the British Parliament—a fine, vigorous, charming old zealot whom I met later in England. In the White House, I was a familiar spirit. Theodore Roosevelt was in the midst of his fight for control of the railroads and for busting the trusts. He had just succeeded in tackling the meat packers. The Pure Food and Drug Act of June, 1906, was on the books, and he was enforcing it with riot and clamor. The people were purging the United States Senate and turning out the conservatives in the state legislatures. We who were the leaders of that day, rejoicing as a bridegroom coming forth from his chamber, we were strong men running a race. How little did we realize that we were merely reflexes of deeper changes.

The rise of commercial credit in the world, made necessary by the introduction of machinery into industry, was remaking all relations between labor and capital. The farmer was beginning to realize that the farm was no longer a way of life but a part of a great agricultural industry. Consolidations were everywhere, great trusts were forming as the result on the one hand of manufacturing units, with wider distribution across the land and over the globe of the products of industry, and, on the other hand, of the need for capital to finance these inevitable growing units of industry. The panic of 1907, the defeat of Chester Long, the rise of the radical magazines, the appearance of Socialists at reasonably respectable dinner parties, the tremendous vogue of Theodore Roosevelt and of my novel "A Certain Rich Man," which was an attack upon the commercial spirit of the age—all of that movement, politically called insurgence in America, was the response of a new stimulant to the life of the world-expanding capital in the form of growing credit. It was all the product of the machine age. How could I, looking in pride that August night of 1908 when a great crowd gathered around the Gazette office to read the primary election returns, how could I know that my victory in Lyon County and in Kansas was not of my doings? If it had not been I, sitting on the cowcatcher flapping my wings and crowing in my heart while I assumed my sweet, modest, Christian attitude, it would have been someone else. For change was abroad in the world. Four linotypes in the Emporia Gazette office, doing the work of a dozen or fifteen printers, the new web press printing Gazettes three or four times as fast as we could print them on the old cylinder press, were merely symptoms of what all the world was experiencing. And here is a curious thing: The same number of people—not a thousand more—who less than two decades before had supported meagerly the Gazette and its rival, the Republican, with not more than twelve hundred subscribers between them, and with an annual gross income of not more than fifteen thousand dollars—now this same population was supporting the Gazette with three times as many subscribers taking a daily paper in Lyon County as had taken daily papers before. And also these same people were patronizing Emporia merchants three or four times as heavily in retail sales.

Advertised bargains were ballooning the size of the Gazette. The dry-goods and clothing stores, which formerly twice a year had received car-loads of merchandise in great wooden boxes, now began to get goods monthly in smaller packages; quick sales, quick turnovers in these stores were making more profits. The living standard in Emporia and all over the United States was rising. Advertising in magazines was assuming com-paratively enormous proportions. All the wheels, cogs, cams and levers of a million mills and industrial machines were rattling away and were becoming the voice of the times. And I, in Emporia, a mere pip-squeak, singing a squawky little political and industrial radicalism, thought I was somebody; fancied I was a part of the chorus that the morning stars sang together. I did not realize until many years later that I had floated—a mere bubble—on the swift-moving current of the change that was coming over humanity, and that was remaking the world.

In 1908, as a reporter, I attended the Republican national convention which named William Howard Taft for President. That was a curious convention, and in reporting it I saw how little enthusiasm those delegates had for Mr. Taft. They cheered the reactionary leaders. Joe Cannon was their idol—not Taft. But they obeyed vox populi, which was the bidding of Theodore Roosevelt in the White House. I sat for several days at odd times during the convention beside Alice Roosevelt, and she knew what a hollow victory was Taft's in that convention. Two years before, she had married a rising young conservative Congressman, Nicholas Longworth. She knew what was going on. She gave me the tip that gave me the beat over all other correspondents in that convention. So I was able to announce that James Sherman, the most reactionary of the Republican Congressmen, would be nominated by the convention for Vice President. It was the revolt of the conservative Republican party against the liberal leadership of Theodore Roosevelt, the young President. If ever a convention was cut and dried, it was that convention. If ever a convention showed its contempt for its master, that convention showed it for Theodore Roosevelt—and his daughter knew the truth. All of the world of change that was abroad in the land, all the new spirit of revolt and liberalism, the Republican party that year rejected in scorn, with the Sherman nomination. They had acted with rather craven obedience to the will of one man, Roosevelt, in naming Taft, but probably with some sort of prescience, instinctively knowing that Taft was of their ilk. They let the President crack the whip—and be damned to him. I doubt if the leadership of the Republican party and the rank and file of that party ever could have changed their attitude. But it was a good place in which to fight. The difference between the regulars of the two parties, so far as the new movement abroad in the world was concerned, was that between Tweedledum and Tweedledee.

In the year 1908 William Jennings Bryan was nominated for the Presidency by the Democratic party for the third time. It was his last race. He had no opposition of any consequence in the convention. His twelve years of leadership in the party, scarcely broken by the revolt against him in 1904, when Parker—a reactionary—was nominated, had a curious similarity to Roosevelt's leadership in the Republican convention. A section of the national Democratic convention was for Bryan—a noisy section. Obviously the sentiment of his party rank and file was for him. But, as a reporter in that convention, I felt a majority of the delegates accepted Bryan, even licked the spoon, but screwed up their faces in some disgust. The party was not yet liberalized. The people of the country and the leaders, Roosevelt and Bryan, were going faster than the party regulars approved. The political machines functioned without conviction. It was so in both parties. Roosevelt cracked the whip. Bryan delivered his ukase. The two conventions were composed of party hacks without much conviction, and naturally the conservatives fell into line. I saw those things as a reporter in the two conventions. I should have liked to believe that the enthusiasm for Taft in the Republican convention at Chicago and the enthusiasm for Bryan in the Democratic convention at Denver represented the conviction of the delegates. But I knew that it did not. What enthusiasm there was, and even that seemed in each case to be a claque, was the mechanical response of the delegates to the voice of leadership and their fear of the rank and file. I thought then that it was the power of the leadership of Roosevelt and Bryan in the two parties. I know now that they were mere figureheads of the two ships. The steam in the boiler room was making them go. The thing that moved the business world in 1907 was moving the political parties in 1908. No real issue divided them. They were curiously similar in their organization and in their intention. And the primary vote of Kansas a few weeks after the two conventions adjourned was a part of the same revolution in the world. My vanity at the vote in Lyon County was absurd. Most vanity is.

That year Jane Addams came to visit us—a large, wholesome, eager earnest woman, with a real sense of humor and a deep purpose showing forth from her glowing eyes and kindly face. Presently, Sam McClure editor of McClure's Magazine, came out for a visit and insulted our hired girl when he left by trying to slip a five-dollar bill into her hand. She was not used to it, and indeed it was not the custom in the West to receive tips from guests. Sallie had trouble explaining to her that Mr. McClure's intentions were entirely honorable. That year we traveled a long summer's day with Taft, when before his nomination he was out going through the rather empty forms of canvassing the country in his own behalf. If ever there was a folksy man in his ways and manners, it was William

Howard Taft. He stood a good six feet two or three, and must have weighed around three hundred pounds. He told us the story about his visit with Mrs. Taft to Moscow, where they had no maid and he had to hook up her dress in the back for a court dinner and ball. He was full of anecdotes that portrayed him as the common man. There was no Yale about him. One forgot he was the son of a federal circuit judge who had married a girl with a rather long upper-class lineage. Neither Sallie nor I realized at the end of that long day that this genial, chuckling, courteous, kindly gentleman was in his heart a deep-dyed political and economic conservative, and bull-headed at that. I wrote a piece about him for McClure's Magazine, portraying him as a sane liberal, and I really believed it. So did millions of followers of Colonel Roosevelt. Mr. Taft's capacity for affection was genuine. His interest in people was unaffected. He wanted them to be happy as he was, and prosperous if they would only go to work. But he was deeply dubious, as the liberals found out too late, of any plan which would ameliorate the conditions surrounding the common man, of any scheme for using government as an agency of human welfare which would make automatic a rise in the general standard of living. Liberalism in the United States, under the leadership of Bryan and Roosevelt, was trying to spread the benefits of mass production from the luxuries of the few to the comforts of all.

The new motor industry was changing many habits of the rich in the United States. But Henry Ford had not come along to democratize the motor car, and it was still a toy of the upper middle class. We, in Emporia, still drove behind our old clop-clopping Clydesdale who pulled the family cut-under surrey with the fringed canopy top. And we lived in a pretty good house in the town, one of the ten best. There were less than a hundred automobiles in Lyon County. I walked over half a mile to work, back home to lunch, back to the office to work and back home at night every day. I met other businessmen on my way going and coming. Only a few sports and an occasional banker rode in motor cars, which were not yet in mass production. But every one sensed the fact that the expensive toy which then cost anywhere from eight hundred to three thousand dollars would soon be within the reach of all. How? No one knew. But they had a hunch, a deep conviction probably based on the fact that we Yankees generally got what we wanted, that soon the motor car would come to all the middle class. It was probably that same hunch that set us marching to Utopia, that gave Bryan and Roosevelt their hold on the imagination of the people. For certainly the Utopia was the evidence of things not seen—but the substance of things hoped for.

CHAPTER LVII

The Europe Which Has Vanished

THE YEAR 1909 was memorable in the life of the White family. It began with a letter from President Roosevelt asking us to come to what his letter declared would be his last and nicest party. This party was to be the White House reception for the Army and Navy. With the letter he sent a gold-embossed invitation, rather gaudy for the Roosevelt of that day. So we packed up and went to Washington, with an incidental trip to New York, where Mr. Howells was exceedingly kind to us, had us in for luncheon with a few fellow craftsmen, and then took us down on Fifth Avenue to a china store where we bought half a dozen gold cups and saucers like those which we had admired in his service. Pretty dishes were always a part of our domestic delights. His daughter, Mildred, bought and presented to us a brown crockery teapot which we have to this day, to remind us of those happy days.

The reception for the Army and Navy at the White House was all that the President had promised. It was a gold-braid occasion—the Army and Navy in full dress, the diplomatic corps in full regalia and their wives dressed to kill. The cabinet was there, a few special members of the Supreme Court, and perhaps a dozen friends like us. As we passed by the Roosevelts on the reception line, the President pulled us out of it, turned us over to a young aide who took us upstairs into the private apartments of the Roosevelt family. There gradually assembled fifty—maybe a few more —special friends. When the line went past and the reception downstairs was done, the President came storming up into the parlor where we were gathered, and I can remember I was standing by a door which led into a toilet somewhere near. I tried to stop him, to say something, and he gave a great "Ugh!" and said: "I'll be back in a minute. I have got to wash my hands." And another "Ugh!" "Shaking hands with a thousand people! What a lot of bugs I have got on my hands, and how dirty, filthy I am!" He came back a few minutes later and resumed where he had broken off:

"Now I am clean. I always do this after a reception. You should remember it. It may save your life some time!"

In a few moments the company formed and went downstairs. There were a score of small tables. On the sideboard was a buffet supper—and a good one, for T. R. loved good, plain, palatable food and lots of it. And this, even for him, was a collation. Justice Holmes took Sallie down. At her table were two members of the cabinet and some admirals and a major general's wife. And at my table were Admiral Sims and General Wood, with "human warriors" in the way of the ladies, God bless them!—probably wives and T. R.'s friends. The talk was leisurely and good. In those last days, as in the last days of any outgoing President, the White House was fairly well deserted. The sycophants were gone, for the outgoing President had nothing to give. The Tafts were forming their own center. In Congress, the President's recommendations were being kicked around and scorned. But he had delivered a scorching message to Congress blasting the idle rich, using the words "predatory wealth" and shocking the daylights out of the Congressional conservatives, particularly Joe Cannon, who publicly damned the President, and Aldrich, who carefully sneered at him, much to the delight of the President. I can remember hearing him snort like an elk in his high falsetto about it across the table to Justice Holmes. The whole occasion was a gay one. It was indeed his nicest party. And as the supper guests were leaving, he put out his arm and called back Sallie and me, and we went up to the White House living room. He stood by the fire, and we sat on a lounge near by. Mrs. Roosevelt came in, probably to warn her husband to bed, but we stood there reviewing the party, talking over the isolation of the White House and the scornful attitude that Congress had assumed toward him. He took it in glee. We talked for a moment about the defeat of Long. He expressed some regret that he had not been able to help, and I gibed that, so far as Congress was concerned and its real appraisal of his policies, he might just as well have fought them in the open. But he contended otherwise. He had no great liking for Bristow, whom he had treated unfairly in a row when Bristow, as fourth assistant to the Postmaster General, tried to oust some crooks from the Post Office Department, crooks who were Hanna's friends, while Roosevelt just before Hanna's death was trying to placate him. In a similar situation McKinley had shown more courage when Hanna had tried to intervene to protect some crooks in Cuba. When Bristow was an investigator, McKinley had called him and told him to go ahead and not be afraid of Hanna. I thought of this that night in the White House as we were talking about Bristow, but saw no need of bringing it up again. We had had that out in 1902, when the President had quarreled with Bristow for being too obstreperous in his righteousness. In a few moments we left. It was our last White House reception for thirty years, and we were thrilled to the core. We were easily thrilled to the core in my earliest forties and Sallie's very latest thirties.

We hurried home to prepare for our first trip to Europe. We were all going—the children and my mother, aged seventy and nine, more vigorous than either of us. She decided to go less than a week before we left. She had some money of her own, and insisted on paying for her ticket. It left her some spending money, which she also carefully conserved. The children were little. Mary was going on five and Bill was going on nine. But we felt they would get something out of the trip, and they did. It was high adventure for the White family. We had been saving for ten years in a building-and-loan, and had scraped together three thousand dollars, with all our debts paid. It seemed like wealth beyond the dreams of avarice. Our boat, a dear old tub called the *Cretic,* which perished ten years later in the First World War, sailed the latter part of March. It went the southern route, stopping at Madeira and the Azores, going through Gibraltar and landing us in Naples. Nothing seemed more romantic to us than this sea voyage. Our only ocean experience had been on the Fall River Line from New York to Cape Cod.

In that far day, when we had less than two score blocks of paving in Emporia and were immensely proud of it, any Emporian's trip to Europe was a matter of town-wide interest. So the week before we sailed our friends gave us a going-away party—a beefsteak dinner of considerable proportions at the Harvey House. All the automobile owners were there, and many of the conservatives, who still drove horses. But the drivers of the more spanking teams—merchants, princes, lawyers, bankers and doctors, that also was a rather spacious group—made speeches at us. There was a lot of kissing at the end, and a few tears as we left for the ends of the earth. I am sure the town was proud of us to go en masse, two children and a grandmother, into distant lands and strange places. The world was smaller then. And maybe happier—who knows?

Probably nothing on the trip impressed the children and their grandmother more than eating on the dining cars between Emporia and New York. My mother got her delight vicariously through the children. They ate a wide swath down the menu card, and she insisted that we give them what they wanted, on the theory that naturally we were stingy, cruel parents who would starve our children but for her. On the dock, as we sailed, were our magazine friends—John Phillips, Ida Tarbell, Ray Stannard Baker; some flowers from Howells, some fruit from the House of Macmillan and a parting floral salvo from Emporia, I think—as I remember it, from the chamber of commerce. How wonderful everything seemed to us on the *Cretic!* I paced the deck and figured that it was as long as an Emporia block, and I was tremendously impressed by the size of the little tub. The passenger list was not large. After two days out I knew everybody. So did the children. And on the third day, Sallie and my mother had become oriented socially. I went below at the first gentle breezes. I always do. Until we got to Madeira I saw more of the pattern of the springs above me in Mary's berth than I saw of the bounding billows. I have always thought that the ocean was a mistake and that God should have fired the angel who made it. It has kept the world apart too long, and it is too wet anyway and a waste of space. Also, it turns my stomach, and I hate it even now after having crossed the Atlantic ten times one way or another, and having traversed the Pacific to the Philippines and back, and to Hawaii. So I lay in my berth and refused the comforts of human society and solid food. But Sallie is a good sailor and my mother was too fond of good food to let a meal go by. The ship's menu challenged her. She ate new food every day. And she came down to my stateroom, roundly scolded me for being a baby, and began recounting what she had eaten, particularly at breakfast—sausages and buckwheat cakes, fried potatoes, hot bread and coffee, starting with cereal and ending with fruit. After she had gone, I lay looking at the geometrical figures made by the springs on the bottom of the berth, until one afternoon when they put Mary to sleep there, and she wet the bed and it leaked on me and the family had a great joke. When she woke, Mary was tickled beyond words. But it did get me up, and that was my last daylight hour in the berth. It made a man of me, and Mary— aged five—claimed great credit for my recovery. We were that kind of a family, if you must know.

When I arose, we were near Madeira. I romped all over the ship. I played quoits. I was the life of the company in the smoking room, though I never smoked and did not drink. But I had enough bounce and foolishness to make up for the lack of alcohol and nicotine. I must have been exuberant, probably pretty fresh in those days, but life was churning in me and kept me on the jump. My mother's Irish energy worked in me like new wine.

I loved people. I remember at the captain's party, a week later, I helped those who were organizing it. Sallie always said to me that when I got on a ship the first thing I did was to go to the captain's quarters and tell him how to run it. I was light on my feet, even on the rolling deck, and when I came out of my torpor I liked to visit around with people in deck chairs who were trying to read. Ocean travelers will recognize this pest easily. I bribed the confidence of the head dining room steward, and was on terms with the deck steward. I talked to the sailors. But I never knew the captain. So far as I can remember, I never saw him. And only at the last of the trip did I know that there was a captain's table and that at it were seated the gentry and nobility of the good ship's company. I was not above whanging away at the piano in the salon, which I perversely called the parlor, for I hated the sea badly enough to avoid nautical terms where I could find landlubbers' synonyms for them. But I did not bet on the ship's run. The five dollars I lost on James G. Blaine in 1884 still rankled in my memory and made me afraid of gambling, so I affected to scorn it.

Little Mary was the only one on the ship who knew more people than I did. She was a cute kid, with pigtails bound in red ribbons. She poked the quoits around. She won a sweater at the children's tournament—or was it a big Teddy doll?—I forget. Bill was decently circumspect and forever disciplining Mary. He was a vigorous chaperon. And he won a prize of some kind at the children's tournament. He was nine, and his mother kept him decently but never gaudily clad, and even at that tender age he loved to snuggle in a deck chair with a book, where he could keep one eye on his wiggling and vigorous sister who adored him openly, shamelessly. Together Sallie and I walked the deck. Together we sat in our deck chairs. Together we roamed the ship and found sunny, warm places near the stacks where she could read aloud to me and we could talk.

In any account of my life this first trip to Europe deserves emphasis. It was a milepost. In the new environment of Europe, I saw myself in perspective. And, as Kipling puts it, "I stood beside and watched myself behaving like a blooming fool," and I enjoyed it.

In Rome we saw the Pope at one of the great spectacles of the Church, the Beatification of Joan of Arc. My mother had been born a Catholic, but had never taken her first communion. A Congregational family took her when she was a little girl, perhaps twelve or thirteen, I don't know, and gave her a home. She went with them to Galesburg, Illinois, where Knox College took her in, a Congregational school. As a child I often heard her talk bitterly of the Catholics around her birthplace in Oswego because they had not helped her when she was helpless. Nevertheless, when she came to Rome, she had one ambition. It was to see the Pope. I could see the old faith stirred in her heart as she stood beside me in the tremendous crowd; and the power of the great spectacle, as we were jammed together in it, was moving her Irish heart profoundly. I watched her. In a way she was a spectacle herself, seventy-nine years old, as vigorous as a woman of fifty, able to do a full day's work at any task she knew. I saw her face light up and then suddenly, just as the Pope was passing in the climax of the day, in mounting passion I saw wrath, deep Irish rage, illuminate her face. I saw her grab a hatpin, though how she got her arms up, Heaven knows. Then a strange thing happened. She ducked slightly, and I saw a man standing near her, in back of her, a weasel-eyed, middle-aged little Italian, suddenly rise up from the throng, a miniature earthquake, and shatter the crowd around her. She had bumped him with her behind, and she hissed as he came down:

"He'll not pinch my leg again!"

I looked again, and Heaven knows how the man disappeared, possibly dissolved in the fury of her wrath, but she certainly gave him a catapult shove from her bottom with a voltage that must have disarmed him, and she waved her hatpin like the sword of a conqueror as the Pope passed on. She did not take her eyes from the Pope through it all. The dual drama of the glorious pageant and the insulted Irish peasant's daughter passed in almost the twinkling of an eye.

She watched calmly while the Pope, in a cloud of glory, was wafted down the aisle. The crowd about her thinned a little. She turned to me after the climax and said:

"These dirty Italians! These dirty Italians!" and that was all.

The heavenly choir resounded in the vaulted doors. The celestial color of a great spectacle still held its form. Ten minutes more the Pope sat on his mounted throne, giving his languid blessing with the two-finger sign that in my boyhood days had been an invitation to go swimming. Except for its utter lack of enthusiasm, the drama of it went on. Joan's spirit would have been called from the farthest star by the joy and beauty of this pageant. It was sustained happily, climaxing in the final act of beatification. In all the world, in all history, no other organization of man's device under God's blessing has been able to put together so much formal richness with such authentic fame and joy, mixed in one high moment of massed ecstasy.

When it was over, my mother and I walked together out of the great building in silence. Never again did she mention "the dirty Italians," and in her life she rarely spoke of that high and holy hour in St. Peter's. I don't know why. She went to the Congregational Church, the church of her girlhood and youth, though she never was a pious person and never seemed in her conscious moments to regret that she had sat under the altar of Henry Ward Beecher and his brother Edward, at Knox College, and had heard the preachments of the great Congregationalists in the first half of the nineteenth century. But nevertheless I am sure that to her dying day that picture in St. Peter's remained in her heart, a sacred memory symbolizing her childhood days.

In Paris, we put up at a little pension in the Cité di Retiro—French to the core, including the unchangeable stinks of a French w.c. For several weeks we radiated from there and did all the tourist things indicated in the guide book. We rode on the Seine. We went to see the graves of poets and dramatists and statesmen in Père-Lachaise, spent a day in Versailles, and several days in the Louvre. And, incidentally, I was conscious of the fact that the Stubbs rebellion was on in France. Labor troubles often broke out. The waiters at the hotels, who spoke English, told us that the struggle for an eight-hour day was on. They also were beginning to realize that old-age pensions were a part of any just establishment of human relations. At that time in Kansas we were wrestling with the problem of workmen's compensation, a law which made an employer responsible for broken men, just as he had to pay for his own broken machinery in the accidents of his business. It struck me as interesting and deeply significant that we found in continental Europe the people perhaps a decade ahead of Kansas and the United States in the matter of labor and agricultural legislation, and my faith was strengthened in the righteousness of the Kansas struggle by finding that it was a part of the world agitation.

One other thing came to me as a part of my Kansas education. In Paris I met an old friend, State Senator James T. Stewart, of Wichita. He was in Paris arranging for funds for a little jerk-line railroad or a trolley system, I forget which. And when I talked to him about his operations, I realized that if the striving of the workers and farmers of Europe was a part of our fight in Kansas, the international network of finance was also a world picture, and part of the same texture and structure at the top, as was the battle for industrial justice at the bottom. Vaguely, it was coming to me that the world was shrinking. We were parts, one of another, in the United States and in Europe. Something was welding us into one social and economic whole with local political variations. It was Stubbs in Kansas, Jaurès in Paris, the Social Democrats in Germany, the Socialists in Belgium, and I should say the whole people in Holland, fighting a common cause. Against what, I was not sure. I only knew I saw a world-wide struggle in the earlier and more peaceful stages of the revolution. I did not remotely understand what was the catalyst that was crystallizing the struggle of the people of the world into one pattern of revolt. I am not sure that even now I know what it was or is. It had something to do with the machines which are changing human habits around the globe, recasting human relations everywhere from the jungle to the university, these strange new labor-saving machines that have in some way revolutionized human life on this planet.

CHAPTER LVIII

Edwardian England

My MOTHER went to England as an army with banners. She could not forget the Irish famine, nor the failure to grant home rule. So she looked with a fishy eye on the glamorous scenes that we loved because they were a part of our racial heritage. For a week or ten days we put up in London at a smart, rather exclusive second- or third-class haunt of the decade's nobility and gentry—the Artillery Mansions. To get in, we had to be introduced. We had pleasant rooms with a fire in the grate in the evening even though it was midsummer. The children played in the courtyards around and in a fountain.

It was in England that we bade farewell to the lilacs, which came upon us first at Madeira in April. They tagged us into Italy and through Switzerland. We saw them in Germany in June, and saw the very ragged last of them in France, and then came upon what seemed to be hothouse lilacs—dark, dark purple flowers—in England.

Mr. Howells had given us a letter to Henry James and another to his brother-in-law, Larkin G. Mead, a dear old man, an expatriated American sculptor with the slang of the sixties still in his mouth. These two letters were the only social letters we presented. I had a sort of letter from President Taft to all embassies, suggesting courtesies, which I never used. I had no desire to make this a plug-hat trip. But at Henry James's invitation I did go on a pilgrimage to his home. He lived at Rye in Sussex—and lived most charmingly—in an old though modest house with a little walled garden back of it. It seemed to me that the house, the garden, and Henry James were all one. We two had luncheon together and a long talk about the United States and about American writers, most of whom I knew, men and women whose work he was enjoying. For an exile he was well informed about American books and writers. We talked after luncheon there in the walled garden under a spreading tree; then we walked about Rye and visited an old church. He told me its history charmingly. He talked, as he wrote, in long involved sentences with a little murmur—mum-mum-mum—standing for parentheses, and with these rhetorical hooks he seemed to be poking about his mind, fumbling through the whole basket of his conversational vocabulary, to find the exact word, which he used in talking about most ordinary matters. He seemed to creak with those murmuring parentheses, but he did talk well, and was altogether a joy. He was of middle height, high-domed, stocky though not chubby; and I fancy his mumbling, fumbling way of talking came because he lived alone so much, an old bachelor. He walked sturdily, with just the faintest swagger to his well set rounding shoulders. The afternoon I spent with him was one of the lovely experiences of that gorgeous summer.

I knew that "A Certain Rich Man" had been published that summer. Macmillan & Company in London brought out a small edition, and we had fancy bindings put on several copies for friend and kin. The company indicated mildly that the book was doing well in the United States, but said it more plainly by inviting us down to the home of one of the Macmillans. It was a typical English country home. The hostess was most scrupulously English in all her domestic arrangements, although she had been born and reared in Indianapolis. We had never seen the service in an English country house before—so many kinds of servants to do so many things. The English scorn of modern plumbing gave great respectability to servants, who did what plumbing did for folks in the United States. I remember a maid brought a shallow tin bathtub and large pitchers of hot water for Mrs. White's bath, and routed me out down a corridor to a stairway to where she said my bath was ready. I wandered about the place for four or five minutes and never could find the bathtub. Heaven knows what they thought of me, but that chambermaid had me cringing. She had come into my room where I undressed hastily, had taken my drawers out of my trousers where I had left them crinkled on the floor, found my undershirt, and put the two together folded neatly on the bed while I cowered under the bedclothes. They had unpacked our valise while we were in the garden an hour after we came, and scattered things about drawers and in closets so that we did not know where to find them. And some way I shuddered to realize that that maid knew everything about us—the undarned condition of our stockings, underwear, maybe buttons missing here and there, for we had been away from home three months and were not in the very pink of sartorial perfection. Sallie had great glee over my embarrassment before the maid and my reservations about letting her bounce me around in my nightgown.

But the Macmillans were exceedingly kind and did not realize our hardships. They had their notions of how life should proceed in a country house, and it went that way. And we, at least and in truth, were as interested in the strange maneuvers of the servants as they must have been amazed at our savage individualistic attitudes. But the talk was good and the house full of young boys from the British public schools and universities—Eton, Oxford, and maybe Cambridge—who were so much more intelligent than the college boys that I had known that I was amazed at what British civilization was doing for upper-class British youth. They talked politics, national politics. The sons and nephews of the family were nicely divided between the Tories and the Liberals, and you could hear them going at it at all hours. My collegiate experience in discussing American politics had been limited to losing five dollars on Blaine in 1884 after which I became, as I think most college boys in midwestern United States were, hermetically sealed to the issues of modern American politics, however we might delve into American history. We did not relate history with life. History stopped for us with the Civil War, or at most the panic of '73. But in England, and particularly there at the Macmillan home, I began to realize the uproar that Lloyd George was causing in that year 1909 with his budget bill. It provided for a tax on land. It carried with it heavy income taxes, for those days; and there was an implication that if the House of Lords held it up too long the powers of the Lords would be curtailed. And imagine discussing such things in a conservative English household a generation ago.

At the publishing house I was invited to luncheon by the Macmillans, and there I met Thomas Hardy. The luncheon was no great shakes—fine rare roast beef, boiled potatoes and cabbage, Yorkshire pudding and a savory dessert. But Hardy, who was then at the height of his fame, was something to write home about. He had a sandy, scrubby, wayward little mustache, blond gray, that had been spoiled too long to be taken in hand in his sixties. His was a ruddy pink skin. He had gorgeous blue eyes which opened sometimes like the lifting of a curfew. His hair was a dark graying brown. His voice was mousy, something almost like a senile tenor. I never knew a man so entirely unconscious of himself. At our luncheon table one of the guests told us that Hardy sat through the first operatic performance of "Tess" smiling, pleased as Punch, but like a wraith, quite disconnected from the world about him. When it was over he sat in the box and clapped his hands for the composer to come out, and then for the singer, and finally for all of the people in the cast. But no one called for him and it did not occur to him, probably, that anyone should call for him. He was just that dear. I remember nothing that he said at that luncheon, for I did not write it down, but I do remember that what he said was impressive and that the way he said it was delightful. He carried conviction as much by his smile and his mien as by his words, and I was charmed. Under direct examination I tried to tell those at the table something about Kansas.

But I must have made a poor fist of it, for they did not believe there was any such country. I tried to tell them about Stubbs and the American insurgents, but there I know they thought I was more than mildly mad. And when I said that Kansas had lived submissively under state prohibition for nearly thirty years without raising an issue in politics worthy of a name, I could see that my reputation as a reporter was wilting. But Hardy was greatly amused. He thought it excruciatingly funny that the same people would endure prohibition whose ancestors one hundred thirty years before had arisen in rebellion against the British government over the little matter of taxes. He strained with inner mirth and would not let himself laugh—probably from habit, but maybe because he wished to be polite to me. But I could see that he was struggling terribly with his risibilities, and I saw the humor of it too, and laughed perhaps as loudly as Hardy would have liked to laugh. The luncheon was really more than a passing event. It was an experience. I really wanted to see Kipling and Barrie, but something happened to prevent our meeting. Perhaps they heard of my desire in time to act. I should not blame them. For I was walking through the vast menagerie of the world gawking wide-eyed and perhaps serving myself too much.

But I did see one British politician whom I particularly wished to see. It was John Burns, the labor leader. I bore a letter to him from either Peter Dunne in New York, or Robert Hunter, who at that time was considerable of a Socialist. He arranged for a luncheon—where, I don't know. I can remember it was in a small room. With him came two or three of the left-wing members of Parliament, men whose names I cannot remember. But he was the soul of the company, a most remarkable man. He must have been in his sixties. He seemed old to me. He had a ruddy face and rugged, covered sparsely by what might be called a scraggly beard, decently kept but thin. His voice was gentle, not the roaring rabble-rousing trumpet that I had expected; and his eyes were bright, lively, illuminating, a blue or gray, which I cannot remember. He seemed to be as anxious to know about American politics as I was to learn about English. I tried to tell him of Roosevelt and about Taft, in whom I was beginning to lose faith. And he told me much about Lloyd George, of whom he had not the highest opinion. He felt that Lloyd George was what in the parlance of politics we called "a double-crosser"—a man who makes too many promises to too many people about too many different kinds of things. Of course Lloyd George was trying to assemble a parliamentary majority and stretch it as far to the right as he could, and as far to the left. John Burns knew this, and he was an uncompromising left-winger. And he hated palaverers, and Lloyd George was one. He was a hand-shaker and a back-slapper, an orator and a politician who liked to please perhaps better than to serve. Most politicians of that type get the notion that their own pleasure is their country's service, that in building up their own strength they are saving their country. From my talk with Burns at that luncheon I gathered that he regarded Lloyd George as just another politician. I knew enough about politics to get Burns' picture of Lloyd George rather too exactly in my heart. Although the terminology Burns used was British, the political atmosphere in which he moved and spoke was universal. Politics from the days of Moses to the days of the second Roosevelt are the same old game. Issues change a little, but men and their weaknesses, the handles, levers and push-buttons by which politicians work and achieve their ends, are well worn through the ages of use.

I suppose I learned more of British politics during that hour or so with John Burns and his left-wing supporters than I had learned in the weeks that I was in London.

But I lost class at the Artillery Mansions when it became known that I was lunching with John Burns. Now that the American boarding house has passed with the coming of the hot-dog stand, the hole-in-the-wall café, the hamburger joint, the cafeteria, the automat, nothing in America remains like the Artillery Mansions. Of course they dressed for dinner there. Of course the meals, although varied, were essentially the same. The cooking was, from any American standard I knew, decent but terrible. The menus adhered scrupulously to an imitation of the table d'hôte of restaurants of a much higher grade. The guests ate in silence, murmured with their food, were exceedingly well bred—more proud of their breeding than they were of the scrimpy, almost stingy respectability of the ménage. I gathered from their uniforms at dinner that many of the men were retired army and navy officers, with an occasional retired Indian civil servant or a county agent in town for the week end, all with their women kind who seemed as lean, as circumspect, as tightly buttoned as the men. They all met in a large salon or parlor after dinner, floating like ice cakes from table to table, where there were magazines and most respectable newspapers, and where also the repressed murmur of softly modulated voices was a constant rebuke to any American. I was branded with the "scarlet letter" when it became known through the head clerk (whom I had asked to get Burns on the telephone) that I was consorting with a left-wing labor leader. If I had introduced smallpox I would have caused less panicky horror than I spread about me after coming back from my luncheon with John Burns. I felt that even the servants—who in America would have been for Burns—deprecated my social misadventure, but in sorrow rather than in anger. One of them, mentioning my transgression, exclaimed, "Ow, him!" and let it go at that. Class runs to the core of British society. It is not a matter of wealth or power. It is a matter of inward attitude of the poor

415

and lowly, the rich and great alike. All these things I learned graciously, happily, but well at the Artillery Mansions.

Once when we were stopping there many years later I spoke of it to H. G. Wells, and he exclaimed, "Ow, there!" Then he caught himself and said that once he had luncheon there, and looked at me shrewdly to see whether I realized whither I had wandered. It was the British Empire on the half-shell.

CHAPTER LIX

We Join a Parade

IN THAT summer of 1909 England received a terrific shock. Blériot, a Frenchman, in an airplane flew over the English Channel. The island was invaded. The ocean barrier that had been England's strength in ages past had been scaled. We first heard about it after dinner one evening, and the dovecote at the Artillery Mansions was all aflutter. We looked at the evening papers in the parlor of the hotel and read the news of the Frenchman's achievement. But those retired military and naval officers and their circumspect frigid wives who bristled with respectability were visibly affected by this first courier of danger that had appeared in England since William the Conqueror. They knew there at the Artillery Mansions that if a man could fly across the Channel, he could carry a gun, or drop a grenade. The whole aspect of total war was in the egg, the innocent-looking egg of Blériot's accomplishment. On the busses the next day we heard the English talk of nothing else. In the stores, the clerks who served us remarked about Blériot in their sales talk. England stood in the presence of something new. And then Selfridge, the American who had established a department store after the Chicago model, Marshall Field, again shocked England by hiring Blériot and his machine and exhibiting the winner on the main floor of his store. The enterprise, the audacity, the advertising innovation that Selfridge exhibited also unsettled the British. And for a week the queue of Britishers who lined up to file past the Blériot machine surrounded the entire block around the Selfridge store and at times curled around another block near by. It must have brought to the store hundreds of thousands of British who had avoided it pharisaically because it was American. We took the children and their grandmother down and joined the queue and edged along for hours with the amazed sightseers who were anxious to see the winner that had come across the sea. Even at the Artillery Mansions there were those so low, so debased, so wanting in proper British pride that they had joined the queue to peek for a few fleeting moments at the weapon that had leveled the walls of their island fortress. But they were tight-lipped about it. They would admit that it was most interesting, but would go no further. But the newspapers were unrestrained, and the men on the street had no compunctions about revealing their consternation. The walls of Jericho were atremble.

A few days before we left England, the children and their grandmother came up from Littlehampton, and we took them on another adventure. For days the newspapers were talking about the great parade that Lloyd George was backing, to demonstrate for his budget bill. The budget bill was, in its way, as revolutionary as the flight of Blériot, for it proposed a tax on land, a deep gouge in income tax on the rich. Moreover—and this is what crashed into the Artillery Mansions like a bomb—Lloyd George's supporters were saying that if the House of Lords opposed the budget, the Commons would take away its power of veto. Revolution was in the air. We were anxious to see the parade, so immediately after lunch one summer's day we hired a rattle-bang old taxi, all of us, and sallied forth. I never saw such a parade before. Organizations from all over England, Wales and Scotland were on the march—laboring men, farmers, farm workers, miners, clerks, the little people of England. They were singing as they marched. Bands were blaring, drums rolling, and it was almost orderly. They even kept step, many thousands of them. Hundreds of thousands were in line. For an hour we rode up and down alongside the procession where the police would let us cruise. I began to see old banners that I had seen in the Populist parade fluttering in the air. Among them were a lot of Jeffersonian mottoes that gripped at our hearts. Pretty soon, in the midst of a battalion of Welsh miners who had bands fore and aft, came, on a purple banner lettered in gold, the Jeffersonian slogan I had heard in the days of the Greenbackers and the Grangers and that I had seen coming down Main Street at Eldorado, and Commercial Street in Emporia, when the Farmers' Alliance and the Populists appeared:

Equal rights to all; special privileges to none.
—THOMAS JEFFERSON

How often my father had quoted that when he talked politics on his hundred forty-four feet of porches around the old White house in Eldorado. It was too much for me. I tapped my taxi driver on the shoulder and said: "Wheel in there behind that banner if you can!"

He could, and did. And that taxi load of Kansans, old and young, rolled slowly into the line and followed the banner for half an hour. We had to stop sometimes. It was a slow pace for a taxi. But I thought of Stubbs and Bristow in Kansas, and of Roosevelt and his fight for seven years in Washington. And I knew that old Bob La Follette would have crowded into the taxi if he had been on the sidewalk. And we were all proud and happy to follow his Jeffersonian flag in the great British revolutionary parade. It was the high day of our trip thus far. Galleries, concerts, strange places and stranger people all paled in significance beside this stupendous parade that shocked upper-class Britain to its foundations. Blériot and Lloyd George were unsettling the footing stones of civilization. Indeed these two harbingers of danger—these two symbols of machine-age revolution that was coming—the revolution, indeed, that was presenting its heralds with trumpets—were waking up, slowly but inevitably, a dazed world. The revolution had appeared. How, few of us knew. I should have known, of course, that the Kansas rebels whom I had fought and who took me in, were a part of this Lloyd George uprising, but I did not realize the unity of the revolt. As we rode in the procession in a rattle-bang old hack, and as I closed my eyes and heard the same old tunes from the bands along St. James's Park that I heard in Kansas: "John Brown's Body," among others, and "The Marseillaise," "Where Has My Highland Laddie Gone?" and "America" set to the tune of "God Save the King," I was stirred to the very roots of my being. Sallie and I held hands and when I opened my eyes through my tears I saw hers. We felt that we were a part of something great and beautiful. We did not know exactly what, except that we knew the under dog had slipped off his leash and this was his time to howl. So in our hearts we gave voice for him and with him.

The children were delighted, their grandmother baffled, by the size and mass and emotional impact of the parade. I think she bragged a little around the hotel when we returned that evening. What with my luncheon with John Burns and the bad odor Americans carried in general, there with the nobility and gentry (junior grade), because of Selfridge's bad form, this countenance of the Lloyd George budget parade was just another evidence that Americans were essentially lower.

In a few days we went to Ireland. My mother wanted to see the birthplace of her father, Thomas Hatten, and she said we would find the register of his marriage to Ann Kelly in the Catholic church there. So we went to Dublin, took a train to Longford, or the station nearest it, and went by an Irish sidecar to the cathedral. There, in the records of 1829, we saw the marriage certificate of my grandparents. They were both young. We rode around the countryside, which was pretty well dotted with Hattens, who were dirt poor, and we talked with some of them, old people who had heard that there was a Thomas Hatten of another generation who had gone to America. But the chickens were on the kitchen table, and there were dirt floors in their cabins, and my mother, who had been brought up with the Yankee Congregational sense of order, thrift and cleanliness, left Longford with no very great idea about the Hattens. She knew that they had come from England two hundred years before, but they were cottage

Irish to her and she left them sadly, and rarely mentioned them again.

We picked up our ship, the *Cretic,* for the home voyage at Queenstown (now Cobh), and our great adventure closed. We climbed up the ladder into the *Cretic* about breakfast time. The decks were lively. Tourists were running about to get a glimpse of Ireland, the last look at land before we pushed out into the ocean. Sallie and I settled the children and their grandmother in their cabin and then after breakfast we came out on deck.

We were parading up and down, arm in arm, and probably hand in hand, when my eye was caught by a New York Times in the hands of Franklin Hurd of Chicago. He was reading the paper, and on the side facing the deck I saw to my amazement—almost to my horror, so close are delight and fear—a half-page advertisement. I caught the words "A Certain Rich Man," and my own name in block type, and then the words "fourth large printing." I grabbed Sallie and we shamelessly stood trying to read the advertisement on the one side of the sheet while Mr. Hurd read the news on the other. He caught us at it. And, seeing our interest, offered us the paper. We tried to protest faintly, but took the paper and there saw the solid evidence that "A Certain Rich Man" was making a hit in the United States. There were highly flattering excerpts from critics; the leading literary commentators of the United States were offering their praises. But that phrase, "fourth large printing," told the tale. Our eyes glistened. We took the paper, folding it almost reverently, and hurried to our cabin. There we sat on the side of the berth and read it all with mounting and mixed emotions. Then almost automatically we turned, because there was nothing else to do in God's wide world, and slipped on our knees and said a little prayer of thanks. That moment was a high moment in our lives. From our wedding day to that day seemed an epoch of itself—clean, clear, definite, and joyful.

We got up smiling, maybe giggling self-consciously at our dramatics, and took the paper into the other room, where the children and their grandmother were reading. We showed it to them. Billy and my mother realized what it meant. If they did not, we got realization to them. And they were happy. The homeward journey began in joy.

At the dock a crowd of friends greeted us: Ida Tarbell, Ray Baker, the John Phillipses (he was editor of the American Magazine then), Lincoln Steffens, maybe Witter Bynner, and possibly Willa Cather (I am not sure) —a crowd of welcomers from the American Magazine met us, helped us through the customs and took us to our hotel. That night, to end the journey in a blaze of glory, we went to Coney Island, and there the children and my mother really had the thrill of the journey. My mother wore us all down, tired out the children, doing everything, riding the Ferris wheel, buying taffy, eating the gala food in stands and cafés, slam-banging through the Crazy-Cat House and riding on the roller coaster. Across one of the avenues of the Coney Island carnival was the great glittering sign "Ain't It Grand to Be Bughouse." We adopted it as the family motto for our coat-of-arms if we should ever get one, and went home limp and weary, with Grandma rampant and still waving the flag of Ireland in her heart.

So in the procession of my life—which had seen Willie White come and fade into Will White; and Will White grow up and become Will A. White, the poet—in that journey across the sea, another—perhaps not a more dignified figure but one a little bit more self-important—William Allen White came to his own and began to merge into still another: a man called "Bill"—Bill White, who was taking more and more part in the politics of his state and his nation. He was somebody. And the struggle of his life in that day was to keep people about him from knowing how keenly he realized it. So I tried to make modesty a protective habit and a mask.

CHAPTER LX

Taft: an Amiable Island

As we came into Emporia, we ran into the town's surprise for us. There was the band. There was a crowd, and as we stood on the platform we began to see men and women in strange old-fashioned costumes. The town and half a dozen friends in the state had worked out some sort of a costume party of characters in "A Certain Rich Man." The costumes were of the seventies and eighties. The characters gathered around us, picked us up— all of us, including the kids and their grandmother—and took us down to the grandstand in the park by the station, and the characters from "A Certain Rich Man" began to make speeches at us. Whereupon Sallie and I bolted. We just couldn't stand it. It was tragic, and funny, and pathetic and absurd and dear. So we ran to the phaeton where Old Tom was hitched near by, climbed in with the multitude trailing behind us. Someone grabbed the hereditary appurtenances of the family, put them in a neighbor's buggy and some way the band got ahead of us and we sailed through the street of Emporia to our home, trailing clouds of glory. There the crowd caught up with us, the band played, and they all sang "Home, Sweet Home." The children made a bolt for the barn and their playthings, and their grandmother went to her home next door and began cooking with all her might and main. And finally all the neighbors left the house and we were alone and happy.

The next morning a funny thing happened—one of those blessed events which have always come along to take the starch out of me. I was walking downtown between Seventh and Eighth when I came upon my doctor friend, whose license to practice had been taken away by the Supreme Court. He felt that I had much to do with it. But we were not personal enemies, did not make snoots at one another. In getting out of his buggy and putting on the sidewalk the leaden weight which served as a hitching post he looked up, and our eyes met.

I said, "Good morning!" He replied pleasantly, and, by way of exchanging a word, I said: "It's good to be home again."

Quicker than a flash he saw the opening I had left and said:
"Oh, have you been out of town? I hadn't missed you!"
I grinned. He snickered. And the episode was closed. It did me good.
needed just that.

But "A Certain Rich Man" was upon us. In New York we had learned
hat the sales were moving along. We had a good contract with the pub-
isher, and the royalties were coming in heavy and fast. In the end, what
vith various editions, including a cheap Grosset and Dunlap edition, a dollar
ibrary edition, and a school reference edition with glossary and notes
(which still sells, by the way), the book sold a quarter of a million copies.
And with the proceeds we immediately went to work enlarging the Gazette
ouilding, and buying a new linotype. I set to work immediately writing a
eries of articles on the political changes that were in the air, afterwards
oublished in a book called "The Old Order Changeth." It was an attempt
to define the issues of the day, new issues then in politics but now a genera-
ion old, and to chart the course of the new movement then under the
eadership of Roosevelt, Bryan, La Follette, and a dozen smaller figures in
he parties, furnishing factional contests within both parties in most of the
northern states. I worked hard on it, and did what I thought was a research
ob writing to official sources in every state, getting a list of the new meas-
ires passed there and really outlining definite trends. Politically the people
vere feeling for new weapons of democracy: the secret ballot, called "the
Australian ballot"; the primary; the direct election of United States Sena-
ors; the initiative, referendum, and recall; a commission form of government in the cities; and other laws amending the registration laws which
orought down part of the control of the citizen. In the economic field the
movement which Theodore Roosevelt was calling "a square deal" advocated
an income tax amendment, postal savings banks, parcel post, regulation of
he railroads, prosecution and breaking of the trusts, a pure-food-and-drug
aw with state laws to support it, extension of laws promoting public health
and hygiene, shorter hours for labor, collective bargaining—and this was the
catch phrase, "with representatives of their own choosing"—workingmen's
compensation laws, state and national extension of the civil service, the
movement for good roads, the regulation and control of insurance com-
anies, banks and savings institutions. These institutions were greatly abused
n some states by scoundrels in charge of them. Along with this movement
commencing at the beginning of the century was the sweep toward national
Prohibition. It was a lively issue during the first decade of the century, and,
peaking rather broadly, progressive state leaders fell in line behind prohibi-
ion. Roosevelt politely rejected it. Bryan was wholeheartedly for it. La
Follette denounced it. But the state leaders, who were canny and probably
never gave it much thought, were for it. Anyway, in the West where the

Puritan tradition still held, they believed that it would work for econom
good. So it was a part of "the movement." This book, "The Old Ord
Changeth," was a sort of standard text and sold along for ten years aft
it was published in 1910. It was used in colleges, and along with "A Certa
Rich Man." "The Old Order Changeth" had its place and did its wor
in its time.

I had more than an academic interest in politics. I had been chairm
and Republican precinct committeeman in the Fourth Ward for a doze
years, had served on the state central committee and on the executive cor
mittee of my county and state organization. When I came home fro
Europe, I began consulting with other independent, progressive-mind
Republicans over the country about President Taft's obvious decision to
with the conservatives. For the most part, we progressives were Republica
who had no use for the Republican party except as we could use it for wh
we thought was the good of the country. We were beginning to form
group across the country. In California, young Hiram Johnson, the refor
governor, was our representative. Half a dozen men almost of his size we
gathered around him. In the Northwest, Senator Jonathan Bourne and W
S. U'Ren were with us. And Senator W. E. Borah often met with our grou
when we were discussing ways and means and policy. In Colorado, Edwa
P. Costigan crystallized the progressive sentiment about his leadershi
In Nebraska, George Norris represented our group. He was the leader of
band of Congressional insurgents who were bent upon breaking down th
rule of Speaker Cannon in the House. In Missouri, we looked to Herbe
Hadley. In Iowa, Senator Dolliver was our local leader, with Cummir
about to be elected Senator, ready to take Dolliver's place. In Minneso
Senator Moses Clapp was our leader; and of course in Wisconsi
La Follette and his supporters became our allies. In Michigan, Govern
Chase S. Osborn stood with us. In Illinois, Medill McCormick, Raymor
Robins, and Harold Ickes were the recognized leaders. In Indian
Beveridge, somewhat coyly and at first rather timidly, sidled into the co
spiracy. In Ohio, James R. Garfield, Theodore Roosevelt's Secretary of th
Interior, agreed with our principles but was a little conservative abo
rough treatment in the Republican party. We thought, and probably I
thought, that President Taft had definitely broken a promise to keep Ga
field in his Cabinet. In Pennsylvania, of course, Gifford Pinchot stood o
as our state leader. In New Jersey, George Record, Everett Colby, and ha
a dozen others, some of whom afterwards rallied around Wilson, gave th
insurgent Republican movement their cordial effective support. In Ne
England, only Massachusetts furnished us with dependable leaders. The
Charles Sumner Bird carried the banner. Around him gathered Albe
Bushnell Hart, of Harvard, and Matthew Hale and Arthur D. Hill

Boston, who were practical politicians and knew how to get results. Of course in New York State, Roosevelt, with his faction, was a tower of strength. But Roosevelt himself was in Africa hunting big game. He had gone there to give Taft a free hand. He had gone with doubts and misgivings, for from the first, immediately after the election, President Taft wanted to make it plain to the country that he was not going to be the shadow of T. R. It takes a tactful man to make that kind of gesture; and Taft was clumsy. He did not know that he had hurt Roosevelt, and in the White House he surrounded himself consciously or unconsciously with men who patronized Roosevelt but did not realize his power. Differing with him on fundamental issues, they belittled him, which is the easiest way to deal with your opponent in politics. And all of this belittlement and aloofness produced an estrangement even before Roosevelt left the country.

With Roosevelt gone, Taft had no restraining influence. He made a definite break with the progressive leaders. In matters of patronage, he recognized the conservative senators, where a Republican insurgent senator had to be rebuked. Senator Bristow of Kansas was set aside, and Senator Curtis was the President's Kansas mouthpiece.

I knew all of these progressive leaders. They had been my friends for several years. Excepting the Congressmen in Washington, I probably knew more of the progressive leaders across the country than most men, and my letter files show that I was writing to them all, stirring up trouble for Taft. I went to the White House to see him before we started our campaign. I hoped I could show him that if he would give us fair treatment, we should be glad to work with him. We met at luncheon. Mrs. Taft was there, and the President's half-brother Charles P. Taft. The President explained that this was the first time Mrs. Taft had come to the table at the White House for several months. She was at that time afflicted with a curious amnesia, but she spoke pleasantly. And yet I felt that she regarded me as a curious kind of horned toad. And brother Charley knew my kind most definitely. I tried to steer the conversation toward my mission. The President knew what I wanted to say. It would be disagreeable, and I could feel him edging away from any serious talk. We had a most amiable time. At one point I began, and said:

"Here is what we want definitely: Support for the income tax amendment, and for postal savings banks, for a railroad regulation law; and we want our Senators to have a—"

And there the President began to chuckle and said: "Oh, White, if you mean Bristow, you know Bristow."

I did. He was disagreeable and tactless and edgy, and I could not help grinning. The President grinned, and said:

"Go talk to Bristow!"

Which was a good answer. It turned away wrath. And either he or h
brother or Mrs. Taft cut in with some irrelevant remark, and the signif
cance of the conference was over—a futile journey, a fool's errand.

I can see Taft now as we sat in the sunshine after lunch on an enclose
porch in the White House. He was a tall man and had accumulated a l
of fat on his long body. To me his legs seemed short for his torso. His fac
was full, long, florid; and he had a light blondish mustache, dark hai
and a chuckling face which deceived many people into thinking that l
agreed with what they were saying. I am sure that Theodore Rooseve
had been completely fooled by Taft's amiable gurgling obbligato whe
they talked, and had really thought, when he left the White House, th
Taft would carry out the Roosevelt policies. He did, but as Senate
Dolliver remarked, "on a shutter!"

That sunny day, as we sat for half an hour talking over everything und
the sun but the thing he knew I wanted to say, I realized how hopele
was the job of weaning him from the reactionary crowd that was surroun
ing him. It was Dolliver again who said:

"Taft is an amiable island; entirely surrounded by men who kno
exactly what they want."

I could not have asked more courtesy, more consideration, more cordi
hospitality, yet occasionally when I referred to Cannon, or Aldrich, wit
the gentle malediction that was in my heart, I could see his eye behind h
smile veiling with almost the hint of a serpentine glitter. The day we ha
spent together on the train in 1907 or '08 taught me to take warning whe
that glitter flashed across his sweet and gentle countenance. When I le
the White House I knew that I and my kind, the whole progressive lc
were anathema—outlawed from his counsel. He would have none of u
Outwardly it seemed that he did not want to be disturbed. Many progre
sives felt that his detachment from our group was a result of a lazy desi
to avoid disagreeable encounters.

It was not that. He was convinced that we were mad. He was a co
sistent, honest, courageous, most intelligent conservative. He believed i
the existing order. He was nice about it, most felicitous, and could at tim
smile at it with indulgent condescension. But it was his world. He deep
resented the hands that would touch the Ark of his Covenant.

Many times after we parted that day I tried by letter and by messeng
to reach him, to make him understand how serious was the uprising again
his creed and crowd. Possibly he knew, for he was sensitive. But if l
knew, he was unmoved. He walked to his doom "a gentleman unafraid.

CHAPTER LXI

The Rise of the Progressives

THAT CURIOUS insurgence in American politics which afterwards was known as the progressive movement was working in both of the parties in the United States in that first decade of the new century, which may well be called the Roosevelt decade. Bryan had appeared in American politics. In the last decade of the old century he had taken the leadership of the Democratic party away from the old silk stockings, and given it to the Populists. They, their heirs and assigns controlled the Democratic party except in its convention of 1904. For a dozen years following 1901, Theodore Roosevelt led the progressive movement in the Republican party. His leadership was challenged by that of Robert M. La Follette, first governor and then United States Senator from Wisconsin. La Follette represented the left wing of Republican insurgents, and an intransigent left wing it was. Roosevelt and La Follette wanted, on the whole, about the same things, but they were poles apart in their methods. Roosevelt would make a noisy fight, and in the end would compromise when he had gone as far as he could. La Follette never compromised. He would prefer to dramatize his cause in failure and take it up later rather than to surrender one jot or tittle of his original bill of contention. La Follette was bitter in his controversies. He was merciless in his attacks. In all my life I have never seen a braver man in politics. Moreover, he made his bravery count. He had come up from the ranks in Wisconsin politics, when those ranks were organized against him. When he came to the Senate, he had a long line of Wisconsin achievements in his baggage, which afterwards went into the platforms and statutes of other states. And the principles for which La Follette fought were known later as the Roosevelt policies.

But Theodore Roosevelt kept pleasant associations with his political enemies where he could. He was bitter enough at times, but I never found him stubborn. He would listen to the populace for compromise. His success lay in a rather large stock of half loaves which were better than none. La

Follette was a "lean and hungry" Cassius to Theodore Roosevelt's Caesar. It was inevitable that they should clash; and, clashing, it was written in the stars that they should never respect one another. And I think, as a friend of both, I am fairly safe and charitable in saying that they were jealous of one another constitutionally, temperamentally, inevitably. I trusted both. I admired both. Probably "admired" is too cold a word; "adored" is too ardent. But between admiration and adoration, I gave each of them a warm heart and I hope an affectionate loyalty. I never was a go-between. I was too smart for that. I should have been ground between their suspicions and probably, in my instinctive desire not to give offense nor to bring pain to a friend, I should have betrayed them both.

But that decade which climaxed in 1912 was a time of tremendous change in our national life, particularly as it affected our national attitudes. The American people were melting down old heroes and recasting the mold in which heroes were made. Newspapers, magazines, books—every representative outlet for public opinion in the United States was turned definitely away from the scoundrels who had in the last third or quarter of the old century cast themselves in monumental brass as heroes. The muckrakers were melting it down. The people were questioning the way every rich man got his money. They were ready to believe—and too often they were justified in the belief—that he was a scamp who had pinched pennies out of the teacups of the poor by various shenanigans who was distributing his largess to divert attention from his rascality.

Reform was in the air. In forging new weapons of democracy in the state legislatures and in the Congress, the people were setting out on crusade. And I was wearing the crusader's armor. A sudden new interest in the under dog was manifest in the land. He was not exalted, but universally the people began to understand what slums were, what sweatshops were, what exploited labor was, what absentee landlordism had become in our urban life, what railroad rates were doing to the farmer and to the consumer. Two-cent railroad fares were demanded in the states. Anti-pass laws were being adopted state by state. Railroad regulation was everywhere an issue—on the stump, in the legislature, in Congress. The protective tariff, as a principle, began to irk the Republican leaders of reform chiefly because it was regarded as the bulwark of "economic privilege"—and those two words were beginning to be common. Roosevelt was coining bitter phrases. La Follette and Bryan in the white heat of their indignation were melting rhetorical maledictions to hurl at the beneficiaries of privilege.

But the point of it all, as I look back upon it now after nearly forty years, is that the leaders—even Bryan, Roosevelt, La Follette—even the state leaders who grew up in more than half the American commonwealths were the product of their times. If it had not been they who rode at the head of the procession in the red sash and gilded epaulet of political powers, others would have come along, for it was a people's movement. The mercy that permeated their hearts, their yearning for justice which sent them to the news stands and bookstores buying by tons newspapers, books and magazines that told them how to be intelligently just and fair in their political aspirations—all published, edited and written by men who took the coloring of their environment—sprang from a widening sense of duty, rather than of rights, moving in the hearts of the American people in that decade.

I did not know at the time how completely I was a product of my environment. If I was a young cocksure reactionary in the nineties, it was because my kind and class were that, and I fear sadly that I must confess that unconsciously I took the protective intellectual, political and social color of my time in the first decade. So we all went together down the road of reform to progress, Bryan, La Follette, Roosevelt; scores of leaders in scores of states—little Bryans, little La Follettes, little Roosevelts appeared in scores of statehouses and countless city halls. They were not conscious hypocrites. Perhaps I had better say "we" than they. We were the people. What the people felt about the vast injustice that had come with the settlement of a continent, we, their servants—teachers, city councilors, legislators, governors, publishers, editors, writers, representatives in Congress and senators—all made a part of our creed and so carried the banner of their cause. Of course demagogues came, many of them, who did not know intellectually nor care emotionally—political paranoiacs who whanged away and did probably more harm than good. But taking it by and large, the representatives of the progressive movement in that first glamorous vigorous decade when America turned the corner from conservatism were the product of the aspiration of the people. They were leaders who were led. Some way, into the hearts of the dominant middle class of this country, had come a sense that their civilization needed recasting, that their government had fallen into the hands of self-seekers, that a new relation should be established between the haves and the have-nots, not primarily because the have-nots were loyal, humble, worthy and oppressed —Heaven knows we knew that the under dog had fleas, mange and a bad disposition—but rather because we felt that to bathe and feed the under dog would release the burden of injustice on our own conscience. We should do it even unto the least of these. We were not maudlin, as I recollect it. We were joyous, eager, happily determined to make life more fair and lovely for ourselves by doing such approximate justice as we could to those who obviously were living in the swamps, morasses, deserts, and wildernesses of this world. It was not religious—at least not pious—this progressive movement. It was profoundly spiritual. And the insurgents,

who were later called progressives, had the crusaders' ardor, and felt f[or]
one another the crusaders' fellowship. They sang songs, carried banner[s]
marched in parades, created heroes out of their own ideals. It was a[n]
evangelical uprising without an accredited Messiah. Because I wrote book[s]
and magazine articles, had my newspaper and sometimes went aroun[d]
making progressive speeches, I was probably in the list of the first hundre[d]
leaders who were thrown into the public eye by this evangelical demonstra[?]
tion. I was one of perhaps fifty Republicans who had the confidence [of]
Roosevelt and La Follette.

I fear I have painted too smooth a picture. All this social and politic[al]
change did not appear automatically in American politics; the spirit [of]
change did not wave a wand and say, "let there be light." In every stat[e]
indeed in every county and city across the land, these progressive leade[rs]
in both parties rose only after bitter struggle. They were the product [of]
more than a lively contest. Sometimes the contests were combats. The co[n]
servatives did not give up control of the party organization in the norther[n]
states, at least, without bloody battle. And it was not all black or all whit[e]
The battles were in gray areas. Demagogues on both sides clamored f[or]
leadership. The conservatives spent money and the progressives spe[nt]
time, energy and sometimes trickery. One side was as good as the oth[er]
morally. Of course men had to change sides if the progressive minori[ty]
became a majority in many states.

As a concrete example, consider the case of my old employer, Be[nt]
Murdock. In the seventies and eighties, Bent had been the righthand m[an]
of George R. Peck, the railroad representative of the state, who ruled it [in]
those decades with an iron hand. Bent Murdock, as a state senator, as [a]
member of the state organization, and as a lobbyist, had served mammo[n]
faithfully, and mammon had kept his ribs well larded. His New Yor[k]
clothes, his bell-crowned silk hat, the boutonniere in his lapel every day, [a]
geranium and at formal times a gardenia, his taste for life at the big hote[ls]
of our cities, his ample table in Eldorado, all cost money. But even in t[he]
nineties, his chains were galling him. He tried to break away, and did, fro[m]
the system which he had done his part to establish. In the early part of t[he]
century, in Kansas, he had joined a group known as the boss-busters. H[is]
group was composed of two kinds of politicians, those who wanted to u[n]
seat the Leland faction—for old Cy was the boss—and those who real[ly]
felt the need for political freedom. Mr. Murdock as a boss-buster was greet[ed]
with laughter. He was the boss of his county, and as a boss he supporte[d]
the big bosses in the state. Nevertheless he was honest about it, I thin[k]
and wanted the boss-busters purged of their self-seekers. He was an insu[r]
gent. In the middle of the century's first decade, Mr. Murdock stood va[li]
antly with Stubbs for all the Stubbs reforms. The Eldorado Republic[an]

430

was one of a dozen Republican papers which supported Stubbs to the limit. And by 1908 when Stubbs was elected governor, Mr. Murdock—Old Bent to the rank and file of Kansas Republicans—was among the first score of Stubbs' trustworthy lieutenants.

I left Kansas in the first month of the Stubbs administration. I knew—for Mr. Murdock had told me, and I had told Stubbs, who received my message blinking hard and grinning rather stonily—that Mr. Murdock would like to be one of the three state railroad commissioners. I knew he had two motives, each struggling for supremacy in his heart, when he asked for that job. First, he wanted to show the railroad politicians who were waning and had seen their best days that he could be a railroad commissioner without their help, and that he could be honest with the people. And second, I knew in my heart that he wanted to be a railroad commissioner because under the law and custom of the state, the railroad commission had its own private car. This car was carried over the state free by the railroads while the commission was assessing the railroad property. Its larder was supplied by the railroads. Its porters were taken from the Pullman service. It was a magnificent equipage. And I knew as well as I knew anything that Old Bent wanted to show Marie Antoinette Murdock that even if he had joined the reformers, he still could command a private car, and stop at Eldorado and take her aboard, queening it as she did in the old and glamorous days. The insatiable pain that gnawed at her vitals still required dulling, and when she had conquered pain Mrs. Murdock was a brilliant and—still, in her late sixties—a beautiful woman. She lowered no flag. She stuck to her lipstick and her rouge and her curls. And for all his side glances down the primrose path, Uncle Bent was terribly proud of Aunt Net when she put on her war paint and went forth from her recluse's chamber into the world for conquest. We Eldoradoans, of whom I was an emeritus citizen, knew that. And if he could be a railroad commissioner as a reward for leaving the fleshpots of conservatism, his cup would have run over.

When I left for Europe Mr. Murdock's candidacy was still on Stubbs' desk. When I came back the first thing I inquired about was Mr. Murdock's status. They told me this story. I forget whether it was Joe Dolley, Stubbs' right-hand man, or Dave Leahy, Stubbs' private secretary, who told it. Whichever one it was said:

"God, Bill, it was awful. Stubbs couldn't do that. He couldn't make a man a railroad commissioner who had been the railroad's footman. It wouldn't do. Stubbs knew and I knew that the old man was earnest and honest and convinced. But it just wouldn't do. So I went to him in the National Hotel last spring and broke it to him. I said:

" 'Bent, we just can't do it!'

"He asked: 'Why? What's the matter with me anyway? Don't you be-lieve I have served Stubbs faithfully, and well?'

"I said to him: 'Bent, can't you see? Can't you see?'

"And he shook his head: 'What have I done?' he cried. And repeated it And I told him: 'Bent, it's your long years with George R. Peck and his dynasty.'

"His face flushed and he cried out: 'Wasn't Stubbs a railroad contractor? Didn't he make all his million dollars feeding moldy beans and wormy dried apples and infected and condemned beef to the railroad construction gangs? Wasn't he a pet of the railroads in his day?'

"And I said: 'Well, maybe so. I don't know. But anyway you know how Stubbs feels about it, and I have told you.'

"And he asked: 'What did he say?'

"And I told him blunt; I said: 'Bent, Stubbs says he can't make a rail-road commissioner out of a man who has been upstairs with every railroad in the state for the last thirty-five or forty years.'

"He looked at me a moment. The tears came into his old rheumy eye and he cried out like a stuck hog: 'Did Stubbs say that? Did Stubbs say that of me, his friend!' And then he put his arm on the table, laid his head on it, and his body shook in sobs for a moment. Then when his grief and anger were spent, he looked up piteously and said: 'Well, I suppose it's all right. Ask him what else he has got.'"

It was a terrible story. I have often thought of it. But Stubbs was kind He made Uncle Bent fish and game commissioner. Stubbs sensed the en-chantment of a private car. The fish and game commissioner had a private car with a fish tank in it which went about the state putting little catfish bass and carp into the streams and lakes. Back of the fish tank were some berths, a kitchen, a dining room, and a club car. Uncle Bent took it, and his spirit was healed. It was his car. He did not have to share it with two other commissioners. It was a bit shabby compared with the shiny office car that the railroad commissioner had, but it was a private car. It stopped at Eldorado and stood on the siding sometimes, receiving the worshipful homage of the multitude.

As soon as I returned home, I sent him "A Certain Rich Man." I sent it in pride, for he had believed in me since I was a child. As a boy I had received his encouragement. With a fatherly affection he jeered and gibed at me a young man. He had witnessed my rise in Kansas politics with real pride He even went to a university commencement once when I was on the Board of Regents.

"You ought to have seen old Mr. Bill," he told the crowd in the Eldorado post office one day, "up there on the platform, a regent, taking three chairs one for his shoulder, one for his big fat bottom, and a leg thrown over the

432

other. God, he looked like an eastern potentate draped over those chairs. You ought to have seen him!"

And I knew when I heard the story that he was very proud of me. So, hearing that he was sick, I went down to see him. I did not realize that it was his deathbed. In his active life he had spanned the chasm between the two worlds: the old world of the pioneers in the Missouri Valley and the new world of their restless, discontented, aspiring sons. In his own way, he had been a triumphant leader in both. In both worlds he had been somebody. He died a fortnight after I saw him.

Not long after the funeral I came down to Eldorado on some errand but really to visit his family, and particularly Aunt Net. She had put her name at the head of the paper as Marie Antoinette Murdock. The two girls were downtown when I called. I sat familiarly fumbling at the piano, waiting for her to buckle on her armor against the pain that was always eating at her vitals; and while I was playing old songs of her generation that my mother used to sing, she came down the stairs in full regalia—a flowing lacy gown with sleeves draped and dripping with lace—and made her usual entrance. After I had greeted her she said:

"Go on, play some more of those old songs."

I did: "Her Bright Smile Haunts Me Still," "Come Where My Love Lies Dreaming," "The Long and Weary Day," "Lorena," and maybe another one or two. She sat in the thronelike chair with carved lions' heads for arms. Her lips moved as she whispered in her heart the old words of the old tunes she dared not try to sing, fearing she would croak. When I got up, she went to the piano, whirled the seat round to fit her torso and sat down to play with a curious rolling style that I had often heard her use when she rendered a flashy polonaise or mazurka. She did not play one of those now, but one of Chopin's poignant nocturnes, as I remember it, a heartrending thing, in her flourishing style, but pathetic. She got up after her performance, smiled deprecatingly, and sat down; and we talked of the old days when she taught elocution in the schools and when Byron now, the town's bad boy, tried to bedevil her and she grabbed him with all the feline strength of a woman in her thirties and shook him so that all over the room we could hear his teeth rattle. It had been the turning point in his life. Later he had become a minister. We had our laugh at the old days, and I told her how she used to scare the daylights out of me when she intoned "The Raven" in her deep resonant contralto. She added gayly, "and the bells, bells, bells" in the same sepulchral voice. Then we fell to talking about the old days, the little Eldorado, the wide place in the road—so rough, so crude, so terrible, which had frightened Alice's mother to death. And we talked about Cynthia, Aunt Net's little girl who came to town with her and died the centennial year, angel child if there ever was

433

one. How strange it was that that town, deeper than Pompeii, should have had erected over it this lovely county seat shaded with elm trees, where lawns encompassed lovely homes, where flowers and shrubs grew down the wide stone walks to the sidewalks in the street, and a decent, peaceful lovely world flourished all about us. She spoke beautifully of me, told me some things Mr. Murdock said after I had gone from his deathbed. For a moment, sitting there in front of her overstuffed hand-carved thronelike chair, I was the Pip to her Miss Havisham as I had been in the early eighties when the Murdocks roomed at our house and I sat on a little oil cloth hassock in front in the gleaming glow of the nickel-plated base-burner as she read to me "The Tide of Enderby" from Tennyson's "Maud." The years had dropped away—thirty of them. I could see at the end of half an hour that the pain was coming back. She rose, shook hands, flowed like a stately stream out of the room again. On the stairway she stood for a moment looking back at me, holding herself against the tug of the pain; then smiling regally, she cried in that dramatic elocutionary voice that I knew as a little child, a deep resonant contralto: "Quoth the Raven, 'Nevermore.'"

And so she made an exit—"the rare and radiant maiden whom the angel called"—Aunt Net. It was as though, with all her frills and frizzes and fur belows, with all her sentimental heart and dear illusion, she represented the past Victorian days, with its cynical prudery, with its fine generosity. A time when things were set and settled, and the social universe molded like a layer cake all tied up in the baker's box with a blue ribbon knotted on top, ready to deliver in a pink cotton and tinfoil world.

"Quoth the Raven, 'Nevermore!'"

CHAPTER LXII

The Roosevelt Rebellion

WHEN ROOSEVELT CAME HOME from Africa, where he had gone directly after the Taft inauguration, he found turmoil in the political air. The opposition of Taft to the insurgents, his open espousal of the Congressional leadership of Cannon and Aldrich, had made the White House a citadel of conservatism. We, meaning half a dozen or so of those insurgents who had Mr. Roosevelt's confidence, had sent messengers into the African jungle to tell him to beware of the change that had come over the leadership of the party. He had sent word back publicly mentioning my name and that of Governor Stubbs of Kansas, as one of those whom he would consult when he returned. He sent our names because they were significant of his left-flank battalion. When he came home he was, of course, pulled and hauled by each side, by conservatives, liberals, reactionaries, and radicals. I found a letter the other day that I wrote to Colonel Roosevelt just after he had come back from Africa, in the spring of 1910. A paragraph or so from that letter will convey my feelings, my political attitude at the time. After explaining why I felt that Taft had failed as Roosevelt's successor, I wrote:

I am against the movement that would make you a Presidential candidate. I have said nothing unkind to President Taft and have not criticized his administration. Yet I may not be classed as an ardent supporter of it. Its intense materialism has saddened me. I have been unhappy many times at the way things have gone. But I believe sincerely that the country would be better off with Taft until 1916 than with you in the next Presidential term. Of course the country would be further along in 1916, with you in the Presidency. You would take us a long way ahead. But as matters stand, the people are not looking to the Presidential office for leadership now. They are beginning to walk alone. They are going ahead themselves in their own way. There is a distinctly growing, automatically organizing public opinion in America today that is the same in every section and corner of the Republic. It knows no class or occupation. It is national. It will triumph over every President, Congress or court that can be found. It is the outgrowth of necessity. With you in the White House, the people feel secure, so the necessity of a self-guarded sentiment is removed. If you were in the office in 1916, we would undoubtedly have better laws and a cleaner administration than we may have without you, but what we would have without you would be net gain, and we would be in a position to fight whatever devils are sent against us in the future with greater success, than if we did the ornamental standing-around for four years while you did the real work.

It seems to me that I expressed the sentiment of a considerable majority of the progressive leaders at that time. We had met often in small caucusing groups and conferences in Chicago, in New York and in Washington. We felt that we could win with La Follette, if Taft had to be overthrown. We were saving our ace. This was in 1910. Events in the two years that followed changed our attitude. But that spring of 1910 the country was politically seething with the yeast of a progressive movement. More people were living under the initiative and referendum when Roosevelt came back from Africa than were living under the direct primary before he left. The direct primary was almost universal. The initiative and referendum was either established or on its way, going to the people as constitutional amendments in twenty states, the more forward commonwealths. In a dozen states, by a primary subterfuge, the people were voting directly for United States Senators. A federal income tax was well on its way. The postal savings bank was all but here. The primary and the anti-pass laws in the various states had broken the sway of the railroads. The national anti-pass law was established, and two-cent-fare laws were working in so many states that the railroads had surrendered to a two-cent fare in large areas of interstate commerce.

That spring in the primaries, conservatives in statehouses and in Congress were being mowed down. It was our job in Kansas, we who worked together politically around Governor Stubbs and Senator Bristow, Victor Murdock and Henry Allen, to bring out Republican candidates for Congress in every district not then represented by a Progressive. I did much of the leg work on that job and in the August primaries we turned up with six Progressive nominees out of eight for our Congressional delegation. It took a lot of work, and as I remember it, I had a lot of fun with it, as I think the others of our group had also. For as I remember them, not only in Kansas but generally everywhere, those progressive leaders were a rollicking crowd—except La Follette. He was grim. So were his followers in the Northwest. But the rest of us on the wrecking crew of conservatism enjoyed our work. The primaries that spring and summer and the election that fall strengthened the progressive minority in Congress and gave us control of half a dozen new statehouses.

It fell to my lot, when the state party council met in Kansas in August, to write the Republican platform. It was regarded as most radical. It preceded the New Deal program by twenty years, and before I submitted it to the party council in Topeka, I sent a draft of it to Theodore Roosevelt, who gave us a green light.

Reading that platform again, I am pleased with the forthright way it goes about its business. The demands and promises of the Republican Party in Kansas are scheduled in the platform as Pledge Number 1, Pledge Number 2, and so down through nearly two dozen specific, unequivocal promises. They were:

A pledge to the Kansas members in Congress to vote for a revision of the Payne-Aldrich Tariff Act, "using as a basis for fixing duties the difference between the cost of production at home and abroad with a reasonable profit for American manufacture." That afterward was the basis of the Bull Moose platform of 1912.

The second pledge was that the Kansas Republican delegation would vote for a tariff commission and that it would also, in revising the tariff, demand a vote on one schedule at a time. Also to vote for a rule that would make membership on the important House committees elective instead of appointive by the speaker.

Pledge Number Five bound the Kansas delegation to vote for a law providing for a jail sentence for the willful violators of the anti-trust law; and a similar pledge to amend the interstate commerce law so that the Interstate Commerce Commission would have power and money to ascertain the physical value of railroads, the idea being that railroads should not use one valuation for taxes and another for rate-making. And the next pledge bound the Republican Congressmen to vote for laws regulating the capitalization of corporations and to give the Interstate Commerce Commission authority over the issue of stocks and bonds of common carriers. This was a vital issue in American politics for twenty years afterward. The Kansas Congressmen were also pledged to stand by the conservation principle, and to support a constitutional amendment providing for the direct election of United States Senators. So much for national affairs.

The Kansas Republicans in the legislature were pledged to vote for a law placing all public utilities, railways, telegraph, telephone, power companies, street railways, distributors of gas, even by retail by pipeline, under the control of a State Board having authority over the issue of stocks and bonds and to value the property of these utilities for taxation on the basis of rate-making valuations. And here is an interesting pledge to compel corporations doing business in Kansas to begin their litigation in the Kansas court and not "to take refuge in the federal courts until the litigation in question has been passed upon by the Kansas Supreme Court." That law was twenty years in appearing, and then it became a federal statute. The party also pledged state constitutional amendments providing for the initiative and referendum and recall, and also a law providing for publicity of campaign contributions as to source and disbursements. And they pledged a Presidential primary in Kansas, instructed the Kansas legislature to vote for the ratification of the income tax, and also promised to take up the practicability of a workmen's compensation law for Kansas. It came a few years later. The state bank guarantee law was pledged in that platform.

It was what might well be called a forward-looking platform. Yet not one demand of the platform was out of line with the general tendency of the times. It was this platform which Colonel Roosevelt made the basis of his Osawatomie speech.

Shortly after the party council, he came West and spoke in Kansas at Osawatomie, the home of the Kansas saint, John Brown. In fact, he dedicated a monument to the old fanatic and in nearly an hour's speech devoted less than seven lines to our hero. But he did get squarely on the Kansas Progressive platform, a position which shocked his friends in the East. They were much more conservative than we were in the West. And many of his old Harvard cronies, who were rallying about him and urging him to oppose Taft, seemed to us in the West to be using the Colonel rather than promoting our cause. Very likely these Harvard patriots had no deep sense of the issues of the hour. They wanted to shout "To hell with Yale," and Roosevelt's candidacy afforded them a beautiful opening. It is hard to bring back today the sense of excitement, almost of tumult, that was in the air over this land in the summer and autumn of 1910. It was revolutionary. Colonel Roosevelt joined it, and despite my qualms and cautions, became the leader of the revolution. He had not yet publicly broken with Taft. But when he endorsed the Kansas Republican platform which was aimed directly at all that Taft stood for, it was plain to the American people that a clash was ahead between the ex-President and the President. La Follette saw it. He was naturally bitter in private and did not conceal his distrust of Roosevelt. They were so different that mutual distrust was inevitable and a break was always a liability to our cause.

The country was on a boom. The short collapse of 1907 had cleaned up many bad debts. Credit expansion was evident everywhere. The railroads were built, but the great industries were just beginning to establish their plants through the East, the middle states, and the Pacific coast. The banks by which one meant the banks of Wall Street, as the core and center of our financial system—were beginning to take over the management of industry. The old founders of American industry, who established the mills and factories after the Civil War, disappeared. Their sons were no bred in the environment which made those old iron men, and their grand sons sold out to chain operators who were financed by the banks. Banker appointed hustling young men from college as managers of the plant and expanded them, for credit was easy. So the boom was on. Emporia wa growing. The Gazette grew with the town and county. We were making six or seven thousand dollars a year from the paper, and I was making as much and sometimes more than that, writing books and magazine articles. I invested everything above our living expenses in Emporia real estate. Never in all my life have stocks, bonds, or mortgages or any evidence of another man's indebtedness to me interested me as an investment. I do not believe I ever owned a bond, a mortgage, or a share of stock, at least not over a few months. But the Gazette building was paid for, our home was paid for, we owned one or two downtown places, and life was secure. I spent no money for liquor, poker or ladies in those years, and so if I cared to put a few hundred dollars into the candidacy of a friend for Congress, or for a state office, I could do so without feeling a pinch. In politics, it is remarkable what you can do with a hundred dollars if you spend it yourself. It is also sad to think of how little you can do in politics with a hundred dollars if you let someone else spend it.

The Little Major, at the bank, was having a sad time with me. Of course he regarded my political activities as definitely insane. But they were successful. I had a little power at that time, more power in the state than he had. For his friends had been mowed down by the rising tide of insurgency. If I had failed, I think our relations would have been different. But I carried a decent deposit in his bank. I owed no money there. So he looked upon me as something like a prodigal son, with sad but none the less genuine affection. One day I went into the bank on some errand, and the Little Major, who by then was in his seventies, and walked like a wiry skeleton with a soft and not very steady tread, came pattering out of his room, took me back and there sat me down opposite himself at his desk. He hemmed ominously as he always did when he was about to relieve his mind, opened a drawer carefully, pulled out a large manila envelope, dumped its contents on the glass top of his desk, again cleared his throat, and said:

"I was going over my papers the other day, clearing up old documents, and I found this which I thought you would like to see."

He shoved it across the desk. It was a letter in longhand, written on the stationery of the United States Supreme Court, signed by an eminent justice, complaining to the Major, who at the time had been the political representative of Senator Plumb in all dubious matters—complaining that the two receivers of the Katy Railroad, whom the writer had appointed when he was a circuit judge, were not, since he had come to the Supreme Court, making their promised and agreed monthly payments to his sister. The justice complained that she was a poor woman and needed the money.

When I read this over and saw the name signed, I remembered the story that Benjamin Harrison told me about Senator Plumb and the nomination

439

of Plumb's candidate for the Supreme Court. How full of wrath Plumb was! How insolent and arrogant he had been with the President. And I saw in a flash the whole system of American politics wherein wealth controlled government, exemplified perfectly with a dozen lines in longhand of that letter before me. There were the courts controlling the railroads through receiverships. There was the Senate controlling the courts through what, in that day, passed not for corruption but for the political amenities of the hour. All that I saw, except the payment of the money to the sister of the justice, I had known as well as one knows anything without the evidence. But to see it there in black and white made me bat my eyes.

The words of Roosevelt's letter to me while he was in the White House about this Supreme Court Justice rose in my mind. In November, 1908, Colonel Roosevelt had written me:

> It is an outrage that a creature like Grosscup should be permitted to sit on the bench. Of course there are few judges who are actually corrupt. . . . But there are many who are entirely unfit to occupy the position they do. Brewer being a striking example of his kind. There is altogether too much power in the bench.

Incidentally, and in parenthesis, let me say that even three weeks after the election of Taft, Colonel Roosevelt began to be suspicious that Taft was moving away from the "Roosevelt policies," and was snuggling up to the conservatives, for in his letter he expressed the wish that I would write "in the most emphatic manner" to Taft. "It could only do good."

I knew the justice. I had met him when he was a circuit judge. In Kansas he was known as our scholar in politics. He had been graduated from Yale. He was a man of wide reading and considerable culture. He believed in the divine right of the plutocracy to rule. He distrusted the people, and his decisions limited their power whenever the question of their power came before the court. It was only when the people themselves rose up, broke the lever which United States Senators held over the federal courts, and by the primary smashed the machine through which the railroads controlled the legislatures and elected the senators; only then did the people erect the machinery by which they could set up free government. When Roosevelt came to the White House, less than half a dozen states had the primary. When Taft left it, the primary was widely adopted in the United States but the core of the group of states that renominated Taft was made up of states that had no Presidential primary, so fast had the revolution spread over this land. It was a real revolution. When the people captured the party machinery they quickly set up economic measures which would broaden the base of every man's social inheritance.

I made some casual remark, but the Little Major could see that he had jarred me. I knew what he was thinking of—that all this progressive non-sense which was engaging me at the time was a passing phase and that my world of reform was built of cardboard, papier-mâché and paste. Then the Little Major opened another envelope and passed its contents over to me. There were three receipts for Wells Fargo Express packages valued at one thousand dollars each, currency. The receipts were signed by John P. St. John, who then, in 1881, was serving his second term as Governor of Kansas. He wanted to go to the Senate and was about to oppose Plumb The Little Major coughed nervously and said: "You know, Will, I went up to Topeka. I talked to St. John. I persuaded him that he had better run for a third term for governor. And I got him to agree. So this three thousand dollars was Plumb's contribution to his campaign expenditures."

He spoke softly, almost in a whisper, as though across thirty years some-one might be listening. St. John was the father of Prohibition in Kansas and in 1884 he ran as a candidate for President of the United States on the Prohibition ticket. Gossip said that the Democrats paid the expenses of the Prohibitionist campaign and sent St. John to New York State, where he gathered up enough votes to defeat Blaine in the Presidential election of 1884. It all came back to me, the story of the loss of New York State, the defeat of Grover Cleveland and St. John's ill-fated candidacy for a third term. I sat there for a moment in silence, looking at the Major's documents. He was about to destroy them, for I think he knew he was marked for death.

He broke the silence, smiling amiably back in his well trimmed gray beard, after moistening his lips.

"Well, Will," he said almost behind his hand and with his soft deprecating voice, "the world has changed a lot in thirty years, hasn't it!"

I could only nod my assent. I wanted to cry out: "God, how it has changed and how you and your kind have passed, let us hope forever, from Amer-ican politics!"

A few months later we buried him. He was my dear friend. Without him I could not have survived the nineties. We saw eye to eye in those days. We were friends to the last. So we gave him nineteen guns in the Gazette and buried him with a page of obituary biography and with editorial heralding trumpets that should have gotten him well past the pearly gates. I set all of this down here to show what a strange world we have, how mixed and confused and baffling it all is. The Little Major, exactly as he was, Plumb's political fence, was one of the best citizens in Emporia, public-spirited, generous, essentially kind, and to those he loved he was sweet and gentle. And yet . . .

441

CHAPTER LXIII

The Battle Begins

IN THE ELECTION of 1910 Kansas went overwhelmingly progressive Republican. The conservative faction was decisively divided. The same thing happened generally over the country north of the Mason and Dixon line. The progressive Republicans did not have a majority in either house of Congress. But they had a balance of power; amalgamation with a similar but smaller group of progressive Democrats under Bryan's leadership gave the progressives a working majority upon most measures. They had seen the conservative Democrats and the conservative Republicans united openly, proudly, victoriously to save Speaker Cannon from the ultimate humiliation when his power was taken from him by his progressive partisans. So in the legislatures and the Congress that met in 1911 a strange new thing was revealed in American politics. Party lines were breaking down. A bipartisan party was appearing in legislatures and in the Congress. It was an undeclared third party. But when the new party appeared on the left, the conservative Democrats and the conservative Republicans generally coalesced in legislative bodies on the right. For the most part the right wing coalescents were in the minority. In Congress, on most measures, the left-wing liberals were able to command a majority. They united upon a railroad regulation bill. They united in promoting the income tax constitutional amendment. They united in submitting another amendment providing for the direct election of United States Senators, which was indeed revolutionary. But they were unable to unite in the passage of a tariff bill. Local interests in regional commodity industries like cotton, lumber, copper, wool and textiles were able to form a conservative alliance which, under the leadership of President Taft in the White House, put through a tariff bill that was an offense to the nation. But otherwise the new party of reform which had grown up in ten years dominated politics in Washington and in the state legislatures north of the Ohio from New England to California.

I was happy following in the train of this new alliance. After the election of 1910 I spent considerable time in January and February of 1911 helping Governor Stubbs with his legislative program. I was errand boy, peacemaker, jollier, fixer, horse-trader, but only one of half a dozen members of the third house who faced similar unofficial representatives from the paid lobby. But in the main we were victorious, although I took a hard licking with the defeat of the initiative and referendum measure and proposed constitutional amendment. But Stubbs came out in the legislature with his program more than decently successful. He was becoming a national leader. He was hobnobbing with men like Hadley of Missouri, Norris of Nebraska, La Follette, Governor Chase Osborn, Gifford Pinchot, James R. Garfield, Senator Hiram Johnson, George L. Record of New Jersey, and was one of the men whom progressives in the nation regarded as a sound and dependable leader. A curious man was this Walter Roscoe Stubbs. He was a Quaker, had attended the state university a year or so, dropped out to go to work; had become a railroad contractor, amassed a fortune in his forties and appeared in his early fifties as chairman of the state central committee in the day of the Boss-Buster's victory over the Leland machine. He was a two-fisted slugger in politics. He introduced the long-distance telephone, spent thousands of dollars calling up leaders, organizing his progressive machine; and he was a good salesman and sold himself and his cause to young men. He talked an hour with me on the phone before I first surrendered. It was a Quaker exhortation to righteousness. I was willing to be righteous, but I hated to desert an old friend like Cy Leland. And within two years after Stubbs was inaugurated, Cy Leland, whose machine had been wrecked, joined us, carrying a banner of righteousness and psalm-singing. It was funny, and the state got many a giggle out of it. Something like that was happening in every state. And the incident has a place here because it was politically typical. Many an old stager who had run with the state machine in the various commonwealths climbed on the hub, threw a leg over the wheel, got into our bandwagon, grabbed a horn and became a progressive tooter. The desire to go with the winners in politics sometimes moves politically minded men with the power of a great faith.

But the contest was not easy. It was not all one way. The regulars on the right did not give up their fight easily. So 1911, despite the progressive victory of 1910, was a year of stress and tumultuous hubbub all across the land in American politics.

All of which I saw; a part of which I was. So William Allen, the novelist, submerged, and I was Bill White, or Old Bill White: a scant forty, carrying my maximum weight, wearing the best clothes I knew how to buy (but often too busy to keep them pressed; still given to the broad-brimmed black hat that was the politician's caste mark. I went East many times in the early part of 1911, saw Colonel Roosevelt frequently, held prolonged and unimportant conferences in Washington with such progressive leaders as Victor Murdock, Borah and Norris could assemble, and we were full of plots and counterplots. At that time most of the progressives I saw were rather for La Follette as our Presidential candidate the next year than for Roosevelt. He also was undecided what he would do. I am sure that he was trying to make peace with Taft. And I am also certain that Taft would have been glad indeed to make peace with Roosevelt. But the courtiers at the White House in those days made peace impossible. Though several conferences were arranged, the result was negligible.

It was heartbreaking to watch that gradual, apparently inevitable estrangement between two old friends, for Roosevelt and Taft had been dearly beloved companions. Taft had risen from the judiciary in Roosevelt's term in the White House. When he came into the Cabinet, he accepted Roosevelt's official leadership. Taft respected rank and authority. He took orders from Roosevelt when Roosevelt could sign them officially. Taft was a man of great charm, who had to be definitely insulted with *malice prepense* to make him mad. And of course his chief in the White House had been tactful and considerate, and their relations were affectionate. When Colonel Roosevelt had pushed through the Republican convention the nomination of Taft, which he did with rather ungracious and unconcealed frankness, he had no idea but that when Taft was elected he would continue to be a Rooseveltian President. All of Roosevelt's progressive friends were dubious of Taft. I was. But I accepted him despite the fact that Taft showed too much concern for the feelings of Joseph Cannon and was too friendly with Senator Nelson Aldrich for my taste. But we progressives, except for La Follette who was an open rebel, went along with the Roosevelt parade to Taft, and in 1911 we were thoroughly disillusioned.

Among others whose support Colonel Roosevelt commanded was W. R. Nelson, editor of the Kansas City Star. He had no ulterior motive. Personally he liked Taft, but he was deeply offended by the Payne-Aldrich tariff law, and being a natural rebel he rallied to Roosevelt. He was one of those responsible for the manifesto signed by the seven Republican governors, asking Roosevelt to run: J. M. Carey of Wyoming, Herbert S. Hadley of Missouri, Chase S. Osborn of Michigan, Robert P. Bass of New Hampshire, Chester H. Aldrich of Nebraska, W. E. Glasscock of West Virginia, Walter R. Stubbs of Kansas. They made a profound impression on the country and hurried along the swift tide that was carrying Colonel Roosevelt to a decision. After that my poor, weak, barbaric yawp, "Nay, nay," was a breath in the wind. I also began to doubt my own position.

If the White House entourage which surrounded Taft was belligerent to Roosevelt, certainly we, his old progressive enemies, were malignant in our bitterness toward Taft. He had snubbed us. He had betrayed our cause. He had aligned himself publicly with Cannon and Aldrich, explaining that he had to go along with them in order to get his way with Congress. But as he never had his way with Congress and as the party was split to its core because of his attitude toward the Republican reactionaries, we, who were Roosevelt's aides-de-camp, saw in Taft's excuses and palavering about his alignment with Roosevelt's political foes only an evidence of Taft's weakness or the proof of his essential duplicity. Which on the whole was probably unfair. Taft was doing his best. He was not a pugnacious personality. He hated combat. Unless he was prodded to work, he was inclined to take life easy. His critics called him lazy, which he was not. But he did put things off. He did take the easiest course for the day and hour, and was the victim of his own desire for peace and comfort. He seemed cold to us because we were bedeviling him all the time into disagreeable positions. He seemed heartless because he delighted in the easy way to get out of the difficulties of a day or an hour. And I remember we progressive conspirators had a saying: "There stands Taft like the statue of Louis XV in the Tuileries Gardens, smiling and formidable, but without heart or guts."

So the quarrel grew. The chasm between the two men widened. A public gibe here from Roosevelt, a bitter private retort repeated over the grapevine of politics from Taft, the innocent recognition of some enemy of Roosevelt by the White House, the constant hammering upon Taft by men near Roosevelt—all the accumulating little jeers and slights slowly grew into the proportions of a cause and a quarrel. Even then the personal friends of the President and Colonel Roosevelt tried to close the breach, tried to make some kind of armistice. The more they tried, the more inexorably the powers of fate, tearing the two friends apart, worked ironically for disunion. Colonel Roosevelt was rather careless of his innuendo. He had a nice gift for ironic persiflage. He said things, sometimes publicly, sometimes in private, that were hard for Taft to forget. And Taft kept making unconscionable blunders that were elephantine insults to all that Roosevelt believed. Temperamentally the two men could not be reconciled once a quarrel had started.

I was for peace with Taft in the latter days of 1910 and the first half of 1911. Indeed, well through 1911 I felt that it would be a mistake for Roosevelt to run in the Republican primaries against the President. In Kansas, Stubbs, Bristow, the Congressional delegation and for the most part the rank and file, while we threw our hats and cheered for Teddy, were politically aligned with La Follette. We were committed to his Presidential candidacy.

And so matters stood in June 1911 when Mrs. White and I picked up the family and went to Colorado for the summer. For more than a year in our hearts we had been mulling over the basic ideas for a second novel. We had talked a lot about it, were seeing glimpses of the characters, but above all had a sense of what might be called the fable of the novel—the backbone, the thing it was to say and be, the spiritual idea behind it. So we rented a cottage in Estes Park from Professor Hodder of the state university; and in early June cut loose from politics, forgot all about Stubbs and Bristow and set ourselves up on the side of a mountain, with the two children, their Grandma White and their Aunt Jessie Lindsay. I set up a tent a hundred feet up the hill, put my cot and a typewriter there, and every morning after breakfast went up to write. It was a summer of pure delight.

When I grew stale I had two books that interested me that summer: Henri Bergson's "Creative Evolution" and Bouck White's "The Call of the Carpenter." White's book was to me most illuminating. I read it and reread it, and bought extra copies and sent it around. Bergson's dissertation was slow going, sometimes three downs and no gain, a pure philosophic treatise, but I could not take it or let it alone. I had to get on with it and get through with it. The theme of the novel which afterwards appeared under the title "In the Heart of a Fool" was that there are no material rewards for spiritual excellence, and no material punishment for spiritual dereliction. So I had two characters: one, a most prosperous sinner, and the other a suffering saint. All that summer I wrestled with those two figures to make them human; to give the saint his peccadillos; to give the villain his decent moments. The plot of the book was intended to be not a struggle between black and white but between different shades of gray. Seven years we were working on that book. But that summer at Estes Park was sheer joy. In the evenings we gathered the children, seven and eleven, around the fireplace and read Dickens until Mary had to be lugged off dead asleep to bed, and Bill, who always wanted more, had to be dragged to his couch; then his mother and I sat up until all hours while she read aloud to me.

The Gazette office was doing well. It did not need me that summer. A few letters came from Kansas politicians; and I remember, and my files show, that I wrote at least twice to Theodore Roosevelt urging him not to yield to the pressure that would make him a candidate against Taft. I still felt that La Follette could win, and still believed in saving the Progressive act.

It is odd to look back at a halcyon day thirty years ago and more when my only cares were falling hair and a rising Presidential candidate. I was doomed to bad luck with both.

CHAPTER LXIV

The Progressives Choose a Leader

WHEN I CAME HOME from Estes Park in mid-autumn, the tragic quarrel between the two major figures in the Republican party, Theodore Roosevelt and William Howard Taft, was opening a big second act. As a spectacle it had all America on the edge of their chairs. For after all it is not every day that a nation can see a popular hero (and Colonel Roosevelt had superseded Bryan as the political idol of the day) and his lifelong friend, who happened for the purposes of the hour to be President of the United States, coming to verbal blows over matters not of personal interest but of public policy. Neither of them wanted to fight, yet each of them was drawn into combat in spite of himself. Each was the center, or representative, or embodiment of what amounted to a political party. For indeed the progressives were not Republicans or Democrats, whatever party they might nominally espouse. Roosevelt's friends kept pricking him with needles, stimulating his anger, knowing that in his wrath he would attack Taft, directly or indirectly—for Taft, after all, was giving aid and comfort to Roosevelt's enemies. In the White House, President Taft's advisers were sicking him on Roosevelt; he was like a great shaggy Newfoundland who did not like to fight. For after all, the two men were dear friends. They and their families had enjoyed years of intimacy. Yet there it was on the national stage, a battle of the giants for all the world to see. I could not enjoy it. I went East after we came home from Colorado.

I saw Roosevelt. We talked over that indefinite, shifting, intangible series of hunches, guesses and hypothetical phantasms which politicians call "the situation." "The situation" demanded that Roosevelt antagonize the White House. Humanity, and my friendship for the two men, made me chicken-hearted. Also, I was committed to La Follette and could not idly set my commitment aside, for I had great admiration, deep respect and a genuine fondness for him. And it seemed to me then that if he could make the fight against Taft in the Republican convention he might defeat any Democrat who would be nominated. But my files show also that in those days I had a subconscious hope that Woodrow Wilson would be nominated by the Democrats, though he seemed a long chance at that time, because he was carrying out a genuinely progressive program in New Jersey; and I felt he would make the same kind of President, with allowance for temperamental differences in men, that La Follette or Roosevelt would make. So when I talked to Roosevelt, giving him what I felt was an honest report of the situation, I was by that very report urging him into the fray, while outwardly I stood pulling at his coattails with reluctant dread of the coming carnage. It has been my life's handicap that I have always been able to see at least two sides to every question, and, not being cocksure of my position, have often lacked the passionate conviction that gives one the fanatic faith necessary to move mountains.

My letter files bulk large in 1911 and 1912. I was trying to play Providence in Kansas for the progressive organization inside the Republican party. My letters show that I was trying to get Congressman Madison to run for governor. I felt that although he was a dependable progressive, he had, as a Congressman in the Seventh District, much strength in the conservative crowd. Stubbs, who would, I was sure, defeat Curtis in the Republican primary—and he did—needed a little shoring up on the right side, and I felt that with Madison on the Kansas ticket Stubbs could win in November. I remember the files show a letter from Ed Madison to me, addressing me as "My dear Warwick," and indicating that he regarded me as the Kingmaker. He was afraid to take the risk of a gubernatorial nomination. So after some shifting we decided on giving Arthur Capper the undivided progressive vote for Governor. That is to say, we pulled out all other progressive candidates who might have divided the Capper vote. The files also show that I was being hectored to run for Republican national committeeman, and that I did not want to do it. But sometime before the convention, I yielded and went after it like a wolfhound. While I did not want the job I also did not want to be defeated.

In the meantime, in the autumn and early winter of 1911, we in Kansas were trying with all our might to line the state up for Senator La Follette as our progressive Presidential candidate. We had three county conventions early in the winter, and La Follette was beaten in all three. It was jarring. Then a strange and terrible thing happened to Senator La Follette.

He was on the program for a speech at the annual dinner of the Periodical Publishers Association of America. Remember that these Publishers were conducting magazines that were anywhere from liberal to radical. There were gathered all of the progressive leaders in Congress and on the eastern seaboard. It was a most important occasion. La Follette knew it. But he came to Philadelphia, where the convention was held, dead tired, dog-tired after a terrible day's work in the Senate. He never spared himself. His place was late on the program. It was after ten at night when the toastmaster came to him. Just before he rose to speak, his secretary told me, he took a great gobletful of whiskey and swallowed it neat, as a stimulant. He was not a drinking man. But, his secretary said, sometimes, to stoke up his machine, he used any stimulant that might be at hand and had no bad consequences, contracted no habits, but had kept his machine going when his normal strength was gone. He had his manuscript that night at the dinner, and for ten minutes or so, perhaps twenty, he read along fluently and well. Then he put his manuscript down for a moment to emphasize a point. The dinner guests noted that he wandered a bit, repeated himself. When he picked up his manuscript he had lost his place and read for five minutes or so paragraphs that he had already read. Then he laid it down again, and the second time he departed from his manuscript he began to lose control of his temper. He came out of his fury maudlin. No one at the table dreamed what was the matter. For nearly two hours, fumbling occasionally with his manuscript, he raged on and on, saying the same things over and over at the top of his voice. It was a terrible spectacle. The progressive leadership of the United States that night received such a shock as it had never had. Senator Bristow wrote me saying he could never again trust La Follette, feeling that he had worked beyond his strength and was nervously unstable. Bristow was the leader of the La Follette group in Kansas. He had no use for Roosevelt, who ten years before had failed to support Bristow when he, Bristow, was cleaning out the Post Office Department. Bristow believed that Roosevelt was too quick to compromise with evil. So when we lost three Kansas counties in our preliminary fight, Bristow yielded to the clamor of his Kansas friends and we made the shift from La Follette. What we did was simple enough. We stopped insisting on La Follette delegates to the national convention, and let nature take its course.

In the meantime La Follette sent a representative to Kansas to see what was the matter. He came on a day when I was leaving for New York. I could not see him. I tried to meet him on the train, but a misunderstanding occurred. It was genuine. But for years, perhaps all his life, La Follette thought that Bristow and I had double-crossed him. We told him frankly what had happened, but he could not understand the weaknesses of his own candidacy, nor did I. Few people in Kansas knew about the Periodical Publishers' dinner episode. The newspapers were most kind to La Follette. Or perhaps it occurred Saturday night after the Sunday morning papers had gone to press, and it some way missed the reporters Monday morning.

Of course the reporters were kind, for they thought La Follette had suffered a nervous breakdown.

But from that hour in Philadelphia, La Follette's candidacy faded. The progressive leadership he had counted on was afraid of him. It never brought opportunity for the Presidency again to La Follette. He lived on a decade and a half as a minority leader, but only that—a great leader, a brave, wise, uncompromising leader who deserved of his country much more fame than it gave him. No other left-wing leader ever impressed upon the laws and institutions of his country and upon the purposes and impulse of the American people in his time so strong, definite and considerable an achievement as Robert La Follette, Sr.

As it seemed to me then, so it seems to me now, looking back a generation and considering all the men who might have been chosen President in 1912, that La Follette would have done more than any other man to guide the destiny of his country through the devastating second decade of this century. I say this realizing that he was a convinced and fanatical pacifist. But he was nonetheless a patriotic American; and in the crisis where Wilson seemed to fumble, to vacillate, to procrastinate and so let war come creeping upon us almost unawares, La Follette—who was a man of decision, a patriot, unafraid even of a majority of his people—would have been a stronger, wiser man. But the United States in that day was not ready to risk itself with a strong, determined, indomitable man. So La Follette stepped aside and fate passed him by.

Meanwhile one group of friends of Roosevelt, and a similar group of Taft's friends, were trying hard to bring the two men together. They met one autumn afternoon at a beach club in New England. But if it was a reconciliation, it was a hollow one. Each of the principal parties had on his mind things that he dared not talk about. Roosevelt felt that the whole attitude of the Taft administration toward progressive policies and progressive leaders was one of implacable hostility. Taft, on the other hand, felt that it was his administration, not Roosevelt's; that a President had a right to express himself, his temperament and his convictions in his own administration, without the bitter gibes which Roosevelt had darted at him, and without the wolfish hostility that Roosevelt's friends and supporters spread around Washington. So they sat talking about unimportant things and each went his way, unhappy. Finally the President's friends made Mr. Taft say some harsh cutting thing about Roosevelt in a public speech. After the speech the President went to his bedroom and lay down and wept, he felt so deeply the breach of their old friendship. It was about this time that he wrote to me answering my earnest plea that he take the people into his confidence. So I'll let him plead his case for himself:

450

The White House
Washington

March 20th, 1909

Dear Mr. White:

I have your kind letter and take pleasure in it. I am not constituted as Mr. Roosevelt is in being able to keep the country advised every few days as to the continuance of the state of mind in reference to reforms. It is a difference in temperament. He talked with correspondents a great deal. His heart was generally on his sleeve and he must communicate his feelings. I find myself unable to do so. After I have made a definite statement I have to let it go at that until the time for action arises, when I seek as sincerely and earnestly as I can to live up to my previous declaration. Hence as business goes on, and as in an effort to accomplish something I deal with the instruments I have, including those whom the country—especially your part of the country—distrusts as reactionaries, I expect to have my position questioned. . . . But I have confidence in the sound judgment of the people based on what is done rather than what is proclaimed or what is suspected from appearances; and if I can make good in legislation, I shall rely on fair discussion to vindicate me as one who does not make a promise without fully considering and apprehending the exact meaning of the promise and the difficulties of complying with it.

Please write me as often as occasion suggests, and believe me to be,

Gratefully and sincerely yours,

WM. H. TAFT

It seems to me this letter gives the curtain lines for the tragedy of the First Act of this sad story of a broken friendship.

Roosevelt was not the weeping sort. When he decided to cut a throat, he generally justified it and rarely regretted it. But as the winter of 1911-12 deepened, the quarrel became obviously irreconcilable.

La Follette was defeated in county after county in Kansas by the Roosevelt workers. We, who were leaders, needed to use very little strategy. And outside of Kansas it became obvious that the Republican nominee would be either Taft or Roosevelt. Of course La Follette could not see this, and a sense of betrayal mantled him like a neurosis.

In February, 1912, I went to Boston to make a speech before the Progressive Club, a group of young left-wingers; and as I always kept Colonel Roosevelt posted about my whereabouts before I went to Boston, he asked me if I would dine with him, the evening after my speech, at Judge Robert Grant's. I had known Judge Grant. He had written several novels that I liked, and we had met in the National Institute of Arts and Letters. He also wrote inviting me. By the time I got to Boston I knew what was in the air. The Colonel had determined to make a formal announcement, that night, of his candidacy. He knew that I still felt he should keep out of it. But also he knew that I was willing to accept Taft to save Roosevelt, for

I had written him a few days before I started East that I felt he should not run, but I would bet two to one that he would be nominated. It was with that attitude that I went to Judge Grant's dinner.

Judge Grant lived in an old-fashioned house on the right side of Beacon Street. He belonged to the Brahmin caste. It had been an elegant house in the middle of the nineteenth century: the living rooms on the first floor, the dining room and the kitchen in the half-basement. A small group of Colonel Roosevelt's New England friends were at the dinner. We read his statement. He knew how I felt about it. I told him that I thought he was sacrificing himself unnecessarily, but that if he was going to make a mistake I would help him with all my heart to make it as terrible as possible. And we had a laugh and let it go at that. He accepted two or three verbal and rhetorical changes that I suggested, and the statement was given to the press fairly early in the evening. I took the midnight train to New York and Washington, full of a bewildered zeal for a cause that I did not then entirely approve.

The next afternoon I was in Washington. The first man I went to see was Victor Murdock. He was amazed and not altogether delighted with the Colonel's statement, for he was not a Roosevelt worshiper. Victor had fathered a Congressional resolution which cut off several million dollars of graft from the American railroads in their mail-carrying contracts. The President, who did not quite understand it, felt that Murdock, Norris and the midwestern anti-Cannon insurgents were not obeying the party signals, and were playing their own game. So when the Cannon crowd started to crucify Murdock, the President did not lift a hand to uphold him. But it was obvious that Murdock was going along with the progressives. He knew that La Follette was hopeless. He thought Roosevelt could win. I remember I greeted him with:

"Victor, the Colonel thinks it's 1860, and it looks to me about like '56. He's not running against Douglas. He's running against Buchanan."

Victor grinned and said: "Bill, he's running against Franklin Pierce. This rebellion has a long, long way to go before it wins."

Victor knew the powers of inertia in the House, and the strength of an organized reactionary minority, well financed, socially intrenched, politically arrogant. He was not afraid; but he was not deceived either. I have always thought that Colonel Roosevelt fooled himself in that February statement. For the clamor in the country for him was maddening. No wonder it turned his head.

Naturally in Washington his statement had given much courage to the insurgents there. They rallied to Roosevelt, and practically all of them left La Follette to drain his cup of bitterness alone. A few nights after, a dozen

452

r twenty Rooseveltians met in downtown Washington—I think in the
Willard Hotel—to discuss ways and means. I can remember only a few
Senators: Jonathan Bourne, Moses, Clapp, Bristow, Johnson of California,
Beveridge, Dixon of Montana, Dolliver, Borah, Victor Murdock. I believe
George Norris brought in half a dozen or more members of the House of
Representatives. We formed a loose organization without a name, devoted
to the Roosevelt primary campaign, for by that time most of the northern
states had Presidential preference primaries.

In the discussion of attitudes, Senator Bourne stood up and said, after we
had made Senator Dixon our chairman:

"Gentlemen, the first thing we have got to decide is a matter of fundamental policy. If we lose, will we bolt? To get this thing before the house,
I move that we agree, here and now, and not be too secretive about our
agreement that if we lose, we bolt."

He had consulted no one, apparently. The motion was a stunner. There
was a moment of silence when Bourne sat down, and the men around the
table moistened their lips and batted their eyes. They were faced with a
proposition which might seal their political doom, and end their Congressional careers.

I had no such career to end. I was thinking only of the Colonel's position
if he should bolt the possible nomination of Taft. This nomination did not
seem possible at that hour. We had forgotten the mercenary southern delegates. We were all hypnotized by the clamoring voices across the land.

As we stood there, with that motion before us, we realized we were at
the near bank of the Rubicon. The discussion was louder than it was sincere, I thought. Too many men were thinking of themselves, and not the
cause. A precious few of them were thinking in terms of what it would do
to their hero. In the end, without a vote, but because it seemed to be the
consensus of opinion, the sense of the meeting was that we should bolt and
make our campaign with that aim in our own hearts and with that threat
hanging over the heads of our adversaries. After that we discussed ways and
means, state organizations, appointed committees to raise funds and did
the usual things that political conspirators do who are organizing a raid
on any political citadel.

But after that meeting, for a day or two I talked with various members
of the conference, and after they had slept on it the proposition to bolt did
not appeal to them. I found no one except Bourne, and perhaps Beveridge,
who was willing to admit that a threat to bolt was good policy. Yet because
every political conference is a sign, the substance of that threat sifted into
the minds and hearts of the friends of President Taft, and instead of terrifying them it gave them the purpose and direction of their campaign. It
was to hold the Republican national organization as it was constituted in

the Republican national committee, and ride the storm even if Taft was de
feated, and win four years later.

A political organization is party-minded. Also it is set eternally in th
heavens. Tomorrow is also a day with the national Senatorial committee o
either party. It functions not by quadrennial but by decades and generations
The threat to bolt gave the conservative Republicans their one hope to win—
not with Taft, but with time. They planned their campaign along thos
lines. Because I sensed that, I redoubled my effort in Kansas to be electe
to the national committee. I did not believe, until the deed was done, tha
Roosevelt would bolt, then or ever. But I did feel, that spring of 1912, tha
on the Republican national committee I could be a troublemaker for th
conservatives, and I took my own campaign rather seriously.

I think I realized then that the progressive movement was joined som
way with the uprising of the liberals in England and that it was a part of th
restless socialist protests in continental Europe, north of the Alps. The Swis
achievements under the initiative and referendum, and all that the Scan
dinavian countries were doing in the way of labor reform and agrarian ad
vancement, cheered me up. The Chinese reforms under Sun Yat-sen wer
coming along in those days, and crowned heads were dropping all ove
the world that first decade and a half of the twentieth century. The editoria
page of the Gazette shows that I sensed the fact that the middle class wa
rising—that something was going on—that we insurgents or progressive
(or whatever name we adopted for ourselves) were moving on a tide; bu
this was all I knew. It was a generation later that I understood the deep cur
rents of that tide. I could not know then that we Republican rebels yam
mering away in the Kansas courthouses and in the band shells of the park
in the public square—we who were clamoring for a dozen mild reform
that spring in our legislatures and in Congress—were lifting strange voice
in a world revolt against the inequities which were rattling away in th
civilization of Christendom.

I suppose the thing that was happening was something like this: For
long time, three or four centuries, man in various places over the planet had
been extending his material outlook, discovering new continents and islands
conceiving inventions that lightened his labor and broadened his horizon—
inventions that made clothes and food and shelter the ordinary social in
heritage of many men. Along with these explorations, discoveries and
inventions, men had been learning to read and write. The printed book
appeared and preserved humanity's knowledge for everyone. Pestilence
which had come out of grinding, filthy, cruel poverty disappeared. In short
life was becoming easier for hundreds of millions of people on the earth
who were working with new machines and gadgets, and who were reading
and writing with stimulated minds. So as men saw life more clearly through

the centuries, they developed a sense of mercy. The natural aspiration for justice in the human heart took definite force. The struggle for liberty widened and became a more intelligent aspiration with a more certain and definite purpose. As the people, the middle class, began to exercise functions in government, government changed. It was established to secure kings and the aristocracy in their privileges. Two hundred years ago, men came slowly to realize they could use government as an agency of human welfare. As the wheels of inventions were multiplied and turned more rapidly, as education spread, as literacy became common, men realized that they could use government to establish justice. The ballot box appeared. Republics were established. The democratic ideal began to grow and blossom. In the middle of the nineteenth century it was the common aspiration of men from the Caspian Sea to San Francisco, as inventions multiplied by thousands and as primary education became all but universal. In the hearts of all the world was implanted the spirit of revolt against a civilization and an economic order which barred so many men and women and little children from the basic blessings of life which the machines had created. Hence the dilettante liberalism of the nineteenth century became in the new century a militant radicalism all over western civilization. It touched everyone. No nation was too backward to deny this stirring in the hearts of men. Even Russia felt the current in 1905. Every nation had its militant leader as, in the United States, every state had its little Roosevelts and Bryans and La Follettes. The conscience of the world was moving. Of course everywhere from the Czar's palace to Potsdam, to Threadneedle Street, to Wall Street, economic and social privilege, entrenched and resisting with cunning and power, made the release of the inner fraternal forces of man a slow and tedious process.

CHAPTER LXV

The Battlelines Form

LOOKING BACK into my life over the year 1912, I seemed to be forever busy about something, stirring around in the midst of tumult and struggle, making decisions that seemed important in that hour, decisions that now seem so irrelevant to anything that persists in the world today. And for me, all this hurrying about, all this tumult, struggle, mental and spiritual pulling and hauling, was about and around Theodore Roosevelt.

I was drawn to him by personal loyalty. I disagreed with him on unimportant matters. I was often annoyed a little with things that he said or did. He made a speech in Columbus, a most radical and indefensible speech, advocating the recall of judicial decisions. I never knew who advised him to make that speech, though at the time I tried to find out. But it hurt him; probably it crippled him more than any other one thing that he did in his life. For the speech shocked millions of his countrymen whom he had gathered about him as followers, and it attracted only the radicals who are never dependable to follow in any man's train nor to pursue any consistent course. I tried to explain that he meant by recall of judicial decisions only the legislative enactments needed to amend the statutes upon which the decisions were made. Probably he meant something of that sort. But the phrase "recall of judicial decisions" set the key of the marching song in the political combat that made the year such a time of clamor and alarm. It was a high key, and too much in falsetto. Colonel Roosevelt from the hour of that speech at Columbus until the election in November, 1912 was forced in self-defense to a position much farther to the left than he should have taken—indeed, farther to the left than he would have taken naturally if in the back of his head he was not always trying to justify the "recall of judicial decisions" to a public that challenged it.

My first job was in Kansas. A dozen Republican leaders who had been supporting the Progressive cause for half a decade or more made it their business to see that the Kansas delegation to the Republican national con vention was composed of men who would support Colonel Roosevelt for the Presidential nomination against President Taft. I was one of those leaders. I traveled about Kansas making speeches where it was necessary, attending county conventions where I could be of any service and district conventions where the battle was raging—sometimes talking, sometimes horse-trading, compromising, working at political combinations that would promote the Roosevelt cause.

In the end, we won. We carried all but two congressional districts, and we carried the state convention. I was the Progressive candidate for national committeeman. Henry J. Allen, of Wichita, headed the Kansas delegation pledged to Colonel Roosevelt. At the state convention we named not only the delegates but the Presidential electors who should vote in the Electoral College for Colonel Roosevelt as the Republican nominee. In the midst of this fight, I went East once or twice, possibly three times, to confer with the Colonel and with his national supporters about national strategy. The Colonel was carrying the primaries in the northern states, decisively; and it was evident that in the southern states, which never went Republican, and in which the Republican party in too many cases was a corrupt alliance between the rich and the purchasable, the organization supporting Taft was naming the delegates. Colonel Roosevelt had carried Massachusetts, Pennsylvania, Illinois, Ohio, the Missouri Valley states, excepting the Dakotas where La Follette's men were named, and the Roosevelt movement swept onward to the Pacific coast. In May, when we held our last pre-convention conference at Oyster Bay, it was plain that we had the Republican sentiment of the country, as it was uncovered by direct vote of Republicans in state primaries, rather overwhelmingly for Colonel Roosevelt. It was also clear that the Republican national committee having the South, one-third of the convention, as its pawn, was instituting contests in convention states which would probably give the national committee an opportunity to organize the national convention. For the national committee named the temporary chairman who named the committee on credentials. The committee on credentials seated such contestants as they deemed worthy or necessary to promote their plans. There you have drama.

On the one side was the national committee. It was supporting President Taft. The national committee had the power to organize the convention, name its temporary chairman and its permanent chairman. First, the committee would have back of it the South, although these delegates represented no possibility of a Republican majority in their states in the election. Secondly, the committee would have, on the early balloting, the strength of its contested delegates. Thus the Taft conservatives, by controlling the national committee, could shape the convention in its image.

Facing this phalanx of sheer political machine power was the sentiment

of the country as revealed by the primaries in the great Republican area
of the nation which were for Roosevelt. Naturally passions mounted
Popular indignation, being thwarted by a hold-over national committee
was faced by the contempt of this national committee as it went ahead with
its plans to nominate Taft, ignoring public sentiment and entrenching
itself for another battle in the Republican national convention of 1916. I
is difficult to imagine now, thirty years and more after 1912, how deeply
the United States was stirred.

Colonel Roosevelt was being staged as a martyr. He did not have a drop
of martyr's blood in his veins. He told me so when we were discussing the
matter late in the spring. He wanted to be a victor. And yet, there he wa
with the stage set tableauing him a pale martyr in his sheet of fire. He go
mad, deeply, terribly angry at the injustice which he faced. He could no
think that a national committee which he had swayed in the White Hous
four years before could treat him with such utter scorn, nor that it would
risk Republican defeat to retain its control of the national Republican
organization. He was a practical politician, was Colonel Roosevelt. He had
fought it out in the caucus at Oyster Bay, as I had. He had stood on a chai
in state conventions and howled with the winners. And on national com
mittees he had gone to the edge of the abysms and backed off before h
bolted.

For Theodore Roosevelt was a party man. He was not a party man be
cause of much conviction. We held about the same ideas of party loyalty
that it was a necessary evil if one gave his principles in government a
chance for a fair trial. In other words he was an expedient Republican, no
a congenital partisan. He had used other people's party loyalty for hi
own ends. And here before the convention opened in 1912 he found the
Republican national committee quite as scornful of Roosevelt in attaining
its partisan ends, quite as contemptuous of the moralities as he had some
times been when he remained regular (as for instance in 1884 when he
supported Blaine, in whom he had no faith). He fought then and ran
away that he might live to fight another day.

He found the national committee playing the same trick on him. He did
not like it in prospect as he saw the forces of politics shaping the tragedy o
martyrdom for him, while the powers controlling his party piled the faggot
of intrigue and corruption around his stake. When I saw him in those late
spring days, neither of us mentioned the possibility of a bolt. Each of u
knew that our Progressive conference had decided upon it. He was unde
cided then, I know, because he avoided the subject when we talked. We
made the too obvious pretense in those days of our party loyalty, whistling
in unison through the tall timber of darkening events to support ou
courage.

I came to the conference as a victor. Kansas was back of Roosevelt. I was the successful candidate for the national committee, although my election had not been formally achieved. But I spoke with authority in the caucuses, and on the board of strategy. I fear I was not too modest in that hour.

It was in those spring conferences of the Progressive Republicans in 1912 that I again met George W. Perkins, who had risen rather suddenly in the Roosevelt councils. He was one of the partners of J. Pierpont Morgan. We met upon the common ground that he had lived in Wichita during the real estate boom of the eighties. He was state representative of the New York Life Insurance Company. We had a score of mutual friends. Personally we got along together rather well. But deeply and instinctively we distrusted each other. He represented money and the power of money. I felt that Morgan had cast Perkins into the Progressive movement as an anchor to windward; that he was Roosevelt's friend—"just in case"! He was a handsome young fellow, slim and trim, rather exquisitely undertailored. He was addicted to gray and white, and I liked a mohair suit he had so well that I came home and got one from our Emporia tailor. Perkins had good habits, mental, personal, political. He made quick decisions, spoke in a soft voice, smiled ingratiatingly, easily, was as careful of the punctilios as a preacher at the front door of the church, and I used to watch him fishing for men with a certain pride in his skill, which I greatly admired. But he was none the less a sinister figure in those conferences, and I knew it. I grumbled to Roosevelt about him, though I rarely made the mistake in politics of warning a man against his supporters. It is unlucky. But I felt that Roosevelt knew Perkins as I did. I hoped and rather believed he distrusted him as I did; but I also sensed that Roosevelt was using him, and I used to wonder which was fooling the other, he or Perkins. George Perkins, in the drama of Roosevelt's life, was to play a major part, and it is necessary in this narrative to set down these details thus early in that story of the rise and fall of Theodore Roosevelt. It is a brave and tragic story, and I must hurry along to the telling.

A part of that story, so far as it affected my life that spring, was the writing I did. The Gazette files indicate I was in the thick of the Kansas fight and I wrote a magazine article or two. Where I published them I do not remember. I only remember that when I was standing hat in hand, in the hall of Judge Grant's house in Boston, after his friends had urged me to prepare a magazine article about the Roosevelt position in the campaign, Roosevelt had followed me downstairs and said:

"Now about that article. Try not to poise it on the knife edge of that balanced, judicial attitude you assume sometimes."

The last half-dozen words slipped up into the falsetto—the gay defensive falsetto which Roosevelt sometimes slipped into in his merrier and more malignant moments. I grinned.

"All right, Colonel. I'll tip the balance a little for you."

He laughed and ran upstairs. It is curious that I remember this dialogue and do not remember the article, or articles; yet I wrote them, and I am sure they were well loaded with Roosevelt faith, for I was burning up for the cause. However much I may have doubted the wisdom of his candidacy it was the only candidacy that dramatized the Progressive cause, the only candidacy that stood a chance to win under the realities. And my feet were so deeply held by the undertow of the strange current that was moving across the world—the urge of civilization for greater justice in human relations, that I was guided more by zeal than by wisdom. Probably after all I had little choice. I was caught in the current of the times, and my kind, full of arduous hopes and the glamorous visions of young men, could do only what I did in the way I did it.

But it was a lot of fun. In the late spring, the Presidential primaries were held in many states. One after another, the great Republican states wheeled into line for Roosevelt. The country was afire with the conviction that he could save the Republican party from the defeat which obviously was awaiting President Taft. In the White House, Taft was such a bungler, so insensitive to the currents of public opinion, so dependent on the reactionary congressional leaders, that he seemed to be putty in their hands. Always, for some strange reason, this country rejects the leadership of a party committee. As a people, we seem to want our leadership personalized, incarnate in flesh and blood. Taft made it plain that he was going along with the organization, a leader who was led. He had faith that the organization would rescue him. The returns from the Presidential primary elections did not shake him. He seemed to have no faith in the Republican rank and file. We Progressives who were in control of the primaries seemed to him like yawping Yahoos whom his organization cohorts would wheel into line the election in November. He trusted to the leadership of the conservative elements in the country. These elements were mostly rich men, well placed, well housed, well fed, well clad, who hitherto for a generation had been able to control American politics, and who, in those days—though Taft did not know it—were dumb, blind, and helpless. But they did control absolutely a good working majority of the Republican national committee and thus could control the convention which could and, Taft was certain would, nominate him.

It was a stone wall that the Republican masses met that spring. Is strange that the leadership of those masses supporting Roosevelt were berserker in rage as they approached the solid, unyielding walls of the fortress? I rode with them, not in the front ranks, but a captain perhaps among generals. And I, for all my misgivings of the year before, for all my hesitancy in the midwinter, raged in the onslaught upon the fortress as we neared the moat. It was a gay, mad hour. Looking over my political letters of that day and turning the pages of the Gazette in the spring and early summer of 1912, I seem to have been as crazy and as happy as the leadership I followed.

In the midst of it all we had bought a cabin on a hillside near Estes Park, Colorado. It was surrounded on three sides by snowcapped mountains that looked down into a valley, a peaceful green valley through which the Big Thompson River wound its way. It cost us only a few hundred dollars. I paid for it out of an advance on a contract to report the Republican and Democratic national conventions that year for a thousand dollars each. George Matthew Adams, who ran a newspaper syndicate, had hired four of us for the two convention jobs: George Fitch, the novelist; H. T. Webster and J. N. Darling, cartoonists; Edna Ferber, a rising young authoress; and me. When I signed Adams' contract and took his advance payment, I paid for the Colorado cabin. And it was to be for all our lives a haven and a refuge. The cabin was only eighteen by twenty-four, with a fireplace in a little living room, two bedrooms and a kitchen. Yet the fact that we bought it and had time to negotiate for it in the midst of the bedlam about us would seem to prove that there were areas of sanity somewhere within us, for there on that hillside we found a place of peace to which we were to withdraw in summers for thirty years and more. I pause to chronicle the beginnings of the house in Estes Park because the episode probably had a larger place in our real lives than had all the clash of the combat which was just before us on the big national stage where I strutted in a little brief authority, an accredited Kansas captain in a wild charge against the impregnable wall of conservative inertia that all the world was trying to batter down.

"Do you want to know about old Bill White?" said Henry Allen, riding on Roosevelt's train through Nebraska one evening late in the spring of 1912. "Well, I can tell you. He is down somewhere in Labette County in some little country town. And he is doing one of two things: He is standing on the rostrum of the schoolhouse assembly room making a speech for you, in a Palm Beach suit, sweating like a horse, stuttering and stammering to think of the word he wants to say, rabble-rousing to get a Roosevelt delegation out of that county. Or else he is sitting on the bed in a room in some dingy hotel at some crossroads town, fixing up a horsetrade so that Labette County can have a Presidential elector or an alternate to the district convention, if they will instruct their delegates in the district convention to vote with the Roosevelt crowd in the district and the state convention. And old Bill's compromising. He is sweating just as hard, but he isn't sputtering for the right word. He knows it!"

CHAPTER LXVI

Armageddon

I WENT TO CHICAGO in a dual capacity a week before the Republican national convention convened. I was to report the convention and its preliminaries for the George Matthew Adams Newspaper Service, but I also went as a successful candidate for Republican national committeeman from Kansas, who would be elected by the Kansas delegation when it assembled. As a politician I went to the Roosevelt headquarters in the Congress Hotel and joined the conference of conspirators. As a reporter, I appeared at the Stratford Hotel where George Matthew Adams had quartered his other trained seals, George Fitch, Harry Webster, and J. N. Darling. Edna Ferber lived on the South Side in Chicago, and we proceeded to form a lively company. To me it was the comic relief of a nerve-tightening experience. We men—most of us old enough to be her father—took over Edna as our "Little Eva." We ate together, worked together, wrote together. Later in the convention we sat together. I took my writing job most seriously. And in that pre-convention week I turned in a story a day, sometimes two stories, one for the morning and one for the evening paper. Adams had more than fifty American daily papers on his syndicate string, the best papers in the country.

Probably waiting for the curtain to rise on the great national tragedy is as good a time as any to introduce Edna Ferber. In that year she was in her early twenties, just shedding the last plumpness of her early and middle teens. She stood five feet three or four firmly on her feet, with a sturdy body whose good lines one who was infatuated might easily have believed beautiful. Her skin was clean, healthy, and her cheeks were highly colored with the youthful glow that knew no drugstore. She was brunette, with a great mop of dark hair, blue-black, wavy, fine—the kind of lovely hair one is tempted to tousle. Her brow was low and broad. But her eyes—from them her spirit shone out. It was an eager spirit—young, curious, demanding understanding, honest, and wiser than a thousand years. I can remember yet across thirty years how we four men romped with her spiritually as with

462

pup, guying her, teasing her, helping her, tripping her, rolling her over, loving her to death. We called her "the angel child," which nickname she pretended to resent. Maybe she did—we could never tell. She was too smart for us. It was George Fitch who called me "Uncle Tom." I was in my middle forties then. And he called George Adams, our boss, Simon Legree. After the hubbub and rancor around the political headquarters it was a comfort, indeed a delight, to sneak off, in the Stratford Hotel, to another planet in another solar system.

That week before the convention opened, the national Republican committee, in its headquarters rooms, was slowly throwing out Roosevelt delegates, some of whom probably had questionable status, and substituting Taft contesting delegates, building up an impregnable majority in the convention for Taft. It was done with obvious *malice prepense,* with a sort of Gargantuan impudence, profligate and heroically indecent, which angered the Roosevelt majority in the country and turned Michigan Avenue, where the delegates milled up and down between the hotels, into a hell's broth of wrath. By Friday before the convention met, the crowds on Michigan Avenue overflowed into the street. The hotels were packed. The Roosevelt headquarters in the Auditorium Hotel consisted of a suite of four rooms, an outer reception room letting into a larger room which in turn opened into a smaller consultation room. Off that was a bedroom. That suite was on one of the upper floors of the hotel. On the second floor was a row of offices near the Florentine Room. The Florentine Room was ordinarily a large dining room, or ballroom. There a platform was erected, and all day long orators were declaiming, men from all over the United States who wanted to relieve their emotions. It was a sort of steam gauge. Senators, members of the House of Representatives, governors, state bosses, all were called to this rostrum and talked to the crowd standing agape around it. When governors or senators spoke, or a leader like Pinchot or Garfield, the Florentine Room was crowded to suffocation. It was full of emotion, and reporters covered the proceedings there.

In the little office badges were distributed, names of delegates listed, workers assigned tasks among the doubtful delegates, if there were any. I never heard of any, for by that time the issues were made. It was black on one side and white on the other. But bands had to be scheduled, and there were scores of them blaring up and down Michigan Avenue, marching through the hotels. Uniformed Roosevelt clubs had to be given something to do, and the turmoil channeled into something like order and purpose. Perhaps half a hundred men were working in those offices. On the lobby floor below, a few desks were manned by minor workers doing the thousand chores that are necessary for the organization of a first-class Presidential candidacy in any convention.

It is hard to reconstruct for this story the emotions of that hour. The mounting hatred on both sides which has dissolved with the years was then a terrible reality. The Friday of the week before the convention, Colonel Roosevelt decided to go to it. The decision broke a long precedent in convention amenities. It just was not done. There again I was not in the group that urged him. I thought it was a mistake. I suppose always my feeling was governed by a desire to shield him from his own mounting passions, whatever they were. Enmity to Taft certainly was one. The fear of defeat, which he did not take easily, was another. Rage, sheer animal rage at the indignity put upon him by the conservatives, and the contempt for him so evident in the course of the national committee, formed no small element, I think, in his decision. Ambition, I am satisfied, was not the governing passion. It was there, but he was a compromiser. He would have compromised at any stage of the game if he could have saved his face in compromising. But no possible compromise was thwarted by his ambition; of that I am fairly sure. At any rate, when we knew he was coming emotions began to rise among his friends and his enemies. The situation was genuinely tense. Yet it was profoundly American. Gags, funny stories, tags evoking laughter ran through the crowds in Chicago. Someone had ten thousand handbills printed the day before he arrived in Chicago which announced that Colonel Theodore Roosevelt would walk on the waters of Lake Michigan at 7:30 Monday evening. And the bands were playing a popular song, "Everybody's Doin' It, Doin' It, Doin' It," which provoked smiles on the too intense faces of the mob that surged along the Avenue. So steam was released; but the engine of public opinion was running there and throughout the country with a too high gauge. I was busy with my daily story for the Adams Syndicate and did not go to the train or try to see Colonel Roosevelt when he arrived; but the streets were packed, and his car moved slowly through miles of cheering citizens. Police had to cordon his entrance to the hotel. They had to move him through the lobby into the elevator. If ever an American was a hero of a hot and crowded hour, it was Theodore Roosevelt that day in Chicago.

He spoke the next evening at the Auditorium. Borah was with him on the platform. I had a front seat and heard the speech. It was one of his very best. Of course it could have been vapid and dumb, and the crowd would not have known it. It would cheer anything he said. So, as he spoke, some way the emotions of the crowd were wound tighter and tighter and released themselves in yells and roars. It was not an altogether pleasing spectacle and I was disturbed, I suppose a little frightened, at the churning which he gave the crowd. He closed with the phrase which has lasted now through thirty years but which then literally sizzled in the hearts of his auditors and winged across the country solidifying the Roosevelt sentiment:

"We stand at Armageddon, and we battle for the Lord!"

That phrase, coming at the end of three-quarters of an hour's diatribe against privilege and of pleading for the cause of the underdog, set the issue of the year. But Roosevelt's underdog was not proletarian. He was a middle-class, white-collar dog. Labor never followed Theodore Roosevelt. He got his share of the labor vote, but he was essentially—and that speech revealed him—the champion of the little businessman, the country lawyer, the doctor, the teacher, the preacher, the real estate dealer, the skilled worker—those whose labor organizations were rich and prosperous, the printers, the railroad men, the hard-coal miners. Speaking broadly, and of course allowing for notable exceptions, his opponents, those whom he had called "malefactors of great wealth," were the bankers and their principal clients, the great investors, the holders of stock in those organizations which formed the conscious "aggrandizement of great wealth." They and their satellites were conspicuous in the support of Taft and the conservative element in the Republican party which backed up the machinations of the Republican national central committee.

Roosevelt was forever inveighing against class. He did not seek labor's support. Nor did he denounce wealth as wealth. He was always, even in his Armageddon speech, protesting against the political expression of class feeling; for he was a middle-class man, upper middle class, but proud of the fact that he could call his program "the square deal." If he denounced the greedy leaders of capital, he was equally quick to cry out against the weakness of tyrannical labor leaders. When he fought for workingmen's compensation laws, when he advocated the eight-hour day, when he tried to stop child labor—all measures which would have affected exclusively the wage-earning class—it was evident that he was doing it not to benefit that class chiefly, but as a matter of justice which would bring indirect benefits to all classes. The point I am trying to make—and I am sure that it was the point of his Armageddon speech—is that that Roosevelt movement of the second decade of this century was not a class movement. It was a middle-class revolt against the injustice of our society, our industrial organization, our economic establishment, our political institutions. In so far as it had a proletarian angle, it expressed a big brother's pity, and attempted to implement his mercy toward the lesser and weaker members of his tribe and clan.

It was universal across Christendom—that feeling of revolt against things as they were. I did not realize that as I sat in the Auditorium, thrilled to my heart with a speech which he was making there before me. Yet now, looking back across the turmoil of two wars and across the folly of a plutocratic peace, I can see and feel the vast differences between the world revolt of the early decades of this century as I saw it decently demonstrating itself in Europe, in England, in that passionate protest in Chicago, and the movement which rose in Russia, in Germany flashed for a moment in the great

465

strike of the middle twenties, flared up in the New Deal and finally set the world aflame in '39. To that circumspect middle-class Armageddon of 191 came all the dynamite that has crashed into the modern world.

After the meeting closed, Borah and I walked for a few blocks along Michigan Avenue, trying to analyze the speech. Borah was an orator, and he knew how Roosevelt did it. He was tremendously impressed with it; but he was a little frightened, as I was. We had no idea of the hidden force beneath our feet, the volcanic social substance that was burning deep in the heart of humanity.

For three days before the Armageddon speech, the leaders on both side of the convention contest had been sedulously organizing their forces. The Roosevelt leaders assumed that La Follette, who had the Wisconsin delega tion and some delegates in the Dakotas and the far Northwest, would join with the Roosevelt forces in organizing the convention against Taft; but La Follette balked. The Roosevelt forces agreed to take as temporary c permanent chairman anyone whom La Follette chose. The Wisconsin dele gation would have been glad to see Governor McGovern as chairman, and he was eager to take the nomination; but the uncompromising spirit of the Wisconsin warrior balked. He could not be coaxed, bluffed, or bribed by offers of convention power to ally himself with Roosevelt. So he went his own way. Rumor said, and it was fairly well substantiated, that he came to a little town outside Chicago where he could be quickly available at the convention, and where he could see his own supporters easily. There he skulked like a plumed-bonneted Indian warrior, while Roosevelt was taking his followers to Armageddon.

Taft's leaders, Barnes, Penrose, Watson, and Mulvane, were swiftly ma turing their plans, recognizing as legitimate their faction in the conteste delegates from district after district, and state after state. Passions wer mounting, and yet, in the crowd of ten thousand people that crowded the sidewalks on Michigan Avenue and stuffed the hotels, there were no fight. In a Democratic convention, with similar emotional differences, the ho southern blood will boil and the Irish temper crack. But these Republican were Yankees at base, professional people, little merchants, bankers, peopl who swallowed insults easily and grinned while they took the money on th counter and went on with their business. Yet they were human enough. The day after the Armageddon speech, it was plain that the Taft faction woul win. Governor Stubbs, who had the Republican senatorial nomination i Kansas, one of the seven governors who brought Roosevelt into the Pres dential race, began to get nervous. He saw ahead. He ceased speaking at th Florentine Room and forum. He was not so conspicuous around the Roose velt headquarters. Then he had a telegram calling him to Topeka. H walked into Colonel Nelson's room and, making obeisance to Buddha, said

"Colonel, I find I have got to go to Topeka. They need me there."

For a second wrath flushed into the old Colonel's face. He looked at Stubbs with Olympian contempt and then let out his great raucous voice. "So you are going to run away from us, are you!" And he left his mouth open for the unspoken God damn, just looking at Stubbs.

Stubbs stayed. He went back to the Florentine Room. He came home from Topeka, joined the Roosevelt bolt, and went down to defeat like a gentleman. That was the way passion worked in the heart of a well-placed, well-bred, air-conditioned Republican statesman when his wrath was ruffled. I put this in here to explain why, with all the ruckamuction and rancor of that week in Chicago, assault and battery were so conspicuously absent.

When the convention opened Tuesday morning, it had no surprises. The Taft men, through the national committee, put forward young Victor Rosewater, editor of the Omaha Bee, as their candidate for temporary chairman, and elected him after a few hours' turmoil and struggle during which time the Roosevelt floor manager and convention spokesman was young Herbert Hadley of Missouri. We were dear and beloved friends. He stood on the platform protesting every inch of the proceedings. He was most courteous. Indeed he breathed an air of chivalry that was pleasant to the heart. In that day he was in his late thirties or early forties. He stood slim and lithe as a movie actor. He had a kindly, resonant voice. His elocution was polished, his gestures pleasant, his manner firm and determined. He captured the imagination of the delegates. He was the gallery idol. Roosevelt was proud of him. We from Kansas and Missouri basked in his reflected light. After the convention—I think it was the next day—I was at the Roosevelt headquarters. When I went in Beveridge was standing on a chair in the outer room making big medicine oratorically to the waiting statesmen. Roosevelt called me into the inner room and asked:

"What do you know about Hadley really?"

I told him about Hadley's determined rise, his obvious but decently repressed ambition; about his capacity for student poker; related the fact that he had been suspended in his senior year at K.U. for some harmless student revelry and had kept up his studies during his suspension and had taken his finals with honor, which amused Roosevelt. I told him about Hadley's escapade with Mamma Bear on Specimen Mountain when he filled the cub's bottom full of birdshot, not knowing that Mamma was around the other side of the rock, and how Hadley ran around the edge of a cliff and dropped fifteen feet and came rushing into camp and fainted—all of this amidst the low murmur of the crowd on Michigan Avenue below us—amidst the tension and the sense of strife about the place, the slowly mounting fever that was all but crackling in our blood. Roosevelt, leaning forward on his chair, heard me, knowing that I was giving relevant testimony and competent about young Hadley. He chuckled as I talked.

"Well, they want to compromise on Hadley. He is going to see me in a few moments." He paused. "That story places him." Again he paused and said, snapping his teeth together as he often did when he was a bit perplexed: "I can take Hadley, but they must purge the roll of the convention if they compromise with me, take off the fraudulent delegates. Let an honest convention assemble, and it can do what it pleases, and I'll help Hadley."

He knew and I knew that that was idle talk. The organized leaders would not trust him. Moreover, they would not trust Hadley after the convention. A few moments later Hadley came in. He and the Colonel talked for half an hour. I saw both the Colonel and Hadley within a few minutes after their conference. They told substantially the same story. It amounted to this: Roosevelt would not compromise on Hadley unless the national committee seated the delegates who Roosevelt honestly believed were fairly elected. The story afterward survived that Roosevelt would not compromise on Hadley, which was not quite true. I should like to be able to remember where I was during that conference. I think that the Colonel asked me to go sit with Mrs. Roosevelt awhile in the inmost room. I know that I was there that morning before the convention met. There she sat knitting, looking out into the street, down the six or eight stories, where the mob was milling and roaring below. I never saw so calm a woman. She reminded me of Madame Defarge, but she was not grim. She was just sweet and unruffled and lovely.

Two or three times that week I was with her. Always the Colonel sent me in to her to store me away when he needed me, or to be a quick witness to some transaction; and I felt that she was like a calm Olympian goddess looking down on the clamoring street with the noisy marching cries, "We want Teddy!" and some way perceiving the gallery mob in the Coliseum, roaring over and over again that slogan, drowning the blare of the bands, lashing the stolid delegates below who were about to nominate Taft. There she sat high above the crowd beside the hotel window, knitting. It was easy to imagine that she might be knitting the pattern of the country's life into that garment, whatever it was—weaving the inevitable destiny ahead of us out of the yarn and skein where it had been wound by the hand of some terrible fate.

CHAPTER LXVII

Climax and Exodus

THE REPUBLICAN NATIONAL CONVENTION was meeting that week under a guard of nearly a thousand policemen. They crowded the aisles. They ranged through the galleries to maintain order. Not that disorder had broken out, but the marchers in the streets, the great throngs in the gallery were so overwhelmingly bent upon the nomination of Roosevelt that his inevitable defeat seemed to be a good reason for the cordon of police that ran through the hall like a blue smear around the buff upturned faces of the delegates. I had been elected Republican national committeeman before the convention met, so I sat for the most part with the reporters where I could look down into the human caldron that was boiling all around me. The committee on credentials had done its work. It had seated enough contested delegates to nominate Taft. The parliamentary question which was before the house in the first day or two of the convention came in a motion to require the contestants on both sides to stand aside and let the uncontested delegates vote on the temporary organization of the convention. That motion, if passed, would, of course, have given Roosevelt control by about the same small majority that Taft had when the committee had seated practically all his contested delegates. There was parliamentary precedent to justify the prevalence of either the yeas or the nays; but with the contested delegates voting for themselves the Taft forces easily controlled the temporary organization which would also set up the permanent organization.

The Roosevelt delegates presented, as their candidate for permanent chairman, the name of Wisconsin's governor, McGovern, whom the Wisconsin delegates heroically deserted. The other La Follette delegates followed the La Follette suit. McGovern was defeated for election as permanent chairman by Elihu Root, who took the chair. He became the symbol of the Taft machine. He was a man then in his sixties, probably the most learned, even erudite, distinguished, and impeccable conservative

Republican in the United States. He had served as United States Senator, as Secretary of State, as Secretary of War. He was the idol of the American bar. He had authority. When he clicked the gavel on the marble block that topped the speaker's table, order ensued almost hypnotically. The gaunt thin-lined features of this man so conspicuously the intellectual leader of a convention which had been melted by rage into a rabble, stood there calm, serene, and sure in his domination of the scene. He looked down upon the sweating wrathful faces in the pit where the delegates sat, swept his eyes around the vast horseshoe of spectators who jammed the gallery until they sometimes crowded the police guards off their feet. But Root's hands did not tremble, his face did not flicker. He was master. He knew probably what we afterwards found out, that the railing approaches to his rostrum were wound with barbed wire, that he was commander of the police, and could have checked a riot by raising his hand. He knew also that hundreds of his outraged fellow Republicans, men who had once been his friends, were glaring at him with eyes distraught with hate. I have never seen mass passion sway men before or since as that great multitude was moved those first hours after Root took command. Then indeed fights broke out, like bubbles on the boiling caldron all over the pit where delegates were so full of the gall of grudge and resentment that they could give utterance to their fury only in their fists. The police promptly stopped the fights and prevented rioting. Root seemed to us like a diabolical sphinx. He pushed the program of the convention through steadily, and as swiftly as possible. Hadley, floor manager for Roosevelt, matched Root's basilisk imperturbability with suavity and charm. He was punctilious where Root was grim. He even cracked a joke now and then.

I knew when I saw Hadley that he was stricken with tuberculosis and often went to his post with a temperature of 101 or 102, and at the climax of his duty he was carrying 103. Few knew that. I told Roosevelt, and he cried out for a moment, shocked and pained at the tragedy of it. But there on the floor of the convention he stood, an idol none the less, because hundreds, perhaps a few thousands, knew that Hadley had been the rejected compromise offered by the Taft delegates.

It is one of the mysteries of democratic action, this mob sentience, which so often in moments of grave portent casts the players on a tragic stage so nicely. Here for two long, hot, melodramatic days these two—Hadley and Root—stalked the stage, perfect incarnations of the opposing forces.

Root in his morning coat and gray trousers, a lean, almost hatchet-faced man in his late sixties, repressed, almost reticent in his stingy use of words exactly chiseled out of the moment's need, was the greatest corporation lawyer in the United States, a man born on an endowed college campus, representing the impeccable respectability of invested capital. All his life he had been on the money side of lawsuits representing the invested economic surplus of a thrifty and not too scrupulous plutocracy. As befitted such a character in such a miracle play as we were staging in those days, Root was probably the most erudite and polished statesman of his day. Foreign travel had made him a cosmopolitan. Service in the United States Senate and in the Capital had given him that gentle, almost wistful cynicism that garbs the American aristocrat who stems back to Concord or to the James River. He was from every angle the perfect symbol of a propertied class struggling for its privileges which it honestly deems to be its rights. It was deeply symbolic that invested capital should be encased in dark-striped trousers and morning coat, wielding the gavel as a king would wave his scepter, with a dignity that made a show of indignation superfluous.

Beside him many times the convention saw the young Rooseveltian leader, Herbert Hadley. He wore a long gun-barrel double-breasted knee-length coat, and often in controversy smilingly pushed back a flap, shoved his hand into a trouser pocket, using the other for gesticulation, and smiled the guileless smile of lingering youth—boyish, disarming, as he spoke for the lost cause. He came to that rostrum because he had been fighting for ten years all that Root had defended for forty years. Hadley was a reformer. As prosecuting attorney in Kansas City he had been the foe of crooks, big and little; and as prosecuting attorney he had flashed on the national screen sharply, effectively, rather mercilessly cross-examining John D. Rockefeller the elder, who was the lion totem of the clan of predatory respectability in American industry. Hadley was the David to Rockefeller's Goliath. As governor of Missouri he had led the state in adopting the current reforms popular in that hour. There they stood in that vast charade that was picturing, *ad lib.,* the conflict inherent in Christian civilization, the conflict between aggrandized enterprise and its various ramifications of commercial and industrial rapacity, on the one hand, and the protest against that pious pillage, man's sense of pity for the exploited, his uneasy sense of wrong that was disturbing the middle class, and the inner urge for justice which has been the motor of human progress as man has struggled for the thing called liberty through the ages. They were old, old forces in an ancient miracle play of human history that were clashing there that sultry June day in the Chicago Coliseum—Root and Hadley, not villain and hero, not the dragon and St. George, but Samson blind in Gaza and Laocoön and his struggle with his snakes.

Slowly, motion by motion, phase by phase, the steamroller crushed its way toward the nomination of Taft. And here is a funny American expression: In the midst of all the rancor and wormwood pumping in the hearts of the delegates, every time a motion was offered by the Taft people, a thousand toots and imitation whistles of the steamroller engine pierced

471

the air sharply, to be greeted with laughter that swept the galleries. An American crowd will have a terrible time behind barricades, or surging up Pennsylvania Avenue to overwhelm the White House. It will probably laugh itself to death on the way. Kipling said it of the American: "His sense of humor saves him whole."

Looking back, I don't remember how I wrote my stories for the newspapers. I did them faithfully, and they were good stories. I can remember hours at the reporters' table as I watched the Taft steamroller crushing its way through its program. I can remember gay mealtimes with the Adams trained seals, and with other newspapermen who always congregated with their kind. I can remember conferences with the Kansas delegation. We stood almost solidly (two districts dissenting) with the Roosevelt forces. Henry Allen, who was chairman of our delegation and our most distinguished delegate, had been picked by Colonel Roosevelt's board of strategy to say farewell on behalf of the Roosevelt delegates to the victorious Taft forces when Taft's nomination was made. And I can remember well how proud our delegation was of Henry, and how delighted I was with his speech which we read together before he spoke it.

I can remember wiggling in and out of the crowded Florentine Room of the Roosevelt headquarters like an overfed ferret, nosing out little inside notes of news for my daily articles. I can remember quiet talks with Roosevelt in his room alone. He was becoming deadly as his defeat approached. We discussed the possible bolt. We discussed the formation of a new party. There again I rejected it; but there again I was determined to follow my leader after I had advised him against a course which seemed inevitable. He knew I would follow. Then a curtain falls, and I do not remember when the decision was made that Roosevelt should bolt the nomination of Taft and run, either with a rump nomination or with the backing of a new party. Personally I favored the new party rather than a rump nomination, but I do not know when the decision was made to take the latter course. I was not present when the Roosevelt forces decided to do so. I heard it secondhand. But I do remember these things: Sitting at the reporters' table I heard Henry Allen's ironic diatribe as he stood before Chairman Root and bade farewell to the Taft majority. It was a masterpiece of amiable sarcasm. And I was astonished to realize that I had not detected, when my eyes had read this speech, the fact that its climactic sentence lacked a verb. No one else had noticed this. Afterwards Henry saw it, and we had a pleasant titter about it. But the hour was too tense for grammar.

When Henry finished his tearless farewell, all Roosevelt delegates marched out of the building with as much dignity as men of wrath can assume in defeat. The Kansas delegates met immediately after the rout and I resigned as Republican national committeeman for two good reasons: First, we wanted to hold the Kansas end of the Republican national committee, and I would not even pretend to support Taft under the wicked circumstances which surrounded his nomination; second, we elected a good smiling Republican, who would go through the motions of supporting Taft with some sincerity, and who was nevertheless politically aligned to our faction in Kansas.

I left the convention after the progressives walked out, but returned an hour later to see the final obsequies. It was a dreary performance, the nomination of Taft, and of James Sherman for Vice President. Those who remained in the galleries stayed only to hoot ribaldly as the delegates on the floor, amid a wilderness of vacant chairs, went through the motions of reading their platform and nominating their ticket. Late in the afternoon they adjourned. I had a long day's story to tell to the readers who were taking my syndicated articles in two score newspapers. I did not drop into the Roosevelt headquarters in the Congress Hotel after the adjournment, but hurried to my room to write.

For some reason I did my own filing that night, which meant that I prepared three carbon copies and the original. I could file to about half of the newspapers with one copy through the Western Union, but maybe a fourth of them required filing through the Postal Telegraph Company on a carbon, and ten or a dozen of them required separate filings. Two of them near by, in cities like Milwaukee or Detroit, received their copies by mail. After I had written my story that night, a two-hour job, I used another hour or such a matter filing what I had written. By that time it was well along into the middle of the evening. I came back to the hotel and sat down alone to have the first good meal I had had since breakfast. All day I had been subsisting on sandwiches and hot dogs at the restaurants under the rostrum at the Coliseum. It must have been nine o'clock, perhaps later, and I was still feeding rather luxuriously and abundantly, when I noticed the dining room filling up. Ed Mullaney, one of the Kansas bolting delegates, came in, sat down beside me, and asked:

"Why weren't you over to Orchestra Hall?"

I told him why, and he began to laugh. "Well," he said, "you missed the big show."

I said, "What show?"

"Oh," he said, grinning and knowing how funny it was, "we have organized the Progressive Party. Roosevelt made a ripsnorting speech, and the crowd tore the roof off and we are on our way!"

And I didn't know a thing about it. Neither did the readers of my story, and I was supposed to be on the inside of the whole Progressive bolt! I had missed the story, and you could have bought me for a nickel. Experiences like that are good for a man when he gets puffed up; and I certainly was puffed up that week in Chicago, what with associating with the great, edging in on conferences and waddling around with a fat man's strut.

It was too late to file another story. I hurried down to Roosevelt's headquarters. The Colonel yelled at me in his high falsetto, asking where I was and where I had been. Then he told me quickly what had happened after I had left the Kansas delegation. The bolt and the formation of the new party had been decided on several days before, but not the meeting at Orchestra Hall. The meeting was most dramatic, as they told it there in the Roosevelt headquarters, everyone sizzling with enthusiasm. Before bedtime I also was pretty well carbonated with hopes for the new party.

I was, of course, made national committeeman, and at an informal meeting of the national committee was elected a member of the national publicity committee. Practically all the rebels who had walked out of the Republican convention that day joined the new party. And the unseated delegates from the Taft states joined the new party, so that it was not hard to organize it on the spot and call a national convention for mid-August. Immediately after the Democrats had nominated their Presidential ticket, I went to bed chagrined and disgusted with myself at missing the birth of the new party. I believe it was an historic event.

I got up the next morning, properly chastened, greatly reduced in size, and went more or less humbly about catching up with the procession. The chief business before the Progressive national committee was organizing the nominating convention. That we did quickly and well, but it was no trouble. The Progressive movement was a ship in the midst of a sea of boiling indignation and surging optimism. I had not been for the bolt. I desired the new party only because I believed it was the fair and honest thing to do to leave the Republican organization, which was hopelessly reactionary; but at the very end, in the afternoon, when I resigned from the Republican national committee, I hoped that Roosevelt would not take the Progressive Presidential nomination. I believed then—and events justified me—that we should have held him as our ace, which would also have saved him from the possible humiliation of defeat at the polls. I felt some way that our party would be the stronger and the longer-lived if it was not a personal party, not too much a camouflage upon a disgruntled bolt. Deep down in my heart, my affection and protective care for the Colonel and his fortunes governed my political judgment, except that I wanted the new party. I did not want Roosevelt to bolt nor to run independently as a sorehead without the new party.

All this seems like raking over old ashes, yet it mattered intensely in that summer day of 1912. I had no thought or hope or political desire except to get the new party started and at the same time to protect my friend from the consequences of his impetuous desire for revenge. He was burned up with it. Rage, futile, thwarted wrath, glowed in his face that night after the party had been launched in Orchestra Hall. He was not downcast; indeed he was triumphant, full of jokes and quips as though the teakettle of his heart were humming and rattling the lid of his merry countenance. But rage was bubbling inside him.

The thing I did not like there at the last was the presence of George Perkins, Morgan's partner, fluttering around the headquarters, smiling and simpering in triumph like a sinister specter—in his gray alpaca suit to match the slightly sprinkled gray of his brown hair and his gray mustache, and it seemed to me covering a steel-gray heart. He was not one of us, the mad mullahs of that selfless effervescing group, the men who had made the battle in the field, those who had carried the primaries in the Republican states of the North. Perkins was too close to the Colonel, and we—perhaps not I, for I had no sense of jealousy, but Beveridge, Bristow, Amos and Gifford Pinchot, Hiram Johnson, Dolliver, Cummins, Senator Clapp, Senator Bourne, Hadley, Harold Ickes, Governor Osborn of Michigan, the New England crowd, and the New Jersey Progressives following George Record and Everett Colby—were not so close as we should have been to the Colonel that day nor, to peek ahead a little, in that campaign.

The only value this part of my story has is in revealing me a rebel against the rebellion, suspicious even in my enthusiasm, but abating no ounce of energy even though I was standing beside myself, watching myself like a big brother. I have always done that. Something in moments of tension has always split my personality. Maybe it was in inheritance, blood, or paternal environment—the calculating Yankee watching the wild Irishman not without amusement and sometimes with qualms. It was so that night and the next day when the Progressives crossed the Rubicon, and I splashed along with them. Heaven knows, we didn't know why we were going. We knew nothing of the deep urge that was drawing us with the time spirit. But we thought we knew. The phrase was pat and apt that marked our destination: "To social and industrial justice."

CHAPTER LXVIII

The Nomination of Wilson

I DON'T KNOW HOW nor when I squeezed in two weeks that summer in Colorado in our newly bought cabin. But the fortnight filled the cisterns of my spiritual and physical energy, and I came back to Kansas full of a dozen maturing plans, mostly political. In early July I went to Baltimore with George Adams' trained seals, to attend and report the story of the Democratic convention.

Adams had rented a three-story house in a good neighborhood half a block back of the Hotel Belvidere. The doctor who lived in it had moved out, and left his cook and maybe a housemaid, both colored. We saw little of the maid, but the cook was our delight. She was a square-rigged, scow-bottomed, easy-going person whom we called Jemima, whether it was her name or not. She laughed easily and cooked like an angel. We bought our own groceries. Edna Ferber and I were the stewards, and we liked company. We were given to breakfasts, held open house and invited the wide world, our world being more or less circumscribed by newspaper people and writers. We had breakfasts at which often ten or fifteen guests dropped in for pancakes or waffles, sausages, and berries then in season—raspberries, strawberries, or huckleberries—or ham and eggs and hot biscuits and honey whatever Edna and I could pick up at the market and tote home in our basket, and whatever Jemima could make for our provender. We liked to have her serve at the table dressed as she was in the kitchen, and we kidded her and courted her and flattered her until she was quite one of us. There was no attempt to "keep the nigger in her place." I think our Yankee manners shocked her a bit. She did not quite understand it. But what meals she served! We stowed Edna on the third floor by herself, where she queened it with her typewriter. But below the third floor a man's bed was his own only if he got it, for our guests were forever coming in at all hours and flopping down on empty beds, as the convention tended to hold night sessions and as Fitch, Webster, Darling, and I were compelled by the irregular

476

sessions of the convention to write our stories at midnight. The ménage in the doctor's house was utterly mad. The hotels were crowded, and often the big overstuffed chairs in our parlor were filled for the night, and the sofas rarely were empty. Washington newspapermen came over, and occasionally politicians. Victor Murdock, a Seventh District Kansas Congressman, was there often, and Gilson Gardner and Billy Hard, and sometimes they brought strangers whom we had never seen.

Curiously we attracted crowds without serving liquor. I don't know why we did not serve liquor. Maybe it wasn't the habit of the day and times. But we had a hilarious time, cold-sober, with good food and good company. Probably it could not be done today; for that was a generation ago. But I know I had no trouble writing my newspaper stories. I was used to writing in the uproar of a printing office, and the riot of other newspapermen and women did not disturb me. Certainly the stewardship of the house under Edna's direction, and she was a kid of twenty-five, did not irk me nor take my time, nor divert my attention from the main business of the day. I roamed through the hotel lobbies and into bedrooms of the political hotels. I often met Bryan and his brother, Charley, and we reporters all knew that someone, maybe it was brother Charley—it might have been Bryan—was promoting a rather futile cabal to nominate Bryan again that made no headway and excited no opposition save tolerant smiles. Bryan was a strange figure in that convention, a ridiculous man with tremendous power.

I was almost as much interested in the nomination of Woodrow Wilson by the Democrats as I was in the Republican nomination of Theodore Roosevelt. For it was obvious that Wilson, who had become the legatee of the Bryan estate in the Democratic party, was having the same fight in his party that Roosevelt had led in the Republican party.

Having a rather sketchy Republican loyalty I was naturally for a situation that would bring liberal victories in both parties. I knew, and I suppose the whole world of American politics knew, that Taft and his following were only a small minority of the Republican party. A considerable majority of the states had, in the half-decade before 1912, again and again supported liberal leadership in one party or the other. Even in the South, the leaven was beginning to work in states like Texas, the Carolinas, Tennessee, Kentucky. Yet the picture of the Democratic party, when the national convention opened in Baltimore, indicated that Champ Clark, Speaker of the Democratic House, had a definite majority of the convention. Under the rules a Democratic nominee had to have a two-thirds majority. That rule, for two generations and more, had given the South the veto power over all Democratic nominations. For the South always held two-fifths, or nearly that, of the delegates in the Democratic convention and, as the South generally voted as a block, the nominee had to suit the South.

Clark was from Missouri. He came out of the southern tradition. He was a Kentuckian with Virginia roots. By an ironic turn of fate, Bryan, who was a delegate from Nebraska, was instructed to vote for Clark. In the caucusing before the convention it was evident that the reactionary forces of the convention would support Clark. Tammany was for Clark and the old-fashioned gold standard. Old-fashioned silk-stocking Democrats symbolized by August Belmont and Thomas Fortune Ryan, were for Clark. So Bryan gave it out before the convention that he proposed to fight anyone whom Murphy of Tammany, Thomas F. Ryan, and August Belmont supported.

The convention had hardly opened before Bryan attacked his foes by name in a rather absurd resolution. It made a sensation, and the Clark forces finally decided to laugh it off by letting it pass unanimously without opposition. They made it ridiculous in the convention, but Bryan made it dramatic in the country.

Bryan was a curious figure in that convention. The sixteen years that had elapsed since the boy orator of the Platte stampeded the convention at Chicago had broadened his girth, thinned his hair, taken youth out of him. He was slightly stooped, and had not the cast of countenance of maturity, but a little too much weight in jowl and belly. He was beginning to dress, of summers, in an alpaca coat with a white vest and wrinkled trousers. He had never paid much attention to clothes, and he had a frowzy look. It was evident from the parliamentary dowdiness of his resolution attacking Ryan and Belmont that his thinking was slightly askew. But his speech supporting his motion certainly had enough fire in it to draw howling approval from the galleries, and also of what was evidently a majority of the convention. It was a sinister exhibition, that response to the Bryan resolution. It was different from the clamor that greeted Roosevelt's leadership at Chicago, more emotional, more unrestrained, more savage. The academic group which was designed to control the Democratic party under the leaders like Wilson certainly had not made over the party. It was still Irish, and the rebel yell still ripped through the applause like a scythe down the swath.

On the first ballot, Clark took the lead. He registered a majority in the early balloting. As Clark was gathering his majority, it became evident that Wilson would be his opponent. Other Democratic candidates lost strength, which generally went to Wilson. After Clark had assembled his majority, he held it for several sessions.

To say that, does not carry the sense of drama. To understand the drama we must realize that, ballot by ballot, the country was standing around the billboards of newspapers in great crowds, watching the Baltimore struggle. The cleavage between progressives and conservatives which had been opened by the Chicago convention was deepened and widened in the hearts of the American people by the spectacle at Baltimore. Clark, who was a better politician than Taft, had not revealed his conservatism. That showed forth in the character of his supporting delegates, and after he held his majority for a day the nation realized, as the convention had realized from the first click of the temporary chairman's gavel, that Clark and Bryan were fighting the battle that Roosevelt had lost to Taft.

I was almost as deeply moved, watching Wilson's strength develop, as I had been at Chicago, where I had a personal stake in the ballot. I had met Wilson at Madison, Wisconsin, two years before. I had watched his career as governor of New Jersey, when he had, by sheer intellectual strength, given his state the primary, the direct election of United States Senators, by the contemporary subterfuge of allowing candidates for the State Senate and legislature to pledge themselves to a candidate for United States Senator. Wilson was for the workmen's compensation law, for child-labor enactments, and for the whole progressive program. He had dramatized himself skillfully, and stood as a progressive Democrat just as La Follette, Roosevelt and other state satellites in the Republican party had become branded with the liberal sign. So I found myself cheering whenever Wilson gained a state in the balloting. I know now from looking back over my newspaper reports that I filed at the convention that I reasoned that the conservative vote outside of the deep South was negligible and that if we had Roosevelt running against Wilson, the country was sure of a progressive President. And in my heart, loyal as I was to Roosevelt, it made no great difference to me whether Roosevelt or Wilson won. Although I was capable of emotional strain and surface prejudice, my ingrained habit of seeing both sides helped me to size up the realities of the political situation, and I gave my loyalty to the progressive cause rather than to the Progressive party.

I had no great personal liking for Wilson. When I met him, he seemed to be a cold fish. I remember I came home from the meeting at Madison, Wisconsin, and told Mrs. White that the hand he gave me to shake felt like a ten-cent pickled mackerel in brown paper—irresponsive and lifeless. He had a highty-tighty way that repulsed me. When he tried to be pleasant he creaked. But he had done a fine liberal job in New Jersey. I liked the way he gathered the Irish politicians about him and let them teach him the game in his gubernatorial fights. In every contest he rang true. So, as the convention dragged on, far past the four or five days that it ordinarily took to hold a national convention, my respect for Wilson grew and my admiration waxed warm. And when the Nebraska delegation, after days and days of balloting for Clark, broke to Wilson, I stood on the reporters' table top and cheered, until I was hoarse, with the galleries; while Tammany and the irreconcilable reactionaries in some of the southern states, and Tom Taggart, the Indiana boss, clung to the spars and lifeboats of the wrecked Clark liner, and all the country knew that Clark's day was done—that the progressives were about to win a victory in Baltimore to offset the defeat in Chicago.

Once at the last, as the convention was balloting until long past midnight, we were routed out of our beds almost at dawn and hurried into the convention to watch the break-up of the wreck that had been the Clark majority. It was then, I think, that I danced on my table and yelled to my heart's content. Wilson's strength in the convention slowly mounted until it tipped over the two-thirds majority needed for the nomination. But I did not exult much after that first demonstration of Wilson's power. It was tragic to see Clark's strength crumbling. I say tragic because it was indeed that disintegration of failure which one sees in well-built drama. Human nature is not always lovely in failure, and I sat watching the rise of Wilson and the fall of Clark—seeing men scurry from the Clark camp to the other to save their political hides, watching them sneak into the Wilson camp or go with banners.

I was not sure, as the Clark forces began to break, what really was back of the collapse. Was it the instinct to climb on the bandwagon? Was it the inner latent belief of those delegates who left Clark that the progressive cause was the righteous cause? Was it fear? What was it? It came to the same thing, that crystallization of the progressive elements of the Democratic convention which we had witnessed in the Republican convention a few weeks before. But in the Republican convention they came convinced, instructed, militant. No votes were changed after the first click of the temporary chairman's gavel on the marble in the Republican convention at Chicago. But there at Baltimore, before my eyes, I saw the thing happen —the formation of a left-wing group led on the floor unofficially by Bryan, who even in victory looked like an adorable old rag baby, but who had steel at the core.

To see that spectacle, in the longest convention I had ever reported, slowly unfold itself, take significance and definite meaning, was something well worth while. I shall never forget the metamorphosis from the mob to the marching cohorts of liberalism following Wilson, led by the spirit of Bryan. One would have said that, with the overthrow of a man like Clark, rather primitively human in his passions, his followers would have made a split in the Democratic party like that I had witnessed in Chicago. The Clark people were mad, but most of them who really understood what they were doing were above all loyal Democrats who believed in party discipline. I have said many times they were Irish and southern; but their party was next to their religion. So Wilson faced no revolt when he took his nomination. And I heard no such deep and bitter damnation for the winner from his beaten opponents as I heard in Chicago when Taft won. The Democratic party was fairly well united. Its wounds healed quickly. However Clark might feel his own wounds (and he did feel them long and deeply—indeed, defeat broke his heart), his fellow Democrats soon became Wilson Democrats, and at the last I could see there, at my reporter's seat at the convention, that Wilson would go before the country with his party phalanx behind him.

In reporting the convention I did not conceal my frank bias for the Wilson cause. I was a liberal before I was a Republican or a progressive, and was proud then of my heart's loyalty to the cause. Certainly I did not try to write a colorless story. I wrote frankly as a partisan of the liberals in both conventions, and while I told the truth as I saw it, my story was the story of the progressive split in each. There was no nonsense about concealing the cause of the rift, or smoothing it over as a personal triumph for either Taft or Wilson. I painted the conservatives black, and probably made the liberals white-winged angels—which they were not. They were only men, two-legged and frail, walking in strange new roads drawn by something they did not quite understand, following a pattern of political conduct that they could not quite resist, in a drama whose lines they improvised out of the promptings of their hearts.

CHAPTER LXIX

The Birth of a Party

IT WAS NO EASY JOB, when I got home from Baltimore, to assume my part
of the leadership which was organized in Kansas from the grassroots for
the Progressive party in the campaign that was looming ahead of us. The
first job was to hold local conventions to nominate delegates to the first
Progressive national convention, which was held in the late summer. Henry
Allen, who had been the chairman of our delegation to the Republican
convention, naturally was the leader of the delegation in the first Progressive convention. I was a delegate—I forget whether from my congressional
district or from the state—but we did hold our caucuses and conventions,
and we did name a strong delegation to the Chicago Progressive convention.

If the Progressives were a party of protest, they were not in the least
proletarian. It was middle-class to the core. It was just as suspicious of
Gompers and organized labor as it was of Rockefeller and organized capital.
We were, of course, careful not to shut the door on labor, and if a Morgan
partner could get into a place of leadership it indicates we were careful
not to shut the door on Wall Street, if it came penitently, seeking refuge.
But the movement which Theodore Roosevelt led in 1912 was in the main
and in its heart of hearts *petit bourgeois:* little businessmen, professional
men, well-to-do farmers, skilled artisans from the upper brackets of organized labor. It was from the ranks of these people that our delegates were
called to the Progressive national convention.

The day before it met, "Bull Moose" became a tag for our party. Reporters
asked Colonel Roosevelt, when he first arrived in Chicago for the convention, how he felt. He called out lustily, snapping his teeth, batting his eyes
and grinning like an amiable orangutan:

"I feel as strong as a bull moose!"

From that hour we, who followed in his train, were Bull Moosers, and
proud of it.

It was when we were redecorating the Coliseum at Chicago that we discovered, underneath the bunting that wrapped the railings around the speaker's stand, the banisters and the steps approaching it, closely wrapped barbed wire. In any struggle to get to the chairman of the Republican convention, Mr. Root, or to take possession by force of the organization on the platform, the attackers would have found their hands lacerated if they grabbed those railings or banisters, lacerated even before they got upon the platform, no matter from what angle they tried to rush the speakers' stand. We were hopping-mad when we discovered that barbed wire. It was a symbol of all the fraud and force and shenanigans and duress which we had encountered in the Republican national convention a few weeks before. When we decorated the Coliseum we took off the barbed wire and replaced the bunting.

The Bull Moose convention had little gallery support, but we managed to fill the delegates' chairs. I had seen many a protest convention. As a boy I had watched the Greenbackers. As a young man I had reported many a Populist convention. Those agrarian movements too often appealed to the ne'er-do-wells, the misfits—farmers who had failed, lawyers and doctors who were not orthodox, teachers who could not make the grade, and neurotics full of hates and ebullient, evanescent enthusiasms. I knew that crowd well. But when the Progressive convention assembled at Chicago I looked down upon it from the reporters' stand and saw that here was another crowd.

Here were the successful middle-class country-town citizens, the farmer whose barn was painted, the well paid railroad engineer, and the country editor. It was a well dressed crowd. We were, of course, for woman suffrage, and we invited women delegates and had plenty of them. They were our own kind, too—women doctors, women lawyers, women teachers, college professors, middle-aged leaders of civic movements, or rich young girls who had gone in for settlement work. Looking over the crowd, judging the delegates by their clothes, I figured that there was not a man or woman on the floor who was making less than two thousand a year, and not one, on the other hand, who was topping ten thousand. Proletarian and plutocrat were absent—except George Perkins, who was too conspicuous. He and his satellites and sycophants from Wall Street and lower Broadway, who had known Roosevelt in Harvard, loved him and misunderstood him; but they had their influence. Sometimes I felt even then the weight of their influence bore too heavily on the scales of his decisions. I told Roosevelt so in those happy moments we spent together, swapping wisdom in persiflage, when he in the lexicon of my felicity was Daniel Boone, the wilderness hunter, and I in his was the Old Boulevardier; and the Colonel knew right well of my distrust of his palace courtiers from New York.

Of course when the convention assembled, George Perkins—spick-and-span, oiled and curled like an Assyrian bull, and a young one, trim and virile—was conspicuous in all the preliminary proceedings. He was a man for detail, and he did a right competent job of stage management in that dramatic hour when the Bull Moose party was born, even though he could not fill the galleries. On the speaker's stand, we had notables from all over the land: college presidents, heads of scientific foundations. Our prize exhibit was Jane Addams. I had something to do with bringing her to the convention, for I had known her many years. She had visited us in Emporia. I had seen her in Hull House several times. When she came down the aisle back of the speaker's stand where the other notables wearing Bull Moose badges were arrayed in proud and serried ranks, the delegates and the scattered spectators in the galleries rose and cheered. Not even the Colonel got much more rousing cheers than Jane Addams, when she rose to second his nomination.

The Colonel was there on the platform, and I saw his eyes glisten with pride and exultant joy that she was fighting under his banner. I have rarely seen him happier than he was that moment. The band played "Onward, Christian Soldiers," which probably Perkins or some of his newspaper friends had adopted as our anthem; and the crowd cheered and began to sing as the band led. When our platform was read, it also was interrupted by cheers and outbursts of the band, probably signaled by Perkins or one of his assistant stage managers. It was all beautifully done, and after the platform had been adopted and the nominations of Colonel Roosevelt for President and Governor Hiram Johnson, of California, for Vice President, we adjourned, singing "Praise God from Whom All Blessings Flow."

We were mighty well pleased with ourselves, filled with a glowing sense of duty well done. We also believed that we had seen a historic occasion, the birth of a party that was destined to rise and take in the country the place that the Republican party had occupied for fifty years. I know this, that a thousand delegates carried home little mementos of the day and hour, effigies of the Bull Moose, pictures of the Colonel, badges identifying themselves as delegates. They hoped that these trinkets would be family heirlooms in another day and time. The occasion had all of the psychological trappings and habiliments of a crusade. We were indeed Christian soldiers "marching as to war"—and rather more than mildly mad.

I went to Chicago nearly a week before the convention assembled, for I was interested more than anything else in the progressive platform. I had been somewhat responsible for the Kansas progressive platform of 1910 which was, I believe, held by Roosevelt as a tentative fighting, trading creed. Indeed at the Republican convention I sat with the progressives who had their committee on platform all named to function if McGovern and not

Root had been the permanent chairman. I tried in the tentative Republican committee on platform to work in as much of the Kansas platform as I could; and at the Progressive convention I sat in the drafting committee on platform and was able to write in many of the ideas that had been embodied in the Kansas platform of 1910. We worked four days and the better part of three nights on that first Progressive platform. Dr. William Draper Lewis, dean of the law school of the University of Pennsylvania, was the chairman of the drafting committee. He had prepared a platform much more conservative than the Kansas platform. Several others appeared with ready-made platforms. Gifford Pinchot, who had consulted with Colonel Roosevelt as his old friend and supporter, appeared with a fine program which he and his brother Amos had submitted to the Colonel. After we had wrangled for a day or so over the Lewis, Kansas, and Pinchot platforms, Dr. George W. Kirchwey, Dean of Columbia University Law School, appeared with the most radical of all the platforms. He also had read it to Colonel Roosevelt. They had gone over it. The Colonel approved it. Apparently the Colonel was ready to approve anything that any responsible Progressive brought to him in sincerity. So by the time Dr. Kirchwey appeared in the committee he had the lasting blessing of our hero; and I should say, looking back over those years, that the Kirchwey draft was followed more nearly than any other draft in formulating the first Progressive national platform. For that day, it was radical.

On the political side of current issues the platform declared for direct primaries, nation-wide preferential primaries, the direct election of United States Senators, the short ballot, and finally the initiative and referendum and recall in states. We declared for civil service reform, the exclusion of Federal officeholders from party conventions, publicity for a limitation of campaign contributions, limitation of armament and two battleships a year while negotiations for limitation of armaments were going on. Our two controversies were over the tariff and the antitrust laws. We were in session two nights and a day. The tariff plank I submitted after a long wrangle. It was written by William S. Culbertson, a young man from Emporia who was working under Dr. Frank W. Taussig of Harvard, whom President Taft had drafted to study a possible tariff commission. The tariff plank pointed the way to a tariff commission.

The antitrust plank divided us even more seriously. We could not agree on the procedure that the government should use in attacking the trusts. One group of us—the left-wing Progressives—wished to catalogue specifically the evils of the trust which could be defined in law and made actionable. The right-wing Progressives wanted a general definition of the kind of antisocial conduct which should be indictable. This side felt that to specify the kinds of indictable conduct would limit the courts in proceeding against the trusts. Colonel Roosevelt knew of the wrangle and the deadlock in the committee. Indeed, in the convention hall the delegates were marking time, listening to speeches, cheering, raising a hullabaloo as all Presidential conventions do while the committee on resolutions is out.

The Colonel called some friends together and drafted a platform which Senator Joseph Dixon brought to the committee. Senator Beveridge came to explain the Colonel's position, and asked us to adopt the plank. There was still a row. We modified the Colonel's plank, and a compromise was reached. But it took time to modify it, so the convention went on and named the Colonel for President, amid wild enthusiasm.

After the nomination of Hiram Johnson for Vice President, Dr. Lewis, chairman of our platform committee, appeared, read the platform. When he came to the compromise plank it was evident that George Perkins was angry. Perkins was a supporter of the plank which did not specify indictable acts. In the compromise, we had left the matter of specific listing of indictable acts rather vague. But Perkins was angry. When Dr. Lewis finished reading that plank, Perkins rose, slammed his chair back, and walked out of the convention, a one-man bolt. It was the contention of Mr. Perkins' friends that the clerk of the committee gave Dr. Lewis the wrong plank to read. That is possible. It is not in my judgment probable. At any rate a sizable row arose behind the curtains. The plank Lewis had read, which in my recollection was the one the committee had adopted, was given to the press. But Mr. Perkins' publicity agent, who was also secretary of the national committee—Oscar King Davis—saw to it that, after the convention adjourned, the morning papers carried the Perkins plank in the platform.

It was a merry row. Nevertheless the platform itself was notable, and vastly more important than the row which it produced. To realize what that platform meant in the way of social and economic advance, one has to go back to 1912, twenty years before the New Deal, and grasp the fact that even then a considerable minority of the American people voting the Bull Moose ticket and another minority supporting the Democratic platform under Mr. Wilson that year voted for the same things. We, in our Progressive platform, declared in favor of workmen's compensation laws for insurance against sickness and unemployment, prohibition of child labor, minimum wages for women, safety and health standards for various occupations, prohibition of night work for women along with an eight hour day for them, one day's rest in seven, and an eight-hour day in continuous twenty-four-hour industries. When the New Deal came with its program, it went little further than Colonel Roosevelt's Progressive party had gone twenty years before. It was no wonder that Herbert Hoover who gave us a thousand dollars in 1912 to promote the candidacy of the

Colonel and this platform, declared twenty years later that the reforms of the second Roosevelt were long overdue.

When the row over the antitrust plank was raging, one of the funniest things I ever saw in politics turned up. I was sitting on a chair in the hall of the Blackstone Hotel, working on my newspaper story, and saw the Colonel pendulating between Perkins' room and Pinchot's room. He would toddle out of one room, looking over the top of his glasses, with the contested plank in his hand, and enter another room—maybe Perkins' room; and then in a few moments, like a faithful retriever, would come popping out, panting across the hall to Pinchot's room, still with the paper in his hand, grinning at me like a dog wagging his tail as he tried to compromise the differences between the pinfeather wings of his new party. Looking back over the years, I realize that the differences between Perkins and Pinchot were purely academic; but they seemed vital at the time. The Pinchots certainly represented the views of the convention. Perkins, with equal certainty, represented the views of Colonel Roosevelt's New York friends, who were with him not so much on economic grounds as because they felt he had been cheated out of the nomination. They did not understand at all why the Republican party was split. They did not realize that the Progressive party, which they were founding, was a part of the middle-class protest (perhaps "revolt" is a truer word) that had begun with the demand for free labor in abolition times—that had bloomed modestly in the agrarian protest of the Grangers and the Greenbackers—that had flowered in Populism and almost fruited under Bryanism in the Democratic party, and was ripening under the Roosevelt policies and the Progressive party into a responsible middle-class rebellion at the slow-moving economic progress made by our government. These New Yorkers regarded the Progressive party as merely a decent machine to get Roosevelt elected without a rump convention of the Republicans and a formal bolt of Taft's nomination. To form a new party was quite another and more respectable thing. And the Colonel, finally becoming conscious of us as he trotted from door to door and back, looked over his glasses and giggled in a falsetto greeting of delight, keenly appreciating the funny figure he was cutting. Finally the Pinchots took the last change the Colonel could squeeze out of them. The compromise, which amounted to little, went back to a subcommittee of the committee on resolutions, of which I seemed to be a member. We went over it and incorporated the changes which Perkins had forced out of the Pinchots, which were, as I say, of no great consequence.

Our social philosophy simmered down to this: The national income must be shifted so that the blessings of our civilization should be more widely enjoyed than they were. To make that shift, what Colonel Roosevelt called "predatory wealth" or "aggrandized capital" should have its claws pared, its greed checked, its rapacity quenched so far as is humanly possible. And the shift or redistribution of national income should be achieved by using government where necessary as an agency of human welfare. Lord, how we did like that phrase, "using government as an agency of human welfare"! That was the slogan, that was the Bull Moose platform boiled down to a phrase.

CHAPTER LXX

Enter a Smiling Villain

THE MORNING after the convention adjourned, I had my first disturbing disillusion about the Progressive party. The platform which our committee had agreed upon was published. But its antitrust section and the Pinchot plank had, during the night, been definitely changed back to the Perkins plank, which appeared in the morning press.

We started a row, and had the Colonel's promise that he would see that the official publication of the platform was corrected. Which was done for one or two editions. But I seem to remember that, in later editions of the platform which the national committee gave out, the antitrust plank was again modified to meet somewhat the Perkins requirements. This was not the way Christian soldiers marched with the "cross of Jesus, onward as to war." It was a detour down a purple primrose path that we starry-eyed martyrs disdained to tread. I set this episode down, trivial though it is, because it shows that human organizations have human faults. Little lies, little greeds, little cowardices appear even in the most high toned endeavors and in the midst of the grandest heroics. We who thought ourselves marching in the gleaming raiment of saints in that day and hour, blamed this diversion upon Perkins. I still think we were not mistaken. I remember this, that the Colonel and I went to bat on the proposition, and he could not believe that Perkins was responsible for the change in the text of the antitrust plank. His soft side was loyalty to his friends, and I thought, as we wrangled, that I should be the last to blame his soft side, otherwise I should have been cast into outer darkness long before. For he had had to defend me from the Perkinses in his life for fifteen years, and still he tolerated me, and we could quarrel in mutual respect and affection.

It may be excusable to pause in this narrative for a moment and write in some account of the Colonel as he appeared to me in that convention. His wrath was submerged. He was ebullient, clicking his teeth sometimes like a snare-drum obbligato to the allegro of his blithe, humorous, self-deprecatory assurance. The squeaking falsetto in which he gently clowned himself was most disarming. He seemed full of animal spirits, exhaustless at all hours, exuding cheer and confidence. His paunch was widening a little. The cast of his countenance at rest was a little grimmer than it had been in those first days when I had known him as Assistant Secretary of the Navy and as a young President. Into him had come not merely the sense of power but the unconsciousness of power. For a decade I had noticed something magnetic about him. When he came into a room, he changed all relations in the room because perhaps all minds and hearts turned to him in some attitude, all differing perhaps, but influenced by him. There in Chicago, in the late summer of 1912, he was in command and yet was forever disclaiming, vaunting his modesty genially. With all his physical virility, he was indeed the Bull Moose charging about the hotel corridors, stalking down an aisle of the Coliseum while the crowds roared, walking like a gladiator to the lions. In those days of the accouchement of the Bull Moose, he was superb. What if he tried to cover and to defend Perkins? What if he was a little obvious now and then as he grabbed the steering wheel of events and guided that convention not too shyly? I felt the joy and delight of his presence and, knowing his weakness, still gave him my loyalty—the great rumbling, roaring, jocund tornado of a man, all masculine save sometimes a catlike glint, hardly a twinkle, in his merry eyes.

The day after the Bull Moose convention adjourned in August, 1912, the national central committee of the party met to organize. It was assumed by his supporters and by many other members of the committee that George Perkins would be made chairman of the executive committee of the national committee. I rebelled. I liked George Perkins personally. He had lived in Kansas long enough to acquire a folksy way. He exuded pleasantly the odor of great power that came from his Morgan connection. He had done a dozen little things to accommodate me and bind me to him which I could not forget. So in my rebellion I was tempted to stop or compromise. But I did not. I went clear through. Oscar King Davis, who was secretary, in his book recalls that "characteristically" I took the floor in the central committee meeting and spoke against Perkins, warning the committeemen against him as a leader of our party. We had elected Joseph M. Dixon chairman, and Perkins was to be the inside mainspring of the party largely because he was furnishing and collecting the funds. My protest was probably crude and angry. O. K. Davis remembered it as a bit quixotic and smiled across the years at it. He wrote in his Autobiography:

* "Released for Publication" (Houghton Mifflin, 1925).

That eminent Kansas Progressive, William Allen White, Editor of the Emporia Gazette, who is so progressive that he never is long in any one place politically, seemed to be the leader of this opposition. He had the courage of his convictions too. He spoke right out in the meeting.

Harold Ickes, on the other hand, in a letter to me thirty years later, cast me as something of a hero, which I was not. I was just a scared but determined, fat and preposterous-looking young fellow in his early forties trying to overcome his doubts by venting his wrath a little too raucously perhaps; but I did look Perkins squarely in the eye, and as gently as I could, being full of indignation, I denounced him and opposed his selection as chairman of the executive committee. A small group, fewer than half a dozen out of the forty, followed me in the ballot. Harold Ickes, who held Jane Addams' proxy among others, and Meyer Lissner, who also took the floor to support me; and one of the Pinchots stood by me.

Then, of course, what always happens to a man who proves he has more courage than judgment, happened to me:

A dozen or twenty of the committeemen who voted against me came to me privately to congratulate me and express agreement with what I said, giving various perfectly good reasons why they did not vote with me. Something like that always happens to men or women who "go too far." Indeed, Perkins, himself, immediately after the meeting adjourned, came over, put his arm around my shoulder, and said he hoped he would prove that I was wrong. We had no personal quarrel. We parted, respected friends. He had his way of looking at things; I had mine. But I refused to follow him, then or ever. I wonder what he would have said in his memoirs about me and my kind. I have grasped the velvet glove of many iron hands, but have enjoyed none more heartily than George Perkins'. I have looked into the gentle, warm, gray, stubborn beam in many eyes, but none more deadly than George Perkins' happy smile. If I have painted him as a villain, I am sorry. He was just. He was playing his game righteously enough from his viewpoint, and I was playing mine. In the Punch-and-Judy show of the moment, we two, a part of the century's struggle to realize humanity's ideals, were puppets in the pageant. We knocked our heads together for the delectation of the angels who saw far ahead the way the tide was washing. And little we knew about it.

From Chicago I went home and devoted the rest of the summer and the autumn until election to helping the Kansas state Progressive chairman to organize Kansas for the Roosevelt ticket. We decided that we would raise our own funds. We wrote to the national committee that we would accept none of its money. We suspected it was Perkins' money—and were right about it. He had donated or collected most of the national committee's funds. So we raised ten thousand dollars, and it was my job to pass the hat for the Kansas campaign. This was all we needed, and we had a little money in the bank when we quit, less than two hundred dollars. We had every county organized thirty days after the Bull Moose convention had adjourned. Early in the campaign I began to feel that we Bull Moosers were playing an unfair trick upon the Taft Republicans. It was this: The Republican Presidential electors which we had chosen at the state convention in late May or early June were all Roosevelt supporters. They were going to vote for Roosevelt, all of them. Yet he was not the Republican nominee. They would be on the Republican ticket. If they remained there, the Taft men would be disfranchised. To me it was an open-and-shut proposition that this was unfair. And somewhat by bull strength, in spite of divided opinion in our party, I took those Rooseveltian electors off the Republican ticket. The Taft Republicans put up their own men as electors, and transferred the Roosevelt electors to the Bull Moose ticket. While I was in the midst of it, before it had been done, I saw the Colonel and told him what I thought I should do, that it was plain, honest, political decency to do so. I knew that in doing so I had turned over the state to Wilson. For what with the confusion about the electors and also with the normal Republican strength of the state divided between the Bull Moose and the Taft men, the Democrats inevitably would win. When I had finished my story, the Colonel looked at me for a moment with his jaw agape; then it clicked shut and he asked:

"White, do you really *have* to do that?"

I answered: "It's only honest, Colonel."

He sighed, and I detected sadness in his voice: "Yes, I suppose so. It's only honest."

But I knew what he thought. Still in the end, I am sure he was glad that I did it.

When we had refused in Kansas to take George Perkins' money and had collected our own ten thousand—of which a thousand came in a check from John M. Landon, father of Alf Landon—U. S. Sartin, the state chairman, and I felt free, and we notified the national headquarters that we did not want any more Perkins pamphlets. Perkins had printed a score of different pamphlets on public affairs, for instance, "What Perkins Thinks About the Tariff," "Perkins on the Trust," "George W. Perkins' Views on Labor," and so on down the line. They came in great bales by express collect to Emporia, and I refused to pay the charges and sent them back, after I had notified the national headquarters not to send them. The next time I saw George Perkins, I told him what I had done, to be sure that he knew, and he chuckled:

"You old devil! You're an Injun. Don't you ever forget?"

Whereupon we sat down and had a talk about the things on which we did agree; and they were many. In that campaign, on my one visit to New York, I heard the funniest political story I have ever heard. It came from Joe Dixon, the chairman of the Progressive national committee. A current story was being whispered about the country to the effect that Mr. Wilson had disrupted the home of a man named Peck. Someone was hawking about a sheaf of letters from President Wilson to Peck's divorced wife, written before the divorce. A gentleman had offered them to the Republican national committee, and Taft's friends turned them down. They came to the Bull Moose committee. Joe Dixon refused to buy them, and then checked it up to Roosevelt. It was a dirty business. I may say in passing that I afterwards saw the letters. I believe, without evidence to confirm it, that some prominent Democrats had bought them. Anyway, I saw them, and they were entirely innocuous. They merely indicated an exchange of intellectual amenities, over a period of a year or two, between two people who liked to play with words. But neither Dixon nor Roosevelt knew of that. They were peddled as salacious and incriminating.

But anyway, when Dixon told Roosevelt what he had done, the Colonel's face lighted up. "Of course you're right." He repeated it and was full of glee.

Joe asked: "Well, now, Colonel, why do you think I was right?"

The Colonel paused for a moment to gather his answer, and said: "Joe, those letters would be entirely unconvincing. Nothing, no evidence would ever make the American people believe that a man like Woodrow Wilson, cast so perfectly as the apothecary's clerk, could ever play Romeo!"

To know the gangling Wilson, grim-visaged, dour, repressed, and as ungallant as a scarecrow, made the Colonel's quip most pat and ridiculous.

During the early part of the campaign, the Bull Moose national committee provided Colonel Roosevelt with a special train in which he toured the country, accompanied by two or three score metropolitan newspapermen. His train came to Emporia one Saturday night, and he stopped with us. The campaign was at its height, and the visit of the Colonel to Emporia was an event of the greatest magnitude. Presidents Hayes and Grant had been here, and Taft had stopped for a few moments while the engine on his train took on water. But at the height and in all the excitement of the campaign, the nation's most spectacular figure spent Sunday in Emporia. The White family still had its surrey with a fringed top and Tom who went *clop, clop, clop* down the street. We had a score, maybe two score, of automobiles in the town, and all the owners—Democrats, Republicans, and Bull Moosers—offered their cars to us. But we loaded the Colonel, on Sunday morning, in the old family surrey, much to the shame of the town; and I took D. A. Ellsworth, the town poet, and Fred Newman, the town banker, with me as I drove the Colonel around showing him the

493

sights of the city. It was supposed that I would take him to our Congregational church, and it was packed to the doors; but the Colonel asked if there was a German Lutheran church in town. There was, and I took him there Mrs. White did not go. She was afraid to leave the preparations for the Sunday dinner. So we four—the poet, the banker, the hero, and I—marched down the aisle of that little church where a score or so of worshipers were gathered, by no means a fashionable church. When the preacher saw what he had, he turned pale. He afterwards told me he felt like dropping dead; but he went through with the service and read his sermon without changing it. He made some slight reference to the Colonel's presence. Of course everyone in the congregation had stared at him in amazement. But the preacher lined out the hymns, and I was interested and delighted to note that the Colonel stood up with the congregation and sang three verses of "How Firm a Foundation, Ye Saints of the Lord," without taking up the book. As a songbird, the Colonel was nothing to brag about. He had a rough bass about a half-tone off-key, and no ear for music, melody, or harmony. But he bellowed through the hymn without "da-daing" on a line so I was proud of him.

Emporia en masse entertained the two carloads of newspapermen on the wide verandas of the country club building and on the golf course and brought two wagonloads of watermelons ripe and just off the vine after cooling them overnight at the ice plant. A few of the sports produced liquor, but not much, and the newspapermen had to spend a dry Sunday But they had a view of a midwestern town with its wide green lawns, its arched elm trees, its two colleges, its country club and its lovely parks.

At our home after church we tried to shield the Colonel. We had put a great heaping platter before him on the table, and we did our own pushing and shoving. Little Mary, aged eight, would not come to the table because she thought she could get more fried chicken, without being noticed, by staying in the kitchen. Billy, his mother, the Colonel and I devastated that heaping platter of fried chicken, mashed potatoes and creamed gravy. The Colonel seemed to enjoy it. After his Sunday dinner, we put him to bed for an hour. He was tired. When he came downstairs after his rest, we three sat in the front room considering the cosmos. The talk drifted to the Republican convention. I asked him if he knew about the barbed wire around the bunting-covered railing that shielded the rostrum. His eyes snapped and he rose, backed himself in front of the living-room fireplace, and I never saw him so wrought with wrath.

"Yes, I knew about that barbed wire. Someone told me the day of the nomination. I wanted to take a pistol and go into the convention, and, if trouble had started, if those policemen had tried to use violence on our men, I think I could have given a good account of myself!" He stopped.

His teeth were set, and he cried: "And, by George, I wouldn't have wasted a bullet on a policeman. I would have got Root and got him quick!"

We sat through a moment's silence and, his rage being spent, he sighed, and smiled, began clicking his jaws, walked back to his chair and exclaimed without passion:

"I suppose it's all right. It's all for the best!"

The talk turned to the current campaign. After that outburst, it is comforting to look forward half a generation and read these lines from Elihu Root, written to me in January, 1928, when I wrote congratulating him on receiving a Civic Forum Medal presentation for his work as directing the foreign policy of the United States when he was Secretary of State:

I have reached the point where my active part in affairs is finished and, to borrow a phrase from W. C. Brownell, I "view the human scene with the dreamy eyes of the ruminants of the field." When a man gets to that point he begins to have some degree of historical impartiality about the events in which he has been concerned; and it is very gratifying to know that you have reached the same attitude by your own road. Roosevelt went through the same process to a considerable degree, for it became possible for us to become friends again without any discussion of the past, and for several years before he died I do not think he made a public speech without first sending me the manuscript for criticism and suggestion.

Curiously enough, I got a new estimate of your character and conduct by reading "The Martial Adventures of Henry and Me." There is a human quality of humor and sympathetic understanding which has made me delight in everything that you have said and done since, whether I have agreed with what you said or not. I like your stirring up of the crust formed by conventions because at the same time you do not abjure the accumulated wisdom of the race, which institutions are formed to preserve and which the same institutions, if they are left alone, will always tend to smother. Just where the line comes between preserving and smothering it seems difficult to determine, and there are constantly honest differences of opinion which nobody has any right to get mad about. That is the essence of liberty.

It seems somewhat pat to lift the veil of the future beyond that angry moment there by the fireplace, to a calmer, wiser day. The Root letter represents on the whole more reality than the rage and wrath that ran riot in men's hearts in 1912.

But at any event, there before the fireplace T. R.'s anger submerged and the talk turned to the current campaign. Ten minutes later he was telling us in his chuckling falsetto that in Denver the patriots referred to diminutive Judge Ben Lindsey—trim, slim, sawed-off dynamo in a Prince Albert coat to give him the dignity of his intellectual capacity—as "the bull mouse"! Then we reverted to his campaign. He was counting his chickens, and felt that he had a reasonable hope to win the election. He counted

Kansas in his column. I doubted it, but at the last I, too, felt Kansas would turn to him, for certainly the vocal part of the population was for Roosevelt overwhelmingly, and he did give Wilson a good race in Kansas. Taft fared so poorly in the election that it was evident that the conservative wing of the Republican party was a distinct, almost negligible minority, though it held great power in controlling the Republican national central committee.

All through the autumn I devoted my time to the election. In the end Kansas went Democratic. Stubbs, who had defeated Curtis in the primary for the Republican senatorial nomination, was defeated by an unknown and inconsequential Democrat. A progressive Democrat, George Hodges, was elected governor, and Wilson carried the state with Roosevelt running him a decent second and Taft a poor third. So it was in all the states of the North and West. The solid South did not crack or crumble. But it was evident that the progressive or liberal movement was overwhelmingly in the majority in the United States. The election of 1912 was the first election in which the liberal movement registered its strength. Bryan had never been able to command so many Democratic electoral votes as Wilson, who definitely inherited Bryan's strength. And no liberal Republican, not even Roosevelt in 1904, when his liberalism was revealing itself, ever before had called out the voting strength that Roosevelt commanded. So I was happy about the election, though I lost my first choice and my heart's political desire. I felt sure that the liberal movement in the United States had come to stay, that a party was organizing to carry its banner and that in some way we should find a permanent vehicle in which to assemble the votes of the liberal majority in the United States. The other day I had a letter from a friend of those days who found the remnants of an old speech of mine of 1911 in Denver, in which I said:

"Only a war can shatter the sure advance of this movement of the people for distributive justice. War is the devil's answer to human progress."

As the year closed after the election, I realized that I had lived a hard and busy year. I had completely neglected the novel we were working on. And Sallie felt that I showed signs of strain, though I was eager to see that our Bull Moose platform pledges should be adopted by the Wilson Democrats. The Colonel also displayed more than passing interest in this idea. The national Bull Moose committee had funds. It set up a Washington office where bills were drafted and lobbying was started to put through Congress the immediately realizable ideals of our platform. And so the year closed without an anticlimax.

CHAPTER LXXI

After the Battle

THE YEAR 1913 found the White family—father, mother, the two children, their Grandma White and our faithful Martha, who was nurse, cook, maid, friend and companion—all settled in a beach house on the Pacific, at La Jolla, California. Mrs. White had uprooted us, bag and baggage, first because she thought I was tired and a new environment would refresh me; and second because she thought the novel we were working on was now ripe.

For four months I fiddled away on it, two morning hours, six days a week. In the twilight we walked together along the ocean, talking over the story, developing the plot, trying to realize the characters. We knew exactly what we wanted to dramatize, but it was hard to fit the fable to fictional reality. Yet it was a lovely time. The children played in the ocean and in the sand by the bathing cove. Sallie and I bought vegetables and fresh fruits of the Chinaman who came to the back door every day. We made friends with the fishermen and got all kinds of rare sea foods— clams, abalone, sand dabs, or smelts that came scurrying into the cove when the whales were outside and wiggled to death on the beaches as the tide went out. From the Mexicans who lived in the villages along the road to San Diego we bought strange hot sausages and Spanish groceries that were good.

The American stage still was a national, not a New York, institution. Every week or so we went to San Diego to see a good play. We saw Maude Adams there, I remember, and Julia Marlowe, and E. H. Sothern, and other stars of the stage who were troupers before the First World War. We had books and magazines a plenty, and just enough of give-and-take in parties to keep us interested in the life about us. Of course we became villagers in thirty days and were absorbed into the village life of the wandering tourist colony, a small but pleasant group—writers in exile, health-seekers, idlers, golf-playing retired professional men, and merchants and farmers from the Middle West. It was our crowd. Probably I missed something then and all my life by a congenital incapacity for enjoying golf, which bored me, poker which overstrained me and taxed my patience, fishing and hunting which required too much exercise, and whiskey, which gave release to no pent-up emotions and so just hurt my stomach. But thus it was, and I had to get my male society around the grocery store, the drugstore, and the barbershop. Yet I have never felt lonely.

In La Jolla, by the time I had got my reading finished—three or four daily papers, the current magazines, and a book or two that were always lying around face down, half finished—and by the time Sallie and I had done our marketing and visiting around on Main Street and taken the children for a walk or a plunge, then enjoyed our meals and our sleep, it was a twenty-four-hour day. Emporia and Kansas and the Bull Moose party sloughed out of my conscience, and I took on the petty satisfying worries of my environment.

Once Kansas intruded in a letter from Governor Hodges telling me that the legislature had adopted, and he had signed, a law introducing the headless ballot in our elections, known then as the mass ballot. The law abolished party tickets on the Kansas ballot and put the candidates in one long row with "R" and "D" initialed after each name. For five years I had been pushing that measure. I had circularized the legislature, fumed in the Gazette, and annoyed editors of other papers asking them to reprint what I had written. Governor Hodges, who as a Democratic state senator had supported my mass-ballot proposition, in his letter gave me credit for the triumph of the measure and made me happy for a week, For, after all, I had no great interest in the candidacy of any man, save as that man was able to help some measure I was sponsoring in local politics. And we had, by 1913, the anti-pass law, the primary, the workmen's compensation act, a minimum wage law for women, the anti-child-labor law, and the Massachusetts ballot on the Kansas statute book, and I felt that I was somewhat responsible for each measure. Of course I could only claim my share of credit, but these measures were my pets. I did not try, while I was working on "In the Heart of a Fool," to give Kansas politics much absent treatment. I kicked off the whole world of Kansas and lived on another planet. It probably indicates a shallow nature that I should be able so entirely to get away from one sphere of activity and into another.

So the winter wore away, and in late spring we packed up our caravan and went home. We found business booming. We needed another linotype for the Gazette. Advertisers were crowding its pages. Often we had six pages and sometimes, maybe once or twice a month, eight pages. The farmers were getting good prices for their grain and livestock. They were to look back on those days from 1909 to 1914 as ideal years when farm prices were relatively just, compared with the prices of labor. The Bull

Moosers in Kansas and everywhere were full of ebullient enthusiasm. Although no election was looming up that year, the Bull Moosers were holding meetings, particularly giving dinners, hearing speeches and singing songs. Our national leaders were hurrying about from state to state addressing these glamorous dinners. It looked as though the Bull Moose party was sweeping everything before it. The Republicans had no such dinners, and the Democrats feeding at Woodrow Wilson's pie counter had no need for them. The thing we should have noticed was that at all these dinners in the county seats, and at the banquets on formal occasions at the capitals, the same group of patriots was gathered around the board. Why that should have fooled us, I cannot imagine. Two or three hundred people at a dinner is a small fraction of the electorate, and we held few public meetings, for no campaign was pending. We could not see that the strength of our cause was waning. We applauded wildly when our speakers demanded social and industrial justice; we were delighted when they talked about "distributive justice" and proved that the country had solved its problem of production of wealth and that the great problem of the distribution of wealth challenged the country. Yet we Bull Moosers—middle-class folks who had received all our share in the "distribution of the national income" and were fat and saucy in our attack upon aggrandized capital, were almost alone in our charge upon the citadel of privilege.

Labor was at work in those years. The farmers' prices were reasonably good. While we sat at our feasts across the land, the whole cause and justification for our attack upon the established order was paling. And the injustices of the distributive system were being corrected, not by laws but by speeding up the wheels of industry in the United States and to an extent around the world.

In our own country a new element had come into the industrial and commercial picture. The automobile age had arrived. Ford's assembly belt was turning out Model T's. A kind of democracy was coming into the world and not through the ballot box, not by marching cohorts in the streets carrying banners, not even out of Congress nor its laws. The thing which was changing our world was the democratization of transportation. The files of the Gazette show that we had our first commercial garage in Emporia at that time. By way of humorous reference we called it "the garbage." In a few months a second garage appeared in the business part of town. We bragged that Lyon County had over fifty motorcars. Soon a motorized truck appeared on Commercial Street. The town was paving rapidly. All over the middle states, the prairie states, where roads had to be laid out on alluvial soil, the King road drag appeared. County and township road officers used it to smooth off dirt roads after a rain. It made going easy for the motorists who ventured to travel between towns. They organized by states and published road maps showing where the roads were dragged. Then suddenly appeared a new advertiser in the Gazette. He was the Buick agent. Then came an advertisement for the Maxwell and the Winston, and the Gazette traded advertising from an automobile manufacturer for a motorcar, thirteen hundred dollars' worth. But we felt the car was too expensive for us to use, so Old Tom continued to clop up and down Exchange Street. We sold the motorcar to a doctor in a neighboring town, and thus got cash for our advertising. Times were good, and even a blighting drought in central Kansas in the summer of 1913 did not check the wave of prosperity. That summer, taking the manuscript of our novel, we went to Colorado.

We had enlarged our cabin, building a fourteen-foot porch on three sides of it. We also built a log cabin one hundred feet up the hill, and two small bedroom cabins, so we were living like princes. The whole flock of cabins and the land had cost us less than three thousand dollars. A magazine article or two had easily paid the bill. The paper was making money —on a guess, ten thousand a year. The Bull Moose party was singing its head off, clapping blisters on its hands at dinners across the country, holding national conferences in Chicago, New York, and Washington, and making big plans to relieve the oppressed, who at that moment were not heavily oppressed, though we did not have sense enough to connect politics with commerce.

So for a couple of months I went up from the main cabin of our Colorado home to the log cabin on the hill and pecked away at my typewriter on the novel. Incidentally I wrote a magazine article or two with which I bludgeoned the wolf at the door. I made some speeches in Colorado at dinners and conferences such as the Bull Moose party was holding in Kansas and across the land, and always I had a book or two at hand. That year it was Jacques Loeb's "Heredity" and one of Henri Fabre's books on insect life. Vernon Kellogg was feeding me Alfred Russel Wallace's books and his own studies with Dr. Jordan, and I was still struggling with Henri Bergson and his philosophy of creative evolution.

It was in those days that I realized what an extraordinary mind Colonel Roosevelt had. He was a page reader. We were on the train going somewhere—Heaven knows exactly where, except that he had a private car and had to go trotting out to the rear platform every hour or so to make speeches, and then ducked into his compartment where I sat watching him as he read a book called "Heredity" by J. Arthur Thomson, an Aberdeen biologist. He was reading it a page at a time. I had read the book. It was tough going. It took me five or ten minutes to turn a page, and he was turning two or three pages a minute. He peered over his glasses at me as I was grinning at him, and said:

"You think I am faking."

I nodded.

"All right. Take the book. I have read to here. Go back as far as you please and examine me."

I did. He was letter-perfect. It was one of the most extraordinary mental feats I ever saw. How did he do it? The vocabulary that Dr. Thomson used in his book had sent me chasing to the dictionary every few minutes. I had to go even to the French and German lexicon; and once in a long while the Doctor would indulge in a Greek word. But the Colonel charged through it all, breasting the big words like high weeds and comprehending what he was reading.

I may say here in passing, perhaps not in pride but hardly in regret, that in all the thirty years in which Sallie and I have been summering in Colorado with the near-by trout brook murmuring in our ears at night, I have never cast a fly, hooked a worm, or yanked a fish from the cooling waters of a bosky dell. But certainly I can eat six crisp fried trout on a platter with great gusto. It has been my good fortune all my life to be surrounded by good fishermen. Bill and my brothers-in-law have only to stand on the banks of a trout stream to have all the trout for a half-mile on either side rush to them and jump for their hooks.

Looking back across thirty years to the century's second decade when I and the boys I knew in college were in their early and middle forties, it seems extraordinary how we kept the bond of our friendship. Kellogg and I saw each other two or three times a year. Funston, when he got settled down to the humdrum of a life as a major general and was commandant of various army posts, I saw sometimes two or three times a year. I remember—to go back a little into the years when Roosevelt was in the White House—Funston, who was rising rapidly in the army, was talking too much. Kellogg and I guessed why: Funston, who to us was still "Timmy," still could not carry his liquor. Roosevelt sent me to Timmy to tell him that he must quit talking, or the President would have to rebuke him publicly. When I told my message, Timmy looked at me and grinned.

"O Billy, look not upon the gin rickey when it is red, and giveth color in the cup, for it playeth hell and repeat with poor Timmy."

In 1914 President Wilson sent Funston to Vera Cruz. President Madero of Mexico had been assassinated, and his unrecognized successor, Huerta, had refused to apologize for an insult to the American flag at Tampico. Vera Cruz was the nearest port to Mexico City, so we put troops ashore there. An international incident was developing. Wilson was being noble and puffing and huffing at the job, treating the Mexican government as though they were little brown brothers; and Huerta was getting madder and madder. Funston was tugging at the bit, taking a lot of Mexican insults he didn't care to swallow. Later he was to command American troops on the border when Pershing's column crossed the Rio Grande to pursue Pancho Villa after his raid on Columbus, New Mexico.

I saw Funston from time to time in those years—often, I suppose, when he came to Kansas to visit his relatives. The last time I ever saw him, he came to the house through the rain. I had not known he was within two thousand miles when I saw the sturdy little figure buffeting the storm; and the last I had heard of him, he had been in command of American troops that landed in Vera Cruz. It was Wilson's idea to bluff Huerta with those troops; then he weakened and ordered Funston to withdraw. When we sat down in front of the fire in our living room, Funston broke out with dazzling, wrathful profanity, Mexican-English-Filipino-Spanish, a fireworks of rage. The gist of it was this (after he had cussed himself into something like repose, tears filled his eyes):

"Billy, you won't believe it. I never thought I would have to do it. God knows it cut my heart out, but I had to retire American troops in order under the sniping fire of those [here he burst into a set piece of pyrotechnic profanity] . . . greasers from windows as we embarked. God, Billy, fancy that! Fancy the American flag, with me in charge of it, going meekly out of a dirty, stinking greaser hole—withdrawing my command under fire!"

After which he calmed down and told his story—not a pleasant story in American military annals. He had no sympathy with President Wilson's bluff; but he had much more respect for Huerta when he called the bluff. Funston was a colorful figure. Probably not since the days of the Civil War generals has the American army had such a commander. And in all my days I have never had a more faithful, loving friend than Funston. We parted for the last time that day as he went out into the rain. He turned back at the sidewalk, saw me lingering in the door, and waved his hand and gave me the old gay smile.

"God bless you, old-timer," I cried as he waved.

"Same to you, Billy, you old hell-raiser!" he answered, and disappeared from my life into the twilight mist.

CHAPTER LXXII

The First Rumble of Guns

W%HEN I saw Theodore Roosevelt early in 1914, I sensed that he was fearful
—perhaps the word "leery" expresses it—of the divine mission of the Progressive party. He began to realize even quicker than I did, and certainly
before most of his crusading followers suspected, the approaching debacle.
For a considerable percentage—anywhere between 40 and 60 per cent—of
the Roosevelt vote in 1912 was a protest vote against the outrageous action
of the national Republican committee. Thousands, perhaps millions, of
citizens who voted for Theodore Roosevelt for President in 1912 as the
Bull Moose candidate had no idea of endorsing the radical Bull Moose
platform. And being loyal Republicans who had sinned, they began to
get most virtuous when they thought of their sins. So they began to be
highly indignant at the thought of a third party. We of the faithful, noted
that we could identify the stray sheep of our party when they said, "Of
course I was for Roosevelt, but—" and called them the "Roosevelt butters."
And what a lot of them there were!

Despite the "Roosevelt butters" in many of the northern states which
Roosevelt carried or where he ran second in 1912, the faithful, of whom
I was one, began to hold national, state, and congressional district conferences or conventions, to find candidates who would fill our ticket in
the congressional and state elections of 1914. It was a tough job. It was
one thing to drum up a crowd, singing "Onward, Christian Soldiers," hurrahing for Roosevelt and booing Taft after the dramatic swindle in the
Convention of 1912. It was quite another to go out in cold blood and get
men to run on a third-party county ticket. The people who want county
offices are timid folk, easily scared about their party standing. Yet my job
as national committeeman, along with the Kansas state chairman, Mr.
Sartin, was to get out a county ticket in every county and to get Bull Moose
congressmen running in every district. We did it, and we also put out a
state ticket with Henry J. Allen running for governor and Victor Murdock,

503

who was a congressman in a safe Republican district, running for United States Senator. I remember that when Henry promised me to run he said:

"There's just one little thing: Will you call up Elsie and tell her?"

So I called up Elsie and said: "Now look here, Elsie, don't be worried about Henry. He won't be elected. Not a Chinaman's chance. All we want—"

Then she cut in: "Now, Will, if he is not going to be elected, why do you want him to run? It sounds foolish to me. No sense in it!"

But he ran, and with Elsie's consent, on high patriotic grounds. And, recalling the telephone dialogue, I know now that I also knew the truth about the Bull Moose party. Probably I knew it in 1912 when I told Victor Murdock in Washington, amid guffaws, that Theodore Roosevelt thought 1912 was 1860 and that it was only '56, or maybe only '52, the days of Buchanan and Pierce, not Lincoln. However, I felt in 1914 that we had the nucleus of a party: that we should not abandon it. In those days, former President Taft was gibing at us by saying we had an army of colonels, which was the ignoble truth. But I felt, if the colonels would stand the fire of 1914, they could rally, not to a victory in 1916, but to a substantial minority that might make a party of real principles four years later. This was before the war had begun to affect the United States. For two years our general staff of colonels had been working with the Progressive members of the Senate and the House of Representatives in Washington, forming a coalition between the liberal Republicans and Progressives on the one hand, and the Progressive Democrats on the other. We sent emissaries to President Wilson persuading him to join us in putting through as much of the federal program as was possible. In his first term, therefore, we had established a Federal Trade Commission. We had set up the Tariff Commission with powers to change tariffs in certain cases in accordance with passing needs. We had established the parcel post in opposition to the railroads. We had written a strong railroad commission law. We had achieved the direct election of United States Senators. We had written a law providing for minimum wages for women and children in industry, and had passed a law prohibiting child labor—both of which the Supreme Court invalidated—and we had furnished public opinion which sustained the Supreme Court in establishing the eight-hour day in the railroad industry. This decision was a large legal hole in the dike upholding what was then the ten- and twelve-hour day. And by the time war, with its reactionary wave, was well under way, we Progressives in the Bull Moose party and under the leadership of Woodrow Wilson, had come a long distance in our first march from 1901, when Roosevelt had entered the White House as the Republican leader after Bryan failed twice in his race for the Presidency. In a decade and a half the progressive movement in the United

States, which was called insurgent (then, under Roosevelt, was called the Square Deal; later, under Wilson, known as the New Nationalism, and finally as the Bull Moose party) was officially the Progressive party and had a definite record of achievement.

It is worth while to set down here briefly the major Federal measures we had achieved in those fifteen years. Here the most important measure was, of course, the Roosevelt-Pinchot Conservation Act which took millions of acres of timber and grazing and mining land away from exploiters and turned it over to the government for conservation. Then in that decade and a half began an intelligent control of the railroads, and practically war on the evils of bigness in corporate business—the antitrust laws and lawsuits; the Food and Drug Act of June, 1916; rural free delivery and the postal savings bank; the direct primary in practically all the states; the initiative and referendum in twenty-two states; and the Income Tax Amendment, and woman suffrage. Certainly in that body of legislation was evidence of a political revolution in the hearts of the American people. They had backed this legislation under three administrations: Theodore Roosevelt's, Taft's, and Wilson's. The people had followed leaders in both parties and established those leaders firmly in public confidence, a score of leaders in the statehouses and in Congress. They had fought to a standstill their conservative adversaries and had won every pitched battle that was waged, except the tariff; but, if they lost the tariff, the forward-looking citizens of the country had backed President Wilson in securing a sound Federal Reserve Act which certainly put the crimp in the pull of Wall Street financiers, who had too much power over the nation's monetary system.

I set these things down here not to write a history of the Progressive party but merely to list the things in which I had been interested—the things that had been a part of my daily life in politics for fifteen years—the things that had brought me into friendly relations with liberal leaders in both parties. I knew them all, and had confidence in them, believed them; and I could work with them without much regard for party affiliation. My letter files of those days are filled with friendly letters, letters which address me as "Will"; with my letters, which called them by their first names, not, I hope, presuming too much, but because we had sat in conferences in hotel bedrooms and around luncheon and dinner tables at night working on the strategy which made many of these measures possible. I had little part in it except as legs, go-between errand boy, compromiser. Probably also my irrepressible tendency to gibe and quip and relate many a wise saw and modern instance furnished comic relief for many a tedious hour in many a brittle situation. As I set down each of these items in a long list of revolutionary measures, it recalls some gay episode or some tense hour, or some long season of anxiety and tension. Each of these measures was a station in my

Via Dolorosa, if you can call a way of sorrow a road down which there was much chuckling and some laughter and in the end certain satisfactions that come with victory. It was not a martyr's path, but I had no personal interest in it. I was not a candidate for any office dependent upon the success or the failure of the program I was supporting. Indeed, I am fairly well persuaded that if one really wishes political power for any considerable time, he should not run for office. Nothing is quite so impotent in politics as a defeated candidate. After his defeat people discredit everything he does, on the theory that what he does is done to promote his own interests. The man who deceives himself into thinking that his election is necessary to any cause is yielding to his vanity or something worse.

In the late summer of 1914, the White family cut loose from politics and went to Colorado, where I worked again in the log cabin above our living rooms there on the novel that had been engaging me for so many years. And into that pleasant recreation plunged the World War. In the mountain valley below us and on the hills around us within a mile radius were half a dozen Kansas college professors and professional men. They gathered on our porch when Bill and Mary brought up the mail from the post office— we were taking four daily papers besides the Gazette—and we sat there with our families and discussed the news as it was blazoned in the headlines. The news was inconceivable. I remember Professor Hodder, of the history department of the University of Kansas, who had a low opinion of newspapers anyway, sitting tight-lipped and grim while we discussed the invasion of Belgium, the fall of Liége, the sack of Louvain, and all the horrors that followed that gray steel wave of Germans that washed over Belgium. For two days, maybe three, Hodder declared:

"It can't be so. They aren't telling the truth. Why, there's a treaty between Belgium and Germany that would prevent it! The newspapers are making it up!" And so on.

When he had to accept the invasion of Belgium as a fact, despite the treaty, the foundations of his faith in modern civilization completely caved in, and he was a heartbroken man for nearly a week. All those first scenes in Belgium in 1914 are associated in my memory with the front porch of our cabin, with the meadow and its waving grasses below, the long lateral moraine rising above the meadow, and over that the snow-clad range, with Longs Peak arching far above the range in solemn majesty, flecked and speckled with white snow down its granite face. We, who were gathered there from the colleges roundabout to read the news and mull over the papers, had no idea of the significance of the war, what it would mean to modern civilization. And I did not remotely dream that this war was a part of the revolution that I had seen gathering in Europe, that I was myself encouraging with all my might and main in my own land. It seemed like a quarrel between the crowned heads of Europe, the Hapsburgs, the Hohenzollerns, the Romanoffs, the Wettins. I realized with sadness that it would affect the United States indirectly, by turning the minds of the people from reform to safety. I did not then even dream how our whole economy would be bent toward making the materials and munitions of war. I did not foresee the boom, though I knew that reform would be suspended. I was that wise. But after the war councils on the front porch were over, I climbed up to my desk in the log cabin and pecked away at my story or wrote letters to my fellow reformers in Kansas and elsewhere, bemoaning the wreck of matter and the crash of worlds.

In the autumn of 1914 the people of the United States must have taken a deep interest in the war. For I remember well that we Bull Moosers in our Kansas campaign for congressmen, senator and governor in November, ascribed our defeat to the war. We had fine audiences, in some cases great audiences, for Henry Allen and Victor Murdock, our candidates for governor and senator. We brought one or two of our national orators like Beveridge or Pinchot or Raymond Robins to the state and had what might be called an outpouring of the masses at every meeting. But the Bull Moose vote confirmed Taft's diagnosis. We were afflicted with an army of colonels, and when I saw Colonel Roosevelt after the election, he was depressed about the third-party movement.

I was not. I still felt that if we would stay with it, and were willing to lose another Presidential election, we could establish ourselves as the second party. But the Colonel shook his head. He had no desire to be cast in the role of General James B. Weaver, the Presidential candidate and leader of the Greenbackers and the Populists who had seen many defeats. Moreover, the war was stirring him. At first he seemed to feel somewhat sympathetic to the Kaiser, but that lasted only a few weeks. The wave of rage in the United States at Belgium's fate in the hands of Germany carried the Colonel along with it, and by early winter he was well established as a Man of Wrath, raging at Wilson for his neutrality. And the more he raged, the more he forgot about the Bull Moosers—orphans in a storm. In his fulminations at Wilson, Colonel Roosevelt alienated many of his Progressive party supporters who agreed with the President that America should remain neutral. In the main, I was more inclined to follow Wilson's foreign policy than Roosevelt's militancy.

At first the Colonel did not advocate American participation in the war. But he clamored for preparedness. For a whole year after the electoral debacle of the Bull Moose, Colonel Roosevelt devoted himself to criticizing the Wilson administration for its attitude on foreign policy, and he was particularly bitter at Wilson for not advocating a policy of armament. Woodrow Wilson, being what he was, Scotch-Irish and temperamentally a Presbyterian fundamentalist, if not theologically such, refused to be budged by the Roosevelt clamor. The President felt that a sudden policy of military preparedness and naval activity would shatter the sincerity of his neutrality policy. During the whole long year of 1915 Roosevelt led the clamor against the administration, hammering away on the need to train and arm men against the time when we should inevitably enter the war. Roosevelt would have armed to prevent war. He and I disagreed, though he probably was right. Whenever we met (and it was often), and when we wrote letters (which was occasionally), we quarreled about Wilson. I did not care for Wilson personally—my one meeting with him had chilled me considerably; and I deeply admired the Colonel, even though I did not join his clamor. Yet our relations remained cordial. He regarded me as a sheep that had gone astray. I might have been the one outside of the ninety and nine, for he was always trying to make me see his light and follow in his path. Probably I typified a wing of the Bull Moose party that was cold to his appeal to arms.

In the summer of 1915 the White family bought, partly for cash but mostly for advertising, its first motorcar. Poor old Tom, the clop-clop, was pensioned in a pasture for life. Bill and a boy friend in the garage from which we bought the car—it was a Chandler made in Cleveland—hitched up and drove us to Colorado. It was a three-day journey, seven hundred and fifty miles over dirt roads. A rain would hold us for hours—sometimes for twelve hours, sometimes half a day—and we were forever tinkering with the car along the way. Those were the days when the driver had to get out and get under. The tires were paper tires, apparently, for they were always blowing up and getting pinched in the rims. The Chandler was no worse than other cars. Man was merely learning how to make motorcars, and in a few years he began to learn how to make roads out of taxes on gasoline. If ever there was an evolutionary process it was going on in transportation, in that second decade of this century.

During the summer when we were in Estes Park, I put aside the novel and began to write a few short stories that a year or so afterwards appeared in a book called "God's Puppets." I was stale on the novel, and that summer wrote a magazine article or so. I was always busy at the log cabin in those days. Yet I had plenty of time for picnics and fish fries and dinners.

It was that year that Bryan, on a lecture tour, came to our cabin and sat on our porch for an hour. I had come to have great respect for Bryan—I still do not know exactly what it was about him. I believe that he was as honest and as brave a man as I ever met, with a vast capacity for friendship. For his was an ardent nature. He was now paunchy. The black wing of hair that had flopped on his forehead a dozen or twenty years earlier was thinning. He was baldish and heavy-jowled. But his voice was fresh and his eyes were keen. His laughter was never quite unrestrained. Indeed, when he laughed heartily he seemed slightly ashamed of himself, as though laughter was a sin. I remember also that after a few casual, rather perfunctory remarks about our view of landscape around, he was not interested in it. That landscape was our pet child—it just had to be admired; but Bryan patted Longs Peak on the head and sent it away with the other snowcapped mountains, which amused me. We talked about the war. I was much nearer his views than Roosevelt's, and I suspected then he and I came more nearly agreeing than Wilson and he; for he was beginning to be irked with Wilson's inner doubts about neutrality. Bryan's peace treaties, which were in his heart and in course of negotiation, seemed to me most wise. Of course I know now that the world was not ready for them. They were face-savers for many of our international neighbors, who must have smiled at Bryan as they were signing his treaties. Why did we not see? Why did he and I, sitting for an hour on the porch of our Estes Park home, talking about peace, run on and on, without ever realizing that treaties alone cannot maintain peace? Why did we not realize that treaties could only define peace which international economic adjustments must first establish?

Bryan did most of the talking. Some friend was with him, and we three walked around like hens in high oats, in the tall grass of the new heaven and the new earth that were spinning out of our hearts' desires. I have never met a man with a kindlier face, with a gentler, more persuasive voice, nor with seemingly more profound ignorance about sophisticated, mundane matters. He was a twelve-year-old boy in many things, yet a prophet far more discerning of the structure of the world that would be, and should be, and even now is (a house not made with hands) than were any of us: Roosevelt or Wilson or La Follette. Bryan saw vaguely the edifice of civilization stretching two decades ahead of him, with something like La Follette's inspiration; but La Follette was vastly more practical. How La Follette scorned the rose-tinted cloud walls of Bryan's noble mansions! La Follette's world-to-be had metes and bounds, a solid foundation, and a reasoned philosophy. He must have inherited with his name the logical processes of a Frenchman. But Bryan as we sat together, his rhetoric full of biblical metaphors and similes, his voice lovely to my ear with its modulating cadences, though he was not an oratorical talker, left an impression on my mind and heart that I have carried, even cherished, through all these years. I am ashamed now, and was ashamed then, that two decades earlier I had scorned him in "What's the Matter with Kansas?" as a boy orator. I wondered, as he sat there, if he remembered it. If he did remember, no rancor held over through the years; for he was most cordial and aglow with friendliness. I tried once to get a picture of that interview over to Mr. Roosevelt, and he stopped me. He could not endure it. Bryan was Bryan to him, the crazy fanatic without learning and without sense. The Colonel's intuitions, which were keen, never grasped the meaning, to this country and to his own cause, of Bryan and his work. Bryan was a voice crying in the wilderness when Hanna sat on Herod's throne, and the high priests and Pharisees burned incense and made obeisance to McKinley, and the plutocracy which McKinley symbolized. Colonel Roosevelt came to scorn that plutocracy and to understand McKinley's weaknesses and limitations; but he could not unsay the things he had said of Bryan, and could never wipe out the estimate of Bryan that came in the campaign of 1896, when the Colonel and I were young acolytes at Mammon's altar. I do not think I ever heard him say once, "I was dead wrong; I am sorry"—seven rather difficult words for the best of us to articulate clearly.

After Bryan left, who should come wandering up to the porch but Clarence Darrow! I had met Darrow in Chicago in 1897, a young lawyer in his forties. He was the perfect antithesis of Bryan, a cynic, a sophisticate and a Sybarite. We talked for an hour. I did not agree with a thing Clarence Darrow said, but I tremendously enjoyed the way he said it. From time to time as he talked I caught his eye delighting in the scenery. Once or twice he cried out in joy at its beauty. In conversation he was a chuckler who talked in wise saws, cheered meticulously, grinned diabolically. He thought he was shocking me, and I believe he enjoyed it. He yearned for peace as much as Bryan, but had no hope for it and would have been angry at the terms upon which it could come. Darrow was off the same emotional piece of goods as Bryan. Bryan sublimated his excess of ardor in what he deemed public service. Darrow let off steam by romance—the woman proposition. He was not an indiscriminate petticoat chaser, nothing like it; but he loved, like the wind, where he listed. And through all the years between that night when I first met him in Chicago, before Chauncey Williams' great fireplace, until the day he died, Darrow belonged to the great brotherhood of pilgrims who tread the primrose path not idly but with zeal and a deep conviction of their rectitude. Bryan, on the other hand, seemed not to know that there was another sex than his. I have seen him in all times and places, in supreme crises, in humdrum hours. I never caught in his eye the wayward spark from a hidden fire in his heart. He was an innocent, intellectually and emotionally—a child in a garden who loved its beauty, enjoyed its perfume, and never crushed a bud.

Darrow was intended by nature to be as tall as Bryan, but he stooped and slumped. His clothes were a mess, wrinkled, untidy—entirely clean but slomicky, if I may coin a word to fit his dishabille. He slouched when he walked, and he walked like a cat. I always thought of him as Kipling's cat who walked alone. For he was essentially a lonesome soul, always seeking the unattainable, I think; hobbled by his own cynicism but always stumbling on, looking for the ideal which he could not accept without quibble or gibe—a complex man, a rebel like Eugene Debs. Curiously, I associated Darrow and Bryan and Debs with the outposts of that American revolution which rose in the last decade of the nineteenth century and was going strong when these lines were written. If Bryan could have had some part of Darrow's capacity for intellectual doubt, if Debs could have had Bryan's indomitable energy and a little of Bryan's ignorance about realities, and if they all could have been rolled into one with the elements of each soul well mixed in the composite, what a man they would have made! I think Lincoln must have been such a mixture.

CHAPTER LXXIII

Drums and Bugles from Afar

IN THE YEAR 1915 the European war was beginning to dominate American politics. It dominated somewhat, I suppose, because the war was beginning to change our national economy. In the middle of 1914 a definite lag had come in business and industry. It disappeared after the Marne. War orders were speeding up the wheels in a thousand mills and lighting the fires in ten thousand furnaces. Accelerated business was increasing our national income. Labor and agriculture were getting more money, if not a larger share of the income, than they had had during the decade and a half before. War was producing in the United States its own intoxication, a kind of economic inflation that had spiritual reflexes. People felt happy because they were busy and seemed to be making money. As we rode to and from New York that year, we could see a change in American industry as we sped through the industrial sections of Ohio, Pennsylvania, and New Jersey. Things were humming. The British and the French were placing tremendous war orders in the United States. The Germans, because of the British fleet, could not get their orders across the ocean; so naturally, as the Allies were our customers, they became our friends. America began to swing away from Germany—all of America, from Hudson Bay to Patagonia—because the Germans, in order to buy our goods, had to run the British blockade.

The Bull Moose party, which was founded upon a demand for distributive justice, using government as an agency of human welfare, lost its cause. Prosperity was cheering up the farmers and the workers. Our little army of colonels drilled lonesomely on the parade ground of a lost cause. Yet during that mid-year of the second decade, we kept holding our conference dinners. We, the faithful, were still white-hot with zeal for our party. We could not realize that when the economic set-up of the country changed, when prosperity came rolling in from the war, we did not touch the realities of the political situation. So we went on through that year like fairies dancing in some sylvan glade, apart from the busy world and its realities. Colonel Roosevelt knew right well what was happening. Our failure at the polls in 1914 convinced him that we were "spurring a dead horse." Those were his words to me and to a dozen others who talked about the party occasionally when he dropped in on a conference; but he was making it rather definitely known that he was done as our candidate. He did not wish to sacrifice himself on the altar of a futile party.

Anyway, social and industrial justice no longer interested Colonel Roosevelt. He had a war, a war greater than even he realized it would be, to engage his talents. He made a tremendous clamor for preparedness. He won back many of his old enemies, the big businessmen who now saw eye to eye with him and applauded as the Colonel raged at Wilson—a rather easy matter, too, because Wilson had won in 1912 when Roosevelt lost; and Wilson's scorn for the loser was something that Theodore Roosevelt could not endure. Roosevelt considered Wilson, the college professor, a theorist; and he always liked to consider himself a practical man. Wilson had never attended a county convention. The only time he had crossed the threshold of a state convention was when it had nominated him for governor of New Jersey. Roosevelt always tried to get along with the organization. In his precinct, in his state, he made broad the phylacteries of his political Republican garments, though he often thought like a mugwump. In the end, he was regular. Moreover, Wilson was a man of letters. While Roosevelt had written many books of which he was proud, nevertheless he liked to think of himself as a man of deeds. So Roosevelt took the warpath against Wilson and all his works, and particularly against Wilson's pacifism, his watchful waiting, his neutrality in Europe, his unpreparedness at home. I had a sneaking admiration for these attitudes in Wilson.

Many Progressives heard Roosevelt's war drums with distaste and uneasiness; but they did make a tremendous clamor, and finally the uproar was so definite that the Democratic national organization and the Democrats in Congress feared that Wilson might lose his leadership. I heard him recant, at a dinner arranged by the Manhattan Club at a New York hotel.

The afternoon before the dinner Bob Collier, of Collier's Weekly, told me what was in the wind. Along with Norman Hapgood, and probably Mark Sullivan, we had a box seat in the gallery, where I was less than thirty feet from the speakers' table. Knowing what was coming, I watched the President closely. I never saw an unhappier face; it was dour. He scarcely spoke to those at his right and left. The gay quips and facile persiflage with which I had seen his countenance shine at the dinner in Wisconsin were missing. When he rose to talk his glum face was a douser on the applause, for it was perfunctory. His voice was strained when he began. It relaxed a little as he went on, and by the time he had come to his climax, announcing the national intention to rearm for national defense, he had cast off his black mantle, and his voice was vibrant and his face was radiant for a few moments. But he was taking his medicine without licking the spoon, and it was a bitter dose. I may have imagined it, but that night, as I watched the President—and I admired his belated stand for rearming, though I had not encouraged it—I felt he had entered a new phase of leadership. Neutrality had gone out of his heart. He was a partisan of the Allies against Germany. He took the country with him eventually.

This was a year before the national Democratic party renominated Wilson with a New York orator's slogan as a platform—"He kept us out of war"; and I was glad in my heart that night that he had made his decision. I slipped down from the gallery before the dinner adjourned, and tried to shake the President's hand. He was already leaving. I only saw him as he passed, waved at him, and was able to stir up a smile on his face as he recognized me. From that hour it was evident that the President had his country with him. Sympathy for the Allies, unashamed, unquenched, glowed in the hearts of the American people. They were beginning to understand the meaning of the war. Perhaps they realized what a wrench it was in the heart of their leader to confess the truth that neutrality was a menacing hypocrisy. Not long after that I saw the President again, from a window of the Macmillan Building on lower Fifth Avenue, marching at the head of the Preparedness Parade. He was in Presidential regalia: silk hat and cutaway coat of the period, dark striped trousers, appropriate tie— a fine figure of a man. His head was thrown back in exultation, for he received a tremendous ovation during the mile and more of the march at the head of the bands, the drum corps, the soldiers, sailors, and civic organizations. And cheers along the line rose to greet him like a flowing wave of deep emotion that seemed to carry him along as one tiptoeing upon clouds. It was a happy day for him, and he turned a happy face to the multitude.

The country was tremendously stirred by the events in Europe—the horrendous battles, the slaughter; the danger threatening Western Europe, to which the United States was bound with many ties, first of blood and then of democratic interest. These were our people—these British, these French, these Belgians, these Portuguese, and, finally, these Italians, who were at war. We were not used to smelling blood from vast human slaughterhouses. Not since our Civil War had the ghastly facts of human butchery come so close to us as they were in those middle years of the century's second decade. The Boer War had not touched us seriously, nor the Spanish War, nor the Filipino rebellion. They were remote, and the casualties were few. But this First World War was in our front yard, and we were horrified, frightened, and angry at the same time.

It must have been on that autumn visit to New York, when Sallie and I were staying at the National Arts Club where Mary Austin was functioning as high priestess, that we met Herbert Hoover. Hoover was looming up as a national hero. He was beginning to feed the Belgians, and was in New York arranging for an American end of the Belgian Relief Foundation. Vernon Kellogg had been with him in Europe, and his letters to us were filled with the glories of Herbert Hoover. Mary Austin had met Hoover when she was living with her husband, who also was an engineer; and she had been in and out of the Stanford community where Hoover lived. I remember that I was shocked, but not beyond a good giggle, when I caught her referring to him as "Bertie"; but you may be sure not calling him that to his face. Kellogg had never used that name—to him Hoover was "The Chief" or "Mr. Hoover." Naturally we jumped at the chance when she invited us to meet him.

At a supper served in one of the studios Hoover sat in the midst of a small company, probably not more than a dozen or fifteen people; and we two Kansans were tremendously shocked when he declared that both the belligerents had treated him badly in his efforts to feed the Belgians. We did not know then that he was constitutionally gloomy, a congenital pessimist who always saw the doleful side of any situation. But we were idealizing the British; we considered them and all their doings highly noble, and to hear him shake a dubious head about their intentions and their essential integrity as it related to Belgian Relief frightened us. Otherwise we found Herbert Hoover a most intelligent person who smiled naïvely with a certain vinegary integrity, and a mild delicious sense of humor like a vague perfume about his aura. In short, we fell for him. He seemed to have an adolescent sweetness with his perverse acerbity, flecked in its texture with an engaging and disarming smile. He was a complex person who curiously drew to him in a steel-bound loyalty the men whom he touched, but a man who never was able to make a mass appeal. After the crowd passed fifty, the influence of his charm began to weaken. That whole group that gathered in the Arts Club that night was mesmerized by the strange low voltage of his magnetism. Sallie and I felt that we had met a Person—a Person of some dignity and power. Of course the fact that Kellogg loved and trusted him made it easy for us to transfer to Mr. Hoover a sort of in-law relationship; but even without it he would have brought us into his camp. He was the link—a real living link—for us with the European struggle. It meant much to us; so the first man we had seen who was in the midst of the conflict was drawn into our hearts and lives. For after all one cannot impersonalize entirely a cosmic human drama like that war. Icons, images, symbols, were all right, but here a flesh-and-blood hero stepped out of the great drama of Europe onto our tiny corner

515

of a stage. We set up a little altar to Herbert Hoover in our hearts—and after thirty years the candle before it is still burning.

When Woodrow Wilson spoke for preparedness at the Manhattan Club and when he had marched on New York's Fifth Avenue in the long Preparedness Parade, the bell tolled for social reform in the United States. The struggle for industrial economic justice and progressive political change had ended. Not that President Wilson had consciously put the period at the close of fifteen years of liberal advance. The war did that. But when he—the liberal leader—was forced away from his liberal goal into the business of rallying his country into the quickstep of war, even though he still sincerely protested against entering the war, we poor panting crusaders for a just and righteous order were left on a deserted battlefield, our drums punctured, our bugles muted, our cause forgotten.

We did not know it. A few thousand of us, maybe a hundred thousand, felt that the need for justice was stronger than the urge for war. And we kept on during the whole year of 1916—indeed for another year beyond that—trying to mend our drums, trying to take the rags out of our bugles and call men to our standards. The party Progressives still conferred in the nation and in the states, but it was harder every season to get enough people together for a dinner in the towns, the counties, and the districts. We party Progressives knew that it was an uphill fight; but if we could hold our party together through another Presidential election, which we realized would return Wilson to the White House, it was worth the effort.

Roosevelt, who hated Wilson and above everything wished to unsaddle him, did not share either our faith or its enthusiasm. He came to the conferences sometimes. He generally spoke bravely; but in private he told us all (at least he told me and many others) that there was not a drop of crusader's blood in his veins and that it would be a crime against our country to let Woodrow Wilson shilly-shally and polyfox along with his watchful waiting on Mexico, and his other cheap policies toward the Kaiser. Roosevelt, in talks with his Bull Moose lieutenants and captains, made it plain that he did not want to be an accessory to the election of Wilson by running as a third-party candidate. And yet he did not say definitely "No," and we—I don't know how many hundreds of thousands of us across the country, who felt that the Progressive party was worth cherishing—kept on hoping and, we feared, vainly hoping, that we could go to the people again as a party, advocating our program of social, economic, and political progress. And all this while Europe was aflame, and the brands were lighting a thousand furnaces in America, turning plowshares into spears and the implements of peace into the material munitions of war. How could we have been so blind? How could we have failed to see that a party, whose aim was to readjust industrial inequities, could not thrive in a day when production of goods and wealth rather than the distribution was the chief business of American life? Yet we did not see it. Certainly I did not see it. Whatever my memory of those days may show, my letter files reveal that I was following a zigzag course. It was largely parallel to the road I took between 1910 and 1912 when I was certain that Roosevelt should not be a candidate against Taft for a year or two, then was overwhelmed by the course of events, presently wrote him that he would have to run, and ended by urging him that he must run.

So after 1914, when it was obvious that the Bull Moose party was a group of leaders without followers, I wrote letters indicating that I had some doubt about what Roosevelt should do. My files and his replies show that I gave him a lot of bad advice; but it varied, and I suppose his files would show that Progressive leaders all over the country veered and shifted as I did. We were not a bunch of crooks trying to use a great leader for our own purposes. Neither were we fools or weathervanes. But changes come fast in wartime, and as facts change opinions change.

About the only letter written from 1912 to 1916 of which I am proud is one in which I said it was "futile to hope to establish a Progressive party in this country without La Follette." La Follette never wavered. He loved martyrdom. If he could have had our support from the election of 1912 to 1916, we should have had a third-party ticket out in 1916 and again in 1920. But he never had behind him the kind of leadership that followed Roosevelt. And he would not follow Roosevelt, nor would Roosevelt follow him.

In the meantime, with Roosevelt in Brazil, Perkins was in charge of the Progressive party; and the more radical of our party leaders began to grow suspicious of him and restless under his leadership. Gifford Pinchot was in open revolt, and they had a semipublic quarrel in which probably each was a little wrong. I was inclined to follow Pinchot, for I knew that he was right and that Perkins' leadership was hurting. Albert Beveridge and I had a set-to in the mails, which came to nothing. I was a compromiser who saw both sides, and tried to bring together contenders who generally agreed on matters of principle and differed on methods of procedure. I was raising money for the party chest in Kansas, and trying to settle a party row in Colorado. I had a finger in political pots in the West, and I was jumping around spiritually, much like a cheer leader turning handsprings and flip-flops. In the midst of these alarms came a letter from Woodrow Wilson thanking me for some support of his foreign policy. During this whole period my relations with the White House were pleasant. It annoyed Colonel Roosevelt that I could tolerate Wilson, whom he loathed; yet our friendship was never shaken. George Perkins and I kept up an epistolary but on the whole rather amiable conflict. I was always telling him I did not believe he should run the show; and he was patient with me, trying to explain why he should. He was right, for he was the treasurer; but he was not my treasurer, and I could talk back to him, which others sometimes could not do. I go into these details of my correspondence because, better than in any other way, it photographs the disintegration of the Progressive party in those four years after the defeat of Taft. A letter to Theodore Roosevelt after one of our numerous conferences at Chicago assured him that the crowd there was "spiritually tired"; yet no one wanted to go back to the Republican party. It was evident that ours was a middle-class group Even in 1914 we had the votes of the professional class but not the farmers— the farmer was too prosperous. And we did not get labor, no part of it. All that I wrote to Theodore Roosevelt about the Chicago conference and our party situation failed to impress him, for in his next letter he called our foreign policies "terrible," and protested, probably thinking I was faltering in the faith, that he never could support Wilson and Bryan.

But in 1916—after I had staggered for two years from the feeling that Roosevelt should not be a candidate of the Bull Moose party in 1916, to the feeling that if he did not run we could not go before the people, and then back to a conviction that he could not win in 1916 even if he ran—I found myself going ahead in Kansas, trying to get out a congressional ticket and pull the party together so that we could have a state convention to nominate delegates to a national convention where a President would be nominated and a platform written. It would be easy to take this correspondence for the eight years from 1908 to 1916 and prove that I was either a vacillating opportunist or a diabolical intriguer. I like to look back at that correspondence and wonder what I really was.

Of this I am sure: I was struggling to cut down my weight. I was counting my calories fastidiously, and I remember vividly and with pride that when I went up to Chicago in 1916 to attend the Bull Moose national convention and to report it and the Republican convention for the three-score American metropolitan papers, a Chicago paper which carried my convention stories printed my picture from toe to top and noted that I had lost thirty pounds! I had what would be called today a new streamlined figure. But it was hard to hold. I had given up trying to hold my hair. In my forties and fifties before I began to wrestle with the physical deficiencies of advancing years, I gave probably too much thought trying to subtract cubits from my stature. The fight with my body was never done, and yet I lived a healthy life, with little sickness and practically no pain. But in my forties, whatever my political caprices, however much I battled with that novel which I was writing at odd times for ten years, my real struggle was to keep down my fat. Three times a day I looked with lustful eyes upon butter, bread, and pancakes, but eschewed them. Three times a day I cut the fat from my meat and shoved it aside on my plate, avoided potatoes, and tried not to look upon the gravy when it was brown and gave color in the gravy boat. Three times a day I passed up sugar and tried to substitute saccharine. And still my girdle stood between forty and forty-two, and still the scales showed me over two hundred.

I liked good clothes. I was exacting about my neckties. I always took Sallie along to pick my hats so that I should not let my own extravagances of taste make me look ridiculous; for Willie White in his blue suit with the braid binding, and Will White with his broad buckskin cowboy hat, and Will A. White, the poet with his Byronic collar and crêpe necktie, and William Allen White in his Palm Beach suit, these, my ancestors, had left their mark upon me. Though I may have been a vagabond in politics, sartorially I tried to tread the straight and narrow path; and, in spite of all my disagreement with George Perkins and his public policies, I deeply and profoundly admired that gray mohair suit which seemed to encase in shimmering steel his trim, slim, agile body. Suppose he was slick and his tailor had made him good-looking—I took thought of him even if I did not follow his counsel. All these things I am sure of, even if I am confused and bewildered about the kind of man I was in the midst of the second decade of the century in matters of state and public welfare.

CHAPTER LXXIV

Decline and Fall

I REALIZE, of course, that ways of thinking and patterns of political conduct do not come bang-up against a certain year or month or day, and then suddenly turn or dissolve or shape new courses, but looking back it seems to me that what may be called the liberal movement in the United States came to a rather definite and catastrophic climax in that summer of 1916. Probably dissolution had been going on since 1912; but certainly in 1916 in two conventions at Chicago—the Republican and the Bull Moose—conservatism definitely and, for that decade, finally won. The story of the collapse of political liberalism that had been known very seriously as the insurgent movement of the Progressive party is so palpably, dramatic definite, and certain in its outward details that it will bear telling here, particularly as my life was so deeply affected by the circumstances that illustrate the change, a change that was for me tragic indeed.

During 1915, in the Republican party and in what might be called the Perkins wing of the Progressive party, two groups were trying to reunite the two parties. They had set the dates for the two conventions in the same week and on the same days of June, at Chicago. The Progressive harmonizers would have been willing to take the nomination of Theodore Roosevelt by the Republicans and accept their Vice President. This suggestion of course was an insult to the Republicans, who still hated Roosevelt bitterly; but it was also offensive to many Progressives, probably to most of them. They hoped to nominate Colonel Roosevelt and adjourn and so, with a third ticket in the field, force Roosevelt's nomination on the Republicans. The Progressives, in their conference before the convention, planned to nominate Roosevelt and then either to empower their central committee to accept the Republican nominee for Vice President, or to nominate a Vice President and empower their committee to withdraw him and accept the Republican nominee, thus effecting a fusion. The weakness of the Republicans was that they had no strong Presidential candidate. Taft was out of the question. He would not accept the nomination, and his nomination would have been futile. Charles Evans Hughes, Chief Justice of the United States, was considered by both parties, but while he made no direct statement, time and again he had indicated his distaste for the nomination. Yet those eastern Progressives who rallied around George Perkins were working with a group of Republicans led by Frank Hitchcock of New Mexico, a national committeeman and former Postmaster General under Theodore Roosevelt. They seem to have been working on Hughes. They had every reason to believe that if Roosevelt was not nominated by the Progressives, Hughes would accept a Republican nomination.

So the conventions opened. The supporters of Hughes in both parties knew exactly what they wanted and fairly well what they could expect of Mr. Hughes. The Progressives did not know what to expect of Colonel Roosevelt. He and I had talked in the spring in Kansas City. I was not sure then that he should make the sacrifice and run, for we agreed, he and I, that Wilson would probably be re-elected and his candidacy would be a sacrifice hit. Again he declared that he did not want to be a martyr, that he might fizzle out as a perennial third-party candidate, and the prospect— looking back at General Weaver of the Greenbackers and Populists—disconcerted him. He had no desire for posthumous glory. He wanted to be a vital part of his times. At parting, as I left the room he said:

"No, White, I just mustn't do it. As things look now, it would be more than the Progressives ought to ask of me!"

For by that time he had persuaded himself that he had been forced to bolt in 1912, when, as a matter of cold fact, he went into the third-party bolt in a rage. No one could have stopped him; I had tried vainly. He had persuaded himself it was a matter of principle, and we all agreed with him after the fact; but in 1916 he felt that he had nobly led an assault upon privileged plutocracy, and had done his full part in the Progressive movement.

We Kansans came to Chicago with what might be called a high-grade delegation. It was not the rag, tag, and bobtail. It was anything but the lunatic fringe. Bankers, lawyers and preachers, ex-judges and highly placed citizens of Kansas (including, perhaps, John M. Landon, father of Alf and receiver for the Prairie Oil and Gas Company) formed our delegation. Watching the crowd gather for two or three days before the convention opened, I saw the same kind of delegates from the Midwest all the way from Ohio to Colorado. The Californians, too, were exceptional men. The South, in anything but a Democratic convention, is generally a pretty scrawny lot. But what jarred and angered me and made me mad was that the delegates to the Bull Moose convention from the East were big businessmen, who had come at Perkins' beck and call. This was not true of Massachusetts, but it was true of the metropolitan area—New Jersey, New York, Connecticut, and Delaware. Their names have faded now from the roll of fame but I remember that a great steel master was one of them. A group of Wall Street brokers and bankers of some renown sat with New York when the convention opened. Obviously, they regarded the western delegates as longhairs, and Perkins was holding fusion conferences with Republican delegates from which Victor Murdock, chairman of the Progressive party, was barred. Perkins was merely head of the executive committee, or something of the kind. After that we held our own conferences. They were anti-fusion in their aims.

My son Bill, aged sixteen, old enough to be interested in politics, came with me to Chicago. I could not take him to the University Club with me because of his age, but he put up at the Congress Hotel; we ate together three times a day and he went with me generally to the interminable series of conferences, caucuses, and committee meetings that I attended. He was a great comfort to me. He ran errands and gave me an extra pair of legs. am sure that he enjoyed it and probably profited by it too.

Early in the week we western Progressives planned to nominate Roosevelt on Thursday and adjourn, after heavily empowering our national committee to work out fusion plans on Vice President or not, as the Committee chose. We elected Raymond Robins chairman of the convention. He was acceptable to both factions. I am sure his sympathies were with us. He was friendly, and I think had some political obligations to Perkins.

The Republicans were bitter. Their permanent chairman was a man I had never seen before, Warren G. Harding. I drifted over to hear his opening speech. He was a handsome dog, a little above medium height with a swarthy skin, a scathing eye, and was meticulously clad in morning clothes with a red geranium as a boutonniere, and he had the harlot voice of the old-time political orator. But he was bitter, scalding-bitter, to Theodore Roosevelt. I distrusted him, and into my distrust came something unpleasantly near to hate; for I thought he was deliberately, cruelly unfair. Of course he represented the tip of the salient on the right. Two or three hundred Republican delegates, men like Borah and the Kansas Republicans, and Will Hays of the Indiana group, were reasonable men. Some of them told me later they were back of the movement which was urging Hughes to accept the nomination. The Chief Justice had met former President Taft in the spring, and they had talked matters over, matters probably being the political terms upon which Hughes could accept the Republican nomination for President. In his three denials in letters, one to Bascom Slemp and another to Henry A. Wise Wood of New York City, and still another to State Senator Charles H. Brown, of Massachusetts,

Hughes protested that he was not a candidate. In the letter to Senator Brown, he used this phrase:

"I cannot permit the use of my name."

Yet his friends kept on using it. And in Chicago the week before the convention, when conferences and councils and committee meetings were being held by both parties, and unofficial backstage bi-partisan caucuses were being held to bring the two parties together, Hughes was the magic word. It was evident to me then—and, looking back over the years in the light of what happened later in the week, I am satisfied—that Mr. Perkins and Frank Hitchcock knew definitely that Hughes would accept the nomination. Their strategy was to keep the Progressives from nominating Roosevelt and adjourning. They wanted the Republicans to nominate Hughes. And our group, the left-wing group in the Bull Moose party, was determined to nominate Roosevelt immediately after the platform had been adopted, even before if necessary, and let the Republicans decide who would be responsible for the reelection of Wilson. This left-wing group succeeded in breaking the Perkins slate which included Walter F. Brown for permanent chairman. The committee on permanent organization returned the name of Raymond Robins, after Robins, as temporary chairman, had made a rabble-rousing speech to the convention when it assembled, and had become the idol of the men who had determined to nominate Roosevelt and adjourn.

It is hard to bring back to these pages the rancor, the strife, the tumult that raged in that Progressive convention the first two days, Tuesday and Wednesday. These men and women—for women had come into the political picture by 1916, from all over the United States—were an earnest lot. They were full of emotion and zealous in their purpose. They were not party-minded. The party was too young for that. But most passionately they wished to see all that they stood for organized into a definite program under the aegis of the Progressive party. And they believed that finally Roosevelt, if he was nominated, would not desert them. In that week more than at any other time in his career Theodore Roosevelt was a little tin god to his idolaters. Not at any time in 1912, not even when he escaped an assassin's bullet, was he so vividly lifted in the hearts of his followers as the hero-god of their hopes.

Perkins was trying to maneuver the Rooseveltians into accepting Hughes as a fusion nominee. I was in many conferences. I do not see exactly how I filed my daily story to the syndicate papers who were paying me so well; but I managed to meet my deadline every day, with an hour out of politics. The other twenty-three hours, it seems to me, were spent walking up and down hotel corridors, sitting in bedrooms that were stinking with stale smoke, serving on committees, intriguing, planning, conspiring to bring

523

about the nomination of Theodore Roosevelt before the Republicans name
their candidate. Harold Ickes remembers * this plan. I was to sit near th
telegraph instrument at the back of the Auditorium stage where the Bu
Moose convention was raging. Over that instrument information wa
ticking in about the happenings of the Republican convention at th
Coliseum. Donald Richberg was to have a similar post in the Republica
convention. He was to advise me, and I was to tell him what was going o
James R. Garfield, the floor leader at the convention, was not in our plo
We felt he would fall in with our plans, but we did not wish to em
barrass him.

Perkins and Ickes had it out one day backstage. Perkins knew what w
were up to, and we knew what Perkins was up to. Knowing Ickes fo
nearly forty years, and having seen Perkins under fire, I can imagine th
dialogue. When I got word that the Republicans were entering the orde
of nominating a candidate—which did not mean they were going to vot
that day but rather make speeches for a time—I sent word (I think b
Ickes) to our fellow conspirators. That was late in the week; it may hav
been Thursday or Friday. We tried to make a premature nominatior
Gifford Pinchot, I believe (or perhaps it was Amos), rose in the conventior
got the chairman's eye, and was about to speak. Perkins, on the platforn
like a terrier at a rathole, instinctively realized what was ahead. He create
a diversion; turned Chairman Robins around. In the diversion, the speake
was silent. A motion to adjourn came and left the speaker standing. Th
motion to adjourn may have been—I have always thought it was—o
signal from Perkins, who feared that we of the left wing would force th
nomination of Roosevelt a day before the Republicans were ready to ballot

That afternoon a messenger from Perkins' room in the Blackstone tol
me that Colonel Roosevelt was on the wire, and I hurried to the telephone
The Colonel began reproaching me for not calling him. Our group ha
tried to call him several times but without success. I told him so. He begar
sputtering in his characteristic way, "Well, well now—here . . ." an
finally settled down to a coherent declaration: "That's strange. Didn'
Perkins tell you last week that this phone was open to you?"

It was a direct line from Perkins' room to the President's library in Oyste
Bay. I had not known that such a line existed, and told him so. Again h
burst into expletives and said:

"I haven't heard from Jim, or Hiram, or Raymond, or Gifford"—mean
ing of course Jim Garfield, Hiram Johnson, Raymond Robins and Gifforc
Pinchot—"and the private wire was put in with the explicit understanding

---

* "Who Killed the Progressive Party?" by Harold Ickes, American Historical Review
Jan., 1941.

hat it would be equally free to you five people. I have not understood why
ou have avoided me."

I told him that I had been talking with the other four during the last
veek probably every hour of the day, and I was sure they did not know
bout it. His irritation was not feigned when he asked me to get each of
hem in the room and on the phone at once. Then he told me that he felt
: would be a mistake to nominate him under any circumstances, and we
rgued that out. There was nothing to say in defense of my position if
ve were considering his future. There was much to say if we were con-
idering the Progressive party. All of which I told him. He was firm but
ot cocksure of his position, and began suggesting names for the Pro-
ressive nomination—names that shocked me. I cried out violently as he
vent over the list: Senator Lodge, John W. Weeks, even Root (that, softly
nd tentatively), and two or three other right-wing Republicans whose
ames would have doused that convention with chill anger. I told him so.
Ve wrangled for a few minutes and then laughed it off; and I told him I
vould have Jim Garfield on in ten minutes, which I did, and the others in
rder, except perhaps Hiram Johnson who at that time had developed re-
ations with Perkins which made it difficult for such a proud man to go
nto Perkins' room, hat in hand, and ask for the telephone.

Among other things that I tried to convey to the Colonel was that our
onvention was a gathering of rather highly placed people. This amazed
im, and he came right back with the statement that I was the only one who
ad told him so, and he understood it was a mob of irresponsibles. It was
pon the basis of the information that came from Perkins' room, from a
roup of bankers, brokers, a few industrialists, newspaper proprietors like
Munsey and Stoddard, that the Colonel had formed his judgment, and
vritten the letter which was in Perkins' hand two days before the nomina-
ion of Hughes. Sometime during those two days I heard of the letter, and
he Colonel may have told me of it over the phone. Knowing of it confiden-
ially, I could not use the information. He may have told Jim Garfield and
Gifford Pinchot, and certainly did so if he told me. The convention was not
n session when we talked to him, and did not convene until Saturday morn-
ng. In the meantime, we gathered the conspirators, a score or two of us,
nd made our Saturday plans.

When the convention opened Saturday morning, our plans were laid.
Bainbridge Colby was to nominate Roosevelt as quickly as possible after
he convention preliminaries were finished. Our platform had been adopted
y the committee. There was no question about it. We were ready to go.
Then Colby from the floor asked for recognition. He was out of order, of
ourse. We were stalling around on some parliamentary subterfuge waiting
or Heaven knows what. Colby was to nominate Roosevelt right out of the

blue. We knew that once the name came before the convention on any kind of motion, it would prevail. The nomination would be made. When Robins recognized Colby, Perkins, sitting on the platform back of the chair, instinctively knew what was up. He literally leaped to the speaker's stand and began crying out in a distrait and almost hysterical voice. Harold Ickes recalls that no one knew exactly what he was trying to say. Robins shoved Perkins back into his chair, and Colby in less than a hundred words put Roosevelt's name before the convention. Such a burst of cheering, so full of joy, so charged with exultation, I never had heard. I had been attending conventions and had heard the claque of candidates roar on sometimes for an hour, but that ten-minute burst for Roosevelt there in the Auditorium was a cry that I had never heard before. Governor Hiram Johnson seconded the Colby resolution. By ayes and nays on the spot the nomination was made. In a few moments the nomination of John M. Parker, former governor of Louisiana, for Vice President, followed.

The nomination of Roosevelt was made at noon—nearly exactly noon. I am satisfied that what Perkins was trying to say before the convention was that he had a letter from Colonel Roosevelt declaring that he could not accept the nomination of the convention. I understood before the convention assembled that morning that Perkins had such a letter. He may have told me. But we, the conspirators, carried out our plot. The job was done. Then a most amazing thing happened. Hughes had not been nominated by the Republicans. Perkins could not be sure that he would be nominated though it was strongly presumed that he would be. But after the nomination of Roosevelt and after our noon adjournment, during which time Hughes was nominated by the Republicans, Perkins still withheld the letter from Roosevelt. We gathered there that afternoon and started a money raising campaign. Still Perkins withheld the letter. We were going on into the campaign. Every hour that we sat there raising money—and we raised something over a hundred thousand dollars and were pledging strongly— I watched the proceedings from a box where I sat with Ida Tarbell and some friends from the American Magazine (probably Steffens and Ray Stannard Baker). I was glowing with a kind of terror such as a train dispatcher might feel who had two engines approaching on the same track. I knew of the letter. From hour to hour I wondered if it had been withdrawn, and tried to think what could have happened that caused its withdrawal. The Republicans completed their ticket and adjourned. We remained in session until late afternoon, raising money, making plans, rejoicing.

At last the collision came. The letter was presented. In amazement that great throng heard it. The last words, "But your candidate I cannot be," fell upon them like a curse. For a moment there was silence. Then there as a roar of rage. It was the cry of a broken heart such as no convention ever had uttered in this land before. Standing there in the box I had tears in my eyes, I am told. I saw hundreds of men tear the Roosevelt picture or the Roosevelt badge from their coats, and throw it on the floor. They stalked out buzzing like angry bees and I followed them.

In the late afternoon a few of us gathered at the University Club. We tried to make plans. We could not. It was a dour and terrible hour, the ebb tide for our cause. We looked out across the stark ugly stretches of the dirty marsh where once our current flowed so strong, and in the agony of disillusion and despair we saw the dark rocks and the crawling things that had been underneath that ebbing tide.

I wrote my story for the papers. Then Bill and I had a light lunch. We dressed and went out to a buffet supper on the North Side given by Janet Fairbank. There was a lodge of sorrow too. A dozen or twenty of our conspirators were there, and one or two of the exultant enemies. It was a ghastly evening. It was nearly midnight when I got back to the club, called Sallie on the phone in Emporia, and spent nine dollars and eighty-five cents bawling like a calf into the receiver. At least I had release and relief. She cut me off when she thought I had spent enough money, and I went to bed at peace, and slept. It was the end of a great adventure, politically and emotionally probably the greatest adventure of my life.

My despair came because I did not realize what had happened. It was merely ebb tide. Since the Civil War had destroyed slavery in this country and the tide went out with Reconstruction and the corruption of Grant's day, a new tide had been flowing in, and for fifteen years since the century's turn had been pounding upon the rocks of privilege, and of social and economic injustice, crumbling them here and there, and making inroads upon bastions and ramparts. This Progressive movement was a part of a revolution. And as I stood there heartbroken upon the shore at ebb tide, I did not realize how soon and how strong the tide would come flowing in, and what rocks and docks and earthworks would melt in that flowing current.

Hughes and Wilson

THE NOMINATION of Chief Justice Charles Evans Hughes by the Republican
followed the nomination of Roosevelt. It was the best nomination the Re
publicans could have made. Most of the Colonel's insurgent friends of 190
favored Hughes instead of Taft for President. The whole La Follette grou
preferred Hughes to Taft. I did, and so did the second- or third-strin
leaders around President Roosevelt.

Hughes had made a great reform governor of New York. He had cleane
out a nest of scalawags in the life insurance business in New York City an
State. He had made a successful fight with the direct primary. Curiousl
enough, in 1907 Roosevelt was not so sure about the direct primary, and i
talking to me based some of his opposition to Hughes (when Roosevelt too
Taft) on the fact that Hughes was too sure about the direct primary. Late
of course, Roosevelt accepted it as he did the initiative and referendum an
recall. But in 1916, eight years later, Hughes was an ideal Republican nom
nee. His gubernatorial record appealed to the Progressives. He had bee
aloof from the two factions in 1912. He was a man of unblemished politic
character and personal integrity. Having been a Supreme Court Justice, h
added distinction to the Republican ticket; but, the day after the nominatio
of Hughes by the Republicans, the Progressive national committee met an
endorsed Hughes by only a narrow margin.

I did not vote. I was too deeply wrought up to abandon even the remot
hope of a Progressive party by joining the Republicans. The Progressive
held their national committee together. I was a national committeeman.
was certain only of one thing: that if the party could be salvaged as a goin
concern I should be ready to join it and do my part in saving it. Of cours
Colonel Roosevelt supported Hughes largely because he bitterly dislike
Wilson and all his works and ways. The Colonel, leading the agitation fo
preparedness, had forced Wilson into a program of armament. When th

Germans began their U-boat campaign on American shipping, the Colonel wanted to declare war, or shoot back in an undeclared war. Wilson's watchful waiting, which seemed to the Colonel to be wishful thinking, deeply enraged him, and he did not suppress his wrath. So, now that he had a candidate of decent size with a fair probability of winning, the Colonel with all his heart joined the Republican campaign. We met two or three times during it. He scolded me, and we fussed and fumed because I would not give more than mumbling lip service to the Hughes forces. I did not support Wilson, but many midwestern Progressives did. I had met Mr. Hughes once or twice some eight or ten years before, and had the highest esteem for him. I conceded every good point which his supporters urged, and which the Colonel pressed home; but I was too freshly widowed to be in a mood for political romance.

The Democratic national committee met in St. Louis the week after the Republican convention, and I attended as a reporter, taking Bill with me. It was a tame convention. Wilson was renominated without much enthusiasm. He had alienated the machine Democrats, but they had to take him. The cogs, levers, wheels, and pulleys of the mechanics which carried the Wilson nomination to consummation creaked, wheezed, groaned, and squeaked painfully as the processes drew to a close. Bill and I lunched, dined, and breakfasted with the newspapermen and the Democratic statesmen. I remember we had one evening with Martin Littleton, a New York congressman who delivered the speech which started the slogan, "He kept us out of war." It was consciously built up, and it reminded me of college oratory. But it did rouse the only spark of enthusiasm that glowed in the Democratic convention, and became the strongest vote-getting feature of Wilson's second campaign. He, himself, never used the slogan nor gave it endorsement—never made the promise to keep us out of war. He was entirely free to go to war if he chose to—meanwhile letting the people be deceived, as they were, by the use of the slogan, which covered billboards all over the land and was the holy text of Democratic orators.

Bill and I came home from the convention. I was low in my mind. We packed up the family and went to Colorado, where I worked hard on the novel that was on the board, and wrote two short stories for the Saturday Evening Post.

In late August, Mr. Hughes came to Estes Park to rest from his campaign. Of course I went to call on him. He had been through the California episode in which his conservative managers had managed his exits and entrances so that he slighted, indeed openly snubbed, Hiram Johnson—who was not a man to be snubbed. Hughes was conscious of his blunder when he came to Estes Park. He and I went for a ride up Fall River and climbed a hundred feet or so among the rocks and sat down for a talk. The Califor-

nia episode came up, and I assured him that the Kansas Republicans wer
not prima donnas, and that Governor Capper heading the Progressive fac
tion, and Mr. Albaugh and Mr. Mulvane representing the conservative
were earnestly trying to harmonize the party there, and that Mr. Hugh
need have no fear to accept any program that either Governor Capper or h
factional opponents proposed. Then Governor Hughes turned to me an
asked:

"What are the Progressive issues? I have been out of politics now so lon
that I am not familiar with it. Just how should I express my sympathy wit
the Progressive movement?"

I knew that Hughes was by instinct Progressive according to the insu
gent standards of 1908 to 1912, but I was amazed that on the bench he ha
not read the papers, that he did not know what we were driving at. Obv
ously he did not; when he walked out of the governor's office with his loc
reforms achieved, he felt the world was finished, all wrapped up in tissu
paper and tied with red ribbons for the millennium. So I recalled the Bu
Moose national platform of 1912 with its demands for "social and industri
justice." I suggested that he take up the matter of the prohibition of chi
labor which the Supreme Court had barred, that he consider the laws limi
ing the hours of work for women and establishing minimum wages; th
he support the eight-hour day, an old-age pension, a workmen's compens
tion law, a tariff commission with powers, the endorsement of the Feder
Trade Commission, and currency reform which was then pending in Co
gress under the leadership of Carter Glass. We discussed these matters rath
fully. He listened with sympathetic intelligence. But I feared that he did n
comprehend how earnestly a considerable section of public opinion ha
accepted and endorsed those issues. Our meeting was cordial, and he w
most considerate of my suggestions; but the pressure from the right w
with him, always, in his campaign, and he had no time nor strength to be
it down. So his campaign did not touch with much emphasis the questio
I had raised when he asked my opinion. Also the war came nearer, and i
issues rose, blotting out social and economic controversy.

I have no doubt that Mr. Hughes desired to keep us out of war as def
nitely as President Wilson. I, in those days, hoped ardently that we cou
avoid entrance into the conflict. And as the campaign warmed up in Se
tember, it was evident that the war issue would not be squarely met. At
national meeting of the German-American Alliance, resolutions endorsii
Hughes shook the Colonel and his friends. Still the Colonel went out in
special train touring the country, particularly the West, speaking fo
Hughes. I joined his train at Kansas City and rode to Emporia with hii
He was angry with Hughes for not taking a more decisive stand in favor
bringing the United States into the war. The German-American endors

ment bothered the Colonel. In one of his gala moments he admitted to me that he was afraid that Hughes was only a pink-whiskered Wilson. I think at that time I had more admiration for Hughes than had Roosevelt who was supporting him. But I had no grievance against Wilson as the Colonel had, or thought he had; and anyway I was still in mourning for the lamented Bull Moose.

One of the few times when Roosevelt cut me to the quick was on that train. I forget who was standing about when we talked, but it was a group of his followers. When he was fulminating against the pacifists, he cried out: "Poor bleeding Jane Addams!"

I could not forget that day four years ago when Jane Addams amid a volcano of emotion and applause had stepped to the platform to second Theodore Roosevelt's nomination as the Progressive Presidential candidate and his eyes were filled with grateful tears. It was not anger at him that I felt there on the train but a deep pitying sadness that a man could so soon forget.

So I left his train at Emporia when he headed west. I did very little in the national campaign one way or another, but devoted the Gazette's political activities to the reelection of Arthur Capper, governor of Kansas. A fortnight or so before the election, Sallie and I went to New York on a business trip. There Colonel Roosevelt invited us to Oyster Bay, and we spent a delightful evening with him and Mrs. Roosevelt at dinner and around the hearth in his workroom. He brought home the day's mail, as was his custom, to Mrs. Roosevelt. She went over it, they discussed it, and we all fell to talking about other days. Politics were adjourned. But just before bedtime, perhaps as we were standing before the fire ready to go to our rooms, Sallie let drop the innocent remark that she was going to vote for Wilson! The roof lifted from the house. The Colonel let out a blast of pain and rage and sorrow. Then we had a laugh and went our ways. We were to take an early train the next morning and have breakfast before sunup. While we were dressing, in burst the Colonel, coatless and vestless, not noticing that Sallie was in her petticoat. He began:

"Oh, my dear, my dear, it can't be, it really can't be, not really, that you are going to vote for Wilson!"

It occurred to him in a moment or two that Sallie was not fully dressed. He threw up his hands and went out, and talked with the bedroom door ajar until she was ready to come out and go to breakfast. Then he and she had it out over the meal, and Mrs. Roosevelt and I enjoyed our victuals. As he waved us off in the car bound for the station, his last words were a welding of imprecation, pleading, and anguish for her not to do a thing like that. It was not that he had such faith in Hughes, but he could not endure anyone whom he loved giving aid and comfort to a man whom he despised.

In that election of 1916, of course, the Democrats made the most of their slogan "He kept us out of war"; but when the returns were all in they proved clearly that Wilson was elected by the votes of the Progressive states: states normally Republican in the Middle West, many of them for Roosevelt in 1912, but operating under the political reform that had come into vogue in that first decade and a half of the century (direct election of the United States Senators, and all the rest of it)—in short, the very states where Roosevelt's leadership had impressed the people in other days.

Hughes was not sufficiently aware of the importance of Progressive issues to appeal to these Republican states. Kansas was typical of them. It elected a Republican state ticket and then voted for Wilson—not because he "kept us out of war," for Kansas when the war came was among the first three states to fill her enlistment quota. Kansas and these other western states were not pacifist. They voted for Wilson because of his progressive achievements in his first term. These states would not, in 1914, leave the Republican party for the Progressive party, but two years later they would not support a conservative Republican against a progressive Democrat. I was satisfied then (and wrote an article for the Saturday Evening Post supporting my belief) that "He kept us out of war" did not reelect President Wilson, but that the defeat of Hughes came about because he did not understand the divisory issues of the day. The war in Europe had submerged them, but it had not obliterated them. The American people were still liberals in 1916.

Early in 1917 General Funston died. He was sitting after dinner in the parlor of the St. Anthony hotel in San Antonio, where he was stationed with his troops on the Mexican border, and was listening to the orchestra playing for the dancers. The orchestra was in the midst of "The Beautiful Blue Danube." He turned to his companion, the lady with whom he had been dining, and smiled as he said:

"What beautiful music!"

Then he closed his eyes, and with a sigh he was gone.

For thirty years of our lives we had met as dear companions. I was always "Bill" to him, and he was "Timmy" to me. We wrote affectionate notes to each other. When he was head of the war college at Fort Leavenworth, he wrote:

Dear Bill:

I am a College President. Break it gently to the boys in the fraternity. Me a College President—my God!

That sort of thing! In his lonely days on the Yukon and under the Arctic Circle, he wrote blithe gay idiocies to me, and I returned in kind. I cannot remember him in a uniform: as a soldier he was offstage in my life. As a young fellow he had been always falling in love. I hope the lady next to him

532

that night had lovely eyes, and I hope that as he fell into his last long sleep with the strains of "The Danube" in his heart he was blessed by some woman's sweet and kindly smile. His death was the first that had occurred in the golden circle that I joined at the university. And it saddened me so that even today as I write across more than a quarter of a century I cannot recall it without a shadow of the sorrow that I felt.

I had probably been closer to Kellogg and Funston than to any other men for a generation, thirty years and more. When Funston died, Kellogg was in Europe with Hoover, feeding the Belgians. He had written, or was writing, a book about the Germans called "Headquarters Nights." When he returned on furlough to visit his parents in Emporia, I saw him. He was eager to get into the war. I had supported in the main the Wilsonian theory that we could keep out of war and should. Yet—and this was characteristic of me, I suppose—I had most earnest views about our duty to be as un-neutral as possible with Germany, and to help the British where we could.

When Wilson took us into the war the Gazette supported every measure which he deemed necessary. And we favored the vigorous prosecution of the war. Kansas and all the midwestern states that had voted for Wilson developed a robust war spirit, and enlistments preceded the draft. We bought war bonds to our full quota. We exceeded our quota for the Red Cross and the Y.M.C.A. Drives and campaigns gave us delight. We treated roughly laggards who withheld their subscriptions to the war effort. We were suspicious of families with German names. And I was on all of the money-raising campaigns, chairman of a "Special Gifts" committee—which means I helped to look after the larger givers. Every country editor's job is to conduct, directly or indirectly, his town's drive for progress and benevolence; and it was no new experience for me to pound the streets of Emporia with a subscription paper in my hand. I had done it for twenty years. Yet for all my patriotic interests, I stood, I hope, rather sturdily for the rights of free expression. The protestants against war throughout the country, the pacifists like my friends, David Starr Jordan and La Follette and Jane Addams, had my sympathy and support. I remember one winter day when Scott Nearing, a pacifist Socialist, came to Emporia to see me. I invited him home for dinner, and Bill, my son, who was in high school, was seriously alarmed lest I should get into trouble harboring an enemy of the government. He went to his mother about it and shook his head with solemn warning. But Nearing was the first of a rather sad little procession of the despised and rejected men in those days who beat a path to our front door. All my life, because in some way I have had to see both sides, I have in my political activities rested under the suspicion of trafficking with the enemy. I could not do much for them except hold their hands, and let them weep on my shoulder. I kept La Follette's picture in the Gazette office, and whenever I would leave town for a day or two I would go back and find it turned to the wall. I never could find out who did it. I did not care much.

In those days when I was supporting Wilson and the war, I came to dislike him—this man who was President—for his cold, mean, selfish policy toward those whom he liked to segregate and hate as his enemies, those who he probably fancied had forced him into preparedness, notably Roosevelt. I can still in my mind's eye recall the picture that I had from the day's press reports when Roosevelt, who more than any other thing on earth desired to fight for his country, walked up the curved pathway to the White House, swallowing his pride—and it was certainly a bitter mouthful—and asked the President to be allowed, under any terms, to recruit a regiment for France. The frigid malevolence with which Wilson denied this strong man's plea, made in what Wilson, being sensitive and wise, knew was excruciating abasement, carved deeply in my heart a picture of Woodrow Wilson that I could not erase when I wrote a book about him. His salving over his humiliation of Roosevelt with the oily pretext that it was in the interest of military discipline was, for me, worse than his real reason, wicked as I felt it to be. As Commander in Chief, Wilson could directly or indirectly have easily curbed any untoward military conduct of Theodore Roosevelt. It was ungenerous and worse—it was stupid—of Wilson to think that Roosevelt would be intriguing and caballing in France. Yet I supported the war and every major move that President Wilson made to wage it. And when he went to Europe to make the peace I supported him in that with what I tried earnestly to make a devoted loyalty. It was not important, what I did. I recite it here only to show what I am: a person pulling and hauling inside, tugging and wrestling with doubts and conflicts, despite my outward faiths and inner constancies.

CHAPTER LXXVI

A World Aflame

IN THE SUMMER of 1917 I went to war. I put on the uniform of a Red Cross lieutenant. Henry Allen of Wichita and I went together. We were designated as inspectors of Red Cross activities in Europe. What we really intended to do was to come home and write articles and make speeches about Red Cross activities. We did not inspect much. We did not have special intelligence enough to help much even if we had inspected the Red Cross activities in Europe. But we did see the American soldier coming fresh off the boat; we did see the front line from the Vosges to Belgium; and we got the feel of the American soldiers in France. Every day I wrote home to Sallie and the children a confidential letter for their eyes only. I had no thought of publishing the letters. But they were impressions hot off the griddle with no attempt at literary flavor.

When I came home Sallie insisted that I sit down and make a book of them. So I wrote "The Martial Adventures of Henry and Me." It was a trivial book, and the theme of it was in the first paragraph: the story of two fat middle-aged men who went to war without their wives. I rigged up a rather cobwebby romance to give the book a backbone; I knew that sketches would not be read. But I felt that if the experiences I had enjoyed —and I really did enjoy them even though I was frightened—were hung on the thread of a tenuous love affair, the book would have a chance. The story was fabricated by taking three or four persons I had met on the boat, in Paris, at the front, and in England, and pasting them like paper dolls on the gossamer story, giving them assumed names, letting them talk in imaginary dialogues, and moving them about most conventionally toward a happy ending. But the tale had its value because of two things: the scenes were described in the colloquial language that a man uses to his family; and it was a book without hate, parts of it funny. It sold well, forty or fifty thousand copies. But the English would have none of it. The humorous parts offended them. They could not conceive of a writer joking with death. The book outlived the war. It remained in print until the need for lead in the Second World War turned the plates into bullets.

Looking back at those days overseas, I remember a few things that I did not put in "Henry and Me." One of these was an episode at a Paris railway station. The Red Cross was there serving refreshments when along came a woman in a Red Cross uniform. She was of high rank, and she fluttered the Red Cross girls and their man captain. She was a tallish, skinny woman, and by country rules would have been called "stuck up"; but she was in trouble. She was trying to get on a train, and nobody seemed to know just what to do with her. I found out quickly what her trouble was, and how to get her to her train far down the platform. It was about to move out. We should have to run for it. I grabbed her bag in one hand, took her by the other, and finally, when she did not have much speed in her, grabbed her around the waist; and we ran like whiteheads down that platform. At first she seemed to resent my arm around her; but it gave us speed, and she settled down in a second or two and seemed to enjoy it. Just as the last whistle had blown, I boosted her into a coach with most undignified but absolutely necessary technique, and she turned back blushing and laughing, and I tipped my hat to her. When I got back to the Red Cross refreshment stand, they said:

"Do you know who that was?"

"No, but I hope I gave her a thrill."

With gasping awe they said: "That was Mrs. Vanderbilt."

It was a Dowager Vanderbilt, high up in the royal family! I hope I left her with a sense that, in emergency, the Kansas peasantry is not without a certain competence!

In England I renewed my acquaintance with the Walter Pages. They were running a simple democratic household there, though Page was a person of great importance as our Ambassador. But I never saw a man who was less disturbed by royal flattery. Mr. and Mrs. Page held that fidelity to democratic tradition in their thinking and in their lives. After the war Page, because he had seen what a German victory would mean, was criticized bitterly for his pro-British attitude. I hope now that his countrymen realize that he could have taken no other attitude if he would be true to the republican philosophy upon which his government was founded, and its civilization erected.

In Paris, Henry and I saw Ambassador William Graves Sharp. Once or twice we went to the Embassy for dinner or a reception. At home he was a politician, an Ohio congressman, and politically smart. Mrs. Sharp never did get us straight, never knew which was Henry and which me, and told us both frankly that she could not tell one from the other. We were both fat, both baldish, both in our late forties; both talked with a midwestern clip, and both kept our giggles on a hair-trigger. The ambassadorial ménage in Paris was much more elaborate, rather more gorgeous, than the household of Page in London. Probably it should have been. But Page's way of doing the job before him was more effective, perhaps because it did not •conform, as did Sharp's, to the European standard.

In Paris I often saw Mr. and Mrs. John Fisher. Mrs. Fisher was Dorothy Canfield, born in Lawrence, Kansas, daughter of my dear college professor, James H. Canfield. John Fisher was driving an ambulance for the French; and Dorothy was in Paris with her family, doing war work and writing a novel. She and I roamed over Paris at times. I was looking for French peasant dishes, coarse, gaudy native stuff, and I bought a boxful. I also bought a great round platter, the biggest platter I ever saw, decorated like a county fair. I did not pack it with the other dishes but took it in my hand, expecting to carry it with my personal baggage back to the States. I went to a millinery store, got the biggest, widest hatbox I could find, and made it the basis of a packing case for my platter. I spent more on the packing than I did on the platter, and was vain and proud of it. When we left for the boat train Henry noted in the taxi that I carried the package in my lap. I put it with my baggage on the platform and went up to the end of the train on some necessary errand, leaving Henry to guard it. As I passed the baggage car on my return my cherished platter was making a parabola through the air, followed by my two grips, and I "saw my fondest hopes decay." When I got back to Henry, he smiled triumphantly and said:

"Will, I found a man who would put all our baggage in a baggage car, and we won't have to carry it."

Just that. He was proud of himself! When I got to London I picked up the package containing my platter. I shook it, and heard it jingle. I left it in the station. And for a quarter of a century, Henry thought I was an inconsistent cuss to go to all that trouble about a platter and then walk off and leave it.

In Rome, the American Ambassador, Thomas Nelson Page, was more than kind to us. Medill McCormick, afterwards senator from Illinois, joined Henry and me, and we went out to the Italian front, a sad spectacle compared with that in France. We were only a week ahead of the debacle which came when the Austrians chased the Italians fifty miles back in a miserable rout. But the Italian front was more picturesque than the French. I seemed to be living in another world there. And one day a cable came from Sallie forwarded from Paris to Rome. It announced in cryptic language that an oil well on our farm at Eldorado had come in dry.

We had been offered two hundred thousand dollars for that farm with a fifty-thousand-dollar advance, before the oil well was started, if we would accept the standard drilling contract. But I waited for a larger royalty, a fourth of the oil. I was willing to take the gamble of no advance and a large royalty, and I am glad I did. But the cryptic language which Sallie used to tell me of the dry well went over my head because my mind was filled with the fantastic spectacle of war and the unbelievable grotesquery of the Italian front. It took me two days to untangle the meaning of her cable, so far was my mind from mundane things. Out there on the front I had almost forgotten that the well was drilling. The half-million dollars that a good well would have meant had receded from my consciousness—war will do those things—though I suppose the half-million did not really mean much to me. It might have disrupted and disorganized my life. I knew that before I sailed. Anyway, what did I need and what did I want with all that money! But there in northern Italy, my life seemed to have got into a new airtight compartment, and I could hear Emporia tapping but faintly on the outer door.

I came home from Europe in the early autumn, and every day kept hammering away at the novel "In the Heart of a Fool." It had taken shape and was being trimmed down. I never worked more faithfully nor harder upon any job. When I write that I was working on the novel, I mean that I was working an hour or two every morning. The day was spent at the Gazette office. The paper was growing. The new press that we had bought a few years before was becoming inadequate to take care of the increasing subscription list.

The Gazette has always been a country paper, interested chiefly in local news. Our subscribers, of course, were all within a range of thirty-five miles from our front door. If I had a hundred thousand subscribers I would have been poor indeed, for, as country newspapers were organized in the second decade of the century, we made our money not out of subscriptions but out of advertising. The home merchant gave us our profits. And what possible good could the Newman Dry Goods Company get out of a circulation that spread farther than their customers could come for their advertised wares? After my morning's work on the novel or on magazine articles I went to the office and did a hard day's work writing editorials, talking over business problems, cheering up the men who sold advertising, writing local stories, and serving on various committees which fostered the town's needs. It was not a lazy man's job as editor of the Emporia Gazette on Commercial Street, a job which has engaged me for nearly half a century. But it has been a happy job, and I have waxed "healthy and wealthy" and, I hope, wise in doing it. The war did not curtail our business. Sugar rationing and meatless days did not trim down the advertising of the Emporia merchants, even though all of us in town who had as much as two thin dimes to rattle in our pockets invested one of them in a war bond and divided a nickel of the other among war activities like the Red Cross, the

Y.M.C.A., and the Salvation Army. Still we had plenty, lived well, and, barring the tension of war, were happy. I suppose I was happy because I was busy.

The year 1917 saw me through my forty-ninth year. I was husky, a bit too heavy, my jowls a little too pouchy. My skin was ruddy, my eyes untouched by glasses, my teeth sound, my ears keen, my love of every good and beautiful thing hearty, and I hope fairly intelligent. My hobby was the phonograph and the classical music I could hear from it. That was before the day of many albums of the symphonies, or the complete parts of musical masterpieces, and I made a point of gathering from all the record makers the various parts of sonatas, symphonies and concertos: an andante from Columbia, an allegro from the Brunswick, a scherzo from the Victor, and so assembled my Fifth Symphony and others. When I was in London, I picked up parts of half a dozen of the classical works of the standard composers and brought them home with me. In the evening and on Sundays Sallie and I played them and enjoyed them, and the children came to know and understand them. So music was a real part of our lives.

During the First World War the moving picture was just beginning to sap the income of the theater in American country towns. The theater was disintegrating. Special railroad rates were being abandoned; it was hard to move scenery and a large company. Emporia's Opera House was gathering cobwebs. But when we went to New York—which was two or three times a year—we saturated ourselves with the theater and its diversions.

In the days of my forties I had no sense ever of being held up. I wrote half a dozen magazine articles every year; and in my forties I published four books: "The Old Order Changeth," "A Certain Rich Man," "God's Puppets," and "Henry and Me." During the war I bought my share of Liberty Bonds, which I promptly sold after the armistice. We lived well at home; traveled decently, never in luxury; enjoyed what the world had to offer, but not extravagantly; watched our pennies and put whatever money we had above our daily needs right back into the Gazette office. We had five linotypes and a well-equipped office. The subscription list had risen to five thousand, all in Lyon County. The county, which in 1895 could afford only two thousand local daily papers, in 1917 was taking five thousand and nearly a thousand copies of the Kansas City Star. The benevolent economic revolution was raging over the United States. Progressive change was touching every avocation, trade and calling. The standard of living, even during the war, was rising. And how I was enjoying it all! Life, as I passed out of my forties, was good. I liked it and it was kind to me. It had preserved my body. It had nourished my mind. It had, I am sure, broadened my spirit, widened my scope and influences and given me a happy home with dear and lovely companions, Sallie and the two children, which were enough to glorify the life of any man. I could not have asked for more and really did not. All I asked for was the strength to do my day's work and enjoy its fruits and its emoluments.

According to Kansas standards I was well-to-do. The Gazette was making ten thousand dollars or so a year. I was making half that much, perhaps, in book royalties and from magazine articles. Money, which never nagged me, was not bothering me, as I was closing my first half a century. I was reading fairly widely in biology, because Kellogg, whom I saw two or three times a year, stimulated that part of my curiosity, and I liked it. And I was reading a lot of books on psychology, normal and abnormal. I had a whole case of books which Bill and Mary called "Daddy's nut books." And of course there was music. Every year we brought to Emporia a symphony orchestra. Once Damrosch came with his orchestra from Minneapolis, and St. Louis orchestras came. And wherever we could find music in New York or Kansas City, we went. At home we spent hours—all of us—listening to the phonograph, familiarizing ourselves rather consciously at first, but later in delight, with what might be called the musical classics. More than all of that, our home was filled with wayfarers, people who came to visit, people who could talk, who knew things and kept us in touch with the world.

In 1917 politics seemed to have sagged nationally, and in Kansas the Republicans were engaged in harmonizing, and held many conferences which I did not attend. I knew that sooner or later I would harmonize. When I got ready, I would try to make my own terms. I often saw Colonel Roosevelt, who could talk of nothing but the war and fumed at Wilson before we got into the war for not getting in sooner, and, after the war came, for not making war more to Roosevelt's liking. I was saddened to see the Colonel so unhappy. Yet he did lead an intelligent and active opposition to the President, and gathered Republicans around him. I am sure that he wished to lead the Republican party in 1920, either to be nominated himself or to control and direct the nomination. Neither of us made any pretense of respecting the Republican party nor did we really have a great interest in its platform and so-called principles. But in the Republican party were obviously millions of men and women who voted with it blindly, and whose blindness could be used to promote the causes which we had at heart—the causes which had been stirring in the hearts of the American people for nearly half a century following the Civil War. If the Republican organization would use the blind party faith of the rank and file for bad ends, why should they not be used for what we esteemed entirely good ends? So the Colonel, who honestly despised Wilson, was not displeased to know that by voicing his low opinion of the President, he, the Colonel, was rising in Republican favor.

So 1917 passed. My novel was almost finished, revised and re-revised, and copied for the fourth time.

In Kansas politics I was busy promoting the candidacy of Henry J. Allen, the Bull Moose leader and my dear friend since college days, who was being drafted as a harmony Republican candidate for governor. I summoned twenty or thirty politicians of both sides to Emporia, and Sallie fed them, and we organized the Allen campaign. I was one of three who agreed to raise the money for it. The standpat Republican leader, Mort Albaugh, who was also Henry's personal friend, set up an office in Topeka. Henry was in Europe in the Red Cross and was to be nominated and elected *in absentia*. It was easy. To raise the ten thousand or so that we needed for the campaign was as easy as picking cherries. The money came from sources which we were glad to publicize, mostly in hundred-dollar contributions or less. This ease and facility on the money-gathering side of the Allen candidacy proved to me, at least, that it was popular, that Allen's political boom was a winner. Speaking generally I should say politicians who want to win should beware of a cause that does not speak fluently in money. People who won't give, won't vote.

CHAPTER LXXVII

A Hero Goes to Valhalla

BETWEEN my late forties and my early fifties came the period during which I began to feel a sense of security, the sense that I was "well fixed," though of course I had, even at the valuation of an inflated dollar, no more than a quarter or a third of a million. My income from writing, from the Gazette, and from rents, was little less than twenty-five thousand dollars, and that was more than we could spend. I had no desire for more income, nor for more property to clutter up my life. I felt that I was over the hill so far as money-making was concerned. Times were easy in Kansas. The farmer was getting good prices for what he had to sell, grain and livestock. The Emporia banks were lending money upon fairly easy terms. The merchants and professional people were doing well. The Gazette's circulation and advertising rates were going up proportionately. The war years were boom years. As a nation we were exporting tremendous quantities of war material and munitions.

After the beginning of 1916 and before the end of 1918 the United States went into a new phase of its economy. It became a creditor nation and not a debtor, and curiously an exporter and not an importer. From an economic standpoint it was a sign of insanity. A nation should not be sending out its capital and its goods at one and the same time. To be a world creditor we should at least have been a world importer, thus allowing our debtors to pay us. But no, we had to have our cake and eat it. We had to be a great exporter nation and a great creditor nation and we began erecting a house built on sand. In Emporia, in the Gazette office and in all the publishing offices where I sold my wares, this economic madness was creating a rather exhilarating delusion of grandeur. We were drunk and dressed up, all of us. I received twenty-five hundred dollars for a magazine article in those days—a short story—and two thousand became a regular price. My books sold fairly well. In real estate, whatever I touched was gilded. My luck in politics was also charmed. Whatever I tried to do I did reasonably well.

I was doing better than I ever believed I could. I was happy at home; useful in the town; serving my country by going forth helping to sell Liberty Bonds by making speeches that told about the war in Europe. Occasionally I made a Commencement address at some of the second-grade colleges and received an honorary degree in addition to a decent stipend. I never used the degree but I was making a collection. By the time I was fifty I had degrees from Washburn College and Baker, the University of Kansas, Columbia University, and Oberlin. And strange as it may seem, considering my average grade of B at the university, I delivered a Phi Beta Kappa address at Columbia and was often invited to talk at academic gatherings. I know I liked that sort of thing. To go to a college for two or three days, talk in chapel, discuss problems with the classes, dine at the faculty club, sit around the fire, loaf and invite my soul—it was flattering. While I talked I laughed and made myself the butt of my own jokes, and so managed someway to give the impression that I was not as puffed up as I really was.

But in those academic shades, talking to men who were far removed from politics as I knew it, I came to have an uneasy but growing sense that the egoistic forces of this country were organizing. I came to believe that the thing or the force or the social stratum which Theodore Roosevelt had denounced as "predatory wealth" was drawing together in some sort of an organization. Talking to college professors who made charts and wrote books around them, the economists, the sociologists, the political scientists, I began to be conscious, if I did not fully realize and understand, that some relation was being established between our expanding industrial life and the direction our country was taking in the world of international politics. I did not see it clearly, but I sensed that in those middle and latter years of the second decade of this century the old ways of our country were passing.

We were moving into a new and strange time. Mark Hanna had tried hard to plutocratize the Republican party around the interests of manufacturers. In his day the National Association of Manufacturers was organized. He worked with them rather than with the bankers of Wall Street, though he was cartooned in a "dollar-mark" suit. Then along came Theodore Roosevelt, who tried to overturn Mark Hanna's industrial empire. The National Association of Manufacturers grew in Roosevelt's day, but its power—first challenged by him—was checked in the first decade of the century. But the war came in the second decade, stimulating our industrial growth; and with the growth of industry came political power. Wilson struggled with it. But by reason of his regal manner, his unfamiliarity with practical politics, his stubbornness and something akin to arrogance, those who hated him and his works were willing to see his policies wrecked, even though wrecking those policies undermined the foundations of their country. Theodore Roosevelt was one of those. He wrote me in those days bitterly about Wilson.

Perhaps these lines from a letter of August 3, 1917 (shortly after the Colonel had swallowed his pride and asked President Wilson to give him a commission to go to France), will summarize the Roosevelt attitude toward Wilson:

Now as to what you say about Wilson. I entirely agree with you that we should stand for whatever good things he does. I stand by him in these matters and stand most actively by him against the La Follette-German-socialism-pacifism combination. But I regard it as the gravest possible moral offense against this country to stand by him *as a whole,* or to use language about him which will mislead people into the belief that on the whole he has done well and ought to be backed. Fundamentally our whole trouble in this country is due more to Wilson than any other one man, and his foes of the stamp you mention are able to attack him now only because of the weapons he himself forged for their use. Everything he has said since April 2nd can be justified only if we not merely unstintedly condemn, but treat with abhorrence what he had done before, and he has *done* badly. As Raymond Robins said to me, "Wilson has spent two and one-half years dulling the conscience of our people and weakening their moral fibre, and then without any change in circumstances he reversed himself while running full speed; and naturally the machinery stops and an immense number of people are completely puzzled and find themselves wholly unable to get up any moral enthusiasm." He won the election on the "He kept us out of war" issue. He had no convictions in the matter. He has no convictions at all although he has opinions and coldly malicious hatreds. He thought, and thought rightly, that this was a good campaign cry until after election. Hughes did not meet the issues squarely, and the bulk of the Republican leaders were but very little better than the Democrats. But the fact remains that it was Wilson who was the great offender, and that the damage he did to our people morally and materially during the last three years will bear evil fruit for a generation to come. Moreover his attitude since the declaration of war has been one of intolerable hypocrisy. It was possible to make some kind of a defense for our going to war on the ground that we were fighting purely for our own interests and rights, and because after two years Germany still adhered to the position about which we had sent her an ultimatum two years previous. Mind you, I say it was *possible* to take this attitude; but it would not have been a *proper* attitude, for there was more justification for going to war immediately after the sinking of the Lusitania than there was for going to war last spring. But what is perfectly impossible, what represents really nauseous hypocrisy, is to say that we have gone to war to make the world safe for democracy, in April, when sixty days previously we had been announcing that we wished a "Peace without victory," and had no concern with the "cause or object" of the war. I do not regard any speech as a great speech when it is obviously hypocritical and in bad faith; nor do I regard the making of such a speech of service to the world. I regard it as a damage to the cause of morality and decency.

So far as concerns what Wilson has done in the past few months, I think on the whole it has been badly done; and, what is more, that it has been badly done because of very evil traits on his part. He was emphatically right about the draft. He was emphatically wrong about the militia and about turning down the volunteer system as a vitally necessary stopgap. He took these attitudes because he was much more anxious to spite Leonard Wood and myself than he was to save the country. He has permitted seven months to go by without making an effective move in the vital matter of shipping, because for political reasons he was not willing to back Goethals. To have appointed Daniels and Baker originally was evil enough; to have kept them on during a great war was a criminal thing.

The greatest damage that can be done to the cause of decency in this country is to stand by Wilson in such a way as to imply that we approve or condone his utterly cynical disregard of considerations of patriotism and national efficiency and his eagerness to sacrifice anything if to do so will advance his own political interests. He has just one kind of ability; a most sinister and adroit power of appealing in his own interest to all that is foolish and base in our people. He not only appeals to base and foolish men; he appeals also to the Mr. Hyde who, even in many good and honorable men, lurks behind the Dr. Jekyll in their souls.

Faithfully yours,

THEODORE ROOSEVELT

Colonel Roosevelt was as eager to see the rising power of industrialism checked, controlled and channeled to the common good as Wilson was. But Roosevelt would not work with Wilson. And I, who disliked Wilson instinctively and admired Roosevelt deeply, though feeling that he was wrong, was disturbed as I went about the country at odd times living with the gentle far-visioned people in the academic world, who saw and were making me see, more and more clearly, how the centrifugal egoistic forces of American life were generating more and more irresponsible power— were hungrier and more insatiable every year to increase that unleashed power. I suppose my lifelong distrust of the principles of the protective tariff was father of my fears. The thing called protection was after all the principle that menaced our Republic. I was uneasy when I realized in those mid-teen years that we were making mountains of exportable things and at the same time lending to our Allies and debtors the money to pay for the things we made. I did not define it, did not even see it clearly in these explicit terms, but I was deeply concerned about the economic unbalance, the growth of predatory power in politics. I was mildly heartbroken that a man like Theodore Roosevelt, who really hated what I hated in our national life, should let his deeper personal hate for Wilson hobble him in the struggle against the enemies of his country—men and forces against whom Wilson was battling with all his might before the war and during the war.

I did not pull a long face. I did not mourn and moan publicly, for I was not quite sure of myself. I did not trust my hunches. And so I went about cheerfully, gayly at times, even though out of the corner of my eye I saw things that scared me out of a year's growth. Those things almost a generation later I was to meet on another battlefield as naked power seeking to convince the world that special privilege, raw, unconcealed and undiluted, was necessary for the common good. But in those days, in the midst of the First World War, and in the economic and political adjustments that followed it, the isolationism which made the beneficiaries of protection isolationists first developed. And I, who was deeply poisoned in my youth in Jimmy Canfield's economics class at Kansas University, fretted and fumed and grinned—but bore it.

On the other hand and at home, the Republican candidacy of Henry Allen for governor of Kansas was symbolic of the harmony movement over the country. The Rooseveltians were moving in. Everywhere men like Allen were assuming local leadership of the Republican party. The regulars were losing control not of the party organization but of popular leadership outside it. Half a dozen former Bull Moosers were going to the United States Senate. Half a score of gubernatorial candidates were appearing from the Bull Moose ranks. The chairman of the Republican national committee, Will H. Hays of Indiana, was a Republican Rooseveltian in the convention of 1912, and he was trying harmony in the party from the Rooseveltian angle. The White House must have been aware of this. There was evidence to convince me that someone in the White House was trying to defeat Allen in the Republican primaries by discrediting him while he was in Europe with the Red Cross. I am satisfied that if I had not been able to persuade Henry Davison, head of the Red Cross, to let Allen change over into the Y.M.C.A., he would have been publicly disciplined for a trivial and altogether sensible violation of rules or orders, in his routine Red Cross work at the front in the spring of 1918. The switch to the Y.M.C.A. saved him. He had the Republican nomination with an easy victory as most of his kind won in Republican primaries across the land. Allen was elected Governor by a decisive majority.

The fact that Allen was the symbol of the rise of a chastened, weary, and disillusioned liberalism in the Republican party did not curb greatly the activities of the greedy, egoistic forces in that party which controlled its organization. They treated us liberals who were getting the offices to liberal helpings of veal from the fatted calf; but, like the elder brother, they kept right on running the farm.

Then came the Armistice! and I was keen to go to Europe and write about the peace. I asked Walter Lippmann to intercede for me at the White House, thinking I might get a passport and a minor place in the President's peace party; but the President did not see it. So I turned to the Red Cross, where John S. Phillips (once of McClure's and the American Magazine) was editor of the Red Cross Magazine. He commissioned me to go to Europe and write some articles on the European postwar demobilization. And he got me a passport when passports were hard to get. Having the passport, I went to the syndicate which had been selling my stuff to newspapers, and they sold my articles from the peace conference, giving me the right to use the cable three times a week. I believe I was to get a thousand dollars a month and some part of my expenses. Sallie insisted—and she was wise—that I take Bill along. He was then eighteen. I was able to get him demobilized quickly from the Student Army Training Corps, and in early December he and I appeared in New York, got into our Red Cross uniforms, and were ready to sail. All this was done in thirty days after the Armistice. It was fast work.

The night we passed through New York before sailing, Bill and I heard Chaliapin in "Boris Godunov" at the Metropolitan Opera House. That fact of itself is set down here only to indicate how much music meant to me in that day and time. Chaliapin was Chaliapin to me, just another man singer. But the orchestra and the choral pieces, in short the harmony and swing and cadence of it, all without the words, which I did not understand, and the plot which I never could make much of, thrilled me deeply. I had heard opera at the Metropolitan before; but it had been comparatively trivial—"Aïda" and maybe "Il Trovatore" or "Faust"—and the light music of those operas did not attract my attention as much as the spectacle of the people in the boxes and the pit. As for the music, I had no great sense of emotional upset as the tunes went through my head like strands of pulling taffy. But "Boris Godunov" did something, left a deep impression.

And the other thing that I remember in New York of that day was not unlike the impression that I had from Chaliapin's Boris Godunov. It was a day with Theodore Roosevelt! Really a day, though I spent only an hour or so with him at the hospital. But let me tell about it.

I had told the Colonel that I would be in New York sailing for Europe, and he wrote asking me to call and see him. When I got to town I found a message asking me to come to see the Colonel at the Roosevelt Hospital at noon. Bill and I showed up at the hospital and the girl at the desk gave us a rather glassy eye. She called the Colonel's nurse, who said that he was not so well that day and was sleeping and could not be seen. While we were talking, Mrs. Roosevelt appeared and said that the Colonel was under the influence of a narcotic. We chatted for a moment, and I asked her to tell the Colonel that General Wood was a bona-fide candidate for the Presidency, and that if the Colonel had any idea of running he should talk frankly to General Wood. That was the chief thing I would have said to the Colonel. Whereupon we departed, and Bill and I took Brock

Pemberton, a former Gazette reporter, to lunch. At that time Brock was an aspiring young theatrical producer.

When we returned to the National Arts Club after lunch, the people in the reception office were in a great flutter. Three messages had come in two hours from the Roosevelt Hospital: one signed by Dr. Lambert, his physician; one by Mrs. Roosevelt; and one by some hospital official. The telephone girl at the club managed to convey the idea that Colonel Roosevelt was more than eager to see me: messages of inquiry had been coming every fifteen minutes for two hours. The Colonel was still an important national figure, and messages from him at fifteen-minute intervals to our rather modest club produced an impression. About four o'clock Bill and I, having placed our trunk in the ship's hold at the dock, appeared at the hospital again.

As we came in the door, the girl at the desk came out into the lobby. She said:

"Mr. White, you don't know how glad I am to see you!"

Before I knew it, an interne had grabbed my hand and said: "Come right along—hurry! The Colonel is anxious!"

Then appeared Dr. Lambert and took me by the arm and said: "You've saved our lives. That man has had this whole hospital upside down for three hours."

Whereupon Mrs. Roosevelt came hurrying down the corridor and cried: "Theodore will be so glad to see you, and it was so good of you to come again."

The doctor cut in: "I would rather see you than any other man in America right now. Maybe we can get that man's temperature down. He seems to have been raising Ned all over the place."

When we went in the Colonel was propped up in bed, sweet as a cherub, reading. It was marvelous to see how that dynamo could send the juice over that hospital, across the town, down to the National Arts Club, and impress a personality through a dozen people most vividly. He seemed to be glad to see Bill, whom he had known since he was a baby. For a few moments Archie and Kermit, or perhaps one of them, I am not sure, appeared, and the Colonel's pride in his soldier boys was a delight to witness. The affection between them was unassumed, and when his sons left he bragged about them with glistening eyes. He did not mention politics until I brought up the matter of General Wood, then he was anxious. I told him how I knew that Wood was running, and my story was convincing and probably disturbing. Finally he said:

"Well, probably I shall have to get in this thing in June."

He told me that Boies Penrose, and also Barnes, his archenemy, had sent word that they would accept him as a candidate. This is what I wrote to Sallie after I went to the club:

He showed me a rather radical article he had written advocating his Republican platform, an eight-hour day, old-age pensions and social insurance. Look it up and copy it. It will be in the Star, I think. . . . Cull from it his program and write a bit of an editorial about it, calling attention to the fact that he is moving forward fast.

I am satisfied that, if the Colonel had lived, he would have been the Republican nominee and the country would have had, in workable terms, from a Republican administration, much of the social program that came a dozen years later under the second Roosevelt. It would have been adopted in normal times. We should have had the little end of the wedge. It would not have disturbed economic and industrial traffic, and a great cataclysm might have been avoided.

We sailed on a small French ship with a crooked beam, the *Chicago,* which listed seven ways from Sunday, and I was seasick much of the time. At the table, Bill and I were seated with librarians, Dr. and Mrs. Willis Kerr, from the Kansas State Teachers' College, and a group of assistants who were going to Paris, to set up a reference library for the American workers at the Peace Conference and for the A.E.F.

Bill and I shared our cabin with Norman Angell, who was also a tablemate, and I came to admire and trust him and have held him in affectionate esteem through all these years. He was going to write about the peace conference, for a string of British papers. As we dropped south toward Bordeaux, our landing place, the weather moderated and we walked the deck a great deal, tromping on shell-pink clouds of iridescent dreams about world peace. There was rumor and gossip about the League of Nations which Wilson was determined to establish, and Angell had a lot of ideas about the League—better ones, I discovered later, than Wilson had. But we talked at the table and on deck in our chairs and afoot, about the League and Europe and the peace, and it was a highly profitable journey. I disembarked with much more baggage in mind and heart than I had in the hold. It was my introduction to international politics.

When we landed at Bordeaux, between Christmas and New Year, I was full of enthusiasm—fired with a desire to see and be a part of what then seemed to be one of the greatest adventures that man had ever embarked upon since he dropped his tail and went to Eden.

At Paris, they sent Bill and me and Norman Angell to a little hotel called the Normandie. Coal was short in Paris that winter, and the Normandie was so cold that it reminded me of the icehouse on the Walnut River at Eldorado. We shivered there for nearly a week; then Norman Angell, who knew Paris better than we did, found out that the Hôtel Vouillemont, across the Boissy-d'Anglas from the Crillon, had recently been occupied by the American Navy, which moved out leaving an ample stock of coal. We found good rooms there, with an adjoining bathroom, and hot water all day and night. So we left the Normandie and tucked in for nearly five months at the Vouillemont. There lived Ray Stannard Baker, who was the President's mouthpiece to the press, and Ida Tarbell, who was writing something about the peace for the American Magazine. Dorothy Canfield used to come occasionally. Half a dozen men who were more or less attached to the American delegation to the conference lived there: James Scott Brown, an advisor on international law; some Quakers who were doing reconstruction work in terms of many millions of dollars in devastated France; and, for a time, Oswald Garrison Villard, and one or two correspondents from the London papers who knew vastly better than I did what the conference was about. I must set these names down here, not in pride but to show how I got what little education I had, as I wrote my stories from Paris for the McClure Syndicate.

I was one of the cable men. I used the cable three times a week, writing my letters in cablese, skeletonized. And I told seriously, honestly and briefly what was going on at the conference in those days. Reading those stories today I see they are dull and unimportant. I realize now that I did not know the truth and that few, if any, of the American correspondents knew it. We had access to the facts. Ray Baker was illuminating when he talked and most obliging when we asked questions. But we did not ask the right questions apparently. We did not comprehend the significance of the conference even if we sensed its importance. And some way, with all the thousands and hundreds of thousands of dollars spent by the American press in cable charges and in reporters' salaries, the American people got only the facts and not the truth. For no one knew the truth. I doubt now if Wilson did; and if Clemenceau and Lloyd George suspected it they did not reveal it.

I suppose it is, briefly, something like this: The French, who were the continental representatives of victory, desired to establish, under the League of Nations, and rather deeply under it, the old European balance of power. They wished to control Central Europe and the Near East. They were willing to give, and England was willing to take, colonies in Africa for exploitation under the fairly decent but always imperial habits of the British, and the French were willing also to give Great Britain freedom in the Far East, in the Pacific, around the coast of Asia. Japan was a stepchild, and China a poor orphan. Wilson had, in the end, to compromise consciously and was forced, by the ignorance of the American delegation, into regrettable positions. He had to agree to things that he knew were bad, to get what

550

he regarded as the larger good; and he often took things that were bad, not knowing how bad they were. He could not play politics as Lloyd George, a professional, could, or as Clemenceau could who had all his life lived in the atmosphere of compromise, intrigue, and debate. Wilson was not exactly an innocent but his life as a college president had not equipped him with political experience. He was sitting in a game with two sharpers who knew the cards, who had marked the decks and knew the value of the chips. Yet he was for all that, by reason of the nobility of his ideals, the brave, fine way he stuck to them, and even for what he achieved, a truly great and noble figure in Europe that year.

The next few chapters will be an attempt to tell something not of what really happened but of the atmosphere of Paris in those days—the Paris of the Peace Conference. No one who was there enjoyed it more than I did. No one, I am sure, took less to it and brought away more. And I am sure that no one grew in strength and grace and, I hope, in wisdom as I did, for few of them started so far back in the muck and mire of ignorance as I. The only thing I took worth baggage room to Paris that year was an open mind.

We had been in the Hôtel Vouillemont only three days when I came down to breakfast and saw in the morning edition of the Paris Herald the news that Colonel Roosevelt was dead. I can remember, across the years, standing there with that paper in my hand; dumb, speechless, and probably tearful. I could not have read that news without sorrow. Again and again I looked at the headlines to be sure that I was reading them correctly. Ray Baker came along, and I cried:

"Ray, Ray, the Colonel is dead—Roosevelt!"

He must have seen the grief in my face. He had the paper in his hands also, for he had read it at breakfast. He put his hand on my shoulder and said:

"Yes, Will, it's a great blow. We are all sorry."

Then he and Ida Tarbell and I sat down to talk it all over, and get used to a world without Roosevelt in it. Not since my father's death had grief stabbed me so poignantly as those headlines cut into my heart that gray, cold Paris morning. In the meantime, across the world, in Emporia, Sallie —who had been all day at the Gazette office working on the Gazette's news story of the Colonel's death—came home at night to Mary our daughter and a glowing fire in the living-room grate and there opened a letter, probably the last letter that the Colonel ever wrote:

December 28th, 1918

Dear Mrs. White:

"Home Fires in France" has come and I am looking forward to reading it. I saw W. A. the other day and that really fine boy of yours. Any mother would be proud of him! I am much discontented about the hurried glimpse I caught of you last October. The real trouble was that I was then well on my way to the attack of inflammatory rheumatism which has since laid me out, and I was so occupied in getting through the campaign without a breakdown that I did not have the sense and intelligence to insist on getting you out to Oyster Bay. I shall hope for better luck when you come east.

Faithfully yours,
THEODORE ROOSEVELT

It was a voice across the black chasm of death. The voice persisted even when his lips were sealed. I have never known another person so vital nor another man so dear.

CHAPTER LXXVIII

The Peace That Passeth Understanding

THE PARIS of the peace conference in the winter of 1918 and 1919 was crowded. Ten thousand civilian visitors must have come there from every nation in Europe. For every nation on this globe had some vital interest at that conference. Each nation sent its delegation and its delegation brought its hangers-on—men and women whose special interest made it profitable, even necessary, to come to Paris so that the special national interests would not be ignored in the conference. Probably nowhere else on earth were ever assembled so many self-seeking visitors who knew, or thought they knew, exactly what they wanted. The air was filled with international horse-trading. The world's great commodity interests there probably for the first time met face to face. And from that Paris conference sprang the inter-national agreements, patent pools, cartels, trusts, interlocking international directorates that began to rise in the third decade and were organized compactly in one huge world-wide compact of plutocracy. That organism—somewhat financial, somewhat social, and of necessity more or less political—was growing conscious across national lines, even across ocean boundaries. Indeed it was passing the equator and spreading the sensitive pocket nerves of the well placed and overweening people of this globe. It was not domi-nant, but it sought unconsciously that world organization—that world sense of the power and glory of the almighty dollar which makes (and which, a quarter of a century later, was definitely beginning to make) a new kind of aim and purpose for the leaders of this world—leaders in business, lead-ers in intellectual affairs, political leaders of all parties, right and left alike.

There at Paris these thousands of representatives of the Nations and those who came to guard them, had to be fed, lodged, entertained, trans-ported around the city, and diverted with the idea that they were achieving something worthwhile. So the air was filled with gayety; theaters were crowded, concert halls played to capacity houses, restaurants within a mile of the Place de la Concorde were always showplaces jammed with people who wanted to be seen. And the two opera houses, the Opéra Comique and the Opéra, were sold out days in advance. Traffic on the boulevards was congested. The city was a place of parties, receptions, teas, conferences, caucuses, secret gatherings. And out of it all, where the horde of visitors went about their foolish futile errands, grew that world which wrecked itself in a quarter of a century; largely, I think, because the same unrestrained forces of amalgamated self-interest found that winter in Paris —in all its gayety and beauty, and outward sense of joy and inner sense of power—the formula of destruction which was to shatter the world.

I did not know this at the time. I worked hard, six or eight hours a day. I attended regular press conferences held by the Americans and by the British. Occasionally I went to the French, who were such obvious liars that their perfidy palled after it ceased to be amusing. And when there was a special conference or a semipublic meeting of any consequence, I made it my business to attend. Every day I saw Colonel Edward M. House, who had been the President's emissary to Europe during the war. I walked with him late afternoons along the banks of the Seine and we discussed the passing show in the various secret conferences. I am sure that he was candid with me. I am certain that he had no guile. So far as he knew what was pending and why it was important, he told me. Much that he told me was in confidence. If he knew something about the undercurrents of the great peace conference I would have known it. More than that, every day Ray Stannard Baker, who saw the President for an hour or so and talked frankly with him as the official press representative of the American delegation, talked with me at breakfast, luncheon, or odd times when we met as old friends; and Norman Angell, who was a good pipeline carrier from the British delegation, told me from time to time what Great Britain was after. I was exposed to all the facts. I should have known the truth. Moreover, every day I saw and talked with the American correspondents; the wisest of them all was Frank Simonds, who was beginning to know the truth, who tried to tell me the truth. But he was such an inveterate pessimist that I could not believe the truth when he told it to me. He saw the rocks and the wreck ahead. He wrote it to his papers. And much thanks he got for it. The President became bitter against him and he lost caste and standing as men always do who proclaim the unpleasant and terrible truth. I remember that Frank Simonds one day in February showed me his cable. The first lines contained the phrase:

"The League of Nations is dead. The treaty of peace is impossible."

That was the burden of his song. After Wilson refused to consider the use of force as a guarantee of the decisions and pronouncements of the League of Nations, Simonds felt that without a common police force to implement the treaty of peace and to make good the decisions of the League of Nations, the League would fall into a political mechanism to promote the balance of power, the old organ of European political stability. He also was sure that without an international police force, the terms of the treaties soon would be violated because no one cared to stop the intrigue of special privilege in and upon the conquered countries which would sooner or later render the peace of Paris a mockery.

But one must not get the impression that I, or anyone else at Paris, was devoted solely to considering and reporting high and mighty matters. Paris was gay. Bill was with me. He was studying French with a tutor four days a week and soon had the language in hand. His two years of French in high school, plus a natural aptitude for language, made him most useful to me. We went together to the theater and to the good restaurants, often picking up friends; and because I was lonesome for the female society of my kind, we generally picked up interesting women of whom there were great lonesome droves in Paris, members of the various reconstruction units, wives, sisters, and daughters of delegates and experts attending the conference, and occasionally the classical detached expatriated American mother and daughter living on the Continent because prices were cheap and domestic duties were few. These women, who were as lonesome as we, were good companions at the theater. They often dropped in to the Vouille-mont for tea. We took them sometimes to the opera.

The French were hospitable. They were forever entertaining the press of the world and were particularly eager to please the representatives of the American press, and especially courteous to those of us who were filing news by cable. So Bill and I saw everything that was going on. The French nation rented a gorgeous palace of a rather vulgarly rich man—a palace he had adorned in the decorations with naked women spreading over fire-places, or standing on the newel posts, or bending over doorways and win-dows. It was a forest of obtrusive nudity, and it became known to the American press delegation as "The House of a Thousand Teats." There the French gave us dinners, shows, lectures, and receptions to meet the great and the near-great. I remember a lovely evening I had there with Henri Bergson, the philosopher whose "Creative Evolution" I had taken two years to read. He was a charming man who reminded me, because he was blond and slight and soft-voiced and with a certain suppressed humor, of James Whitcomb Riley. We three—the merchant, my host, and Bergson (and possibly Bill)—ranged over the whole earth and the fullness thereof in our talk at the dinner, and I went home late with my head in the stars.

However, I do not wish to give the impression that I was so terribly in-tellectual. Bill and I made the rounds of the best restaurants of Paris for dinners and ate every variety of food that the broad Republic of France could provide. I balked at snails but Bill got them down without a quiver.

The Chinese gave to the foreign press—particularly the British, Americans, and the French—the most elaborate dinner I ever tackled. It began at eight and they were still serving food at midnight. Between the courses there was talk, and we correspondents kept expecting the Chinese to announce the purpose of the meeting, to tell us their side of the peace negotiations. The quarrel over Shantung was up, and the Chinese had vital interests. One course followed another; and between courses, the Chinese hosts—I think Wellington Koo was one—and half a dozen other Chinese gentlemen who spoke beautiful English, talked gracefully about many things, and never once mentioned pending matters in the conference. After the food stopped coming, we all politely lingered. It became one o'clock. The Chinese still talked, and one by one the American correspondents made their apologies, leaving one of their colleagues to stay and report what happened. And somewhere after half past three I was left as a sentinel to report to Tom Johnson, Herbert Swope, Larry Hills, Edwin Hill, and Arthur Krock what, exactly, the Chinese had invited us there for. I staggered home, sober enough, but weary and heavy laden in my digestive tract, at the crack of dawn. I was the last American to leave, and I never learned—and no one ever learned—the purpose of that dinner. The Chinese were just that polite. Moreover, I had to be on hand at noon the next day to a most formal and gorgeous luncheon given by the Mexicans, and they made short shift of saying what they wanted. It was aplenty, and of course they did not get it. But they did put on a food show that was the wonder and admiration of the American press for a long gustatory week.

For all the festive face of Paris, in her heart of hearts turmoil was raging. It was man's first experience in organizing world affairs. The Roman Empire, after all, was mostly a Mediterranean concern. Napoleon scarcely left the boundaries of Europe. The British Empire represented only a minority of mankind. But here for the first time man was trying to organize the whole globe into some kind of political entity. These thousands, perhaps hundreds of thousands of men and women who were gathered there in Paris in the early winter and spring of 1919, were literally of "every kindred, every tribe on this terrestrial ball." With their self-interests, which were unrestrained, was their satellite special interests which were greedy and unashamed in their greed; and they were trying to integrate, trying sincerely to form, some kind of unity. But it is evident now that something more than good will is needed. Their noble emotions which might have united them were not matched, there in Paris in those days of the winter and spring of 1919, by their minds. The problem was too big for man, acting in his collective capacity with his limited knowledge and experience, to solve.

I gathered from day to day, talking with Colonel House, Ray Stannard

Baker, and a score of others who were nearer to the American delegation than I was, with what terrible earnestness Woodrow Wilson was trying to comprehend the problem. I think he knew—he must have known—his limitations, any man's limitations facing that problem. In the end, the problem was checked up to three men, to Wilson, Clemenceau, and Lloyd George. The preliminary work—what might be called the predigestive process—was done in scores of committees, and by these committees checked up to a rather large council of the Allies. There the work of the committees was digested. But giving the blood, putting on the flesh, and making the bone of the world structure was in the womb of The Big Three. Premier Clemenceau represented the continent of Europe. He knew it as well as one man could know it. He was a cynic but not a pessimist, for he had a great faith. But chiefly his faith was in France and the French way of life. At first probably he despised Wilson as a canting Presbyterian moralist. He sneered at him in several public utterances before he met him at the conference at the Table of Three—sneered politely with a gay French touch, but nevertheless his sneers were poison barbs. Lloyd George was a horse-trading Welsh politician—expansive, emotional, but canny in the deep and bitter experiences of a lifetime in the peculiarly shady politics of the British parliament. He knew little about continental Europe and apparently cared less. His eyes were greedy for advantage to the British Empire. He wanted colonies. He wanted British mandates which were quit claims rather than fee simple deeds to possession. Lloyd George knew Wilson and his kind better than Clemenceau, for Wilson was a Scotch-Irish parson in his eyes. He understood Wilson's aspirations, shared them with a sort of academic enthusiasm. Lloyd George, in the Council of the Three, worked more often with Wilson than with Clemenceau; but when the interests of the British Empire were at stake he deserted Wilson with the sweet and lovely complacency of the courtesan who has her children to support.

Wilson proclaimed during the war, at the end of the war, and when he went to Europe, that the United States wanted no territory, desired no colonial influence, hoped only to establish an organization to guarantee world peace. For that he would do anything; indeed his stern Presbyterian morality once in a long while was bent to what he thought was a larger good. The difference between the complacency of Lloyd George and the surrender of Wilson was that the Britisher knew he was harloting, and Wilson believed he was serving the will of God. The secret treaties which the Allies had made before America's entrance into the war, with Italy and with Japan, rose to meet President Wilson early in the sessions of the conference. After the Convenant was drawn and he came home, the President denied that he knew of those treaties until he went to Europe. There again I think the Scotch-Irish parson was telling the truth. He had heard of them. They seemed trivial at the time they came into his ken. Other matters, which seemed much more important to him than the text of the treaties which were published in the New York papers, were worrying him deeply. So in the conference there at Paris, when the treaties rose and stood in his path as he walked sternly toward his ideal of justice, he was concerned with these complications, bedeviled by their consequences in the work before him, and necessarily detoured more or less around the straight path to his objective. Woodrow Wilson was fundamentally honest, a man of high and noble purpose at that conference. And he sat there at that cosmic poker game with the fate of humanity in the run of the cards. He made his bets with his hand face upward on the table for all to see. He really had only one chip in the game, to secure justice for humanity in some kind of vital political organism that would live and breathe with the righteousness that was in his own heart. But alas, the thing he fathered had his own weaknesses. He begot it too good for this world.

Now all these things I sensed, suspected vaguely, understood but did not quite know as I went about my job in Paris in those days. I knew as much as any other reporter. I did not have the sense that Frank Simonds had, or that Oswald Garrison Villard had. I could not coordinate my facts and integrate them on the thread of wide international political experience. After all, I was just Republican precinct committeeman in the Fourth Ward of Emporia, Kansas, who had been on the state committee and had been on the National Committee, and so walked with what I thought was a heroic tread. But the vast complexity of European politics, built on centuries of tradition, usage, prejudice and conflicting desires, was not even remotely in any corner of my consciousness. So I wrote the day's story without realizing the larger story of which the report of the day's routine was a small and insignificant part. It would have done me no good to turn blue-stocking, and study seriously to find the mainspring of European politics which guided Clemenceau and which in a measure was the basis of what Wilson must have felt sometimes was the treachery of Lloyd George. Probably I caught a better sense of it all by hearing good music, listening, where I could understand them, to plays, seeing all the pictures that I could, talking night after night and day after day at luncheons and dinners with men and women who knew the truth, better than I could have done if I had delved into books and devoted solemn hours querying historians and philosophers. Anyway, as the reader will know who has followed this story, I was not one to get my education out of books. I have read many books. In college I read many, but they were the obbligato and not the theme that I pursued in seeking wisdom.

CHAPTER LXXIX

Versailles Puzzles over the Soviet Republics

I suppose the story of the Commission to Prinkipo belongs here. Certainly it is a part of my primary education in European politics. It was an insignificant affair and it fizzled. Yet in its pattern and in its failure lay all the evils and tragic weaknesses that made the Peace Treaty of Versailles a mockery. Here is the story, the personal story of what was to me an illuminating and exciting adventure.

I began to realize early in January that the fundamental clashes in the conference were between the French demand for security against another German invasion, versus the feeling of Wilson and Lloyd George that the best security France could have would come if the Allies treated Germany fairly, and if the conference left a fairly free Europe, free to organize itself as a going civilization. This clash explains much, though of course not all, of the political maneuvering at Paris in the winter and spring of 1919. France desired to control eastern and central Europe. France feared Bolshevism in that area with a jibbering terror. Lloyd George and Wilson were uneasy about the Bolsheviks but the whole political policy of France at the peace table was to put a ring around Germany and erect a barrier against Russia. Preferably France would have liked to overthrow the Bolshevik regime and restore, if not the Romanoffs, at least some semblance of the Kerenski Republic. Clemenceau was willing to trade security against Russia and Germany for anything that Great Britain desired, or that Wilson cared to put into the bargain. So, in the end, the British extended their colonial empire. Wilson got, with certain reservations, his League of Nations, France the establishment of a balance of power in central Europe, and a free hand to deal with Russia either by diplomacy or force.

These things I learned, talking with Colonel House and with Ray Stannard Baker, and occasionally discussing the problems of the day with

Tom Lamont of the House of Morgan, and from Norman Angell who knew what was going on in the British delegation. It was in late January that Ray Stannard Baker told me that Lloyd George and President Wilson had persuaded the French to set up a conference with the Russians at Prinkipo in the Sea of Marmora, an island off Turkey where Lenin and Trotsky would either send envoys or go themselves, and where they would meet representatives from the little nations that had broken off from the Bolshevik rule, Estonia, Latvia, Lithuania, an Arctic Republic under the leadership of Tchaikovsky and, as I recollect, a government more or less on paper in the Ukraine. Perhaps one or two other White Russian governments were included. It is unimportant to list them. The idea of the conference at Prinkipo was to bring these small nations to a definite agreement with Russia which should guarantee the peace of the Baltic and afford a certain amount of security to the Allies of France in her scheme of European balance of power, the Balkan countries, Rumania, Austria, Czechoslovakia.

After explaining the purpose of the conference to me, Mr. Baker said:

"Will, would you go as one of the American representatives to that conference?"

I was bowled over. What did I know about European politics except that in a general way I knew, or thought I knew, those matters that I have just related. I was abysmally ignorant. In politics one must know two things: the issues at stake, and the men who dominate those issues and dramatize them. I knew vaguely about the issues, but not how they affected each of the principalities, and I knew nothing of the Powers. But here was a chance to serve and to learn. With some proper protestations of modesty which probably I really felt, I yielded. Baker told me that my American conferee would be Professor George D. Herron and asked me if I knew him. I had never met him, but I knew about him. Baker told me the names of the men who were being considered as the French delegates to the Prinkipo Conference and the names of the British. I did not know the Frenchmen, but the British names were fairly familiar. I have forgotten them now. Which makes no difference, for the episode was a mere bubble on the stream of contemporary events. But I was pleased and in my pride cabled Sallie.

The Conference was set for mid-February and a day or so after the announcement was made of my appointment and Herron's, Professor Herron appeared in Paris. I saw that he was lodged at the Vouillemont where we could talk things over.

I just pause here to draw a picture of Professor Herron, for he was a vital part of this little story. Look: A man in his early sixties, with a square French beard, a soft but almost tragically insistent voice, an overwhelming (at least to me) self-assurance, cloaked by a quiet, repressed, and rather deadly manner, and utterly humorless. A dozen years before the Paris Conference, he was teaching sociology and economics at a small but exceedingly well considered Iowa denominational college, a Congregational school like Yale, Oberlin, Knox, Beloit, which had gradually passed out of Congregational control and denominational imprisonment into a dignified independence. He had a wife and a family. He fell in love with a pupil, a Miss Rand; but he justified himself so entirely that he could not imagine anyone questioning him or his motives, and walked boldly into this love affair. It rocked the campus like an earthquake, and he left the school with Miss Rand and her mother, whom he had talked with his insistent voice and steely assurance into accepting the situation. To the newspapers the story had all the elements of a juicy scandal; and wherever Herron and the girl and the mother went, the spotlight played upon them. There were demonstrations in the street, and they had a rather miserable time. The family in Iowa submerged and ran away from the spotlight with becoming dignity. Perhaps because Herron was a disciple of Wilson's academic political theories, Woodrow Wilson, then president of Princeton, tried to befriend him. Herron's gratitude must have been deep and abiding. America would give him no peace, and Herron, Miss Rand, and her mother finally went to Europe. His wife gave him a divorce, and he married Miss Rand and settled in a university in Switzerland. There she died; and he married another woman, an estimable middle-aged lady of considerable means who died in short course. As I recollect it, he was now living with his fourth wife. All of these things I knew.

At home, the announcement that Herron had been appointed one of the delegates to Prinkipo caused the newspapers to revive the story, and made the conference a joke. I heard later (I cannot remember whether House or Baker or Lamont told me) that the President was greatly annoyed at the way Herron's name had been received by the American newspapers. Why he did not sense it in advance, Heaven only knows.

In Switzerland, Herron had become a figure of some importance in Wilson's successful invasion of Germany by propaganda. The President, two years before the Armistice, had used Herron as his liaison officer between the Allies and the German Social Democrats and liberals. The Weimar Republic was set up by men with whom Herron had been corresponding. He was a sort of superspy, and his diplomatic ability may not be questioned. He was a real person, whose love affairs were the reflex of a serious and overwhelming belief in himself. He was like one of those poor American boys who, taking the egoistic road at its fork, made great fortunes—solemn, one-gallused aristocrats. He was a solemn one-gallused intellectual, and his ability should not be discounted because of his surviving idiosyncrasies. What strange yoke-mates we were! I often wondered, as we tried to team up, what he thought of this off-ox.

I was given to quips and jests and jollity, to quick and sometimes illogical decisions. I was utterly ignorant of things that were commonplace in his erudition and his practical political experience in Europe. I chattered persiflage. I adorned my speech with what seemed to be comic references, metaphors, illustrations. I liked parties. I must have been a cross to poor Herron, who never left a sentence unfinished nor a logical process incomplete, to whom all food was alike, and all social gatherings where men met in camaraderie were a pain in the neck. But he knew the situation which we were tackling. Almost the first thing he told me after he had been in town two or three days was that the French were working on the delegates from the White Russian countries who were to sit with Lenin and Trotsky's delegates in the Prinkipo Conference, trying to get them to refuse to go to a conference with the bloody Bolsheviks. The French persuaded these delegates that it would be terrible to sit at a table with representatives of robbers, murderers, and arsonists who had overthrown the Russian government and brutally murdered its Czar. But they were bewildered and impoverished, living at mean, smelly little hotels or pensions, and I had the bright idea, which worked well for a few weeks, to round up each delegation and feed it. So two or three nights a week Herron and I picked out a good gay restaurant and invited the delegates from some of these countries to dine with us, taking along a friendly interpreter. Having given them a square meal, we sailed in, and in most cases undid the work of the wily French, and pledged these delegates, one by one, to come to Prinkipo. At the dinners, Herron was most competent. He knew the best restaurants in Paris, though he ate with no discrimination. But he talked convincingly, and I was a sort of snare-drum obbligato to his tuba solo, and added the condiments to our conversations.

In the meantime Lloyd George and Wilson had sent emissaries—Lincoln Steffens and Bill Bullitt—to Russia to find out whether or not Lenin and Trotsky and Tchicherin, their foreign minister, would send delegates to Prinkipo. The chief objection which the French raised to the recognition of the Lenin government at the conference was that Lenin had repudiated the national debt of the Czarists. Steffens and Bullitt succeeded in getting the Bolsheviks to include a discussion of that debt in the agenda of the Prinkipo Conference, which was something of a diplomatic victory.

They were in Russia two weeks and came home full of strange tales. Steffens, in particular, was bug-eyed with wonder. I had known him for nearly twenty years, since we had worked together on McClure's Magazine, and he had visited us in Emporia; and now he and I talked many a long hour about the strange and wonderful things that he had seen. Bullitt was more or less a stranger to me. I liked him. He was a man of great charm; but he came from a different star, moving in a different social orbit, and we had to let mutual admiration rather than understanding grease the machinery of our relations. I never doubted his sincerity. His courage was obvious. He had a quick brain, a precise, logical process, and knew many things in many books which I only suspected and often profoundly doubted. So I had my story of the Bullitt-Steffens mission from Steffens. Like the ancient mariner, Steffens was always stopping the wedding guests and telling them his Russian story until they beat their breasts in despair. One day at the Crillon, six or eight of us were sitting in the big fat leather chairs in the lobby around Steff, listening to his Marco Polo story. One of Steff's favorite phrases in that stirring tale was, "I have seen the future, and it works!" It was an impressive sentence. I had heard him spring it several times, and I liked it; but it was beginning to pall on the other newspapermen, and so was the whole wonder tale of the Russians' social miracle. Respecting Steffens thoroughly, knowing him for an accurate even if graphic reporter, none the less they were just a shade weary; and probably envy for his luck tinged their skepticism. At any rate as he talked—and certainly Steffens talked well—they were prone to prod him now and then with poisoned darts of doubt. The prodding did him good, for a little irritation put him on his mettle. At the climax, or near the climax of his story, to prove with a sentence the reality of his Utopia, he exclaimed:

"Gentlemen, I tell you they have abolished prostitution!"

I do not remember whether it was Larry Hills of the New York Sun, or James of the New York Times, or Herbert Swope of the World, or Arthur Krock—but one of them held up his hand, stopped Steff, and cried:

"My God, Steff! What did you do!"

Steff, who was never a philanderer, blushed like a beet and rose and trotted away, for he was too little to stalk; and the Crillon forum broke up amid triumphant cackling which purged us all of envy.

When I told this story to Herron a few hours later, he did not crack a smile. His only comment was, "It was most unfortunate."

For some reason or other, Samuel Gompers was against the Prinkipo Conference. America never had a labor leader so conservative politically as Gompers. One day Herron and I in our missionary endeavors invited Gompers and William English Walling, his friend and ideological interpreter, to lunch at the Vouillemont. I never saw Herron perform more brilliantly. He had Gompers, who was a first-rate talker and a man of conviction, on the mourners' bench ready to concede that a meeting with the Bolsheviks at Prinkipo might be a good thing. I could understand as I watched Herron coopering Gompers and Walling, how Herron did so much—and he really did important things—to start and establish the German upheaval that gave Germany the Weimar Republic. I could appreciate President Wilson's estimate of Herron, and his confidence in Herron's capacity as a diplomat.

The whole failure of the concept of the League of Nations as Wilson presented it to the Peace Conference that winter was epitomized in this little cyclonic gust of wind that moved across our plans for a Conference at Prinkipo. The United States had changed its economy from a debtor nation to a creditor. France believed that Paris had permanently replaced Berlin as the economic and industrial and even political capital of Continental Europe. She could not endure the thought of a Russian giant menacing France in the Middle East and Near East. The Prinkipo Conference, which Lloyd George and Wilson sought to arrange in the interest of a decent perspective for the power of Russia, France sought to destroy. She was greedy for colonies but chiefly for European dominance in a world held together by a balance of power, the old diplomacy of man, since he began forming dynasties and nations. I sensed this then but not so clearly as it is evident today. Probably Professor Herron helped me to see these things, for he, with all his solemnity, often approaching intellectual pomp, did know Europe. I do not wonder that Wilson sought his counsel. I wish Wilson had heeded it more often.

In the meantime, despite the frustration which the French delegation to the conference was throwing around the Prinkipo meeting, I was having a good time. I had found where the Sunday symphony orchestras were playing. By the grace of Professor Herron and the Paris-wise American and British newspapers, I had, like an old dog, located some pretty good slop-route restaurants of quality which I could afford to patronize, and when we took the straying Estonians, Latvians, or Lithuanians, or Tchaikovsky's Arctic Republicans to these restaurants to bring them into the Prinkipo fold, my conscience let me enjoy to the full the delights these restaurants offered. I also got great pleasure from the method which Professor Herron used, careful, conscientious, logical, diplomatic, and wise. Mostly he was my interpreter; but I doubt if he could translate my jokes adequately. Time passed, and with it the date for the conference. President Wilson and Lloyd George kept trying to get the French to set a new date. They were slippery. No new date was ever set. And so the conference just fizzled out.

It was one Sunday during that winter that Ray Stannard Baker, Ida Tarbell, and I commandeered—how, I do not remember—a Red Cross car and went in the early morning down to Barbizon. I only knew Barbizon as the scene of some of Corot's landscapes, but I crammed up on the Barbizon School of painting and was ready for my day. Bill's method was to wait until he saw a place and then cram up on what he had seen. Either

564

method is good. The Forest of Fontainebleau is most beautiful. Barbizon is a dear, smelly old French town where Baker and Miss Tarbell and I had a friend lying ill, Auguste F. Jaccaci who had been with us on the American Magazine and on McClure's; he was now doing a relief job, working with the French children. He had been stricken with pneumonia in our hotel and taken for convalescence down to Barbizon. We wandered about the town and the forest for the greater part of the day. Bill and I picked up an old battered potbellied five-gallon copper teapot which rode us like the old man of the sea for four months until we got back to Emporia. It is strange how some objects resist the packing case and pop out in your lap whenever you finally decide to move. I think, for the final leg of our homeward journey in August, we stuffed the old thing with dirty clothes and jammed it in a trunk. But it stands at home, as these lines are written, proudly perched on a bookcase, a monument to the persistent folly of man.

We started back from Barbizon almost at dusk; along the highway we turned in behind two or three government cars, apparently traveling together, with another car behind us. The car behind us speeded up and passed us and then slowed down, and as we were in a hurry we passed the passer and the next car. Our French chauffeur felt that he should show off the Red Cross car we were using, and after we got by the second car, the third car began speeding up and then both cars behind us entered into an exciting race. One passed us. We passed it. Then two passed us and we passed them. The car ahead of us kept going faster and faster. Finally we saw the cars were government cars and thought some smart-aleck colonel was trying to show off and take the road from us. Bill and the chauffeur in the front seat stepped on the gas and with a mighty spurt we passed the car which was just ahead of us when we began the race. The boys in the front seat gave our car the gun and just as we passed the speeding car at something like sixty miles an hour we looked to see what particular smart-aleck old colonel was trying to make us eat his dust, and Baker and Miss Tarbell almost fainted. It was the President and Mrs. Wilson. We were probably supposed to be assassins thirsting for his blood, as we both were going fast. We were something like a quarter of a minute getting around his car, and he got a good look at us; but we went ahead just the same and passed his two forward escort cars. There was no use pretending pious penance after the deed was done; but I imagine that Baker and Miss Tarbell had a rather sad journey back into Paris. Anyway the President's delegate to Prinkipo, who was not particularly eager to hold his job, chuckled a vest button off as we hurried home. It isn't likely that Woodrow Wilson, after coming to the White House, had ever endured such vast impudence as we bestowed upon him there in the gloaming on the Paris road.

The next day I asked Baker if the President had called him down at their next meeting. He grinned and said: "No, but he knew about it."

The press conferences of the American delegation at the Peace Conference were for the most part rather dismal affairs. Once or twice President Wilson came to us for a formal interview; but the second time his confidence was betrayed by a Hearst reporter, and the President never appeared again. The matter which the Hearst man revealed was entirely trivial, but Wilson could not stand it. So generally we had Secretary of State Lansing. Our press conferences were held late in the morning in a room at the Crillon. The Secretary always was in formal garb, a tailcoat with silk binding, a double-breasted watch chain, dark gray striped trousers, gray spats, and shiny patent leather shoes. His game was to convey absolutely nothing as pleasantly as possible. He was always visibly frightened in the presence of newspapermen and did not relax. Certainly he never unbent, and certainly he never gave us the slightest bit of news. In contrast to him, Henry White tried hard to entertain us. Once he had a choice morsel of news, some decision that his committee in the conference had made the evening before, and he told us about it with detail. When he had gone, several of the reporters who had been on the job early that morning revealed to us the fact that the President had overruled Henry White and that the news he gave us was utterly useless. The President had not thought it worth while to notify him what had been done. His humiliation when he found the truth was properly painful and unnecessary. We did not blame him. We knew the President and his "tricks and manners."

To make up for this, Henry White chartered busses and took the entire press conference over Paris, showing them the old Paris of the seventies which he knew in the days of Empress Eugénie. He gave us two or three beautiful hours that had as much relation to the Peace Conference as an astrologer's chart. General Bliss, one of the President's delegates to the conference, was cordial and extremely anxious to impart news; but he did not have the President's confidence, and when he saw how ruthlessly the President had treated Henry White he ceased to be of much service to the press. We of the American press got more from the British press conferences than we did from our own. They were generally in charge of Lord Robert Cecil, who mouthed and mumbled his words in that one-legged non-rhythm which high-class Britishers use when speaking formally. But he did know what was going on, and he did tell us. It generally checked with the truth. Certainly he never tried to deceive us. The American press respected him.

CHAPTER LXXX

Occupied Germany: 1919

I HAVE A strange feeling as I begin to write about a trip Bill and I took in Germany in late January of 1919. As I sat down to write this story, I had the clippings from the Emporia Gazette of articles that I wrote for my syndicate; I had before me family letters that Bill wrote and I wrote to his mother and sister and grandmother. These articles and letters represent accurately what we saw and felt on that trip. It is a picture of American troops quartered in the Rhineland, and reflects, strangely enough, an attitude which must seem strange today. For the American soldiers of that day, quartered there in the Rhineland with the German people, lived not as conquerors but as guests and without hate. General Headquarters had to issue an order forbidding our soldiers to fraternize with the populace, and the order had about as much force as if they had posted a notice commanding the wind to be quiet, the water to be still, and the sun to change its course. It seems to me worthwhile to present that picture of the Rhineland sixty days after the Armistice, as we saw it on our hasty journey from Paris to Coblenz in the Rhineland, with a day in Cologne. With us in our car was Burge McPhall, a former Gazette reporter who had been with Pershing's army for the Associated Press during the last three months of the war and on the front when the Armistice was signed. Cyril Brown, a reporter for the New York World, was also with us; and we picked up a reporter for the London Daily Mail and another for the London Daily Express. We had no trouble with the German language. Two or three of the reporters who had been war correspondents spoke German well. I had a smattering of college German and could get along limpingly, with a vocabulary that widened from use. These details are set down because they indicate our competence as witnesses.

Near Coblenz was the headquarters of General Joseph T. Dickman, who lived at general headquarters for the Third Army, the army of occupation. We found him a fine old German-American with a deep contempt for French works and ways. I was introduced to him as the correspondent of the McClure Syndicate. Neither my name or that of the syndicate registered, but he banged away at the French with gusto and profane eloquence. Apparently the casual way the French take the universe got him, for he was a methodical old boy who had a place for everything with everything in its place. He believed in promptness and accuracy and was most unhappy not to find it. The French genius, which is of another sort, irked the old man.

Quite apart from him as a museum piece was the building wherein he held forth. It was a modern office building, a sort of federal building, which had been occupied by the German government. On the walls of General Dickman's office were pictures of Bismarck, the elder Kaiser, and Kaiser Wilhelm II, and steel engravings showing various days of triumph for the German army. Not a thing had been changed. The war maps of Germany hung on the walls alongside the pictures of their idols. When the Germans moved back into that office they found the building as they had left it. For the Americans observed a biting, scrupulous honor about things all over Germany. We noticed as we rode about that no German sign was painted out, no German monument was changed. The Americans put up their own military signs and painted upon them their own military instructions. They touched nothing that the German armies had established. Those engravings on the walls of General Dickman's office were a part of the American psychology of occupation. I was interested in one print in particular. It represented a long triumphant file of troops marching past Blücher, who was mounted stupendously on a stallion reviewing the file as it passed down the hill into the Rhine Valley. It was all most German, most military, quite definitely Prussian, and in the foreground of the print we saw a German soldier dropping out of line, kissing a struggling woman while the others, soldiers and bystanders, smiled. Imagine a painter from the North putting that kind of an episode into a picture of Sherman's march to the sea. Then imagine that picture hanging in the office, let us say, of the governor of Kansas. The only comparable picture I know in American art is the famous picture of General Tom Ewing's "General Order Number Eleven," painted by a southerner, a Missourian, George Caleb Bingham. It is a hate-rouser showing the Union soldiers devastating a wide area on the Kansas-Missouri boundary. In that picture the conquerors are shown with scorn and contempt, and that picture has been popular in the Missouri Valley for two generations. But it is not shown to glorify the lust of conquerors—rather, to hold it in obloquy.

We bunked up one night at an American army post in a little town where a company of our young soldiers were quartered in a cloister. They

insisted that the nuns had invited the soldiers to come as guests. The nuns
kept house for the boys, who were as happy and comfy as bugs in a rug.
The nuns moved about the place cheerful and happy, and when one remembers the stories that were told, either true or false, about the nuns in
Belgium, one gets an idea of the deeply different relations between the
American army of occupation in Germany and the German army of occupation in Belgium.

That non-fraternizing order from G.H.Q., of course, was posted all over
the place in that village where the nuns were hostesses, and the priest in
the village had spoiled all the fun for the boys and the town girls by calling
all the girls together and warning them about the wiles of our boys. But
in the next village the priest had taken no such precautions, and the boys
were having the time of their young lives, all quite against regulations.
They were popular in that village even though the order against fraternizing was strict.

The company band played in the public square two or three times a week,
and we saw the populace turn out to listen. The whole village crowded
about. Certainly we could see no aloofness, no fear. There was, of course,
a little shyness. They were village people, these were strangers, but certainly not conquerors. The soldiers played with the children and smiled
at the girls, who were clearly on amiable terms with the village. Yet, at
that same village—and I set this down to indicate how strictly the rule
against fraternizing was sometimes enforced—an M.P. tackled a British
newspaperman in British correspondent's uniform who was talking with
Bill and me. He wanted to know why he was walking the streets with a
civilian, for I wore no uniform and the M.P. naturally assumed that I was
German.

We left the village that morning with the band in the public square
playing ragtime, and climbed the hill to the castle, where General Muir
had his headquarters. He was in a typical castle on the Rhine, even though
it was on the Moselle. It was an old castle from which the robber barons
in the old days could see their prey coming and rush down upon the caravan to overpower it. The castle was owned by a wine merchant who had
restored it most faithfully and fitted it out for a summer home. In a most
feudal manner, the General had added the military hereditaments thereunto appertaining, with guards and outriders like the old barons' henchmen. In restoring the place they scrimped on plumbing, so amid the feudal
splendor the doughboys in khaki hovered over the American oil stoves
which stank up the place gorgeously and smeared the splendor with
splotches of smoke here and there; and the baronial halls were heated with
huge gas logs.

The General came in, rather a large mahogany piece, I should say a collector's item, a perfect example of the old army.* The soldiers about him seemed bored to death. We talked to them in the corridors and around the grounds, and they were like all soldiers, keen to have it over with, then to get home and go to work. Probably in this modern world no soldier likes his job.

Leaving the General, we went into the back areas, up the hills above the Rhine. There, in little villages miles from the railroad, our boys were quartered. The gray gloomy villages were not spotlessly clean. Water ran down the gutters, in which the natives washed tons of turnips—apparently the chief fodder item for their cows. Sometimes we stopped and talked to the villagers along the way. Politically they were all Centrists and Catholics, and they were against the Kaiser and the Bolsheviks. Amidst our soldiers, by the thousands, women were walking these lonely roads, as carefree as the men—which probably more than anything else indicates how little our army is a conquering army. We asked a woman along the way if she was not afraid. She said, "Afraid of what?" I replied, "Well, afraid of the soldiers, for instance." The pretty woman smiled back and answered, "Why?" Then she said, "They are a nice lot." One German peasant asked us, "We notice always your American officers talk with the men, play games with them." It was baseball and basketball mostly, for in order to get up teams the G.H.Q. had commandeered all college and professional baseball and football and basketball players even up to colonels. The peasant said, "Your soldiers treat the men as though they were folks. We do not understand that. With us the men are not folks, only officers are folks. The rest are cattle. We see your men obey their officers in the drill, and our soldiers tell us your men have fine discipline in battle. We do not understand this!"

Then we undertook a difficult job of getting it through that peasant's head that our men obeyed their officers because they respected and admired their officers, not because they feared their officers. Then, by way of trying a little missionary work, we tried to explain that to bring obedience based on respect rather than fear into the world was what brought us into the war. All this greatly puzzled him. He made us repeat it over and over, and looked at us like a smart collie dog, as though he almost understood, and he went away repeating the phrase, "obedience based upon respect rather than fear," chewing it all over. I wonder if he ever got it.

We came to one dreary gray village above the mountain, where a captain and his company were stationed in a kind of a hotel. One hundred boys were billeted in the village with two hundred people. The soldiers were

---

* Our meeting ground was the fact that he had a brother living at Harper, Kansas, whose son was just appearing in Kansas politics. Afterwards he ran for governor.

crowded into bedrooms, sometimes two in a fat German bed. They lived in little low-ceilinged rooms never heated, and the homes were bleak, ugly and meagerly furnished. I should say a Kansas farmer's house was vastly more comfortable. The boys were not supposed to sit around the stove with the family—that was fraternizing—so the boys went out of doors and, with nothing to do, got the harness on the horses and proceeded to dirty the harness and then came back and cleaned the harness. Or else they would go out and dirty up their guns, then come back and clean their guns. One or two nights a week they had boxing matches in a neighboring village, and the regimental band played every few days. But generally the boys sat around in the stable messroom. Their food was good, and they were, on the whole, cheerful and happy, except that they wanted to get home. They had their daily drills and their games—football, baseball, and basketball—and they were full of ginger and needed no bucking up in their morale, except that they were deathly homesick.

In most of these peasants' houses, one still saw pictures of the German royalty. Apparently no one had taken these pictures down. As we went along those ten days or two weeks in Germany, I never saw a clean place on the wall where the Kaiser's picture once hung. In one little village we had dinner at a home where four Americans were billeted. They ate with the family, but at their own end of the table. The mother and father of the house sat at the other end. They told us that they had ten children, all living. Seven boys were machine gunners in the war. One boy was only sixteen. The four machine gunners were at home, eating with the family at the other end of the long table. This apparently irked the American boys. It was hard not to fraternize. I noticed that when the father and mother took the shade off the lamp and carried it over to a picture in the corner and threw the light on one of their chief treasures, a gilt-and-white-framed enlarged photograph of a big strapping German in full dress regalia, the soldiers at the American end of the table were apparently as full of pride as the old people. This household was Catholic, and they also had a low opinion of the Kaiser, as most Catholic peasants had in those days—not so much because he had brought on the war as because he had borrowed all their money and then run away to Holland without paying it back.

In due course we came to Cologne. There was another area, and along the whole broad countryside around Cologne was a series of gay bright peasant villages, very different from the gray bleak places in the hills around Coblenz. This Rhine country apparently was Germany's Colorado and California combined—their spare bedroom. Along the way on the hillside were sunny homes of the rich Berliners and Hamburgers. Every village had its restaurant. Even then, in the midwinter of 1919, the restaurants were open with little food. Yet every town was spick and span and modern, and for the first two hours out of Cologne everywhere American soldiers colored the landscape. The children seemed to take to these grinning cheerful-looking American boys as big brothers. They had no trouble with the civilian population, for they were natural-born fraternizers and couldn't help it. Certainly they were guests and not conquerors. The hosts and the guests were as polite to each other as a basket of chips. The American soldiers tipped their hats to the old men and the women, and even the officers got off the walks for the women and the old men. They played with the young girls on the sly in spite of all the rules of the G.H.Q. The G.H.Q. might as well post a trespass notice against the coming of the warm spring winds. For these American boys loved female society, and their blood was stronger than orders from G.H.Q.

As we were passing up the Rhine Valley, we came to the headquarters of General Douglas MacArthur. Burge McPhall had known Douglas MacArthur in Washington and also at the front before the Armistice. So we stopped, and before we knew it we had accepted the General's invitation to lunch.

He had commandeered a beautiful home—larger than Al Gufler's in Emporia, and most exquisite, high above the road overlooking the Rhine and the hills beyond. It sat on five or six acres of grounds. Very old grounds they were, with formal plantings of evergreens which were, I should say, a hundred years old. Yet the house was most modern and most comfortable. It was a grand contrast to the castle where General Muir lived on the Rhine peak. This house was a home. Inside, everything was white, very severe, all straight lines, all repressed, as if the architect had said to himself, "I'll not be French; I'll not be French," a thousand times over. The draperies and hangings were severely plain but beautiful to a degree; and every form of house luxury that you ever heard of was found there, but always hidden, suppressed, covered from ostentation. The repression of it all was Spartan. With the General and his staff was the household of the owner, an old man, a baron, I believe. He looked like David Warfield, lisped like him, hesitated like him, and was exceedingly well bred. I found the young men of the General's staff (all staff officers here were in their twenties and thirties) playing a solemn game of billiards with the old man; very sedate, very dignified, very much on his behavior—always the host, never the companion of the men. They met the family formally, exchanged daily compliments, were pleasant but not cordial, punctilious but never familiar; and so their relations were little better than frigid, somewhat warmer but not at all comfortable.

Into this austere and formal situation flashed General Douglas MacArthur, aged thirty-eight, a bachelor, with the grace and charm of a stage hero. I had never before met so vivid, so captivating, so magnetic a man.

He was all that Barrymore and John Drew hoped to be. And how he could talk! He was a West Pointer, son of the old General, General Fred Funston's friend, and was widely read. He stood six feet, had a clean-shaven face, a clean-cut mouth, nose, and chin, lots of brown hair, good eyes with a "come hither" in them that must have played the devil with the girls, and yet he was as "he" as Chapman's bull in the Estes Park meadow. His staff adored him, his men worshiped him, and he seemed to be entirely without vanity. He was lounging in his room, not well (an ulcer in his throat), and he wore a ragged brown sweater and civilian pants—nothing more. He was greatly against the order prohibiting frat-ernization. He said the order only hurt the boys. He told of going out for a Christmas visit to the troops. In one little town of a thousand people, the boys had rigged up a Christmas tree in the town hall. They had deco-rated it beautifully and were solemnly having a stag dance, while outside looking in at the windows were two hundred girls. The General danced around with a sergeant to show his good will, and went on to the next town.

He felt that the common people of Germany had had war crammed so far down into their bellies that it had gone into their legs, and they were done with it and all who advocated it. He said the German women were all voters and were studying politics in a thorough-going scientific manner. He said the women of his household were solemnly going into their duties as voters, and that they all despised the Kaiser. He knew; no man with his eyes and face was going to be fooled on the woman vote. He said—and we found it to be true when we got to Cologne—that the German army was practically demobilized in the last few weeks and that there was no attempt to reorganize it except upon a volunteer basis. He had the new army regulation which provided that no German officer could hold a com-mission when a majority vote of his command opposed him; and he said all the young blades of aristocratic Germany were getting out, looking for jobs outside the army, because of that regulation. Also he said that our reports were that Hindenburg was getting very few volunteers for the expedition to Poland; no one cared what happened to Poland. He thought Baker and Wood would be the presidential nominees, and he was greatly interested in the radical movement in America. We visited with him for two hours.

After leaving MacArthur's headquarters, we went into the British area. There we met the Canadians. They seemed bigger than our men, and possibly their mustaches made them seem older. Also they were not living under such severe discipline as our men—no daily drill in many divisions, only a hare-and-hounds game twice a week—and fraternizing was wide-spread among the Canadians. But on the other hand, they were not having the easy time that we were having. They lived as conquerors rather than as guests. There had been clashes with the German population—both sides were hotheaded. A demobilized German officer tramped on the Union Jack and got ten years for it. He had torn the flag down from the statue of the first Kaiser Wilhelm. The Canadians had put it there because the Germans had covered the base of the statue with wreaths. They had done this because some gay young Canadians at pistol practice had shot off the old Kaiser's nose. What prompted them to shoot off the old man's nose, I don't know; but something came out of the house of hate that Jack built, and the rest was inevitable. It didn't happen with our boys, and so men were saying in Paris that we were becoming propagandized. I thought so myself until I saw the situation. Given our American boys, and the docile German people, the result was foredoomed. They simply had to function as they were functioning.

As we came into Cologne I saw with astonishment that the men were practically all back from the German army. Never before in my life had I seen so many men. The streets were black with them. They were not at work, I was told—at least, only on part time—and the soup kitchens were running at full blast. They were being fed, but they were demanding work. The walls were covered with political posters, and little knots of men and surrounding spectators gathered on every corner. No big public meetings were allowed, but it was evident that northern Germany was seething. The whole population was fighting the Reds. The Catholics were the strongest anti-Red group, the regular Socialists were next strongest, and the Social Democrats and the Democratic People's party seemed next. The walls were bristling with proclamations, and politics was red-hot. Men, women, everyone, was talking politics, and the streets were crowded. But the queerest thing of all was that in all that crowd—and we looked for two days—we did not see one cripple. Burge said they simply didn't appear. Maybe they were being reeducated; maybe some public policy kept the cripples hidden—but whose or what policy? It couldn't be the old regime; its power was suspended if not gone. But the cripples—and there were hundreds of thousands, probably millions of them—were nowhere to be seen in Germany. Some other day they might come out, but now they were absent or cured or hidden.

The strongest contrast I saw on this trip was in the stores and shops of Cologne and of Strassburg. The windows at Strassburg were full of food; Cologne's windows were absolutely barren of food. Not a sausage did I see in Cologne, not a piece of candy. No cheeses or butter or rubber goods or shoes were on display. The windows were filled; the great department stores flashed women's apparel, the picture stores and the book stores and the music stores had alluring windows. Canes, umbrellas, furs, furniture, antiques—expensive articles, rich and luxurious, gleamed on every side; but the bakeries and butcher shops and confectioners were filled with a sad camouflage of boxes and gimcracks to hide the truth from the casual eye. The bulging fatness of Strassburg was nowhere duplicated. France was making her new possession feel the glory of France. Germany in her shop windows was showing more than anywhere else the hopeless shame of a conquered people.

Otherwise, Cologne was a splendid city. They had built it according to modern city planning. In the dry-goods districts some architect had done marvelous things. The store buildings were modern Gothic and conformed to a plan which bound the commercial exterior of the town to the cathedral. The hotels were wonders of comfort—New York had nothing more gorgeous. The whole place seemed to be the expression of a spirit of the times; and there on those beautiful buildings and about in the squares were bas-reliefs of great hulking giants breaking clubs, statues of the Hohenzollerns showing their power, or Bismarck with his sneer, and one saw the worm in the bud. Their crass philosophy was imprinted everywhere, for them to bow before. Possibly all these placards on the walls, these angry street crowds and the gaunt windows of the food shops might turn the Germans from their idols of wood and iron and stone. I didn't know, but I seriously doubted it.

We stopped for lunch at Bonn and went out to visit Beethoven's birthplace. It was a place of pilgrims, and they had a museum full of records. They seemed very proud of Beethoven in Bonn, and they had done him well in the museum; but a little steam heat would have helped. A dozen Canadian soldiers were with us and seemed intelligently appreciative of everything—more so, I thought, than Americans might be.

It is curious to go back to the notes, the letters, and articles I wrote in January, 1919, about this trip to the American front in Germany. It is evident that the people of our country felt that a policy of kindness toward the German people in their humiliation and distress would bring response in kind. The soup kitchens which were running full blast in Germany were for the most part financed by Americans, entirely by the Allies. Germany was prostrate, and our soldiers, who obviously represented the attitude of the people of the United States, were on German soil not as conquerors but as guests. Their attitude was entirely misunderstood. Apparently the Germans felt that our kindly consideration was the result of fear. When the German peasant was puzzled by seeing commissioned officers playing baseball or football or basketball with the enlisted men, our explanation apparently did not explain. He went away muttering the phrase "obedience based on respect and not on fear." That, he could not comprehend. Also we were fooled by his phrase *Herrenvolk,* which we thought meant "folks"—folksy folks, common people, when apparently he referred to a master race; and we could not understand how commissioned officers (*Herrenvolk*) could command obedience based upon admiration, respect, and affection. It was too much for him. The German mind in 1919 was not ready to receive the ideas of democracy. It was not a part of their tradition, and the conduct of their conquerors could not be explained in terms they could comprehend.

We, the victors of 1918, made our blunder by assuming that the language of democracy was understood by a people who had never in all their history fought for the freedom of the common man, for the rights of the people. We thought that liberty could be passed around as alms or material benefits. We did not realize that men can have freedom only when they have found it worth the sacrifice. Ours was a sad and tragic blunder in 1919, and for a generation the world paid for it. Maybe the debt is not paid yet.

CHAPTER LXXXI

Through the Valley of the Shadow

When I returned from Europe in 1919 the fight upon the League of Nations was raging. It was led by "a group of irreconcilables," most of whom were Republicans. Lodge was their leader. A majority was visible in the Senate, through many informal ballots, for the League of Nations with reservations. The reservations were supposed to be written and submitted by a group of Republicans: Nicholas Murray Butler, Charles Evans Hughes, Elihu Root, and William H. Taft. It was obvious that Wilson was deeply irritated by the reservations. When he came home in February, certain modifications were suggested by this group or by their Republican senatorial representatives, and he accepted them. To surrender again was temperamentally impossible for him. He was equally angry with the reservationists who had a majority in the Senate and with the irreconcilables who were in a minority but who, voting with the reservationists, made a decisive senatorial majority against the League. The treaty with the League attached was pending in the Senate. I felt it my duty under the auspices of an organization quickly created for the purpose (called, I believe, "The League of Nations Association") to go out and make speeches favoring the adoption of the League. I paid my own expenses.

(I mention this fact not because it indicates any high moral principles but because it was smart. Nearly a quarter of a century before, as a poor young newspaperman, I let Cy Leland give me a hundred dollars for my expenses on a trip to Washington. Afterwards he boasted he had bought me. On both my trips to Europe under Red Cross auspices I paid my own railroad fare, steamship fare, hotel bills; and I have never gone on any political mission that I did not pay my own expenses. During the First World War I paid my railroad fare and hotel bills while making speeches for the Red Cross and the Liberty Loan, although each of these agencies offered to pay my expenses. In politics it is most important that a man pay his own way. And in mentioning this fact here in connection with my word for the League of Nations, I set it down only to warn young men against the temptation of letting anyone pay any expenses when one is on any kind of a political or propaganda mission. One surrenders his freedom while he is in service and his right afterwards to change his mind and criticize or even denounce the cause he has espoused if it goes wrong or if he discovers that it is making mistakes. In politics, a man must pay for his freedom with his own checkbook.)

I went into Wisconsin and, as I recollect it, into Michigan; made a speech or two in Missouri and in Kansas. It was obvious that I was fighting for a lost cause, which did not discourage me. But I found everywhere that the rigid belligerent attitude of the President toward the reservationists was weakening his hold upon the people. Soon after I came home from my speaking campaign, the President was stricken. We did not know at first how heavy the blow was, but as the autumn deepened and the winter opened, it was obvious that Woodrow Wilson's work was done.

The syndicate which had been employing me in Paris asked me to cover the story of a conference which President Wilson had called in Washington to consider the twelve-hour day in the steel industry. The large commodities industries under the influence of labor leaders like Samuel Gompers were forcing the abandonment of the ten-hour day. The eight-hour day was largely adopted by industries like transportation, communications, textiles, copper, mining and smaller manufacturing concerns. A Supreme Court decision in 1917 had established the eight-hour day as a legal day for American railroads, but steel was on a twelve-hour day; this was a national disgrace, so Wilson called a conference. He named delegates to represent the steel industry. They were under the leadership of Elbert H. Gary, who was the head of the so-called Steel Trust. Labor was represented by Samuel Gompers, head of the American Federation of Labor. The public was represented by a number of distinguished citizens who were not public officials, among others young John D. Rockefeller, Jr., and my dear friend, Ida M. Tarbell. I must have met Rockefeller before this conference, for we were on pleasant terms. I had often met Gompers at various national conventions where I was a reporter, and we were friendly. Gary, I think, I met for the first time there, but we soon settled down into pleasant relations.

The first or second day of the conference, while I was at a window of the conference room (held, I think, in the Pan-American Building) looking over the lovely formal garden, young John D. Rockefeller, Jr., came up and our elbows touched. After some casual conversation he batted his eyes, grinned, and said: "You know Miss Tarbell very well, I believe." I was glad to say that I did, and after some sparring he indicated that he was a bit puzzled as to what attitude he should take toward her. Young

John D. essentially was a gentle person, a kindly, warm-hearted man. It was evident, even if he had not said so in terms, that his natural instinct to be friendly with people in general was making it rather difficult in the case of Miss Tarbell; for, after all, her book about his father and the methods of Standard Oil in the seventies and eighties and nineties was an unpleasant fact which gave him something more than pause. These two were in the same section of the conference; both were bound to be leaders in the conference; in the main and on the whole their views about the steel industry were the same. Also their two figures were conspicuous: Miss Tarbell as the archenemy of Standard Oil; Rockefeller as the son and heir of Standard Oil. When we had cleared away the formal rubbish of our preliminaries, he indicated that he was in a rather delicate situation, and seemed to want my advice. I told him that personally she was a sane common-sense person with really as much sensitivity about the situation as he had, and that he could afford to go ahead, meet her casually and naturally, and they two could find a path of approach to a pleasant relationship and a useful cooperation. I believe he really was trying to find out what kind of person she really was.

Shortly afterwards I met Gary, whom I knew was fond of Miss Tarbell. I told him about young John D.'s uneasy feeling, and the Judge and I had a quiet chuckle, knowing that the two, who had been antagonists, could, if they were thrown together and used their common sense and their instinctive kindness, find a way of approaching the job before them easily and naturally. One noon, when the conference was in recess, we saw young John D. hurrying out in the street to hail a cab for her. Franklin Lane, Secretary of the Interior, who gave a dinner for the delegates, placed the two side by side. I always thought Judge Gary put him up to it. At any rate, as the dinner proceeded the Judge enjoyed the spectacle of the leaders of the right and the left chatting amiably together; and Miss Tarbell told me afterwards that he nearly winked his eyelids loose at her and at Rockefeller, over the beatific picture they made, each trying to outdo the other in politeness as the evening wore on.

The last session of the conference was notable. I sat at the press table not twenty feet away from one of the most dramatic public spectacles in what might be called a Grade C drama that I witnessed. On the front seat sat Judge Gary, who upheld the twelve-hour day and had defended it through the long conference. Samuel Gompers, the leader of organized labor, had attacked it during all the conference. Gary had summed up his final word in a formal but not convincing speech. He knew precious well that the debt was against him and that his position was untenable. Gompers was on the program to reply to Gary.

Let me pause here to set down my impression of these two powerful men who, perhaps more than any other two men, represented, typified, and spoke for the differences between labor and capital in the first quarter of the century in the United States. They were powerful men, leaders who had real following and spoke each for his class. Judge Gary was the most notable figure in the conference. At that last meeting he sat in the midst of the group representing the public, watching the convention with a cold gray eye and an exceedingly bright one—terrier-bright. He uttered never a word. He was the dapperest man in the room. Sometimes he wore a light brownish gray suit with a splendid light vest; generally in his buttonhole there was a boutonnière. He dressed as if sitting for his portrait, with clothes creased, linen immaculate, and hands manicured. They generally rested clasped together in his lap as though sustaining his stomach, which was not large and needed no support. He impressed one as being a nerveless man. He sat there for thirty minutes without moving a muscle except once or twice to brush his chin while Samuel Gompers stood arraigning Judge Gary's Steel Trust and all its men in a powerful speech. The whole conference, fifty reporters and a roomful of spectators, stared curiously at Judge Gary while Gompers spoke. Gompers was glaring at Gary with a fiery eye. But never a twitch moved Gary's face. Not by a movement of a foot or a hand did he indicate that he was under the slightest nervous pressure. The cold, determined, indomitable physical nature of the man never had a more grilling test than that afternoon under the Gompers arraignment.

Gompers himself was something of a figure, probably on the whole the most interesting figure in the conference, if not so conspicuous as Gary. Gompers was a little man, five feet three or four, stocky, almost fat but not quite, with moth-eaten hair, and a smooth-shaven face. He had leathery pink skin, sloping shoulders, and was long-armed and short-legged, an old gorilla of a man! He was Judge Gary's antithesis. During the conference Gompers rarely sat still. One might know how the conference was going by looking at his half-bald head, which flushed pink and paled white like the bulb of a barometer as the proceedings went forward, pleasing or displeasing. He did not fidget, but he rarely held the same position ten minutes at a stretch. He had his group well in hand, indeed he was the soul of his group. There was not much consultation in public, but Gompers sat by Frank Morrison, his chief lieutenant, and kept running-fire whispered talk to him. Gompers was nervous: he liked to sputter in speech. His face was mobile, his mouth was large and strong, his jaw was brutal and indomitable. He had the big nose of the ruler; but his eyes—there was mystery! They were sheathed with thin saurian lids; when he opened them wide they gave a flaming effect to his face. Generally they were half closed, and back of the eyes sat the Jew, the quiet, inscrutable oriental—grim, purposeful, imaginative—the eyes of a man who saw great visions. The soul behind them dreamed huge dreams—an old man's dreams, not a young man's glowing visions. And yet the face around the eyes was a mask, mobile, but secretive, furtive. Gompers looked curiously unwestern, curiously oriental, curiously like a Persian potentate. All he would have needed that last day in the conference was the front-hall rug and a fez, to simulate the sheik in his power. Yet Gompers was the ideal of the doughty bunch of Irish labor men who surrounded him, and his will prevailed without discussion or argument. They believed in him; they knew they could trust him. He was absolutely true, genuinely square in his relations to those about him. For all the furtive oriental cast to his face, his character was western, fundamentally American.

I wrote the story of Judge Gary's ordeal under Gompers' fire (I think for Collier's), and the story was a picture of two iron men at a moment of crisis. I hope I made a good picture of the old Judge, meticulously tailored, white of hair, with an iron-gray mustache, and Gompers, aging but resolute, with mangy hair, splotched face and unpleasant features, dressed slouchily but with an unmistakable male vanity, displaying much more than ordinary talent in his diatribe, and carrying the conference with him. After the story had been published I received a letter on rather elegant stationery in that angular hand writing that was fashionable for women at the turn of the century:

Dear Mr. White:

I read what you said about the imperturbability of Judge Gary under the lash of Gompers. You spoke of his color not changing and of the control he had over his features.

Well, you missed the point. You should have watched his ears. When the Judge is moved, his ears turn white. I am sorry you didn't watch his ears.

So was I. That letter, which was anonymous, remained photographed in my memory, and the handwriting, so obviously of the fashion of the late nineties, stuck in my memory. Only three years later I was to see it again with amazement. But the conference added two friends to my sheaf: John D. Rockefeller, Jr., and Judge Elbert H. Gary, both strong men, earnest, sincere, intellectually honest, and each brave, intrepid in his own way and after his own manner.

It was in the autumn of 1919 that Will Hays, chairman of the Republican national committee, began trying to work for harmony in the Republican party. He set up a harmony platform committee under Ogden Mills, which would try to work out before the Republican Presidential convention of 1920 a set of Republican principles that would be acceptable to the progressive and the conservative wings. He named me on the committee.

It was a good committee, if I do say so. On it were open-minded, intelligent men from both wings of the party. We worked hard on a short simple definite statement of Republican issues and were fairly well agreed upon it.

While I was busily engaged with work on the Hays harmony platform in January of 1920, one of those major breaks in one's life occurred. A fire broke out one evening at dinnertime in the roof of our house. It destroyed the third floor. We had to move out in less than an hour. And here is something I am putting down as a warning against accepting circumstantial evidence. For six months before the fire, we had been thinking of remodeling the house. Frank Lloyd Wright worked on a set of remodeling plans. They were too devastating on the old house and destructive, so we paid him his fee and accepted the plans of a Kansas City firm of architects, Wight & Wight. We were about to leave the house, and the day before the fire I had bought a house eight blocks west of ours where we would have been moving in a week. I closed the deal the very day of the fire. Our house was well insured. A few weeks before, I had seen that the policies were renewed. There was perfectly good circumstantial evidence that I had set the fire to get the insurance covering the five or six thousand dollars' damage to help remodel the house. I told the insurance adjuster the facts about the fire and the house and the architect and our plans. But nothing happened. The claim was paid. And for the next year and a half we lived outside our home watching the workmen remodel it. As these lines are written, we have lived here on this town lot, one hundred fifty by one hundred thirty feet, for nearly forty-five years, a long time for anyone to dwell on one spot.

At that time, I decided to be a candidate for delegate to the Republican convention in my district, the Fourth Congressional District. I won easily. Governor Allen dominated the Kansas delegation and by common consent committed it to the Presidential candidacy of General Leonard Wood. I had known Wood since the early Roosevelt days of the McKinley administration. I liked him. He had visited at our house and we had been entertained by him. On most matters of internal policy and foreign policy we were in fairly close agreement. I disliked his military showmanship; but if he could tolerate my pacifism—and he did—I could get along with his showmanship. At the time those matters were largely academic. Everyone believed that the peace of the world was secured for a generation or two.

So I went as a delegate to the national Republican convention of 1920. The Kansas delegation elected me to serve on the committee of resolutions, the platform committee. But before the convention assembled it was evident that the national Republican committee, which had wrecked the party in 1912 by nominating Taft, was dominated by the Senate group who had fought Wilson on the issue of the League of Nations. The United

States Senate and the Republican national committee united forces. It was a strong combination. The liberal group still known as the Progressive crowd made its first fight in the convention to control the committee on resolutions and to write the platform which Chairman Hays had asked Ogden Mills to arrange. Mills was defeated as a candidate for chairman of the resolutions committee by Senator James Watson, an avowed spokesman of the reactionary senatorial group. We Progressives were able to muster less than a dozen men in the committee who represented our faction in the Republican party. William E. Borah was with us in most matters, though he took an independent course in the committee on the matter of foreign policy. We worked together on domestic issues. We managed to slip into the platform five demands of the National League of Women Voters, most of which have been granted. Senator Medill McCormick was with us on these domestic issues. But we were overwhelmed on most of our suggested planks by reactionaries. For two whole nights and a day and part of two other days we worked on the platform. In the meantime I was writing a story every day and sometimes two stories, one for the evening and one for the morning papers of the syndicate which was taking my stories. I had a good string of papers from Boston to Los Angeles, the best in the country, it seemed to me. And I think I am fairly modest in saying that I covered the convention well in those three days and nights while the Resolutions Committee was working on the platform. I was fifty-two years old. I was strong as a bull and loved a scrap. I had plenty of them, all the fights that I could handle.

In the meantime, Governor Allen had been chosen by General Wood to put the General in nomination for the Presidency and Henry was working on his speech day and night. He wrote at least two, and if I am not mistaken three, speeches which were inevitably rejected by the Wood forces. I say inevitably because any board of political strategy supporting a candidate wants nothing forthright, no commitments. They desire circumlocutions. One of the troubles with Governor Allen's orations was that they were too eloquent. A story began to creep among the delegates that the reactionary forces in control of the convention would like to nominate Allen for Vice President to appease the Progressives; so the Wood people watched every syllable of his speech to see that he did not glow and lure the delegates. It was a funny proceeding, which I watched out of the corners of my eyes from time to time as I worked in the committee room and on my stories, for Henry and I were dear and close friends and could laugh at the tragedy of his position: temptation glittering before his eyes, the suspicion of the Wood supporters clouding every moment, and the final acceptance by Wood's supporting strategy of a dull, unconvincing, purely political speech which gave Wood no standing. Whereupon Wood's friends blamed Allen for not rousing the convention. The governor's position was one of those seriocomic predicaments which no dramatist can originate but which arise out of the play of human ambitions, temperaments and untoward circumstances, to drive earnest men and women and sometimes strong ones into distraction and folly. Henry and I, while this situation was forming like a cyclone on the horizon, had our moments of giggling and rather detached interest in its inexorable approach, dooming Wood's candidacy and Henry's ambitions alike. The only way to enjoy politics is to do your serious best, take the consequences, and not bewail your loss if it comes.

In the meantime I was watching two interesting games while I worked in the resolutions committee, one the building of a platform, the other the backstage machinations of what was known as the Senate cabal. It was in control of the convention. I have never seen a convention—and I have watched most of them since McKinley's first nomination—so completely dominated by sinister predatory economic forces as was this. It was controlled by a national committee representing plutocracy and United States senators, the political representatives of what Theodore Roosevelt had called amalgamated wealth.

One day Henry Allen came to me and said that he had been called to a room in a business block and taken onto a high mountain by a group representing oil, who questioned him closely about his views on foreign policy and particularly Mexico. This was in relation to his possible candidacy for Vice President. That candidacy was one of those things that he did not encourage, and so far as he could he let it alone. But his name was buzzed about in high places, so that oil thought it worth while to probe him. Every delegation that I knew much about was loaded with one, two, or half a dozen representatives of national commodity interests—oil, railroads, telephones, steel, coal, and textiles. We had been warned five months before the convention by Harry Daugherty, an Ohio lobbyist, that Harding would be nominated in a "smoke-filled room" after the delegates had been allowed to play for a while with their own candidates. I saw Harding, one day, at the elevator of our hotel.

Harding wore, on the day I saw him, a two days' beard and was disheveled His eyes were bloodshot. He evidently had been drinking. He looked little like the fine statuesque figure, all tailored, pressed, the "oiled and curled Assyrian bull," who had stood with a red boutonnière in his lapel, four years before, and abused Theodore Roosevelt to the yipping delight of the Republican convention when they were trying fusion in 1916. There was the front-window model for President. But the model I saw there at the elevator door looked like the wreck of the *Hesperus*. He was discouraged. His friends told me, then and after, that he had at that time given up hope for the permanent deadlock between Wood and Lowden which presently developed in the convention. The situation did not seem to furnish his friends the opportunity they wanted to take the nomination from the floor of the convention and give it to the Senate cabal. Harding, I learned later, had been shooed away from Chicago when it began to look as though the "smoky room" manipulators would have their way. But in the preliminary days of the convention, while the representatives of organized capital were pulling their wires and bringing the convention to heel, they managed to put on a show or perhaps were gathering strength for a show, which deeply discouraged Harding and the personal coterie about him, the Ohio gang, a bad lot.

The convention waited a day for the report of the platform committee. Senators Borah, Medill McCormick, and I managed to wangle into the platform a phrase granting to labor "collective bargaining" in labor disputes with "representatives of their own choosing." That was Gompers' phrase. He presented it to Borah and me, and by persistence and horse-trading we managed to get it in. Also we managed to get in something that Gompers did not like, a promise pointing to the recognition of Russia, and a mild endorsement of what was then known as the World Court. But the committee deadlocked and spent most of its time on a plank relating to foreign relations. Borah was an out-and-out isolationist. So was McCormick. We— and there were a dozen of us active and determined in the committee who favored the League of Nations Covenant as it was amended by the reservationists—tried all sorts of formulas, some frankly compromising phrases, others slick and greasy, which might get by. But Borah's eye caught our subterfuges and finally we asked Senator Lodge to take the matter up with Elihu Root, who was sailing for Europe.

Root was an internationalist; but he realized the problem before him to get any formula into the Republican platform that would not close the door absolutely to negotiations to join the League. He sent back a plank. It was fearfully and wonderfully made. It meant nothing except that it frankly did mean nothing, and we accepted it. It was that, or defeat on the floor. For the Republican party of 1920 had the same bitter hatred of Wilson and anything Wilson stood for which twenty-four years later was to mark the Republican party as it entered the campaign of 1944. It was "isolationist" for spite and hatred, governed by its emotions, and not amenable to reason. Out of that witch's pot of mad malice rose the stench which produced Harding's election and became the Harding administration. I do not think that the propertied interests of the country deliberately started this wave of wrath against Wilson to create in Chicago the situation which gave them control of the Republican party. Things are not so simple. Wilson had his blame in the matter, and the anger and bitterness of the Republicans only met Wilson's suspicious jealousies, bitterness, and cold malevolence toward his opponents. Perhaps even without that vicious quarrel the result in 1920 would have been the same. As we rose out of the war, the world's creditor nation, custodians of the world's debt, we had not learned as a people how to behave as a creditor. Perhaps our own pride and fear and newly acquired and not quite understood leadership of the world gave us a vulgar, rapacious arrogance which dramatized itself in the idolatry of the power of money. If it had not produced Harding it might, indeed probably would, have expressed itself in some other way as evil, as tragic, and as shameful. I do not know.

I only know that I was unhappy as I watched the convention, as I sat night after night until dawn in the resolutions committee, and as I sat with the Kansas delegation in the great hall where the thermometer rose to 100, to 101, to 102 degrees Fahrenheit, and the multitude sweated, stank, and lifted from the floor sheeplike faces which fell under the hypnosis of the American madness of the hour.

For two long days the deadlock between General Wood and former Governor Lowden gathered strength. Then it clinched and set like a bone. Kansas was more or less pledged to Wood, and we voted generally as a unit for Wood. Saturday morning, the morning of what was to be the last day of the convention, Senator Curtis came to the Kansas delegation and told us frankly that it had been decided (the phrase was his) to give Harding a play, after trying for a ballot or two to name Wood. The delegation was for the most part glad enough to take orders. I sat in the meeting of the delegation in our hotel that morning, and when the Curtis order came, I blew off. I cried:

"If you nominate Harding, you will disgrace the Republican party. You will bring shame to your country."

James Stewart of Wichita, who more than anyone else represented property—I had met him in Paris trying to raise funds to build a railroad—sneered across the room:

"Ah, White, you are a dreamer. Try to be practical once."

And then I blew off again. But in my malediction I was prophetic and did not quite realize it. The end of the whole business was that I got practical, and I told the leader of the delegation that I would go along with them to Harding to make it unanimous if, and only if, they would promise to go with me to Herbert Hoover if Harding could not make it. It was a long chance. They took it. Early in the afternoon, when Wood failed to take the necessary gain in the balloting, Curtis came to our delegation and told us that now was the time to break for Harding. Kansas was to lead the break, and I was up against it. I remembered sitting there sweating, fanning myself with my new twenty-five-dollar Panama, with my coat over the back of my chair, in a blue-and-white striped silk shirt of great pride, re-faced, perturbed, and most miserable in body and spirit. I didn't want to vote for Harding.

I had warned the delegation that morning against Harding, and yet these were my friends. Some of them had run errands for me in politics, others had done me many favors, and Mulvane, who was my only real political adversary in the delegation with influence there, had promised to go to Hoover if Harding failed. If Harding succeeded, my opposition would not head him off. I was torn, as I often am in politics, between the desire to jump in the fiery furnace as a martyr, and the instinct to save my hide and go along on the broad way that leadeth to destruction. In the end I toddled along, followed the Kansas banner in the parade, ashamed, disheveled in body and spirit, making a sad fat figure while the bands played, the trumpets brayed, and the crowd howled for Harding; and in that hour the Republican party bade farewell to the twenty years of liberalism which had grown up under the leadership of Theodore Roosevelt. As I marched, I saw Harding in Chicago back in 1916, in the measly opportunist convention where the whole desire of the party had been to head off Roosevelt; I saw that figure of Harding, all properly tailored, with suitable dove-colored trousers and morning coat, with a red geranium in his lapel, mouthing those mean miserable strafings at "T. R." which gave him his first prominence and distinction as a national Republican leader. And indeed, as I trudged along in the Kansas delegation leading that parade to Harding, my heart was bowed down with a weight of woe. I kept feeling that I should have looked better sulking in my seat, letting the hope of Hoover, with which I licked my spiritual wounds, go glimmering. I kept asking myself, "Is the long chance of Hoover worth this?" And my striped blue silk shirt and my red necktie, all bedraggled with sweat, didn't revive my drooping spirits as I marched and the crowd yelled and danced on the grave of the Colonel who had been my leader and my friend for a quarter of a century. A sad spectacle I made, and time has not softened the shabby outlines of the picture in all these long years.

I have often wondered, looking back over the years—nearly a quarter of a century now—why I faltered that hot afternoon in Chicago. The promise of Mulvane to support Hoover if Harding failed should not have held me in the Harding parade. But there I marched! I believe now that the death of Theodore Roosevelt and the rout of his phalanx of reform, together with the collapse of Wilsonian liberalism when America rejected the League of Nations, the eclipse of the elder La Follette's leadership, all created in my heart a climax of defeat. My purpose was enervated. Indeed, the whole liberal movement of the twentieth century which had risen so proudly under Bryan, Theodore Roosevelt and La Follette, was tired. The spirits of the liberals who called themselves Progressives were bewildered. The fainthearted turned cynics. The faithful were sad and weary, however bravely we shouted. I did not sink low enough to carp; but as I trudged up the aisle of the convention hall, when Kansas took her banner to Ohio for Harding, I was too heartsick to rise and fight. I hope now, looking back to that sordid hour in Chicago, that I am not merely rationalizing my conduct to justify its turpitude!

And so, in the heat and confusion and insanity of that afternoon, Kansas voted for Harding. The Kansas banner led the Harding parade. I marched with the Kansas delegation hoping in my heart that Harding would fail in a ballot or two, and that I could collect my promise. I think it might have been done. Anyway, on the next ballot and the final ballot I cast one of the nine votes in that convention for Herbert Hoover and tried to purge my soul. I was being practical, God help me, and I was greatly ashamed.

In the meantime Henry Allen had delivered his dull, unemotional speech nominating General Wood. It had fallen flat. He and I knew it would. It was a terrible speech, as edited down by Wood's board of strategy. Men who did not know this said that Allen had deliberately made a poor speech to cripple Wood and promote his own candidacy, which was silly, for such an obvious betrayal would have injured, and did injure Allen, and he knew it; but, being a gentleman and a practical man, he took up his cross and went his appointed way.

Harding was nominated and Senator Medill McCormick told us in the Kansas delegation that on the slate it was written that Lenroot should be nominated for Vice President. Curiously, the delegates in the convention revolted. They had taken orders from Harding. They were disgusted. They knew in their hearts what it meant. And they rose and flouted the bosses and nominated Calvin Coolidge for Vice President. Moreover, the convention resolution named me as chairman of the committee which would formally notify Governor Coolidge of his nomination. When I heard my name I presumed, of course, that someone had misread it or I had been confused with Henry Allen. Afterwards, I learned that it was Charley Curtis who hoped to bring me into line, to put me into the party harness, by giving me this distinction. But I left the hall that night thinking that the next day the error of the committee would be corrected and Henry Allen would of course undertake the job of notifying Governor Coolidge in the formal exercises which would take place in mid-July at Northampton, Massachusetts. I gave the matter no further thought. I wrote and filed my story that afternoon. Sallie and I packed our trunks and left on the evening train for Emporia.

Before we left, Henry and I held a long lodge of sorrow, walking along Michigan Avenue in the twilight with our coats over our arms, mumbling at the ingratitude of republics and the treachery of great wealth. Prob ably we were not unlike the caveman before the hole in the hill that was his home, looking at the clouds, at the mystery of the weather, at the changes that follow the precession of the equinoxes, the coming of the spring, the glowing splendor of the autumn. Man must have come a long way when Solomon found only these things that he could not explain: a ship in the midst of the sea, an eagle in the air, a serpent on the rock, and the way of a man with a maid. We have learned much in a thousand years about even those mysteries, and maybe in another thousand years we will begin to understand those laws of spiritual gravitation which govern the mysterious workings of democracy in the heart of Man. Anyway, the ticking of the vast machinery there in convention hall and in those political hotels of Chicago—the machinery erected by a modern republic to do its will and way and work—was so loud that we could not tell the time it told, and we trudged on, two middle-aged balding fat men in badly sweated shirts under our bright new Panama hats, looking at the fading sunset and the evening stars, not unlike the caveman before his door, marveling at the doings of his Gods.

CHAPTER LXXXII

Mostly Personal

TWO OR THREE weeks later, the Democratic convention was meeting in San Francisco; and my contract with the newspaper syndicate required me to go there. Of all the national conventions which I have attended in the last forty-four years, that convention at San Francisco was physically the most pleasant. Of course, the weather was irreproachable. The San Francisco restaurants are the best on the continent. The San Francisco people are most hospitable. They chinked in the spare time of the newspaper correspondents and the visiting delegates and statesmen with parties and excursions all over the Bay region. Then, of course, around the Bay were two or three large universities and most of the visitors from the East had friends there in the student body or on the faculty. I had the Sutliffe girls and Ed Franklin, my university friend, and his wife, with whom I had kept up an affectionate friendship through the years. And then among the other newspaper reporters covering the convention was Edna Ferber who was always a delight. Together we went to the long string of parties that the townspeople were giving to their visitors. And we knocked around town together. I remember one afternoon when the convention had just adjourned, walking two or three miles from the hall to the hotel, down the broad gay streets, each of us holding a sack of ripe juicy cherries, eating the fruit and snapping the seeds into the air while we discoursed of the many strange things in the heart of nature and of man. Also an old friend and defaulter from a wrecked bank of Emporia, living in the Bay region in most conspicuous anonymity (for he was still wanted) looked me up and we spent an evening together at a restaurant overlooking the sunset and the sea, and had a fine time reminiscing about the old days in Emporia. The convention also was a delight.

We who reported it saw, or thought we saw, many evidences, unmistakable evidences, that President Wilson, stricken as he was, hoped for

590

a third-term nomination that would vindicate him and give him a chance to rescue his discarded and discredited League. He was met, of course, by the Democratic bitter-enders who had opposed him in the Senate. Senator Jim Reed, of Missouri, was much in evidence and to my delight I heard Helen Sutliffe, sitting behind me, give him a piece of her mind. I had known Helen ever since we were in Kansas University; and when a girl has lived, as she had, fifty-four years of maiden meditation, she has thought up a lot of things and a lot of ways to say a lot of things that blister and burn. Helen turned on her fireworks though she had never laid eyes on old Jim before.

But the delegates paid no heed to Wilson's desires. Later evidence has indicated that the callousness of the convention hurt him deeply. But there was a gay debate between Bryan and Bourke Cockran about Prohibition; and young Franklin Roosevelt, in his prime, a state senator from New York State, stood before the convention and made an impassioned plea for the nomination of Governor Al Smith, which also the convention ignored after some rather obvious clack and a considerable real enthusiasm for the man who had dared to oppose Prohibition when it was young and strong. In the end the convention made a synthetic nomination: Governor James M. Cox, a newspaperman in an Ohio country town, who made his living as Warren Harding made his. Cox was more of a person than Harding and has survived with much more repute than his fellow Ohio editor; but his nomination did not stir the convention or the country profoundly. I had no use for Harding, but I could not get excited about Cox. Both had obvious faults. Let me go forward four months, and say that every time I considered voting for either of them I decided to vote for the other. I ended by thinking hard about Cox as I went into the election booth and so managed for a moment to justify a vote for Harding. I could have done it the other way quite as easily.

That summer I went to Estes Park and when they told me that I was supposed to notify Calvin Coolidge officially of his nomination with a speech at the ceremony, I said no, and someone else did the job. I lost no caste with Coolidge, who knew about it. Maybe he respected me, who knows? For he was always more than kind to me.

The summer in Estes Park was pure joy. The two children, Bill and Mary, and their mother and one of her sisters and, I think, my mother and Sallie's mother. It was a gala time by day. Up in a log cabin, one hundred feet above the living quarters, I hammered away at my typewriter, writing something, perhaps a part of a book, perhaps a magazine article. But Bill was twenty and Mary was sixteen, and they were forever going out to parties and dressing, and little dances were springing out of the cracks of the boards on the wide porches and in the living room. The phonograph was forever chirping its Gargantuan cricket song, either for dance or diversion, for I brought some records out of the big box of classical records that had come from London. Friends were continually coming and going. We gave a tea for Jane Addams, I remember, and had faculty people from the neighboring valley crowding on the front porch, and Mary was there, lovely, being a child and stuffing herself with food in the kitchen but being quite a young lady on the porch serving our guests. And Bill was fishing and supplying the frying pan and tramping all over the hills, sometimes gone for a day or two camping. The Estes Park markets in the village were filled with fresh Colorado fruits and vegetables, and we rarely sat down to a meal without company. It was a gay, boisterous summer, the last we were ever to have as a united family.

I began working on a book of short stories that summer and fall. Some of them were published in the Saturday Evening Post and in Collier's. But the book was never gathered, the series was never finished.

That summer in Estes Park, where we had been going regularly for nearly a dozen years, and where Bill and Mary had grown from childhood into rather mature adolescence, we saw more of them and came to know them better than ever before. Bill had come to the park when he was eleven years old and loved overalls and wanted to go barefoot, which was impossible in the sand and pebbles and stones and cactus of Colorado. Mary had come to the park when she was a five-year-old. We turned them loose then as children with the children of the academic people from Kansas University on the hillside and in the valley. We could locate Mary with our field glasses by the little red-ribbon topknot on her towhead, a mile away in the meadow by the brook that played through the grass. Bill, like all the Lindsay men, was an expert fisherman. Mary tried it and gave it up. He had patience. She was highly energized and could not slow down for fishing. As the summer passed, Bill began to climb mountains. Mary's heart was wedded to the burros. We had, at one time, three which she picketed and fed; and by the time she was a dozen years old, she was in overalls renting her burros out to tourists and cottagers. Bill, when he was sixteen, had climbed all the mountains there were, had gone over the range, could guide parties, and did, to remote places, and knew all the fishing holes of the region. Both were mad about Dickens. In the evening they used to lie on the floor before the fireplace and listen to their mother reading "David Copperfield," "The Pickwick Papers," "Our Mutual Friend," "A Tale of Two Cities." Both were bookish children, and both inveterate newspaper readers. I don't think I ever saw either of them look at the comic strip, although Bill, before he could read, loved a Sunday supplement figure called Little Nemo. I used to bring home to him the Sunday supplement of the New York paper that printed Little Nemo's story in colored pictures

For two or three years he marked Tuesday on his medal calendar as the day of Little Nemo. But in the park, where we took many newspapers and had magazines forwarded from Emporia, the children, as soon as they could understand them, pawed over these things; and we kept suitable books about, which they devoured and read over and over. By the time she was sixteen, Mary had read all of Mark Twain's books, some of them many times: "Huck Finn" and "Joan of Arc" were her favorites. When Bill had read a book he had read a book, and did not want to read it again. Instead he read another book and still another. There in the park they were allowed to dress as all children wish to dress, like little ragamuffins. Bill wore overalls, galluses, and black shirt. Mary wore something of the same costume, and it was hard, even when she was sixteen, to get her into dresses. She hated women's hats. Always, until her last day, her mother had to drag her almost by the hair, screaming, into the millinery store; a new dress was the bane of her life. But that last year in the park we did trim her up like a Christmas tree for the cowboy dance at Stead's Ranch. Bill took her, I think, with something like pride, though it was well concealed in an elder-brother patronage, to the dance; and Mary afterwards reported that he really danced with her once or twice, which was extraordinary under the circumstances. All their lives their mother and I had been candid with them. They seemed to know rather earlier than most children where babies came from, and we accepted their knowledge and they accepted our acceptance of their knowledge; it was a rather pleasant relationship lacking strain and promoting confidence.

One day when Mary was almost seventeen, a girl in high school had to quit school to get married only a few months before her baby came, and naturally it was a tremendous scandal. The poor child had been afraid to tell her parents. We were walking downtown about that time, and I said rather casually:

"Mary, don't ever be afraid to come to me, no matter what happens to you, good or bad. You can always depend on me understanding, and I will always help you, no matter what." There was a pause. "Don't forget this, Mary, ever!"

The little she-devil snapped her eyes and looked at me. "Do you mean if I am ever going to have a baby?" We both giggled and then laughed, and the tension was broken.

Another time, I brought home Sherwood Anderson's "Winesburg, Ohio." We never forbade the children to read any book; but Sallie was out of town or two or three days with a sick brother. When she returned she took the book to bed with her to read; and the next morning, seeing Mary eyeing the book, she said:

"Now, Mary, here's a book that sometime you ought to read; but not now. You aren't quite ready for it. Two or three years from now you wil comprehend it better, and I wish you would wait."

Mary grinned as she looked her mother in the eye and said:

"Yes, Mother, I feel as you do. I have read it, and I think it is hardly the kind of a book I would put in the hands of a young mother like you!"

So they had a laugh. That was the way we lived with her.

Bill at sixteen we treated as a man grown, a father of children. At twenty he was generally supervising us in a pleasant parental attitude. He read everything, and we talked about everything. Barring the fact that he had the adolescent habit of lying in bed late in the morning and had to be shaken out, had to be stood on his feet and cuffed around before he would wake up, he was a model son and gave us no trouble. He made good grade at school. Mary's grades were uneven, depending on her attitude toward the teacher; but she got no sympathy at home about Teacher. It was our attitude at home that all children were wrong and all teachers were essentially, fundamentally, and everlastingly right when the children complained about them. So Mary's poor grades were not the occasion for going to the schoolhouse and complaining about Teacher. Bill went his scholarly way through high school, and we never heard of his devilment until years after he was graduated; but Mary, who was no hand to tread her winepress alone, brought home her troubles, advertised her adventures at the top of her voice, bewailed the deep damnation of her teachers without echoing parental response, and ended by laughing at them. That summer of 192 in the park, we knew that Bill was going to Harvard, and that the family would be rather badly battered. So Sallie and I cherished every happy day of it. Mary came home for meals after spending her mornings in the Y.W.C.A. grounds, half a mile away, and spouted a fountain of miscellaneous and generally useless information about that citadel of morality—the term was hers, though she was really a devout little person and, the told us sometimes, led the exercises of the young women of the Y.W.C.A gathered for state convention. But she had lively and devilish comments to make on everything. Bill packed his lunch and his fishing outfit ar came home with his creel full in the afternoon and had little to say abo strange adventures which we heard from others. He certainly never tattle on the gang he ran with; and by the same token we knew that he was sa and sound and fine in his relations with them and with us.

It is odd how two children out of the same womb with the same er vironment could be so different and yet so dear. That summer in the par where we all huddled together in three little cabins around a living-roo cabin, was a fair and sunny one which we shall cherish through the yea as our brightest memory of the family. Above everything else, from chil hood on, I have been a family man. An event has never happened in n

594

life that I have not waited for its completion by milling it over and finally giving it substantial reality in the family. Then it became set in its proper direction and place in my life.

So, when we went home in September, Bill left for Harvard. Here is how he came to go to Harvard. One day, in the spring before we went to Estes Park, Bill came to us and said:

"I don't want to go back to K.U. In the Fraternity House"—he was a member of Phi Delta Theta, my own fraternity—"there are only two books, 'Tarzan of the Apes' and 'Joan and Peter'; and the man who owns 'Joan and Peter' is trying to trade that off for a pony to 'Hannibal in the Alps.' I want to be where folks talk things over; I mean politics and things like that. And it seems to me Harvard is the place I need."

So long as he had that much wisdom, we trusted his judgment as we always have trusted it in matters relating to his own affairs and his own destiny. So the Harvard decision had been made before we came to the park. He took his year and a half's grades from the Kansas University and easily made a freshman entrance to Harvard. It was lonely at home without him, though he wrote with regularity, and no one could have asked for a more devoted child.

His Harvard experience was a liberal education for his parents too. He went to Boston often and from Boston and its remote environments we got some sense of New England, how it hangs together, what makes its wheels go round. Riding through rural Massachusetts and seeing illimitable stretches of white houses with green blinds, all neat and trim, kept and tended, with a thrifty woodpile in the rear, and the outbuildings on all the farms and in the country towns of about one size and character, we felt the democracy of it. Here were no unpainted houses such as we knew in the West, or slatternly barns and farm buildings. Here were no shacks and great houses as we had seen in the South, for New England's essential democracy shines forth in the homes and farms of New England, and in the country towns for that matter, though the big house on the hill in the industrial town and the factory barracks in the valley certainly shatter the democratic ideal in spots. Bill's Harvard days were the making of him, and we took a sort of postgraduate course in sophisticated living, for we had to see his coonskin coat, his ramshackle Ford, his unbuttoned sophomore galoshes, his tail coat and white tie in his junior year, his success as a co-author of two Hasty Pudding Club musical comedies, his course with Professor Copeland, affectionately known as "Copey," and his editorial work on The Lampoon and his blossoming into some of the college clubs. All these things came to us intimately and with a freshness that was amazing and delightful. He certainly earned his way through Harvard with the joy he gave his doting parents.

CHAPTER LXXXIII

Harding and Cox

AFTER we came home from Colorado in the fall of 1920, I was faced with the unpleasant duty of either supporting Harding or bolting him. I did neither. Perhaps one editorial may be found in the files of the Gazette faintly indicating my support of the Republican national ticket, though I bore down hard many times on the need of electing the Republican state and congressional tickets, and I was always strong for the Republican county ticket. It generally carried with it the election of a county commissioner. This board distributed the county printing, which was not a rich plum, but palatable. During that campaign I was one of those who signed a letter to Harding asking him to support a League of Nations. The letter was written and was passed around among the signatories by Herbert Hoover. It was signed by Root and Hughes and, as I recollect it, by Taft and a rather substantial group of conservative Republicans.

Harding naturally made an equivocating reply, and even if he had answered it with a straightforward "Yes" it would have meant nothing. His "Yes" would have been based on expediency rather than conviction. He probably had no conviction. He had passing opinions, poor fellow. He was densely ignorant. At best he was a poor dub who had made his reputation running with the political machine in Ohio, making Memorial Day addresses for the Elks, addressing service clubs—the Rotarians, Kiwanians, or the Lions—uttering resounding platitudes, and saying nothing because he knew nothing. During the campaign I had a long letter from George Harvey, who was chaperoning Harding at Marion for the national Republican committee, asking me why I did not support him. I answered with a long letter which I knew Harding would see, explaining as one editor to another why I just could not do it.

In the end, even on the morning of the election, I did not know exactly how to vote for President; but I screwed up my courage and voted for

Harding, thinking of the shortcomings of Cox. I fear those shortcomings were exaggerated. I did not realize how bad Harding would be; but it was not in the stars to elect anyone in 1920 who advocated anything seriously. The country, after eight years of Wilson and the four short years of breathing space with Taft before Wilson, and seven years of Roosevelt—almost twenty years in which people were keyed up to principles, years in which causes were followed and battles fought for issues rather than men—was tired of issues, sick at heart of ideals and weary of being noble. Nations get that way as people do. In 1920 also, the fact that we were a creditor nation sobered us down. Our vast national debt of twenty-four billion gave us anxious pause. And we kicked off our pilgrims' shoes, unbuttoned our strait-laced raiment with the odor of sanctity about it, and slumped. Maybe I slumped too. For twenty years I had been following Roosevelt, and when he died I was carrying his banner:

> 'Mid snow and ice
> A banner with the strange device.

Maybe I was footsore and weary, as all the old liberals were. However, it was Harding who was elected rather boisterously, and the gaudy, bawdy, hell-roaring third decade of the century opened.

After Harding was decently seated in the White House, an ironic thing happened. In his first message to Congress, he ignored practically all of the five demands which organized womanhood of the country had been able to slip into the Republican platform, and recommended specifically the one demand which Senator Smoot had rejected, the demand for federal aid for maternity hospitals and nurses. Nothing could illustrate more beautifully the breakdown of party government. Nothing could prove so clearly how little relation a party declaration has to actual party performances. The planks which we liberals had slipped into the Republican platform were ignored. A short, equivocal plank on the tariff had embellished the Republican platform, and most of the first sessions of Congress, when the Republicans came in, were devoted to the tariff. Our egregious compromise on the League of Nations resulted in a number of curious feints from President Harding toward adherence to the World Court. But he backed, sidestepped, and sparred for position so obviously that nothing came of his foolish gestures. He was sadly beset. Secretary Hughes and Mr. Hoover in his cabinet, and Republican leaders like Taft and Root outside of the cabinet, were urging him to join the World Court. And in the Senate the irreconcilables bedeviled him incessantly to keep out. He did not know what to do. So he went flutter-ducking around, trying to satisfy both sides, and fooled no one.

But President Harding did one important thing. He called the Disarmament Conference. In November, 1921, the response of the people to that call, a glorious flare-up of faith which Wilson had fanned to flame in 1917 and 1918, was lovely to behold. Probably the American people even then would have followed some strong leader into a crusade for organized world peace. The nation rejoiced in pride at America's part in summoning the conference.* I went to the conference as a reporter for a group of twenty-seven newspapers with something like the exultation of spirit that had taken me to the peace conference at Paris. In Emporia, between the call of the conference and its date of meeting, everywhere I met joyous comments. The Democrats were, of course, saying, "I told you so," and the Republicans also pointed with pride to what Harding had done.

As I sit writing these lines here in my middle seventies, my memory goes back down the long line of political spectacles that I have seen in thirty years, beginning with the nomination of McKinley in 1896 when the free-silver delegates from the mountain states, after appointing Senator Teller of Colorado, and Fred Duboise of Idaho, as their spokesmen, bade farewell to the Republican party and marched out, while the delegates, standing on their chairs, chanted the "Battle Hymn of the Republic." Fifteen national conventions of the major political parties I have seen in these thirty years, nearly all of them. On the American continent, speaking generally, there is no more dramatic gathering of men, outside war, than in those great concourses of our national parties. Bryan, who in conference was not important, on every convention floor was a dramatic figure, and excepting his first national appearance which gave him the Presidential nomination in 1896, I have seen Bryan at every major performance he has given. I saw the Progressive bolt at Chicago, the organization of the new party, its anticlimax in the same city four years later; and I have seen the grinding tragedy which came in 1924 when Governor Smith and W. G. McAdoo, each representing a phase of American civilization, ripped at each other like two battling stags in a forest until both sank exhausted in the death grip. In Paris, I saw the Covenant of the League of Nations first read to the assembled delegates in the Room of the Clocks. I saw the spectacle at Versailles when the Germans came in a plug-hat phalanx, preceded by the diplomats of the world, to hear the Versailles Treaty—a sort of exalted dance of wooden soldiers. I saw the nomination of Wilson in 1912 when the liberal spirit of the nation definitely overthrew conservatism in the Democratic party, a lively but somewhat dedramatized spectacle. But of all human conclaves I have ever witnessed, the gathering of the Disarmament Conference in Washington furnished the most intensely dramatic moment I have ever witnessed. It is worth describing, for what it might have been.

That Disarmament Conference might have been the beginning of a new era in man's life upon this planet. But alas, humanity was not ready for the dream of peace which tried to take shape in reality that misty morning in the autumn of 1921 in Washington. All the gorgeous visions of a peaceful world that stirred that day, and rose in the dramatic outburst of that hour, did not come to birth. Yet those aspirations stirred deeply in men's hearts, not only in that room where the delegates to the Disarmament Conference were gathered but all over the world. I feel that I should try to make a record of the scene.

It lacked the color of pageantry. A small room seating fewer than three thousand people held, in encompassing galleries, the American Senate, the American House of Representatives, the American Supreme Court, the diplomatic corps from the various foreign embassies and legations, a fringe of newspapermen, and a group of distinguished sons-in-law from the State Department. The spectators were mostly clad in conventional black. A few women wearing blues and crimsons made bright flecks in the somber tones of the galleries. The delegates in the pit assembled about a U-shaped table. They also wore the conventional black of the statesmen, excepting a few turbaned East Indians and less than half a dozen admirals who speckled the drab scene. Democracy, which rejects distinctions among men, rejects the colors which mark the distinctions, and so it is for the most part drab. The U-shaped table at which the delegates to the Disarmament Conference sat was a solid affair of walnut, constructed for the occasion, which gave an air of sincerity and permanence to the scene—an air which the Paris Conference lacked, where green baize was thrown over pine boards supported by obvious sawhorses, giving the conference a temporary, makeshift appearance. Otherwise, the delegates sitting at Washington, in November of 1921, looked much as the delegates looked in Paris, drafting the Treaty of Versailles. But the Washington gathering had even less gold braid, tinsel, and military rooster feathers than the Paris scene displayed.

One conspicuous delegate appeared in America who was entirely absent, conspicuously ignored, and rather bitterly snubbed at Paris. It was God. No one, not even President Wilson, introduced God to the delegates at Paris.

After a Baptist minister at Washington, in a formal invocation, gave official credentials to God in the Disarmament Conference, President Harding opened it with the words, "Inherent rights are of God and the tragedies of the world originated in their attempted denial." Later in his speech, the President asked: "How can humanity justify or God forgive the World War unless its fruits shall be fruits of permanent peace?"

The speeches of all the delegates, that first day of the Washington Conference, were couched in language filled with biblical allusions, and the eloquence of every speaker had an evangelical swing, peculiarly American, middle-class American, the patois of King Demos indicating a deep emotional conviction, a religious conviction about the business in hand.

For all the high hats of Congress, the Supreme Court and the diplomats, the Washington Conference was at heart deeply middle-class, thoroughly democratic. The ancient instinct of American politicians to cheer broke out early in the first meeting of the conference. President Harding, groomed within an inch of his life, made the opening speech of the conference. A handsome figure was Harding; the slouch was all gone. He walked to the desk like "a bridegroom coming out of his chamber," said his little speech —which was unimportant, rather stilted, and delivered in a throaty oratorical voice, lacking somehow in sincerity; but the cheering arose as he sat down. The Senate had the temerity to begin the cheering. The House joined, and the Supreme Court, the diplomatic corps, and the reporters respectfully followed in the clamor. The European delegates were shocked. Cheering is bad form at diplomatic functions across the ocean.

Then followed Hughes, and it was from Hughes' speech that the thrill of the day emerged. Here were delegates from England and her colonies, from Japan, from France, from Belgium, from America, summoned to hear a disarmament proposal, and the American spokesman, Charles E. Hughes, Secretary of State, rose and threw into the conference a sharp challenge of sincerity. Excepting President Harding and one admiral present, no man in the hall knew how deeply Hughes proposed to cut the armament of the world.

Compared with the President, Hughes was slighter, and his face, ruddy with health in his mid-fifties, glowed with the kind of spiritual exultation which gave tone and timbre to his voice. No throaty oratorical nonsense was there. His words rang out with a trumpet clearness of a challenge. As he went into the details of his proposal, the sheer audacity of his deliverance— an audacity backed by the financial power and economic resources which gave America the leadership of the world—created a genuine hush of awe in the room. The well masked faces of the diplomats cracked under the impact of Hughes' speech. One could see them moistening their lips, craning their heads forward. One knew that the American Secretary of State was reaching their spirits as men, not as diplomats. With characteristic American dignity and self-respect, Hughes had not communicated to the representative of any other nation an inkling of the American proposal. Just before the conference met, Secretary Hughes talked for three hours with Mr. Balfour, the British leader, about affairs of the convention, giving him no intimation of his intentions. Balfour, of course, knew that he was going to fire a bomb, but not that the bomb would blow nearly two million tons of war craft out of the waters of the world. The gloomy British reporters seated in the press galleries, who came to America peddling pessimism, were shocked to a faster heartbeat, and when the Senate led the galleries, standing to release its exuberance by cheering for ten minutes, the British delegates led the visitors from the Allies in a mad chorus of approval, like a great political convention. The drab lining of those galleries, looking down upon the pit where the delegates sat, was resonant with enthusiasm. The greeting which the crowd gave to President Harding was perfunctory. The response which came to Hughes' promise that America would sacrifice a considerable part of her Navy, was an outburst of acclaim. Into the outburst of the crowd spilled the joy that had tightened its nerves as it listened. Hats waved, handkerchiefs fluttered, men shook one another's hands, hugged one another, slapped one another, exhibited every kind of animal delight of which human beings are capable in their high moments. There was an agenda or program of the conference; but after Hughes had spoken democracy took charge of the rules and order of business, and as the cheering died the galleries—after the ancient fashion of American political conventions—began calling out for speakers. First of all, the Senators insisted upon hearing M. Aristide Briand; and when the other parts of the room had quieted, from the Senate sections came cries of "Briand, Briand." The Senators pronounced it with a long *i*, and the French did not understand that the Senators were calling for "Breeand." Such is the difference in pronunciation of vowels among our Allies. I sat next to William Jennings Bryan, former Secretary of State and three times Presidential candidate of the Democratic party, who was a fellow reporter. When the Senate called for "Briand," my colleague thought it was he who was called for. He whispered:

"White, shall I get up?"

I said: "No, they don't mean you."

"Yes," he said. "But they are calling my name."

"They mean Breeand, the French Premier," I said.

"Do they pronounce it that way?" said Bryan.

And when the clatter for "Briand, Briand, Briand," spread over the hall and became a roar, William Jennings Bryan rose up beside me and started to lift his hand. I gave his coattail an awful yank, for the Senate, seeing him, broke out in a raucous:

"No, no, no! Sit down, sit down! No, no, no!"

What with the yank on his coattail and the shock of those riflelike noes, Bryan fell back into his chair smiling kindly, but dazed and confused. Arthur Balfour rose when order had been restored, spoke in the exact but hesitant British manner, with no emotion, in splendid English, perfect taste, and real distinction, and so quieted the crowd. When the meeting adjourned, the American reporters—perhaps a hundred of us—went to our press headquarters in a near-by building to write the story of the morning.

One after another entered the room, literally bubbling with happiness. I have never before seen newspapermen thrown off their feet in a mass as they were. These were old stagers in the craft, for no callow youth was assigned to this important task. Here I met men whom I had been seeing at conventions and conferences for thirty years, the most skillful newspapermen of America, inured to all sorts of excitement and generally emotion-proof. But they went about shaking one another's hand, slapping one another's back, delighted beyond words, not merely with the splendid drama of the Hughes speech, but with the deep implications for peace that came in the Hughes proposal. It was from this gathering of newspapermen that I had realized how tremendous had been the drama of that moment.

Looking back nearly a quarter of a century upon that scene, I can understand why, with all the enthusiasm in the heart of mankind for peace, the efforts of the Disarmament Conference failed. In brief, men wanted peace, but were not willing to pay the price of justice—and peace without justice is a mockery. Men thought that by disarming the world peace would come. Delegates to the Disarmament Conference from all over the earth, who for a few moments rose and cheered with unquestioned sincerity as Charles Evans Hughes made his great speech, represented millions of people who were not ready for peace. Their national plans and aims were bars to peace on earth because those aims and aspirations were not based upon good-will to men. No one can doubt that the world wanted peace. The 1920's were full of manifestations of man's desire for a peaceful world. But also the nations of the earth and their leaders, political, social, industrial and financial leaders, had dreams of wealth and power, plans narrowly centered in nationalism. And the whole bright bubble of peace by disarmament, which gleamed and glimmered in the hearts of men in the 1920's, was a sad illusion and mirage that had no reality.

We who were pacifists, and I was one, believed that it was only the Admirals and Generals and the armament makers who brought war to the world. We did not know that war came inevitably out of the hearts of greedy men who led nations into the paths of potential conquest and exploitation and oppression and deep injustice; we could not know—we whose voices were lifted in cheers that day in that little room in Washington. How the angels must have wept or smiled, God knows which, as we lifted our voices in that futile cheer which was a prayer for peace that could not come to the world because of the evil deep in our own hearts. Still the yearning was there, the ancient hope of the Hebrew prophets for that day when men would turn their spears into plowshares and their swords into pruning hooks, and war should be no more. But man was not yet ready. He had not yet purged his heart nor prepared his life for peace.

CHAPTER LXXXIV

Mary White

THE WHITE FAMILY was busy rebuilding its home after the fire. Bill came home from Harvard for Christmas. Mary, well along toward her seventeenth birthday, was going out to little high-school dances. She had passed through the riotous period of her life while Bill and I were in Paris, when her mother got her first gray hairs keeping vigil over the child with her rollicking, irresponsible habits which hid a great tenderness under a vast humorous impudence that was not so easy to curb and channel as it seemed. But the worst was over. That winter of 1920 and 1921, she was tremendously interested in music, good music on the phonograph, the classical symphonies and sonatas. She had passed out of the Wagnerian stage into Beethoven and was getting some notion of Brahms. She was reading O. Henry, Morgan Robertson's adventure stories, Mark Twain—still, again, and always Mark Twain—and Dickens, and was trying to bury her little snoot in the New Republic and the Nation! They were a little beyond her, though she had passed out of the St. Nicholas and the Youth's Companion stage and was interested in Collier's, the Saturday Evening Post, and a stamp collection. Also she read books of popular science and the poets of the new century. For a girl of seventeen, she was intellectually fairly well developed. She was a born tomboy. When Bill, who was gentle and maybe a little shy, went to the common schools in Emporia wherein were a dozen colored children, among them the usual number of bullies as among white boys, we were a little sorry that he had to take rough treatment on the school grounds from these colored boys who had not the environmental restraints of the white boys. But when Mary went to the same school, we were sorry for the colored boys. For Mary was a scrapper. She would slap twice her weight in trousers and had the skill in combat to defend herself after she had made an assault. Once when Mary was a freshman in high school, Bill and the family were covered with shame by a story that Mary had thrown a boy about twice her size in one of the corridors and got on his chest and was punching his countenance when the older boys got her off.

At home, her excuse was: "Well, he'll never pinch me again!" And she batted her eyes and grinned, realizing probably that there were certain things that a girl has to take. And that sort of thing never was repeated.

She rode her horse, first a Shetland pony, then a spirited single-footer, all over town and was a familiar figure everywhere. She shared; whenever she saw bug-eyed kids on the other side of the track looking wistfully at her she got off her horse, she put them on and led her horse by the bridle, or let them ride around the block. She hated special privilege instinctively and once told her teacher with welling eyes,

"I'm so tired, so darn tired of being William Allen White's little girl!"

And she meant it. She wanted to be Mary White in her own right. She was five feet three, and disliked that too. She wanted to be as big as her ideas. I never knew how my father, who was only an inch or two taller than Mary, felt about being a little sawed-off man until I noticed in the early spring of 1921 that Mary was beginning to walk with the same curious little swagger, bending her body not from her hips but from her dorsal vertebrae just a little bit, and it was amazing how much her back view looked like his. She was constantly, in those days, reminding me of him in physical habits, and sometimes in her bubbling humor and impish mischievousness. Because of this odd physical and spiritual resemblance between the ancestor and the descendant, I often dreamed of my father in those days—vivid and generally joyous dreams. I did not understand it then. Now I can see that it was natural enough. The dreams came because Mary was continually dropping little hooks of reminder into my subconscious mind, and in sleep the images took form.

In May, 1921, I was called away on business—among other things, to make a speech in the East and to see La Follette. I went away in the late afternoon, and Mary and her mother drove me to the train. They stood on the platform while I hurried back to the observation car and waved them out of sight. The picture they made there, with the background of the sunset behind the roundhouse, has always remained with me. They were smiling and waving, and stood until after the train had passed entirely out of their sight. A week later perhaps, a telegram from Sallie told me that Mary had fallen from her horse and was hurt, but not seriously. She told me to go on with my engagements. I went to Atlantic City where I had promised to speak at the annual American Booksellers Association convention, and there received a telegram to hurry home, that Mary was in danger. When I changed cars at Chicago, Harold Ickes and Edna Ferber were on the platform to tell me that Mary was dead. It was a long, sad, agonizing journey home. The Santa Fe stopped the train for me at Exchange Street so that I should not have to go clear to the station, and there Sallie met me. Her face was brave, and her heart was staunch; and when I kissed her I knew it was all right.

Bill came home from Harvard a few hours later. The day after the funeral I knew that I must write something about Mary. Sallie and I walked down to the Gazette office together, and I hammered out her obituary. We went over it together, and revised it three times in the proof before the type was put into the forms. I had said my say and felt eased in my soul.

The town was deeply moved by it. I could tell that. As I walked about I could see in the faces of people, even without their telling me, how the editorial about Mary had touched them. In a day or two, of course, the town forgot the editorial. Then the Kansas City Star picked it up. And Franklin P. Adams reprinted it in his "Conning Tower" in the New York Tribune. From there it went through the daily press of the country. And then a woman's magazine repeated it, then another and another. Christopher Morley was making an anthology and asked to include it. Alexander Woollcott put it into his first "Reader" and read it over the radio. Other radio entertainers used it and within a year it appeared in four books of reading for high schools and colleges.

Mary had been entered at Wellesley before her death; and in 1926, which would have been her graduating year, her class adopted her and dedicated the Wellesley Annual to her. She was carried on the rolls of the class of 1926 for many years. In the meantime, year after year, the piece appeared in innumerable anthologies. We kept tally on it for twenty years and it had been in more than forty of those school readers or anthologies of Americana, in the best of them and in the humbler ones. It has been a comfort to her mother and me to know that for a decade, at least, Mary will survive. She would now be in her forties. If the article never appeared in another book, she would survive in the hearts of youth well into her fifties. Hardly a day, never a week, passes that boys and girls in high schools and colleges do not write to me about "Mary." Teachers often write, and whole classes sometimes join in a letter to her mother and me about her. The youth of today will remember her well into their maturity. She has a certain extension of her life in the lives of others. She survives, I think, as she would like to survive—in the hearts of her kind, high-school and college students. It is a strange immortality. Probably if anything I have written in these long, happy years that I have been earning my living by writing, if anything survives more than a decade beyond my life's span, it will be the thousand words or so that I hammered out on my typewriter that bright May morning under the shadow and in the agony of Mary's death. Maybe—when one thinks of the marvels of this world, the strange new things that man has discovered about himself and his universe, it could well be true—maybe in some distant world among the millions that whirl about our universe, Mary will meet her mother and me and, just as she grinned and looked up at her mother that evening when we climbed the mountain in Colorado, with her hand around my finger, she will grin:

"Daddy and I have had an adventure!"

It would be a gay and happy meeting.

MARY WHITE

May 17, 1921.

The Associated Press reports carrying the news of Mary White's death declared that it came as the result of a fall from a horse. How she would have hooted at that! She never fell from a horse in her life. Horses have fallen on her and with her—"I'm always trying to hold 'em in my lap," she used to say. But she was proud of few things, and one of them was that she could ride anything that had four legs and hair. Her death resulted not from a fall but from a blow on the head which fractured her skull, and the blow came from the limb of an overhanging tree on the parking.

The last hour of her life was typical of its happiness. She came home from a day's work at school, topped off by a hard grind with the copy on the High School Annual, and felt that a ride would refresh her. She climbed into her khakis, chattering to her mother about the work she was doing, and hurried to get her horse and be out on the dirt roads for the country air and the radiant green fields of the spring. As she rode through the town on an easy gallop, she kept waving at passers-by. She knew everyone in town. For a decade the little figure in the long pigtail and the red hair ribbon has been familiar on the streets of Emporia, and she got in the way of speaking to those who nodded at her. She passed the Kerrs, walking the horse in front of the Normal Library, and waved at them; passed another friend a few hundred feet farther on, and waved at her.

The horse was walking, and as she turned into North Merchant Street she took off her cowboy hat, and the horse swung into a lope. She passed the Tripletts and waved her cowboy hat at them, still moving gayly north on Merchant Street. A Gazette carrier passed—a High School boy friend—and she waved at him, but with her bridle hand; the horse veered quickly, plunged into the parking where the low-hanging limb faced her and, while she still looked back waving, the blow came. But she did not fall from the horse; she slipped off, dazed a bit, staggered, and fell in a faint. She never quite recovered consciousness.

But she did not fall from the horse, neither was she riding fast. A year or so ago she used to go like the wind. But that habit was broken, and she used the horse to get into the open, to get fresh, hard exercise, and to work off a certain surplus energy that welled up in her and needed a physical outlet. The need has been in her heart for years. It was back of the impulse that kept the dauntless little brown-clad figure on the streets and country roads of the community and

606

built into a strong, muscular body what had been a frail and sickly frame during the first years of her life. But the riding gave her more than a body. It released a gay and hardy soul. She was the happiest thing in the world. And she was happy because she was enlarging her horizon. She came to know all sorts and conditions of men; Charley O'Brien, the traffic cop, was one of her best friends. W. L. Holtz, the Latin teacher, was another. Tom O'Connor, farmer-politician, and the Rev. J. H. Rice, preacher and police judge, and Frank Beach, music master, were her special friends; and all the girls, black and white, above the track and below the track, in Pepville and Stringtown, were among her acquaintances. And she brought home riotous stories of her adventures. She loved to rollick; persiflage was her natural expression at home. Her humor was a continual bubble of joy. She seemed to think in hyperbole and metaphor. She was mischievous without malice, as full of faults as an old shoe. No angel was Mary White, but an easy girl to live with for she never nursed a grouch five minutes in her life.

With all her eagerness for the out-of-doors, she loved books. On her table when she left her room were a book by Conrad, one by Galsworthy, "Creative Chemistry" by E. E. Slosson, and a Kipling book. She read Mark Twain, Dickens and Kipling before she was ten—all of their writings. Wells and Arnold Bennett particularly amused and diverted her. She was entered as a student in Wellesley for 1922; was assistant editor of the High School Annual this year, and in line for election to the editorship next year. She was a member of the executive committee of the High School Y.W.C.A.

Within the last two years she had begun to be moved by an ambition to draw. She began as most children do by scribbling in her school books, funny pictures. She bought cartoon magazines and took a course—rather casually, naturally, for she was, after all, a child with no strong purposes—and this year she tasted the first fruits of success by having her pictures accepted by the High School Annual. But the thrill of delight she got when Mr. Ecord, of the Normal Annual, asked her to do the cartooning for that book this spring, was too beautiful for words. She fell to her work with all her enthusiastic heart. Her drawings were accepted, and her pride—always repressed by a lively sense of the ridiculous figure she was cutting—was a really gorgeous thing to see. No successful artist ever drank a deeper draft of satisfaction than she took from the little fame her work was getting among her schoolfellows. In her glory, she almost forgot her horse—but never her car.

For she used the car as a jitney bus. It was her social life. She never had a "party" in all her nearly seventeen years—wouldn't have one; but she never drove a block in her life that she didn't begin to fill the car with pick-ups! Everybody rode with Mary White—white and black, old and young, rich and poor, men and women. She liked nothing better than to fill the car with long-legged High School boys and an occasional girl, and parade the town. She never had a "date," nor went to a dance, except once with her brother Bill, and the "boy proposition" didn't interest her—yet. But young people—great spring-breaking, varnish-cracking, fender-bending, door-sagging carloads of "kids"—

gave her great pleasure. Her zests were keen. But the most fun she ever had in her life was acting as chairman of the committee that got up the big turkey dinner for the poor folks at the county home; scores of pies, gallons of slaw, jam, cakes, preserves, oranges, and a wilderness of turkey were loaded into the car and taken to the county home. And, being of a practical turn of mind, she risked her own Christmas dinner to see that the poor folks actually got it all. Not that she was a cynic; she just disliked to tempt folks. While there, she found a blind colored uncle, very old, who could do nothing but make rag rugs, and she rustled up from her school friends rags enough to keep him busy for a season. The last engagement she tried to make was to take the guests at the county home out for a car ride. And the last endeavor of her life was to try to get a rest room for colored girls in the High School. She found one girl reading in the toilet, because there was no better place for a colored girl to loaf, and it inflamed her sense of injustice and she became a nagging harpy to those who she thought could remedy the evil. The poor she always had with her and was glad of it. She hungered and thirsted for righteousness; and was the most impious creature in the world. She joined the church without consulting her parents, not particularly for her soul's good. She never had a thrill of piety in her life, and would have hooted at a "testimony." But even as a little child, she felt the church was an agency for helping people to more of life's abundance, and she wanted to help. She never wanted help for herself. Clothes meant little to her. It was a fight to get a new rig on her; but eventually a harder fight to get it off. She never wore a jewel and had no ring but her High School class ring and never asked for anything but a wrist watch. She refused to have her hair up, though she was nearly seventeen. "Mother," she protested, "you don't know how much I get by with, in my braided pigtails, that I could not with my hair up." Above every other passion of her life was her passion not to grow up, to be a child. The tomboy in her, which was big, seemed loath to be put away forever in skirts. She was a Peter Pan who refused to grow up.

Her funeral yesterday at the Congregational Church was as she would have wished it; no singing, no flowers except the big bunch of red roses from her brother Bill's Harvard classmen—heavens, how proud that would have made her!—and the red roses from the Gazette forces, in vases, at her head and feet. A short prayer: Paul's beautiful essay on "Love" from the Thirteenth Chapter of First Corinthians; some remarks about her democratic spirit by her friend, John H. J. Rice, pastor and police judge, which she would have deprecated if she could; a prayer sent down for her by her friend, Carl Nau; and, opening the service, the slow, poignant movement from Beethoven's Moonlight Sonata, which she loved; and closing the service a cutting from the joyously melancholy first movement of Tchaikovsky's Pathetic Symphony, which she liked to hear, in certain moods, on the phonograph; then the Lord's Prayer by her friends in High School.

That was all.

For her pallbearers only her friends were chosen: her Latin teacher, W. L. Holtz; her High School principal, Rice Brown; her doctor, Frank Foncannon;

her friend, W. W. Finney; her pal at the Gazette office, Walter Hughes; and her brother Bill. It would have made her smile to know that her friend, Charley O'Brien, the traffic cop, had been transferred from Sixth and Commercial to the corner near the church to direct her friends who came to bid her good-by.

A rift in the clouds in a gray day threw a shaft of sunlight upon her coffin as her nervous, energetic little body sank to its last sleep. But the soul of her, the glowing, gorgeous, fervent soul of her, surely was flaming in eager joy upon some other dawn.

CHAPTER LXXXV

Deflation

SITTING in a mahogany-paneled room in New York, the national directors of the Federal Reserve Bank, in 1921, decided by formal resolution to deflate the currency. After the war, labor troubles broke out all over the country. The high wages which prevailed during the war, wages symbolized by silk shirts on workers and a great herd of new and secondhand Fords stampeding over the country, persuaded the American banking interests that their job as vicegerent of God in the United States required them to do something about labor. They felt that deflation would take the crimp out of the arrogant labor leaders and help Harding restore the country to normalcy. But they made a bad guess. Deflation did not hit labor but it did hit the American farmer, and it hit especially hard the cattleman of the Middle West. For they operated largely on borrowed capital. The cattlemen who banked at Emporia typified the beef-growing industry from the Alleghenies to the Rocky Mountains. They bought their stock largely in Texas or southern New Mexico—yearlings or two-year-old steers—kept them on grass for a summer, fed them in barns or sheltered cattle lots, and put them on the market in the second summer, well fattened and ready for slaughter. The operation was a transaction covering a year and a half. Often, they rented their pasture; generally, they bought and fed and, in most cases, borrowed money to carry them. They had been doing this since the Civil War. Their credit at the bank was good; their notes were carried in the bankers' portfolio as A-1; but when deflation came, when credits were crimped and the bankers had to build up reserves, this cattle paper could not be renewed and literally tens of thousands of cattlemen all over the West went to the wall.

The credit structure which reached small-town merchants cracked. Stores closed, banks were tottering, business slacked. Car loadings on the railroad dropped. Railroad men were laid off. The railroad business slackened and in the summer of 1922 a shopmen's strike was called in the Middle West.

The outlook for the strikers was never hopeful. Remember that the farm boy, who was learning as much about the car and the tractor as he used to know about the horse, had been coming into town to work in the garages since the war. The Federal Reserve was deflating the farmer as well as railroad labor, and when the workmen walked out of the shops, the boys from the garages walked in, and more farm boys walked into the garages. There was an exhaustless source of fairly skilled labor at hand, to break the shopmen's strike. Whatever justice there may have been in some of their demands, the strike was ill timed. Also there was a silly terror of Bolshevism in the hearts of the American people. The cruel raids of Attorney General Palmer had been continued somewhat by Attorney General Daugherty, who persecuted reds and radicals far beyond the danger which they threatened.

In Kansas, we had enacted an Industrial Court to adjudicate labor disputes in essential industries. Railroad labor was obviously an essential industry. And although this was a national strike and the Kansas Industrial Court could have done nothing to settle it, Governor Allen, under the impulse of terror which filled the hour when the strike was called, set out to use the machinery of the Industrial Court and the strong arm of the state. Troops were sent to various railroad division points, and considerable flurry was manifest over the state.

The strike affected Emporia, for we had one of the largest shops on the Santa Fe system. The railroad had installed a company union. The men didn't like it. They wanted to join a union that would be recognized by the Railway Brotherhoods, and when the strike was called the leaders of the Emporia shopmen came to the Gazette office to talk the thing over with me.

I assured them that we would print the news, that we would always give them a chance to present their side through the Gazette, and that when any statement came from the railroad we would show it to them and print their answer with the statement, which was only fair. I said that frankly I could not advise them one way or the other about striking, but if they struck we certainly would not criticize them and would see that they had every chance to present their case to the people of the town and county. They struck. We printed the news. Bill, who was summering in Emporia, was put on the job of covering the strikers' meetings. They admitted him to the meetings and he made a full, honest, and intelligent story of what happened. The strikers were pleased. No violence of any kind occurred in Emporia. In other towns where the newspapers hooted at the strikers and refused to give them space to present their side of the case, cars were tipped over and heads were bashed, and there was trouble in the wind. Trains were delayed. In the meantime, Governor Allen had taken the railway side of the case. He believed that the strikers were stirred up by labor agitators. He felt that the strikes should be suppressed because of the violence that was evidently rising as a result of them. In all the towns, a considerable group of merchants had been carrying the shopmen on their credit books for anywhere from thirty to ninety days. They knew these men. Ordinarily in Emporia they paid their debts, as in the other country towns. The shopmen met the merchants in the churches and lodges, and they all were on friendly terms. Over the state the strikers distributed a large placard about two feet long and one and a half feet wide, on which was written, "We are for the strikers 100 per cent." The strikers asked merchants to put these placards in their windows as a neighborly act. The placards offended Governor Allen. He felt that they heartened the strikers and justified them in their violence. He issued an order demanding that the merchants take the placards down. I told him over the telephone that I thought it was pretty awful, but he couldn't see it that way. I also told him that I was going to put a placard up in my window, not indorsing the strikers 100 per cent but at least giving them encouragement in struggling for what they regarded as their rights. We were affectionate friends all during the controversy and remain so today. He said, "Bill, if you do that, I'll have to arrest you." And I said: "Come on and arrest me and we'll test this matter in the courts. I think your order restricts the liberty of utterance."

There it stood. The next day, after Sallie and I thought it over and slept on it, I put a placard in the Gazette window which read:

"So long as the strikers maintain peace and use peaceful means in this community, the Gazette is for them 50 per cent, and every day which the strikers refrain from violence, we shall add 1 per cent more of approval." Then I signed it.

It was a poster of the size which the Governor had ordered down, and of the same character except in degree. The fact that we were friends and political associates made my action news. The next day photographers were down from Topeka and Kansas City, snapping pictures of the poster. It became a national episode. The Kansas press was largely with Governor Allen. The national press, and particularly the liberal press, was with me. And a great hullabaloo occurred across the land.

In the meantime Governor Allen came down to visit the Kansas State Teachers' College; and of course I invited him to lunch, and of course we had our pictures taken together, for the photographers followed him to Emporia like trailing clouds of glory. This made national headlines and first-page news. But it also raised a doubt in the minds of labor as to my sincerity. Men who are striking and risking their jobs don't like to see their friends fraternizing with the enemy. I, on the other hand, and Henry on his part felt that each of us had to do what he was doing. We were of different temperaments and looked at life, in this strike, from different angles. I only wanted the matter tested in the courts. If necessary, I intended to go to the United States Supreme Court, and said so. I never denounced the governor, but had made it clear that I felt his action was unfair and unconstitutional. And he, on his part, said what he thought of my attitude.

It is difficult at this time to revive the picture presented by our controversy. For a moment it was a national cause. I received scores, probably hundreds, of letters and telegrams endorsing my position, and a few of course denouncing me. I received offers from lawyers to take the case to the United States Supreme Court, and I was vociferous about one thing: I wanted the case tried on its merits and started on its way through the courts. In the meantime, at the height of it, the Kansas gubernatorial primary occurred. I was supporting my old friend Roscoe Stubbs, who was trying to come back as a candidate for governor. I was his most conspicuous supporter. Middle-class opinion in Kansas said thumbs down to my poster. Poor old Stubbs went to slaughter, in the primary, and I was sorry.

About that time an old friend whom I had known and worked with for many years, a former Bull Mooser, Fred J. Atwood of Concordia, Kansas, wrote me a warm and sincere letter of protest. It was kindly and came out of the affection in his heart. I answered him and then it occurred to me that my answer to him would be my answer to everyone who differed with me. I took the carbon copy of my answer, marked it for the editorial page and headed it "To an Anxious Friend." Two or three days after the letter had gone to Atwood, I worked over the phraseology of that editorial. I cut out every adjective and used a verb instead, which greatly strengthens one's style. I shortened it, avoiding repetition, and finally ran it out. I think I transferred it from the editorial page to the front page.

Here it is:

TO AN ANXIOUS FRIEND

July 27th, 1922.

You tell me that law is above freedom of utterance. And I reply that you can have no wise laws nor free enforcement of wise laws unless there is free expression of the wisdom of the people—and, alas, their folly with it. But if there is freedom, folly will die of its own poison, and the wisdom will survive. That is the history of the race. It is proof of man's kinship with God. You say that freedom of utterance is not for time of stress, and I reply with the sad truth that only in time of stress is freedom of utterance in danger. No one questions it in calm days, because it is not needed. And the reverse is true also; only when free utterance is suppressed is it needed, and when it is needed, it is most vital to justice.

Peace is good. But if you are interested in peace through force and without free discussion—that is to say, free utterance decently and in order—your interest in justice is slight. And peace without justice is tyranny, no mattter how you may sugar-coat it with expedience. This state today is in more danger from suppression than from violence, because, in the end, suppression leads to violence. Violence, indeed, is the child of suppression. Whoever pleads for justice helps to keep the peace; and whoever tramples on the plea for justice temperately made in the name of peace only outrages peace and kills something fine in the heart of man which God put there when we got our manhood. When that is killed, brute meets brute on each side of the line.

So, dear friend, put fear out of your heart. This nation will survive, this state will prosper, the orderly business of life will go forward if only men can speak in whatever way given them to utter what their hearts hold—by voice, by posted card, by letter, or by press. Reason has never failed men. Only force and repression have made the wrecks in the world.

It went over the country like wildfire. Editors supposed that I had written it to my friend Henry Allen, although there was nothing to indicate this in the editorial. The moderation and strength of this boiled-down, concentrated, passionate reply to my opponents gave it wings. Like "What's the Matter with Kansas?" It went all over the country. In due course it received the Pulitzer Prize for the best editorial of the year.

In the meantime, the strike ended. Late in the autumn the attorney general of Kansas moved to dismiss the governor's suit. With all the earnestness of a hardened martyr, I tried publicly and privately to stop the dismissal; but when the attorney general refused to prosecute there was nothing else for the court to do. But the court did accompany its order of dismissal with a statement that I had appeared and demanded a trial insistently and with obvious sincerity. The court was aware that I was anxious to settle the constitutional question raised by my arrest. Then the court dismissed the case. And of course hundreds of Americans, including many of the shopmen whose rights I had tried to defend, refused to believe that the suit was anything but a publicity stunt, a put-up job between two friends to get our names in the newspapers. Which didn't matter, so far as I was concerned. I had done what I had to do, had presented the case, and had won it as far as I was concerned, and lost as far as the governor was concerned. No rift ever came to our friendship. Each thought he was right and still thinks he was right, and there was never any question of hard feeling on either side; which is the way, it seems to me, all controversies should proceed to settlement under the democratic process.

CHAPTER LXXXVI

An American Tragedy

AT THE END of Harding's first year in the White House it was evident that the man tremendously desired to do what he regarded as the right thing, that he saw—as clearly as he could see anything—an opportunity to make a name in history. But he was forever striving between those forces about him who were pointing him to a high course, and those other forces to whom he gave his love and loyalty, which were taking his administration down to an abysm of political dishonor which has rarely been reached in the history of the American Republic. This latter influence, which had been about Harding in Ohio and in the Senate, was not conspicuously dominant at the end of his first year. The public could see that he had done some good and notable things. The Emporia Gazette printed an editorial on the first anniversary of the Harding regime, calling attention to the conspicuously decent things which had been accomplished. It pleased him. It pleased Mrs. Harding also. Both of them wrote letters of grateful appreciation. Once or twice later they sent or wrote friendly messages, and in midwinter of 1923, when I happened to be in Washington for a few days before sailing with Sallie and Mr. and Mrs. Victor Murdock for a Mediterranean cruise, the President sent for me. I do not know how he learned that I was in town. Certainly I did not seek to see him.

But I went over one Friday about nine o'clock. It had been more than four years since I had been in the White House. The last time, it was to see President Wilson during the war. I was impressed then by the steely keenness, also coldness, of Wilson's figure. He had stood to greet me in the room where I had seen Taft and Roosevelt and McKinley before him —a spare, ascetic, repressed creature, a kind of frozen flame of righteous intelligence. When I had begun explaining some proposal (I had just returned from Europe), he parried and countered quickly, as one who had heard the argument I would present and was punctiliously impatient. He presented another aspect of the case and outtalked me, agreeing in nothing. I could not tell how much he assimilated. He afterward did exactly what I had suggested, and never remotely put into action the theory which he advanced to me. But upon the visit to Harding I was haunted by the Wilson ghost; perhaps because I met some of the old White House employees on the visit to Harding. I came a few moments early expressly to visit with my old friends, Ike Hoover and Jud Welliver, before the time of my appointment with the President. Welliver was employed in a secretarial capacity. We talked about Harding, and Jud broke forth after a moment's preliminary sparring with something like this:

"Lord, Lord, man! You can't know what the President is going through. You see he doesn't understand it; he just doesn't know a thousand things that he ought to know. And he realizes his ignorance, and he is afraid. He has no idea where to turn. Not long ago, when the first big tax bill came up, you remember there were two theories of taxation combating for the administration's support. He would listen for an hour to one side, become convinced; and then the other side would get him and overwhelm him with its contentions. Some good friend would walk into the White House all cocked and primed with facts and figures to support one side, and another man who he thought perhaps ought to know would reach him with a counter argument which would brush his friend's theory aside. I remember he came in here late one afternoon after a long conference, in which both sides appeared, talked at each other, wrangled over him. He was weary and confused and heartsick, for the man really wants to do the right and honest thing. But I tell you, he doesn't know. That afternoon he stood at my desk and looked at me for a moment and began talking out loud:

" 'Jud,' he cried, 'you have a college education, haven't you? I don't know what to do or where to turn in this taxation matter. Somewhere there must be a book that tells all about it, where I could go to straighten it out in my mind. But I don't know where the book is, and maybe I couldn't read it if I found it! And there must be a man in the country somewhere who could weigh both sides and know the truth. Probably he is in some college or other. But I don't know where to find him. I don't know who he is, and I don't know how to get him. My God, but this is a hell of a place for a man like me to be!'

"He put his hand to his head, smiled at his own discomfiture, turned, and walked heavily away. I see something like that going on in him all the time; the combat between folly and wisdom. I never knew a man who was having such a hard time to find the truth. How Roosevelt used to click into truth with the snap of his teeth! How Wilson sensed it with some engine of erudition under the hood of his cranium! But this man paws for it, wrestles for it, cries for it, and has to take the luck of the road to

616

get it. Sometimes he doesn't, and sometimes he does, and much he knows about it when it comes."

At the end of our talk I went into the Presidential office, where the President stepped forward cordially to greet me. He had been sick. There was a dark cast to his olive skin. He was dressed with exact sartorial propriety, with exactly the kind of boutonnière he should wear, with precisely the gray stripe in his trousers that the hour required, with a proper dark four-in-hand tied most carefully. For a moment or two, while he was offering cigars and moving festively out of the preliminaries of a formal conversation, he was socially and spiritually erect. But as we sat in the south sunshine flooding through the windows of his office, he warmed and melted and slouched a little. I had no idea why he had sent for me. I have precious little idea now, only a theory. I have a notion that he was lonesome, and that he wanted to talk about the newspaper business. At least he talked of little else. He began by asking me what we were paying for print paper, where we got it, how many carloads we used a year, going into the terms of our contract which by some miracle I had in my mind.

Then he began rather abruptly: "Here's another thing. What do you do with all the people that want to subscribe to your paper outside of the trade territory of the Emporia merchants? I am being swamped by subscribers from Oregon and Maine, who want to read the Marion Star every day, on the theory that I knock off two or three hours down here and write the editorials for it. If these subscribers don't let me alone, they will bust the paper. The white paper and postage costs more than the subscription price. They are no good to the Marion dry-goods stores. They don't buy anything there, and I can't raise my advertising rate. And I can't reorganize my whole business to make a paper that would interest the advertising agencies in New York and Chicago to bring me a lot of foreign advertising."

By "foreign advertising," he meant advertising from outside Marion—chewing gum, pianolas, pipe organs, tooth paste, Grand Rapids furniture, life insurance, and the like.

He went on: "Yet the boys down there tell me we are getting a big list of these expensive subscribers, and I don't know what to do. What is your plan? Don't you have a lot of subscribers to the Gazette all over the country who want to see what you write, and who are not worth a penny to your town merchants?"

I told him that we had a little weekly, four pages, without any advertising, and we charged enough for the weekly to pay for the white paper, and let it go at that. This weekly contained the editorials and a little local news for people who had moved away from Emporia, and just about paid expenses. The idea struck him as worth considering, and he talked a little more about it. Then he went on to ask about our profit-sharing plan, of which he had read something in the trade papers. He outlined his plan of distributing stock in the Marion Star to his employees, and explained that it worked well. He went into the matter of wages for reporters, linotype men, floor men, and the foreman, and we compared notes. While one of the White House servants was putting wood in the grate, we both watched him critically. Then the President rose and walked over to the fire, stood with his hands behind him warming his back. One could see that he was physically subnormal. He had a powerful frame, strong, rather sloping shoulders, with just a hint of a stoop that tall men often need to get their eyes in focus with the common world a few inches below them. As he stood there by the glowing fire and mused a moment, he said:

"Well, when I first took this job, I had a lot of fun with it. I got a kick out of it every day for the first six months or so. But it has fallen into a routine, more or less."

He spoke slowly, dropping into a reminiscent mood, and went on: "You know every day at three-thirty, here in the midst of the affairs of state, I go to press on the Marion Star. I wonder what kind of a layout the boys have got on the first page. I wonder how much advertising there is; whether they are keeping up with this week last year. I would like to walk out in the composing room and look over the forms before they go to the stereotyper. There never was a day in all the years that I ran the paper that I didn't get some thrill out of it."

He grinned and paused, and it wasn't for me to talk. I fancy he was getting out of me exactly what he wanted—an audience who would understand the touch of homesickness which had come to a man away from his life's work, a man who had been confined to his room and was a bit under himself physically. Suddenly he broke a minute's silence, left the fire, came over, sat down, crossed his legs, and asked abruptly:

"Say, how do you get the county printing?"

I told him that there was a gentlemen's agreement between the Democratic paper and the Gazette that when the Democrats elected the county officers, whose business it was to let the county printing, we would not bid; or, if we did bid, we bid the full legal rate. So the Democrats let the printing to the Democratic paper. And when the county was Republican, the Democrats decently refrained from disturbing the legal rate by a cutthroat bid.

"That's fine, fine!" he answered, and a querulous strain rasped in his voice. "Do you know how we used to get it? Well, we all go in and bid and choose among ourselves the low bidder before we bid, and he adds enough to his bid to give us all a little slice of the profits above his low bid."

He paused a second and then turned toward me a troubled face, and he cried: "And that's the hell of it. Right now, at the moment, there is a bunch down at the Willard Hotel coming up here to see me this afternoon, good friends of mine from Ohio, decent fellows that I have worked with thirty years. Some of them have supported me through thick and thin. Well, there is an energetic young district attorney down East here—maybe New York, or Boston, or Philadelphia, it don't make any difference where—and he has gone and indicted those fellows; is going to put them in jail for violating the antitrust law or some conspiracy law for doing exactly in crockery what I have done in printing for twenty years. *And*," he added, "they know all about my method, and they are going to ask me to dismiss the indictment. I can't do that. The law is the law, and it is probably all right, a good law and ought to be enforced. And yet I sit here in the White House and have got to see those fellows this afternoon, and explain why I can't lift a hand to keep them from going to jail. My God, this is a hell of a job! I have no trouble with my enemies. I can take care of my enemies all right. But my damn friends," he wailed, with a sort of serio-comic petulance, "my God-damn friends, White, they're the ones that keep me walking the floor nights!"

He rose, stretched, and went over to the fire, which mellowed him again, and learned that I was going to Constantinople. He asked me to see a boyhood friend, a Dr. Bowen; gave me a card to him. Bowen was a preacher, the head of the American Bible Society in the Near East.

"We were boys together," the President explained. "His father was the leading lawyer of the town—mine, the doctor. We used to run together, go out sparking together, fought together, roamed the woods and fields like two young dogs together; and in the last two or three years, with all the hurry and trouble and excitement of this job and the war, I have lost track of him. I have let him drop. And I want you to tell him that I think of him and think of the old days together lots of times when I am alone and sick—go over it all. Hunt him up, and give him this card, and tell him that Warren wants to know if there is anything he can do. Bowen was an awful nice boy—decent, you know, square, that kind of a boy. He helped me a lot."

So we talked on, never touching politics; talked of homely country things for the better part of an hour. And then a doorman announced that the cabinet was gathering. He took me out and introduced me to a number of members that I had not met, and there for the first time I saw Secretary Fall. The man's face, figure, and mien were a shock to me, that such a man could be in a President's Cabinet; a tall, gaunt, unkempt, ill visaged face that showed a disheveled spirit behind restless eyes. He looked like the patent medicine vender of my childhood days who used to stand, with long hair falling upon a long coat under a wide hat, with military goatee and mustache, at the back of a wagon selling Wizard Oil—a cheap, obvious faker. I could hardly believe the evidence of my eyes. How he must have twisted the nerves of Secretary Hoover! How Hughes must have sensed him and pitied him! The rest of the cabinet, except Hughes and Hoover and Hays, were for the most part starched-shirt-fronts, human bass drums, who boomed out in front of the plutocratic sideshow with bellying banners, shouting the wonders of the fat boy of prosperity and the octopus of big business, and the fire eater and sword swallower of a starved but greedy militarism. Obviously, the relations between the President and his cabinet were meticulously polite, punctilious to futility; there could not have been camaraderie that Taft knew, nor the joyous enthusiasm between the men which Roosevelt inspired, nor even the deference which Wilson required. Harding and his cabinet looked to me like a lot of pallbearers who never once got down to the truth about the deceased.

I left the White House with a feeling that it was the scene of a terrific struggle. Fall was the symbol of one of the forces, Hoover of another, that were grappling for supremacy with the confused mind of the President. His heart was all right. His courage was fairly good. But his confusion lay in his lack of moral perceptions. He did not know where to place his loyalty. He was deeply fond of his friends the grafters—the petty politicians in every state, who were looking for pickings through the Republican national committeemen, or through some subterranean avenue to quick easy money, or a soft cynosure. The President was under many obligations to Harry Daugherty. Daugherty's standing in the Republican national committee and his acquaintances gained as the attorney for a number of great corporations in various states, had given him easy access to delegations under the senatorial control in the Chicago convention. Over the protests of a powerful group of highly respectable Republicans, the President had appointed Daugherty, and the latter's friends had moved into the Attorney General's office, making it a rendezvous for questionable characters and a nest of scandal. Cheap and sometimes corrupt little men were using the powerful leverage of Daugherty's name for unbelievably corrupt semipublic transactions. The spy service of the Department of Justice was set upon those who protested against the dubious transactions of the Attorney General, or indeed upon those who protested against any irregular practices anywhere in the Federal government. On the other hand, Secretary Hughes, Secretary Hoover, and half a dozen of the younger eastern senators who were close to President Harding, notably Frelinghuysen and Wadsworth, men of unquestioned conservative convictions but pure motives, were appealing to another loyalty in the President—his loyalty to his position, his loyalty to the people, his resolve to do well in his high cause.

The hour I had spent with Harding convinced me that he realized the conflict around him and that, in so far as a man with his sordid background could, he was trying to line up with the righteous forces, striving to break away from the hands of the past that were drawing his administration down to shame. I remember well walking down the avenue from the White House, troubled in my own heart about the proper attitude to take toward him. Obviously, I could not sit by, grinning at the tragedy. It was a question whether or not to join those who were trying to destroy him in order to expose the corruption which his friends were shielding, with his too obvious acquiescence if not connivance, or whether to join the forces that were trying to win him from his old ways, his vicious companions, and strengthen his purpose to serve his country. It was plain that his purpose needed strengthening. The Washington of the newspapermen—the writers, the liberal senators, the western congressmen—was abuzz with a thousand little stories, rumors and suspicions of irregularity, sometimes amounting to crookedness, often merely the petty performances in the various departments, the Interior Department, the Navy Department, the War Department, the Attorney General's office. But there were counter stories, little hero tales of the President's kindness, of his dawning consciousness of the truth and his growing resolve to serve it. And at the end of my walk I decided to line up with the Hoover-Hughes crowd, and try to salvage something from the threatened wreck. I remember talking to Secretary Hoover two or three times at his office and in the home of Vernon Kellogg. Hoover was under no illusions, but he believed that the President, like the Prodigal Son, would come to himself and cease living with the swine. I wrote a piece about Harding emphasizing his good intentions, his kindly nature, his lonely position, his country-town view of life; spoke of his associates in Ohio, of the Saturday night poker game in Marion, and the good fellowship which organized it and kept it going, and tried to explain him in terms of the leading citizen of a country town moving cautiously and rather alone in a new, unfriendly environment. In a day or so Mrs. White and I joined the Victor Murdocks on a Mediterranean cruise. When we came to Constantinople I tried to find his old friend Bowen, but learned he had died two years before. I saw his widow and told her of the President's thoughtfulness. And when I came back to Washington Mr. Harding sent for me and learned for the first time of his old friend's death. In the sad moment that followed, he said:

"God, have I been that busy, that I let him die without knowing it! What a life!"

He asked about the consuls I had seen or heard about along the Mediterranean. I told him about Consul General Ravndal, of Constantinople, and said that he was of ministerial size. The President's face clouded for a moment and he said:

"Yes, I know there are a dozen of those consul generals who are of ministerial size. But we can't appoint them. They are barred by the mean salarie which the United States Government pays to its diplomatic service. A consul general, Ravndal and his kind have few social duties. As minister he would need money. No provision is made by the government for thos necessary social obligations. George Harvey has been trying to come hom for six months. The best men we have in the ministerial service find th social drain too heavy upon them."

Then he told me what the British and French ambassadors were getting how much contingent fund they were allowing, and contrasted our ow pinchpenny salaries to those which other governments paid. We talked alon; for half an hour, and as I rose to leave he said:

"Well, White, I liked your piece about me. You have sensed it. I mus have the support of the decent folks in this country. God knows I hav got to fight, and I suppose I am to blame for it if any man is to blame fo his own past. But it was a good piece, the sort of thing that ought to b written."

We were standing in the doorway, and a broad grin rose out of a kin heart as he said: "Mrs. Harding liked it too, but she said: 'Warren, wh did he drag in that Saturday night poker game?'"

I made no reply, and he broke a short pause by saying kindly: "It's a right. That was part of the picture. I told her it should go in."

And we parted. Some time that spring while I was in Washington I met on the sidewalk in front of the White House, a group of friends. The seemed to be in charge of Oswald Garrison Villard. Monsignor Ryan wa in the group. They stopped me and I learned that they were on their wa to meet President Harding by appointment, to plead with him for th pardon of Eugene Debs. They insisted that I should go along. I knew Debs I believed that he had been unjustly imprisoned, so I joined them. In th White House office we stood in a group, and just as the President cam in Villard said:

"White, you speak first."

I tried under my voice to say I had formed no speech, but I cut loose The President listened attentively, and obviously with more than casua interest. Villard followed me, and Monsignor Ryan followed Villard. W spoke briefly three or four minutes each. The President asked questions and as Ryan closed at the end of a dozen minutes and our time was run ning out, the President said pleasantly that he was glad to have the matte presented, that he thought he understood the Debs case, and that he woul give it his immediate attention. Whereupon a woman, one of those huma hellcats who have no sense of the proprieties, stepped forth and cried:

"Mr. President, that's no way to answer us. We demand a yes-or-no answer now!"

We were shocked. One of us tried for a second or two to disavow the woman's outburst. But the President straightened himself up. The stoop seemed to come out of his shoulders. A certain gentle dignity enveloped him. He said:

"My dear woman: You may demand anything you please out of Warren Harding. He will not resent it. But the President of the United States has a right to keep his own counsel, and the office I occupy forbids me to reply to you as I should like to if I were elsewhere!"

A little flutter of applause came from our group. He smiled and nodded for me to stay after the others were gone. I started to congratulate him. He laughed quietly.

"I hope you thought I got away with it all right. Of course, I want to do something for old Debs. I think I can." After a pause he grinned and said: "But, God, that was no way to get it!"

After that we chatted for a second, and I left him. I saw him next and finally a few months later in the West—first at Kansas City and then on the train crossing Kansas on his way to Alaska. He was cordial, kindly, extremely courteous, but obviously under some strain. Three times he said:

"White, I want to have a long talk with you."

It did not seem to be easy to arrange it that day, but I felt that something was on his mind. Nicholas Murray Butler told me that just before Harding left Washington for this Alaskan trip he sent for him, and they spent a Sunday together; and all that day Harding was trying to nerve himself to tell something. Heaven knows what! Probably the same thing that he wanted to tell me, for the meeting at Hutchinson had been only a few days after the Sunday he and Butler spent together—futilely. I remember sitting in the private car between Emporia and Hutchinson, and he again said this: "I have no trouble with my enemies. I can take care of them. It is my friends." And he repeated it again, "My friends, that are giving me my trouble!"

The night before, I had seen Harding in his Kansas City hotel. He had tried to get me to come to dinner with him. I sent to the hotel at dinnertime, explaining that I could not come because I should have to turn down an old friend who had prepared a dinner. Harding, Mrs. Harding, and Senator Capper were dining alone in the hotel suite. As I came in Harding rose, came from the little dining room of the suite carrying his napkin, and greeted me most cordially. He invited me on the trip that I took the next day. While we were talking Mrs. Fall, the wife of the Secretary of the Interior, came to the door. He excused himself a minute, took her into an adjoining room, and did not return. Finally I made my excuses to Mrs.

Harding and to Senator Capper and went on my way. Senator Capper told me afterwards that Mrs. Fall and the President stayed closeted in that room until the very moment he went to make his speech, and that he came out obviously frustrated, worried, and excited. What she told him must have been on his mind when he saw me on the train the next day. What he suspected was probably on his mind when he sent for Nicholas Murray Butler, and he could not bring himself to make a clean breast of it. Is it a wonder that he died that summer? How could the doctors diagnose an illness that was part terror, part shame, and part utter confusion! For the first time in his life he had encountered a moral issue that he could not dodge.

I left him at Hutchinson with an uneasy feeling. He had no sense of his physical strength. He went into the wheat field on a hot day, not to boast as a farmer, but to prove himself a good fellow. That was the strength and the weakness of him—his unquenchable kindness, which too often shadowed his higher loyalty.

CHAPTER LXXXVII

The Downhill Pull

SALLIE AND I CAME HOME in midspring of 1923 to Emporia, after three months abroad, to find the town in a building boom. The Ku Klux Klan had captured the City Building at the spring election, and the paper, having been defeated in the mayoralty fight, was enjoying that complacent advantage which every newspaper enjoys when it gets licked. Its friends are fairly sure it was right, but its adversaries are in that moment of disillusion which always comes to a majority in an electorate when it finds that its hero is a man, an ordinary, two-legged man who cannot do many of the things he promises to do and does not do the few things that he can do. Generally speaking, a newspaper is better off losing than winning a fight. When it wins, the newspaper has to console the disillusioned majority, and so loses caste. That is why nothing fails like success in politics. The advertising patronage of the paper was growing rapidly, crowding extra pages in every day. A new linotype which we had bought in the previous year did not relieve the pressure in the composing room. Merchants were spending their money freely to attract buyers. And from the East came thousands of dollars in advertising, calling attention to national products—automobiles, radios, phonographs, tobacco, oil, transportation— a long list of things which once were luxuries and were becoming the common comforts of the people. The economic revolution was going full tilt. A whole class was moving up in its standard of living, in its self-respect, in its attitude toward life. The serving class in America was passing. The machine was becoming the servant. The servant was joining the master class. New houses all over Emporia were replacing the old houses and the character of every street was changing. The odd thing about this building boom that came to the country towns in the early part of the third decade of this century was that the big houses, which might be called the three-girl houses, were practically extinct in country towns. The one-girl house, or the no-girl house, was rising on the outskirts of every town in the smart

625

suburbs. The girls who thirty years before went out to service were working in stores or offices, having graduated from high school either in their rural neighborhoods or in the nearest town. They were marrying clerks and office men and skilled workers, and the wages of women doing housework were rising faster than the wages of men in the stores and offices.

Our first three-story, brick apartment building in the town was ready for occupancy—another sign, a social sign, that the economic revolution was achieving its purpose. The home was changing. Old America, the America of "our Fathers' pride," the America wherein a frugal people had grown great through thrift and industry, was disappearing before the new machine age. Mass production was accumulating and distributing wealth by some inner automatic process quite beyond government and law: as though the mass of machinery on this continent was one vast machine spewing out of its hopper a glittering shower of goods, chattels, and material hereditary appurtenances which were being carried by tubes and wires and shafts and funnels and trolleys to all parts of the earth, to all estates and conditions of men; distributing it by some prescience accurately, if not quite justly, to the homes of the multitude. The Gazette was, of course, one of the little cogs of the distributing machine. It was a different organization from that I had come to a generation before, with a forty-five-dollar weekly pay roll, a bookkeeper and a reporter, each of whom did more or less of the other's work, when advertising—like kissing—came by favor, and subscribers expressed their politics in their preference for a newspaper. Our politics had nothing to do with our subscription list, and our advertisers cared precious little personally for the editor or his views on any question except the price of advertising. Journalism was ceasing to be a profession and was becoming a business and an industry. That also was a fruit of the revolution.

The miracle of the radio was becoming a commonplace in the humblest home. Kansas was presently to have enough automobiles to put every man, woman, and child in the state on wheels at the same time. Everyone was working, and the country, spiraling upward toward the Coolidge bull market, throbbed with a new youth. But alas, where was mine? I was already into my sixth decade, which by any definition you care to take, is the downhill pull.

A milestone in my life had been that bright, crisp day in February, 1918, when I celebrated my fiftieth birthday. It shocked me. Sallie had arranged a dinner for a dozen of our old friends. Before they came I went upstairs to dress and, coming down before the guests were assembled, I amazed the family by sitting down midway on the stairway landing and bursting into tears. To be fifty was definitely to leave youth and young manhood, and to begin to be an old man. Always I had dreaded the responsibility of maturity. I mourned because I was grown up. For I had liked to hide my blunders and my conscious idiocies behind the shield of pretense that I was young, naïve, inexperienced. I was given to impish mischief, and under fifty it might be excusable. But I felt, there on the stairs, that I had crossed the deadline; that the whole gay panorama of childhood, boyhood, youth, young manhood, and mature adolescence was gone. Fifty years meant something so new and so sad that I felt upset in bewilderment and something like sorrow. I had crossed the meridian, and I did not like the new country.

And where, in these glittering twenties, were the hopes which I and my kind had held so high in the first two decades of the new century? Looking around me in the gathering roar of prosperity, the only rising political force seemed to be the dark bigotry of the Ku Klux Klan. And other sinister forces of oppression to the free human spirit seemed to be gathering across the seas. Where were our hopes and dreams of yesteryear?

Looking back now more than thirty years, I can shut my eyes and see that Bull Moose convention of 1912, see their eager faces—more than a thousand of them—upturned, smiling hopefully, with joy beaming out that came from hearts which believed in what they were doing; its importance, its righteousness.

It seemed to matter so very much, that convention of zealots, cleansed of self-interest and purged of cynicism. I never have seen before or since exactly that kind of a crowd. I impressed it on my memory because I felt as they felt—those upturned, happy faces.

And now they are dust, and all the visions they saw that day have dissolved. Their hopes, like shifting clouds, have blown away before the winds of circumstance. And I wonder if it did matter much. Or is there somewhere, in the stuff that holds humanity together, some force, some conservation of spiritual energy, that saves the core of every noble hope, and gathers all men's visions some day, some way, into the reality of progress?

I do not know. But I have seen the world move, under some, maybe mystic, influence, far enough to have the right to ask that question.

THE LAST TWO DECADES

BY W. L. WHITE

I HAD HOPED to tell the story of the last two decades of my father's life not in my own words but largely in his, making it a mosaic of the letters and editorials he wrote on the fast-changing scene, hoping that the contrast would not be too great between my selection and his narrative.

I find that this last hope is impossible. For in his account of the previous five decades he tempers what he then wrote and thought with that mellowness which only comes with the years, at some times because they had taught him tolerance, at others because time had drained off the emotion of the hour and he could look back with kindly detachment.

Often the value in what he said lay not in its permanence but in his saying aloud, in earthy phrases and with the terrifying frankness of a child, what many thought but few dared whisper.

So, for instance, with his epitaph of Frank Munsey, the newspaper proprietor whose consolidations had thrown thousands of reporters, editorial writers, and printers out of work. In the Gazette (December 23, 1925) he wrote:

"Frank Munsey, the great publisher, is dead. Frank Munsey contributed to the journalism of his day the great talent of a meat packer, the morals of a money changer and the manners of an undertaker. He and his kind have about succeeded in transforming a once noble profession into an eight per-cent security. May he rest in trust!"

So, also with his more mellow four-line epitaph on Woodrow Wilson:

"God gave him a great vision.
"The Devil gave him an imperious heart.
"The proud heart is still.
"The vision lives."

Early in the twenties, at about the time his own narrative leaves off, he fired the Gazette's first editorial gun against the inevitable rise of postwar prejudice:

629

"An organizer of the Ku Klux Klan was in Emporia the other day and the men whom he invited to join his band at ten dollars per join, turned him down. . . . To make a case against a birthplace, a religion, or a race, is wicked, un-American and cowardly. The Ku Klux Klan is based upon such deep foolishness that it is bound to be a menace to good government in any community. . . . American institutions—our courts, our legislators, our executive officers—are strong enough to keep the peace and promote justice and good will in the community. If they are not, then the thing to do is to change these institutions and do it quickly, but always legally. For a self-constituted body of moral idiots who would substitute the findings of the Ku Klux Klan for the processes of law, to try to better conditions, would be a most un-American outrage which every good citizen should resent. . . . It is to the everlasting credit of Emporia that the organizer found no suckers with $10 each to squander here."

However, this prediction was wrong, and the following week he had to admit:

"The Ku Klux Klan is said to be reorganizing in Emporia. It is an organization of cowards. Not a man in it has the courage of his convictions. It is an organization of traitors to American institutions. Not a man in it has faith enough in American courts, laws and officials, to trust them to maintain law and order. . . . It is a menace to peace and decent neighborly living and if we find out who is the Imperial Wizard in Emporia, we shall guy the life out of him. He is a joke, you may be sure. But a poor joke at that."

The tide, however, was too strong at this point to be checked. By 1924, Emporia had a Ku Klux mayor, and in the primary elections for governor, Klan-endorsed candidates had won both the Republican and the Democratic nominations.

So, on September 20, my father announced that he was entering the race as an independent for governor, because:

"I want to offer Kansans afraid of the Klan and ashamed of that disgrace, a candidate who shares their fear and shame.

"The issue in Kansas this year is the Ku Klux Klan above everything else. It is found in nearly every county. It represents a small minority of the citizenship and it is organized for purposes of terror, directed at honest law-abiding citizens; Negroes, Jews and Catholics. These groups in Kansas comprise more than one-fourth of our population. They menace no one. Yet, because of their skin, their race, or their creed, the Ku Klux Klan is subjecting them to economic boycott, to social ostracism, to every form of harassment, annoyance and every terror that a bigoted minority can use.

"Kansas, with her intelligence and pure American blood, of all states should be free of this taint. I was born in Kansas and lived my life in Kansas. I am proud of my state. And the thought that Kansas should have a government beholden to this hooded gang of masked fanatics, ignorant and tyrannical in their ruthless oppression, is what calls me out of the pleasant ways of my life into this disgraceful but necessary task. I cannot sit idly by and see Kansas become a byword among the states. . . . I call to my support all fair-minded citizens of every party, of every creed, to stop the oppression of this minority of our people. It is a national menace, this Klan. It knows no party. It knows no country. It knows only bigotry, malice and terror. Our national government is founded upon reason, and the Golden Rule. This Klan is preaching and practising terror and force. Its only prototype is the Soviet of Russia."

As the campaign progressed, my father warmed up his vocabulary to pay his respects to the Republican candidate:

"The gag rule first came into the Republican Party last May. A flock of dragons, Kleagles, Cyclops and Furies came up to Wichita from Oklahoma and called a meeting with some Kansas Terrors, Genii and Whangdoodles. . . . A few weeks later, the Cyclops, Kleagles, Wizards, and Willopses-wallopuses began parading in the Kansas cow pastures, passing the word down to the shirt-tail rangers they were to go into the Kansas primaries and nominate Ben Paulen."

Although Paulen was presently elected, my father received about the same number of votes as the Democratic candidate; and he felt that the hundred and fifty thousand-odd votes which he had piled up had demonstrated to politicians that the Klan endorsement was, in fact, a handicap as there was in Kansas a larger anti-Klan vote than there were Klansmen. At all events, the Klan presently disappeared from Kansas politics; and on May 5, 1926, my father fired in the Gazette his parting shot:

"Doctor Hiram Evans, the Imperial Wizard of the Kluxers, is bringing his consecrated shirt tail to Kansas this spring, and from gloomy klaverns will make five Kansas speeches. We welcome him. Enter the wizard— sound the bull roarers, and the hewgags. Beat the tom-toms.

"He will see what was once a thriving and profitable hate factory and bigotorium now laughed into a busted community; where the cock-eyed he-dragon wails for its first-born, and the nightshirts of a once salubrious pageantry sag in the spring breezes and bag at the wabbly knees.

"The Kluxers in Kansas are as dejected and sad as a last year's bird's nest, afflicted with general debility, dizziness on going upstairs, and general aversion to female society."

But there is deeper wisdom in that analysis of the Ku Klux Klan which he presently wrote for the magazine World Tomorrow, and which has a sobering similarity to the postwar years of World War II. He felt that:

"We who think we have grown-up minds have our own mental distempers. We are going through our own years of bitter disillusion. The great guns of the Western Front smashed so much more than the little French towns and the flesh and blood of the soldiers.

"They [the people] counted on the faith of the world, the ideals of the world, the high hopes of the world. Amid the ruins, they are all broken and sad. We should not be angry if the child minds about us show a strange perversity and a wicked bigotry which is bound to pass as humanity readjusts itself after the breakdown of civilization."

But even with the passing of the Klan my father was not happy in the Roaring Twenties. As early as 1926, he saw the times of the Big Bull Market with sad clarity:

"What a sordid decade is passing! It will be known in American history fifty years hence as the time of terrible reaction. . . . It will not be the story of a weak man like Harding nor a silent and unemotional man like Coolidge. They are mere outer manifestations of the inner spiritual traits of the people. The spirit of our democracy has turned away from the things of the spirit, got its share of the patrimony ruthlessly and gone out and lived riotously and ended by feeding among the swine.

"Corruption is rampant in high places. Special privilege is unleashed and shameless. The fourth-rater is coming into prestige and power in business, in politics, in religion. . . . Perhaps the whole thing is epitomized by the rise and fall of Harding. The story should not be written now. It would hurt too many hearts. But when it is written, it will be a bitter and awful thing.

"If Roosevelt had lived [my father, of course, refers to Theodore] it might have been different. But who knows? Times are made more or less by leadership, but there is the other half of the equation, which is that times develop leaders. It would have been an uphill and terrible struggle, possibly a fruitless and tragic struggle, ending in sad defeat for the old Colonel had he lived in these times. Perhaps if he had lived, he would not have permitted public sentiment to sag as it has sagged. One doesn't know. Nothing is as futile as the ifs of history.

"We have not come to the turn of the lane. The manifestations in Iowa, in the Dakotas and in Wisconsin are sporadic,—little isolated dust storms on the desert, whirling fitfully, meaning little except as evidence of a gathering storm which is not yet even upon the horizon.

"The nation has not yet been shocked out of its materialism. Of course, Coolidge is a tremendous shock absorber. His emotionless attitude is an anesthetic to a possible national conviction of sin. . . . We have just got to grind along and develop a leader and it is a long, slow task calling for all our patience. How long, Oh Lord, how long! *

"What a joy it would be to get out and raise the flaming banner of righteousness! Instead of which we sit in our offices and do unimportant things and go home at night and think humdrum thoughts.

"What a generation!"

It is on the whole not surprising that this malcontent, who so clearly rejected the validity and the permanence of that Best of All Possible Worlds, should have been blacklisted in 1928 by the D.A.R. along with a list of liberals and pacifists which included Dean Roscoe Pound of the Harvard Law School, President Mary E. Woolley of Mount Holyoke College, Felix Frankfurter, then a professor in the Harvard Law School, Clarence Darrow, Rabbi Stephen S. Wise, Norman Hapgood, and David Starr Jordan.

This temporarily roused my father out of his discontent to produce the following gentle pastoral idyll on the subject of the good ladies of the D.A.R. whose leaders were:

"developing a taste for those idle, apoplectic old gentlemen in red flannels who escape the boredom of their rich wives by sitting in club windows in Washington and bemoaning the decadence of a growing world. The nice old girls of the present D.A.R. administration have been hypnotized by the brass buttons of the retired Army officers and lured into this red-baiting mania by the tea-gladiators of Washington."

When Mrs. Brosseau, then the D.A.R.'s president, retorted with spirit, he charged that she had:

"put the entire D.A.R. membership list on the sucker list of the super-patriots [because her black list had singled out] organizations affecting colored people, Jews and Catholics . . . the peculiar enemies of the Ku Klux Klan. The D.A.R. has yanked the Klan out of the cow pasture and set it down in the breakfast room of respectability, removing its hood and putting on a transformation. Mrs. Brosseau is a lovely lady with many beautiful qualities of heart and mind, but, in her enthusiasm, she

---

* When this editorial, more than a decade later, was published in an anthology, my father added the following footnote: "Well, six years brought the man! And when he came, I some way did not 'get out and raise the flaming banner of righteousness.'"

has allowed several lengths of Ku Klux nightie to show under her red, white and blue."

The year 1928 also saw the nomination of Herbert Hoover (my father had been one of his early western supporters) and his campaign with Governor Smith in which the most noisy issue was Prohibition, combined, in the South, with a seldom-voiced anti-Catholicism. My father was, of course, a deeply convinced Prohibitionist. There were bigots in this movement, but I wonder if any subsequent generation can understand that there were also many most earnest, if mistaken idealists who poured into the movement the enthusiasm of a deep hope that Prohibition could abolish alcoholism, and that it would be a tremendous step forward in human happiness. No Marxist ever poured higher hopes and more selfless energy into his panacea than did the Prohibitionist of the last generation. Furthermore, my father, who had so often and so brilliantly interpreted to the nation the hopes and fears, aspirations and prejudices of the Middle West and of country towns, shared their deep and instinctive distrust of the big-city political machine which was epitomized by Tammany.

All through the economic storm which broke six months after President Hoover's inauguration, my father's basic faith in his old friend remained unchanged. But even as early as 1930 he began to doubt not Hoover's program, but his ability to hold popular confidence. He felt that Hoover, who

"has some sort of shrinking horror of connecting his office with causes, should be told by his advisors that in extraordinary times of turmoil and panic, the Presidential office must take leadership in the country.

"He must . . . appeal to the people. He must dramatize his cause or the cause loses, and with the cause his fortune falls.

"Go to the people, Mr. President. They are dependable. Lincoln, Roosevelt and Wilson found the people a tower of strength and of refuge. Whoever is wise and honest and brave, they will follow to victory. But their leader must take them into his councils. They will repay candor with confidence."

And this same note is sounded in his political epitaph on Herbert Hoover written just after the Roosevelt landslide in 1932. He felt that Herbert Hoover had:

"suppressed the drama which another man, with a politician's instinct for heroizing himself in any crisis, might have turned to his own advantage. If he had any illusions, and certainly the President had few, . . . one was a blind faith that some way democracy in the end would be able to see with its own eyes the truth. He believed that the people could see it clearly and logically without drama, without a hero in whose struggles

634

they could see a story, and so feel their way to the truth. But, alas, the President was wrong in attributing a logical habit of mind to men in the mass. They must emotionalize their thinking. They need a story. They learn their truth in parables.

"He will be known as the greatest innocent bystander in history. But history will also write him down an earnest, honest, intelligent man, full of courage and patriotism, undaunted to the last.

"Here is tragedy . . . a brave man fighting valiantly, futilely to the end."

My father's first reaction to the New Deal was bewilderment. A month after the inauguration of President Roosevelt, he was writing:

"Strange things are moving across this American world of ours. The country seemed to want dramatic action. Roosevelt is supplying the want.

"It isn't in the books. The Constitution is straining and cracking. But, after all, the Constitution was made for the people, and not the people for the Constitution. We are toying gayly with billions as we once played cautiously with millions. We are legerdemaining a huge national debt which is to be paid Heaven knows when or where or how. It is bewildering—this new deal—the new world. How much is false, how much is true, how much is an illusion of grandeur, a vast make-believe, only time will tell.

"In the meantime, the wizard in the White House works his weird spell upon a changing world."

But by 1934 he found compensation because,

"for thirty years, now, the Editor of the Gazette has been hammering away for a larger participation of the average man in the wealth of this nation—less for superintendence, interest and profits,—more for wages. We have clamored for higher income taxes, for devastating inheritance taxes, for workmen's compensation, unemployment insurance, old-age pensions, for all the measures which Colonel Theodore Roosevelt used to call 'social and industrial justice.' President Roosevelt's new first assistant secretary of the treasury is described as believing in the following social reforms:

> Higher income and inheritance taxes.
> Federal grants for the unemployed.
> A more equitable distribution of wealth.
> Unemployment and old-age pensions.
> Minimum wages.
> National economic planning.
> Public works and mortgage relief.

635

"Franklin Roosevelt has packed his whole government in Washington full of men like that. Congress has given him broad powers. He surrounds himself with leaders like Eccles, Tugwell, Ickes, Wallace, Frances Perkins and Morgenthau who believe in all these reforms. It is plain as a barn door that we are getting our revolution through the administrative arm of the government, without legislation.

"Well, in these sad days of depression, the Gazette gets a great laugh out of this. In fact, you may catch us grinning at any hour of the day or night to think of what has happened in this land of the free. We hope the conservative Democrats who were lambasting Hoover a year and a half ago are enjoying what they got.

"These are great days—if not happy ones."

In the summer of 1933, as a reporter for the North American Newspaper Alliance, my father attended the London Economic Conference, witnessed the short-lived struggle for power between Raymond Moley and Cordell Hull, and at the end of the conference, with my mother, took a short trip to the Soviet Union avoiding Germany where Hitler had just come to power. In Moscow they spent most of their time with the veteran reporters —Maurice Hindus, Walter Duranty, Eugene Lyons, Louis Fisher and William Henry Chamberlin, who even then had varying points of view. Russia in 1933 was undergoing not a depression but a famine in the south as a result of the collectivization of the land and the liquidation of the Kulaks. The American reporters in Moscow knew that an estimated three million people were dying in the Ukraine, although no reporters had visited this region nor could news of the famine be cabled abroad.

Back in Emporia, my father was making up his mind about Roosevelt. He was greatly pleased when the President came out foursquare for the Child Labor Amendment, pointing out in the Gazette:

"It is that sort of thing that makes the people love him. He may make mistakes—loads of them, but the folks know he is brave and honest, and that he is never going to be caught . . . hesitating in a crisis. Roosevelt has his weaknesses, but his strength is so fine and fair that the people will forgive him when they find he is wrong; and he can start all over again with new confidence."

As the New Deal's economic program came into view he felt:

"Evidently the President is aiming at something of the same target at which both the fascists and the communists are shooting; that is to say, the socialization of capital, the regimentation of industry and agriculture, and, finally, a more equitable distribution of wealth, a guarantee of a minimum standard of living for all who have worked honestly. . . . Obviously, he is not greedy for power. No one can deny that he is seeking the larger good of the American people. It is evident that he is no dictator. He has none of the faults and few of the virtues of a tyrant. Instead . . . a yearning for peace, for justice and for self-respect, for the people of this country and for the world."

He also felt:

"In all this tremendous change from the old democracy of individual laissez faire to the new democracy of socialized capital, no question of honesty, no scandal . . . has come to the American people."

And yet:

"Far be it for the Gazette to carp. We are supporting the administration and the whole alphabet thereunto appertaining. But are the American people ready for the revolutionary change, the fundamental break with our American past that is necessary if this revolution takes hold permanently? Today, it is a palace revolution which has captured Washington. How far and how deeply in the hearts of the American people has it gone? These questions are not asked by an impertinent enemy but by a sincere friend whose fond and fervent hope is that the day he long has sought is really here."

Yet occasionally, my father had honest doubts as to whether this long sought day was really desirable:

"Roosevelt's greatest problem can be stated thus: Can government chain its dollars, harness them to the common good, and still retain free men and free institutions? It has never been done before. Political liberties always go down when economic liberty is circumscribed. But this is a new world. Our democracy for a hundred years has been a new order, but it is more deeply rooted here than in Europe. Probably America can do this strange thing—establish a new revolution of free men with their dollars in shackles."

It was a question which later was to trouble the economist Hayek, who gave a different answer. In these years, my father's occasional criticisms of the Roosevelt program were always friendly. In sounding the knell of the NRA, he pointed out that its mistake was

"taking all business at one fell swoop, which recalls the epitaph on Bill Nye's famous dog, Epaminondas, who in his insatiable thirst for gobbling everything, gobbled off a plasterer's mixing board a bellyful of plaster of paris, which hardened; when he died, Bill Nye took the dog from around his monument and wrote these soulful words: 'Here lies Epaminondas, interior view. He bit off more than he could chew.'"

Meanwhile, Alfred Landon was looming over the flat prairie horizon as a probable Republican Presidential candidate. He had been elected governor of Kansas in 1932 and again in 1934 in the face of Democratic landslides, somewhat because of his abilities and largely because in both campaigns the independent candidacy of John R. Brinkley (a goat land doctor who had been barred by the State Medical Board from practicing in Kansas) had subtracted many thousands of votes from what otherwise would have been a Democratic majority, with the result that Landon emerged in 1935 as the only Republican governor in the land to survive two Democratic landslides.

Landon was the son of an old Kansas Bull Mooser who had been my father's friend since the golden days of 1912. He was supported by what remained of the Roosevelt Progressives in Kansas. The reader has seen that my father's old Kansas political friends meant much in his life, and so can understand that in this situation he had little choice, whatever he may have felt and written previously about Roosevelt. For Landon was as yet unknown outside the state. Over the nation, my father was probably the best known Kansan, and his opposition at this stage would have been fatal. Furthermore, my father, who was personally fond of Landon, wanted tremendously to believe that Landon was a true Bull Moose Progressive; and there was a considerable body of evidence to justify this hope.

Yet his praise of Landon, while generous, could hardly be criticized as hysterical. Late in 1935, he editorialized on the Landon boom, pointing out that Landon's Kansas friends

"will not claim him to be a superman. They will not point to him as a miracle worker.

"But he will go forward and not back. That we know. . . . We make no bond for anything else. Take him or leave him."

Early in 1936 when the private cars of prominent Republicans on pilgrimage were already a familiar sight in the Topeka switchyard, my father wrote his first serious editorial estimate of Landon, pointing out that he:

"is now going into that rarefied atmosphere where the great currents of American politics run swift, capricious and mercilessly cold. . . . Political geography has taken him where he is; a successful Republican governor of a midwestern state who, as La Follette's Monthly declares, is not too progressive to offend the conservatives, and not too conservative to lose the support of the liberals.

"But political geography does not make a man President. He must measure up to certain spiritual requirements. He must have moral courage, or, if not that, the backing of great material forces—money for instance. He must have intellectual strength—or, lacking that, a great charm which to the moron mind substitutes for intellectual endowment. He must have insight—instinctive and canny. Or to make up that lack, he needs a crafty political acumen and a manipulating ability that amounts to genius. . . . Every man has latent forces. . . . In the next three months, only one man can make Governor Landon President, and that man is Alfred Mossman Landon. He, himself, must make each great and final decision.

"But if he does not have these extraordinary qualities—if some hellborn breed of events thrusts him luckily into power without the strength to do the job, God help his country in a time like this.

"In the meantime, all of Kansas is proud to see him take the upward journey, proud and happy that their friend and fellow Kansan is on his way. And as he goes, he has their blessing.

"But in the high bleak thin air—he walks alone."

However, my father followed him to the Republican convention at Cleveland, at which he was a Landon delegate and also a member of the platform committee. His principal contribution to the campaign was a small book "What It's All About," in which he gave outsiders a picture of Governor Landon. However, he hit at the President in a ringing Republican editorial when Roosevelt invaded Kansas to speak at Wichita two weeks before the campaign's close. Pointing out that

"our old American smiler declared that Kansas would not have pulled through the last few years of drouth and depression if it had not been for 'federal aid in many fields of endeavor,'"

he charged that the President's logic was

"slick as goose grease and false as hell. . . . Who in the world thinks 'it is wrong to give federal assistance'? We Republicans are just as much for . . . it as the slick old thimble-rigger who passed so felicitously through Kansas yesterday. . . . Where the Republican plan differs from the Democratic practice is in our promise that this federal aid shall be administered by the states, counties, and cities . . . following local knowledge and wisdom. [Otherwise you] build up a great political machine centered in Washington and pay for it with waste and extravagance. . . . It's sensible if you are a Democrat but mad as a hoot owl if you are a taxpayer."

It was on this Kansas trip that the President, when his train paused in

Emporia, told the crowd that, anyway, he was appreciative of "Bill White's support for three and a half years out of every four."

The next two years of my father's life were fairly well occupied with the preparation of his book "A Puritan in Babylon," published in 1938, which was actually a political and economic study of the 1920's done in the form of a biography of Calvin Coolidge. It was, from the standpoint of scholarship and research, perhaps his most important book to date.

Meanwhile, war was approaching, a subject on which he had few illusions. Certainly not many are to be found in his editorial of November 11, 1933. Here he pointed out:

"Fifteen years ago came the Armistice and we all thought it was to be a new world. It is! But a lot worse than it was before.

"Ten million men were killed and many more maimed, fifty billion dollars' worth of property destroyed, the world saddled with debts.

"And for what? Would it have been any worse if Germany had won? Ask yourself honestly. No one knows.

"Is this old world as safe for democracy as it was before all these lives were lost?

"There is no democracy east of the Rhine. Tyrants have risen where constitutional monarchs ruled twenty years ago. . . . The boys who died just went out and died. To their own souls' glory, of course—but what else? . . . Yet the next war will see the same hurrah and the same bowwow of the big dogs to get the little dogs to go out and follow the blood scent and get their entrails tangled in the barbed wire.

"And for what?

"Look at Russia, ruled by the proletarian tyrant!

"Behold Germany, governed by paranoiac sadists!

"Italy has lost her liberty to fill her stomach and enthrone the rich!

"Poland, the Balkans, and Central Europe—a super powder magazine —waiting for the match to blow civilization back to the dark ages!

"What a glorious war! All wars are like that. The next one will be worse.

"War is the devil's joke on humanity. So let's celebrate Armistice Day by laughing our heads off.

"Then let us work and pray for peace when man can break the Devil's chains and nations realize their nobler dreams!"

This was probably the prevailing American viewpoint in the late twenties and middle thirties. It was to change with events, as was his own. When, after signing a pact, Russia and Germany closed in on Poland, he became chairman of that committee which presently secured the repeal of the American embargo on arms, thus enabling the British and French to buy munitions in this country. Of all this I know little at first hand since I had already left for Europe as a war correspondent; but the committee was substantially the nucleus for the more powerful group which, as America, stunned by fear, watched the fall of France, was later to rise under his chairmanship as the Committee to Defend America by Aiding the Allies.

While the first German tanks were fumbling through the Ardennes Gap, he was writing:

"As one democracy after another crumbles under the mechanized columns of the dictators, it becomes evident that the future of Western civilization is being decided on the battlefield of Europe. . . . Terrible as it may seem, the people of our country cannot avoid the consequences of Hitler's victory and of those who are or may be allied with him. . . . It would be folly to hold this nation chained to a neutrality policy determined in the light of last year's facts. . . . America must spend every ounce of energy to keep the war away from the Western hemisphere by preparing to defend herself and aiding with our supplies and wealth the nations now fighting to stem the tide of aggression. . . . It is for us to show the people of England, of France, of Belgium and Scandinavia that the richest country on earth is not too blind or too timid to help those who are fighting tyranny abroad.

"If they fail, we shall not have time to prepare to face their conquerors alone."

It is superficially a most curious fact that the "William Allen White Committee," then so bitterly denounced by Bundists and Communists as a group of irresponsible interventionist war-mongers, should be headed by a man who believed with a great earnestness that this country should not enter the war, nor, in aiding the Allies, take any step which would give the Axis casus belli.

Actually, a minority of the committee, which toward the end may have become a majority, believed (I happened to share its view) that the sooner American soldiers were sent overseas, the better chance we should stand of preventing an otherwise inevitable and permanent Axis conquest of Europe.

This was never my father's view. If his name was of value to that committee because it savored, not of the war-fevered eastern seaboard, but rather of the traditionally isolationist Midwest, they had also to accept the handicap that his own convictions represented the average opinion of America more accurately than any Gallup Poll, and this average opinion was presently to reach a state aptly characterized by Mark Sullivan as "a case of split personality—mass schizophrenia" in the conflicting beliefs that

Hitler's defeat was a matter of life and death for America, but that under no circumstances should we declare war.

Probably his principal service to the committee was in connection with the campaign of 1940 when, on several occasions, he served as a liaison between Willkie and the President in a largely successful attempt to prevent the Roosevelt foreign policy from becoming the principal issue of the campaign. But early in 1941 he resigned as active head of the committee after a somewhat heated and complicated dispute as to whether or not it should favor American naval convoys for our Lend-Lease aid to the British. His position, presently expressed in a letter to one of the committee's members, was:

> "When the President is for them, I'm going to support them, of course. But I do not believe that our organization should keep nagging him and needling him while he is hesitating. I do not believe that he and Secretary Hull have changed their minds since they both spoke to me about convoys, and both protested against their use. Perhaps they should change their minds; I don't know. But I don't think our organization is doing any service to the President in building up public sentiment that will force his hand."

In May, he was writing to his old friend, Oswald Garrison Villard:

> "I hoped I would never see another war. I shall never encourage the coming of another war. But if it comes, this summer or next summer . . . I see nothing to do but to fight it with all our might and all our hearts. And that's not a pleasant prospect for a man who realizes the utter futility of wars in the past and who can only hope rather vainly that, out of this war, men may learn wisdom in the end.
>
> "But how can they learn wisdom through hate and rancor and suspicion and all the hell's mint of counterfeit coins of wisdom that will be spread across the world in the currency of our spiritual commerce? . . . I should like to postpone it for another year by any device that will keep England afloat while we prepare. In that year, much might happen. . . . Possibly the Nazis will not be able to go through another winter. That may be wishful thinking. . . . I'm hoping rather than thinking."

Even on the eve of Pearl Harbor, he was writing:

> "I am one of those in the 75 per cent of Americans who, for a year, have been ringing up in the Gallup Poll as favoring the President's foreign policy. I am also of the 95 per cent who have been ringing up in the Gallup Poll for this same period as wishing to avoid war."

Meanwhile, Russia had come into the war. Possibly because, when he headed the committee, the American Communists had so viciously attacked him, one can detect a note of cautious restraint in his salute to this new ally. Writing for the Gazette two days after Hitler's attack, he pointed out that between Stalin and Hitler,

"the two dictators who are clashing along the long boundary line between the Slavic and the Nordic civilizations in Europe, it is small choice. . . . Both are conspicuous international liars. . . . Both have betrayed and murdered their best friends. Both are tyrants, ruthless of human life, utterly impervious to the claims of dignity for the human spirit. So both hate democracy with a craven hate."

Although he felt that Stalin's "lust for power was fairly well confined in the boundaries of his country," and that he was "at the moment fighting America's most dangerous enemy," his conclusion was that America, England, Scandinavia, Holland, Belgium, and France, "indeed all honest men who love freedom all over this globe," could now take a deep breath and "wish that it shall be a battle to the death"—a grim view which he modified two days later, when the Russians seemed to have halted the German attack:

"What a miracle it would be if those slab-sided, gawky, bewhiskered Bolsheviks stand-up-and-fall-down steppers on their own feet—should hold the Nazi champions long enough to let the people in Germany know that their omnipotent Führer was just a dub of common clay. Then, indeed there would be a celebration; a shindy as the old-fashioned posters used to say, 'platform dancing in the grove and fireworks in the evening!' "

Yet some mistrust still persisted, for still later he was writing to an old Kansas friend of isolationist tendencies that the world would never be safe until Hitler was licked—

"and, if you ask me, this world won't be safe even then . . . unless Joe Stalin is shoved back in his corner."

My father was still preoccupied with his estimate of Roosevelt and, in a letter to another correspondent, found the President

"a great puzzle. I am fond of him. He has done everything I ever asked, but I have asked for precious few things. In the summer of 1940, because I was chairman of the Committee to Defend America by Aiding the Allies, he talked in utmost confidence with me and let me talk in turn confidentially to Wendell Willkie, which I did and I hope with some effect. At least we kept the foreign issue out of the campaign as far as possible.

"I knew the President nearly twenty years ago and have liked him. I suppose he knows my weaknesses, and I am sure he knows that I know his, and we have put up with each other. Each of us probably feels in his heart that in certain matters he tolerates fools gladly. On that basis we have erected what might pass for a friendship. But I miss what I found in Theodore Roosevelt—a certain ruggedness, the ability to quarrel bitterly with a man and then take him to his heart and forget the quarrel. . . .

"Yet he has done so many fine things. He has started us down so many roads that long had been blocked by an arrogant plutocracy that I cannot ask perfection and I am glad he came."

Now and then in these closing years, he glanced shrewdly into the future, as in his letter to Alfred M. Landon in mid-July of 1942. Landon had sent him a proposed speech, to which my father replied, objecting:

"You emphasized the difficulties rather than the needs for some kind of world organization to save the peace. I have no plan. I don't string along with Clarence Streit. I follow Hoover closer than any other one man as he set forth the case in his book. But it is wiser to prepare the popular mind to accept as inevitable some kind of organization rather than to raise the obstacles . . .

"When I look into the future, even two or three years, I am shocked, indeed horrified, at the inevitable spectacle that rises before me no matter who wins the war. The duties of a decent victor will be burdens and not tokens of triumph."

Some flavor of the placid routine of these closing years is given in a letter to Edna Ferber written in July of 1942:

"I am working on my autobiography. Every morning at half past seven the stenographer comes out to the house. I lie on the porch in the hammock and dictate fifteen hundred words or so, and by half past eight or nine go down to the Gazette office, take care of my letters, then come home and sleep, do my editorials in the afternoon for the next day's paper, and knock off at half past five and call it a day.

"I get up as much copy as anyone around the shop and, of course, have my finger in a lot of local pies. Just now I'm helping to nominate a governor and am busier than a man falling out of a balloon without a parachute. But it would be pretty terrible not to be a part of things.

"Of course, the war has got me down, and I know it is a long war, terrible next year and maybe worse the year after. But by 1945 I think we can see daylight if we can just keep out of inflation. That is the hell fire and damnation that looms ahead of us, and I am scared stiff."

My father's fatal sickness began in the fall of 1943, but in the earlier part of the year the time he could spare for active politics was devoted to an attempt (it was unsuccessful) to organize the Kansas Republican delegation for Wendell Willkie in the 1944 convention and election. He had previously written Justice William A. Smith of the Kansas Supreme Court:

"I'm 100 per cent sold for life on Wendell Willkie and if I am the only man in Kansas who is following him . . . I am going to do it. I have made my living by being a pretty good judge of men, and never since Teddy Roosevelt have I known a man on whom I have pinned my faith as I pinned it on Wendell Willkie. I think one of the most courageous things any man ever said in public life was Willkie's 'campaign oratory' statement. It was not discreet, but it was deeply honest. Only three times in public life have I seen such honesty. The pretension that a candidate's utterances are omniscient when everyone knows he is talking damned nonsense is one of the large reasons why the American people lose faith in democracy."

So in May of 1943, he was writing to Thomas W. Lamont that:

"Of course, I am for Willkie. I still have faith that he will be able to breast the tide and buck the isolationist reaction against him. . . . This is a hunch and a guess. I have no facts to support it and have been wrong before; I may be wrong this time."

During the same spring, he paid his respects to another Republican candidate in a Gazette editorial in which he said:

"The same forces in the Republican party that gathered about Taft in 1912 and that nominated Harding in a 'smoke-filled room' in 1920, . . . seem determined to force the nomination of Governor Bricker of Ohio as Republican Presidential nominee. And who is Governor Bricker? Alice Roosevelt is said to have defined him in five words: 'Bricker is an honest Harding.'

"That leaves little more to be said. He is a man who is trying to capitalize the tremendous discontent among Republicans and among Democrats who hate the New Deal. . . . He hopes to get by without saying anything, without getting on either side of the momentous questions of the hour—domestic and foreign.

"A man who can stand in American politics, aspiring for a high office, without the intelligence, the courage, or the honesty to make some declaration upon the most important issue that has ever faced this old earth, certainly is not the kind of man for the Republicans of this country to rally around. . . . Surely the Republican party, which came to power more than eighty years ago under Abraham Lincoln by saving the country from disunion and by freeing 4,000,000 slaves, the Republican party which guided the country while a continent was settled, . . . cannot be so craven that it would conspire to steal into victory with no issue but Bricker and a bellyache."

This tribute he presently sent to Willkie with the comment that it had "raised hell clear across the continent," as a result of which he had received

"a stack of letters as thick as a hired girl's leg. I just had to take a sock at that bird, and I hope this will find you the same."

In addition, that spring, he sent Willkie several letters of strategic advice, arguing that he should

"avoid the President when you possibly can. Don't wisecrack at him, but when you have something to say, don't pull your punches or slap his wrist. Sock him with all you've got, but with a dignity that becomes a patriot and a great cause."

In general, however, he urged him to:

"Attack the fundamental domestic policy of the New Deal and not the President. Handle him with tongs. Explain why deficiency spending will bring us to the brink of ruin. Tell the people that the extension of governmental powers into planned economy in time of peace is the denial of liberty inevitably. For the very theory of planning requires that man shall become a wooden figure without will, without individuality, that he shall be, in short, that powerless human sheep, the economic man, a social and political eunuch.

"The people are ready to hear this. They are yearning for new leadership. We are entering an interregnum. Either Hitler and the storm troopers, the boys in the pool hall under the leadership of Ham Fish, Martin Dies, Gerald Nye and Colonel McCormick will come out and take leadership and bash the heads of liberals everywhere, or you will take leadership, and the time is short."

To another Republican leader who asked his opinion on a new Republican platform, he wrote:

"We should . . . denounce all government coddling, either to capital in the form of protective tariff, or to labor in the form of special privileges. And we should not be mealy-mouthed about either. The strength of the Republican party is the middle class—the small businessman, the independent operator in any line of mercantile or industrial business. He is the man who should be considered in writing our platform. I'm getting pretty sick of the pussyfooters who try to catch the WPA and the National Association of Manufacturers with the same kind of talk. Personally, I want neither of them."

He was also looking ahead toward the end of the war, which he had predicted for 1945, and in another letter says:

"After unconditional surrender . . . we are in for a ten-year struggle in which we must put our American energies, our American production, and the full strength of American credit—not into a grand do-good adventure, not into making the world beautiful and utopian, but into a cold-blooded, hardboiled attempt to put world civilization back on its feet. The capitalist system must not break down. Unless capitalism is willing to organize, to sacrifice, to envision its own self-interests in the renewal and revival of civilization, war will be a failure. . . . And a weary, disheartened world will turn to some totalitarian tyranny and we shall regiment mankind in inevitable economic slavery."

Something of the same note is in his letter to Mr. and Mrs. Raymond Robins in which he says:

"As we approach the peace, . . . we are standing in slippery places. I get more and more frightened at the limitations of our political institution and the tremendous, unbelievable size of the political job before us, and the economic commitment we must make in the next two or three years if the peace shall become really a victory and not a prelude to a debacle.

"And the fourth term bothers me. . . . Every year that Roosevelt is in the White House he deteriorates physically and also . . . in leadership due to the natural distrust of the country for a man who has such faith in himself and so little in God that he believes he is indispensable. People know, deeply and instinctively, that when a man becomes indispensable to a democracy it is no longer a democracy; and that weakens the President for the greatest task that has ever faced any man on this planet.

"It may take another false peace and another war to develop the stern qualities in the people that will make them worthy of the great leader who is necessary to do the work ahead of us. I suppose we should not be silly and expect it to be done overnight . . . but be grateful if it could be done in a century."

His criticisms of the President, while frequent, were never bitter. On his return from the Teheran Conference, my father, in an editorial, pointed out:

"He saw more of an amazing world than Marco Polo. He saw in North Africa alone as much conquered land as Alexander saw when he wept for new worlds to conquer. He performed a feat so strange even in

647

modern war, so amazing and unbelievable, that if it had been prophesied fifty years ago men would have stoned the prophets for impiety.

"Biting nails—good, hard, bitter Republican nails—we are compelled to admit that Franklin Roosevelt is the most unaccountable . . . President that this United States has ever seen. He has added a vast impudent courage to a vivid but constructive imagination, and he has displayed his capacity for statesmanship in the large and simple billboard language that the common people can understand; moreover, that the people admire, even when it is their deadly poison. We have got to hand it to him.

"Well, darn your smiling old picture, here it is! Here, reluctantly, amid seething and snorting, it is. We, who hate your gaudy guts, salute you."

Still later, he was writing to Henry J. Allen:

"The President is a baffling case. For ten years he has been staging himself as the champion of the underdog. But I doubt if he really understands the underdog well enough to love him intelligently in spite of his faults. And from now on out, if I was the underdog, I should bury my bones against the day of hunger.

"He is too many for me. Like you, I think he inordinately wants a Fourth Term, but I don't know why. You think he wants power. I think he wants to sit in, to win hand after hand, and maybe take quite a pot with him as he passes through the portals of history. Theodore always had one eye on history; . . . he played a bold hand, did what he thought was right, and defied the world, the flesh, and the devil, which is something that F. D. R. just can't do. He can defy Wall Street when Wall Street is groggy, and anyway Wall Street doesn't have many votes. But he has never offended any minority that has supported him when that minority was wrong and when any intelligent man must have known it was wrong.

"And yet, if he can die before 1944, he will leave a great name in history. Lincoln was beloved of the gods, who took him just before he started to fight the Republican radicalism led by Thaddeus Stevens on reconstruction. If Lincoln had gone into that fight, God knows how he would have come out at the inevitable defeat."

And in late August of his final year he was writing to Harold B. Johnson:

"It is the tragic weakness of the Roosevelt administration that after twelve years he has so entirely denuded the Democratic party, that it has not one available leader who can carry on the work which he has started. As you know, I have never been greatly excited about Roosevelt as a dictator. He laughs too easily. He is too soft-hearted in many ways. . . .

But he has functioned much like a dictator in chopping off the political heads of possible rivals—not with a snickersnee, not with a machine gun, but with soft soap, kicking them upstairs or choking them to death on taffy."

So often, in those final months and weeks, as old age was closing relentlessly down on him, my father was trying to peer into the future. "We must," he wrote in a cautioning letter to Roger Straus, a devoted Dewey supporter,

"pick a man of size this time. . . . For the peace will bring problems as urgent and as important as the problem of war."

Yet always he could bring his gentle irony to bear on himself, even on his own eager interest in the future. For he concludes:

"This started out to be a note of gratitude and here it is, an old man, babbling about those years when he will be merely a ripple under the daisies."

Index

Note.—The abbreviations T.R.=Theodore Roosevelt; W.A.=William Allen White.

Landon, John Manuel, father of the preceding, 492, 521
Lane, Franklin Knight, Secretary of the Interior, 579
Lang, Andrew, his "Ballade in Blue China," 246; 145, 271
Lansing, Robert, Secretary of State, 566
Larriway, Orin, convicted of murder, 135
Lawrence Journal, W.A. becomes reporter, 141, 144–45, 153–54; Vernon Kellogg made editor, 155; 157, 166, 244, 256
Lawrence Tribune, W.A. made editor, 155
Lawson, Thomas William, his book on Wall Street, 388
League of Nations, Wilson determined on its establishment, 549; declared dead, 554; fight on it raging, 577; 555, 559, 578, 582, 585, 591, 596–98
Leahy, David, 431
Learnard, Col. Oscar E., owner of the Journal and Tribune of Lawrence, 154 ff.
Lease, Mary Elizabeth ("Mary Ellen"), 218–19
Leavenworth Times, 84
"Leaves of Grass" (Whitman), 195
Le Bon, Gustave, his story "The Crowd," 271
Lee, Gen. Robert Edward, 359
Leedy, John W., governor of Kansas, 198
Legate, James, soldier, and a bribe, 89–90
Leland, Cyrus, Kansas political boss, 191–93; in McKinley-Bryan campaign, 273–74; 222–23, 248–52, 255, 257, 291, 293, 295, 303, 321, 343, 352, 388, 430, 443, 577
Lenin, Nikolai, 390, 560, 562
Lenroot, Irvine Luther, 588
Leon (Kan.) Indicator, 396
Leonidas at Thermopylae cited, 354
Leslie's Monthly, name changed to American Magazine, 387
Leslie's Weekly, 104
Lewelling, Lorenzo D., elected governor of Kansas, 228–29
Lewis, Dr. William Draper, chairman of Bull Moose platform committee, 485–86
Liberty Loan, speeches for it by W.A., 577
Liége, its fall, 506
Life, magazine, 287–88
Limiting hours of labor for women, 530
Lincoln, Abraham (16th Pres. of the U.S.), 7, 9–10, 72, 86, 231, 359–60, 504, 511
Lincoln-Douglas debates, 7
Lindsay, Capt., father of Sallie, 242
Lindsay, Jessie, 446
Lindsay, Milton, bother of Sallie, 245
Lindsay, Sallie, meets W.A., 214; warns him on liquor, 224; marries him, 241–43; honeymoon, 244–46; society editor of the Gazette, 264; declares her intention of voting for Wilson, 531; 216 passim
Lindsey, Judge Benjamin Barr, 495
Lippmann, Walter, 546
Lissner, Meyer, 491

Liszt, Franz, 248
Little, Edward, 198
Little Nemo in colored pictures, 592–93
Littleton, Martin Wiley, originator of "He kept us out of war," 529
Lloyd George, David, 390, 413–15, 418–19, 550–51, 557–58, 560, 562, 564
Lobdell, Charles Elmer, lawyer and banker, 135–36
Lodge, Henry Cabot, senator from Massachusetts, 525; leader of the attack against League of Nations, 577, 585
Loeb, Jacques, his "Mechanistic Conception of Life," 500
London, White family in, 411–20
London Daily Express, 567
London Daily Mail, 567
London Economic Conference, 636
London Illustrated News, 104
Long, Chester Isaiah, wins fight for U.S. senator, 351–53; back of Judge Blub Blub, 353–54; defeated for reelection, 394–97, 399–400, 405; 366, 389
Long, Nathan, boy friend of W.A., 49
Longfellow, Henry Wadsworth, 101
Longworth, Nicholas, married to Alice Roosevelt, 401
Loomis, Nelson Henry, railroad lawyer, 233
Lord, Louie, actress, 69
Lorimer, George Horace, editor of Saturday Evening Post, 313, 326, 346, 372
Louvain, its sack, 506
Louvre, 409
Low, Marcus A., railroad lawyer, 232
Lowden, Frank Orren, in deadlock with Gen. Wood for Presidential nomination, 584, 586
Lowell, James Russell, 230
"Lucille," 79
Lynching of Negroes, 156
Lyons, Eugene, 636

"M Quad" (pseud. of Charles Bertrand Lewis), 95
MacArthur, Gen. Douglas, 572–73
Machine age, comes to the U.S., 319
Macmillan Co., of New York, 399, 406; of London, 412–13
Madden, John, Populist, 302
Madero, Francisco, President of Mexico, assassinated, 501
Madison, Edmond Haggard, 448
Madison, James (4th Pres. of the U.S.), 358
Mafia lynching in New Orleans, 341
"Main Travelled Roads" (Garland), 217
Maine (U.S.S.), sinking of the, 312
Manhattan Club of New York, 513, 516
Manhattan (Kan.) Mercury, 256
Mantell, Robert Bruce, plays Romeo, 153–54
Marat, Jean Paul, mentioned, 278
Maria Theresa, Empress, mentioned, 92
Marion Star, President Harding's newspaper, and its problems, 617–18

Vandergrift, Frederick, city editor of Kansas City Star, 210, 234
Van Horn, Col. Robert Thompson, and his Sunday editorial, 207–8, 212
Van Schaick, John, 287, 302
Vera Cruz, Mexico, Gen. Funston lands with American troops, 502
Versailles, 409
Victory dinner (McKinley) at Zanesville, Ohio, 289–91; called the Feast of Belshazzar, 292
Villa, Francisco (Pancho), his raid on Columbus, N. M., 502
Villard, Henry, 268
Villard, Oswald Garrison, pleads for pardon of Debs, 622; letter from W.A., 642; 550, 558
Virgil's "Aeneid," 106, 125; "Elegiacs," 125

Wadsworth, James Wolcott, Jr., senator from New York, 620
Waggener, Balie Peyton, railroad lawyer, 232
Wagner, (Wilhelm) Richard, heard in Kansas City, 234
Walker, Francis, textbook on Sound Economics, 187
Wallace, Alfred Russel, 500
Wallace, Henry Agard, 636
Wallace, Gen. Lewis (Lew), his "Ben Hur," 245
Walling, William English, 563
Walnut Valley Times, 89
Waltzes, 75, 94
"Wandering Jew," by Eugène Sue, 101, 106
Warder Grand Theater, Kansas City, 211–12
Ware, Eugene, his "Rhymes of Ironquill," 91, 190; 223–24, 279–80
Warfield, David, a likeness, 572
Washington, Booker Taliaferro, 292
Washington, George (1st Pres. of the U.S.), a comparison, 231; 358
Watson, Carrie, librarian, 153
Watson, James Eli, 466, 583
Watts, Jack, 156
Way, Irving, of Way & Williams, Chicago publishers, 288
Way & Williams, 266, 273
"We want Teddy!" marching cry in Chicago streets after the Roosevelt bolt, 468
Weaver, Gen. James Baird, one-time leader of the Greenbackers and Grangers, 189, 218, 507, 521
Webster, Harold Tucker, cartoonist, 461–62, 476
Wedding story mixed with Kipling, 264–65
Weeks, John Wingate, 525
Weimar (Germany) Republic, 561, 564
Welliver, Judson Churchill, his story of President Harding's troubles in the White House, 616
Wells, Herbert George, 416

Wells, Mortimer, his ice-cream parlor, 149, 180
Western Artists and Authors Society, 223–24
Weyler, Gen. Valeriano, 306
"What It's All About," W.A.'s book in the Landon campaign, 639
"What's the Matter with Kansas?" an editorial, 280–85, 287, 291, 297, 323, 328, 336, 347, 364, 509, 614
Wheeler, Ella, mentioned, 324
White, Dr. Allen, father of W.A., 3; graduates from medical school, 6; meets Mary Ann Hatten at a dance, 8; woos her in letters, 12–19; their wedding, 19; his aid in a drought and grasshopper year, 30; his treatment of a drunk, 33; buys house and has housewarming, 42; dies, 82; his funeral, 83; 236
White, Bouck, his "The Call of the Carpenter," 446
White, Daniel, uncle of W.A., 6, 31, 52
White, Freddie, brother of W.A., died in childhood, 25, 30, 36
White, Henry, at Paris Peace Conference, 566
White, John, great-grandfather of W.A., 4
White, John, grandfather of W.A., 4–5, 34, 235
White, Mary, daughter of W.A., 372, 391, 406–8, 446, 494, 540, 551, 591–94, 603; dies, 604; her father writes her obituary, 605–8
White, Nicholas, ancestor of W.A., 4
White, Union, uncle of W.A., 5n.
WHITE, WILLIAM ALLEN:
his birth and babyhood, 3
his experience with Indians, 23–24
hatred of his baby brother Freddie, 25; his death, 25, 30, 36
goes to school, 37
politics enters his life, 39
learns to swim, 45
banker for marbles, 47
breaks shoulder blade and ends sporting career, 48
his fighting career, 48–50
gives up smoking, 51
his desire to become a circus performer, 51
gives up card-playing, 52
evolution into boyhood, 57–58
learns to play the organ, 58–60
works as a bootblack, 64
as a cigar merchant, 67
beginning of his newspaper career, 68
the schoolboy, surveyed, 75
tries to write poetry, 79
death of his father, 82
finishes high school, 96
goes to college, 100
on the Eldorado Democrat, 109
celebration of Grant's funeral, and its results, 114–16